The editor

James Park has worked for a film producers' pressure group and the American showbusiness weekly *Variety* as well as writing screenplays. He wrote *Learning the Dream: the new British Cinema* in 1984, and *British Cinema: the Lights that Failed* six years later. Editor of *The Film Yearbook* for the past four years, he has also written *Shrinks – the analysts analysed*.

ICONS

STYLE MAKERS AND BREAKERS SINCE 1945

EDITED BY JAMES PARK

BLOOMSBURY

This book is dedicated to Janet Vaughan

First published 1991
by Bloomsbury Publishing Limited, 2 Soho Square, London W1V 5DE

This paperback edition published 1992.

British Library Catloguing in Publication Data

A CIP record for this book is available from the British Library

ISBN 0 7475 0743 0

Designed by Geoff Green
Typeset by Florencetype Limited, Kewstoke, Avon
Printed in England by Cox & Wyman, Reading, England

10 9 8 7 6 5 4 3 2 1

Contents

Acknowledgements

The nightmare that producing this book became would never have been begun had not Cat Ledger and Jon Savage thought up the idea. Some initial research was carried out by Adair Brouwer and John Hare, who then sensibly left the project. The editor is grateful for the assistance he received from Ondine Upton, Clare Downs, John Alexander, Jonathan Moody and Robert Sandall.

Contributors

Mark Sinker was born in Shrewsbury. He has written about music, films and TV for a variety of publications, including *Wire*, the *Observer*, *Music Week*, *Marxism Today*, *NME* and *Elle*. He has also taught mathematics, philosophy and scientific logic, and is the occasional editor of the underground critical journal, *Virtual Space*.

David Quantick is a regular contributor to *Spitting Image*, *New Musical Express*, *City Limits* and *Punch*.

Robert Silver trained as a barrister and now writes for a wide range of publications. Special interests include legal issues, modern history, the Middle East, international relations and elections. He is doing a PhD at Cambridge on British public opinion and foreign policy 1938–9.

Trevor Willsmer has written a TV series on the Children's Crusade. Following the publication and subsequent pulping of his first novel, *Jessie*, he formed Lone Wolf Productions, through which he has produced and directed several short films.

Robin Rimbaud is a noise investigator/researcher who has written music for films, acted as an exhibition curator and founded Peyrere Indent, an independent publishing group.

Markus Natten is a retired poet currently co-writing two screenplays, *The Winter Man* and *Circuit of Nerves*. He writes regularly for *Fear*, lives in the New Forest and dreams of having his own cookery programme.

Don Watson is a writer and performer. He was a staff writer for *New Musical Express* and is currently poetry editor on *City Limits*. His first novel, *The Fear of Heaven*, was published by Fourth Estate.

Andrew Chitty studied anatomy and psychology in London, neuro-psychology in Saint Andrews and film in Bristol before moving into television. Finding himself completely unemployable, he decided to become an entrepreneur.

Caroline T. McCabe has worked in the fashion department of the *Sunday Times* and as a freelance assistant stylist for various magazines.

Stephen Dark is a journalist who writes about the media, property and finance.

Caroline Heslop has researched contemporary music in Bali and Indonesia, presented television programmes and written a weekly theatre column for a London freebie.

Danica Ognjenovic writes for *Creative Review*.

Nigel Wheale is co-editor of *Shakespeare in the Changing Curriculum* and editor of the forthcoming *Post-Modernism: A Theory in Practice*.

Signs and Symbols

Translations

Books written in languages other than English are indicated by their translated names, then the dates of the original publication and of any translation.

Death Signs

➳	murder, assassination, execution
†	suicide
✈	fatal confrontation with car, lorry, plane or other piece of modern technology
✣	Excessive consumption of alcohol, cocaine, heroin or other substances

Symbols

❍	Of global impact
▲	Downbeat
■	Dull, solid, middlebrow
▥	Jailbird
▯	Almost ended up behind bars
∀	Primitivist/Fundamentalist
&	Post-modern
✍	Wiggy genius
⚢	Significantly gay
$	Super-rich
❃	Chameleon tendencies
⊸	Known drug user
❞	Self-publicist/Chatshow regular
♥	Necromantic love-icon
✌	Politically engaged
✚	Conspiracy/Cult connection

☆	New Age
☞	Astringent, difficult, modernist, élitist
✖	Recluse
⇔	Retro
♦	Innovator
✎	Precocious
❀	Late bloomer
[punk symbol]	Deconstructor/Subversive/Punk
[thumbs-down symbol]	Out of fashion
✓	Survivor

The Contemporary Carnival

Living through the late twentieth century has been, for most people in the developed world, an experience of rapid, accelerating change. Secure patterns of belief and organization collapsed long ago, and contemporary existence can be likened to sitting at the centre of one of those pictures representing the city at night, in which moving cars have become luminescent streaks of light. Philosophers now emphasize the idea of flux with as much glee as Heraclitus did over two millenia ago: everything is constantly changing.

Icons offers a route map through this postwar world. It aims to encapsulate the essence of what 1000 or so key individuals said, wrote, did or endured in order to justify some claim to fame. In the process, the book tries to illuminate most of the significant shifts that have taken place over the past 45 years in architecture, philosophy, physics, rock music, biology, literature, fashion and almost everything else.

The entries are ordered alphabetically, so that the book can be used as an ordinary reference book in which one might hunt a name that has been mentioned in an article, or dropped into the previous night's conversation. But *Icons* can also be used to discover surprising connections between diverse areas of activity, taking into account the fact that, whether they were pop musicians, philosophers or politicans, everyone who has been included was a participant in the same stretch of history.

Horror marked the beginning of the late twentieth century. The bones and ashes found behind the doors of the gas ovens scattered across Central Europe showed humanity's potential for inflicting misery on its own kind, while the mushroom clouds over Hiroshima and Nagasaki were soon etched in the modern consciousness, providing conclusive evidence that science would not always work for the betterment of humankind.

The desire to prevent both sorts of horror from happening again led to an alliance between Europe and the US which was directed against the Soviets and the expansionist desires with which the latter was mistakenly credited. The result was a stand-off between the US and the USSR, the two superpowers, which for four decades built up nuclear arsenals and fought proxy wars across the globe. Only at the end of the 1980s did the desire of those in the east to enjoy the prosperity of those in the west, and the inability of the Communist system to give it to them, bring down the Iron Curtain that had divided the world into two ideological blocs.

After the Americans had taken on responsibility for the globe, caution rapidly gave way to idealistic optimism. Where others saw nuclear weaponry as a terrifying harbinger of the apocalypse, the US authorities welcomed the bomb as a mechanism for blackmailing the world into the 'American Way'. The confidence of the US in technology was total. Having devised a means to obliterate the planet, American scientists set about conquering the stars, but successive international crises brought home how limited was the effectiveness of nuclear might once others had secured the same technology. Military setbacks in south-east Asia suggested the limitations of firepower against an enemy, while the 'smart' bombs used in the Gulf War did nothing to rid the Middle East of Saddam Hussein.

It was the failure of the planned economy that led to the end of the Soviet Union in 1991. The Americans had long been promoting the free market and unbridled consumerism, encouraging more and more people to drink Coca-Cola, drive Fords, eat McDonald's, watch Hollywood movies and sitcoms on their television sets. They encouraged trade with everyone and, along the way, helped Western Europe and parts of the Far East to affluence, until eventually the US was forced to admit that Japan had beaten them at their own game.

With access to new economic resources, governments learned to sugar the pains of modernity through welfare state measures — paying for education, health care and housing as well as providing cash for those who could not find work. And prosperity fostered a culture which represented people to themselves as ever-hungry consumers, endlessly seeking out new goods and commodities. That, at least, was the message advertisers proclaimed via hoardings alongside roads, spreads in magazines and carefully honed television commercials.

Commerce drew the world together in new ways. Multinational companies scattered factories and shops across the globe, paying little attention to local regulations or the interests of local communities. They took advantage of developments in travel, electronic communications and computer technology, all of which broke down the distances between peoples and the boundaries between nations. Just as money could move from Frankfurt to Tokyo in a fraction of a second, so were musical trends, architectural styles and clothing fashions no sooner unveiled in London, Paris or Rio de Janeiro than they were picked up and propagated around the globe. While the United States imported architects, philosophers, literary theorists, designers and film-makers to ensure its own culture stayed at the top of the pile, Western culture in general opened itself up to enriching influences from Africa, South America and the Middle East.

So completely did the process of change obliterate earlier patterns of human solidarity that many sociologists predicted it could not go on, that the human psyche would crack. But men and women turned out to be, for the most part, fairly adaptable, although they might still debate whether their material comforts were worth the psychological hunger that product advertising and endless novelty seemed to breed.

In impoverished Communist nations and the Third World they could still have revolutions, as was demonstrated in Central America, the Philippines, Poland, Czechoslovakia, East Germany, Romania and the Soviet Union, but the discontents of life in the developed nations no longer bred the sort of anger that toppled governments. People weren't hungry enough to want to launch themselves against the citadel; they were having a good time.

Too good a time, in the eyes of some politicians, who

started to argue that the host of benefits aimed at ensuring nobody would go hungry or sleep without a roof over their heads had all but destroyed communities which previously knew how to look after their own. The New Right that came to power in Britain and America during the 1980s took an axe to this 'dependency' culture and the post-war consensus, labelling the poor spongers and making them suffer because, they argued, it would do them good.

Those who predicted uprisings in Nottingham or Pittsburgh overlooked just how far the state had gone in taking the sting out of life. The rhetoric of revolution was now confined to the study-bedrooms of students and occasional romantics on the dinner party circuit. Politics no longer worked to the grand plan, but was reduced to a series of struggles by those who considered themselves oppressed on the grounds of colour, sex, sexuality or religion.

Television nurtured this sense of individual impotence by turning all forms of protest into audiovisual events that flickered across the screen and faded away, caught up in a never-ending flow of information, entertainment and infotainment. TV was the shaping fact of culture from the mid-1950s. Offering to tell people all about the world, it also pumped them full of jargon, nonsense and simplistic ideas. Existence for some was reduced to a solitary sojourn with the TV set, and in the west it was certainly the new opium of the masses. But in Romania, among the most oppressive of Communist nations, television became, in 1989, the agent of revolution.

The multifariousness of the world encouraged nostalgia, as well as the search for simple solutions to complex problems. Economists proposed a new monetarist creed, which held that fixing the money supply was the only requirement for continued prosperity – bliss to politicians worn out by economic fine-tuning and the difficulties involved in running a welfare state. Meanwhile many architects gave up trying to express the modern spirit and took to incorporating pillars, pitched roofs and masonry in their designs; fashion worked the styles of previous decades as 'looks'; and pop music seemed for a time hooked on reviving the 1960s.

Disillusioned idealists gave up the political process altogether and took to planting bombs or murdering judges under the banner of organizations such as the Baader-Meinhof gang in West Germany or the Red Brigades in Italy, revealing in the process the new powers of supervision and control with which modern technology had supplied modern police forces. Others sought refuge in the emotional warmth of numerous cults brought from the East by figures ranging from the relatively benevolent Bhagwan to the sinister Reverend Moon. Attempted modernization of Middle Eastern states led to the fundamentalism of the Ayatollah Khomeini, just as free love in America fed a backlash organized by television evangelists. But the worst evidence of just how deadly nostalgia could be came from Cambodia, where Pol Pot did away with cars, doctors, modern irrigation, machinery and books, and put to death anyone who could boast a smidgeon of education.

The old dividing line between popular and highbrow crumbled as writers, musicians and artists tried to embrace the contemporary flux and the omnipresence of the new mass culture. For many, creation became a celebration of chance and absurdity, and the aim of tapping into deep emotions or changing people's way of looking at the world was abandoned. Many artists welcomed culture's new position as just another commodity in the marketplace.

The inhabitants of the post-war academy included structuralists hoping to classify all the symbols out of which stories were created, and practitioners of the 'new history' aiming to give a total account of previous mental states. However, these were gradually displaced by a new outlook, more humble in the face of a complex reality and emphasizing the impossibility of enclosing everything within a fixed intellectual frame. Some philosophers came to describe the world as a place of purposeless systems, arbitrary structures and random events, embracing disorder and instability. Scientists offered an account of nature in continuous flux, and began to wonder whether there was anything out there to describe. Was not any description simply an emanation of their own inner consciousness?

Nothing more clearly illustrated the inability of scientists to predict the consequences of their own actions than the ecological payoff from 45 years of economic growth and scientific innovation. Although the effects of pesticides on marine life had been exposed in the early 1960s, the total impact of modern science on the environment only slowly pushed its way up the international agenda. The panic button was finally pressed in the mid-1980s, after at accident at the Soviet Union's Chernobyl nuclear power plant scattered fall-out from Kiev to Lapland and beyond. The gases in refrigerators and hairsprays, it was revealed, were blasting holes through the ozone layer around the globe, while emissions from coal-fired power stations and car exhausts were warming the planet's climate. As drought gripped grain-growing areas around the world; as dead seals were washed up on the shores around Britain, and the snows did not come, people began to ask whether, far from controlling nature for their own ends, the scientists might not be destroying the very basis of human life. With fears further stirred by the development of AIDS, a devastating virus, it seemed to many that the prospect confronting the international community at the end of the second millenium was nothing less than the extinction of its own species.

As the twentieth century draws to a close, everything seems to have been put in question. The technologies in which many placed their hopes have polluted our waters, poisoned our food and wrecked our immune systems, while new developments in the labs offer the awful prospect of numerous genetic mutations being launched upon the world. No political system can any longer claim a monopoly of virtue: Communism has collapsed, unable to deal with the complexity of modern consumer desires; socialism is seen as leading to economic stagnation; while rampant capitalism has been responsible for coarsening human sensibilities and nurturing inner-city violence. Religion is once more centre-stage – not only in newly democratic Eastern Europe and among liberation theologians in Latin America, but also, menacingly, among the varieties of Islam in the increasingly volatile Middle East. It is at once the most dangerous time in history and the safest; one is torn between despondency and ebullient optimism *Icons* offers itself as a way to understand how we got here, and aims to provide some sort of guide to the way ahead.

A

Alvar Aalto 1898-1976

& FINNISH ARCHITECT, DESIGNER

Drawing his inspiration from the granite rocks and dense pine forests of his native Finland, Aalto challenged the notion of a universal architectural style, one that would be as appropriate to an affluent American city as to the rural hinterlands of the Third World. His designs broke with modernist orthodoxies of purity and unity, featuring curves as well as contrasting textures and shapes. He never made a lot of noise about his ideas but, thanks to his genius for relating buildings to landscape, secured commissions to put up schools, churches and libraries in cities from Oregon to Tehran. For his Town Hall at Säynätsalo (1950-2), he characteristically used brick against timber around an open courtyard through which, between gaps in buildings, there are views over forests and lakes. The Otaniemi Institute of Technology (1955-64) has a fan-shaped auditorium at the centre of a series of rectangles which house the administrative offices and teaching departments. Although Aalto's style was too idiosyncratic to be imitated directly, his affection for interlacing curves influenced Danish architect Jörn Utzon's plans for the Sydney Opera House (1957-65), with its series of upright shells set on a promontory jutting out into the harbour.

Chinua Achebe

(Albert Chinualumgu) born 1930

♦ NIGERIAN NOVELIST

Things Fall Apart, Achebe's 1958 fable on the tragic collapse of Nigeria (and all Africa) in the face of colonial aggression, is generally regarded as the beginning of modern African literature. The novel shows the inevitability of disaster when alien cultures collide: the losers too inflexible to deflect the threat; the winners too arrogantly ignorant to know why they have won, what is being lost and how to continue. There is a double irony in the title Achebe chose – first, that the opening salvo in a continent's literature should take its pessimistic title so brazenly from Yeats; second, that such an inauguration should put the whole idea of Western literary superiority in question. After expanding the tale into a trilogy that led from his grandfather's day to the fall of colonialism, Achebe went on to prove himself a front-rank satirist with *A Man of the People* (1966), answering critics who had suggested that the rough and simple style of his first books marked the limit of his ability. In 1987, after 21 years of relative silence, he published *Anthills of the Savannah*, a bitter but witty reassessment of Africa's progress under self-rule. Neither nostalgic for the past nor sentimental about the present,

Achebe's honesty has been a thorn in the side of successive Nigerian regimes.

Dean Acheson 1893-1971

AMERICAN POLITICIAN

Son of an Episcopalian bishop, Acheson became, after legal training and official service, a major figure in US diplomacy, who stirred up much bluster in the UK when he said: 'Great Britain has lost an empire and not yet found a role.' He helped to plan economic warfare against Germany and Japan during WW2. Then, as ☛Truman's under-secretary of state in 1947, he masterminded the '15-week revolution' of US foreign policy, which involved plans to take active steps against genuine (and imaginary) Soviet aggression, pledges of aid to states under threat and the Marshall Plan to revive Europe's war-torn economy. He was a major force in creating the North Atlantic Treaty Organization (NATO) as part of a plan to 'contain' Communism. The failure of the US to do this in China and Korea led to forceful right-wing attacks being launched against him in his final days at the State Department, although his over-hawkish analysis of North Vietnam's relationship to the USSR at about this time led, within a decade, to the Vietnam War. He returned to advise Kennedy over the war, and later presented such a gloomy picture of America's position that ☛Lyndon B. Johnson was shocked into de-escalating the conflict and declining to stand for a second term as president.

Kathy Acker born 1948

❞ AMERICAN NOVELIST

Until Acker no woman had set foot in ☞the luridly dismal corridors of the World According to ☛Genet, ☛Céline, ☛Foucault and ☛Bataille, with its power-fix cruising and violent hostility towards the settled order. *Blood and Guts in High School* (1978) drew on the emotional battlefields of her own relationships, turning them into an unnerving weave of extremism and obscenity. Jarring disruptions of identity merge autobiography with plagiarism to such an extent that neither reader nor writer can tell which is which – the point being the degree to which human character is made up of the fragments of previous fictions. She studied with ☛Robert Creeley, and worked for a time in a sex show, but she was shaped as a writer by ☛Burroughs. Since moving to England in 1985, her work has adopted a different tone – a series of unstable characters pass through melancholic and romantic landscapes of decay. Peopled by sailors, pirates and other (almost) stock outsiders, her narratives throw up questions about power, sexuality, desire and conventional storytelling. The British critical establishment seems to see her as all spiky hair, tattoos and swearing - their helplessness is probably a sign of Acker's artistic success, though it is increasingly tiresome to continue making this allowance.

Ansel Adams 1902-84

AMERICAN PHOTOGRAPHER

Adams' technical contributions to photography are so important that the symphonies of light and shadow he made of his pictures have also tended to receive lavish critical praise. But his images of the mountainous, deserted vistas of the American West or the Sierra Nevada's rock formations suggest such an aridly immaculate vision of nature that younger, less reverential observers now tend to dismiss him as a would-be landscape painter – inhumanly exact, spiritual, poetic, escapist. His sense of America as a shrinking natural paradise pushed him towards conservation issues, and he talked about his camera as 'an instrument of love and revelation', despising the photo-journalist's modernist machine-gun brusqueness. Having once studied to be a concert pianist, he was given to describing variations of light in the language of music theory, and to arguing that photography deserved the same respect as great art, literature and architecture.

Charles Addams 1912-88

AMERICAN CARTOONIST

A cartoonist with one endlessly flexible gag, Addams created a world of deadpan menace that provided a welcome antidote to the cloying blandness of Norman Rockwell's visions of the perfect nuclear family. Addams's America is a melting-pot New England suburb or Manhattan apartment block where witches, ghouls, phantoms and monstrous one-eyed deviants have settled into a life of solid citizenship. His grotesque Family, inhabiting a crumbling gabled ruin of a house with a shambling, seven-foot zombie of a butler, spawned two popular TV sitcoms, *The Addams Family* and *The Munsters* (both 1964-6). At that point, William Shawn, the severely patrician guardian of *The New Yorker*, stopped running Family cartoons, and they were not resumed until the spring of the year Addams died. His sense of the macabre, which was born somewhere between the foggy swirl of Universal horror movies and the clearly etched shadows of *film noir*, survived into the age of 'body horror', although by the end nostalgia had obviously softened it.

Konrad Adenauer 1876-1967

WEST GERMAN POLITICAL LEADER

Adenauer was prominent in German politics from his election in 1906 as a Cologne city councillor until his forced exit from the post of chancellor in 1963 – the result of his characteristic restraint during the Berlin Wall crisis. As an opponent of Hitler in the 1930s, he was pushed out as mayor of his native town and became caught up in plots against the Nazi regime. After 1945, he emerged as head of the centre-right, Catholic-run Christian Democrats, who ran the country, either on their own or as coalition leaders, until 1969. He defined the central lines of West Germany's post-war foreign policy: strong backing for NATO, co-operation with the US and participation in the European Economic Community , under French hegemony, as a counter-weight to American influence. His domestic policies were geared to re-election; the primary interest was foreign affairs. 'No experiments – Konrad Adenauer', his slogan for the 1957 election, can be taken as a verdict on his period in office.

Theodor Adorno 1903-69

▲ GERMAN PHILOSOPHER

✌ Since Adorno's project amounts – ☞ whatever his intentions – to making the 'sceptical critic' a model for the twentieth-century political activist, it is unsurprising that his work remains both of visionary importance and widely ignored. The Frankfurt School practised a non-Stalinist Marxist analysis that began as a cross-disciplinary research programme working through the sceptical strands of High German metaphysics from Hegel to Heidegger . Its most learned voice was provided by Adorno's austere, difficult, sometimes snobbish neo-Marxism. Increasingly

Nazism interposed itself, and much of Adorno's later work is dedicated to finding a way to continue after Auschwitz. The faults and the strengths of his approach are best seen in his writings on music. Believing passionately that Germanic culture represented the pinnacle of humanity's aesthetic achievement, he gave lifelong endorsement to Schoenberg's abstractions (wherein formal self-consciousness and the embrace of dissonance imply a social critique). With music from outside the Western tradition, he could only snipe at its trivial immaturity. Confronted by jazz, for example, or much of the output of the pop and mass-media era, Adorno simply talks nonsense. A victim of his early Marxist convictions, he struggled throughout his life to recast them as a flexible, critical-analytical tool that would never harden into killing dogma. As a result, Frankfurt School Marxism is free-thinking, old-fashioned, insightful and, ultimately, a failure: it never quite turns to face the present situation.

Abel Agenbegyan born 1932

SOVIET ECONOMIST

Soviet central planning has, traditionally, been laboured and physical. The multiple decisions that are vital to make it work have overwhelmed the system, creating endless log-jams and bottle-necks. Agenbegyan has been director since 1967 of the leading centre for research into the 'socialist market economy' and, in 1983, sent a highly critical report to the Politburo on the workings of the Soviet system. He became one of ☛Gorbachev's closest advisers, playing a key role in his schemes for economic reorganization. He does not favour 'market socialism' – the alternative espoused by some Soviet thinkers. Instead, he wants to see *better* planning, co-ordination and administration, seeking to inject tough Western analysis into the way the economy is run, without Western institutional mechanisms. Thus, he stresses management skills, the adroit application of economic levers and up-to-date methods of production control. His critics argue that the system itself is flawed, partly by tensions between workers and managers, partly by conflicts between the party and the managers or technicians. As the Soviet Union's economic problems worsen, advocates of fullblown free-market economics have pushed Agenbegyan to the sidelines.

Gianni Agnelli born 1921

$ ITALIAN BUSINESS EXECUTIVE

Italian governments come and go, but this car manufacturer goes on and on – the most powerful businessman in Europe today. FIAT (*Fabbrica Italiana di Automobile di Torino*) was founded by Agnelli's grandfather Giovanni, who supplied arms to the Italian government in both world wars and backed Mussolini's regime. The grandson, by contrast, is an internationalist and enlightened liberal, with well-established links to the Italian socialists. He has helped to sponsor a training centre for Third World manufacturers, and set up domestic welfare programmes, especially in Turin where he is based. His policy at FIAT is to establish the firm as the leader of Europe's car industry to rival Detroit's General Motors: in 1970, he opened a car-making plant in the USSR. In addition to his position as chairman of FIAT, Agnelli controls two of Italy's three national newspapers (*La Stampa* and *Corriere della Sera*) as well as holding substantial interests in periodical and book publishing. Trained as a lawyer, Gianni, after heroic war service, followed grandpa's advice and 'had a fling for a few years': a playboy, he featured regularly in gossip columns and became addicted to car racing. His own son and putative heir, Edoardo, embarrassed his father by speaking publicly, in 1986, about his search for a religious alternative to materialism, and then by getting himself arrested in Kenya four years later for possessing heroin.

Chantal Akerman born 1950

☞BELGIAN FILMMAKER

Akerman learned from her male mentors – ☛Jean-Luc Godard , ☛ Michael Snow and ☛ Stan Brakhage – that film could be both experimental and personal, and went on to develop a new approach to feminist cinema. Her films articulate personal history through a language of isolation and contemplation. With minimal narrative content, they feature long empty corridors, hotel rooms, unbroken train journeys and silences punctuated by few words. Akerman's is an internalized world, where the viewer has to look for the characters' emotions behind the face they present on the screen. Her concentration on space, both visual and aural, creates a fractured urban world where the spectator can observe and assess the relationship between alienated personality and bleak landscape. Many find her films self-indulgent and, as a result, apart from her first art-house success *Saute ma ville* (1968), she has built a reputation rather than a following.

Brian Aldiss born 1925

BRITISH WRITER AND CRITIC

Aldiss has been one of science fiction's foremost critics and analysts since the early 1960s, writing a comprehensive critical history of SF – *Trillion Year Spree* (1986) – and ensuring that this often self-ghettoed tradition retains some kind of place in public regard without losing too much of its uniqueness. As a novelist, he has played a solid and consolidating role, taking such exotic New Wave/Inner Space subjects as alienation, identity and illusion, and setting them in what amounts to prosaic, glum England – even his tales of Helliconia, a far distant solar system of his own invention, carry touches of day-to-day Home Counties life. In the tradition of John Wyndham , he is not the kind of stylist to scare off the less adventurous reader, and as a result of this reserved suburban clarity, he is easy to underestimate. His resistance to pulp standards and most lowest-common-denominator considerations have probably divested the UK contribution to SF of a certain low-grade energy. For two generations, though, the best and most daring writing from Britain and abroad has carried approving and appropriate review-quotes from Aldiss in his capacity as literary editor of the *Oxford Mail*.

Muhammad Ali

(Cassius Clay) born 1942

❞ AMERICAN BOXER

✎It is hard to imagine any of the black pugilists who came before Ali so brazenly declaring themselves to be 'the greatest' – whatever anger was eating away inside, they presented themselves to the American public as humble, deferential and patriotic. But Ali, who secured the world heavy-weight title in 1964, was boastful, proud and willing to take a stand on issues. A natural showman who attracted public attention by baiting his opponents and predicting in which round he would secure victory, he joined the Black Muslims (a group advocating the establishment of a separate black state in the US), changed his name, refused to serve in Vietnam and became a folk hero to rebellious blacks everywhere. The outraged boxing authorities took away his title in 1967, leaving him free to address rallies and star in a short-lived Broadway musical, *Buck White*, and in his own Hollywood biopic, *The Greatest* (1967): he later lent his name to a syndicated children's cartoon series. In 1974 he grabbed back his title by defeating George Foreman in Kinshasa, Zaïre, and then retired from boxing in 1978. When his speech became slurred and he started to show signs of mental confusion – all symptoms of Parkinson's disease from which he suffers – most assumed these to be the consequences of the punishment his head had endured.

Richard Allen

▲ BRITISH PULP NOVELIST

The exploitation novel has a respectably sleazy history from the Victorian penny dreadful to ☛Mickey Spillane's sado-Fascism, but the books of Richard Allen are pure pulp. His runaway success was *Skinhead* (1970), which hit on the formula of brutal violence combined with brutal sex and and wild right-wing moralizing, and spawned such successors as *Suedehead* (1971), *Skinhead Girls* (1972) and *Dragon Skins* (1975). Even Allen's world of blunt prose and even blunter heroes blanched in the face of punk: his book *Punk* (1977) was even more ridiculous than his attempt at glitter rock, *Glam* (1973). The novels serve now as a particularly garish memory of a farcical decade – at the time, they formed the staple reading diet of a significant section of bored youth, whether devoured under desks or behind the bike-sheds. It is important to note that they were passed around, so were communally experienced. And the moronically blank hatred they propagated underpinned punk's iconography and some of its early drive.

Woody Allen

(Allen Konigsberg) born 1935

AMERICAN FILM-MAKER, SHORT STORY WRITER, ACTOR, CLARINET PLAYER

Allen fuses immensely literate comedy with surreal vaudeville – much in the manner of S. J. Perelman. Where the early films were little more than compilations of sketches, the more recent offerings have narrative and character. It is as if Allen began by hating himself and ended up liking everyone, except perhaps those who prefer his earlier (funnier) films such as *Sleeper* (1973) or *Love and Death* (1975). In his time, Allen has worked in the tradition of ☛Bergman and parodied Bergman. He has also created slapstick comedy out of Dostoyevsky and Tolstoy alongside such garish satirical comedies about sex, neuroses and being a short, smart Jewish New Yorker as *Play It Again Sam* (1972) and *Annie Hall* (1977). Despite making more than ten films about his own sex life, often co-starring a current or recent lover, he is apparently too modest to go and collect his Oscars. He has also written short stories: in one, 'The Kügelmass Episode', his hero gets into *Madame Bovary* and

Woody Allen

marries Emma, thus saving her from what the novel has in store; and in another, a private eye is hired to find God (provided Nietzsche has not already killed him). Footnote for obsessives: Allen has used the same joke – the one about becoming ill by sitting next to estate agents – in both his books and in at least one film.

Salvador Allende

(Salvador Allende Gossens) 1908-73

➳ CHILEAN POLITICAL LEADER

✌ ♥ A Chilean Marxist leader, Allende was toppled by a US-backed military coup in 1973 and died in the attack on the presidential palace – a martyr to Yankee imperialism and anti-Communism. Trained as a doctor, he was from an upper-middle-class family, and his Cabinet experience began in the late 1930s. In 1952, he ran for president, but his own Socialists expelled him for accepting Communist aid. He came a close second in 1958 but was successful only at his fourth attempt in 1970. (There is an analogy with France's ☛Mitterrand, who tried and tried again, finally winning as he built up a left-wing coalition.) Allende then set about reshaping Chile on socialist lines as the first ever elected Marxist: he took over US copper interests, without compensation; he redistributed landed estates to peasant co-operatives; he also printed currency to make up a budget deficit, causing foreign investors to lose confidence and Western credit lines to dry up. Output, by 1972, was stagnant as inflation boomed and bourgeois resistance grew. Although he increased his majority in an election, his regime came under attack both from far left and far right. Unlike Mitterrand, he did not compromise or change tack on the economy, and despite his experience, he probably lacked the political skills to defuse the crisis or control the real powerbroker – the Chilean military. US destabilization left Chile to endure Pinochet's vicious despotism until the late 1980s.

Louis Althusser 1918-90

✌ FRENCH POLITICAL PHILOSOPHER

▯ ✍ ☞ The post-war era in the intellectual life of Paris came decisively to an end with the dismissal of homicide charges against Althusser, its leading philosophical light, on the grounds that he was insane – he had admitted strangling his wife Hélène. An earlier indication that something was seriously wrong had been his appearance at a meeting of ☛Lacan's Ecole Freudienne, where he surprised everyone with a declaration that he had been summoned 'by the libido and the Holy Ghost'. Althusser's mental problems went back a long way, setting up struggles within his own psyche which helped define the character of the 'return' to Marx for which he argued. The problem with then-contemporary Marxism was, for Althusser, its emphasis on economics as a determinant of all social reality; he argued instead that politics and ideology were only slightly less important than economics. Working at such a high level of abstraction that he was not aware of how he was influencing structuralism (by positing ideology as the discourse by which we live our lives), he laid down the seedbed of a new cultural politics and put forward a view of theory as a significant determinant of social change that tickled intellectuals who wanted to see themselves as participants in the class struggle even while they stayed snugly within book-lined studies. The realities of history and economics did not figure a great deal in Althusser's analysis, nor did the vital issues of post-war Europe as they presented themselves to Communists in Bologna or Barcelona.

Robert Altman born 1922

♦ AMERICAN FILM DIRECTOR

'If you try your luck, you could be Donald Duuuck! Hooray for Hollywood!' blares a weird and tinny little jingle over the closing credits of *The Long Goodbye* (1973), Altman's remake in which Elliott Gould plays an anachronistic version of Philip Marlowe in the sleazy, lazy 1970s. Altman is so capable a film-maker, so natural a weaver of art, oppositional politics, almost-mundane narrative and deep American mystery that he has often failed to make the film on hand, and what has been released seems more like provocatively inconsequential sketch-notes. He *can* film the unfilmable: *Come Back to the Five and Dime, Jimmy Dean, Jimmy Dean* (1982) turned a piece of derivative, trapped-in-a-room theatre into something incisive and weirdly cinematic. Altman invents his own techniques (e.g. the camp-broadcast as incomprehensible Greek chorus in *M*A*S*H*, 1970) to entertain himself – one film in two, he stuns everybody. As cinema seems set to enter its worst period for decades, Altman may prove one of its salvations – simply by continuing to confound expectations.

Idi Amin Dada born 1925

❞ UGANDIAN POLITICAL LEADER

▯ Idi Amin was to the 1970s what ☛ Gadaffi has been to the 1980s – the Third World leader whom the West loves to hate. Amin was funnier. He was also a vicious tyrant who killed his Ugandan opponents, expelled the Asians and made war on Tanzania, leading to his downfall. A trusted army chief when he toppled Milton Obote in 1971, his accession was initially welcomed by Britain. The adoption of an anti-British stance won him friends in the Organization of African Unity (OAU), which he chaired in 1975. But he did not appear to have any coherent ideology – not even sharing the OAU's often utopian pan-Africanism. His absurdly inflated ego – he made himself a field marshal and claimed he was heir to the throne of Scotland – plus an eye for the gallery, meant that many did not take him seriously. He was a rugby enthusiast and held the title of Ugandan heavy-weight boxing champion for nine years. Amin fled in 1979 to Gadaffi's Libya, and later to Saudi Arabia, after the Tanzanian army invaded Uganda. Today he waits in the wings, an obscene footnote to history, quietly preparing to return in triumph to his former domain.

AMM formed 1965

♦ BRITISH EXPERIMENTAL MUSIC GROUP

AMM's extraordinary mesmeric drone-improvisations prefigure a whole marginal genre of music – the 'Industrial Noise' branch of New Age. Although they share with New Age music-makers a concern for collectivity, psycho-acoustics and sound without event, they are, in fact, a more isolated grouping with an actively provocative edge to their playing. Coming out of 1960s British experimental music – with its roots in Free Jazz, psychedelia and the ideas of ☛John Cage – they aim for music to be a source of hypnotic fascination. Radical socialist composer Cornelius Cardew was an important member until his death in 1981. Since then they have continued to play, at rare intervals, and to win unexpected converts to their method. The questions they raise – about human responses to abstract sound – are no more answered by their own politics than anyone else's. As they say, 'Ultimately, AMM will fail. There may be rare moments when we, or others, sense a kind of success, but there can never be "ultimate" success.'

Laurie Anderson born 1947

& AMERICAN MULTI-MEDIA ARTIST

Probably the most successful multi-media performance artist of all, Anderson's entry into the pop mainstream – with the freak hit 'O Superman' in 1980 – appeared to coincide with a move towards a milder, more saleable version of her multi-media celebrations of America. In fact, her smiling face, her spikey hair style and her gently cooing half-singing have never been particularly unpalatable, and the attitudes she has adopted towards her single, vast subject have always been somewhat ambivalent. The only confrontational aspect of her *United States* (1983) was its length (eight hours), with more criticism being read into it than was ever there in the first place. Apart from being one of the few people to invent a new musical instrument (she put tapeheads on a violin and strung the bow with stretches of recorded spool-tape), her saving grace is that she is genuinely funny – coolly and lightly – which, coupled with her popularity, makes it easy to underestimate her intelligence and her capacity for exact observation. She reaches audiences that performance art and its 1960s ancestor 'The Happening' always wanted and never attained.

Lindsay Anderson born 1923

▲ BRITISH FILM DIRECTOR

Although he is enamoured of the lesser works of John Ford, Anderson's films are as remote from traditional Hollywood as ☛Stanley Kubrick is from Michael Winner. His early documentaries revealed a concern to integrate social issues into cinema, but his resistance to narrative drive or compassionate characterization often renders his work somewhat antiseptic. Outside his commercially disastrous début feature, *This Sporting Life* (1963), the protagonists are often ciphers, as in his 'State of the Nation' trilogy, in which Malcolm McDowell plays a recurring Everyman: rebelling against social constraints in *If . . .* (1968) by opening fire on the parents and old boys gathered at a school speech day; an emotionally blank coffee salesman in *O Lucky Man!* (1973); and in *Britannia Hospital* (1982), a reporter assuming different roles to get his story. His most recent film, *The Whales of August* (1987), is a melancholy performance piece, suggesting less a fresh direction than a new willingness to compromise and tone down his own brand of anarchy.

Carl André born 1935

❞ AMERICAN SULPTOR

The objects – fire bricks and metal squares – which André arranges in cubic or rectangular forms, used to be part of his daily grind when he worked as a brakeman and conductor on freight trains. This may be why his work conveys more emotional content than that of such rival minimalists as ☛Sol LeWitt, ☛Don Judd or Dan Flavin. He turned (New York) art galleries into vast ambient spaces with 'things' on the floor (he does not approve of height), and he is one of the few modern sculptors known to the wider British public – people travel for miles to visit London's Tate Gallery and laugh at his work – achieving this by aggressive self-promotion and such catchy declarations as 'Art is what we do. Culture is what is done to us.' The bricks are not typical, and his best work achieves a kind of grandeur. Artistic controversy was crowded out by more sinister events in 1985, when his wife of eight months, Cuban artist Ana Mendieta, died after falling out of a window on the 34th floor: André was tried for her murder and acquitted.

Maya Angelou

(Marguerite Johnson) born 1928

AMERICAN WRITER

Angelou's lyrical autobiographies have developed from a straightforward account of a black woman's growth 'from being ignorant of being ignorant to being aware' in *I Know Why the Caged Bird Sings* (1970) to a wider telling of what American society is and has been. Opening in the simplest confessional mode (Angelou as a teenage madame in a whorehouse), her confidence and understanding of what she can make of her life's tale has deepened as she sees more, and as wounds and rejections begin to organize themselves into patterns. The black woman, hitherto silent, learns to speak in a voice – perhaps halting at first – that starts to take pride in its intelligence and its ability to speak, first for others but finally for all. Angelou, working at the level of the archetype, allows her characters to become focal points for a more collective consciousness – articulate black women recognizing and seizing the right to define themselves.

Kenneth Anger born 1929

AMERICAN UNDERGROUND FILM-MAKER

A former child actor, Anger went on to become one of the most influential figures of US avant-garde film, combining in his work the influences of 'magickian' Aleister Crowley and Jean Cocteau with symbolism drawn from mythology, astronomy, alchemy and the iconograpy of American popular culture – movie stars, comic books, etc. *Fireworks* (1947), which he made when he was just 17, is a homoerotic fantasy submerged in dream imagery: a penis explodes into a firework display, a man waves his plaster hand. He anticipated the pop video with *Scorpio Rising* (1962-3), playing a ritualistic soundtrack against violent, homoerotic images of bikers. Shortly thereafter, Anger decided to retire, placing an advert in the *Village Voice*: 'In Memoriam. Kenneth Anger 1947-1967.' Today he is probably best remembered for his book, *Hollywood Babylon* (1975), an anthology of scandals involving Hollywood stars.

Michelangelo Antonioni born 1912

ITALIAN FILM DIRECTOR

Antonioni's films are deeply introspective and concerned with questions of how we see ourselves, how we see others and how others see us. The attention of critics was first drawn to a trilogy of films about restless women and their pathetic men – *L'Avventura* (1960), *La Notte* (1961), *L'Eclisse* (1962). *Blow Up* (1966), the elliptical tale of a photographer who may, or may not, have photographed a murder, moved Antonioni into the nonconformist mainstream. The film's mysteries stay unresolved, but its shadows of doubt are enough to destroy the fragile pop-culture world of its uncommitted hero. The follow-up, *Zabriskie Point* (1969), was a self-conscious embarrassment (and led to his being charged in the US with transporting females across the state line for immoral purposes), but *The Passenger* (1975) – in which a reporter assumes the identity of a dead man, only gradually to take over his memory and become him, or realize that perhaps he was the dead man all along – offered enough food for thought to make up for its lack of entertainment value. Antonioni's protagonists create images of the world – photographs, poetry, films, architecture – but in their attempts to explain and understand their lives, they seem to be wasting them. To the charge that his films are, like his characters, overly intellectual, Antonioni retorts that they come neither from his head nor from his heart, but from his stomach.

Kenneth Appel born 1932

O AMERICAN MATHEMATICIAN

Wolfgang Haken born 1928

O GERMAN-AMERICAN MATHEMATICIAN

In 1976, Appel and Haken presented a proof of the 'Four Colour theorem', which proposes that any map on a plane surface could be tinted with just four colours in such a way that no two adjacent regions would be coloured the same. This was a remarkable result, not just because it had taken a long time to resolve (first formulated in 1856, it had become famous as an unproven conjecture), but because it was the first significant mathematical theorem whose proof relied on the speed of a computer as it ran through thousands of essentially different configurations (a task that a human would take hundreds of years to perform). The result remains controversial insofar as it challenges accepted philosophical judgements about what constitutes a proof. The classical proof was repeatable – sceptics could take a piece of paper and work it out for themselves. An independent check of Appel and Haken's proof can only involve running another program on another machine. In a crucial sense, the length of the calculation is beyond human capacity.

Yasir Arafat born 1929

PALESTINIAN POLITICAL LEADER

Chairman of the Palestine Liberation Organization (PLO) since 1969, Arafat is one of the more remarkable political figures of our time. He does not smoke. He is 'married' to his movement. He consumes gallons of mint tea. He chooses to dress like a cartoon of the radical nationalist Arab. As a civil engineer in the Gulf during the early 1960s, he ran four cars and lived the life of a playboy. Now he is a deadly serious figure who appears, increasingly, to be able to turn his high visibility to advantage – carrying on the extraordinary balancing act that appears to hold together a disparate, dispersed, dispossessed would-be nation of factions through all disagreements over ends and means, violent and non-violent. War with Hussein's Jordan, the demand for exclusive recognition of the PLO by the UN as the Palestinian people's representative, the presence in Lebanon and the unexpected diplomatic volte-face at the end of 1988, when he renounced the PLO's traditional aim of destroying Israel, have all been reactive responses to the situation at hand and not apparently linked to tightly focused political ends, but effective beyond anyone's expectations 20 years ago. (But Arafat's refusal to dissociate the PLO from Saddam Hussein's invasion of Kuwait in the summer of 1990 may have damaged support for the Palestinian cause.) The PLO is not a one-man show and Arafat has been forced to perform another balancing act between the demands of world opinion and the passions of his revolutionary factions. But the verdict on the PLO's strategy over two decades, largely determined by Arafat's decisions, must be that it has been coloured by the self-dramatizations of a national movement in its infancy.

Diane Arbus

(Diane Nemerov) 1923-71

† AMERICAN PHOTOGRAPHER

▲ Whether the people that Arbus photographed were genuinely odd – a human pin cushion, an albino sword-swallower – or just ordinary – middle-class women dripping with jewels – she peeled away the image that her sitters wanted to convey, revealing the humanity and horror beneath. Everyone who came within range of her camera was shown as damaged, resulting in a succession of unhappy stares aimed at questioning our ideas of normality. The occasional image that stands out from the others, based on a genuinely fresh observation of the strange world through which Arbus wandered, suggests the constraints of her world view.

Hannah Arendt

1906-75

❀ GERMAN-AMERICAN POLITICAL THINKER

A Jewish refugee from Germany, who left for Paris, then America, after Hitler came to power, Arendt made a striking impact on the world of political ideas, despite a career of only a dozen years (her last) as an academic in New York. Like other German-Jewish exiles in America, she was deeply committed to the 'life of the mind'. Erudite (she had been a favoured pupil of Heidegger) but never solely a scholar, her work was marked by insight and vision, although she was sometimes weak on disciplined analysis. Sociological themes – alienation, atomization – are central to her grasp of humanity's current situation, as she drew analogies between the Nazi and Communist terror systems and between the French and American revolutions. But it was her account in *The New Yorker* of Eichmann's trial by the Israelis in 1961, more than any other piece of work, that made her name. She saw the camp commandant as a bureaucrat in a moral vacuum – 'the banality of evil' – and not as a demon, and claimed that Europe's Jews contributed to their own fate. This thesis deeply angered US Jewry, but appeals to those intellectuals who see the Nazi holocaust as the work of an uncontrollable machine.

Dario Argento

born 1943

ITALIAN FILM-MAKER

Argento's strident deployment of shock and his deft editing put him firmly in the pantheon of Italian horror directors of the 1960s and 1970s, alongside Mario Bava , Lucio Fulci and Riccardo Freda. Intent upon provoking fear in the audience, Argento supervises the writing, directing and frequently the music for all his movies – the last generally a jarring, cacophonic rock orchestration. Although his early work – graphic and clever thrillers such as *The Bird with the Crystal Plumage* (1968) – secured him a reputation as a competent scare-merchant, Argento's own myopic world view and opulent visual tableaux (very often no more than a supremely adroit, disturbing succession of set-pieces) began to suggest that he was a true *auteur*, especially with *Suspiria* (1975), which shares themes with all his subsequent movies: a central figure is threatened by an unseen person or force, usually from some such conventional location as Hell.

Giorgio Armani born 1935

$ ITALIAN FASHION DESIGNER, BUSINESS EXECUTIVE

One of the new breed of fashion heroes, Armani has evolved a skill in cutting cloth into a genius for marketing his name. Formerly a medical student, he set up on his own as a designer in 1975 and now runs a corporation with a turnover in excess of $350 million. A celebrity who rides in a bullet-proof car, his white cropped hair and casual clothes deliberately convey the aura of someone who is cleaner than clean. Armani's style consists of perfect, fluid, simplistic tailoring, and unlike many of today's designers, he gives his personal attention to each of the designs that emerge from his company – not only clothes, but also umbrellas, suitcases and suchlike. Others use his name illegally in a desperate attempt to add a certain cachet to their mass-produced wares from sweatshops in the Far East.

Neil Armstrong born 1930

AMERICAN ASTRONAUT

On 21 July 1969, former fighter pilot Neil Armstrong took his famous 'one small step' and became the first human being to set foot on the moon (although many Scientologists and the Flat Earth Society dispute his claim). It had been his success in executing the first manual space-docking procedure in 1966, together with his all-American looks, that had led to his being chosen for the Apollo 11 mission. When its lunar module, the Eagle, landed on the moon three years later – narrowly avoiding a boulder-filled crater – hundreds of millions of people watched on television sets all over the world. Armstrong and fellow astronaut Buzz Aldrin cavorted about the moon's dusty surface, collecting samples, and took hundreds of photos just like any American tourists. Having spent fewer than 24 hours on the moon (at a cost of several hundred million dollars), the two astronauts returned to the command module where they rejoined the unfortunate Michael Collins , who had missed all the fun, and set off on their return journey. Although ☛President Nixon fatuously spoke of 'the greatest week in history since the Creation', and many compared the astronauts to great explorers of the past, the moon landings were, above all, triumphs of technology and planning, and also represented an attempt to assert national virility at a time when US soldiers were making no headway in the jungles of Vietnam. Armstrong was involved in some later projects, and became director of numerous companies, but he did not evade the depression that affected many other astronauts – why wish for the earth when you've had the moon?

We're required to do these things, just as salmon swim upstream.

Neil Armstrong

Eve Arnold born 1913

AMERICAN PHOTOGRAPHER

Establishing her photographic approach while covering fashion shows held in Harlem's bars, churches and abandoned cinemas as part of a class assignment for ☛Alexey Brodovitch, Arnold has mediated ever since between Hollywood glamour and the hardships endured at society's lower strata. Working in the US during the 1950s, her portraits of such glitterati as Marlene Dietrich, ☛Marilyn Monroe and Joan Crawford emphasized their sensitivity over the glamorous veneer (she famously photographed ☛Andy Warhol sitting on a toilet and lifting weights), while her coverage of incipient civil unrest – the Black Muslims or the training facilities for civil rights activists – exposed inner resilience rather than the effects of oppression. Her light touch invites the viewer to empathize with the characters she photographs rather than summoning anger, pity or envy. She moved to the UK in the early 1960s, where she produced photo-essays of secluded women, including the Brides of Christ, a group of Franciscan nuns in Godalming, and Muslim women living *Behind the Veil* (1973), about whom she also made a film. The impact of *The Unretouched Woman* (1976), for which Arnold drew on 25 years' work, comes from its contrasts – Britain's queen faces a nursing mother across the page; Lady Spencer Churchill is set in opposition to a nomad woman.

Raymond Aron 1905-83

FRENCH POLITICAL THINKER

Aron spoke, as a French sociologist and political writer, from the centre-right. (The labelling still helps, even though Aron himself was hostile to any superficial mapping of 'left' and 'right'.) His comments gain conviction from the roles he played in the major events of his time, as a columnist on *Le Figaro* and a participant in the French Resistance. Aron, a mix of Gallic logic and Jewish objectivity, was detached enough from the mores and fashions of his own society to develop accounts of world trends that were later shown to be extremely perceptive – thus, his epigram on the Cold War, 'Peace is impossible, war is improbable.' A political independent, he called for an end to French control of Algeria and fiercely attacked academic 'cowards' in 1968, resigning from his university chair. His guiding principle – loyalty to the ideals of Western civilization – inspired his attacks on ☛Sartre for failing to understand the motivations of Stalinist Russia, and his defence of the United States' role in NATO . His reputation as a writer rests on his lucid essays about the fathers of sociology and the non-technical part he played in strategic studies, as he charted the shift in the nuclear situation from balance of power to balance of terror.

Art Ensemble of Chicago

formed 1969

AMERICAN EXPERIMENTAL MUSIC GROUP

The AACM (Association for the Advancement of Creative Musicians) was started in the early 1960s as a community music project that would dedicate itself to exploring the futures and pasts of great black music. The Art Ensemble was its popular front – theatrical, experimental and, for the first 15 or so years of its existence, wildly innovative. All five players – Joseph Jarman, Roscoe Mitchell, Lester Bowie, Malachi Magostus Favours and Famadou Don Moye – are accomplished multi-instrumentalists, composers and comedians. Mitchell's influence, in particular, led to their extended play with sounds in silence and 'little instruments' (bells, gongs and whistles). All of their records feature surprise, although they rarely now break ground in the way they did in the late 1960s with *People in Sorrow*, *Reese and the Smooth Ones* or *Message to Our Folks*. Their shows, for which they still don elaborate quasi-tribal face paint, are now more about fun than revolution, but a touch of Dada improvisation still obtains.

John Ashbery born 1927

& AMERICAN POET

Ashbery's knowledge of French literature (he lived in France for ten years from 1955) and interest in fine art are reflected in his poems, which have a distinctive sophistication that can be labelled 'post-modern'. Early collections, such as *Some Trees* (1956) and *The Tennis Court Oath* (1962), experiment with traditional poetic forms and fragmented, fantastic narratives, but the wit and lyricism in his poetry compensate for all the surface difficulties it sometimes presents, and subsequent collections have extended Ashbery's range to embrace great humour and a meditative poignancy. He is also one of the most compelling readers of poetry that you might hear.

Laura Ashley

(Laura Mountney) 1926-85

⇔BRITISH DESIGNER AND BUSINESS WOMAN

Ever since the south-east of England became a tangled network of housing estates, office blocks and intensively farmed agricultural land, the belief of the English that they are essentially a rural people – living in thatched cottages, keeping chickens and milking cows – has been available for commercial exploitation. Laura Ashley started off with rustic-style table mats and tea towels, but it was the clothes she produced in the 1970s that turned the small factory she set up in Carno, a small village in mid-Wales – with printing technology and business strategy developed by husband Bernard – into the centre of an international business empire. While Laura Ashley garments stood out rather oddly against an urban backcloth, the long dresses with flowery patterns and high necks were welcomed by some as an antidote to the pastiches of pre-war Continental styles that were then popular – although concurrently mocked for their retro-rural associations. The company went public shortly after Laura's death, and shops bearing her name now sell home furnishings and smocks for urban milk-maids across Europe and the US. Its seven factories along the Welsh borders were closed in mid-1990 as manufacture was shifted to the Far East, marking Bernard Ashley's final break from his wife's idealism.

Isaac Asimov 1920-92

■ RUSSIAN-AMERICAN SF AND SCIENCE WRITER

Perhaps the best-known SF writer of all, Asimov developed his hard-science style and his subjects through discussions with John W. Campbell at *Astounding* magazine during the form's Golden Age, then stuck to them for some 50 years. His *Foundation* novels are built round a naïve version of social determinism, transplanted to a (rather dull) trans-galactic community. His *I, Robot* series introduced his famous Three Laws of Robotics (the first of which states that 'A robot may not injure a human being or, through inaction, allow a human being to come to harm'), and became notorious for the strangely mechanical dialogue from its all-too-robotic human characters. Asimov is readable, well-meaning and easy to mock: he never contributed any stories to ☛ Harlan Ellison's *Dangerous Visions* collections because he felt his talent, suited to the stolid 1950s, would no longer pass muster in the 1960s, 'and I didn't want to prove it.' A one-time professor of biochemistry, he was also famous for his substantial contribution to the popularization of science (most of his 300-plus books are nonfiction): his faith in the potential of technology to bring order to society was never shaken.

Clement Attlee 1883-1967

■ BRITISH POLITICIAN

Attlee was Britain's first Labour prime minister with a clear majority of his own, winning nearly 200 seats in the 1945 election. He was a 'quiet revolutionary', who puffed his pipe and gave wily, terse replies at press briefings between glances at the crossword or the cricket scores in *The Times*. He gave freedom to India, took major industries such as coal, gas and railways into public ownership and introduced the National Health Service. A conventional figure from a professional middle-class family, he was conformist in style, radical in views. He was a traditionalist who led from 'left of centre' and a leader who got his way in a Cabinet of stronger personalities by his tight grip on common sense, brisk approach to the Cabinet agenda and strong air of integrity. He had entered politics through work for a public school slum-mission, Toynbee Hall, in the East End and was soon caught up in the fight for better social conditions. Social issues remained his priority, not economics or foreign policy, where he was a realist and pragmatist. He gave the traditional English virtues of fair play and efficiency a socialist slant.

Margaret Atwood born 1939

▲ CANADIAN NOVELIST, POET

Atwood's reputation was built with novels that portray strong, clever and independent women in the throes of some sort of crisis along the road to liberation from their men. She is also a poet, and the quality of her narratives derives from the intensity with which they explore the inner worlds of her characters. The vision is so firmly rooted in one woman's consciousness that the rest of the world seems to exist only as some mental projection. What makes Atwood special is the way she works outwards from this subjective space – her womanhood, her Canadian roots – to a broader perspective, taking in the whole of a world where men and women are in the business of tormenting each other. *The Handmaid's Tale* (1986), her most ambitious novel to date, depicts a society that has been organized like a nightmarish girls' school after a series of nuclear accidents and other environmental disasters have rendered most women infertile.

J(ohn) L(angshaw) Austin 1911-60

BRITISH PHILOSOPHER

The analysis of language, which Austin helped to establish as the main current of Oxford thought, has helped to render British philosophy largely irrelevant to a broad public, while Continental philosophers, willing to take on the 'big' issues and develop complicated metaphysical systems, have been able to hold a position at the centre of intellectual discourse. But Austin's insight – that much of what passes for disagreement about fundamentals is, in fact, only a reflection of the way people use words in subtly different ways – is a valuable antidote to sloppy thinking. He thought that if one could define words, phrases and metaphors with due attention to all their possible gradations of meaning, many of the traditional problems of philosophy would just disappear. The question of free will, for example, is seen in a different light if one recognizes that some actions are performed carelessly, inadvertently, absent-mindedly or aimlessly. He is said to have been a brilliant teacher and, while his analytical mind may have terrified some into silence, his influence on those such as ☛ Isaiah Berlin , who 'rebelled' against his precepts, should not be underestimated.

Richard Avedon born 1923

✎ AMERICAN PHOTOGRAPHER

It was as the boy wonder of fashion photography in the late 1940s that Avedon made his reputation, with pictures of fresh young girls caught climbing from taxis, visiting night-clubs or simply jumping over a puddle and laughing. Then, just when everyone else seemed to be imitating his approach, he abandoned the outdoors for the studio again, pleading that, in a world of 'Hiltons, airports, supermarkets and television', the outside world was irrelevant. His models, however, lost none of their exuberance – running, jumping and giggling against the white backgrounds and harsh light that became Avedon's hallmark. He also works as a portraitist, placing cultural superstars and political power-dealers in the same white-enshrouded environment. Although for two decades, glamour photography has fed off his innovations, an Avedon picture could never be mistaken for the work of any other, and the large prints he produces, probing the finest expressive details of hair and skin, bring out strong tensions in his subjects. A series of harsh photographs showing his father's face as the life drained away achieves an intensity that hovers between elegance and cruelty.

Tex Avery
(Frederick Avery) 1907-80

AMERICAN ANIMATOR

♦ A director of cartoon shorts in the 1940s and early 1950s, Avery was present at the birth of Bugs Bunny , but can only actually claim to have fathered the monumentally deadpan Droopy and the strikingly unlovable Screwy Squirrel – one-gag toon-stars in a mayhem of archetypes, not-so-sly puns, innuendo and unrestrained sexual frenzy. First at Warner Bros, later at MGM, Avery dispensed with the Disney tradition of moving drawings as cute homilies and translated the pyrotechnic slapstick of the silent comedies into funny and/or nightmarish surrealism, which was marshalled round shattered expectations, precision storyboarding and split-second timing. Eventually, when the short cartoon became an unnecessary expense to the major studios, he went into commercials. The best of today's adverts carry a shadow of his daftness.

A(lfred) J(ules) Ayer 1910-89

BRITISH PHILOSOPHER

Ayer never lost confidence in his belief that charlatanism (metaphysical, theological, ethical, political, etc.) could be evaded if only we all spoke correctly, grounding everything in the scientific fact of empirical verification; but he

Margaret Atwood

did abandon the argument that meaningful communication entailed testing every thought against the standards of mathematical logic. Making his name in 1936 with *Language, Truth and Logic* as the first proponent of logical positivism in the UK, he was, like his Viennese teachers, intensely suspicious of such recondite theorizing as Heidegger's *Being and Time* which he considered nonsense that led to Nazism. But by ruling out any potential challenge not expressed in common-sense language, he allowed his attitudes to degenerate into a hale-and-hearty, insular stubbornness, wherein anything he did not immediately grasp must be Continental, meaningless and wrong. He was not as dim as he sometimes pretended to be, and his hostility to florid expression and jargon was valuable – his pragmatically huffy lack of patience actually carried him close to positions taken by the far more abstruse ☛Derrida. But in an age when the common-sense treatment of politics and ethics has been distorted by British tabloid attitudes, it is clear that accessibility does not necessarily preclude emptiness.

Albert Ayler 1936-70

❍ AMERICAN JAZZ MUSICIAN

∀ ♦ Ayler's deliberately primitive group sound and the emotional intensity of his tenor saxophone marked the end of a particular line of development in Free Jazz, a movement that derived its power from the open-ended possibilities of unstructured improvisation. Ayler played as if the schooled traditions of bebop harmony had never even existed, and certain jazz critics, in particular ☛Leroi Jones (Amiri Baraka), read this as a reaffirmation of the spiritual roots of African American art. Ayler appeared to be reaching back towards a mythical dawn-of-jazz era of collective invention, when blues, folk and march-band styles first collided. Some rock critics, led by ☛Lester Bangs, used Ayler as an approval model to justify their pantheon of underground idiot visionaries, starting with ☛Iggy Pop and ending with punk (a connection less extraordinary if we recall that Ayler recorded on the ESP label alongside the Fugs, scabrously political rock-poets, and the Godz, long-forgotten ancestors of ☛ Sonic Youth). Ayler took music along a route where few dared to follow but, towards the end, seems himself to have shied away from its more terrible aspects. The totalized howling hells that he created are unlikely to be easy listening at any time in the near future.

B

Baader-Meinhof Gang

† **Andreas Baader** 1943-77
† **Ulrike Meinhof** 1934-76
† **Gudrun Ennslin** 1940-77

✚ WEST GERMAN TERRORISTS

Their Red Army Faction (RAF) aimed to bring down the 'West German Fascist state'. What they achieved was a climate of high-intensity surveillance where the police broke the law to the hysterical applause of a scared and cowed public. Their political positions were incoherent, but they closely resembled the terrorist groups that emerged from 1960s' social dissent in Japan and Italy, the two other defeated countries of WW2 (the tag 'Hitler's Children' was accepted by the RAF's supporters as well as their enemies) – which suggests that there was more to the phenomenon than bored rich kids with guns. Baader was a confirmed nonconformist: he had served minor jail terms before being drawn into quasi-political action. Meinhof, an intelligent woman of passionate Christian beliefs, had previously been associated with the Social Democrats. Ennslin, the most vicious of the group's leaders, was the daughter of a Protestant pastor. They started off as pranksters, angry at the respect accorded to politicians who backed the war in Vietnam, but the savagery of the ☛Springer press and the assassination attempt on ☛Rudi Dutschke persuaded them that only armed struggle could purge Germany of its inherent Nazism. After amateur attempts at fire-bombings, they went to Jordan to study under Al-Fatah, a Palestinian revolutionary group, and returned with sufficient bomb-planting skills to sow hysteria throughout the German state. Arrested in 1972, they treated their trial with contempt, badmouthing the judges. Meinhof was found hanged in her cell in 1976; Ennslin and Baader died in 1977, in what was announced as a simultaneous suicide – it coincided with the storming of a plane at Mogadishu airport in Somalia, where passengers had been held hostage against the release of all three. The RAF still exists, though further arrests and deaths have reduced its effectiveness, and few Middle East arms and expertise suppliers would now bother to get involved. However, in 1989, as the Berlin Wall crumbled amidst almost universal jubilation, they staged a political assassination that served to remind the soon-to-be-reunited Germany that not all its underground tensions are resolved.

Francis Bacon 1909-92

▲ BRITISH PAINTER

☋ 'For Bacon,' ☛John Berger once remarked, 'the worst has already happened.' His paintings are nightmarish displays of horror – atrocities, butchered meat, caged animals, screaming mutants – and an attempt to come to terms with the brutality of the twentieth century. Distorted figures are confined in doorless rooms or cubes of glass. Suffering in silence, they writhe in pain – provoking sensations in the spectator similar to those that might be stirred by witnessing an execution or ritual torture. Bacon returned repeatedly to the same obsessions: portraits of martyred popes based on Velázquez's *Pope Innocent X*, the studies of movement by photographic pioneer Eadweard Muybridge, Van Gogh's self-portraits. Bacon painted these harrowing images in a refined style that belies the thorn beneath the flesh. He made a late start, painting his first significant work at the age of 40, and seemed to have more in common with contemporary film-makers than his artistic contemporaries – the baby in ☛David Lynch's Eraserhead could have erupted straight out of a Bacon painting.

Abstract painters have thought: why not throw out all illustration and all forms of recording and just give the effects of form and colour? It hasn't worked out, because it seems that the obsession with something in life that you want to record gives a much greater tension and a much greater excitement than when you've simply said you'll just go on in a fancy-free way and record the shapes and the colours.

Francis Bacon

Joan Baez born 1941

✓ AMERICAN FOLK SINGER

Baez made herself into a totem of student radicalism by singing simple ballads about a world without war and conflict. Launched into public recognition at the Newport Folk Festival of 1959, she soon made it clear that her ambitions extended beyond singing. Her participation in civil rights campaigns and anti-war demonstrations – she worked with ☛Martin Luther King and in 1972 endured ☛Nixon's bombardment of refugee camps in Cambodia – led to two terms in jail, and caused her albums to be banned from army bases all over the world. Permanently associated with the most simplistic politics of the 1960s, she has said that 'there'll always be a cause for people like myself'. Having set up Humanitas International to campaign against human rights abuses, she flies around the world (Poland, Northern Ireland, Spain, Ethiopia, Argentina, etc.) hectoring world leaders on their record. To mark her persistence in holding on to the spirit of the 1960s, she was invited to open the Live Aid concert in 1985.

Rudolf Bahro born 1935

✌ GERMAN POLITICAL ACTIVIST

For a while in the late 1970s, Bahro was East Germany's most celebrated dissident precisely because he seemed to be outflanking the Eastern bloc's most orthodox state in his commitment to fundamental Marxist analysis. When *The Alternative in Eastern Europe*, on which he had worked throughout the 1970s, began to circulate privately, he was immediately imprisoned. An international campaign for his release succeeded in gaining his expulsion to West Germany, where he became one of the most eloquent and influential exponents of Green politics as a 'third way' which could move beyond the shared East-West obsession with productivity, development and growth towards a philosophy of sustainable resources. A founder member of the Green Party, he became increasingly troublesome and critical over what he saw as its tendency to compromise for the sake of attaining realistic goals. His writing during this time became more spiritually oriented, apocalyptic and even mystical, so that his break with the party in 1985 surprised few and relieved many. Still a significant force in the deeper reaches of Green thought, he is probably too accustomed to thought as an astringently solitary quest ever to find an organization he can support without periodically having to take it to task.

David Bailey

born 1938

❞ BRITISH PHOTOGRAPHER

At a time when photo-journalism was exposing back-street slum-life in Britain, famine and war atrocities abroad, Bailey was becoming involved in fashion photography as a way of getting close to glamorous women and glamour itself. He bracketed the Swinging Sixties with two brittle, brilliantly empty celeb-collections: *David Bailey's Box of Pinups* (1965) and *Goodbye Baby and Amen; A Sarabande for the Sixties* (1969). These juxtaposed crooks and pop stars, millionaires and models to make a classic pop statement – everything that all these people do is of equal value, and so of no value. All that matters is that they are famous, and what makes them famous is the fact that their faces are collected here. Model Jean Shrimpton was Bailey's lover for a while; he took cover photos for Rolling Stones albums; he claimed to be classless (the then-fashionable codeword for working class and rich). In the 1980s, when first generation pop stars were looking for moves that would keep them in the public eye, and many of them hit on mass spectacles of global concern, Bailey gravitated towards the course he had spurned some 20 years before, taking photos of starving children in the Sudan for Live Aid, and shooting a cinema commercial for the Lynx anti-fur campaign that splattered blood over a fashion catwalk. His photography is hard-edged and cold-hearted – his cynicism and smiling self-promotion mark him out as a natural survivor.

Derek Bailey

born 1932

✍ BRITISH MUSICIAN

☞ Although Bailey's reputation as a guitarist has spread quietly around the world, he is still likely to be found playing to tiny audiences in insalubrious venues. A vital force behind all developments in European improvised music, he has expanded on ideas hinted at by ☛John Cage and ☛Ornette Coleman, creating the basis for a music that can exist entirely without pre-set forms or framework, abjuring repetition of any sort and making itself new from moment to moment. At first very hard work for the listener, his sound becomes addictive thanks to its bizarre chromatic austerity and dry wit. Bailey now has disciples and devotees everywhere – including such (relatively) bankable names as ☛John Zorn, Eugene Chadbourne and Bill Laswell – but this seems unlikely to change him. A significant original, his insane and stubborn resistance to all blandishments has not brought him much money, and every once in a while even his most ardent supporters lose patience with him, but he has changed the way (some) people think about music.

Any attempt to describe improvisation must be, in some respects a misrepresentation; for there is something central to the spirit of voluntary improvisation which is opposed to the aims and contradicts the idea of documentation.
Derek Bailey, Improvisation: Its Nature and Practice in Music

Mikhail Bakhtin 1895-1975

✓ SOVIET LITERARY THEORIST

From the 1920s onwards, Bakhtin refined essentially the same set of ideas, but late publication ensured that his work was fresh enough to attract Soviet intellectuals in the 1970s. They applied his thesis – that art should provide a forum for diverse points of view – to their calls for political pluralism; dissolving the single voice of absolutism into a babble of alternatives. South American novelists such as Jorge Amado and ☛Carlos Fuentes took from him the idea that comedy could have revolutionary implications, turning the world upside down as in a medieval carnival and knocking the veneer off political icons. For Bakhtin, the cultural form that best expresses the heterogeneity of human experience is the novel, providing an arena where characters, from various social contexts and historical times, can meet and challenge each other. He advocated combining styles, and was attracted to the eccentric, bizarre and profane elements of popular culture. A non-Marxist with Orthodox Christian beliefs, his life was largely uneventful; he was arrested in 1929, but a sentence that would have sent him to a labour camp for five years was commuted to internal exile on account of his bad health.

George Balanchine
(Georgi Balantchivadze) 1904-83

♦ SOVIET-AMERICAN CHOREOGRAPHER

One of the great ballet radicals, Balanchine had a huge influence on modern dance. Leaving the Soviet Union for Paris in 1924, he arrived in New York in 1933, where he linked up with critic Leonard Kirstein to establish the troupe of dancers that became the New York City Ballet. While working with Diaghilev in the 1920s, he had formed an association with Stravinsky, which later led to *Agon* (1957), an uncompromisingly abstract ballet considered by many to be the greatest dance work of the late twentieth century. Balanchine also influenced dance in subtler ways: clearing away fussy sets to highlight the dancer; wisely subjugating the tyranny of narrative to the power of shape; and freeing that shape from the orthodoxy of the traditional straight back and hips. His wit and choreographic brilliance were known to his company as the 'Balanchine double whammy', but the 'whammy' was bigger than that: Balanchine's alteration of conventional ballet tactics changed the way an audience *looks* at a dancer.

James Baldwin 1924-87

AMERICAN NOVELIST WHO SETTLED IN EUROPE

'I wanted to prevent myself from becoming merely a negro, or even merely a negro writer.' Baldwin, defiantly gay and coldly honest, was the black American who moulded a style that married Henry James with the cadences of a gospel preacher to argue that American blacks and whites were embarked on a similarly perilous marriage: their relationship had started in the deepest of evil, and would have to grow to love or fall back there. Baldwin was not treated well in the era of Black Power; he posed too many awkward questions and his rage had different modalities. His own rhetoric had given birth to a generation of apocalyptic ranters who turned his anger into something they could kill Dad with, and he was never quite as daring after ☛Eldridge Cleaver attacked him with the claim that intellectualism was the same as homosexuality and both were betrayals of black culture. He broke rules – the ambivalent sex-development of *Giovanni's Room* (1956), for example, includes no black characters – to make new ones. And he used what he thought of as his ugliness ('pop-eyes') as a way to intensify, explore and dissipate several levels of black self-hatred.

Lucille Ball 1911-89

AMERICAN TV COMEDIENNE

Ball became the most popular American television comedienne of all time as the scatterbrained bubble-head sitcom wife of *I Love Lucy* (1951-5). Costarring her husband, former bandleader Desi Arnaz , with whom she shared creative control, the programme was soon regular viewing for two-thirds of the nation's viewers. Its content seldom transcended slapstick, and the success it enjoyed was largely due to Ball's own idiosyncrasies: the Lucy character was never docile although her frequent attempts at reform were acceptable to an America that claimed to love the eccentric individual while actually embracing conformity. She was wholesome enough to represent American womanhood, and she confronted recalcitrant electrical goods and formidable department store managers with a zeal that helped make the sitcom as much an American institution as rock 'n' roll, McDonalds and the electric chair.

J(ames) G(raham) Ballard

▲ BRITISH NOVELIST born 1930

Ballard, the suburban poet of the high-rise and the flyover, has also become the poet of the psychology necessary to love such a world. His attainment of critical approval only arrived with the semi-autobiographical *Empire of the Sun* (1984), which was based on his childhood in a Japanese POW camp outside Shanghai. His dreamy, obsessive work turns around a tiny set of fascinations (empty swimming pools, the erotic car crash, floods, heat, men called Mallory), coupled with technical innovations, both clinical and surreal, that make him seem the least English of writers. On top of this, his pathological urbanity of tone is sometimes thoroughly disorientating. The grey lyricism of his deadening effects owes more to the French anti-novelists ☛Alain Robbe-Grillet and Michel Butor than to anything in English (even ☛Burroughs, an obviously valuable influence, is somewhat more at home with humour and humanity). Ballard was part of ☛Michael Moorcock's New Wave, but science fiction, much more settled these days, now disowns him.

Lester Bangs 1948 - 1982

AMERICAN WRITER ON MUSIC

Championing Cro-Magnon punk rock before it was either popular or profitable, Bangs developed a peculiar, addictive élitism fashioned round anti-élites and backwoods incompetents. This ran defiantly against the tide of the times – the early 1970s – when rock was being hurried into 'growing up' and useless respectability. He lived to see punk prevail over other values, but not long enough to watch it become an orthodoxy. He was an intense, verbose, wild critic, incapable of writing to length. He railed furiously at the idols who failed him, and none more so than Lou Reed , to whom he returned again and again. His reviews and profiles were subjective, impassioned, moralizing rants, but his aesthetic was acute and highly selective. He detested the middlebrow, or anything that sugar-coated the joys of noise and the dysfunctional stupidity that makes great rock great. He convinced many that intelligence was something you had to bring to music, not something you took out of it. An understanding of the politics and potential of 1960s Free Jazz gave his punk soapboxing an authority other back-to-basics ideologues never found,and a sense of continuity that took him beyond nihilism, without ever distancing him from the primitive, adolescent honesty of the music he knew was best.

Amiri Baraka

(Leroi Jones) born 1934

∀ AMERICAN POET, PLAYWRIGHT

✌ Black playwright and activist, Leroi Jones was the provocative political analyst who articulated in the 1960s the still-unbroken links between Free Jazz and Black Power. His writing has a rhythm that gels with the confusion and fury apparent in the playing of ☛Albert Ayler, ☛Ornette Coleman, ☛John Coltrane and others. Subsequent developments tend to suggest that Free Jazz was more a confluence than a movement: by the early 1970s, when Jones had taken the name Amiri Baraka, his writing already seemed to be pushing in a different direction from the universalist spiritualism of Coltrane's heirs. The tragedy of his later work is that although he's still an intelligent, dissident commentator, openness to other ideas and traditions has muffled his unique force. Whereas a collection such as *Blues People: Negro Music in White America* (1963) jammed an incisive new voice up before both hostile and receptive readers, the essays in the more recent *Daggers and Javelins* (1984) – strewn with invocations to take up, for society's salvation, 'Marxism-Leninism-Mao Tse Tung thought' – blur their own maturity. The younger Baraka would have recognized this endlessly reiterated phrase as unmusical intrusion, rather than the African-American chorus he assumes it to be.

Joseph Barbera *see* Hanna-Barbera

Christiaan Barnard

born 1922

SOUTH AFRICAN SURGEON

When Barnard, in 1986, provided endorsement for Glycel, a facial preparation said to provide a 'natural way to younger-looking skin' (but which chemical analysts proved to be a mix of distilled water and sheep's grease), he lost the last traces of the credibility acquired through performing the first human heart transplant. Evidence that he was as much showman as surgeon had been available from the early 1960s when he carried out an attention-grabbing operation to attach a second head to a dog. His transplanting the heart of a young car accident victim into the chest of Louis Washkansky in December 1967 anticipated a surgeon in New York by only three days, but it was Barnard who won the prize that came from being first. He embarked on a worldwide tour, made countless TV appearances and posed for cameras with popes, presidents and movie stars. Barnard went on to make his bid for eternal youth – having himself injected with various animal cells in the hope of restoring various bodily functions, and marrying a succession of women in their early twenties. He did, however, turn a face to reality in a book, *Good Life/Good Death* (1985), in which he argues that doctors are too concerned with preserving life at all costs, irrespective of quality.

Jean Barraqué 1928-73

☞FRENCH COMPOSER

Barraqué was one of the angry young composers, led by ☛Pierre Boulez, who had studied with ☛Messiaen and sought to shake up the post-war musical establishment. The serial music of Schoenberg was fundamental to his technique and, like Boulez, he despised the cult of personality, feeling that the new path for music lay in far-reaching logical developments of serialism. In the 1950s, he turned his attention to *musique concrète*, which used transformations of natural sound which were then composed on to gramophone records. His work took another turn in 1955 when he encountered Hermann Broch's *The Death of Virgil*, whose epic tone echoed what he sought to achieve through his own music. Using this text as a starting point, he planned a gigantic project to create a 'drama having neither actors nor action'. The planning took many years and, although three fragments appeared, the work remained unfinished at his death. An enigmatic loner, Barraqué once said that he detested daylight, the concert-going public (whom he called asses and imbeciles) and his own music. His serialism was said at the time to cause the distinction between dissonance and discord to collapse, a final step that Schoenberg had argued against, and which Boulez, locked into music as ultra-scientific sound exploration, was not interested in taking. However, what were extremes of noise some 20 years ago seem mild enough now, and the dissonance-discord distinction, central to the understanding of pre-war atonal classicism, no longer makes much sense.

Syd Barrett

(Roger Keith Barrett) born 1946

✍BRITISH ROCK MUSICIAN

⊸The archetypal cult figure, Syd Barrett's period of fame lasted about eight months – from the time Pink Floyd, the group he led, had their first hit single, to his quitting the group in March 1968, completely addled by LSD. Two years later, he recorded a pair of moderately successful solo albums, then disappeared into legend. Invariably referred to as either a 'genius' or a 'nutcase', his music tended towards the twee and the obscure, and thus had immense appeal to people looking for something wilfully difficult to listen to. The *aficionado* also revels in Barrett's mysterious status. Does he live with his mother in Cambridge? Is his mind completely ruined? Did he really walk in on a Pink Floyd session in 1975 – 'fat and profusely sweating' – to play on a song the group had written about him? Barrett remains gloriously mysterious to all but a few fans, themselves so mad as to make further investigation fruitless.

John Barry born 1933

BRITISH FILM COMPOSER

Barry is a paradox. Although one of the few film composers with a wide reputation, the cornerstone of his fame is a piece he did not write. His orchestration of the James Bond theme for *Dr No* (1962, credited to Monty Norman) led to his long association with the series, producing a string of upbeat jazz soundtracks, then lush instrumentals for the increasingly exotic locations. Quickly established as one of the top film composers of the 1960s, his melodies are both simple and innovative. The score for *The Lion in Winter* (1968) incorporates Latin lyrics, while the sex scenes in *Midnight Cowboy* (1969) were backed by Wild West rhythms. A more romantic quality became apparent with *Walkabout* (1970), *The Last Valley* (1970) and *Robin and Marian* (1976). Unfortunately, Barry has contributed much of his best work to such outright turkeys as *Hanover Street* (1979), *Raise the Titanic* (1980) and *Howard the Duck* (1986) – scores that will be listened to long after the films they enhanced have completely faded from memory.

Lynda Barry born 1956

AMERICAN CARTOONIST

A contemporary of the post-punk school of American cartoonists, which includes her close friends Matt Groening and ☛Gary Panter, Barry has reached and touched a wide audience with her nationally syndicated *Ernie Pook's Comeek* strip. She dramatizes the odd, enclosed world of a southern childhood somewhere between the beginning of affluence in the 1950s and the late 1960s, complete with the tiny pre-teen tragedies of family discord, friendship strategy and unattainable fashion ideals. Deeper unstated tensions, both racial and social, are narrated earnestly and uncomprehendingly by her kid-mouthpiece Arna Arneson. Perceptive and unsentimental, Barry has the same eye and ear for the weird strengths and endless strangeness of off-mainstreet America as her punkier confrères, although she avoids any hint of their modernist anomie, deliberately focusing on a moment in the unhip past. She's extended this same storytelling to novel form, with *The Good Times Are Killing Me* (1988), but the strip, with its deliberately childish line and scrubbed compactness, is far more powerful.

Roland Barthes 1915-80

FRENCH CULTURAL THEORIST

This singular, entertaining and infuriating critic is best remembered for converting half the intellectual world to structuralism , long after he himself had tired of its unwieldy semi-scientific methodology. He cruised critical positions and analytical methods with a witty exactness; a low boredom threshold always ensured that he was first in and first out. He is largely responsible for the dispatch of existentialism from French intellectual life and for its replacement by the free-thinking Gallic version of post-modernism, and thinkers as diverse as ☛Baudrillard, ☛Kristeva and ☛Derrida are in his debt (as much for his restlessly analytic tone as for any shared insight). His great bugbear was the concept of the 'natural': throughout his many books, he hunted down ways to end such an idea, whether it was to be found hidden in the intellectual baggage of bourgeois society, in the positions taken up by his fellow structuralists or in this or that Marxist attack. The early work is the most systematic; his later writing, through becoming more capriciously subjective, gains in power. A hard act to follow, his disciples in various countries offer pale copies of his intensely mannered ruminative writing style, and imprecise second-hand run-ons of his best observations. His opinions seem to reflect his own sexuality on and off the page – he recognized early on that any thought resting on ideas of 'authenticity' offered a deep threat to the homosexual. Without such a critical distancing from the concept of the natural, his aesthetic would probably have shrivelled long before the fateful laundry van spun round the corner – as it was, the sense that he had been knocked down with great work still to do was inescapable.

Georg Baselitz born 1938

∀ GERMAN ARTIST

It used to be the case that every catalogue featuring Baselitz's paintings contained an apology for the reversal of the image. It gradually became apparent that Baselitz intended them to be presented in this manner, having turned the world upside-down and his subjects head-over-heels. The aim was to direct the focus away from the subject itself, pointing up the discrepancy between art and reality. Although critics tend to dwell upon this inversion, Baselitz brings to his canvases a genuine sense of menace and fear, in the tradition of German Expressionism. There is an aggressive energy and urgency that subsumes the 'direction' of the painting. Though essentially a painter who must sacrifice reality to meet his own demands, Baselitz has since 1980 widened the scope of his output to take up both photography and sculpture. One critic has suggested that his pictures are intended as 'cave paintings for the end of the millenium'.

One is always very surprised when something is excavated from the earth and how modern it is.

Georg Baselitz

Jean-Michel Basquiat 1960-88

✣ AMERICAN ARTIST

∀ No protégé of ☛Andy Warhol is ever ✎ going to escape accusations of hype, however talented they may be. This is to underestimate canny Andy and, in this case, to miss the fact that Basquiat, no *naïf*, had sought out the partnership himself. When graffiti art erupted out of the subways into Manhattan's galleries, he was the (young, black, important) artist that the art world allowed to out-stay the novelty and enter its bizarre, hollow, monied domain, Basquiat having already won significant attention on the Mudd Club post-punk circuit and exhibited as 'Samo' at the influential 'New York New Wave' show. His slash-and-burn iconographic energy is three-year-old childish, a joke on its own primitivism. His raw scrawls, cartooned visual aids and playful techniques could have been distilled from 50 years of 'modern art', but seemed instead to short-circuit straight back to mythical Latin American styles and subjects. Irritated by the way he was being patronized and absorbed, he still played along until it was too late – preferring spectacular burnout, and ending, after Warhol's death, as a heroin addict and a misunderstood success. His own death occurred as he was about to leave New York for the Ivory Coast, in the hope that he could turn his life around.

Georges Bataille 1897-1962

& FRENCH SOCIAL CRITIC

Emerging from the fringes of surrealism, Bataille was a founder of short-lived magazines and 'groupuscules' who played the role of anti-Sartre in post-war Paris; when the existentialist mocked his addled mysticism, Bataille retorted by describing ☛Sartre as the 'sleekest' of all bourgeois literary 'parasites'. ☛Susan Sontag championed his early novel *The Story of the Eye* (1928) as revealing the aesthetic possibilities of pornography. For Bataille, evoking disgust was not just a surrealist shock tactic, it was the heart of his philosophy. He saw the extremes of horror and desire as experiences at the frontiers of consciousness that would open a way to the 'sacred', that which lies beyond existence, and argued in *The Accursed Share* (1948) that individuals should direct their excess energies into transgression. A permanent revolutionary, his scepticism about knowledge – he saw life as a condition of permanent ontological dissatisfaction in the face of ungraspable, unsatisfiable aspirations – establishes Bataille as the apostle of post-modernism.

Jean Baudrillard born 1929

& FRENCH CULTURAL THINKER

❞ Baudrillard argues that a new culture has emerged from the proliferation of new media, dominated not by objects or truth but by simulations. We live in a 'hyperreality', where a television newscast, for example, creates the news for the sole purpose of being able to narrate it. Baudrillard's arguments, never methodologically rigorous, have become increasingly polemical and hyperbolic. Individuals, he says, are no longer liberal citizens trying to increase their civil rights, nor Marxist proletarians engaged in class struggle; rather, they are consumers, vulnerable to the desires created by the media. The mass media only pretend to be processes of communication – in fact the traffic is all in one direction. The only way to fight back is to shut up and refuse participation. It is not really possible, as Baudrillard supposes, to extrapolate a representative view of the whole of society from a study of television advertisements, and by comparison with the related work of ☛Foucault or ☛Derrida, his methods are shaky. It is to be hoped that more rigorous thinkers will pursue the questions he has raised.

We are surrounded by an ecstasy of communication and that communication is sickening.

Jean Baudrillard

Pina Bausch born 1940

GERMAN CHOREOGRAPHER

Bausch fills her Tanztheater Wuppertal with the most extraordinary-looking performers and has pioneered the breakdown of the barriers between theatre, performance and dance. In *Kontakthof* (1978), a series of the sort of small gestures you might make to fill an embarrassing silence are built up into a dazzling display of self-consciousness, expressing the divide between the sexes through the different body languages used by men and women: Bausch's men straighten ties and pull down jackets, women adjust bra straps and check petticoats. She was not always so restrained, and the black humour of some of her early pieces effectively captured the dynamics of desire. Among the English companies to have adapted Bausch's ideas are Lumière and Son, Impact Theatre, DV8 and Extemporary Dance. In addition, Jan Fabré, in the epic (or epically tedious, depending on your viewpoint) *The Power of Theatrical Madness* (1986), clearly drew on her work.

Leo Baxendale born 1931

BRITISH CARTOONIST

Baxendale staked his claim to be the dominant creative figure in British post-war comic art when, in 1953, he introduced Minnie the Minx and The Bash Street Kids to the *Beano* – unsaccharine versions of an urban working-class kid's world in a format that comics have ruthlessly exploited (and exhausted) ever since. His ageless children were engaged in an everlasting war with all authority; for the first time, stories could and did end with Teacher's or Dad's discomfiture and ensuing benign comic reversals. As important were *Little Plum* and *The*

Three Bears, with which Baxendale began to tie together, to increasingly surreal effect, the blobby characterization, squelchy slapstick and peculiarly digressive sense of humour which became his trademarks. Other artists moved in and tamed his invention, while he moved on, leaving a trail of silly mayhem in various now defunct comics such as *Sweeny Toddler*, *Jonah*, *Grimly Feendish*, *Bad Penny* and *The Banana Bunch*. In the 1970s he moved into book sales, and eventually embarked on a major legal action against D. C. Thomson, the notorious Dundee-based publishers of the *Beano*, over the copyrights to his original groundbreaking strips. An out-of-court settlement was reached in 1987.

André Bazin 1918-58

FRENCH FILM THEORIST

Through the magazine, *Cahiers du Cinéma*, which he founded in 1950, Bazin shaped post-war film theory and enabled the likes of ☛Truffaut, ☛Godard and ☛Chabrol to develop the ideas which ensured that none of them ever became fully mainstream directors – and through them he influenced the New Wave film-makers who emerged in other countries during the 1960s. Bazin promoted a cinematic style that aimed at the direct recording of reality: it is just as well that he did not live to watch the gimmicky, fast-flash features now being produced by music video-trained directors. Around his admiration for the work of Jean Renoir, Bazin built a philosophy that valued long takes, deep focus, natural lighting and naturalistic acting over the expressionism of Fritz Lang or the montage editing of Sergei Eisenstein – although he could bend the rules sufficiently to find good things to say about ☛Orson Welles and Erich von Stroheim. Bazin is often associated with the *politique des auteurs*, which was really a promotional platform for the ambitious young turks he gathered as disciples. Observing that the 'genius' of Hollywood lay in a production system that could coax good films out of mediocre talents, he perceptively warned against unconstrained creativity. Suffering from ill health throughout his life, he ran a private bestiary in which he kept several crocodiles.

The Beatles 1960-70

John Lennon 1940-80
Paul McCartney born 1942
George Harrison born 1943
Ringo Starr (Richard Starkey) born 1946

BRITISH ROCK GROUP

Always stranger than their infinite biographers could acknowledge, the Beatles were a rock 'n' roll group rooted in depravity who became family pop entertainers; a group led by middle-class art students who came to epitomize cheerful working-class laddishness; and the only pop group to interest both ☛Harold Wilson and ☛Charles Manson. The Beatles were so big that, in the end, they represented anything you could think of – rebellion, domesticity, sex, innocence, art, commercialism. They wrote their own songs, had high production standards, revived the energy and sexiness of pop just when the solo teen idol had made it innocuous, and had a knack for initiating or taking on innovation. The Beatles, for better or worse, were responsible for the return of groups, the pre-eminence of the album over the single and the studio over the tour, the idea of rock stars as artists/writers/actors, and the subsequent elevation of pop into an 'adult' music. By simply having the ability to invest almost anything they did with melody and invention, they enabled pop music to continue when it was being battered by triple album instrumental concept operas. They survive in memory because, despite ☛Joe Orton's unmade movie screenplay which depicted them as incestuous quadruplets, the Beatles – through good marketing and their own personalities – always operated as individuals, dislocated parts of the Beatle image. Ringo Starr is a children's TV personality; George Harrison is a film financier and minor pop star; and Paul McCartney still maintains the 1963 Beatle image through his family entertainment tunes and films. John Lennon – in legend the uncomfortable Beatle, political, rebellious and rude – either achieved an inner peace or lay around all day taking drugs (it depends on whose account you read). The chance to see the group as anything but mirrors of the 1960s disappeared in 1980 when Lennon was shot.

Simone de Beauvoir *see* de Beauvoir, Simone

Samuel Beckett 1906-89

▲IRISH PLAYWRIGHT, NOVELIST, ☞SETTLED IN PARIS

✖ The citation accompanying his 1969 Nobel Prize for Literature stated: 'He has transmuted the destitution of modern man into his exaltation.' The only winner of that accolade to be listed in Wisden's *Cricketer's Almanac*, Beckett was a compulsive explorer of words and internal worlds. The people in his plays and novels, who inhabit some desolate spot between an unwillingness to end it all and a lack of desire to exist, live off memories whose retelling lights up the passing hours – several commentators have suggested he drew on the boredom and danger he endured while working for the French Resistance. The humour (and the anger) behind the absurdity only becomes fully apparent in performance: *Waiting for Godot*, first presented in 1952 in Paris (where Beckett lived from 1937), abandons conventional structure and plot development for its account of two tramps, indecisive and lacking in motivation, who suffer and wait hopefully for the help that will never come; in *Krapp's Last Tape* (1959), an old man listens without comprehension to the recordings he made as a young man. Beckett's reputation is international – *Endgame* (1957) has been translated into Eskimo and performed in a transparent perspex igloo. He was drawn to brevity: his last book *Stirrings Still* ran to little over 1500 words, and some indication of Beckett's status was indicated by the retail price of the first edition – a cool £1000.

Captain Beefheart

(Don Van Vleit) born 1941

∀ AMERICAN MUSICIAN, PAINTER

Some of Beefheart's stunts seem less impressive now than they did in the dippy 1960s, but his highly individual amalgam of swamp blues, Free Jazz and country soul remains unique. He's a loner-survivor, able to slip from nutcase Dada to deep blues-primitivism without the listener ever supposing they were not the same thing. *Troutmask Replica* is the 1969 double album that pushed his lustily abstract animism furthest upfront, but despite the presence of such legendary names as Zoot Horn Rollo and The

Samuel Beckett
Photo courtesy of Editions de Minuit

Mascara Snake, the band on that record are not a patch on the one he put together for his 1980 comeback, *Doc at the Radar Station* – musicians who had grown up with his 1960s music in their bones, and could make his alien rhythms and structures seem as natural as breathing. This must have been all he wanted and more, because he immediately gave up music for ever to concentrate on his painting.

Menachem Begin 1913-92

ISRAELI POLITICAL LEADER

Begin's role as political head of the Irgun Zvai Leumi guerrilla movement fighting against the British in Palestine was often seen as the explanation for his later intransigent Israeli nationalism. The true picture is more complex. Unlike many other Israeli leaders, he went through the experience of waiting for Hitler in pre-war Europe (most of the rest were born in Israel or arrived much earlier), and clearly his personal response to the Holocaust played a vital part in his evolution. So did nearly 30 years out in the cold as Israeli opposition leader, against the pioneering (socialist) establishment from which other leaders mostly hailed. That gave him a kinship, in his own mind as in theirs, with those other outsiders, the Oriental Jewish immigrants of the late 1940s and early 1950s. But the key may have been his background as a lawyer. Histrionic advocacy significantly underlined the rhetoric used to establish a special rapport with Israeli audiences: Begin, like Trotsky, was defined by his oratory. Revisionist Zionism – the view that Jews only survive, in the end, by fighting – appealed to a tough, trained advocate who singlemindedly pursued the claims to justice of his client, the Israeli people. The legal background also explains his *volte-face* over Sinai; as an advocate, he knew when to withdraw, gracefully, under pressure. However, he is likely to be remembered for Israel's 1982 invasion of the Lebanon – a disastrous mistake from which both countries have yet to recover. In the wake of the furore that followed, abroad and at home, Begin's oratory faltered and he resigned his leadership of the Likud Party. Despite the histrionics, he always had the dignity and bearing of a professional bourgeois from Warsaw; thus his refusal to appear publicly, after his retirement, when he suffered from a disfiguring skin problem.

Daniel Bell born 1919

AMERICAN SOCIOLOGIST

American sociologists generally love static academic models, but Bell, a former journalist, has been caught up in the passions and traumas of his era as he predicts changes in Western society. His overall predictions may be wrong, but they are full of particular insights. His *End of Ideology* (1960) anticipated an end to the war between basic political ideas as the debate on issues was increasingly carried out within a context of shared basic values – the mixed economy, the welfare state. His next major book, *The Coming of Post-Industrial Society* (1973), looked at the problems that arose when experts came to enjoy a monopoly of knowledge, as goods manufacture gave way to data services. His flair for titles was also evident in his 1976 book *Cultural Contradictions of Capitalism*. This argued that free economies only work through disciplined patterns of prudence, planning and self-denial, but these virtues are dissolved by the hedonism that economic success excites. His conclusion – that hyper-inflation is always built into capitalist growth – is a dubious one. The provocative pessimist had failed to see the mid-1970s in context.

Frank Bellamy 1917-76

BRITISH COMIC ARTIST

In the 1950s, the Reverend Marcus Morris launched the *Eagle* in an attempt to wean British youth off a torrent of weird, sleazy, violent American comics. *Eagle* was staid, over-wholesome and preoccupied with promoting worthy hobbies, but it also had Dan Dare (and even though Dare was, at this stage, also staid and over-wholesome, he quickly entered the popular subconscious). Bellamy, who had worked as an independent illustrator (for *Mickey Mouse Weekly*, among other things) until he joined *Eagle* in 1956, had already proved himself innovative and dynamic in the way he tackled page layout, using dramatically cinematic techniques and expert handling of colour to enhance stories (which he never wrote himself). In 1960, he was asked to take over Dare from fellow-*Eagle* artist Frank Hampson, and his redesign pushed it up into a heaven of 1960s SF-fantasy iconography, influencing the course that DC and Marvel would take, under ☛Stan Lee, for two decades. He worked on other strips, mostly historical and historical fantasy, as well as strip-versions of *Thunderbirds* (in *TV 21* magazine) and the long-running (and unreadable) Nietzschian fantasy *Garth* (in the *Daily Mirror*).

Saul Bellow born 1915

⇔CANADIAN-AMERICAN NOVELIST

The characters in Bellow's novels are city dwellers pining for the old values and railing against the new even while being sucked into the compelling vortex of vigour and violence that makes up life in the modern metropolis. In synopsis, the books may sound sour, but they are enlivened by Bellow's intellectual sharpness, feel for low life, taste for vibrant language and the energy with which he conveys a general sense of crisis. Born in Canada and brought up in Chicago, he came to international prominence with a wave of Jewish intellectuals in the late 1950s and early 1960s. He locates the angst of the twentieth-century American in the dissolution of a clear sense of personal identity, a condition deriving from the takeover of the communal realm by the television set, bureaucrats and sociologically trained experts. At times elegiac, suggesting that the new barbarians are plunging us into a 'moronic inferno', the tone of his books is more often one of comic perplexity, as when he describes the efforts made by the hero of *Mr Sammler's Planet* (1970) to dodge nymphomaniacs, pickpockets, exhibitionists, violent madmen and schizophrenics on the streets of New York, or the realization of a character in *Humboldt's Gift* (1975) that his sophisticated delicacy carries no weight against the tough machismo of his gaolers. Bellow's achievement has been to turn the cosmopolitan *schlemiel* into a universal figure. He won the Nobel prize for literature in 1975.

When a Zulu writes a great novel I'll read it.

Saul Bellow

Alan Bennett born 1934

BRITISH FILM, TV, THEATRE WRITER, ACTOR

Bennett's greatest talent is an ability simultaneously to mock and mourn the past. The sermons he delivered in *Beyond the Fringe* ('Life is like a tin of sardines, I often think. . .') in the early 1960s, his first major play *Forty Years On* (1969) and his numerous televised attacks on the brutish mundanity of daily existence all contain an admiration for real or fictional pasts, whether they be more refined ways of serving tea or the great Edwardian country houses. Bennett's ear for a certain kind of surrealistic/inane conversation is superb, while he maintains a unique ability to put complete drama into monologue. Of late, his affection for the past has crystallized into a disdain for the current state of the UK, resulting in sympathetic portrayals of the spies Anthony Blunt and Guy Burgess. The latter seems to speak for Bennett in *An Englishman Abroad* (1983) when he says, 'I can say I love London, I can say I love England, I can't say I love my country because I don't know what it means.'

David Ben-Gurion 1886-1973

ISRAELI POLITICAL LEADER

A socialist Zionist who helped fix the now-tarnished left-progressive image of Israel, Ben-Gurion was premier for most of the period from the country's winning of independence in 1948 to his political exit in 1963. Having left Poland for Palestine in 1906, he formed a force to guard Jewish farming settlements and soon became the organizational strongman for the Zionists and the Jewish state, making the labour movement key to a local nexus of social and political institutions. In the 1950s, he attacked 'Anglo-Saxon Jews' who adopted Israel's fight but did not settle there. Right through his career, he had to handle tense situations that gave little room for manoeuvre. During the war against the British and after, he was caught up in a contest with right-wing terrorists for the hearts and minds of Palestine's Jews. As prime minister, he was always forced to rely on coalitions – his party never had a majority on its own. His major error was to support the Anglo-French landing at Suez in 1956; it is hard now to see how that expedition could ever have secured the exit of ☛Nasser, Egypt's leader. Ben-Gurion was a tough, warm, practical survivor, under whose aegis Israel emerged and survived.

Émile Benveniste 1902-76

FRENCH LINGUIST, BORN IN SYRIA

Benveniste was a comparative linguist, like Rousseau, Nietzsche and Heidegger, but in place of resonant rhetoric he offered doggedly scientific exegesis. *Nouns of Agent and Nouns of Action in Indo-European* (1948) is one of his titles where snappiness has clearly been discarded, and generally his style and subject matter (usually historical Iranian) were less iconoclastic than his findings. Influenced by de Saussure, and thus an influence both on semiotics via ☛Barthes and ☛Kristeva and on deconstruction via ☛Derrida, he challenged standard beliefs about the structure and genesis of Indo-European languages in ways that have had profound philosophical consequences. He noted, for example, in *Categories of Thought and Language* the degree to which the make-up of the Greek language was to determine Aristotle's system of categories, a system which survives to influence modern societies. Benveniste, as much as any of the philosophers he influenced, challenged the idea that meaning came *before* language.

John Berger born 1926

∀ BRITISH NOVELIST, ART CRITIC,
✌ BASED IN SWITZERLAND

Since his articles, written during a spell as the *New Statesman*'s art critic in the 1950s, in which he defiantly argued for a return to socialist realism in art, Berger has made a virtue of being out of step – taking an isolated, almost eccentric stand against the neglect of the social dimension that commercial criticism seems to entail. His target then was the new wave of abstract expressionism; he has subsequently tempered and developed his world view with increasingly subtle understanding of anti-realist techniques and purposes. *Ways of Seeing* (1972) made provocative connections between Sunday supplement advertising and the subjects and styles of the great paintings of the past; it was also significant as a landmark in the art of television advocacy. As a writer, he combines an attractive common-sense approach to fiercely technical and abstruse subjects with an ability to highlight the way cultural pressures force artists to make decisions. He demystifies art, making it earthy without devaluing it. Over the years, he has also gained a reputation as a writer of fiction, often in unorthodox and experimental forms, although the degree of respect he gives to peasant life and experience is almost certainly not shared by many of his readers. More recently, Berger's perhaps well-intentioned criticisms of ☛Salman Rushdie, taking the side of outraged Islam, seemed a betrayal of his earlier pleas for a broadening of systems of interpretation, and confirmed the suspicion that he was developing an uncritical and romanticized view of Third World cultures.

The pursuit of individual happiness has been acknowledged as a universal right. Yet the existing social conditions make the individual feel powerless. He lives in the contradiction between what he is and what he would like to be.

John Berger, Ways of Seeing

Ingmar Bergman born 1918

○ SWEDISH FILM-MAKER,
▲ THEATRE DIRECTOR

Bergman shaped the art cinema of the 1960s and 1970s by showing that serious personal films made in a minority language could nevertheless reach an international market. With a feel and look quite distinct from Hollywood's traditions, his pictures typically deal with characters undergoing crises of doubt and self-loathing – grim subjects leavened by memories of a happier past and visions of alternative imaginary worlds. Even if, at root, almost everything he does is a fantasy rewrite of his own life, there is considerable narrative diversity in the 43 films he has made since 1946. He is the film-maker whose virtues everyone wishing to call themselves an *auteur* must seek to emulate, and it is unfortunate that his easily parodied vices have probably done immeasurable harm to this same group of people (with ☛Woody Allen first among the victims); for a long while European cinema seemed to be retreating into a stereotype of vapid high seriousness. Bergman's energy derives straight from the primitive showmanship of theatre and conjuring tricks, and a child's happy astonishment at these, and his greatest work, from *The Seventh Seal* (1956) to *Fanny and Alexander* (1983), makes this connection directly. Glum middlebrow suffering is burned away by the brightness of the dream-play images, created from a love of light and landscape, as well as the extraordinary charged performances he extracts from his players.

Today the individual has become the highest form and the greatest bane of artistic creation. The smallest wound or pain of the ego is examined under a microscope as if it were of eternal importance. The artist considers his isolation, his subjectivity, his individualism almost holy. Thus we finally gather in one large pen, where we stand and bleat about our loneliness without listening to each other and without realizing that we are smothering each other to death.

Ingmar Bergman, Introduction to The Seventh Seal

Luciano Berio born 1925

& ITALIAN COMPOSER

Berio's cheerfully polyglot 'modern' music was so far ahead of its time – when everybody around him, including his national *confrères* Dallapiccola and Nono, were charging off into the far reaches of serialism or, after ☛Cage, challenging the very definitions of art, performance, meaning and so on – that he seems to have been left behind. Adept at pastiche, he now looks a fine candidate for adoption into the post-modern canon. He shared with ☛Boulez and ☛Stockhausen, his immediate mentors, a need to break completely with much of the recent European past. but in the early days at least, these two were last-ditch modernists with designs on the Way You Listen, whereas Berio seems to have anticipated a world where the from-all-sides inbleed of many musics – and random noises – turns from cacophony to excitement as you learn to read it. Married for a while to avant-garde singer Cathy Berberian, for whom he wrote several pieces, his own eclecticism developed under the demands of her prodigious range (Bach, ☛the Beatles, Berio); since her death, he has moved into the same semi-analytical fabulist groove inhabited by such writers as ☛Italo Calvino and ☛Umberto Eco (with whom he shares an unlikely Italian love of James Joyce). As we become increasingly attuned to this top-level stratum of Italian intellectual life, we should make some retroactive space for its earliest post-war ambassador.

Isaiah Berlin born 1909

LATVIAN-BRITISH POLITICAL THINKER

A lucid writer about political thinkers, particularly those active in Russia before the Revolution, Berlin brings a valuable objectivity to the analysis of moral questions. Political thought, in his view, divides into two camps: at one extreme, the delusive attraction of philosophies that subordinate all moral and social questions to a single goal (Marxism is the most important example); at the other, the more difficult route imposed by a pluralist vision, which accepts that men have a multitude of conflicting desires and interests. This is most famously set out in his essay of 1953 *The Hedgehog and the Fox* (so-called because, while the fox knows many things, the hedgehog knows one BIG thing), in which he examines Tolstoy as a writer in whom the intellectual's desire for a universal principle of life would not yield to the novelist's stubborn awareness of diversity. Berlin is one of several British-based thinkers who dedicated themselves after WW2 to analysing the siren-calls of political systems that offer 'freedom' but bring totalitarianism, and he has argued forcefully for systems built round the diversity of the individual social subject. Unfortunately the versions of these systems which have begun to flourish so violently in America and the UK have made misery for the losers while boosting the earning power of the winners.

Enrico Berlinguer 1922–84

✌ ITALIAN POLITICAL LEADER

The radically new 'Euro-Communist' direction in which Berlinguer led the Italian Communist Party in the 1970s heralded similar moves by Communist parties in Spain and Portugal, though not by the Stalinist party in France. 'Euro-Communism' meant a willingness to attack the USSR, repudiate classical revolution and, in the Italian case, offer co-operation with progressive forces in the centre-right Christian Democrats – the 'historic compromise'. Born in Sardinia to middle-class landowning parents, Berlinguer was arrested and gaoled after street protests against Fascism in 1944. He joined the Communist Party's central committee as a very young man, but he was not a dazzling performer – only a competent speaker, hard-working and realistic as a leader. Under his control, the Communists gained votes – reaching, at best, 34 per cent of the poll – and seats, plus the right to run major cities, including Rome and Milan. But they never made the decisive breakthrough which would have allowed them to form a coalition with the left-wing members of the Christian Democrats, and Berlinguer was not able to squeeze the smaller Socialist Party hard enough to create a real polarity of forces at Italian elections. He did, however, make Communism a respected alternative within Italian politics and his death elicited genuine regret from opponents as well as supporters.

Silvio Berlusconi born 1936

$ ITALIAN MEDIA MOGUL, BUSINESS EXECUTIVE

A former hotel crooner and building contractor, Berlusconi moved into television by providing a special cable service for the 10,000 residents of Milano 2 and 3, satellite cities he had built on the outskirts of Milan. The formula worked, and he shifted into the entertainment big time in the late 1970s after Socialist prime minister Bettino Craxi, Berlusconi's buddy, had given permission for the establishment of a series of regional television stations – the intention being that RAI, Italy's public service broadcaster, should retain its national broadcasting monopoly. Berlusconi set up stations in key cities throughout the peninsula, had them run the same combination of imported American mini-series, game shows and soft porn (most notoriously with *Colpo Grosso*, the show on which housewives and their mates stripped for cash prizes) and – hey presto – he had a network. Thanks to Craxi, a special law was then passed to legalize what Berlusconi had already done. His television channels now take almost a half share of the Italian viewing public, and the mogul's eyes are set on broader horizons: to this end, he has taken stakes in French, German and Spanish television networks and has his eyes on a UK franchise. He also owns AC Milan football club, as well as the Standa supermarket chain, PublItalia advertising group and various real estate operations. However, a sharp brake was recently applied to Berlusconi's expansion when his bid to win control of Mondadori, Italy's largest publisher and owner of the anti-establishment newspaper *La Republica*, was checked by Olivetti's Carlo de Benedetti.

William Bernbach 1911-82

O AMERICAN ADVERTISING EXECUTIVE

Bernbach put wit into advertising, replacing hard sell with understatement and self-deprecating humour. In the process he gave advertising agencies licence to run creatively wild by showing that sometimes they knew better than the clients how to sell their goods. 'When you're only No. 2, you try harder – Or else.' boosted the image of the Avis car hire company, and his 'Think Small' campaign of the 1960s established a cult for the Volkswagen Beetle car among Americans who repudiated conspicuous consumption. Bernbach had a genius for drawing the best out of those who worked under him and, at a time when art directors were copywriters' lackeys, he encouraged them to work in teams, with no rules as to who contributed what. After his death, his company Doyle Dane Bernbach linked up with BBDO International and Needham Harper Worldwide.

Eric Berne 1910-70

AMERICAN PSYCHOLOGIST

Spurned by the American psychoanalytic establishment, Berne went on to develop his own user-friendly therapeutic system – transactional analysis (TA) – based around easy-to-understand accounts of the psychological traps that people lay for themselves. The wit and clarity with which he expounded these ideas in *Games People Play* (1964) turned that book into a bestseller. His aim was to demystify psychoanalysis; in the process he undermined the Freudian theory that the causes of psychological upset lie deep in the unconscious. TA attempts to bestow 'autonomy', leading the analysand to discount past hang-ups and make decisions about the present acts in line with his or her true feelings. What stops this from happening normally are patterns of programmed behaviour aimed at securing the desired recognition from others. Although people would rather have positive 'strokes' – love, affection, understanding, respect – they may learn to make do with negative ones and indulge in games that secure reactions, even though the payoff is always pain. TA is a useful way of sharpening up those who let bullies get the better of them, but it can also put manipulative tools in the hands of hard-hearted souls who enjoy playing around with the psyches of others, and attracts 'this is the cure for everything' proselytizers. Like too many American therapeutic systems, it flatters patients rather than challenging them.

Chuck Berry

(Charles Edward Berry) born 1926

AMERICAN ROCK MUSICIAN

Berry's songs put humour, youth and fun into rock music; his lyrics celebrate teenage love and frustration; and his personal guitar sound is exciting and almost jolly. So it has always been a disappointment to discover that Berry has a reputation as one of the sourest, most miserable old skinflints who ever demanded the money upfront before going on stage. Even a recent film, *Hail! Hail! Rock 'n' Roll* (1987), specifically designed to eulogize Berry, succeeded largely in confirming his public image as a sour old miser. His autobiography blends his rampant self-obsession and delight in dollars with his love for rhymes and catchphrases; it is a dull, rambling book, occasionally enlivened by the intelligence and wit that, combined with the first precise singing voice in rock, made the music more than raucous calls for sexual intercourse or dancing around clocks.

John Berryman 1914-72

† AMERICAN POET

A seminal figure in the generation of American poets which included such brooding, doomed characters as ☛Delmore Schwartz and Randall Jarrell, Berryman's technical sophistication brought a new depth to American poetry. His masterpiece was the collected *77 Dream Songs* (1964), for which he won the Pulitzer Prize. It starts as a fragmentary diary of a battered alcoholic and evolves into an act of mourning for those whom he had lost – writers who had died before him and a father who committed suicide when he was a child. Altogether he wrote 385 Dream Songs, some of which were published posthumously in 1977. His poems exploit a style formed by its eccentricities, where other voices than the poet's intrude, debate and depart. A manic, charming personality, Berryman's battles with alcoholism, drugs and the morality of his adultery reflected an often-tortured psyche. He finally threw himself off a bridge into the frozen Mississippi.

Bernardo Bertolucci born 1941

ITALIAN FILM DIRECTOR

Bertolucci's films of the early 1970s suggested that he might carry forward the energy and innovation of the flagging 'new waves' that had been launched during the previous decade, but as his landscapes have broadened to take in Italian rural history and the life of China's last emperor, so his films have lost their original intensity. All centre around characters whose search for some sense of belonging, whether through sexual congress or adherence to a totalizing political system (Fascist or Marxist), involves a journey away from their social origins. The exotic camera movements, baroque settings and complex structure of *The Conformist* (1970), his masterpiece, provide multiple perspectives on a character locked into the angst he derives from his homosexual longings, his mother's nymphomania and his father's madness – strains whose cumulative effect lead him to marry a dippy lady and travel to Paris on a mission to assassinate his former professor. With *1900* (1976) and *The Last Emperor* (1987), Bertolucci set his characters' psychological traumas against grander historical backgrounds. Both films have their moments, but one suspects that the act of abandoning Italian for English, Rome for London and Cinecittà for Hollywood has diminished Bertolucci's creative powers – and, depressingly, his 1982 film *The Tragedy of a Ridiculous Man* showed that he could no longer find particularly resonant material in Italy either. Morocco is the setting for his latest film, an adaptation of Paul Bowles' *The Sheltering Sky* (1990).

Bruno Bettelheim 1903-90

† AUSTRO-AMERICAN PSYCHOANALYST

Briefly imprisoned in both Dachau and Buchenwald concentration camps before WW2, Bettelheim became a psychoanalyst who successfully treated children with serious emotional disorders at the Orthogenic School in Chicago. His writings investigate extreme situations, how people cope with them and what happens when they cannot. The internees who survived life in the camps were those confident enough of their identity to retain self-esteem; children become autistic who feel they have no control over what happens to them. Bettelheim also wrote, as a Freudian, of the way in which literature and other cultural forms build an individual's inner security. In *The Uses of Enchantment* (1976), he showed how fairy tales help children to deal with barely articulated desires, and the consequent ineffectiveness of bowdlerized versions that have been purged of gore and violence. He also suggested that the mass media, when it offers crude and simplistic images of the world that make no contact with the psyche's inner turmoil, inadequately prepares the individual for the complexities of modern life. In an age when the culture of affluence offers countless distractions and temptations, without providing much guidance as to the meaning of life, individuals must work harder than before to understand their own unconscious needs and desires. Despite his grim analysis of modern times, Bettelheim's writings expressed optimism about humankind's potential to overcome its problems. But having suffered a disabling stroke, he seemingly gave up his life-long struggle 'to invest life with meaning' and took his own life on the anniversary of the Nazi invasion of Austria.

The tedium and dissatisfaction with life are becoming so great that many are getting ready to let freedom slip out of their hands. They feel it is all too complicated, too difficult to hold on to it, and to themselves. If meaning has gone out of their lives, then at least they wish not to be responsible for it, to let society carry the burden of failure and guilt.

Bruno Bettelheim, The Informed Heart

Joseph Beuys 1921-86

∀ WEST GERMAN ARTIST

✍ Even though, for Beuys, the folk-myth nightmare of modern art actually came true – a cleaner mistook one of his sculptures for garbage and threw it out – he remains one of those performer-creators who were able to transform lives and outlooks with a single piece. A brilliant teacher and communicator, and a remarkably prolific creator, his own life had been transformed during WW2, when the plane he flew was downed by Soviet gunfire in the Crimea. He was badly burned but nomadic Tartars saved his life by wrapping him in fat and felt. A kind of nomadism subsequently pervaded his work and attitudes, while his obsessive return to certain materials and themes, such as fat-sculptures and felt-installations, was quite deliberately imbued with shamanism and a sense of the primitive. He linked up with the Fluxus group, and began to operate as a free-form performance artist, using Dada provocations to expose the over-rigid lives of his audiences to their unconscious processes. On one occasion, he smeared his head with honey and gold leaf, took a dead hare in his arms and carried it around an exhibition of his drawings and paintings, letting it touch the pictures with its paws; then he sat on a stool and spoke to the animal for three hours. More famously, he spent a week caged with a coyote. In the late 1960s and 1970s, he became associated with the radical German student movement that would grow into the Green Party, then in a very experimental stage itself, and took to fomenting an almost abstract aesthetic discontent in his own conception of revolutionary politics. He was criticized as much by the traditional left as by the right – and also by the German academic art establishment. He was not above deriding himself as 'the idiot in the felt hat'.

Aneurin ('Nye') Bevan 1897-1960

BRITISH POLITICIAN

Son of a miner, Bevan was a leading figure on the left of the British Labour Party from the late 1930s, when he was briefly expelled for backing a Popular Front with the Communists. His warm Welsh oratory (strengthened by a stammer), generous personality and incisive mind gave him an instantly quotable niche among British radicals. His zest for expensive dinners, at which he often spent the little cash he had, led to his unfairly being dubbed a 'champagne socialist', but he was willing to be unpopular. He held the view that nothing was too good for the working class, who had been held back by the 'poverty of their aspirations' – thus his establishment of the National Health Service. In the 1950s, after resigning as minister, he led the party's 'Bevanite' wing, whose arguments with the right added drama to politics. Loyalty and betrayal are the key themes of his life and times. Reconciled to the right-wing leader ☛Hugh Gaitskell, he defended British nuclear weapons in 1958, declaring that 'no foreign secretary should walk naked into the conference chamber'. He was never forgiven for what was, to many on the left, a betrayal.

Ernest Bevin 1881-1951

BRITISH POLITICIAN

British foreign secretary in the post-war Labour government, Bevin played, with ☛Truman, a significant part in the formation of NATO as an answer to the USSR's takeover of Eastern Europe. As a young union leader in 1920, he had threatened major strikes if Britain backed Poland, then at war with Bolshevik Russia, but after 1945, he soon saw that talking to the Soviets was not enough, as they menaced Western safety. He did not appreciate that economic difficulties back home meant that Britain's days of imperial greatness were over, but his tough line on British interests and his rough, unpretentious manner won over the British Foreign Office, which had initially been unsettled by the shock exit of Eden, his suave forerunner. Patriotic pragmatism, tested by results, meant an ability to cut through to the central issues of foreign policy. Outside Europe, his grasp was less happy. He failed to see that Palestine could not be held in the long term as a British base and sought vainly to prevent a Jewish State by turning back refugee ships from Europe and interning survivors of the death camps. Bullishness, arguably, turned into anti-Semitism.

A. C. Bhaktivedanta *see* Swami Prabhupada

Benazir Bhutto born 1953

PAKISTANI POLITICAL LEADER

Years of house arrest, imprisonment and exile following the execution of her father, the former prime minister of Pakistan, Zulfiqar Ali Bhutto, turned this pampered scion of a wealthy family into a determined politician – her lookalike is dubbed 'The Virgin Ironpants' in ☛Salman Rushdie's novel *Shame* – and the modern world's first woman leader of an Islamic nation. But the high profile Bhutto acquired in the West through her youth and promises of liberal reforms – freeing political prisoners, lifting controls on the media and trade unions – didn't translate into effective action and, within 20 months of her appointment as prime minister in December 1988, she was out of office. Bhutto always faced an uphill battle at home, where the military establishment, which had ruled for 11 years, retained control over the country's considerable defence expenditure, including a nuclear defence programme, but that didn't excuse her failure to push for a political settlement in Afghanistan, stop ethnic violence within her own borders or defuse tensions with India, Pakistan's neighbour and longstanding enemy. Her inability to deal with the country's ongoing economic crisis, together with evidence of corruption on a huge scale – some 26,000 state appointments went to members of her Pakistan People's Party, and Bhutto's husband, Asif Ali Zardari, used cheap bank loans to build up enormous personal wealth – helped to wipe out her popular support.

Elizabeth Bishop 1911-79

AMERICAN POET

Bishop's poems were generally distilled out of her experiences of foreign travel – from Nova Scotia to Jerusalem, from New York to Mexico. She had a zest for the natural world – seascapes, rivers, country lanes – which was reflected in the titles of her collections: *North and South* (1955), *Questions of Travel* (1965) and *Geography 3* (1977). Her strength was the purity of her language, which tended towards the conversational and colloquial, and a diversity in approach that animated her experiments with ballad form, blank verse and even songs written for ☛Billie Holiday. Each poem seems to represent a fresh discovery of the world, and an awakening to the terror within the familiar. Bishop urges her readers to appreciate the little things in life – the family, the home and the community.

Peter Blake born 1932

BRITISH ARTIST

Where some Pop Art can be seen as an ambivalent criticism of consumer society, Blake's version used commercial packaging and cheap toys to celebrate the recent past. Fascinated by badges and other pop music ephemera, he created postcard and pin-up collages filled with a nostalgic longing for a passing world. Blake's best-known work – the sleeve for *Sergeant Pepper's Lonely Hearts Club Band* – is the perfect Pop Art comment on commercial celebrity – putting ☛The Beatles (as cartoon Edwardian circus beaux) next to their own waxwork simulacra, in among a crowd of notables, including murderers, saints, poets and dead film stars: the first LP-release-as-art-event, it altered for ever public perceptions of both pop and art, but left Blake's own ambivalence towards celebrations of popular culture intact. He also created homages to rock 'n' roll stars such as ☛Elvis and ☛Buddy Holly. In the early 1970s, he retired to the country with a group of painters who took up subjects that the pre-Raphaelites would have found familiar (such as Shakespeare's plays) and were dubbed the neo-Romantics.

Harold Bloom born 1930

AMERICAN LITERARY ART CRITIC

'The meaning of a poem can only be a poem, but *another poem, a poem not itself.*' Bloom's criticism seems prescriptive and densely reactionary at first; he seems to argue that the Romantic is the only poetry, Milton's Satan the only poet. In fact, his genius for titles ought to alert us to the radically dissociative programme that is being effected: *The Anxiety of Influence* (1973), *A Map of Misreading* (1975), *Ruin the Sacred Truths* (1989). Bloom's contention – for him it is a fact – is that all that matters is strong writing. His intention is not to interpret poems but to present a history of their birth in the struggle of poets with their precursors to write new poems, when all that is left to be done is rewriting. His poets are monomaniacs, locked in an Oedipal war with their own influences. His avatars are Freud, Nietzsche and Gershom Scholem (a friend of Walter Benjamin and student of the Kabbalah). In fact, Bloom's critical method was once dismissed as 'psychokabbalahism', a description he at once happily embraced. The canonic lineage of (English-language) poetry that he accepts is highly traditional, but he gives an account of it as a 'history of anxiety and self-saving caricature of perverse, wilful revisionism' which is dense, knockabout fun, whether or not you believe in it.

Anthony Blunt 1907-83

BRITISH ART HISTORIAN, SPY

Surveyor of the Queen's (initially the King's) Pictures from 1945 to 1972, Blunt was revealed in 1979 as the last in a quartet of British spies, which had also included ☛Philby, ☛Burgess and Maclean. Everyone had been looking for a fourth man; no one guessed it was this distinguished art historian, an expert on Poussin. Under investigation continuously since 1951, he had actually confessed in 1964, but was granted immunity after he agreed to supply information to the British security services. As a fellow of Trinity College, Cambridge, he had been recruited by Burgess to keep an eye out for likely talent, and during WW2, while serving with MI5, he supplied the Soviets with current British intelligence about the Germans. It is unlikely that Blunt ever learned anything as a palace functionary that could have been of interest to the KGB, despite all the breast-beating that followed his exposure, but he did help ☛Philby and Maclean to escape in 1951. With Andrew Boyle about to spill the beans in his book *The Climate of Treason*, ☛Margaret Thatcher broke the pact that had kept Blunt's past hidden and brought about his public humiliation – his knighthood was annulled and he was stripped of his Trinity College fellowship. For observers of this bizarre ritual, it was difficult to believe this clipped, glib High Tory could ever have declared allegiance to the revolutionary cause.

Steven Bochco born 1943

♦ AMERICAN TV PRODUCER

Starting out as a screenwriter on *Columbo*, a literate, witty, psychological cop show, Bochco's later achievement was to take the ensemble acting of classic British soap opera and the bravura crowd-framing abilities of American directors such as ☛Robert Altman, then weld them into the long-running TV series, *Hill Street Blues* (1980-8). This broke all the then-current rules of viewer accessibility: the frame was often filled with irrelevant off-centre action; minor characters crossed in front of leads; speaking characters moved on and off screen; there was a constant hubbub of background noise; and the hierarchy of the police force was not related to the hierarchy of character importance. It was startling, and ultimately very popular (after some 'improvements' had been made to Bochco's original conception – such as having the crimes under investigation actually solved). The gains in energy and dramatic possibility were obvious, and it should have signalled the end of flood-depth lighting and endless head-and-shoulder shots, the dreary staples of American soaps. But after seven consecutive series, and no very apparent changes in the rest of the mainstream, Bochco lost interest and went off in 1986 to set up his own company – making entertaining, but distinctly less demanding, shows such as *LA Law* (from 1986) and *Hooperman* (from 1987). Without him at the helm, MTM cancelled *Hill Street Blues*.

Ivan Boesky born 1937

✚ AMERICAN FINANCIER

Preaching the creed that 'greed is good,' Boesky earned a reputation as 'Ivan the Terrible' for the ferocious tactics he employed in takeovers. He went on to justify the appellation fully by co-operating with the US Justice Department in the exposure of Wall Street corruption and in the process terrorizing members of the financial community on both sides of the Atlantic (he had been a big player in the battle between Guinness and Argyll for control of Distillers in the UK). He had made his fortune by buying stocks in companies for which another outfit was bidding, calculating that he would be able to sell them for a higher price – for example, he bought $100 million worth of shares in Getty Oil and handed them on to Texaco for twice that value. So far so legal, but Boesky had a mole at Drexel, Burnham, Lambert, the company responsible for financing many of the corporate raids of the early 1980s, and *that* was insider trading. Arrested in 1986, he was fined $100 million, but not before he had agreed to tape conversations with other market operators and hand over details of his transactions. He made further displays of repentance – pursuing Talmudic studies and working with the homeless under an assumed name – and although receiving a three-year gaol sentence, he was soon released on good behaviour. Boesky, who inspired the Gordon Gekko character in Oliver Stone's *Wall Street*, is now disbarred from operating a securities firm but can still advise clients on personal investments.

Marc Bolan

(Mark Feld) 1947-77

✈ BRITISH ROCK MUSICIAN

♥ Bolan was one of pop's great triers. He wandered through the 1960s desperately hoping to be noticed, going from mod to hippy, making the odd dreadful record, until his group, T. Rex, acquired some cult status as faerie rockers. Then, as *Top of the Pops* began to beckon, Bolan ditched half the band, along with most of its hard-core following, and picked up on old rock 'n' roll and R&B. Early T. Rex is the best of 1970s pop thanks to Bolan's sex-pixie look, his peculiar voice singing even more peculiar lyrics, and a strange mix of ☛Eddie Cochran and ☛J. R. R. Tolkien. For some reason, most male British pop stars of the 1980s seem to have discovered both sex and pop while watching T. Rex on television. Bolan, meanwhile, spent the next five years running out of ideas and putting on weight. His death is the usual rock irony: a slight comeback, a cult position, followed by a car crash, in the year ☛Presley died.

Heinrich Böll 1917-85

WEST GERMAN NOVELIST

A deserter from the Russian front in 1944, Böll became the chronicler of West Germany's transition from disorientating defeat to complacent affluence. He distrusted all manifestations of state power and took the side of the 'lambs' against the powerful materialists whom he dubbed 'buffaloes'. Böll's positions were reflected in his laconic prose style and the strategies he employed to avoid speaking with a fixed authorial voice: none of the characters in his novel *Where Were You, Adam?* (1951), set amid the chaos of the disintegrating German army in the last days of WW2, is held in focus long enough for the reader to identify any one in particular as a 'hero'. And the short but incisive *The Lost Honour of Katharina Blum* (1974/5) is presented in the deceptively direct style of a police report, about a woman who murders one of the journalists who have been hounding her. Böll was a consistent critic of Germany's corrupt tabloid press and the sensation-hungry public which supported it, and he defended the individual's privacy against an encroaching state during a period of increasing repression. During 1972, the year in which he became the first German since Thomas Mann to win the Nobel prize for literature, the Soviet authorities turned on Böll for his criticism of literary censorship (he used to smuggle ☛ Solzhenitsyn's manuscripts out of the USSR), while the German right lambasted him as 'a spiritual instigator of terrorism'. In the early 1980s he supported the Green Party and joined demonstrations against US bases.

John Boorman born 1933

BRITISH FILM DIRECTOR

Boorman gives the impression of never being quite happy with his place in the cinematic mainstream, even though he is determined to hold on to it. He can be impressive when he works with a strong narrative and a defined locale: the antiseptic Los Angeles of his first feature *Point Blank* (1967), in which Lee Marvin searches for the fellow crooks who cheated him of his cash; the Appalachian Mountains where three characters take a bloody canoeing trip in *Deliverance* (1972); or, more recently, the suburban London of Boorman's own childhood in *Hope and Glory* (1987). But too often his desire to make a big statement about the fragility of social structures – what stops us from tearing each other apart? – or the ways in which modern technology and urban life have distanced us from nature, leads him into waffling pretentiousness. While sitting through *Zardoz* (1973) or *The Emerald Forest* (1985), it is sometimes very hard to keep from sniggering.

Jorge Luis Borges 1899-1986

& ARGENTINIAN SHORT STORY WRITER, POET

Towards the end of his life, as Borges waited for the Nobel prize that never arrived, he had become such an iconic figure that when in the US he got up to speak and the microphone failed, no one dared to adjust it for him; he talked on, blind, inaudible, quavering, oblivious to a deathly quiet audience straining to hear every word. Having realized that Argentina would never have a written identity of its own, in spite of its mythic colour, he drew on his readings from world literature to turn this apparent defeat into a victory and convince the rest of us that all writing is colonized by its past. Latecomers were clambering around in ruins, not cutting paths through virgin forest. Magical realism existed before him (think of his unlikely hero G. K. Chesterton), but Borges gave it an unsettling and condensed blueprint, and effected – in single, resonant phrases and perfectly abstract story construction – a detonation of the tricks in stories that lead us to confuse the universe with the library. A brilliant succeeding generation of Latin American writers – usually far more politically engaged – have seized on these devices, often in ways that belie Borges's original cultural pessimism. His own run-ins with politics were demeaning (☛Peron sacked him as a librarian and put him in charge of chickens), but his description of the Falklands War – 'Two bald men fighting over a comb' – remains unforgettably exact. Much harder to trace is his ghostly influence on the theorists of structuralism and deconstruction, whose admiration forced them into thought formulations that would accommodate his mazed worlds and persuasive paradoxes.

Pierre Boulez born 1925

☞ FRENCH COMPOSER, MUSICAL THEORIST

A pupil, like ☛Stockhausen, of the mystically inclined ☛Messiaen, Boulez chose to make a religion out of structure, developing for a while the total serialism he embraced in the early 1950s as a break from tainted pre-war culture – not only was the pitch of a note to be subject to dodecaphonic rigour, but also its duration, intensity, volume, timbre and attack. The purpose of this controversial approach was to realign composition as a form of aesthetic research which could then be conducted along scientific and logical lines. Each work, he insists, should contribute a major innovation to the study of music, and as a result, his own output comes under constant self-critical revision. Even though he has come in for extreme criticism as a composer and theorist, there is little disagreement about his authority as a conductor-interpreter of late classical composers, including Wagner, Debussy, Bartók and Stravinsky. An exceptional musical analyst as a student, he was quick to detect original craftsmanship and had no patience for musicians whose renown rested on anything less substantial. He has written, 'Any musician who has not felt the necessity of the dodecaphonic language is *of no use*' – a remark which is probably best understood as a plea for those involved in music today to be aware of earlier classicism's failure to see beyond itself. Boulez has used serialism's structural clarity as a jumping-off point to introduce the non-European methods pioneered by his friend and theoretical opponent ☛John Cage into an increasingly astonishing, suspended, delicate sound-style. Since the 1970s, he has been the prime mover at the Institut de

Recherche et Coordination Acoustique/Musique – the fabled IRCAM, hi-tech home of avant-garde exploration where computers improvise and the future is tentatively notated.

Despite the skilful ruses we have cultivated in our desperate effort to make the world of the past serve our present needs, we can no longer elude the essential trial: that of becoming an absolute part of the present, of forsaking all memory to forge a perception without precedent, or renouncing the legacies of the past, to discover yet undreamed-of territories.

Pierre Boulez, at the opening of IRCAM

Nicholas Bourbaki formed c. 1930

☞ FRENCH MATHEMATICAL GROUP

As a result of a half century of doubts and debates about the foundations of mathematics, a group of French mathematicians came together and named themselves, apparently, after a French general whose contribution to the Franco-Prussian War had been almost entirely disastrous. Their formation was a reaction, some suggest, against the brilliant but notoriously unrigorous French mathematical genius Henri Poincaré, and also to the loss of a whole generation of mathematicians in WW1. The group intended to work up and publish an encyclopaedic series of books – *Eléments des mathématiques* – that would provide an axiomatic basis for all of mathematics past and present: to date more than 20 volumes have appeared. Aridly formalist, and impenetrable to all but the most dedicated mathematical academics (it appears, for example, that Bourbaki regards the diagram as the height of imprecise levity), they were, none the less, immensely influential in the years immediately following WW2, particularly in encouraging the abstract study of structure. Membership is limited, retirement at 50 mandatory and known participants have included André Weil, J. Dieudonné and Szolem Mandelbrot (whose nephew ☛Benoit Mandelbrot fled to America, taking particular exception to the group's strictures on diagrams, to pursue his study of fractal geometry and computer visuals). Bourbaki can claim responsibility for the New Math in America, for the substantial improvements in standards of maths teaching worldwide and for the total inability of countless parents to help the kids with their homework. The group's dominance has now waned.

Louise Bourgeois born 1911

✓ FRENCH-AMERICAN SCULPTOR

Bourgeois provides a link between French surrealism of the 1920s and New York's punk movement. As a child in Paris, her father took her around the cabarets of Montmartre to see 'life'. Having moved to New York with her American husband in 1938, she became, in the 1970s, a noted habitué of SoHo's Mudd Club, and expressed the contemporary mood through a performance piece, *Confrontation* (1979), in which raucous punk models, sporting enormous latex private parts, shouted verbal abuse across a huge table heaped with breasts and sexual organs. A fascination with food, sex and death, as well as an urge to express rage and conjure nightmares, run through Bourgeois' work. The group of paintings, *Women House*, with which she made her name in 1947, make a characteristic connection between women and the traps men build around them; in each case, the heads of women were replaced with images of houses. In the same vein, a marble of 1969, *Femme contra*, shows a seductive woman evolving into an elongated knife. Her first sculptures were life-size wooden figures, and *The Marchers* (1973) featured over 1000 separate marble columns, representing the serried ranks of individuals rising in mass protest.

Habib Bourguiba born 1903

TUNISIAN POLITICIAN

Leader of Tunisia, first as head of the Cabinet, then from 1957 to 1987 as president, Bourguiba was, with Kenyatta, one of Africa's longest-lasting political leader. A critic of French colonial rule and, from 1934, leader of a new nationalist party, he was jailed by the French three times before Tunisia won its independence in 1956. Even so, when Germany released Bourguiba from a Vichy prison in 1942 and sent him to Rome, he still refused to endorse the Axis. Despite tensions with France during the war in Algeria, when Tunisia helped the rebels, Bourguiba maintained a bourgeois republic and brought in social reforms. He always pursued an independent line with the Arab League, withdrawing his delegation on one occasion and acting as a mediator with Israel. Very high unemployment and stagnant food output produced major tensions. Electoral forms survived, but the opposition boycotted assembly elections and Bourguiba, an ageing figure, evolved dictatorial habits, having been made president for life. He was ejected as anger rose and riots spread – a case of a man who had clung to power too long for his nation's interest or the good of his own reputation.

David Bowie

(David Jones) born 1947

BRITISH ROCK MUSICIAN

✓ Watching Bowie on a Pepsi television advert, it is sobering to reflect that he chose his surname to avoid being mistaken for the lead singer of the Monkees. Bowie's quarter-century career has included a bad R&B group, Carnaby Street Edwardian music hall pop, elfin Dylan-type hippy, Nietzschian heavy metal, apocalypse science fiction, cocaine-drained Philly soul, cocaine-drained European Nietzschian heavy metal soul, alienated European electro and, most recently, healthy but wistful dance rock. Between transformations, he has acted in films, recorded duets with everyone from ☛Marc Bolan to Bing Crosby, revived the careers of Lou Reed, ☛Iggy Pop (twice) and Mott the Hoople, espoused philosophies from Fascism to anarchism, written some astoundingly silly lyrics and launched glam rock, futurism, Eurodisco and a myriad other musical movements. David Bowie, therefore, is not one to make a virtue of consistency. His incessant adopting of images flies in the face of rock music's obsession with 'authenticity', and the convincing music Bowie makes in each of his chosen fields questions the validity of that obsession. In recent years, he has presented a 'straight' image, all suits and parenthood; as a result, the quality and sales of his records have suffered. David Bowie's talent lies in finding ideas, collaborating and creating the new from the wreckage of the old.

John Bowlby 1907-90

BRITISH PSYCHOANALYST

'He took the poetry out of analysis' was one listener's response to Bowlby's 1958 paper on 'The Nature of the

Child's Tie to His Mother'. He went on to cause further outrage among his psychoanalytic peers by suggesting that ☛Konrad Lorenz's work with animals could add something to what had been learned from patients in their consulting rooms. Lorenz's discoveries, he said, suggested that children who were separated from their mothers for any length of time would suffer permanent emotional damage: 'Mother love in infancy is as important for mental health as are vitamins and proteins for physical health,' he solemnly advised any woman who might be planning to stray from the cot or the playpen, 'If you don't do your five years' hard labour when the child is young, you do it later . . . ' Bowlby argued that children, like those animals, are biologically programmed to stay close to the most available adult, and that mothers are subject to a similar drive. These views had a considerable influence on mothering in the 1960s, but children are more resilient than Bowlby suggests; they can form emotional ties to several people and endure temporary separations, without necessarily ending up as life-scarred neurotics.

Boy George

(George O'Dowd) born 1961

BRITISH POP MUSICIAN

When his pop/soul/reggae single 'Do You Really Want to Hurt Me?' charted in 1982 and a nation discovered they had bought something by a clear- and high-voiced transvestite in dreadlocks, they responded admirably by buying even more of his records. Boy George – significant for ever because he once said, 'I prefer a cup of tea to sex' – became the first outrageously homosexual pseudo-drag act to win family approval. He was ambiguous, saucy, cheerful and colourful, but he did not realize that career stability lay in stasis. Many years of chat-show appearances might have been his if he had not changed his hairstyle and become a heroin addict. His creative muse now seriously trashed, he found himself on the tabloid front pages and became the first pop act since The Bay City Rollers to suffer the Fleet Street mallet. With his tiny comeback singles and his knack of hovering in the background of tabloid photos, Boy George has come to exemplify the marginalized eccentric, trapped in a minor corner of the entertainment world because he could not adjust to its rules.

Ray Bradbury

born 1920

AMERICAN WRITER

Once referred to as the 'Mom's apple pie' author of science fiction, Bradbury's alien worlds are riddled with a Waltons-style folksiness. The only author ever to confuse Mars with the Old West, his imagination is littered with front porches and old men chewing tobacco, as well as sunny, Norman Rockwellish depictions of possible presents and futures that only point up the nameless horrors lying in wait – as in the nightmarish price the dark carnival of *Something Wicked This Way Comes* (1962) exacts for making the dreams of the small-town folk come true. His most famous book, *Fahrenheit 451* (1953) is, strangely, the converse to all this; it can be seen as the most heart-warming and cosy book ever written about the evils of book-burning – a sort of *1984* written by Li'l Abner – or as a passionate attempt to convey the joy of reading to an increasingly mechanized, novelty-obsessed and disinterested world. Bradbury's reputation derives, in part, from his deliberate association of his own stories with great American literature – in particular, the works of Poe, Ambrose Bierce and Walt Whitman.

Stan Brakhage

born 1933

AMERICAN EXPERIMENTAL FILM-MAKER

Brakhage was the most important figure in the American cinema underground of the 1960s, a film-maker who broke the taboos of method and subject as he sought to reveal what happens behind personal events – the birth of his first child, love-making with his wife. He would scratch film and apply paint to it and use distorting lenses or superimpositions in an attempt to match the processes of thought, dreams, memories and fantasies. He has also abandoned the camera altogether – taping a line of moth wings on to a strip which is then taken through an optical printer. There is no immediate narrative – the fiction of the film-maker behind the camera is the subject. In *Scenes from under Childhood* (1967-70), for example, images of children at play are incorporated alongside memories of his own childhood, with links provided by images of pure colour. *Dog Star Man* (1961-4), which was shot in a year and released in five parts, is built around Brakhage climbing a hill and cutting down a tree. Often the objects, the buildings, the people seen through the lens become so abstracted that they remain as only pure rhythmic patterns of light and colour. He still produces his intimate sketchbooks from his home in the Colorado mountains.

Marlon Brando

born 1924

AMERICAN ACTOR

Had it been Brando who died in 1956, James Dean's personality cult would not have had a chance. Brando was the actor Dean always wanted to be, exploding on to the screen in a torrent of anger, frustration and unrestrained sexual energy. Starting a gay fashion craze with the leather jacket and cap he wore in *The Wild One* (1954), he became the personification of the working-class white rebel – every father's nightmare, every good girl's wet dream. He made Shakespeare sexy, Nazis sympathetic and 'Luck be a Lady Tonight' . . . well, interesting. But a string of flops in the 1960s turned his erratic and unpredictable behaviour into complete eccentricity: rather than learning his lines, he would have them taped to the scenery or other actors' backs; he would act with cotton wool plugs in his ears to ensure that his concentration was not interrupted by the other actors. Meanwhile he developed a passion for ice cream that led to a chronic weight problem. He made a comeback in *The Godfather* (1972), then shocked Mrs Grundys everywhere and sent the sales of butter skyrocketing with his performance in *Last Tango in Paris* (1972), but the renaissance was shortlived. There was a cameo in *Superman* (1978), a rambling performance as Kurtz in *Apocalypse Now* (1979) and a few days' work on *The Formula* (1980), after which he retired to his tropical island and increasing obesity. Following offers of work from almost every name director in the business, he resurfaced after nine years on the set of *The Freshman*, promptly walked out amid a flurry of insults against films in general and *The Freshman* in particular, then returned to finish the role. He also appeared in *A Dry White Season*

(1990). His influence lives on in actors such as Mickey Rourke and Al Pacino.

'What you rebelling against?'
'What you got?'

Marlon Brando in The Wild One

Bill Brandt

1904-83

BRITISH PHOTOGRAPHER

Brandt studied with the surrealists in Paris and showed that, even on reporting assignments to grimy locations, the photographer need not only record 'what is there'. Brandt's dark, heavily contrasted pictures of 1930s life in the East End and the North of England have a poetic suggestiveness that takes them beyond reportage to expose the misery of Depression Britain – a world of smug toffs, glum parlour maids and cheerful Cockneys. His post-war interpretations of 'Literary Britain', covering authors as varied as Chaucer and Shaw, caught the sense of a place's influence over the writer – images of moody clouds, prominent moors and isolated dwellings to evoke *Wuthering Heights*, for example. He had a striking ability to put his subjects into their emotional, social, historical and political context – as witnessed by his 'London Child' of 1955 or the portrait of a trenchcoated Peter Sellers peering solemnly over the top of a newspaper on a park bench. He also managed to push photography into near-abstraction through distortions achieved with a box camera and wide-angle lens. Whether depicting twisted nudes, or an enormous ear set against a beach, these images seem still to represent the furthest point that photography can go.

Willy Brandt

(Karl Herbert Frahm) born 1913

WEST GERMAN POLITICAL LEADER

Brandt fled Nazi Germany in 1933 – very early – for Scandinavia, where he worked as a journalist and changed his name. After WW2, he gained global fame as mayor of West Berlin from 1957 to 1966. Chairman of the Social Democrats (SPD) from 1964, he was West Germany's foreign minister from 1966 and chancellor of his own party's government from 1969 to 1974, when he resigned over a spy scandal; he retained a senior role in the party until the late 1980s. He was the first German left-winger in power with a clear majority of his own. He improved relations with Eastern Europe, including East Germany and Poland , as well as playing a key part in the expansion of the European Economic Community and arguing for additional aid to the Third World as chairman of the Brandt Commission. At home, the SPD's renunciation of Marxism in 1959 was largely his idea. He was an idealist, looking outwards, who gave way to the harder-headed Helmut Schmidt .

Fernand Braudel

1902-85

FRENCH HISTORIAN

A Frenchman who spent much of his time abroad, Braudel has had a massive influence on the writing of history, inside and outside his native country. Like his teacher Lucien Febvre, he was a major exponent of the *Annales* school of French history, which drew on concepts from other social sciences as well as statistical analysis and aimed to determine the basic structure underlying the events of a particular epoch. Unlike its other members who focused on the mind-set of particular periods, Braudel opted for a study of their material culture. His interest in the experiences of living in the past – how did it feel to be a forest dweller in Burgundy, or to run a barge along the Loire? – saves his writing from dessicated abstraction. Works about the Mediterranean in the late sixteenth century, the history of capitalism and the identity of France display his vast command of detail. He often surprises as he rejects, not only orthodox political narrative, but also the 'socio-economic' strait-jacket. His focus is on the interaction of man and his habitat and on the *longue durée* – the unconscious, medium-term factors that shape human evolution. A striking recall explains a dazzling feat of memory – he wrote his best-known book, *The Mediterranean and the Mediterranean World in the Age of Philip II* (1949, 1972-3) without notes, in a German POW camp. An ambiguous love affair with France, yet a hostility to European centralization, may be at the heart of his work.

Wernher Von Braun 1912–77

♦ GERMAN SCIENTIST, WHO SETTLED IN US

Hitler's master rocket builder, Von Braun advanced missile science enormously in the final months of WW2. In particular, he led the development of the V2, the closest the Führer ever came to his threatened secret weapon of salvation, which superseded the earlier 'doodlebugs' by flying faster than sound and thus rendering itself more or less unstoppable by any then-current defence system. The innovations this required involved construction of elaborate built-in steering, stabilizing and timing mechanisms and the solution of fuel injection problems. Various cities in the UK suffered its ministrations. Controversially, but perhaps unsurprisingly, he was spirited away to the US after Germany's defeat, and went on to apply his expertise to the design of rockets that would eventually put the US ahead in the space race – including the massive Saturn rockets which put the Apollo programme into oribit. Soviet rocket science was helped at least as much by its cultivation of several of Von Braun's former colleagues and underlings from the Nazi development sites at Peenemünde. When Von Braun's life story was filmed as *I Aim at the Stars* (1970), several critics responded by completing the title with '. . . But Hit London'.

Richard Brautigan 1933-84

✣ AMERICAN NOVELIST

Likely to figure as only a minor figure in the annals of 1960s' American literature, Brautigan was for a time bracketed with Hesse and ☛Tolkein as an underground favourite on America's campuses, where his collections of inconsequential verse and four novels, starting with *Confederate General from Big Sur* (1965), were widely read. He espoused the attitude that, however horrible and cruel life may be, nothing matters except having fun: a typical Brautigan character in *Trout Fishing in America* (1967) seems more interested in eating some potato salad than grieving over a discarded mistress who has just hanged herself. Brautigan's novels contain barbarism and absurdist humour within rambling, incoherent plots. But *Hawkline Monster* (1974), which he dubbed a Gothic western, was pure pastiche, and he wrote himself into a formulaic corner from which he seemed unable to escape. Feeling that both public and critics had betrayed him, he took to drink.

Anthony Braxton born 1945

✍ AMERICAN MUSICIAN

☞ More respected than heard, Braxton's problems with critics, the industry and the public stem from a commitment to creating music that exists between two incompatible modes: classical after Schoenberg , jazz after ☛Charlie Parker. His examination of the tensions and affinities between these two worlds is rendered further impenetrable by the adoption of an arcane and highly symbolic system of notation and titling, which he surrounds with a dense and difficult critical-descriptive language. From the start, however, Braxton's music has been easier on the ear than its trappings perhaps suggest. His own multi-instrumental reed-playing has its roots in the late 1950s' near-pop styles of Paul Desmond and Dave Brubeck , even though his fascination with form and development can take him into peculiarly un-pop territory, especially when he plays solo (a performance staple he pioneered along with the saxophone quartet). While certain of his compositions, requiring simultaneously broadcast orchestras in different galaxies, may not be properly performed in the immediate future, Braxton's importance is starting to be acknowledged.

Robert Breer born 1926

FRENCH EXPERIMENTAL FILM-MAKER, SETTLED IN NEW YORK

An experimental film-maker and animator from the third wave of the film avant-garde, Breer's work features a succession of moving shapes – some identifiable, some abstract – which play tricks with the imagination but never fail to please the eye. He took the concept of the child's flip-book and pulled out of it the hyper-modern notion of film as blitzed image-rush some 30 years before it would become a video commonplace. He first came to attention with *A Man and His Dog out for Air* (1958), which appears to be full of abstract shapes, although both man and dog eventually materialize. His resistance to the conventions of what films can and cannot be like is just about total – *Un Miracle* (1954), for example, is only 14 seconds long. Breer linked up with ☛Claes Oldenburg's performance art group in the early 1960s, providing home-movie documentation, with *Pat's Birthday* (1962), that would help broadcast Claes and Pat's fun-pop 'happenings' fast and effectively.

Robert Bresson born 1909

☞ FRENCH FILM-MAKER

Bresson has carved out his career by pursuing a single theme – dying with grace. His films make considerable demands on his actors (invariably amateurs instructed *not* to act in the traditional sense) and on his audience, unthrilled by his slow-moving, hypnotic style of direction. Building an elaborate interchange of glances, close-ups and subtle camera movements into an exploration of meaning, his films shape their finely drawn narratives with utmost simplicity and precision, offering in the process an indictment of all cinema that confuses bravura performance with artistic seriousness and muddies its trivial messages with blasting soundtracks and fast cutting. Bresson invites the viewer to look through the blank faces of his characters, whether saints or perpetrators of evil, to the feelings building up within. However great the inner turmoil, the journey the characters undergo in his films is always towards an acceptance of their fate, marked by suicide in *Mouchette* (1966) or the sense of redemption at the end of *Pickpocket* (1959). Although some viewers find Bresson's harsh philosophy difficult to comprehend, any film-maker who can show his audience the range of human vices through the eyes of a donkey (in *Au hasard Balthazar*, 1966) merits attention.

Breyten Breytenbach born 1939

SOUTH AFRICAN POET, PAINTER, POLITICAL ACTIVIST, SETTLED IN PARIS

It is unsettling to discover that Breytenbach – who was incarcerated for over six years in South Africa's disarmingly-named Beverly Hills Prison, where blacks were taken to the gallows in batches – has a brother who at the time commanded a unit of anti-guerrilla black commandos. Breyten's marriage to a non-white (the daughter of a one-time South Vietnamese finance minister) forced him to go into exile in Paris in the early 1960s, whence he inveighed against apartheid in prose and poetry that is dense with rancid disgust and collected under such titles as *Catastrophes* (1964) and *The House of the Deaf* (1967). Allowed to return briefly to his homeland in 1973, he told his fellow Afrikaners that their racist society was doomed. Two years later he returned, and the authorities exacted their revenge, nabbing the insufficiently disguised writer as he made for the border, and locking him up on the grounds that he was the founder of a (non-existent) white wing of the African National Congress (ANC). After over 18 months in solitary confinement, he was tried again on a series of charges that included, incredibly, planning a Soviet submarine attack on Robben Island, where many of the ANC's black leaders were imprisoned. In 1982, under pressure from ☛President Mitterrand, Breytenbach was released. He recounted his prison experiences in the extraordinary, horrific *Confessions of an Albino Terrorist* (1984).

Leonid Brezhnev 1906-82

SOVIET POLITICAL LEADER

The first Soviet leader to head the party and the state simultaneously, from 1977, Brezhnev held real power from 1964, when he replaced ☛Khruschev as party secretary – he was the safe, conservative appointment who promised stasis after a period of political liberalization and agricultural reform. He had climbed the Soviet hierarchy, via regional posts, from his background as a steelmaker's son, rising fast in the era of Stalin's Great Purge and becoming a major general during WW2. His style of leadership was collegiate: the 'Brezhnev doctrine' – that the USSR had the right to intervene in order to obviate a threat to Socialism in any of the other countries that made up the Warsaw Pact, as in 1968 with Czechoslovakia – was widely supported in the Soviet élite. Under his control, the USSR reached arms parity with the West. This was the basis for détente, a policy he pursued in the 1970s, as relations with China worsened; even so, he intervened in Afghanistan in 1979. Because of the arms build-up, the Soviet economy was in bad shape at the end of his tenure. Another significant feature of his reign was the extension of Soviet influence into the Middle East and Africa , often in the search for air or sea bases. A cuddly-seeming figure, he ran an erratic, grim, dull, repressive and stagnant regime. He was a heavy smoker who suffered from insomnia, and said he felt happiest at the wheel of a car.

Benjamin Britten 1913-76

BRITISH COMPOSER

Britten created his first major work, a choral piece around the Christmas theme, at the age of 18. The innocence embodied in this youthful work gave way later to a sense of its loss. He worked a great deal with children, involving their dramatic and artistic potential as still unformed performers and singers, as well as exploring the possibilities of (often religious) operas written especially for children (most successfully in *Noyes Fludde*, 1958). His first large-scale work, *Peter Grimes* (1945), highlighted the souring of his romanticism with its story of a hero who is driven to destruction by the corruption and depravity of this world. Mature works such as *War Requiem* (1962), which articulates a vision of WWI as the destroyer of England's innocence, show Britten at his darkest. Compared to European music of the time, Britten's is profoundly conservative in conception – lyrical, but essentially of the nineteenth century. Although he was enormously popular with middle-class audiences and never challenged the musical establishment (unlike the pacifist ☛Tippett), he was none the less denied unreserved acceptance. Notwithstanding this, his considerable commercial success incurred the resentment of certain otherwise more daring composers, who tried to use against him the open secret of his relationship with tenor singer Peter Pears.

Alexey Brodovitch 1898-1971

SOVIET-AMERICAN ART DIRECTOR, TEACHER

After a colourful early career, which included a stint as a captain in the Soviet army and fighting Bolsheviks in Odessa, Brodovitch joined up with Diaghilev's nomadic Ballets Russes as a set designer, also taking photographs of their performances which were acclaimed for their innovative use of blur to capture movement. Settling in New York in the early 1930s, he was appointed art director of *Harper's Bazaar* in 1933, a post he held for 25 years. There he showed how an integrated approach to pictures, typography and text could produce layouts that enhanced the original material. ☛Andy Warhol and ☛Irving Penn served as his assistants, and he provided photographers such as Robert Doisneau, ☛Robert Frank , ☛Richard Avedon and Roman Vishniac with opportunities to showcase their work. Perhaps his most remarkable feat lay in persuading the whole-frame fetishist ☛Henri Cartier-Bresson to allow his pictures to be cropped. For over 30 years, Brodovitch's Design Laboratory classes provided photographers, art directors and others with an opportunity to learn their craft. And his influence went wider: 'All photographers,' Penn once remarked, 'are, whether they know it or not, students of Brodovitch.'

Joseph Brodsky
(Josif Brodsky) born 1940

SOVIET-AMERICAN POET

Sent into involuntary exile from the Soviet Union in 1972, Brodsky is a lyric poet who writes from his experience of loneliness, pain and brutality. His troubles with the Soviet authorities started in 1963 when he was denounced as a 'semi-literary parasite'; the following year, he was sentenced to hard labour for refusing to become a 'socially useful' citizen. Released 18 months later, he was then harassed for being a Jew and eventually settled in the US. Although cosmopolitan in his poetic interests – he had translated John Donne and ☛Czeslaw Milosz while in the USSR – and sufficiently fluent to have recently translated some of his own work into English, Brodsky has also described how the 'bread of exile' quickly proves 'stale and weary'. The images of death and oblivion that often recur in his poetry run parallel with his love for the best that is man. While the imagery is frequently sinister and wrapped in melancholy – symbolic images of street lamps in a lonely city, minute laborious physical details accentuating decay and imminent torpor – it is accompanied by a streak of black humour.

Prosecutor: What is your occupation?
Brodsky: I am a poet.
Prosecutor: Who included you in the list of poets?
Brodsky: Who included me in the list of human beings?
Exchange during Brodsky's trial for 'parasitism'

Neville Brody born 1957

BRITISH GRAPHICS DESIGNER

☛Jamie Reid distilled three decades of Situationist philosophies and Dada nihilism into his ☛Sex Pistols work, bringing about a design explosion that more or less swept him away. Brody emerged in the aftermath, energized to believe that anything was possible, that there were no rules except the ones he made up himself. Best known for his role in designing the influential style magazine *The Face*, Brody's attitudes to his brief have always been contradictory. Because he seems to value subversive twists to design norms more than textual content, he has often seemed more prepared to harm than to enhance the legibility of whatever article he is working on. He mixes bold and light, serif and sans serif in different words and in the characters in single words; words often run both up and down the page; large type is mixed with small photographs. The subtle unfamiliarity of his layouts slows readers down, a disconcerting undertow to the forward-moving thrust of a piece. The effect in his work has occasionally been startling, the effect on imitators almost always disastrous, as they follow him into territory where rules no longer apply. When anything goes, those without aggressive confidence are lost. Already this jittery state is calming – magazines now mostly look like static imitations of *The Face*'s blandest back pages, as do adverts, shop fronts and newspaper mastheads. Less influential, but as important, his work on record sleeves in the post-punk era is notable partly for his choice of subjects – almost all 'industrial' electronic groups operating via noise, ritual and general weirdness.

Peter Brook born 1925

BRITISH THEATRE, FILM DIRECTOR, SETTLED IN PARIS

Seeking to create a theatre that goes beyond language, and that communicates to a global audience, is seen as blasphemy in British theatrical circles. Unsurprisingly, Brook now lives and works in Paris, despised by narrowly political directors who see the company he runs as a gang of jet-setters peddling

Joseph Brodsky

amorphous, meaningless and sensational images. 'I am looking for something more volcanic' is Brook's retort. Although he made his name with productions of Shakespeare, he began to feel the pull of Artaud as 'total theatre' in the mid-1960s. Some of his experiments can seem like the work of a crazed mystic, but the productions that emerge from long periods of improvisation and deliberation at his International Centre for Theatre Research – such as *The Mahabharata*, a retelling of the Hindu epic premiered at the Avignon festival of 1985 – suggest new possibilities for theatre, deploying a language of gesture and movement to make a direct appeal to emotions that quasi-political diatribes delivered from London's West End stage can never hope to touch. Brook's forays into cinema, at least since *Lord of the Flies* (1963), have lacked the vitality that his work displays on the stage; on film it seems merely solemn and ritualistic.

James Brown born 1928 (allegedly)

AMERICAN SOUL SINGER

Brown stands apart from any other performer in his longevity, originality and urge to self-aggrandizement. Important both for his musical innovations (he remains the most ripped-off performer in the history of soul) and his startling personality, Brown is remembered as the space-quiffed collapsing suitor of 'Please Please Please', clambering to his knees from under an emperor's cape. The man who is known both for fining musicians who had played a wrong note and for being called on by presidents to stop race riots, Brown personifies certain mythic elements of the R&B star: arrogance, extravagance and sexuality. Unlike his peers, however, he was almost a theoretical musician, so alien and rootless did his ideas and rhythms appear (to white middle-America). Even now that he is in his sixties, it does not seem strange that Brown is still a renowned dancer and hot performer, and that he should continue to brag and create. But his performing career was cut short in December 1988 by a six-year sentence for assault, resisting arrest and possessing an illegal firearm — he had been apprehended only after a car chase across two states, which ended when the police shot out the tyres on Brown's pick-up truck. He was released in 1991.

Norman O. Brown born 1913

AMERICAN LITERARY CRITIC

At a time when critical exegesis of the dissolute has reached considerable sophistication (if that is the word), and the field of study stretches from the Butthole Surfers back to De Sade, it is sad that the writer of the essay 'The Excremental Vision' is not better attended to. He has been quietly shuffled off the map, along with his West Coast sparring partner ☛Herbert Marcuse, for too-conspicuous metaphysical silliness in support of the 1960s. *Love's Body* (1966) was literary criticism that called for an end to repression – throwing off our inhibitions and ending wickedness in the commonality of a great Aquarian love-in. Brown is a Freudian with distinct Esalen tendencies, an unreconstructed Reichian with Christian mystical flourishes, an anti-literalist sort of Marxist, apparently a dabbler but none the less providing intriguing insights into all his conflicting influences. He probably should be read more now – without being wide-eyed about it – but this is a bad time for informed innocence or for visionaries.

Sterling Brown 1901-89

AMERICAN LITERARY CRITIC

A pioneering African-American literary critic, Brown's 1931 essay 'Negro Characters Seen by White Authors' challenged a state of things that is hard now to understand, and spurred on a generation of black writers to meet head-on the weight of stereotypes then common in novels: the contented slave, the comic negro, the brute negro, the tragic mulatto and the exotic primitive. He put together the first serious collection of African-American writing, and significantly helped his pupils – who at various times included ☛Toni Morrison, Sonia Sanchez and ☛ Amiri Baraka (LeRoi Jones) – to dispense with the narrow pantheon of mythical black characters that had peopled writing before them; to evade clichés of protest and naturalism; to hear and use instead the many conflicting rhythms and cadences in black speech.

Trisha Brown born 1936

AMERICAN CHOREOGRAPHER

Coming out of ☛Merce Cunningham's classes via the legendary Judson Dance Theatre, Brown soon developed her own view of dance. In 1968, she began creating her 'equipment pieces', task dances dependent on external support systems, the tasks including moving up walls or walking down the sides of buildings. Brown also evolved accumulation pieces in which each dancer adds to an accretion of gestures, sounds or words until a complex system is built up. Brown, continually imaginative, now choreographs for her own group, the less excitingly named Trish Brown and Dancers; the name is the only concession to dull convention.

Lenny Bruce (Leonard Schneider) 1927-66

AMERICAN COMIC

'His only offence was that he dared tell people the truth,' said ☛Ingmar Bergman after a rare visit to the world of stand-up comedy. Bruce caused offence almost daily (notwithstanding his unpublished children's stories and often touchingly naïve sentimentality); he was the first modern comedian to base his act on sex, religion, politics and, inevitably, obscenity. Eventually, the subject of his act was his act, as he moved from discussing the hypocrisies of popes and rabbis and lovers and the Lone Ranger into the minutiae of his own trials for obscenity. Imprisoned on obscenity charges in 1961, he was under continuous observation by the authorities from then on. Comedy since Bruce has rarely used his ideas; he once admonished Peter Cook for the softness of English satire, a softness that has not altered much. Although Bruce's rampaging honesty and examination of personal motives, particularly regarding sex and love, have been taken up by various comedians, most of them have mistaken self-examination for a *carte blanche* to spatter an audience with their own misanthropy or, more generally, misogyny.

Jerome S. Bruner born 1915

AMERICAN PSYCHOLOGIST

The behaviourist approach to psychology, which hoped to dispose of ideas such as consciousness, mind and emotion in order to explain behaviour purely in terms of the interaction between internal stimuli and their receptor's previous experience, now seems absurdly mechanistic. Psychology has largely moved on, while retaining some of behaviourism's rigorous experimental method. *A Study of Thinking*, which Bruner published with two associates in 1956, helped launch the 'cognitive' approach, studying the mind as a complex information-processing system and attempting to show how information passes through a medley of mental processes. The cognitive 'revolution' is one of those intellectual shifts that should not have taken so long to happen – ironically, it had to wait until the arrival of cybernetics, the study of machine systems, and the new understanding that this brought to information technology.

William Buckley born 1925

AMERICAN POLITICAL COMMENTATOR

Buckley has been a gadfly outsider on the wiseguys' right of US politics since the early 1950s, both as editor of *National Review* and presenter of a television interview programme. But his line, even though not dead centre under ☛Reagan and Bush, has now become an insider's one. In any case, his views are not always shocking, given past stances, but they buzz with wit, zest and mischief – it is the way he says it. A mercurial figure, at odds with East Coast progressive, liberal values after WW2, he is dialectically a 'conservative', not just a right-winger; his creed rests on a faith in a Christian moral order. He defended McCarthyism in 1954, violently attacked the neo-Fascist John Birch Society in the early 1960s, gunned for President Ford over his lapses from anti-Communism, sought legal relaxations on hashish, backed Pinochet's Chile and espoused Carter's Panama treaty. He has been a US delegate to the UN General Assembly, a transatlantic sailor, a CIA agent in Mexico City, a spy writer and a candidate for mayor of New York. A millionaire's son, his manner is, a critic has said, an irresistibly 'precise blend of the aristocratic and the faintly vulgar'. The latter aspect of his character came to the fore during a stint as a television commentator at the 1968 Democratic Convention in Chicago. Repeatedly taunted by his fellow commentator ☛Gore Vidal, Buckley hit back: 'Now listen, you queer. Stop calling me a crypto Nazi or I'll sock you in your goddam face and you'll stay plastered.' He sued Vidal for libel, but didn't take the case to trial.

Charles Bukowski born 1920

AMERICAN NOVELIST, SHORT STORY WRITER

A disciple of the Beats who captured the disillusion following in that movement's wake, Bukowski has turned a ten-year drinking spree, which ended in the charity ward of LA's General Hospital, into a steady stream of poems, short stories and novels about that city's lowlife. These centre on a hard-drinking, pot-bellied character called Henry Chinaski, Bukowski's alter ego, who staggers alongside gutters that yield an occasional fallen angel, but more often only liars, losers and dyspeptic old hags. Bukowski is observant with details, and the best of his short stories have a raunchy humour, but he is also immensely repetitive and has a tendency to ramble. Romanticizing his own lifestyle to transform himself into an icon of the writer-as-drunken-genius, he sees self-destruction as the only reasonable response to a ridiculous world. His screenplay for the semi-autobiographical *Barfly* (1987) showed that he has become cynical enough to trade off his own public image.

Claus Von Bülow

(Cecil Borberg) born 1926

DANISH-AMERICAN JET-SETTER

A Crippenesque celebrity, this imposingly tall Dane, once assistant to oil billionaire John Paul Getty, married into a substantial fortune and then glided into public attention when he was arraigned for attempting to murder his wife Sunny with excessive doses of insulin. Found guilty in 1983, he was retried two years later as a result of evidence uncovered by his lawyer, Alan Dershowitz, and acquitted. It was the indifference of both Von Bülow and the jet-set trendsetters whose parties he attended that built the media's fascination. His antics displayed all the hallmarks of the most sensational, trashy soap opera, including avarice, adultery and murderous ambition. Bülow-watching became an active media pastime, reflecting a never-ending fascination with the proclivities and deceit of jet-set players. Somewhere along the line, Sunny's fate – she is in a coma; medical care costs $500,000 a year – was forgotten. Von Bülow's urbane manner and chilling dapperness were the perfect front for a society enamoured of fame, regardless of its cause.

Luis Buñuel 1900-83

SPANISH FILM-MAKER, SETTLED IN MEXICO AND PARIS

Buñuel, the director who brought surrealism to the cinema, was, like his one-time friend and occasional collaborator Salvador Dali , a very Spanish artist – even though most of his films were made in France or Mexico. Brought up in a rural village known for its miracles and processions, religion – or at least the urge to offend its principles – became a central aspect of his work. In *L'Age d'Or* (1930), his second collaboration with Dali, he depicted Christ as the leader of the Marquis de Sade's libertines, while in *Simon of the Desert* (1965), he mocked Catholic dogma about mortification of the flesh. Nevertheless, he seems to have been attracted to the extremity of Catholicism and to the underlying eroticism of its pageantry. After his early celebrity as a surrealist in Paris, he went to Mexico and churned out some commercial pap before producing *Los Olvidados* (aka *The Young and the Damned*) in 1950, a bleak and violent vision of the lower depths. From then on, he made films which exploited his fascination with the incongruous and the fantastic to question all claims of authority and knowledge; the clergy continued to receive a bad press. He was a serious-minded game-player, with a superb mastery of narrative and visual construction, who made mordant comedy out of bourgeois efforts to constrain human reality. He loved to baffle serious-minded critics who wanted to over-explain his imaginative flights.

Wilfred Burchett 1911-83

AUSTRALIAN JOURNALIST

The first reporter into Hiroshima (and the only one to report the horrors inflicted on the civilian population) and the man who exposed British outrages during the 'free' Greek elections of 1946, this radical Australian journalist was at different times cultivated as the Western powers' only reliable link to the Viet Cong , vilified as a traitor to civilization and exiled from the country of his birth in an era when Australian passports were stamped 'NOT VALID FOR RED CHINA'. Born to severe hardship, in a family which would be ruined and then humiliated during the Depression, he took bitterly against the vagaries of capitalism, and developed into one of only a tiny number of Western journalists prepared to report what Eastern bloc politicians actually said. This led to Burchett himself being treated as the ultimate Communist fellow-traveller. But he was too good a contact – intrepid and resourceful – for other journalists to avoid turning to him as Cold War policies twisted and turned, and alliances formed and collapsed. In Central Europe and the Balkans after WW2, he questioned the Stalinist party-line. Thereafter, throughout the Korean and Vietnam wars, he was unaligned enough to become intimate with both ☛Ho Chi Minh and ☛Henry Kissinger, although his unapologetic willingness to expose what he took to be lies from the Western powers at the onset of the Korean War would always be held against him. His dogged support for embattled Third World countries never faltered, and increasingly after the mid-1960s, he wrote as an advocate of the Hanoi line – turning against the US for the savage way it was pursuing its anti-Communist war, and also against the USSR for its reluctance to support liberation struggles worldwide. His last despatches covered the Vietnamese invasion of Cambodia in the aftermath of the ☛Pol Pot regime.

Chris Burden born 1946

AMERICAN PERFORMANCE ARTIST

When ☛David Bowie sang 'Nail me to your car and I'll tell you who you are,' he was referring to the highly publicized exploits of this Californian performance artist, son of a sheet metal worker, who had himself pinned to the roof of a Volkswagen. Burden's early work – he locked himself in a locker for five days and survived on water piped in to him – was mild compared to the unpleasant things other mutilation-fixated performance artists were doing to themselves: Gustav Metzger, the developer of Auto-Destructive Art (and ☛Pete Townshend's art teacher), exacted a fierce revenge on animal carcases; Fakir Musafar took to assaulting his own body with clamps, daggers and surgical belts; and Rudolf Schwarzkogler of the Vienna Group actually died as a result of deliberate self-destructive 'performances'. But Burden graduated from endurance to damage with 'Shooting Piece', in which a friend shot a bullet at his arm, intending only to graze him but, in fact, taking away a large piece of flesh. This encouraged Burden to further dicing with death, which included lying wrapped in a canvas bag in the middle of a busy street. His more recent work is more sculptural, including a piece called *Samson* (1985-6), for which two 23-foot pieces of timber were arranged like a mousetrap at the entrance to a gallery, under pressure from a jack. As each visitor filed through a turnstile, so the trap was cranked tighter until one day . . . Burden was the inspiration for a whole generation of American cowboy artists who sensed a new frontier of macho.

Anthony Burgess (Anthony John Burgess Wilson) born 1917

❞ BRITISH NOVELIST, COMPOSER BASED
■ IN EUROPE

In a Burgess novel, God is a vindictive bungler who affords humanity as much contempt as that which the author metes out to the characters in his books. A latecomer to literature, Burgess was only stirred to write when his doctor mistakenly announced that, at the age of 42, he had developed a brain tumour and had only one year to live. He has kept up the pace that his imminent demise forced upon him for the ensuing 30 years of good health. Non-political in his diatribes against socialism, Fascism and all liberal ideas that purport to progressiveness, Burgess shares with ☛William Burroughs a distaste for rampant consumerism and the English. His much-vaunted verbal pyrotechnics suggest the self-taught working-class boy who found less solace in human friendship than in a dictionary, and he hangs his wordplays around rather routine narratives and never seems particularly engaged in what he writes – which may be why he can write so much, as well as being omnipresent on television chatshows and as a newspaper columnist. Among his more celebrated novels, *A Clockwork Orange* (1962) pitches an aggressively violent gang of youths against the equally amoral violence of the state, while *Earthly Powers* (1980) evokes ☛Greene and ☛Waugh in its satirical lattice of misguided power, distrust, death and spiritual dissolution. The people in Burgess's universe are smart, though fatalistic, because they realize they will never have the time to attain their own strictly defined goals. Burgess is also a not completely unsuccessful composer, with symphonies and operas to his credit.

Guy Burgess 1911-63

BRITISH SPY, SETTLED IN THE SOVIET UNION

In the early nineteenth century, Burgess might have gone off to Africa, performed dastardly deeds and claimed new territory for the British empire. Born a century later, he worked for the BBC, MI5 and the Foreign Office at a time when British power was on the wane. Burgess blamed the decadence of the nation's aristocracy for this betrayal of Britain's imperial past and became a Marxist committed to the idea that Britain's future lay with the Soviet Union, and that a revolution would enable the country to regain its place in the world. His scruffy appearance, filthy habits and drunken rowdiness created an image contrary to the self-effacement normally associated with spies and prevented him from rising very high up the information-access ladder (whereas Maclean, for example, was in on high-level discussions with the Americans about atomic policy and the Korean War). In 1951, Burgess was recalled from his post in Washington and asked to resign because of disorderly conduct. The net was beginning to close around Maclean, and the two men fled to Moscow.

James Burnham 1905-87

AMERICAN POLITICAL THINKER

A leading intellectual of the American right and a founding editor of the *National Review*, Burnham was a political scientist who proposed the perceptive idea of a contest for power between managerial élites – East, West and elsewhere – as a way to view post-war international relations. He saw these élites as running supranational blocs that were in the end neither capitalist nor socialist but bureaucratic or technical. He was attacked by ☛Orwell in two notable essays of the late 1940s: Burnham's view of evolving political trends within societies was right, Orwell argued, but his predictions were often wrong – he said Germany would win the war – and he saw future events in lurid terms. Like ☛Bertrand Russell briefly, after 1945 Burnham advised the US to take the intitiative and be prepared to use nuclear weapons before the USSR had a chance to expand further. His fixation on power turned into a misleadingly global guide to the many-sided patterns of human conduct, reflecting a distorted caricature of America's love of size. 'Power' is for Burnham what 'class' is for some Marxists – the key to social behaviour, dictating options which we must adopt if we want to be on the winning side. His titles, such as the *The Web of Subversion* (1954) and *Suicide of the West* (1964), have the tense air of the ☛McCarthy era.

William Burroughs born 1914

AMERICAN NOVELIST

This mordant chronicler of our worst imaginings defined himself unapologetically in the early 1950s with his never-to-be-forgotten/forgiven takes on the hobo-drunkard's confessional Beat novel, *Junkie: Confessions of an Unredeemed Drug Addict* (1953) and *Queer* (1955): unapologetically, but also somewhat misleadingly, since Beat is self-pitying in ways that Burroughs has never needed to be (he comes, perhaps not surprisingly, from a wealthy family). From *The Naked Lunch* (1959) on, his homoerotic imagery has become so coldly precise, his cut-ups so drained of conventional moral cause-and-effect, that his writing has contracted into appalled views of the present from an alien future. Desire has mutated from the search for true love, and once-and-for-all absolution has been replaced by endlessly repeated hunts for the quick fix – sex, the needle or any other momentary power displacement. Belief has been replaced by addiction, science by paranoia, classical narrative-as-quest by this cycle of fragments. His dreamlike, vicious lyricism builds a morality out of the knowledge that systems destroy morality – to him, as society tends towards the condition of the police state, we might as well be cruising teen-gang (gay male) outsiders. He plays this for sardonic laughs, but it never compromises the essential bleakness of his vision. Many by-products of his nightmarish SF speculation have entered popular myth, and a more honest appreciation of his gifts (and defects) has begun to emerge, after years of hyperbole and bigotry, thanks largely to the efforts of his most significant reader/disciple, ☛Kathy Acker.

Cyril Burt 1883-1971

BRITISH PSYCHOLOGIST

A pungent contributor to the debate about the respective roles of nature and nurture in determining intelligence, Burt's reputation has been wrecked since his death by the discovery that he fabricated some of his evidence. A brilliant clinical psychologist, he saw heredity as the key determinant of IQ levels and argued for an education system that separated those with high potential from others; he also developed sophisticated statistical techniques to codify IQ numerically. His aims were not unworthy – he hoped to use IQ tests to enable bright, but poor, children to be admitted to better schools – but implementation of his proposals played a part in turning the tide of intellectual fashion against him. Intelligence is multi-faceted rather than a single measurable

William Burroughs
Photo courtesy of John Calder (Publishers) Ltd

attribute; it is possible to be good at creative writing or dealing with people, and bad at maths. Dividing people between grammar schools and secondary moderns on the basis of a particular bundle of capabilities, and thus marking those who went to the latter as having less potential in life, began to make less and less sense. Burt claimed his central thesis was based on the largest-ever study of separated identical twins, but a study of his notes after his death suggested he had invented many, if not all, of these all-too-rare case studies. But it is also possible that Leslie Hearnshaw, who 'exposed' him, may have fabricated evidence too. Burt's interest in intelligence reflected his own need to be seen at the top of the intellectual ladder. Like many others with large egos to support, a terror of being revealed as a sham may have driven him to self-destructive unscrupulousness.

The Byrds 1965-73

Roger McGuinn born 1942
Chris Hillman born 1942
Gene Clark born 1941
David Crosby
(David Van Cortland) born 1941
Michael Clarke born 1943

AMERICAN ROCK GROUP

They took ☛Bob Dylan's clanking, hoarse folk ballads and made them into Beatlesque wisps of pop, taking George Harrison's ringing guitar sound and developing it into the strange pseudo-Indian sound of 'Eight Miles High' and then, after Gram Parsons joined up with Byrds leader Roger McGuinn , the group 'discovered' their country roots. Finally they faded, as American rock loudly entered the 1970s in a slew of fuzz guitars and pedal steel. The Byrds began as Carnaby Street streamlined for the West Coast – all tiny Lennon shades, Brian Jones haircuts and Seekers-style English folk – but later became more American than even presidential candidates are required to be. In that time, they explored notions of style, psychedelia, America and the past more effectively than most.

C

Cabaret Voltaire formed 1975

BRITISH ELECTRONIC MUSIC GROUP

Part of the wave of British electronic experimentalists whose emergence ran parallel with punk but whose musical effects were more far-reaching, Cabaret Voltaire took their name from the Swiss café-cabaret used by the Dadaists during WW1. Fascinated by the idea of chance in art, they translated it into industrial rock terms. Their early singles helped define the sense of diversity and dark adventure of the immediate post-punk period, while their album, *Voice of America* (1980), with its use of taped cut-ins of voices from the media, established a form that influenced a broad range of contemporary music, from Frankie Goes to Hollywood in the pop mainstream to early hip-hop. With *Crackdown* in 1983, they made a bid for pop acceptability that initially had its seductions but ultimately lost direction.

Amilcar Cabral 1924-73

GUINEA-BISSAU POLITICAL LEADER, REVOLUTIONARY THEORIST

Italy's Red Brigade terrorists read Cabral's writings (he has been called the African ☛Che Guevara) but did not take much note of his slowly-but-surely approach to revolution. If they had, the Red Brigades might have been kicking their heels for so long that their fervour would have died: the factories of Turin were less ready to rise than the backward villages of Guinea-Bissau under less-than-formidable Portuguese rule. Cabral's African Independence Party of Guinea-Bissau and Cape Verde (PAIGC) initially pursued independence through peaceful action but took up arms following the violent repression of a strike. Advisers from China and the USSR urged Cabral to strike fast; he said he would move only when he had built a base for support. He established a democratic government centred upon peasant communities – setting up schools and health teams in the steadily expanding area under PAIGC control. His revolution was based upon a realistic knowledge of his people, an avoidance of wishful thinking and an acceptance of gradualism. The Portuguese killed him, but not the political system he had built.

John Cage born 1912

AMERICAN COMPOSER, THEORIST, MYCOLOGIST

☆ One of the most influential avant-garde artists of the century, Cage has had far more effect outside music than in it; even in it, and through the legacy of his immediate pupils – Morton Feldman, Earle Brown, Christian Wolff and David Tudor – his theoretical writing has had as much significance as any of his compositions. None the less, *Imaginary Landscapes 4* (1951, for 12 radios continually re-tuned) and *4'33"* (1952, the one where nothing happens) dramatically presented his call for the introduction of chance elements and indeterminacy into composition. A pupil of Schoenberg (who praised his technical skill, but not his attitudes), conversion to Zen Buddhism pushed his music towards an approach that was the opposite of serialism – hoping by example and invocation to alter what constitutes a composer's purpose and what counts as music. Jazz musicians obviously preceded him, but he was the first composer from a classical background to recognize the changes that sound recording brought to aesthetics, and the first to return to any tradition of improvisation. One of the most likeable of artistic extremists, Cage's gentle anarchism has always extended to the performer's relationship with the audience – his anti-aesthetic insists that music is a thing of wider possibility than was supposed. Not one to stand on his dignity, he became a well-known figure on Italian television, answering questions about mushrooms on a popular quiz programme.

Maria Callas
(Maria Kalogeropoulou) 1923-77

GREEK OPERA SINGER

The archetypal operatic diva, whose virtuosity was breath-taking, Callas displayed a temper off-stage as short as her range on-stage was wide. Opera house managers were driven to distraction by her demands, while their audiences were transported by her talent and striking appearance. Although she was capable of an occasional ostentatious flurry of sheer technical ability, she never lost the emotional focus of her voice. Initially favoured for Wagnerian roles, she later acquired a greater reputation for her interpretations of Verdi, Puccini and Bellini. The uniqueness of her voice lay in its combining the power of a dramatic soprano with the lightness appropriate to more frothy operatic concoctions. The record of her personal life included a tumultuous marriage to Italian industrialist Meneghini, who also acted as her manager, and an affair with Aristotle Onassis, who cast her off in favour of Jacqueline Kennedy.

Italo Calvino 1923-85

& CUBAN-ITALIAN NOVELIST

Calvino could have been just one among the many post-war writers who wanted to rebuild the world through all the flurry and weirdness of words. Instead, combining Italy's underrated cultural confidence and his own remarkable anti-narrative ability, he ended up outstripping them all. A Communist in the 1950s, he began as a novelist locked into the clarity of the same anti-Fascist sensibility as Italy's neo-realist film-makers. Later he became a significant collector of folk-tales, and worked from a resilient realism-of-the-moment out towards an astonished variety of takes on the cosmos, its purpose and its possibilities. At the heart of his technique is the erotic reader-writer complicity in storytelling – with a book such as *If on a Winter's Night a Traveller* (1979/1981), he converts the standard device of the stylistically striking opening chapter into an infinitely receding series of new beginnings that the reader can never get beyond, inspiring meditative surprise rather than the frustrated irritation that caused ☛Nabokov, for example, sometimes to lose his readers. Well versed in the outer reaches of science and its paradoxes, Calvino opened up more possibilities for writing, social or aesthetic, than any other artist of his high book-world reputation since the war.

James Cameron 1911-85

BRITISH JOURNALIST

It was characteristic of Cameron's luck that, in the course of a 1966 interview with the prime minister of North Vietnam, ☛Ho Chi Minh should arrive unexpectedly, keen to chat despite having earlier refused. 'Let's leave that to the PM,' Cameron reports him as saying about anything to do with politics. 'Tell me what the Haymarket looks like these days.' Once dubbed the prince of journalists, Cameron was tough, vulnerable, sentimental, embattled, liberal and impeccably honest. Having worked his way up from paste-boy on a local Scottish paper, he sent reports to *Picture Post* on the first underwater detonation of an atom bomb, at Bikini, and the huge Korean coastal assault at Inchon; then lost his job for sending outspoken accounts of the treatment of North Korean POWs by South Korea's venal and violent leader ☛Syngman Rhee, an ally of the West who had not been criticized till then. He went on to work for the ill-fated *News Chronicle*, the *Daily Mail*, the *Daily Herald*, the *Evening Standard* and the BBC. A massive heart attack then forced him to give up globe-trotting and into a twilight decade of highly subjective, emotional, intelligent columns for the *Guardian*. Cameron's abiding humanity helped him talk hard sense to the high and mighty in an age when such a thing was still possible. Circumstances, and newspapers, are different now.

Joseph Campbell 1904-87

AMERICAN MYTHOGRAPHER

Campbell took the totality of surviving pre-scientific myths and boiled them down into a single story, in the process offering a 'scientific' vindication of America's obsessive individualism. The 'monomyth' he describes in *The Hero with a Thousand Faces* (1949) relates how a heroic individual, after a period of study with a wise old guardian, sets out on a protracted journey, endures many trials, wins a battle against a sinister enemy and, following self-discovery, emerges to revive an ailing community. This book so influenced the young George Lucas that he was to thank Campbell for having been the accidental progenitor of the 1977 film *Star Wars*. As with the infinitely more sophisticated work being done by ☛Lévi-Strauss, Campbell's approach largely ignores what particular myths meant to particular people. And while his four-volume *Masks of God* (1959-68) makes important points about the way in which myths have been used to orientate people in relation to their inner selves, their societies and the universe, whenever Campbell tried to relate his ideas to the contemporary scene, he drifted into incoherence – a result of his wanting to believe he was living in the best of all possible times. Three years after his death, Campbell acquired guru status in the US when a series of television interviews, *The Power of Myth*, was broadcast on PBS. In the UK, the programmes caused barely a ripple.

Albert Camus 1913-60

FRENCH NOVELIST, PLAYWRIGHT, PHILOSOPHER

Although often associated with ☛Sartre and ☛de Beauvoir as a post-war existentialist and advocate of 'commitment', Camus' pitch was radically different. Unimpressed by summonses from middle-class radicals to take to the barricades, or flights of abstract thought, he opted for the celebration of simple human pleasures. Sartre was a philosopher who wrote novels, plays and almost everything else; Camus was essentially a novelist, who used metaphor to express his ideas about broader issues. Analytically in *The Rebel* (1951/3), allegorically in *The Plague* (1947/8), he argued that totalitarian organizations set up for the general good can liberate no one and destroy no injustice. Brought up in the slums of Algiers, his view of life was based on an acceptance of human suffering. Human beings should simply acknowledge that the world is irrational; there is no way out. Just as Sisyphus rolls his rock uphill again however many times it slips back, so life should be lived for all the pleasure and pain it offers. His celebrations of physical and emotional intensity, combined with an acceptance of human imperfection, make him a more attractive figure than Sartre, with whom he quarrelled over an essay by ☛Merleau-Ponty that justified the use of violence for political ends; less attractively, he also differed from him over the future of colonial Algeria, which he did not want to see fully independent.

Elias Canetti born 1905

☞ BULGARIAN-BRITISH WRITER

The first 'British' citizen to win the Nobel prize for literature (in 1981), Canetti's life might have been invented by ☛Borges. Born in Bulgaria to Spanish-Jewish parents, his first language was Ladino. He began his schooling in London and wrote much of his work, from a Hampstead flat, in German – the 'secret language' used by his parents when they did not want little Elias to understand. In 1927, he became caught up in the running mob responsible for igniting the Justizpalast in Vienna, and all his major writings reflect his subsequent fear that flames would consume everything he lived for. His only novel *Auto-da-Fé* (1935/1946) culminates, like ☛Eco's *The Name of the Rose*, in the burning of a library – the core of existence for a catastrophically unworldly Sinologist who has been tricked into marrying his rapacious housekeeper and then expelled into an underworld of grotesques. Canetti's preoccupations were further developed in *Crowds and Power* (1960), his musings on the way people lose their individuality in a crowd, and the various forms of interaction that result. His weird, obsessive imagination is also on display in his original travel book, *The Voices of Marrakesh* (1967/87), which has such chapter headings as 'The cries of the blind', 'The maraboul's saliva' and 'The donkey's concupiscence', and in a play, *The Numbered*, set in a totalitarian state whose citizens are named by numbers representing the ages at which they must die. Canetti fathered his first child at the age of 67.

Truman Capote

(Truman Streckfuss Persons) 1924-84

AMERICAN NOVELIST, JOURNALIST

A leading progenitor of the New Journalism, Capote's creed – that the truth was best served with a dash of invention – helped him form a genre as it destroyed him. His dandyish novels and his brilliantly captious glamour-profiles of the 1950s, for *Vogue*, *Harper's Bazaar* and *The New Yorker*, set the agenda for the 1960s with their flip, precise celebration-dissections of stardom, sex and their respective discontents. But his phenomenally successful 1966 examination of a vicious and senseless small-town murder, *In Cold Blood*, seemed to drain something from him, as if the truth of genuine violence destroyed his faith in revelatory invention. For the next 18 years, Capote sold himself on the promise of his never-to-be -finished novel, *Answered Prayers*. The fraction that survived, not much more than what had been excerpted in *Esquire* almost ten years before his death, showed that his imagination had turned ugly and his once-legendary ability to connect had long vanished. He became an increasingly eccentric media parasite, living off his reputation – the need to question life through his work having given way to the desire for celebrity.

Ernesto Cardenal born 1925

✌ NICARAGUAN POET, POLITICIAN,
∀ RELIGIOUS LEADER

Cardenal has challenged state violence through writing, preaching and politics. His best poems blend chronicles and myths with the rubble of city life – shop signs, newspaper headlines and advertisements – and aim at political targets; thus *Hora O* (1960) depicts the sorrows inflicted upon Nicaragua by dictators and interventionist foreign powers. Cardenal retreated into a monastery following his first brutal encounter with radical politics as a student activist in the early 1950s, and after becoming a Roman Catholic priest, he set up a community on the island of Solentiname in Lake Nicaragua, where the poor discussed the Bible in relation to their own lives. Initially an advocate of non-violence, Cardenal came to argue that the Church would have to play a role in liberating the poor from oppression, and gave his support to the guerrillas fighting the dictatorship of ☛Somoza. Eventually becoming minister of culture in the now-dismissed Sandinista government, he has had several run-ins with ☛Pope John Paul II, who believes that holding office in a revolutionary government is incompatible with a pastoral vocation. Cardenal's recent poetry is a powerful articulation of Latin American liberation theology, the dream of a 'new human being' integrated into a loving community.

Pierre Cardin born 1922

$ ITALIAN-FRENCH CLOTHES DESIGNER,
✓ BUSINESS EXECUTIVE

Of all the designers who have diversified out of haute couture, Cardin has ventured furthest – the 800 or so products that carry his name range from cigarettes, chocolates and toilet seats to dolls, skis, pens and toothpaste. Having worked with Dior at the time of the New Look, Cardin launched his own label in 1953. He was first to make designer clothes available as a ready-to-wear collection, a step which led to his expulsion from the couturiers' professional body in 1959. During the 1960s, he became renowned for hard geometric shaping and for gimmicky innovations such as incorporating vinyl into his 1964 'Space Age' line – homage, he said, to the Apollo space programme. Fearful of his standing in the less innovative 1970s, he made his first move out of clothes, initially into furniture and then into practically everything else. Cardin is now big business, with 840 factories in 102 countries, together employing some 190,000 people. He has expanded into Eastern Europe, China and the Soviet Union.

Stokely Carmichael

(Kwame Touré) born 1941

✌ TRINIDADIAN-AMERICAN POLITICAL ACTIVIST

Black Power – a term Carmichael invented – represented in the mid-1960s no more than a call for black citizens to take up arms in self-defence and a refusal to let the process of enfranchisement be negated by reactionary violence. But at the time, when the right to vote in several parts of the US was still new enough not to be certain of survival, the situation was probably too fragile to tolerate such a summons. Carmichael, born in Trinidad and educated in the US, made his name in the rural South as president of the Student Non-Violent Co-ordinating Committee (SNCC), which fought segregation through direct action. From 1966, following the murder of ☛Malcolm X, SNCC took over as the radical wing of the civil rights movement. However, their subsequent espousal of black nationalism coincided with a withdrawal from the rural roots they had fostered so intelligently, and from 1967, Carmichael's flair for street rhetoric got the better of him. He declared – from Cuba – that revolution in the US was necessary and urged the torching of Washington DC. From the late 1960s, he linked SNCC to the Black Panthers, who saw themselves as a Viet Cong force in urban America, but their aggressive style only accelerated their decline from organizational politics into street theatre – the fact that they were permanently armed gave police a direct excuse to shoot first. In 1969, Carmichael broke with the Panthers and the Left generally; the situation was out of control, and he was being harassed constantly on all sides – by this time he had been banned from entering any Commonwealth country (he still is). He moved to Guinea in Africa with his then-wife, the singer-activist ☛Miriam Makeba, changed his name to Kwame Touré and started to work for the pan-African movement. Carmichael was no angel of coherence or consistency, and his militant style scared, and still scares, many white observers – but what SNCC achieved in the South attests to his early political vision.

Anthony Caro

born 1924

BRITISH SCULPTOR

'Sculpture can be anything' was the insight with which Caro moved British sculpture away from the monumental bronzes of ☛Henry Moore, his former teacher. Although his practice of scavenging raw materials in the backyards of factories and among demolished buildings has been compared to ☛Warhol's raid on the iconography of the mass media, Caro's sense of his work as an 'expression of feeling' is a long way from the pop artist's camp sensibility. After a trip to the US, where he learned about abstraction from ☛Clement Greenberg and welding from ☛David Smith, Caro started to make ground-hugging pieces out of prefabricated metal – including aluminium tubes, the tops of boiler tanks, propellor blades and the like. Despite the hint of the shipyards evoked, the results are elegant celebrations of abstract shape displaying lightness and fine precision of line: *Early One Morning* (1962) is a bright red construction of beams and steel rods, while *Month of May* (1966) consists of magenta, orange and green aluminium rods flung over a supporting framework of beams. Caro used colours to express distinctive 'moods' and to take away the weightiness from the parts in his pieces, but abandoned the practice in the early 1970s as his sculptures became more austere and geometric. The extent of his influence as a catalyst of Britain's new sculpture movement is partly due to his having been a teacher at St Martin's School of Art in London (1953-64), where he taught Philip King, Barry Flanagan and Peter Hide, among others.

Rachel Carson 1907-64

○ AMERICAN MARINE BIOLOGIST, WRITER

♦ It was through studying the complex ecology of the sea, and the equilibrium sustained by endless competition between marine species, that Carson became aware of the ways in which science threatened to destroy the balance of the natural world. 'It is our alarming misfortune that so primitive a science has armed itself with the most modern and terrible weapons,' she wrote, 'and that in turning them against the insects, it has turned them against the earth.' Her *Silent Spring* (1962) was the first eco-shocker, detailing the toxic effects of agricultural chemicals on wildlife and human beings. It led to an immediate toughening of the laws on pesticide use – although it was ten years before the US banned DDT (which was still legally on sale in the UK until 1984). A lot more poisonous filth has, of course, been pumped into the earth's air and waters since Rachel Carson brought its dangers to the world's attention.

John le Carré *see* le Carré, John

Angela Carter born 1940

BRITISH NOVELIST

Carter is a writer of adult fairy tales whose subversion of the romantic originals provides entertainment for girls and boys who like their De Sade mixed with Suchard chocolate. A fascination with violence, be it tattooing, mutilation, castration or cannibalism, has exerted an abrasive influence over her feminist character studies. These include *The Magic Toyshop* (1967), a parable about an orphaned girl who is visited by horrors when sent to live with her uncle, and *The Sadeian Woman* (1979), her non-fiction dissection of the new pornography. Though sometimes coy and aloof in her symbolism, Carter produces horror fantasies worthy of ☛Burroughs and ☛Ballard, and serves as a precursor to ☛Kathy Acker. Her ideal seems to be 'to let the sleep of reason beget monsters'.

Elliott Carter born 1908

☞ AMERICAN COMPOSER

Although he attended the first performances of ☛Varèse's music in his youth and became enthralled by modernism, Carter felt for some time constrained to maintain the Stravinsky-style neo-classicism he had acquired from his teacher, Nadia Boulanger. His personal style made its first appearance in his Cello Sonata of 1948, and since then he has explored atonality with a robust independence, creating music characterized by an inventive energy as well as great textural and metrical complexity. Working in all substantial instrumental forms, his tendency to cast instruments as characters in an abstract drama is most apparent from the concertos. The result is a music of restless motion, in which contrasting waves of sound clash against each other.

Henri Cartier-Bresson born 1908

FRENCH PHOTOGRAPHER

Although the way he used to talk about his hunt for subjects – prowling the streets, 'very strung-up and ready to pounce' – suggested an image of Cartier-Bresson as a photographic mugger, his approach depends upon the non-presence of the photographer in the picture being taken. Just as the sitters in the portraits were asked not to acknowledge what was being done to them, so the people he captured on the streets had either forgotten, or were unaware, that a camera was being pointed in their direction. Cartier-Bresson's aim was to capture the 'decisive moment' when an action achieved formal perfection. This led him to talk about the 'pure pleasure of form' in a way that invited attack on the grounds that his pictures were *only* beautiful. In fact, his painterly eye brought home with greater force the realities of life for those who lived at the centres of modern cities, or in slums and brothels across the world. Producing his first major reportage from Spain in 1933, Cartier-Bresson subsequently worked in Africa, Mexico, the US, India and elsewhere, and was one of the founders of Magnum, the agency that represents the world's top photo-journalists.

John Cassavetes 1929-89

✣ AMERICAN FILM DIRECTOR, ACTOR

'I consider myself an amateur film maker and a professional actor' was Cassavetes' account of himself. Generally regarded as the founder of alternative cinema in the US, his 1960 film *Shadows* offered a challenge to the mainstream that was low in budget but high in authenticity. His films resembled his acting performances – gutsy, rough and slightly wild. After a brief, unhappy flirtation with Hollywood he held to his own line in the making of movies. This involved building up his loosely plotted explorations of human relationships in association with a regular team of performers – Ben Gazzara, Peter Falk and his wife Gena Rowlands. Cassavetes' characters in films such as *A Woman under the Influence* (1974) and *Gloria* (1980) start on the edge, gradually exposing even more of their frailties, faults and contradictions. Some films contain scenes of emotional barnstorming that stretch on so long, like extended jazz improvisations, that the performing virtuosity exhausts the viewer. The reward, particularly in *A Woman under the Influence*, comes from moments of intense revelation.

Carlos Castaneda born 1925

☆ PERUVIAN-AMERICAN

ANTHROPOLOGIST

Academic-turned-mystic, Castaneda acquired counter-culture popularity with his accounts of his five-year period of training as a 'man of knowledge', guided by the possibly fictitious Don Juan Matus, which gave intellectual justification of a sort for the use of hallucinogenic drugs. His first bestseller, *The Teachings of Don Juan: A Yaqui Way of Knowledge* (1968), offers an esoteric casserole of Yaqui Indian doctrines and drug-induced psycho-babble. During the early 1970s, several sequels to this pop-psychology bible appeared, drawing comparisons with the widely-publicized hype of Cyril Hoskins, the British plumber and novelist who purportedly transcribed the spiritual edicts of Lobsang Rampa – a Tibetan monk who was either an alter ego or an expedient literary device. Don Juan's tabulations appealed to a muddle-headed generation who did not like the way things were and sought an easy ride to some form of separate reality. No one else has ever reported meeting Don Juan.

We are both beings who are going to die. There is no more time for what we used to do. Now you must employ all the not-being I have taught you and stop the world.

Don Juan to Carlos Castaneda

Leo Castelli

(Leo Krauss) born 1907

$ YUGOSLAV-AMERICAN ART DEALER

It is necessary to understand the Castelli philosophy in order to understand why, ever since ☛Clement Greenberg was left holding up the tattered flag of abstract expressionism, art dealers have eclipsed art critics as arbiters of artistic reputations. For Castelli, whatever artists do is art, and the job of an art dealer is to find the 'leaders of a new movement' – artists who do things differently – but such ideas lead inevitably to the avant-garde being equated with the latest artistic gimmick. Once an insurance broker in Trieste, Bucharest and Paris, Castelli worked in US army intelligence and set up a company manufacturing sweaters before he established the first of his two galleries in 1957. There he built his reputation as a spotter of new talent with exhibitions of ☛Jasper Johns' flags and targets and the combine paintings of ☛ Rauschenberg, and he went on to promote the careers of ☛Frank Stella, ☛Roy Lichtenstein, James Rosenquist and ☛Andy Warhol. More recently, he has been responsible for the puffery surrounding the work of such critically execrated neo-expressionists as ☛Julian Schnabel and ☛David Salle.

Fidel Castro

born 1926

CUBAN POLITICAL LEADER

Son of a middling-rich sugar plantation owner, Castro led a revolution from the hills against the Cuban dictator Fulgencio Batista, who fled in 1959. It was Castro's second try; the first, in the early 1950s, had led to two years in jail. He has now been a Communist state leader longer than anyone else, but he only emerged as a Marxist-Leninist in 1961 after the US's failed 'Bay of Pigs' invasion attempt – a response to his confiscating $1 billion worth of US property. Like Egypt's ☛Nasser, once rejected by the West he turned to the USSR; unlike Nasser, he became a Communist. Noted for his beard and his cigar – the CIA tried to bump him off with an exploding version of the latter – he has long been a heart-throb for revolutionaries everywhere. In the 30 yearssince the revolution, Cuba has instituted a highly developed health service and literacy programme and become one of the most racially integrated societies in the world; it has also become increasingly reliant on the Soviet Union for aid, and acted as the USSR's military surrogate in Africa. Castro's Cuba is a nasty dictatorship with political prisoners, a personality cult and torture for opponents – seventh from the bottom in the global league table devised for Charles Humana's *World Human Rights Guide* (1983).

Nicolae Ceauşescu

1918-89

ROMANIAN POLITICAL LEADER

The execution of Nicolae Ceauşescu and his wife Elena on Christmas Day 1989, only ten days after Romanian troops had massacred unarmed protesters in the city of Timisoara, was the most significant and unexpected event in a year of Eastern European revolutions. As president of Romania, Ceauşescu put brothers, sisters, nephews, nieces, cousins and in-laws into senior posts, gaining a reputation as the most repressive head of an Eastern European society. He forced residents of 7000 villages into modern 'agri-complexes' (a process officially termed 'systematization'), thereby setting aside considerations of humanity, taste and tradition; and because many of those affected were ethnic Hungarians, this caused intense friction with Romania's Eastern bloc neighbour. This was an example of the sort of independent behaviour that had earlier made him something of a Western hero. He set out, from 1965 when he became party secretary-general, on a path of his own, fostering ties with the West, China and Israel; opposing the Soviet invasion of Czechoslovakia in 1968, and once mobilizing Romania's forces against the risk of Warsaw Pact attack. Ceauşescu's downfall followed a stage-managed rally in Bucharest where the obligatory waving of flags gave way to boos and catcalls seen by millions of television viewers. In the ensuing unrest, the army changed sides and anti-Ceauşescu forces captured the television centre, although many died as members of the Securitate militia fought on. The new leaders were left with the formidable task of rebuilding a devastated economy and democratic institutions after 40 years of one-party rule.

Paul Celan

(Paul Antschel) 1920-70

† ROMANIAN-FRENCH POET

Celan lost both his parents in the concentration camps and was himself subjected to internment in a Romanian labour camp in 1944, experiences that haunted all his post-war work. Prior to the war, he had made a few tentative forays into verse, but it was amid the aftermath in Paris that he forged his reputation. Language, he said, was the only thing that remained intact for him. His imagery is often restrained – some of his work has been criticized for laying an aesthetic veneer over the camps – but it gains tension from the gulf between the refinement of its form and the terrible reality it is describing. His meditations on the possibilities of speech acts or of abstention from them, together with his personal and poetic involvement in the Holocaust, have resulted in a flood of commentary.

Claude Chabrol

born 1930

FRENCH FILM DIRECTOR

Chabrol, like other less likely members of the French New Wave, made criticial obeisance to ☛Alfred Hitchcock as the master of suspense, but welded this genre to the intellectual concerns of the art film, resulting in thrillers that fascinate as much as they chill. His stories of calculated violence and repressed sexuality gain their force from the way they are rooted in French provincial settings. The action of *Le Boucher* (1969), for example, is placed so securely among the rituals of marriage and death, and against the calm symbolism of a flowing river, that the discovery of a mutilated body by a group of schoolchildren is a shattering intrusion. But the chills are regularly highlighted against the scenes manifesting the director's pleasure in food: the first thing the heroine of *Violette Nozière* (1978) does after committing murder is to eat her way through a chunk of beef, and Chabrol is said to be himself a first-class cuisinier. As a director, he seemed for a while content to play variations on the same theme, relying on cinematic plausibility rather than psychological veracity. As mellowing age has thawed his icy intensity, the films have become more discursive and less intriguing – only the posters promise a return to the form of *Le Boucher*.

Lindy Chamberlain

born 1948

AUSTRALIAN VICTIM

Chamberlain became the focus of an Australian witch hunt, where justice was defined by public opinion, the media and circumstantial evidence. In 1980, the Chamberlains' nine-month-old child disappeared from a camp in deserted bushland; Lindy claimed she saw a dingo running from her tent, with the baby clutched in its jaws. Initial sympathy turned to scepticism as a result of the mother's apparent indifference – actually a reflection of her religious convictions as a member of the Seventh Day Adventist Church. Malicious speculation was further fuelled by police failure to find the baby's body. A trial for murder in 1982 condemned the mother to life imprisonment, for cutting the baby's throat; subsequent appeals were unsuccessful until new evidence emerged. It took seven years to transform Lindy Chamberlain in the public eye from hated killer to victim of social prejudice. The case pandered to the crudest Australian passion for the chase – hunting the detached, isolated figure through the courts because she failed to make a public display of maternal despair. Although the Chamberlains were judicially exonerated and their story was made into a feature film, *Cry in the Dark* (1988), Chamberlain and her family received no compensation from the Australian government and they filed for bankruptcy in 1989.

Charles, Prince of Wales

born 1948

BRITISH HEIR TO THE THRONE

The look of anguish on his face as Prince Charles speaks about the fate of unemployed youth, the state of the nation and the future for the planet may reflect his discomfort at speaking about such things from a position of high privilege. Constitutionally unable to direct imprecations against those actually responsible for coarsening the nation's heart, he has diverted most of his attention, and his substantial influence (no one finds it easier to secure press attention for his pronouncements), towards determining the future shape of British architecture. Just as an order from his wife, Princess Diana, can make the reputation of a fashion designer, so Charles has made certain that planners throughout the country will bear him in mind when making their decisions. To hear the Prince bleating on about the destruction of Wren's skyline, or praising the film-set buildings constructed by Quinlan Terry on the banks of the Thames at Richmond, you would sometimes imagine he did not know that the last two centuries had happened. By his attempts to become involved in contemporary issues, Charles shows just how far removed he is from the realities of his subjects' lives, and just how irrelevant the monarchy has become. Although he is sometimes depicted as battling against current orthodoxies, his dislike of bureaucracy (of the sort that tells people what kind of housing is best for them) and intellectuals (with their high-flying ideas about modernist architecture) can be assimilated into trends within contemporary conservatism.

Ray Charles

(Ray Charles Robinson) born 1930

AMERICAN SINGER, MUSICIAN

Blind from the age of six, Ray Charles was the first, as singer and piano player, to fuse the conflicting traditions of blues and gospel – secular sorcery with religious fervour – and endless imitations of his vocal cadences now litter the history of popular music. His contribution is almost too basic to register: it is the ground on which pop walks. White artists spent two decades trying to appropriate his energy, and a further decade trying to escape his influence, but it was not until the first wave of punk that they succeeded in evading him. As with many of the R&B generation, Charles has latterly been much acknowledged, although public awareness has not allowed him to do more than regurgitate his early triumphs. While it is true that none of the work he has done since the early 1960s matches the fruitful shock of that initial synthesis, his broad re-examination of the roots of country soul affirms his intelligent mastery.

Bruce Chatwin 1940-89

∀ BRITISH WRITER

Chatwin's writings reflect an interest in remote places and idiosyncratic patterns of thought, but the approach goes far beyond that of even an observant travel writer. His underlying theme is distaste for the noisy city, and the uniformity that modern life fosters. Once head of the Impressionist department at Sotheby's in London, he left to study archaeology: when an academic award took him to New York, he found he could not write and fled to Africa. Chatwin's work pursues his interest in characters who enclose themselves in the past, living in a state of suspension while everything around them changes. Among the bizarre people he found on his wanderings around southern Argentina and Chile, which became *In Patagonia* (1977), was a German farmer who, when he raised a glass, would toast the mad nineteenth-century king, Ludwig of Bavaria. *On the Black Hill* (1983) concerns twin brothers, born in 1900, who live the century as farmers in the Welsh hills, largely unaware of the outside world until an aeroplane takes them soaring above it on their eightieth birthday. His last novel, *Utz* (1988), focuses on a porcelain collector in Prague who works on, unaware that history has destroyed the Central European culture which was the source of the values to which he still subscribes.

César Chávez born 1927

MEXICAN-AMERICAN UNION LEADER

Coming from Arizona, Chávez transformed trade union campaigns for migrant Hispanic farm workers in California into a national issue. Written off as a failure at school, he went on to become, in 1968, a national hero who was fêted by all three rivals for the US presidency, receiving especially strong support from Robert Kennedy. His targets for unionization were people to whom US labour laws were of no help and who needed unusual forms of aid. Chávez used not just strikes and pickets, but also marches, consumer boycotts and hunger fasts, as he injected ethnic self-help and Catholic zeal into the bid to organize and win better conditions. Another creative idea was to seek group contracts for workers, enrolled as a self-employed bargaining unit, not just a union. By encouraging voter registration, he played a significant role in building Hispanic self-awareness while he turned their interests into a countrywide issue through the 1968 boycott of Californian grapes, aimed at bringing to the negotiating table those grape-growers who would not negotiate with the United Farm Workers Organizing Committee (UFWOC), the group that Chávez led. In the 1970s and 1980s, UFWOC was a declining force, and Chávez became known for eccentrically trying to foist his own enthusiasms – holistic religion, vegetarianism, faith healing – on union members.

Judy Chicago
(Judy Cohen) born 1939

✌ AMERICAN ARTIST

Since 1969, when she turned away from her 'mainstream' work – hard, shiny, minimal sculptures – Chicago has outraged and delighted her (mainly feminist) audience by painting vulvas that look like exotic flowers and carry evocative titles such as *How does it feel to stretch as far as you can?* She helped to found the Feminist Studio Workshop in Los Angeles, and in the mid-1970s, her position at the centre of a female subculture and interest in china painting led to *The Dinner Party*, a three-year ensemble project involving ceramicists and embroidery experts. These traditional female crafts were applied to a huge dinner-table setting which Chicago described as 'a sort of reinterpretation of the last supper from the point of view of those who had done the cooking'. It was also a celebration of famous women, fictional and non-fictional; 39 famous women guests were 'expected', and a further 999 names were inscribed on the floor. First exhibited in March 1979, it was the source of instant controversy – many museums have refused to house it. Much mocked at the time, the piece formed the emotional focus of a new wave of feminist art, flouting taboos and rupturing conventional histories.

Nancy Chodorow born 1944

✌ AMERICAN FEMINIST

Chodorow's distinctive feminism derives from her answer to one question: why do women want to be mothers? She believed this desire should not be credited to innate instinct, or ideological conditioning, but had to be seen rather as part of a complex system of psychological patterning, developed within the family. Little girls remain 'attached' to their mothers at a stage in development when boys are driven by the workings of their Oedipus complex to see Mum as someone 'other'; from then on, women define themselves in relation to others, while men seek to mark out their separate identities. This not only makes women good mothers, it also gives them the desire to re-create their infantile experience within the family. For Chodorow, women's acceptance of the domestic position lies at the root of their oppression. If men could learn to take an equal role in parenting, they would also acquire the benefits that flow from defining oneself in relation to others, and sexual inequality would disappear. Although reducing 'maleness' to destructiveness quickly becomes simplistic, Chodorow reaches her conclusions through a subtle deployment of psychoanalytic findings.

Noam Chomsky born 1928

AMERICAN LINGUIST, POLITICAL ACTIVIST

The cold eye that Chomsky has cast over executive lies, not-so-covert superpower activities in the Third World, and the Fourth Estate's failure to report (let alone criticize) the same enters a third decade undimmed. The founder of generative grammar and a respected academic who has done much to clarify the underlying forms of language, he has, since the beginning of the Vietnam war, also pursued a career as 'watcher at the gates' of our moral consistency. In the tradition of ☛I. F. Stone's *Weekly*, he condenses official releases – and press reports – to tease out the ludicrous and ugly contradictions in position-taking, and to lay bare the implicit racism and explicit arrogance that inform high-level decision-making. The link between his politics and his linguistics is a belief that, since all languages operate with exactly similar root power and sophistication, the assumptions of cultural or social superiority made by leaders of the free world are wholly unjustified. His unremitting lack of humour beyond a bitterly polemical sarcasm can make his writing impenetrable but, given that his typical subject matter includes unreported murders, massacres and assaults on comfortable First World apologists for tyranny, the dry tone does not seem entirely inappropriate.

Henri Chrétien 1879-1956

FRENCH INVENTOR

Chrétien changed the shape of films, if not forever, at least for the best part of two decades. In the mid-1920s he experimented with an anamorphic lens process that projected an image twice as wide as that of a normal cinema lens, but it was only in 1952 that he sold the patent to a major studio, Twentieth Century-Fox, which was eager to possess a rival to the three-projector Cinerama system that had briefly knocked television for six. Boasting greater depth, clarity and colour balance than its competitor, while using considerably less film stock, Chrétien's invention was launched in 1953 as CinemaScope, turning *The Robe*, a mediocre backlot sword-and-sandal flick into the studio's most successful film of the decade. Directors such as John Sturges, Stanley Donen and Vincente Minnelli elevated the invention beyond the level of a mere gimmick by taking advantage of the opportunities it offered for playing with perspective and background detail, in such films as *Bad Day at Black Rock* (1954) and *Seven Brides for Seven Brothers* (1954). The increasing significance of television and home video funding for the film industry has led to a decline in the use of anamorphic widescreen, but it can still bring out the best in directors as varied as John Carpenter, ☛Steven Spielberg and ☛Robert Altman.

Christo

(Christo Javacheff) born 193

BULGARIAN-AMERICAN SCULPTOR

Like ☛Carl André, Christo is an artist whose work has engulfed its creator: even those who do not know his name are aware of 'the man who wraps things up'. His work is about what does and does not constitute an art work, and how it can be the absence of the thing that creates the work, as in the wrapping-up of the white cliffs of Dover. It is also about spectacle – to wrap up an object on the scale of his work takes a highly co-ordinated team, working on a definitively

Noam Chomsky
Photo: John Cook

unproductive final piece. Space and its significance also figure, as in his proposal to wrap up the Reichstag, Germany's old parliament building that straddles the Berlin Wall. The Christo approach is probably best known from the television advertisement for Silk Cut cigarettes, in which a huge purple curtain is hoisted across a range of mountains, to the soundtrack of wittering art critics.

Church of the Sub-Genius

formed 1978

AMERICAN UNDERGROUND GROUP

Owing to its peculiarly fissiparous bent, the elusive and bizarre Sub-Genius foundation admits disciples only on the understanding that they break with and subsequently work to destroy the mother church. Largely founded by Paul Mavrides, a prankster who runs Anarchy Comics and illustrates *The Fabulous Furry Freak Brothers* strip with Gilbert Shelton, as well as contributing to such underground information projects as *Re/SEARCH* magazine and ☛Survival Research Laboratories, their worshipped icon is the face of a glibly smiling, pipe-smoking man, one J. R. 'Bob' Dobbs, who was supposedly shot to death at the 'Night of Slack', his first public appearance, in San Francisco, on 21 January 1984. Their purpose shrouded in direct-mailing mystery, they have become known as the anti-cult cult. In a country which has always thrived on conspiracy cultures, and the thrills and threats of shared arcana, it may or may not be a relief to hear Mavrides say, 'You're a mark if you send money in. You're a true Sub-Genius if you bother and say, "Send *me* something! Send *me* money!" '

Eric Clapton

born 1945

BRITISH MUSICIAN

It seems an age since anyone thought to spray 'Clapton Is God' on anything; graffiti, at least, has come a long way. Clapton appeared for a while to represent everything that British pop could be: he was its rough diamond pinnacle, obsessed with recasting a blues past into a more-than-just-repro present, as the crushed heart of that bizarre trio, Cream. When people talked about white blues-men, they either meant backroom traditionalists, or they meant Clapton, pointing to his obvious if diffident misery and working-class roots to convince themselves that he was London's Delta Robert Johnson. This was nonsense, and to his credit, Clapton knew it. After Cream collapsed into a stupidity of warring egos, and a couple of years of super-group activity that culminated in the still-impressive song 'Layla', he spent a drug-marred decade pretending to be just another backroom traditionalist, emerging occasionally with a cool and apparently deliberately dull album to prove he was still alive. He effectively destroyed the illusion that he was the black man's respectful ally with a notorious drunken outburst on stage in the late 1970s that led directly to the formation of the pressure group Rock Against Racism, and subsided thereafter into even greater somnolence. An idol to some for his supposedly masterful 'musicianship', his significance is endlessly over- or underplayed. Talented, tortured, his contribution to rock now seems ephemeral compared to that of his own best idols.

Michael Clark

born 1962

BRITISH CHOREOGRAPHER

The *enfant terrible* of dance, Clark is often remembered for daring to shock the stalls at London's Sadler's Wells theatre by appearing with nothing but an artificial phallus to conceal his modesty. Emerging from traditional ballet schools and dancing initially with the Ballet Rambert, he set up his own company at the age of 19 and soon attracted a cult following with his innovative pieces. Dismissed by critical purists, he wanted 'to make people see that the way my company works and the sort of dancing we do is as valid as anything else.' The work mixes high street glittery punk chic and camp design, by the likes of 'free art' icon Leigh Bowery and fashion designers Bodymap, with a propelling rock soundtrack, featuring the work of Laibach, Wire and The Fall (the latter sharing equal billing with Clark in his 1988 show *I Am Kurious Oranj*). The entertainment value in his cabaret-ish shows has lured a new audience to contemporary dance, but while one cannot deny Clark's prodigious talents as a dancer, some of his shows have suggested a contest between the scene-stealing acrobatics of his brash collaborators and the dance itself. *Heterospective* (1989), the piece with which he ended the one-year sabbatical he needed to recover from a knee injury, is a softer piece, albeit not without a few hi-jinks.

Arthur C. Clarke

born 1917

■ BRITISH WRITER

The man who wrote *2001: A Space Odyssey* (1968) and who presents television series about weird things, Clarke has promoted the idea that SF should be about 'big' ideas. He presents SF utopias, as well as 'warnings about the future of our planet' of astoundingly hippy-style vagueness, but which are generally backed up by substantial technological knowledge. ☛Kubrick's film, with its blank spaces and blanker faces, summed up the failure of Clarke-style writing as literature peopled by humans and most SF as lists of great visual images with epic bits. The 'sequel', *2010* (1982), directed by Peter Hyams, nailed the point home further. Clarke is one of the four top-selling SF writers, with ☛Robert Heinlein, ☛Isaac Asimov and ☛Frank Herbert. At his best, he can genuinely evoke a sense of wonder in the face of space, science and other weird things. He also has a sense of humour: his short story 'The Nine Billion Names of God' tells of a sect of Tibetan monks installing a computer to list all God's names, which are generated by a complex letter permutation; when this task is finished, the universe will end 'Overhead, without any fuss, the stars were going out.' At his worst, Clarke turns into a lobbyist for his own far-sightedness – the man who predicted the unmanned satellite has never let us forget it.

The Clash

1976-83

Joe Strummer (Joseph Mellor) born 1952
Mick Jones born 1956
Paul Simonon born 1956

▲ BRITISH ROCK GROUP

✌ The first Clash were among the best of early punk. Formed simply as a Sex Pistols/Ramones-type teenage rage band, around the nucleus of Joe Strummer and Mick Jones, they quickly took on a vaguely political aspect. Always ready to confuse rebelliousness with revolution, they wrote songs about unemployment, racism, urban alienation and jail. They played benefits and refused to appear on *Top of the Pops*. When punk's initial charge faded, The Clash made uncertain forays into heavy rock and self-justifying gang anthems, but they were saved from an ignominious end by their reputation as an excellent live group and their easily assimilated dress sense. They became increasingly popular in America, where audiences viewed The Clash as part of an unbroken line of rock leading from the Rolling Stones to Springsteen, and accepted their political posturing. The Clash – with their hotchpotch of imagery gleaned from James Dean, *Apocalypse Now*, *Taxi Driver*, Jamaican culture, old rock 'n' roll and cowboy films – stayed true to the roots of R&B, at a time when innovative groups such as ☛Talking Heads, ☛ Joy Division, Public Image Ltd and others were questioning the dominance of such music. They also favoured small venues as a reaction against the trend for US promoters to push groups into the stadium.

Eldridge Cleaver born 1935

AMERICAN WRITER, POLITICAL THEORIST, ACTIVIST

'Black power to black people; white power to white people; all power to all people' was the theme of Cleaver's speeches during the 1960s. Dubbing himself 'the apotheosis of the American nightmare', he had been brought up in the slums of Los Angeles, and spent periods in various penal institutions from the age of 12. He became a rapist as his way of 'defying and trampling upon the white man's law', only acknowledging the error of his chosen course during nine years of imprisonment between 1957 and 1966, and a period of self-analysis that led to a collection of essays published as *Soul on Ice* (1968). While on parole he joined up with the Black Panthers and became their minister for information. Looking to the radicals of the New Left to ally themselves with black demands for access to political and economic power, Cleaver stood for US president in 1968 and gathered some 30,000 votes. After becoming involved in a fight with the police, he was ordered to return to jail, but he fled to Cuba and then Algeria. Later, in Paris, he became a 'born-again Christian' and a conservative. Taking no further part in US politics, he toured America as an evangelist and rewrote his memoirs. ☛Jesse Jackson, another preacher, may be the active expression of a similar link between black awareness and Christian zeal – what Cleaver might have become had he resumed his radical career.

Patsy Cline

(Virginia Petterson Henley) 1932-63

AMERICAN COUNTRY SINGER

Cline formed the female archetype for the struggling country singer, moving up from poverty through tragedy to success. She was the first female country singer to find her feet in pop, first with 'Walkin' after Midnight', and later – classically – with 'I Fall to Pieces' in 1961. Later that year she was badly injured in a car crash; within two years, she was dead in a plane accident. Her light pure voice still keeps her popular, but her death has been turned to sleazy marketing advantage in Nashville – never more so than in the release of posthumously dubbed duets with Jim Reeves (also long dead by then) in the early 1970s.

Chuck Close born 1940

AMERICAN ARTIST

Close's work confounds critical categories and the expectations of viewers. His portraits convey no more information about his subjects than a mug-shot from a photo-booth. He works from photographs, solemnly including the blurs and spatial distortions on the resulting canvases. This suggests he should be dubbed a photo-realist, but the grid he places over the image puts the viewer in mind rather of ☛Sol Le Witt and other apostles of abstraction. Much of the impact of Close's portraits come from their size: there is something shocking in the contrast between the human watcher and the large-scale representation painted by Close, and it is difficult to get far enough back to see anything other than a blurred nose or ear. Close moves around his canvas on a forklift truck, fitted with a television that broadcasts a steady stream of soap operas and gameshows to relieve the tedium of his work.

Eddie Cochran 1938-60

✈ ♥ AMERICAN ROCK 'N' ROLL MUSICIAN

Technically important as the first white act to combine youthful references in his lyrics with a raunchy spirit, thus setting himself apart from his soda-pop rivals, Cochran achieved real fame by dying in a car crash. It was a time when the purer rock 'n' roll played by Cochran and his co-passenger Gene Vincent (who survived the crash, although his career did not) was being replaced by a saccharine substitute. His death, so soon after that of ☛Buddy Holly, sealed off the 1950s as a musical period, enabling rock to start seeing the past as mythical. He also brought in the first touch of the macabre to rock history by recording a song called 'Three Steps to Heaven' just before his death.

Nik Cohn born 1946

BRITISH ROCK WRITER, BASED IN US

Somewhere between a wild music critic and a rock 'n' roll-obsessed author, Cohn is nearly famous for being the man who wrote the article from which they made *Saturday Night Fever* (1978) and the man who inadvertently gave Pete Townshend of ☛The Who the idea for *Tommy*. (In his own defence, Cohn remarked, 'Pete Townshend is great at understanding half of an idea'.) Cohn began writing novels at 17, moved on to write the first great history of rock – *Awopbopaloobop Alopbamboom: Pop from the Beginning* (1969) – at 22, wrote a book about clothes and style, captioned the startling *Rock Dreams* (1973) collaboration with Guy Peelaert, moved to America and wrote a piece for New York magazine, 'Tribal Rites of the New Saturday Night', which eventually inspired *Saturday Night Fever*. He was one of the first rock writers to capture the feel of the music in his writing, and he was the first to understand the importance of rock's mythologies and romance. His best writing brings out all the glamour, seediness, sexiness and violence of rock music, and on occasion, it is better than the music it describes.

Daniel Cohn-Bendit born 1945

✌ ☜ GERMAN-FRENCH STUDENT LEADER, ECOLOGIST

'Danny the Red' bridged Franco-German divisions as a student leader in 1968, having been born in France to German-Jewish refugee parents. The French Communist paper, *L'Humanité*, called him a 'German anarchist'. French students identifying with him cried, 'We are all German Jews.' Influenced by socialist and anarchist ideas, he was an anti-Stalinist, and the aim of Group 22, which he led, was to unite all the groupuscules of the extreme left when student riots in France, initally against rule-bound traditionalism in French education, opened out to wider spheres. Short, with red hair, Cohn-Bendit spoke explosively in three languages, forcing academics and establishment figures to respond on his terms. His base was the West German Students Group (SDS), headed by ☛Rudi Dutschke. 'Our action went ahead of our theory' was his explanation for the failure of the movement. Cohn-Bendit was exiled to the UK, then settled in Frankfurt, where he edits *Pflaster-strand*, a bi-weekly current affairs magazine, and plays a leading role in the Green Party. An attempted comeback as a student leader in 1986, when he addressed French students, in revolt against a law that would have introduced selection to the universities, was an ignominious failure; the students preferred to make their own revolution.

Ornette Coleman born 1930

❍ AMERICAN JAZZ MUSICIAN

∀ ✍ ♦ Coleman's appearances in the late 1950s scared many people into dismissing his music as 'anti-jazz', a description which seems less insulting now than it did at the time. He learned his trade playing alto saxophone in R&B scratch bands and never lost his ear for haunting blues-directness and simple melody. He refused to become caught in bebop's macho downside, and quickly broke with its rigid chord-proprieties and competitive manner. In the mid-1960s he took up trumpet and violin, without tuition, and added them to his repertoire, arguing that learned traditions of technique restricted his range of expression. He took this to outrageous extremes when he added his ten-year-old son's defiantly 'unspoilt' drumming to his small chamber ensembles. Coleman transformed popular and improvised music so profoundly that the change is still poorly understood, even by its first advocates, and at a time when few doubt his significance as a saxophone player, composer and theorist, his work since the early 1970s is largely ignored. The untapped possibilities of electric rock led him to form Prime Time, a strange, noisy, space-age R&B group that recaps the deepest of his innovations and irritates almost everyone who loved him before. Otherworldly and gentle, Coleman has never learned to push for the recognition that his aesthetic deserves, but every new generation throws up a few more disciple-addicts.

John Coltrane 1926-67

❍ AMERICAN SAXOPHONIST

♦ For many, Coltrane was the greatest saxophone player ever, and his achievement probably caused more people more problems than any other contribution to music this century. A driven perfectionist and master technician, his sheer strength of will intimidated two generations of saxophonists – especially tenor players – into weak and pointless imitation. Free Jazz, to which he had lent critical credibility when its leading explorers were being accused of charlatanism, faltered significantly after he died. He transformed the language of his instrument, but his commitment to maximum impersonal expression seems to have misled most of his overwhelmed commentators. He had the ability to inspire sidemen to astonishing empathy in territory they would not have reached on their own but it sometimes seems that his music is revered rather than understood, as i its turmoils and conflicts are too disturbing to be understood in human terms. His quest for the holiness of intensity took him beyond entertainment *and* art – he ended up talking to himself.

Comme des Garçons *see*
Kawakubo, Rei

Richard Condon born 1915

✚ AMERICAN NOVELIST, SCREENWRITER

Condon's mordant, convoluted political thrillers have probably spawned more conspiracy paranoia than the most astutely subversive underground tracts. A Hollywood scriptwriter until the late 1950s, who worked for both Walt Disney and Howard Hughes, his books weld the black pulp-cynicism and nutty cliff-hanging complications of *film noir* to the elaborate dynastic convolutions of the paperback bestseller – with the result that almost all his books have been successful, and most have made good films. The best, and certainly the most notorious, is *The Manchurian Candidate* (book 1959; film 1962), which was ordered to be withdrawn by its star, ☛Frank Sinatra, in the wake of ☛John F. Kennedy's assassination, reflecting concern perhaps that the delirious amorality of Condon's script would no longer be to the public's taste. Condon's recent trilogy (*Prizzi's Honor*, 1982; *Prizzi's Family*, 1986; *Prizzi's Glory*, 1988) has made much of the similarities and connections between mob family life and US domestic politics, but his masterpiece, *Winter Kills* (1974), takes the idea furthest, when a transparently Kennedy-like president turns out to have been murdered not by the mob (or even the CIA), but by his father, for almost comically classical reasons of sexual threat and jealousy. In the climactic scene, the father falls to his death out of a skyscraper window. On his way down, he grabs hold of a Stars and Stripes that has been allowed simply to rot; it falls apart in his hands and he plunges to the street below. The scene is typical of Condon's gleefully absolute cynicism and also his perverse inventiveness.

The whole thing – politics, terror, what have you – seems to come and go like a tide. I don't think we'll ever be able to do much more than simply observe the kinds of beings that actually succeed in the process we call politics. It's no use kidding ourselves that they're ordinary people just like us, because they're not. For all the similarities, they might as well be from another planet. Probably are.

Richard Condon

Terence Conran born 1931

BRITISH DESIGNER, RETAILER

A design guru who has had a significant influence on Britain's retail industry, Conran dreams of transforming the British consumer's awareness of design and aesthetic taste. He first made his mark on the high street with Habitat, a chain of shops that made interior style available to the middle classes at prices they could afford (until the late 1950s, modern design had come from Italy or Sweden, with a large price tag). Emphasizing furniture that was devoid of unnecessary decoration, Conran's total-concept approach did for shop interiors what ☛Barbara Hulanicki had already done for fashion through Biba. His grounding in design was apparent in the importance he attributed to the product and his genius for detail (it is said that, even today, he has to approve everything, from sofas to toilet-roll dispensers). The high profile that grew up around his entrepreneurial flair was further developed as he built up his Storehouse retail conglomerate through a series of purchases (Mothercare, Heal's, British Home Stores). But the group suffered from poor management, leading to Conran's resignation from the company in early 1990 and his retreat to the Conran shop in west London. A proselytizer for modernist design, he set up the Conran Foundation which lavished £7 million on the world's first Design Museum, based in London's Docklands, which was opened in the summer of 1989.

John Horton Conway

BRITISH MATHEMATICIAN, SETTLED IN US

An eccentric and well-liked academic mathematician (first at Cambridge, then Princeton), Conway has pushed games theory into bizarre areas by combining a talent for provocative simplicity of exposition with seductive mental subtlety. He is best known for the invention of the computer game 'Life'; it consists of pieces on a chequered board, which are intended, subject to the most elegantly basic of rules, to model cell propagation. A player creates a pattern of pieces and sits back to watch it evolve (it eventually dies out, or else returns to the original configuration). The attraction of this simplest of games is the quite unexpected richness and complexity of development possible, making it phenomenally popular across computer faculties worldwide in the early 1970s. Conway has also made significant – and often typically elliptical – contributions to combinatorials, knot theory and the analysis of sporadic groups. He has also worked on the remarkable non-periodic tiling of the plane discovered by ☛Roger Penrose in the mid-1970s, helping prove that it genuinely never repeats itself, and clarifying its fractal properties – so that it has an air about it of ☛Borges's infinite library. Conway's highly entertaining 1976 book *On Numbers and Games* further adds to modern mathematicians' sense of the uncanny – the basic materials they work with (numbers) are increasingly revealed to be far stranger than we are used to supposing.

Sam Cooke 1931-64

➽ AMERICAN SOUL SINGER

Cooke was one of the first singers to move from gospel to pop, creating the idea of 'soul music' which blurred the differences between the secular and the sexual. He also helped to introduce the notion of 'the voice' into pop, being remembered for his vocal ability more than his material, despite the latter's importance. His songs pose questions about the merits of recording 'worthy' material next to overt bubblegum such as 'Cupid'. Cooke was murdered by a woman when he entered the wrong hotel room, and the verdict of justifiable homicide added credence to the view that rock singers led unstable and wild private lives. The fact that Cooke could lead a morally dubious life style and record material as sublime as 'You Send Me' and 'A Change Is Gonna Come' adds complexity to a music once regarded as simplistic. In a brief career, Sam Cooke pointed at more contradictions than the myth of the popular entertainer normally allows for.

Francis Ford Coppola born 1939

AMERICAN FILM DIRECTOR

If Coppola had been gifted with rather more entrepreneurial nous and managerial skill, he might have had a greater influence on the way Hollywood now operates. His best films resonate with a vision of the family that is part of his Italian inheritance, and with his now-defunct Zoetrope studio, he sought to establish some sort of creative enclave in which the film makers he admired could down cups of coffee and exchange ideas, as an alternative to the impersonality of the Hollywood system. He is a writer as well as a director, and a good enough one to ensure that even the scripts he puts together on the run, such as *Apocalypse Now* (1979), have an inner coherence missing from the work of many *auteurs* with more time for deliberation – a skill he probably learned during his low-rent apprenticeship with ☛Roger Corman. His fascination with new image-making technologies resulted in some of the most visually striking movies to come out of the US during the 1970s and 1980s, without leading to the empty-headedness that marks the work of other 'movie brats' such as ☛Spielberg and Lucas. Many Hollywood directors like to talk about their personal 'vision': Coppola was able to put his on the screen – simply because he had also directed *The Godfather* (1972), one of the biggest-grossing movies of all time. The irony of this is that the two *Godfather* films (and a third one was released in early 1991), which were sold as glamorized gangster movies based on a bestselling pulp novel, present a far more complex, dark portrait of the underbelly of American history than any of his more recent, more personal projects. The ambivalence in his relation to Hollywood – which he feels kept his post-*Godfather* masterpiece, *The Conversation* (1974), from the audience it deserved – kept him sharp during the 1970s, but it has been a worryingly long time since he produced his best work.

Anton Corbijn born 1955

DUTCH PHOTOGRAPHER BASED IN UK

If the *cinéma-vérité* films of the 1960s helped define and drive rock's first golden age, the work of a group of daring British-based photographers set the tone for what some regard as its second: the post-punk surge of the early 1980s. Corbijn's dark, rich portraits of ☛Captain Beefheart, Siouxsie Sioux, Ian Curtis and others gave notice that rock was capable – against even its supporters' best expectations – of evolving into a complex, shadowed, mature language. In the event, these pictures probably reached further than almost anyone pictured in them knew how to, as if the distance this Dutchman's laboured English put between him and his subjects gave him access on a more intuitive level to their inner thoughts. A series of portraits of ☛Miles Davis turned the jazz man's ageless face into a living African mask, not hiding the fierce intelligence, but closing in on something else – a primeval, sorcerer's spirit. Corbijn has also directed short promo-films for rock groups – usually elliptical and expressionist, always in black and white.

Le Corbusier *see* Le Corbusier

Roger Corman born 1926

AMERICAN FILM DIRECTOR, PRODUCER, BUSINESS EXECUTIVE

This one-man movie industry was the mogul of 1950s trash movies, many of which have now attained cult status. Churning out up to five movies a year, he had the knack of knowing exactly what he could get away with, providing ludicrous movies for ludicrous times. Early attempts to develop the most ridiculous monster-movie nasty ever to reach the screen, with titles such as *The Monster from the Ocean Floor* (1954) and *Attack of the Crab Monsters* (1957), gave way, with the arrival of the Teenager, to such late-night rerun fodder of the future as *Carnival Rock* (1957), *Teenage Caveman* (1958) and *T-Bird Gang* (1959). He swung away from trash to some extent with a series of Edgar Allen Poe adaptations, beginning with *House of Usher* (1960) and culminating in *Masque of the Red Death* (1964). Through the 1970s, following the failure of his revisionist flying ace drama, *Von Richtofen and Brown* (1971), he was content to nurture the talents of film school graduates who would work for peanuts – Peter Bogdanovich, ☛Francis Ford Coppola, Jonathan Demme, ☛Martin Scorsese and others – a list that shows that Corman's talents are deceptively maverick for a man often dismissed as an exploitation-movie hack. It was not until the late 1980s that he regained the nerve to direct, with the gleefully bizarre *Frankenstein Unbound*.

David Cornwell *see* le Carré, John

Gregory Corso born 1930

AMERICAN POET

All the Beat movement writers laid claim to being outsiders. But ☛William Burroughs was a Harvard graduate, ☛Allen Ginsberg was equally academic in background, and even ☛Jack Kerouac, the prophet of the road, was a mother-loving boy. Only the fourth, younger member they recruited as their D'Artagnan genuinely came from the wrong side of the tracks. Gregory Corso had spent most of his life in a series of homes, both institutional and downbeat. With his semi-literate Italian father, he graduated to the penitentiary, and made his way from there as a petty criminal before meeting Ginsberg. Corso's poetry reflected the direct aggression of his personal manner, and he became internationally famous for his abusive manner as much as for his muse.

Julio Cortázar 1914-84

ARGENTINIAN-FRENCH SHORT STORY WRITER, NOVELIST

Although his first story was published in a magazine edited by ☛Borges, and the influence of his fellow Argentinian miniaturist is felt in the title of his first collection, *Bestiario* (1951), Cortázar did not feel as content as his mentor within the confines of a library. He said as much in an epic novel, *Hopscotch* (1963/6), about an Argentinian intellectual who rampages through Paris and Buenos Aires in the hope that he can slough off his cultural baggage – 'the stupid pride of the intellectual who thinks himself equipped to understand'. Cortázar seemed unhappy with the idea that readers might become ensnared in his stories and overlook their wider implications: 'The Continuity of the Parks' features a man so involved in a novel's plot that he allows one of its characters to creep up behind him with a knife. Although the fantastic that so often irrupts into the everyday in Cortázar's short stories parallels the excited involvement of reading, the tales are constructed to leave the reader with a sense of disenchantment. In later stories, the effect is often overtly political, as in 'Apocalypse at Solentiname' (1976), where the photographs that should reveal brightly coloured paintings made by members of an idealistic Christian community show instead a massacre on the streets of Buenos Aires. It was another Cortázar story about what photographs reveal that ☛Antonioni adapted for his film, *Blow Up* (1966).

Lucia Costa *see* Niemeyer, Oscar

Elvis Costello

(Declan MacManus) born 1954

BRITISH MUSICIAN

Costello became popular at a time when almost everything he represented – melodic construction, an understanding of American rock forms, singing about relationships – was anathema to the punk enthusiasm he rode in on. His peculiarly unattractive image helped endear him to millions, who latched on to Costello's 'cleverness' as an alternative to punky nihilism and disco chirpiness. Subsequently, Costello's moods have mellowed – a little – and he has become part of the respectable rock coterie, collaborating with ☛Roy Orbison, ☛George Jones and Paul McCartney, as well as The Pogues, Christy Moore and Squeeze. He is valuable for his intelligence, his use of pop knowledge – he can juxtapose moods simply by pastiching two or three contrasting pop songs at the same time – and his ability to exist just outside the pop charts. Often taken a little too seriously, Costello is still a great deal more than the pub-rock ☛Dylan fan who got lucky. Overburdened by superlatives, he still deserves most of them.

André Courrèges born 1923

FRENCH FASHION DESIGNER

Courrèges produced 'gear' for 1960s' 'chicks' that became so ubiquitous (thanks to plagiarism by other designers) and was so much a part of its time that it now looks as if it must have been a compulsory uniform. That's partly because Courrèges's styles both reflected and influenced the way SF film-makers anticipated that costuming would develop in the next millenium. His 'moon' girls, dressed all in white, wore the first mini-skirts to be paraded on the streets of Paris, together with geometric hairstyles, white plastic glasses with thin slits for vision, white flat-heeled boots and stylized white baby caps. Like ☛Mary Quant, with whom he shared a concern with freedom of movement, he created a 'little girl' look, comprising short skirts, flat shoes and little caps, but despite the similarities, his style was always crisper and smarter than Quant's. After the decade of retreat, skirt lengths started dropping in the 1970s. That didn't suit Courrèges, whose approach began to seem dated. In the early 1980s, L'Oréal, the French cosmetics company, sold rights to his name to a Japanese operation, Itokin, who then applied it to everything, from cameras to telephones, thus ensuring that 'Courrèges' became a name that nobody could ever again associate with real style.

Robert Creeley born 1926

AMERICAN POET

Creeley's poetry follows ☛William Carlos Williams' dictum that 'Language is a thing within the world, the world is not a thing in it.' His early work, collected in *For Love: Poems 1950-1960*, is intensely formal, compact and insular. Much preoccupied with marital themes, it depicts women as both necessary to sustain male consciousness and as sexual partners. More recently, Creeley has dissolved these formalisms to create more fluid work in the manner of ☛Charles Olson and Robert Duncan, and with *Away* (1976), he signalled an end to his preoccupation with marriage crises. One of the founders of the Black Mountain Poets, Creeley's poetry betrays the influence of philosophy and linguistic theory, particularly that of ☛ Wittgenstein : critic and poet Eric Mottram has linked Creeley's work to a statement in that philosopher's *Philosophical Investigations*, that it is 'the field of force of a word that is decisive'. Most of Creeley's poetry is vividly introspective, as if its aim is to define what can be said to be real, starting with itself.

Francis Crick born 1916

BRITISH MOLECULAR BIOLOGIST

♦ Crick was the mathematical mind in the double-act (with ☛James Watson) that proposed the double-helical structure of DNA, with two chains running in opposite directions, and particular bases in one chain being paired with other base molecules in the other. Once this structure was elucidated, the genetic code followed: the way certain basic sequences in the chains form a code for the different amino acids that make up the body's proteins. Crick also postulated what has become known as the 'central dogma' of molecular biology, suggesting that genetic information could only pass one way – from DNA to RNA to proteins. More recently, however, it has been shown that some viruses contradict this prescription, invading a cell with RNA, which then hijacks the cell into producing DNA. Crick went on from investigating the secret of life to studying the problems of the brain. Despite his former partner saying that this would be a great help because there were not that many smart people working in neuroscience, Crick has yet to find the holy grail. Perhaps the time is not yet right, or perhaps other people have not yet done the right experiments for him to interpret.

David Cronenberg born 1948

CANADIAN FILM DIRECTOR

Once a biochemistry student, Cronenberg broke away from the horror-film view of evil as an external force to espouse a vision drawn mainly from ☛William Burroughs and ☛J. G. Ballard, in which evil is something internal, almost pathological: Burroughs' *Naked Lunch* and Ballard's *Crash* are on Cronenberg's list of possible future projects. His early films, including *Shivers* (1975) and *The Brood* (1979), plunged straight into a world of gynaecological menace to which he has always returned. In the early 1980s, his critical reputation received a boost with better-made shockers such as *Scanners* (1981) and the deranged *Videodrome* (1982), which developed the then-new idea of pirate video networks into an exploration of social prohibition, fantasy, censorship and control. He used his first mainstream break – a remake of the 1950s B-movie *The Fly*

(1986) – so effectively that it actually enlarged his cult following (an almost unheard-of situation with cult figures of any kind). His second, *Dead Ringers* (1988), which told the story of twin psychotic gynaecologists, proved him capable of using Hollywood to his own ends. His iconoclastic visual metaphors present a view of humanity's evolution as still primarily physical, presented within narratives that are more interested in ideas and thematic explanation than glib, theatrical execution. Mainstream audiences will always elude him: his movies are too intellectual for the less-discerning slice-and-dice consumers (who only went to see *Scanners* for the exploding heads), while art-house critics are repelled by his graphic symbolism.

Walter Cronkite born 1916

AMERICAN TELEVISION NEWSCASTER

As anchorman of CBS TV news for 20 years from 1962, he was described as 'the most trusted man in the US'. Like ☛Eisenhower, both political parties asked him to run as a presidential candidate; unlike Ike, he said no. It was his vital role as a programme chair in presidential elections that gave him his position as a symbol of neutrality. His status was such that, when CBS decided to pension him off, they gave him $1 million a year for seven years. In the 1940s, he had been a war reporter, and it was his eye for exciting stories – he had an informed enthusiasm for space travel – that marked his journalism. He always signed off: 'And that's the way it is.'

Anthony Crosland 1918-77

BRITISH POLITICIAN, THEORIST

An active member of ☛Harold Wilson's governments, Crosland's 1956 book *The Future of Socialism* helped shape the Labour Party's thinking on welfare and economic management. He argued that new conditions had rendered the old goals of the socialist left out of date. In particular, the main aim of ☛Attlee's post-war government – the state takeover of major industries – was no longer useful. Instead, he advised planning for growth through state access to 'the commanding heights of the economy' as a way of funding his central goal: more generous social services leading to more equality. This 'revisionist' view of democratic socialism, with its emphasis on equality over nationalization and state influence over state control, is often termed 'social democracy'. Although his key aim of equalizing wealth and incomes was not consistently pursued, his general approach was in line with that followed by Germany's social-democratic SPD party, which in 1959 abandoned state control of industry as a key aim. An ex-paratrooper, Crosland was famous for his arrogance and his sense of humour: he insisted on a lounge suit, rather than formal dress, for diplomatic dinners.

Robert Crumb born 1943

▲AMERICAN COMICS WRITER

✍ A small, short-haired, neurotic bundle of irony, Crumb evolved from a sometimes enthusiastic, sometimes cynical chronicler of West Coast counterculture into a hopeless Mr Grouch, out of sympathy with everyone else. Self-taught, he established himself, at a time when comics were called 'comix', by taking the simple virtues of the all-American funny pages into uncharted sex-territory, with an autobiographical fantasy-honesty that still earns him amused rebukes from many feminists. His rounded, basic style is a folk art, however self-conscious, and so holds itself above the shock-mechanisms of super-hero pulp, thus helping to create space for new-comers such as *Yummy Fur* and *Love & Rockets*. In spite of his acknowledged pre-eminence, he prefers to stick with the underground and the freedom it allows – since 1981, he has published *Weirdo*, one of the most respected outlets for non-mainstream talents. To his chagrin, he will, of course, never overturn others' ageing-hippy fondness for his earliest creations – Fritz the Cat, Mr Natural and the 'Keep on Truckin'' poster – and he is now unjustly regarded as an anachronism.

Johan Cruyff born 1947

♦ DUTCH FOOTBALLER

By the mid-1970s, the economic need for footballers not to lose had driven the game towards an increasingly gridlocked, violent spectacle. While the English team was perfecting the art of the 'professional foul', Italian football had (in reaction to the threat of bought-in superstar strikers) developed a positional strategy devoted entirely to defensive play-safe attitudes – deploying four backs and a sweeper – which was being widely copied throughout Europe. In complete contrast, the Dutch team Ajax, then captained by Cruyff, and the teams that Holland sent to the World Cup (which Cruyff also led), startled and entertained everyone by committing themselves to what was dubbed 'total football' – all ten outfield players were designated both defenders and attackers and were given the whole field of play to cover. Although this required phenomenal alertness, stamina and intelligent teamwork, it (literally) ran rings round any rigid position-play and man-to-man-marking strategy. Cruyff was the nerve-centre of any ten that he captained – a brilliant, innovative player who once noted that he expected to be hard-fouled five times a match just to get him out of the way. Impossible for any team that can't field a full complement of wholly flexible players, total football has not caught on in the way some commentators hoped it would – it has never been adopted in England at all – but it still hangs on as an unfulfilled idea. Cruyff is presently the manager of Barcelona (to which he was transferred in 1973) while the dread-locked Ruud Gullitt, who holds down Cruyff's position in the Dutch team, has acquired something of the same reputation.

Celia Cruz born 1930 (approx)

✚ CUBAN-AMERICAN MUSICIAN

The Queen of Salsa, Cruz is also the music's backbone outside Cuba. The greatest and most regretted of the island's exiles, she is a glittering, ageless, hard-nosed star whose music embodies all of salsa's danger, anger and glamour. An improvising showbiz goddess, with a grip on a song that allows her maximum theatrical movement within it, her asides and dramatic departures stir audiences into frenzies of adoration. Coming out of a poor Havana neighbourhood, she has been on the road almost permanently since 1949. By the time she reached New York in 1960, she already had a strong reputation. At home with the glitziest Vegas routines, as well as the distant Yoruba blood-roots of her music, she has worked with most of salsa's top artists: the veteran Tito Puente, Willie Colon, Johnny Pacheco, Daniel Ponce, the Fania All-

Stars. She conceals details of her age, and continues to deny the rumor that she is a priestess in the African-Cuban cult religion of Santiera – mystery suits the grand vamp side of her style.

Merce Cunningham born 1919

☞ AMERICAN CHOREOGRAPHER

Chance meets dance in Cunningham's hugely influential work. Trained by ☛Martha Graham, he went on to develop the ideas of ☛John Cage, abandoning the classical narrative approach for a repertoire of movement out of everyday motions, such as walking, standing or leaping. Randomness was brilliantly exploited in *Sixteen Dances for Soloist and Company of Three* (1951), where the order of the sequences was determined by the toss of a coin. He worked memorably with Cage in the 1952 Black Mountain College collaborations: while ☛Robert Rauschenberg, who went on to design for the company, provided a soundtrack with an old gramophone and Cage read a text on 'the relation of music to Zen', Cunningham danced through the aisles, pursued by a dog. Cunningham's company, though dogless, went on to spawn most of the leading figures of the 1970s avant-garde – notably Karole Armitage. Among British dancers, ☛Michael Clark has been heavily influenced by Cunningham.

Renato Curcio born 1945

ITALIAN TERRORIST LEADER

Curcio was leader of the Red Brigades, which in the early 1970s conducted a series of kidnaps and murders of significant figures. His breach with the student radical movement in the late 1960s was probably due to distorted religious fury, transferred to the political sphere and acquiring violent features. The Red Brigades broke with the orthodox Italian Communist left (which had already broken with the USSR and made its peace with non-revolutionary Western democracy), savagely attacking it for betraying the working class. Based on factory cells, they played on the unhappiness of southerners in northern Italian cities, who were working for low wages and living in slums. It began as fun and games, as with much of radical politics at the close of the 1960s – an executive would be seized and tried, and then freed after 30 minutes. 'No one among the functionaries of the anti-workers' counter-revolution,' claimed Curcio, 'can sleep soundly again.' He was arrested, freed by a 'commando' group (which his wife may have led), recaptured and, after the murder of a judge delayed his trial, received a 43-year gaol sentence (and an additional term for an outburst during the court proceedings). The Red Brigades, like other terrorist groups of the same era – the Weathermen or the ☛ Baader-Meinhof gang – have been turned into a romantic pop cult, but they played out the roles of Fascist thugs and did not aid the people they claimed to be fighting for. Instead they tried to take the Italian political system back 50 years, and their undisciplined, demagogic violence enabled the Italian state to discredit the far more significant threat from such autonomist Marxist critics as Toni Negri, who was also gaoled, without justification, for supporting terrorist action.

D

Roald Dahl 1916-90

■ BRITISH NOVELIST

Dahl dominated the post-war children's novel – creating a world of revolting rhymes and fantastic tales where witches spit green, greedy children are swallowed by the machinery of a chocolate factory, Little Red Riding Hood turns the Big Bad Wolf into a fur wrap and parents can be eaten by an angry rhinoceros in a crowded shopping street. In the process, he infuriated moral guardians and delighted kids through his empathy with the most absurd reaches of their imagination. While classics such as *James and the Giant Peach* (1961), *Charlie and the Great Glass Elevator* (1973) and *The BFG* (1982) kept him at the top of the children's bestseller lists (even when no new titles were forthcoming), his short story collections and the subsequent TV anthology *Tales of the Unexpected* (from 1979), originally introduced by the man himself, as well as his anecdotal memoirs, *Going Solo* (1981) and *Boy* (1984), ensured attention outside the playground. He listed his principal leisure interest as 'picking mushrooms'.

Ralf Dahrendorf born 1929

✎ GERMAN-BRITISH SOCIOLOGIST

Receiving a professorship in 1958 when he was only 29, Dahrendorf went on to become a member of the West German parliament in 1969 and then director of the London School of Economics in 1974. Subsequently, he was called back to Germany by the Free Democratic Party to reinvent their policies. His academic field has been the progress of the European democracies in the post-war years. He has argued against both the right-wing notion that wealth creation should take precedence over quality, and against the social democratic vision of planning as the way to prosperity; instead of just the bigger-pie-at-all-costs approach, or a concentration on sharing out what we have, he wants both. Modern life offers unrivalled opportunities, and if anyone is excluded from them, that diminishes everyone. Yet the post-war state, which offered to take care of everybody and provide a sense of belonging, did not come up with the goods. By relying on bureaucracy, a client group was created which relied on the state for employment and worked more for it's survival and extension than for the principles of fraternity. Dahrendorf argues that we need to reinvent the concept of citizenship, with a society of people well enough educated to defend their own freedoms and extend them. His description of Britain's now-defunct Social Democratic Party as offering 'a better yesterday' sums up Dahrendorf's attraction – anyone who can coin aphorisms in a foreign language deserves affection – but it is still uncertain whether his vision of a better tomorrow can win minds.

Dalai Lama

(Lhama Dhondrub) born 1935

☆TIBETAN RELIGIOUS LEADER, BASED IN INDIA

Believed by Tibetans to be the fourteenth reincarnation of the popular Buddhist deity Avalokitévara (impressive ears were among the tell-tale signs), the Dalai Lama remains, after 30 years of exile, Tibet's spokesman in its confrontations with the Chinese. His following in the West (he can fill London's Royal Albert Hall three nights running) largely derives from his message that material things can never satisfy people's inner desires. But neither the genealogical credentials nor the arguments have yet done much to win him support from the world's leaders, or to restrain China's persecution of the Tibetans. He fled to India in 1959 and set himself up with a large band of followers at Dharmsala in the Himalayan foothills. Despite attempts by the authorities in Beijing to negotiate his return to Lhasa, and his own offer to concede sovereignty and control of foreign policy to the Chinese in return for complete internal autonomy, a return home seems unlikely in the near future. But the award of the Nobel peace prize to the Dalai Lama in 1989 did boost international awareness of the Tibetan case.

Richard Daley 1902-76

AMERICAN POLITICIAN

As mayor of Chicago, Daley ordered local police to 'shoot to kill' during riots that followed the 1968 assassination of ☛Martin Luther King, and he applied the same tough line, later in the same year, to demonstrators at the Democratic Party Convention. He lived in the same blue-collar, Irish-American area all his life, and worked in a stockyard to put himself through law school; but politics was his career, beginning in the 1930s as a Republican but soon becoming a Democrat. His moment of fame in party annals came when, probably through ballot-rigging, he arranged for enough votes to be cast in his base, Cook County, to swing Illinois, a key state, in ☛John F. Kennedy's favour during the tight 1960 presidential election. 'He made dead men vote,' the line went. As Chicago's mayor, he was a tough, contentious figure who weathered scandals. He cleared slums, reformed the police and built highways, but did little to halt segregation in schools and encouraged office skyscrapers. A symbol for self-made blue-collar workers, he wanted dynamic management, a crackdown on crime and no compromise with liberals on the race question. His son, Richard Jnr., became mayor in 1989 after the death in office of Harold Washington, a black Democrat; although Richard the younger has certainly picked up much of his father's vote, his record on race is, to date, far more attractive.

Erich von Däniken born 1935

✍SWISS PSEUDO-HISTORIAN

For a while Von Däniken's poorly written, ill-researched books sold so well that genuine historians began to wonder if they ought to bother. Starting with *Chariots of the Gods?* (1968/9), he sought to convince his readers that the wonders of the ancient world were all far too sophisticated for our stupid ancestors to have had a hand in their design or construction. Spacemen must have done it for them (and the clues are there if you examine the evidence – religious texts – in the 'right' way). Our ancestors were so lacking, obviously, that they could only worship beings they had actually run into. Millions of readers lapped this up. For many, of course, it was simply the first time that these artefacts had been brought to the public's attention, and they looked on in genuine curiosity at what the Incas had made and done, probably paying little attention to their guide's crackpot explanations. Books which debunk him – and there are many – take a lofty tone, but our deep past fascinates and unnerves us and we do not want it crushingly demystified.

Peter Maxwell Davies born 1934

BRITISH COMPOSER

Maxwell Davies visited the Darmstadt seminars sponsored by ☛Stockhausen and ☛Boulez and other composers of the European avant-garde, but judging their serial techniques an insubstantial basis for a new music, he set out to build his own approach around the polyphony methods of medieval plainsong, to which he has added a taste for complex rhythm. While working on an opera about the life of Renaissance English composer, John Taverner, he began to explore areas of extreme experience (self-betrayal, blasphemy, madness), and subsequent music theatre works, such as *Eight Songs for a Mad King* (1969), took expressionism to the point of self-parody. However, following his move to the remote Orcadian island of Hoy at the beginning of the 1970s, where he still spends six months of every year, his music became calmer and more elegiac. He also returned to large-scale composition, writing symphonies and symphonic works for chamber orchestra.

Finding a grammar and syntax is a very basic problem for a composer today, but many of them don't even seem to realize it.

Peter Maxwell Davies

Angela Davis born 1944

✌ AMERICAN POLITICAL ACTIVIST

▯ An eloquent advocate of black and women's rights in the late 1960s, Davis was unusual in that she was also a member of the American Communist Party. She had become a radical after the homicidal fire-bombing of a church in Birmingham, Alabama, by white racists, which persuaded her that the Marxism of the Algerian student revolutionaries she had met in Paris provided the correct political solution to America's grim social deficiencies. A brilliant student, her politics lost her a job as a philosophy lecturer at UCLA, but she was soon transformed from a political advocate to a political cause. In 1970 when Jonathan Jackson attempted to secure the release of his brother ☛George Jackson and the two other 'Soledad Brothers' by kidnapping a judge from a California courtroom and killing him, the guns used by the abductors, three of whom died in the attempt, had been registered in Davis's name. Picked up in a New York motel after a nationwide hunt, she was charged with conspiracy, murder and kidnap. The New Left were then pushing the line that, in the absence of a non-racist judicial system, all black prisoners were political prisoners, and this move against Davis – clearly a political rather than a criminal figure – was widely taken to prove it. 'FREE ANGELA DAVIS' badges began to appear worldwide. After a celebrated 13-week trial, she was acquitted of all charges. Davis promised to work for a social revolution that 'would encompass the great majority of the working people' in the US, but would be 'led by people of colour'. She has continued to write and teach, though somewhat more quietly.

Miles Davis

(Miles Dewey Davis Jnr) 1926-91

AMERICAN JAZZ MUSICIAN

♦ The 'Cool' in jazz has been so oversold in recent years that it is easy to overlook the fact that Miles Davis meant far more than smoky nightclubs and thin men in suits. During the 1970s, this most aristocratic of street musicians led what some regard as the finest rock band of the time – a dark and violent funk-metal ensemble that combined the vast concert-hall noise arguments of ☛Stockhausen with the folk-intensity of Bartók. At the heart of these charred workouts was the integrity of his own still-small-voice trumpet, itself electronically distorted, etching its always private emotions. It is true that his subtly hypnotic chamber-group took on classic jazz in the mid-1960s, which led to the neo-conservative bop of the ☛Marsalis people, but this only demonstrated Davis's own ability to move on, where others might stamp an idea into the ground. From the 1980s, Davis stepped back from the edge and used Marcus Miller's exemplary wide-screen funk for the lightest sound-painting. This one-time protégé of ☛Charlie Parker proved adept at discovering and drawing out players, and somehow turned whatever he was doing at the time into a significant sideshow to the mainstream.

For me, music and life are all about style.

Miles Davis

Richard Dawkins born 1941

BRITISH ETHNOLOGIST

In the 1930s the various strands of thinking about evolution were brought together in the 'new synthesis', but since the early 1970s, the resultant neo-Darwinism has again been challenged. Enter Richard Dawkins, defending the true faith against Marxists and assorted philosophers of science and, in the process, securing huge sales for his sociobiological book, *The Selfish Gene* (1976). His argument goes like this: At a certain point in time, replicative molecules emerged, and the most successful of them co-operated to build themselves into survival machines. Humans are just one type of such a machine; while our genes are immortal, they cannot constantly control the survival machines. For most of our lives, therefore, survival is up to us, and it is for this reason that 'behaviour' has developed, via natural selection. Consciousness is merely the culmination of a sort of behavioural deception that appears to make us autonomous from the pressures of gene replication. For properties that emerge from more complex social structures, Dawkins coined the neologism 'memes': as genes propagate in the gene pool, so 'memes' propagate from brain to brain. A sort of natural selection favours those 'ideas' which exploit the cultural environment to their own advantage. As an example of the reductionism that dominates evolutionary thinking, in which even social processes must be modelled on DNA, Dawkins' model is ingenious but so mechanistic that it ends up positing genes as our ultimate controllers, and chemical process as the explanation of everything.

Richard Deacon born 1949

BRITISH SCULPTOR

Deacon, who calls himself a 'fabricator' rather than a sculptor, manipulates a variety of materials to produce pieces remarkable for their swelling, curved forms and fastidious symmetry. Beginning with laminated wood, he moved on to linoleum, cloth and galvanized steel – flaunting the way his rather skeletal works are made by studding them with nails, rivets and screws, and allowing the glue to run freely over the joints of the disparate materials. It has been suggested that Deacon is influenced by his father's background in medicine; his work does sometimes seem to echo anatomical drawings. The organic forms are also reflected in the rather clichéd titles with which Deacon christens his suggestive shapes – *For Those Who Have Eyes* (1982-3), *The Heart's in the Right Place* (1983), *Tall Tree in the Ear* (1983-4). Deacon also makes 'art for other people' – an ongoing series of small works that cheekily echo his larger pieces.

James Dean

(James Byron) 1931-55

○ AMERICAN ACTOR

✈ Dean depicted teen angst in *East of Eden* (1955) and *Rebel Without a Cause* (1956), and went on to become a legend. Dying in a car crash shortly after completing work on *Giant* (and on a commercial for road safety), Dean left a career, untarnished by failure, that could be held up as a romantic ideal without fear that he would someday become unworthy of adulation by evolving into an unfashionable left-winger or putting on weight and being vastly overpaid for cameos, as happened to Dean's own idols, John Garfield and ☛Marlon Brando. Age had no opportunity to wither him or stale his infinite variety – or stretch it either. Behind the myth lay a difficult but natural actor with that indefinable spark of stardom, who cultivated his nonconformity for professional reasons but had difficulty in coming to terms with the gap between his image and his affluent but remote upbringing (he was undergoing psychoanalysis at the time of his death). The television appearances, the bit parts in second features and even the impact of his three starring rôles are gone. All that remains are the books, the posters, the T-shirts and the legend.

Laura Dean born 1945

AMERICAN CHOREOGRAPHER

The dances Dean choreographed in the 1970s were rituals constructed out of repeated gestures and simple shapes. Controlled spinning was her hallmark, suggesting the movements of a mystic seeking inner peace. They were pieces of bald simplicity, carrying such names as *Stamping* (1971), *Dance* (1978), *Music* (1980) and *Space* (1988), and conducted to a rhythmic pulse – the music provided by herself, ☛Steve Reich or ☛Terry Riley. She was known in New York, with Lucinda Childs and ☛Trisha Brown, as one of the 'three sisters' of minimal dance.

Having once turned away from ballet, Dean gradually found ways to combine her idiosyncratic style with more traditional modes. Depicted by some as apostasy, this is a natural progression.

Anastazio Somoza Debayle *see*

Somoza Debayle, Anastasio

Simone de Beauvoir 1908-86

FRENCH FEMINIST, NOVELIST

De Beauvoir made a unique contribution to feminism and wrote six semi-autobiographical novels about women suffering amid the ebb and flow of intellectual life in post-war Paris, but she will be remembered largely as another writer/philosopher's sidekick. For this, she had mainly herself to blame: her account of their final parting only confirmed the impression given in other books that her relationship with ☛Jean-Paul Sartre was an obsessive one. The exact nature of that partnership remains the subject of intense speculation. Some thought their pact of 1929 – in which a distinction was drawn between their 'essential life', which would unite them for ever, and 'contingent' affairs which allowed him to keep his own harem – just a con which he imposed on her. But not only did she keep her freedom (they lived apart), but she produced in *The Second Sex* (1949/53) a book which, while drawing upon 'Sartrean' ideas, articulated concerns that were very much her own. From the existentialist position that human beings find meaning in life by defining themselves in opposition to others, she argued that men exploit a difference of biology to dump their sense of disaffection upon women, defining them as the supreme 'Other' in a move that amounts to psychic oppression; women have been conditioned to accept this state of affairs, refusing to embrace the fight for their freedom. The book quickly became a feminist bible.

Guy Debord born 1931

FRENCH SITUATIONIST

The one member of the Situationist International (SI) to endure through its fractious 15-year history, Debord should be seen – with sometime members Asger Jorn, Gil Wollman, Michèle Bernstein and Raoul Vaniegem, as well as Marxist theorist/heretic Henri Lefebvre – as a primary influence not only on the near-revolution of May 1968 in Paris, but also on the ethos of London's underground press and even certain aspects of punk ideology. The SI developed out of an earlier (even tinier) Left Bank twitch of avant-garde politics, Isidore Isou's Lettrist International, and continued its programmes of provocation, graffiti and anti-party revolutionary outrage. The Situationists were concerned to articulate a 'theory of moments', propagating ideas of pleasure and depicting the personal as intrinsically political ('boredom is always counter-revolutionary' sneered one of their mottoes). They anticipated later shifts in the emphasis of leftist thought, while remaining bitter and perceptive critics of the delusionary sideshows that capitalism built for itself. Debord's *The Society of Spectacle* (1967-70) became a central text, influencing more academic thinkers such as ☛Barthes, ☛Foucault and ☛Baudrillard. The Situationists' obsession with the future of architecture tied in uneasily with their celebrations of teen-rage and near-nihilist refusal of any organizational discipline, but by the time

Debord dissolved the SI (proclaiming its 'victory over history') in 1972, their subterranean impact had been assured.

Régis Debray born 1940

FRENCH POLITICAL THEORIST

If there is something comic about any traveller from the pampered West hitching a ride on someone else's revolution, that was doubly so in the case of Debray, whose father was a rich, right-wing lawyer. Breaking with his parents' politics at the time of the Algerian War, the young Debray secured audiences with both ☛Castro and ☛Guevara thanks to an introduction from ☛Sartre. He became an enthusiastic spokesman for their version of Marxism and, in *Revolution in the Revolution?* (1967), developed the argument that revolution in Latin America would be achieved by independent bands of guerrillas with the ability to outsmart larger military forces. In April 1967, Debray was arrested by the Bolivian government as he came away from six weeks in Guevara's mountain hideout, and they ridiculously charged him with rebellion, murder, robbery and assault. Sentenced to 30 years in gaol, he became an international celebrity, even attracting ☛de Gaulle's friendly protests. Debray was released after three years and went on to write a book about Chile, in which he seemed to abandon some of his earlier insistence on 'total class warfare' in deference to ☛Salvador Allende's success through the ballot box. He joined the French Socialist Party in 1974 and, following the 1981 election victory, served for a time as ☛Mitterand's adviser on Third World affairs.

Charles de Gaulle 1890-1970

FRENCH POLITICAL LEADER

De Gaulle was an eternal rebel: against the French army in the 1930s, as he argued for tank offensives to counter the German threat; against the French establishment in 1940, as he set up a Free French movement in London; against prevailing orthodoxy after the Liberation, as he opted out of public life; against his own nationalist backers, as, now president, he withdrew from Algeria despite his backers' deepest desires, and his own ambiguous promises. De Gaulle's view of France was shaped by his family's aristocratic, scholarly army background, singling him out from the urban, bourgeois politicians of French history and contemporary politics. A search for *la gloire*, shaped by his own aloof sense of grandeur, was behind his exit from politics in 1946, as well as his sudden, triumphal return during the Algerian crisis of 1958, as paratroops threatened a coup. An outdated vision of France as one of the world's great powers also explains his policies for the next decade – anti-federalism in the EEC, refusal of Britain's entry, taking France out of NATO, building up a French nuclear deterrent and resigning after the events of 1968 had forced him out of Paris and he had lost a shock referendum. In economic affairs, which did not interest him, he was a pragmatist. He was always an outsider, with a sense of mischief.

Len Deighton born 1929

BRITISH NOVELIST

Deighton changed the nature of the espionage genre with his first and most famous book, *The Ipcress File* (1962). Where spy fiction had been about glamour and public school toughs, Deighton introduced the notion of espionage as a tedious form of desk work, giving his books instant realism and shock value. His use of a small-time Cockney criminal as a hero (called Harry Palmer in the film adaptations) was not only later to make Michael Caine even more famous, but also exploited the 1960s' interest in working-class anti-heroes. Palmer slotted in easily among the Joe Lamptons and Billy Fishers of fiction and the ☛David Baileys and ☛John Lennons of entertainment. Deighton's fascination with realism was to influence the likes of ☛John le Carré and Frederick Forsyth, who would take the genre into a new stupor in the 1970s.

Willem de Kooning born 1904

DUTCH-AMERICAN PAINTER, SCULPTOR

During the 1950s, De Kooning was a dominant figure in the 'action' area of abstract expressionism. His concern was with the physical act of painting, formulating an approach to art that was direct, physical and immediate. The painting was an object over which the painter did not dwell, and De Kooning would have six or seven canvases on the go at any one time. At first glance, his paintings resemble conventional figurative paintings that have been spat out from a blender; they combine a series of splintered, rhythmic and confused gestures with distorted, broken images that are still recognizable – most commonly, a buxom lady in a skirt, her grinning mouth a mere slash cut across her face. It was not until De Kooning shocked his admirers by exhibiting a series of monumental women that his earlier abstract paintings of 1948-9 were seen to contain references to the human figure. Other abstract expressionists, including ☛Pollock and Kline, reacted with contempt, as if De Kooning had let the side down. He went on to outrage them even more by admitting that he thought his work was humorous. De Kooning has also taken to making clay sculptures of nudes, which are then cast in bronze, and his more recent paintings demonstrate a calmer, meditative return to abstraction.

Samuel Delany born 1942

AMERICAN WRITER

Calling himself a 'favourite faggot uncle' to the Cyberpunk generation, with whom he shares many concerns and a junk-lyrical style, Delany's books display greater inner range and technical skills, and are far less easy to categorize (or, indeed, to read), than those of the younger authors he has undoubtedly influenced. The basic pitch is space opera – high, distant and pan-galactic, or near-future, urban and scarily close – but his masterpiece, *Dhalgren* (1975), could pass for dystopic social (and racial) realism: tribal street gangs on the loose in a collapsed city society. One of the few black writers to make a mark in SF, Delany also works as an academic lecturer and critic, and his knowlege of literary criticism, semiotics and linguistics makes him the SF novelist most capable of writing a great work of 'straight' fiction. However, this knowledge also probably provides him with all the reasons he needs for retaining the mannerisms that consign him to his unrespectable ghetto.

Gilles Deleuze

FRENCH PHILOSOPHER

Co-author, with radical psychoanalyst Felix Guattari, of *Anti-Oedipus: Capitalism and Schizophrenia*, a monumental textbook to the ideas thrown up by the student unrest of 1968 which remains much discussed but little read (☛Foucault advises in the introduction that you do not really have to read it, just dip in as you think fit), Deleuze is a mischief-making assassin of hierarchies, dedicated to tracing 'lines of flight' from the Fascism of interpretation to a fluid 'schizo-analysis' that refuses to be bound by a unified higher purpose. Not especially influential abroad (it cannot be that he is too 'difficult': he is a breeze compared to ☛Lacan or the more elliptical reaches of ☛Derrida), Deleuze is a playful polymath who plays the subversive aspects of Nietzsche against the restrictive and/or normative tendencies in Freud, Marx, Hegel and others. Part of the problem must be his association with the 'back-to-nature' primitivism of such British radical analysts as David Cooper and ☛R. D. Laing. In fact, Deleuze, like Foucault, is canny enough to acknowledge that society is a web of power structures and productive repressions – the point is to learn how to move within them, not suppose they can one day be blown away. His legend is further enhanced by apocryphal stories; such as the one about the secretary sitting in a darkened room who takes dictation in long-hand by the light of a star-shaped hole in one of the blinds that cover all the windows, while he sits and chain-smokes, his uncut fingernails now so long and entwined that he cannot hold a pen.

Don de Lillo

born 1936

AMERICAN NOVELIST

De Lillo's preoccupation with conspiracies feeds a paranoid vision of an America infiltrated by covert organizations, threatened by terrorists and humming with electronic listening devices. After tracking the lawless offshoots of the intelligence community in *Running Dog* (1978), he moved on to examine the amorphous collection of Cuban exiles, Mafia hit-men and CIA officers who have been implicated in the assassination of ☛John F. Kennedy. A complex multi-layered construct, *Libra* (1988) evokes the sensation that power has been displaced from democratic institutions to some more dangerous place. From the beginning, De Lillo's characters have struggled to establish a sense of self in the face of proliferating conspiracies and deadly technologies. Linking quasi-journalistic concerns to the sense of a dark, sometimes occult, 'background' world, his novels present a forlornly comic account of the American psyche.

'I understand the music, I understand the movies, I even see how comic books can tell us things. But there are full professors in this place who read nothing but cereal boxes.'

'It's the only avant-garde we've got.'

Don De Lillo, White Noise *(1984)*

Jerry della Femina

born 1936

AMERICAN ADVERTISING EXECUTIVE

Della Femina horrified and amused fellow admen with his irreverent wit. Perhaps a fitting tribute to his bravado is the advertisement he devised for Isusu cars: when most other American automobile advertisements were

Don de Lillo

offering only bland hype, Della Femina's commercial featured a car salesman telling outrageous lies about the vehicle behind him, while subtitles on the television screen gave the true story. He worked his way up from newspaper messenger-boy to become chairman and chief executive of his own ad agency and the most famous advertising man in the world. In the mid-1960s, he produced his best-known wisecrack: while sitting in an agency meeting with his Japanese client, Panasonic, he suggested that the headline for their new advertisement should read: 'FROM THOSE WONDERFUL FOLKS WHO GAVE YOU PEARL HARBOR.' He later used this line as the title for a bestselling book which successfully debunked the advertising world and its excesses. His agency, Della Femina Travisano, sold out to UK advertising agency Wight Collins Rutherford Scott in 1986.

John de Lorean born 1925

AMERICAN BUSINESS EXECUTIVE

Son of a Romanian-American car worker, de Lorean became the 'golden boy' of General Motors – a marketing dynamo who brought 'muscle cars' to US youth. Claiming to be shocked by the immorality of big business, he resigned at the apex of a company career. Setting out to build his own 'ethical' car, he talked British officials into giving him a $97 million aid package and, promising peace in Northern Ireland among other lavish pledges, established a factory in Belfast. The firm crashed, disastrously; many workers lost their jobs. A political scandal ensued, with the government being attacked for failing to spot the crook in de Lorean, who, set up by the FBI, was later arrested on multi-million-dollar cocaine charges (and acquitted). A recent biography argues that he was corrupt right through, diverting other people's cash into his own bank account through a complex network of holding companies. Yet – clearly a con-man, who opted to exploit liberal, enlightened values, and not just narrow commercial interests, in a jungle hedged by rules – he is also a man of real zest and charisma, who has won loyalty from many.

Paul de Man 1919-84

BELGIAN-AMERICAN LITERARY THEORIST

Until the discovery that he had written several collaborationist articles for a Belgian paper – none actually pro-Nazi, one certainly anti-Semitic – in the early part of WW2, Paul de Man's coolly provocative analyses of rhetoric seemed set to dominate, without fear of challenge, every Eng. Lit. faculty in the US and a fair few in the UK. His theory of interpretation insisted on attention to the rhetoric used in writing, because it is inevitably at odds with the direction of the arguments. Opponents argue that, since everything de Man wrote subsequently is now tainted by his initial betrayal, deconstruction's alleged nihilism is basically anti-political and deeply suspect. His defenders, who include ☛Derrida, a Jew, point out that all de Man's later writing argued for resistance to totalizing ideologies, in particular seeking to discredit for ever the organicist metaphors that those articles relied on, as if he had decided to make the substance of his life's thought an atonement for his shameful misdeeds. This position requires close reading, but then that is what deconstruction is all about.

Deng Xiaoping born 1904

CHINESE POLITICAL LEADER

Taking over in China after ☛Mao's death, Deng's enthusiasm for economic modernization led to friendly relations with both the US and the USSR, encouraging many observers to treat this chain-smoker of no great height (4 ft 11 in) as a pragmatic liberal. But Deng tried to implement economic reforms without corresponding changes to the political system, and his petrified ideological hard-core was horribly exposed in June 1989, when he sent troops into Tiananmen Square to massacre supposed 'counter-revolutionaries' – actually they were disaffected students and workers. For Deng, as for Mao in the past, keeping political control in the hands of his wing of the Communist party was an absolute priority. 'We cannot do without dictatorship. We must exercise it when necessary,' he remarked in 1986. Western misconceptions were fostered by the vicissitudes he had endured under Mao, when he argued for economic reforms in opposition to traditional Communist idealists. Sent for re-education during the Cultural Revolution, and subsequently in such ill favour that he had to spend a year in hiding, he nevertheless negotiated his way back to power. The year of most apparent liberalism was 1979: private farming replaced the collective system, leading to record harvests; a new criminal code was introduced, to prevent the persecutions characteristic of the previous decade; real economic growth, rather than simple productivity increases, became an aim, with 'market socialist' ideas borrowed from Hungary and Yugoslavia; and intellectuals were no longer to be regarded as 'bourgeois' but enrolled into the 'proletariat'. His epochal trip to the US in that year highlighted new problems: television-images beamed back to China fed awareness of Western freedoms and prosperity. In Deng's case, a lack of genuine ideological imagination ('Who cares what colour a cat is as long as it catches mice?'), combined with an old man's callous indifference to human life ('What are a million deaths in a population of one billion?'), caused him to turn his back on the rest of the world, only days after a historic rapprochement with the USSR. Following Tiananmen, Deng ceded power of the party and the army to others, bringing to an end his programme of economic reforms.

Robert de Niro born 1943

AMERICAN ACTOR

While De Niro's box-office success is paltry compared to many present-day screen-superstars, his notoriety is considerable – quite simply, because no one else has pushed himself so deep into Method techniques, or gone so far into the roles he has played, the extreme being when he gained 70 pounds to play the overweight ex-boxer Jake LaMotta in *Raging Bull* (1980). The significance of this is more than attention to detail – De Niro has turned a personal fetish into a performer's business all his own, taking empathy well beyond shared pleasure in a fiction and keeping the audience hanging on with the threat that, at any moment, he will somehow lose his own personality in a part, whether it is the Italian-American street-hoodlum in *Mean Streets* (1973), the confused assassin-vigilante in *Taxi Driver* (1976), the romanticized patriarch-as-a-young-man in *The Godfather Part II* (1974) or the comic-devoid-of-personality in *The King of Comedy* (1982). In lead roles or well-telegraphed cameos, in great and daring films, or in strangely run-of-the-mill productions, the cipher that is De Niro hovers behind the all-too-real-parts he plays, America's rootless Everyman suspended in a permanent highwire act. Younger imitators – Mickey Rourke, Richard Gere, Nicholas Cage and Matt Dillon – have absorbed aspects of his technique in various ways, with varying degrees of success.

Dan Dennett born 1942

AMERICAN COGNITIVE SCIENTIST

Cognitive science has a problem explaining how the electrical impulses that carry information from the outside world are actually interpreted inside the brain, without resorting to the idea of homunculi – little people looking at the electrical pictures in the same way as we watch television (which wouldn't take us any further because each homunculus would have to have another homunculus and so on, in an infinite regression). Dennett has tried to combine philosophy, artificial intelligence and humour to provide a way out of this dilemma. Start with the whole person, he says, with their beliefs and desires, expectations and fears. Instead of thinking about an interpreter who deals with everything, break the information down into sub-systems. Exchange the one little person in the head for a committee; each member of the committee is a narrow specialist, more stupid than the whole because they 'think' about less. Dennett compares the mind to the CIA – each bit operates on the 'need to know' principle, receiving only the information it needs in order to get on with its own tasks. Which member of the committee do we identify with when we are thinking? Does there not have to be a boss? Dennett's skill at extending metaphors mops up those problems easily: Think of the mind as a company; what we identify with is the director of public relations, the expert in charge of dealing with the outside world. Dennett has further jokes, parables and stories for questions about consciousness, the mind-body problem, identity. It is so much fun that you would have to be a real bore to ask if it really works.

Eugene Dennis 1905-61

AMERICAN POLITICAL ACTIVIST

Leader of the American Communist Party, Dennis was put in gaol in 1949 for advising the overthrow by force of the US government just before the climax of Cold War anti-Communism. He came from an Irish-Norwegian family in Seattle, where he was active in the 1919 general strike organized by the Industrial Workers of the World (IWW, or 'Wobblies'). He had an adventurous, up-and-down, all-over-the-place career, which included stints as a lumberjack, a truck driver, a longshoreman and an economics teacher, financed by the Communist party. Arrested several times – as a trade union organizer – for public order offences, he went on to spend several years in South Africa, the USSR and China. On NATO's formation in 1949, he helped prepare a statement that 'We Communists would co-operate with all democratic forces to defeat the predatory war aims of the US.' He claimed that his trial was a bid to suppress the party, whose leader he remained until 1959, arguing for partial de-Stalinization after ☛Khruschev's rise.

Maya Deren

1908-61

∀ AMERICAN EXPERIMENTAL
☞ FILM-MAKER

Together with ☛Kenneth Anger, Deren was a pioneer of the second wave of experimental film-making. She co-directed and starred – alongside her husband, documentarist Alexander Hammid – in the legendary Los Angeles underground movie, *Meshes of the Afternoon* (1943), a soundless dream-nightmare study of psychological dysfunction in a suicidal woman. The film was the still remarkable opening shot of a specifically American avant-garde, using quietly fantastical montage and rhythmic editing to illuminate inner worlds, rather than the outer social-political images to which these devices had previously been applied. Although she only made half-a-dozen more films, many of them dealing with dancers or ritual, she had an unparalleled impact, partly as a teacher and propagandist for avant-garde cinema as an alternative to the mainstream, and partly as an organizer, arranging venues for screenings and film-makers' mutual support groups in New York. It is certain that the generation who came to maturity in the 1960s owed her a huge debt. Intriguingly, Deren was as deeply involved in voodoo as Kenneth Anger was in Crowleyan 'magick' – between them, they brought into being a genre that has survived thanks largely to a self-imposed and ever-renewable cloak of esoteric mystery.

Cameras do not make films; film-makers make films. Improve your films not by adding more equipment and personnel but by using what you have to the fullest capacity. The more important part of your equipment is yourself: your mobile body, your imaginative mind and your freedom to use both.

Maya Deren, Amateur vs Professional

Jacques Derrida

born 1930

○ FRENCH PHILOSOPHER,
❞ LITERARY THEORIST

The three long, interrelated texts that Derrida published in 1967 – *Speech and Phenomena, Writing and Difference* and *Of Grammatology* – presented his reappraisals of then-current attitudes so forcefully that he was immediately hailed as the first post-structuralist. This was true without meaning very much, and his influence began to spread faster than the extreme difficulty of his writing could justify. Developing a far more radically ambivalent understanding of how language and metaphor shape the world than that of most of his structuralist contemporaries, he argues that the most profound (and sometimes most respected) arguments in metaphysics actually contain their own refutation because of the way they are built up from certain basic assumptions. Often regarded as frivolous, obscurantist and apolitical, Derrida is certainly the first two: he would argue that the proprieties of argumentation are only there to defend orthodoxy. The last adjective is more difficult. Deconstruction continues and deepens a profound tradition of provocatively dissident close reading – Derrida resembles Nietzsche, in playful rigour if not immediate lucidity. The question 'Who makes these rules, and what is in it for them?' is behind every word he writes, and his strategies have been invaluable to other philosophies of the silenced voice (particularly feminism). Such Third World critics as Gayatri Spivak and Sunday Anozie have developed his ideas in important ways. Given that none of his critics – and few of his rabid supporters – has really come to grips with the full implications of his thought (which they take to be merely a species of radical scepticism concerning the possibility of meaning, communication or knowledge), it is probably too early to say that he is the most significant thinker of the century, but he is unarguably one of the most original.

Philip K. Dick 1928-82

▲ AMERICAN WRITER

Dick's writing so encapsulates 1960s' SF – its formal invention, its paranoid obsessions, its struggles to redraw sordid reality and to redefine lapsed humanity, as well as its submission to the mass-production schedules of pulp fiction – that, while his originality is now taken for granted, his wider importance is minimized. Because of the pressure of deadlines (*The Penultimate Truth*, *Simulacra*, *Martian Timeslip* and *Clans of the Alphane Moon* all appeared in 1964), even his best work is not as fully realized as it could have been, but some of the energy ensuing from desperation works for his themes. The plain greys of his future-shock pessimism and his schizophrenic parallel time-structures achieve insights that no mainstream novelist has matched (even ☛Burroughs, a richer stylist, has a far narrower range). Dick's protagonists are saddened, crushed little people, struggling to retain integrity in technologically alien worlds. The feeling that this was his story too is inescapable. *Do Androids Dream of Electric Sheep?* (1968) was filmed as *Blade Runner* (1982), but the philosophical core of the book was worked into a nightmarishly brilliant surface that annoyed many of his readers by turning philosophical argument into the perfectly realized imagery of an imperfect world. His errant children, the Cyberpunks, have adapted rather well to the amoral tech-jungles he feared and resisted – they like it there – rather as the characters in his posthumously published 'black comdies' of the 1950s (including the brilliant *Confessions of a Crap Artist*) find themselves accepting the nightmare of life in ☛Eisenhower's America.

Joe DiMaggio born 1914

AMERICAN BASEBALL PLAYER

Non-Americans, lacking the deep insight into the mysteries of baseball that is only bestowed on citizens of the US, possibly imagine that it was marriage to ☛Marilyn Monroe which turned this New York Yankee into an iconic figure. Not so. DiMaggio is the man who, in 1941, made at least one hit in each of 56 successive games, the greatest accomplishment in the history of baseball. Consistency on that level takes such an extraordinary combination of skill and luck that statisticians argue that it just should not have happened. It is a record to fuel the dreams of any gambler, and no player has come close to matching it since. DiMaggio's legend was given new life by Simon & Garfunkel's song 'Mrs Robinson', which was the theme song for *The Graduate* (1967).

Dorothy Dinnerstein

✌ AMERICAN FEMINIST

Dinnerstein seeks to make child-rearing, and men doing as much of it as women, into a question of planetary survival. Smudging somewhat the complexity of the love-hate that grown-ups feel for mum and dad, she argues that, through taking most of the responsibility for bringing up children, women have made themselves scapegoats for all the ills of human existence. Kids grow up to find that their lives are, in the nature of things, unsatisfactory – happiness is a scarce commodity. They blame those who reared them, women for the most part, and react by excluding them from many areas of life. Left to themselves, men seek to master the world and are on the way to transforming it into one large machine. The result is increasing misery. In her argument for a pact between male 'minotaur' and female 'mermaid', she differs from some other feminists in acknowledging that there can be no 'solution' to the inner turmoils of the human psyche.

Christian Dior 1905-57

FRENCH FASHION DESIGNER

Dior's 1947 collection – characterized by low necklines, tight waists and generous bosoms – was instantly dubbed the 'New Look' by American journalists, and it established him as the fashion king of Paris, and Paris as again the centre of world fashion. Yet, although his abundant use of fabric provided a shock-contrast to the styles imposed by wartime conditions, Dior was actually reviving pre-war trends in French fashion, as well as offering a nostalgic glimpse back to the *belle epoque* of the early years of the century. Dressmakers in austerity England complained at the extravagant use of cloth, and argued that practical women preferred 'sensible' clothes, but it was rustling petticoats and full skirts that women were buying. For his 1948 collection, Dior made jackets that were cut with loose, fly-away backs and stand-up collars, and he went on to develop the coolie hat, worn low over the eyes and trimmed with bows. He had an undisputed eye for elegance.

Milovan Djilas born 1911

YUGOSLAV POLITICIAN

One mark of progess in Eastern Europe during the 1950s was the difference between the treatment of Trotsky by Stalin, and that of Djilas by ☛Tito. Stalin forced his arch-critic into exile, where he had him killed. Tito sent his former comrade-in-arms (who had held senior posts in the Yugoslav élite) to gaol on three occasions, but in the end, he set Djilas free and permitted him to write for foreign publishers, as a commentator on affairs in Eastern Europe. He was gaoled for the first time in 1956, when already on probation for earlier attacks on the one-party state. His view, put forward in *The New Class* (1957), that an aristocracy had been formed in Marxist societies by those with status in the official machine – the *apparatchiks* who had privileges, if not much property – is now a cliché of media analysis. Djilas was able to work out his ideas from a senior niche in the hierarchy, as he evolved from Communist to social democrat. Unlike other dissidents in the Eastern bloc – ☛Walesa, ☛Solzhenitsyn, ☛Sakharov – he has developed an alternative to the ruling ideology which is not just a response to specific issues such as labour conditions or human rights abuses.

Bernardine Dohrn born 1942

AMERICAN POLITICAL ACTIVIST

A University of Chicago law student who ended up on America's most-wanted list, Dohrn became, for a period in the late 1960s, a radical youth celebrity – the counter-culture pin-up who led the Weather Underground as they were driven from their original anti-establishment prankishness to self-destructive near-terrorism. She began as an optimistic New Left activist campaigning with ☛Martin Luther King but, after ☛Malcolm X and King had been murdered, and the state had begun to deliver more and more harsh retribution for civil rights and anti-war dissidence, reasoned non-violence no longer seemed adequate to her. The working classes would never rise on their own; only direct and deliberately irrational youth-action against the machinery of surveillance and the increasingly vicious backlash was appropriate. The Weathermen, named from a line in a Bob Dylan song, began to garner a confused reputation as the wing of the counter-culture that would go furthest – the New Left's impassioned, loopy, quasi-Maoist id, cruising out beyond the most ultra-militant groupings of the increasingly fragmented movement and heckling for everyone to break with everything except ☛Ho Chi Minh, the Black Panthers and permanent (social, cultural and sexual) revolution. They mocked their own outlaw extremism. They 'smashed monogamy' and then preached celibacy, fomented 'kids' lib' in schools and began to assault the ordinary (counter-revolutionary) American citizen, while railing against the obscenity of the war in Vietnam, eventually working themselves up to the 'Days of Rage' week of Chicago street-wars in late 1969. And then in March 1970, three Weathermen were killed when a nail bomb they were making accidentally went off, and their remaining comrades were now outlaws for real. They spent the next decade on the run, setting off more bombs, killing no one and converting no one. Dohrn, who wrote the oddly dignified Weather-communiqué that identified the three bodies, gave herself up in the late 1970s. A few more held out until 1981 when, the name of the Weathermen long forgotten and their ideals long withered, they were captured, tried and gaoled for a robbery and triple murder committed earlier that year.

Eric Dolphy 1928-64

♥ AMERICAN JAZZ MUSICIAN

Although it seemed possible, in the months before his tragically premature death while on the road in Europe, that Dolphy would have become one of the prime innovators in 1960s' jazz, he never quite had the chance to fix his development beyond a position as the most advanced reinterpreter of all that had gone before. His fluid non-linear takes on bebop are utterly distinctive and he was much sought after as a sideman working, in particular, with ☛Charlie Mingus, but also, famously, on ☛Ornette Coleman's epochal *Free Jazz* double quartet set (1960). Jazz playing being a personal and intensely intuitive kind of travelling, unfinished journeys tend not to be followed up: Dolphy's impressive talents as a multi-instrumentalist (working on flute and bass clarinet as well as saxophone) have probably been more influential than any ideas about where he might have been leading jazz. He is remembered as an inspirational presence, and his album *Out to Lunch* (1964) is one of the masterpieces of jazz recording.

Alexander Dubček born 1921

✓ CZECHOSLOVAK POLITICAL LEADER

Leader of Czechoslovakia's Communist party in 1968, Dubček introduced the 'Prague Spring', a season of reform allowing for a relaxation of censorship and extended debate within the party, which, in turn, led to the Soviet invasion. During WW2 he had been active in the anti-Nazi resistance, and he rose steadily through party ranks after the war. As head of the Slovak party, Dubček led opposition to the national party leader, Antonín Novotny, who was slowing the pace of economic reform. In 1968, he took over power, planning measures that would lead to economic decentralization and political change. Despite a Czechoslovak pledge to stay in the Warsaw Pact, the Soviets insisted on a meeting. Dubček would not budge and, as Soviet tanks rolled into the country, the Czechoslovak leaders were seized and taken to Moscow, where they were forced to make concessions. Dubček, progressively isolated from sympathizers, struggled on until April 1969. Briefly Czechoslovak envoy to Turkey, he refused to defect, was brought home and given a forester's job. His initial statements on ☛Gorbachev's changes in the Soviet Union gave hints of a sad, disappointed man. Nevertheless, following the peaceful toppling of Czechoslovak Stalinism in 1989, he was installed as head of a new-style Federal Assembly, working with the president, playwright ☛Václav Havel, to implement a programme of political and economic reforms.

René Dubos 1901-82

▲ FRENCH-AMERICAN IMMUNOLOGIST, ECOLOGIST

Dubos's life's work was mapped out when he read in a journal that microbes evolve in radically different ways, depending on whether they are in the wild or in a laboratory. He went on to pursue the idea of organisms realizing optimal growth in a friendly habitat, and extended this to take up the fight against pollution. He argued that biology omitted environment as a factor in the formation of human conduct, so that, for example, it did not look into the way children are shaped by their early surroundings. 'Humanness' was his expression for the interplay between human nature and the environment, and Dubos became increasingly worried by the risk of human decay, not humanity's exit. His 1969 book *So Human an Animal* was almost as influential on proto-ecologists as ☛Rachel Carson's earlier *Silent Spring*. Dubos became a naturalized US citizen, and spent his later life planting and caring for trees on his 88-acre home beside the Hudson River.

Jean Dubuffet 1901-85

∀ FRENCH ARTIST

❀ Fired by his rage at the German occupation of France, Dubuffet developed a form of primitive art which he called *L'art brut*, combining influences from Dada, surrealism and psychiatry, and also drawing on his fascination with the art of children and psychotics. He used a strange mix of materials – plaster, putty, concrete, sand, mud and gravel combined with oil paint – and produced canvases that seethed like a tray of maggots, exploiting the texture and weight of such eclectic ingredients. These almost fossil-like creations examine a number of obsessive themes – landscapes, cities and stick figures – and, in their naïve way, reveal a grotesque sense of humour and a sophistication that goes beyond street art. Though a relatively late starter – he tended the family wine business until he was 41 – Dubuffet demonstrated both in his own work, and in his collection of the work of others (psychiatric patients, gaoled primitives), that within the so-called insane and uncultured there lurks a source of unrestricted, imaginative visions.

John Foster Dulles 1888-1959

AMERICAN POLITICIAN

The son of a church minister and a staunch anti-Communist, as US secretary of state under ☛Truman and ☛Eisenhower, Dulles helped shift policy from 'containing' Soviet expansion to taking the initiative against it. He spoke of 'rolling back the Communist world empire,' 'liberating the captive peoples of Eastern Europe' and defending Berlin by military force. Arguably, this was all a pose. Dulles was just talking tough out of a conviction that conflicts such as the Korean War had come about because the Communist powers misjudged US intentions, thinking they would not respond to aggression. While Dulles barked – he threatened to lob nuclear weapons at the Chinese – President Eisenhower's image as a man of peace was enhanced as he negotiated with emissaries from Peking and tied up an accord in Korea. Even so, by intervening in Lebanon and Guatemala, and proposing that American troops be despatched to Vietnam, Dulles prepared the way for the later escalation of US involvement in South-east Asia. He also blackmailed the French into the European Defence Community, hoping to see Europe politically and economically united, and forced the British to withdraw from Suez, by his refusal to prop up sterling. In his zest for moral absolutes, he saw the British as colonialists seeking to reassert their power, just as the Soviets ran an evil empire: Americans, by contrast, were idealists and friends of freedom.

There is no use in having the stuff, and never being able to use it.
John Foster Dulles on nuclear weapons

Marguerite Duras

(Marguerite Donnadieu) born 1914

☞FRENCH NOVELIST, SCREENWRITER, POET, FILM-MAKER

Duras provided the script for ☛Alain Resnais' Hiroshima *Mon Amour* (1959), linking her suspicions of conventional narrative to his obsessions with time, memory and alienation in a story that exploited the subversive topicality (between Korea and Vietnam) of all things Eastern. With its then-remarkable (and still-uncomfortable) political subject – cross-cultural love in the shadow of the bomb – as well as its dense layering of images and laconic, elliptical style, the film put Duras at the heart of the French cinema's New Wave, and helped secure for that movement a central position in the French avant-garde. Born and brought up in French Indo-China, Duras was already associated with the heightened psychological studies of the *nouveau roman* (although at first as a neo-realist rather than an 'anti-novelist' like ☛Sarraute or ☛Robbe-Grillet). Although active in the Resistance and a supporter of anti-colonial politics, she had been expelled from the Communist party in 1955, and has since moved increasingly further away from her youthful

embrace of the Marxist idea of history's ineluctable progress. Her subject over the years (in novels, films and theatre) has been the failure of narrative, its impossibility and its dishonesty. Her work has been unstintingly experimental, and her films, such as *Destroy She Said* (1973) and *The Truck* (1977), have been well-received by feminist critics.

Rudi Dutschke 1940-79

GERMAN POLITICAL ACTIVIST

A West German student leader of the 1968 era, Dutschke was born in East Germany, the son of a postal worker. Refusing military servce, he went to West Berlin's 'Free University' and, by the late 1960s, had emerged as the leader of the extra-parliamentary opposition, protesting against Vietnam and the rightist West German government. An assassination attempt – he was shot in the head in April 1968 – followed a vicious campaign against him by the Springer press and triggered a wave of student riots, first in West Germany, later elsewhere. Soon after, he travelled to the UK to seek medical aid, but when he was expelled in 1971 for illicit political activity, another scandal ensued. Going to Denmark, he made a new start as a politics lecturer. His days of active radical leadership were over, although he played a role in the emergence of the German Green Party. His early death was a direct result of his head wound, which had left him crippled.

Andrea Dworkin born 1946

AMERICAN FEMINIST

Large in bulk, huge in rage, New York working-class, radical feminist Dworkin is unquestionably the most aggressive critic of all aspects of male sexuality and patriarchy. In such books as *Pornography: Men Possessing Women* (1981) and *Intercourse* (1987), she has taken a furious (but very specific) position in the politics of representation, drawing roughly equal degrees of admiration and rabid dismissal from every party to the feminist/anti-feminist debate. Since her position rests fundamentally on a subtle if contentious understanding of the (political) nature of language and the function of symbolism, and since she has openly admitted that her writing is as much polemical intervention as 'fact' – she is a *provocateuse* rather than a theorist or historian – there is little to be gained from advancing the criticism that her commitment steamrollers the complexity of the questions she raises. She argues that pornography is innately, ruthlessly anti-women, that to be 'male' is to be power-seeking and violent, and that a feminist-based censorship is essential for the health of future societies, and she does so with such rigid fervour that some feminists regard her as an unbalanced liability. She ripostes by suggesting that many so-called feminists are no more than collaborators and gender-traitors. Her semi-autobiographical novel *Ice and Fire* (1986) confuses the issue still further, by documenting violent male sexuality with such relentless realism that some readers reportedly find it a mildly porny turn-on.

Ronald Dworkin born 1931

AMERICAN POLITICAL THEORIST

Since the late 1960s, Dworkin has been one of the toughest and most able advocates of liberal positions in relation to legal rights, arguing from a subtle understanding of American jurisprudence as enshrined in the US Constitution. When ☛President Reagan attempted to raise the deeply reactionary Robert Bork to the nine-strong US Supreme Court in 1988, it was articles by Dworkin which really *proved* that Bork's elaborate theory of 'original intent' (which aims to interpret the Constitution and its amendments in terms of what the people framing it had in mind *at the time*) was incoherent, contradictory and ultimately a far-right smokescreen for shifting a delicately balanced judiciary against many of the civil rights gains of the 1960s and early 1970s. Dworkin is concerned particularly with the question of what judges are, or should be. He argues that they do not simply make decisions based upon a series of rules, or make new rules to fill gaps in the law but, in fact, invoke a consistent set of moral and political principles to determine the rights of the individual. From an analysis of these rights, Dworkin argues the liberal case that there is no significant conflict between individual freedom and the search for equality, and opposes the left-wing argument that general welfare should be the ultimate justification for all political and legal action. Each person, he claims, has the right to equal concern and respect – the state cannot tell citizens how to live their lives – but Dworkin can still argue from this position in support of measures of economic redistribution and reverse discrimination. He has made the point that, in a modern state, arguments over the nature of human purpose are fundamentally incapable of settlement, and that rules for the public good cannot be framed with any such higher goals in mind.

Bob Dylan

(Robert Zimmerman) born 1941

❍ AMERICAN SINGER, SONGWRITER

✍ Appearing in Greenwich Village just at the time when beatnik protest was beginning to connect with deeper social discontent, Dylan more than anyone forced rock 'n' roll to grow up, in spite of itself. His buzzard's cackle of a voice defines the term 'unmusical' and his writing, which his fans call poetry, is arguably self-indulgent, repetitive, naïve, confused and second-hand. Nevertheless, he was immensely significant in the way he fused arrogant teen-energy and folk, apparently speaking out against things. He usually was not, but his audiences were anyway more interested in the hip, snide attitude than elaborate oppositional politics. Beholden to no one, Dylan has travelled his own path, through religion and out again, and no one should deny that he has transformed rock's attitude to singing. He was the first in a line of vocalists whose expressiveness resides in purely personal modes of articulation, a line that includes ☛The Beatles' John Lennon, ☛The Velvet Underground's Lou Reed, ☛The Sex Pistol's John Lydon, David Byrne of ☛Talking Heads, Mark E. Smith of ☛The Fall, ☛Patti Smith, and Kate Bush. (There are also hordes of performers who have made a living by copying Dylan's own mannerisms, which pretty much misses the point.) He has done little of note in the past two decades, but the memory of those few years in the mid-1960s, when he lived off speed and his wits, seems to have been enough to ensure him a permanent place in the pantheon.

E

Charles Eames 1907-78

AMERICAN DESIGNER

Eames conceived designs for film sets, fabrics, toys and buildings but made his name as a creator of chairs that were simple, comfortable and technologically modern. In 1940, together with Eero Saarinen, he moulded plywood into a chair that would fit the human body – a revolutionary concept at the time. Mass-marketed after WW2, the chairs became increasingly sophisticated technically – shock absorbers, for example, were adopted from engine design – but all were developments of essentially the same idea. They acquired their status as design classics partly through the way Eames exploited combinations of textures to striking effect, such as wood against metal or leather against wire. Eames' philosophy of comfort with simplicity is evident also in the house he built for himself in 1949, using factory-produced windows, structural beams and sliding doors to construct what he described as a 'variable container for objects and living'.

Umberto Eco born 1932

& ITALIAN NOVELIST, LITERARY THEORIST

Attractively honest about how many people have actually read his complex monastery whodunnit, *The Name of the Rose* (1980/3), Eco claims that William Weaver's English translation is better than the original, and that he loves the hacked-about film version. He carries the burden of his role – popular intellectual without precedent – pretty well (certainly better than the more fashionable ☛Baudrillard), with the added fillip of Vatican bans on both *Rose* and his latest novel, *Foucault's Pendulum* (1988/9). A Joyce scholar (he collaborated with ☛Luciano Berio on a homage-project in the 1950s) and an expert on systems of thought in medieval Europe, as well as one of the first and most influential semioticians and pop-culture theorists, he is untainted by the disdainful élitism some code-breakers seem to tumble into: he takes obvious pleasure in the worlds he uncovers for a living, especially in the area of film theory. He forms one of the most important links between writers such as ☛Borges and thinkers such as ☛Barthes; although probably less inspired or provocative than either, he is more consistent – a natural teacher rather than an iconoclast. For him the post-Saussurian cliché of 'the dispersed economy of the sign' comes to underpin a politics of multi-cultural tolerance. Distaste for narrow fanaticism provided the core of *Rose*, where the villain is a man who destroys books – and murders – to save souls.

Anthony Eden 1897-1977

BRITISH POLITICAL LEADER

Foreign secretary before WW2, the most obvious feature of Eden's career is the dozen years he spent as Winston Churchill's heir-elect, waiting for the ageing premier's retirement. But then Churchill probably realized that Eden did not have the imagination or the resolve to make much of a stab at being prime minister: he was neurotic, indecisive and inclined to uncontrollable fits of temper. Whereas Churchill had always been a realist when it came to assessing the balance of power, Eden was motivated by the resentment he felt against the Americans, who had usurped Britain from its position as a leading world power, and fired up by his implacable opposition to the idea (actively espoused by US secretary of state ☛John Foster Dulles) that the UK should now see itself as part of Europe. A resolve to stand up for himself, and make Britain count in the world, may explain the débâcle of Suez when, with the French, he chose to use the chance of a ceasefire between the Egyptians and the Israelis as the excuse for an invasion to topple ☛Nasser. Eden's personal psychology, plus the British obsession with retaining control in the Middle East, explains the sudden move – not, as he argued in his memoirs, the belief that Nasser had to be stopped, as the Axis powers had not been in the 1930s. Boosting the British economy should have been his real task, not vainly trying to delay the end of empire at its peripheries. His intense absorption in the 1956 crisis led to his wife's cry that the Suez Canal flowed through her sitting-room.

John Ehrlichman born 1925
H. R. (Bob) Haldeman born 1926

✚ AMERICAN POLITICIANS

These 'two Germans' were ☛President Nixon's sidekicks and two of the most powerful men in America until a colleague, John Dean, decided he was not going to be the Watergate fall-guy and dropped them in the shit. Haldeman was overseer to the Committee to Re-elect the President (the fabled CREEP) which provided the funds to pay for break-ins by 'plumbers' such as ☛G. Gordon Liddy and the wiretapping of political opponents. He had been with Nixon since the early 1960s, when he had run the Nixon campaign for governor of California, and came to be known for the ferocious efficiency with which he managed the White House. Ehrlichman, a former lawyer, had also worked for Nixon on previous campaigns, and in the White House was his principal assistant for domestic affairs. He and Liddy inaugurated a wide-ranging regime of illegal surveillance and dirty tricks – everything from burglary to having 500 unwanted pizzas delivered to a Democratic campaign stopover. When five 'plumbers', including Liddy, were caught at the Democrats' HQ in Washington, DC – located in a complex that just happened to be named Watergate – in the middle of the 1972 election, the whole story started to unravel. Haldeman and Ehrlichman, the archetypal middle-management can-do yesmen, both spent a short time in jail – since when Ehrlichman at least has earned a good wage as a writer of books and very thinly disguised screenplays on the saga, and as an after-dinner speaker.

Einstürzende Neubauten

formed c. 1980

∀ GERMAN MUSIC GROUP

Their name translates as 'collapsing new buildings' and their shows are violent, torch-lit, metal-beating spectacles: more than any other group, Einstürzende Neubauten exemplify the urge in the European underground to take popular music beyond the reach of Anglo-American influence. Forming an uneasy alliance between punk primitivism and an earlier generation's anti-art destructiveness, they draw ideas from the Vienna Group, the extremist performance art movement which was committed to total realism to the point where performance and life merge. (One member, Rudolf Schwarzkogler, became addicted to self-mutilation and killed himself.) Einstürzende's programme exalts the creative force of destruction – one of their records is called *Strategies against Architecture* (1984) – but they have moved considerably back from this extremist brink. Their music, which retains its clashing percussive base, has become far more textural, melodic and sophisticated, to the point where it has been adopted in the UK both by the avant-garde Test Department and by chart-pop act Depeche Mode – two versions of EN-sound that are almost entirely different. Einstürzende's former frontman Blixa Bargeld, a charismatic pop-eyed stick-figure, is now a cornerstone of ex-Birthday Party singer Nick Cave's group, The Bad Seeds.

Dwight D. Eisenhower 1890-1969

■ AMERICAN POLITICIAN

Eisenhower's presidency of the US – from 1953 to 1961 – is often seen as a vacuum in recent American history. Even so, the polls say that he was intensely popular – a genial, conciliatory, golf-playing father-figure to the nation. Although he deferred to advisors, he managed to distance himself from ruling forces in the political establishment – thus his warning, as he left office, about the development of a 'military-industrial complex' that menaced democratic control. He fumbled for words and wasn't a political in-fighter, despite a military background which had led to his masterminding the D-Day landings in 1944. Sought in advance by both parties as a potential candidate before 1952, he first resisted appeals, then opted for the Republicans. Clearly not a man of strong political beliefs, he did little to end ☛Joseph McCarthy's anti-communist witch-hunts, even though they marred his early years in power. His responses to Eastern bloc suppression of revolts in East Germany and Hungary were only verbal. He kept US troops out of Indochina, unlike his successor ☛John F. Kennedy, and stopped Chiang Kai-shek from counter-attacking Red China. A clue to his approach is that he brought in a minute's silent prayer to begin Cabinet meetings; he had never been known for his piety before he became president but, in a political world where he wasn't at home, he was set on complying with what he took to be the proprieties.

Elizabeth II

(Elizabeth Windsor) born 1926

$ BRITISH MONARCH

Most celebrities cultivate charm to excess, but the most celebrated person of them all seems reluctant to smile or dress to please. Being able to handle television well is now essential for lesser mortals who hanker after celebrity: Britain's most famous lady comes across poorly on the tube, yet she has real staying power in the popularity stakes. The monarchy has become trivialized, with the exploits of younger royals now part of a soap opera that runs and runs in the world's tabloids, yet the Queen attracts respect, however grudgingly given in some quarters, from even her more radical subjects. She thrives, in part, because she is an enigma. Every British prime minister since Churchill has had regular meetings with her, many have spoken (admiringly) of her sagacity, but what does she think about them? More interestingly, did their joint status as powerful women create a 'special relationship' between the Queen and the grocer's daughter from Grantham? The Queen is said to turn off unnecessary lights in Buckingham Palace (one could imagine ☛Margaret Thatcher doing the same at Downing Street if cameras had been in sight), but how does she really feel about being the richest person in England? Since she guards the secrets of her private life so jealously, what passed through her mind when she found a strange (unattractive) man sitting at the end of her bed? – he had climbed over the wall and penetrated the palace security cordon. The press regularly contain speculation on these and other topics, but the only views she will express in public are those concerned with horses, dogs and her affection for the British Commonwealth.

Harlan Ellison born 1934

AMERICAN WRITER

As editor of the *Dangerous Visions* anthology (1967), Ellison hoped to transform science fiction, pushing the New Wave into experimental and socially critical directions that were both controversial and highly productive. As a writer himself he is talented, aggressive and highly subjective, with a pulp intensity and an ability to use (and abuse) pulp subject matter. Gaudy and garrulous in tone, acid in attitude, he has never moved outside the short story format. His work is often overwritten and always overlength, but these faults are probably inseparable from his strengths – energy, commitment and self-dramatization. He retains a comic-book sensibility and has no bigger fan than himself, but the all-American, anti-American black humour in a novella such as *A Boy and His Dog* (1969) is uncomfortably prophetic. Even at his worst you would rather he was there than not – at his best, Ellison sees and says things no one else dares to.

Ralph Ellison born 1914

▲AMERICAN WRITER

Ellison's reputation rests on a single novel, *The Invisible Man* (1952), about a young black in New York, which garnered such an intense reaction that black fiction was transformed from that moment. The novel mapped an anguished racial self-awareness in a narrative which, though often very funny, appealed directly to then-popular existentialism. Ellison was born in Oklahoma, but moved to New York as a young jazz musician and composer, where he met the black novelist Richard Wright who was to become a life-long friend. Wright was the epitome of the protest artist, taking his lead from the social realist school of the 1930s. Ellison's *Invisible Man*, though semi-autobiographical, is more concerned with a psychological portrait of the inner self, using techniques of monologue and surrealistic fantasy, as well as a great deal of translated folkloric elements. While the approach was much praised by some for being 'universal' rather than 'racial' in thrust, Ellison also came in for considerable criticism from the left and from certain black critics for not writing genuine protest novels, and for presenting a distorted picture of black American life. This point may have stung; certainly Ellison has since said of the book that he 'failed of eloquence', and he has written nothing of length or lasting import since. During the 1960s and 1970s he was much criticized for this, though rumours of the imminent arrival of a new and massive (three-volume) novel seem to have quietened the hubbub.

The blues is an impulse to keep the painful details and episodes of a brutal experience alive in one's aching consciousness, to finger its jagged grain, and to transcend it, not by the consolation of philosophy but by squeezing from it a near-tragic, near-comic lyricism.

Ralph Ellison

Jacques Ellul born 1912

FRENCH POLITICAL SCIENTIST

Ellul is a student of institutions whose books are shot through with theology as he writes about humanity's relationship to technology. The conflict he studies is between 'technique' and 'freedom'. What he means by 'technique' is not just the sum of the scientific processes used for industrial output; it also takes in techniques of persuasion – advertising, politics, education. The milieu, created by technique/technology, is self-determining and nihilistic; it acts by cause-and-effect connections, but is empty of ends. The way people adjust to their milieu is to understand the propaganda they are surrounded by and, thus, to understand the society itself; from there, they can move on to devise goals that they can zealously pursue. 'Technological rationality' is a potent threat, but it can be mastered, turned round and by-passed once it has been analytically grapsed. Ellul, a trained lawyer from a culturally rich family background – poor, artistic, aristocratic, part-Italian, part-Serbian – is caught up in movements to defend France's Atlantic coast and to help drop-outs, and he writes prolifically. Given roots and passions so strongly focused, he is tantalizingly abstract.

Brian Eno born 1948

(Brian Peter George St John Baptiste de la Salle Eno)

BRITISH MUSICIAN

In the early days of Roxy Music, Eno rivalled lounge-lizard star ☛Bryan Ferry for the public's affections, a fact often forgotten later when critics sought to label Eno the pretentious egghead. In fact, Eno's appearance, tape-work and self-confessed 'squeaky' voice were almost as much a part of the wit and strangeness of Roxy as Ferry was. Eno's departure from the group – the rival thwarted – led him first into hilariously perverse and melodically accessible rock. Subsequently he has developed interests in ambient music (unobtrusive sound conducive to certain moods), experimental video, African music, primitive sampling and even Russian rock, all of which have become immensely influential as enough time has passed for Eno's involvement to be forgotten and the British embarrassment at intellectualism to be expunged (actually it may still be an uphill struggle with Russian rock).

Eno's production work for ☛Talking Heads and ☛David Bowie was, doubtless, mutually helpful; the same cannot be said for the contribution he made to ☛U2. Millions of hipsters find him enormously attractive and he is reputed to know more dirty jokes than anyone else in pop music.

Werner Erhard

(John Paul Rosenberg) born 1935

✚ AMERICAN CULTIST

Those who experimented with mind-expanding drugs and disciplines in the 1960s were described as 'dropping out'. However, some came back in the 1970s to build commercial empires upon what they had learned in the underground, and few were more successful than Werner Erhard, founder of Erhard Seminars Training Inc., the purveyors of *est*. This consciousness-training programme developed out of the self-hypnosis techniques that he had taught, as a used-car salesman, to his team of hustlers. Those who submit to this process – generally people who feel they would be more successful if they could 'get it together' – are locked in a room and submitted to verbal aggro until, as the long minutes turn into hours, the banalities propounded from the platform come to seem profound. *est* teaches people to focus on the present moment, and what they want to achieve from a given situation. It is a debris-clearing operation, designed to replace guilt, anxiety and self-doubt with an abiding sense of purpose. Those who go through it feel transformed; but, divested of their soft edges, they immediately alienate all their friends.

Erik Erikson

born 1902

DANISH-AMERICAN PSYCHOANALYST

Traditional Freudian psychoanalysis sees life as one long and lonely struggle to come to terms with the psychosexual experiences of childhood. Erikson, however, divided the life cycle into a series of transitional phases, each of which presents new challenges to the individual self; showed how the dynamics of particular societies helped or hindered passage through each period; and coined the term 'identity crisis' to describe the role-confusion of adolescence, the fifth of his phases. This interest in problems of identity he traced back to his own experience of being deceived about the identity of his father, and the difficulties of growing up as a Danish Jew in Hamburg. Analyzed in Vienna by Freud's daughter, Anna, Erikson moved to the US in the mid-1930s, became Boston's first child psychologist and carried out research at Harvard. It was while working with veterans after WW2 that he developed his notion that psychology should help deal with 'the vicissitudes of normal life', resulting in his 1950 book, *Childhood and Society*, which outlined his eight psycho-social stages. Some of Erikson's most intriguing work explores the psychological development of innovative historical figures, suggesting the parallel social and political developments which created an audience for their particular message. A 1942 paper, showing how Hitler's speeches deployed childhood experiences to strike chords in the psyches of his countrymen, was followed by books on *Young Man Luther* (1958) and *Gandhi's Truth* (1969).

Elliott Erwitt

born 1928

AMERICAN PHOTOGRAPHER

Although he is a noted commercial photographer, and has received major commissions such as one to photograph American architecture for the US Pavilion at the 1970 Osaka World Fair, the pictures Erwitt is best known for are the funny ones. He delights in undermining the solemn and the serious, from weddings to military training, from US rockets to the rituals of Catholic training, but the effect is always life-enhancing. His collection of dog 'snaps' – *Son of a Bitch* (1974), which featured an introduction by P. G. Wodehouse – was a bestseller. Classic Erwitt celebrations of incongruity include a couple involved in an intense conversation amid the shrivelled mummies of Guanajuato; a man pushing a pram alongside three bridesmaids dressed in white; and a group of naked painters at their easels, working on pictures of a fully clothed model.

M(aurits) C(ornelius) Escher

1898-1972

& DUTCH GRAPHIC ARTIST

Inhabiting the same universe as ☛Borges, Escher's pictures – almost all in black and white – present a series of optical illusions (some famous, some developed by Escher himself, two discovered by mathematician ☛Roger Penrose) in which every component of the picture is organized around the optical illusion. People and animals – resembling nothing so much as animated rubber models – live and work, without apparent concern, in the vicinity of impossible structures and tricks in perspective; only the observer is disturbed as two dimensions seem permanently on the point of ballooning out into three. Escher's interest in cosmology, mathematics, the contradictions inherent in representation and mosaics (or, to use the precise mathematical term, tesselations) with cartoon monsters that owe something to Islamic art, give his work an abstraction that is coolly dreamlike, but there is also a fascination with detail and miniaturized grotesqueries that adds its own niggling energy.

Gil Evans

1912-88

AMERICAN JAZZ MUSICIAN

Evans' contributions to jazz – and, indirectly, to pop – came in the field of orchestral arrangement: he had an uncanny ear for 'sensurround' tone-painting that enhanced the improvisations of the performers he worked with. He was first noticed in the late 1940s, when he joined trumpeter ☛Miles Davis, pianist John Lewis and saxophonist ☛Gerry Mulligan to develop a system of texturing that turned into *The Birth of the Cool* (1949-50). A touch too formal, Cool Jazz would become an arid genre, but Evans' orchestral touch was always ahead of fashion. Several other collaborations with Davis, including the remarkable *Porgy and Bess* (1958) and the perhaps over-regarded *Sketches of Spain* (1960), cemented his reputation at just the wrong time: jazz was moving into its most anarchic phase. In the late 1960s, he was drawn to the fierce electric freedoms of ☛Jimi Hendrix, and throughout later years, he would return to wrestle with the problems they presented for his craft. Records never caught the full impact of his music: it breathed best at volume, with full use of space, and this only rarely registered in the studio. Apparently ageless, and certainly remarkably youthful in outlook, aesthetic and otherwise, Evans died at a moment when pop music, entering its own Cool period, had begun to favour him with belated attention.

Hans Eysenck born 1916

BRITISH PSYCHOLOGIST

Eysenck became famous when he was hounded off the lecture platform at the London School of Economics because he argued that racial differences in intelligence test results are largely due to genetic factors. But this most controversial aspect of his writings is also the least original, being largely a restatement of the work of his former student ☛Arthur Jensen. More significantly, he has developed his own theory of personality types, based on statistical analyses as well as physiological and behavioural data. Eysenck postulates a biological basis for personality, rooted in the ability of different brain-types to deal with stimulation. While most of this is scientific, the results are generally inconclusive or uninteresting. An advocate of using 'scientific' research methods in psychology, and such behavioural devices as aversion therapy to cure disorders, Eysenck has fiercely criticized psychoanalysis for producing untestable theories to explain neuroses, making suspect claims for its healing powers and producing results that are no better than would probably occur as a result of spontaneous remission. His refusal to consider cultural bias in the framing of IQ tests has rendered much of his work on 'intelligence' as unscientific as any of the non-behavioural psychologies he criticizes so exactingly.

F

The Fall formed 1977

Mark E. Smith born 1960

▲BRITISH ROCK GROUP

They appeared with punk, but never quite belonged to it. Crushing together arcane references to medieval history and casual Saturday night violence, they embody a spread of British mythologies, ancient and modern, like no other group. Their tattered sprawl of a sound is a mutant descendent of The Troggs, ☛The Kinks and mis-remembered Northern Soul. Rock's basic pitch has always been imminent ecstasy; The Fall's has, from the beginning, been immanent terror, and their one remaining founder-member, Mark E. Smith, is best understood as a 1970s' disco-misfit descendant of Victorian fright-writers such as M. R. James or Arthur Machen. He runs his group like a displaced medieval Lord of the Manor, by turns loopy and cunning, and writes in an eerie, distorted, splenetic argot all his own, which perfectly encapsulates his contempt for, and his fascination with, a world he did not make.

Oriana Fallaci born 1930

ITALIAN JOURNALIST

The child of anti-Fascists in Mussolini's Italy, Fallaci learned early to treat the claims of all power-brokers with proper cynicism. Her interviewing style recognizes that those into whose presence she has been ushered – ☛Henry Kissinger, ☛Yasir Arafat, ☛Golda Meir, ☛Ruhollah Khomeini, ☛Lech Wałęsa and others – have personalities which can only be discovered through provocation. A polemical stance undoubtedly secures insights that would be denied to more cautious, objective reporters, and her pieces have retained their value as analyses of the psychology of power long after they have been published. Her aim is not to scale down these modern icons, but to show the very human bases on which they make decisions with enormous consequences. Her flair for large landscapes and 'big issues' is also manifest in her books on the paradoxes of space exploration and on the Vietnam War. Never a 'reporter' herself, Fallaci's writing shows up the limitations of most here-are-the-facts journalism. But her approach, much imitated, seems less original now than it did in the late 1970s.

Jerry Falwell born 1933

✌ AMERICAN LOBBYIST

☟ A promising athlete at college, Falwell gave up an offer to play baseball for the St Louis Cardinals when he hit on God and moved to a Bible college. He was the man behind the 'Moral Majority', a force which sought to

erry Falwell
Photo courtesy of Old Time Gospel Hour

influence American elections by blacklisting candidates who had voted in favour of abortion, pornography, homosexuality and equal rights for women. His technique was suave and sly; he did not use threats of hellfire. Although claiming not to favour the Democrats or Republicans, he was probably deceiving himself, since his efforts usually helped the Republicans – he called ☛Reagan's triumph in 1980 'the greatest day for American morality' in his adult life, even though Reagan never did more than pay lip service to the religious right's calls. A key to the Moral Majority's gains was its use of the electronic media: it was said to reach 18 million people a week. But corruption scandals increasingly hit the movement – while still at college, it was revealed, Falwell had fiddled meal tickets – and the agenda was widened from 'moral' issues to include high defence budgets and the Panama Canal issue until it became a broadly right-wing force in American life, even if not always listened to: in 1980, Falwell told Reagan not to pick Bush as his running mate. And it was the accession of Bush, more pragmatic than his predecessor, that led to the dissolution of the Moral Majority in mid-1989, some ten years after its founding. The announcement was made in Las Vegas, America's sin city.

Frantz Fanon 1925-61

FRENCH POLITICAL THINKER

Fanon constructed a psychological and philosophical interpretation of colonialism out of his experiences in the struggle for Algerian independence. As a black 'citizen' of France from the colony of Martinique, he had sought to become assimilated into the middle-class black élite of the French system, volunteering for the French army in WW2. But while studying medicine and psychiatry in Lyon, he realized that, for the French, he would remain simply a negro whatever his level of education and culture. He charted the mechanisms by which black Algerians developed a sense of inbred racial guilt and the ways in which the French progressively dehumanized their colonial subjects. Working as a psychiatrist, Fanon found that, among Europeans, just as money and cunning had symbolized the subversive potential of Jews, so sexual potency symbolized that of negroes, but where blacks shared with Jews the characteristic of being defined as 'other', they were also 'the servants'. As an angry and articulate voice expressing the search for self-definition of peoples freeing themselves from colonialism, Fanon's writing has been an inspiration for Third World psychology and critical discourse, and has influenced broader debates about the ways in which individuals define and change their identities in society.

Rainer Werner Fassbinder 1946-82

WEST GERMAN FILM DIRECTOR

Fassbinder's films captured the disillusioned pessimism of his generation, cutting away to the despair and the cruelty that lay behind the material affluence of post-war German society. Apparently not the most pleasant of characters, some said he drew his persona from Biberkopf ('cabbage-head'), the brutish anti-hero of the modernist epic *Berlin Alexanderplatz* (1984), which Fassbinder went on to film for television. Starting out in fringe theatre, in the early days he would hole up in a house with hi actors and shoot a picture in a couple of days, and even when he moved on to bigger budgets, he would often turn out two or three films in a year. Among his works are *Fear Eats the Soul* (1973), a moving portrayal of the love between an old German woman and a Turkish immigrant 'guest worker', and an indictment of German racism; *In a Year with Thirteen Moons* (1978), the tragi-comic tale of a transvestite who decides she wants to change back; and *Third Generation* (1979), a satire on middle-class flirtations with terrorism. His final film was a version of ☛Jean Genet's *Querelle of Brest* (1982), an inflamed story of sex and death in which flagellatory religious processions wind through streets littered with drunken sailors, and a burned-out torch singer chants Oscar Wilde's line: 'Each man kills the thing he loves.'

Jules Feiffer born 1929

AMERICAN CARTOONIST, SCREENWRITER, NOVELIST

Feiffer's jagged cartoons – agonized, starkly furious, mournful, probing, bitterly funny – are among the hardest, unpolished reflections of New York Jewish rad-lib anger at corruption, deceit and weakness in public and private life. Working at the *Village Voice* from its beginnings in the mid-1950s, he was part of a rising underground of political and social criticism. The inventive discipline he put into his 6-8-panel strips was attached to a scratchy expressionist minimalism: some strips featured eight repeats of the same picture, with only the dialogue evolving. Author of several plays, novels and screenplays (including the 1971 film *Carnal Knowledge*), he has never really found a way out of 1970s' subjects – sex and relationships – sticking with classic dramatic construction even when the rest of the world began to want something more fluid, more surprising. His fierce self-discipline is explosive in his strips; in anything more discursive, it is self-torture that does not travel.

Federico Fellini born 1920

ITALIAN FILM-MAKER

Fellini began his career as a cartoonist, developing his tendency to exaggerate human foibles while still keeping them within recognizable distance of real life. Even in such early works as *I Vitelloni* (1953) and *La Strada* (1954), he reacted against the prevailing Italian neo-realism to create a cavalcade of sexuality and imaginative imagery, culminating in his first major success, *La Dolce Vita* (1960), which depicted a shallow journalist's progression through the empty debauchery of Roman high society. Inventing more and more outlandish ways of telling the same story in subsequent films, his subjects ranged from Roman corruption (*Fellini Satyricon*, 1969; *Fellini's Roma*, 1972) and meditations on the nature of the artist (*8 1/2*, 1963), to nostalgia spiced with Fascist anecdotes (*Amarcord*, 1973). As his reputation as an *auteur par excellence* grew, so he found himself working on more introspective films that failed to find favour with audiences. But amid the vulgarity and over-indulgence, Fellini still has magic to spare.

Jerry Della Femina *see* Della Femina, Jerry

Lawrence Ferlinghetti born 1919

AMERICAN POET, PUBLISHER

A central figure in the revitalization of American poetry in the early 1950s, Ferlinghetti ran the City Lights bookshop in San Francisco which provided a meeting place for ☛Kerouac, ☛Ginsberg and ☛Corso. His editorship of the City Lights publishing company covered a legendary period which began with the publication of his own *Pictures from the Gone World* (1955) and continued with Allen Ginsberg's *Howl* (1956) and Corso's *Gasoline* (1958). His own work is actually closer to a form of American surrealism than it is to what is considered 'Beat' poetry.

Bryan Ferry born 1945

BRITISH ROCK MUSICIAN

After a past in teaching and soul bands, Ferry formed Roxy Music in 1970 as a conceptual package combining pop-art pastiche, rock music of several eras, artifice and – best of all – a strong opposition to the 'authentic' fake-hippyishness of the early 1970s. With a sense of humour rare in rock, the band produced music that was innovative and commercial. Ferry took his irony into solo records, producing a non-political version of 'A Hard Rain's Gonna Fall', a deadly and joyless 'The In Crowd' and a powder-dry camp 'It's My Party'. Ferry could move from distanced, stylized caricature to high, doomed passion in moments, and he displayed a classic combination of disdain and affection for pop. But the decline of Roxy Music as a creative and commercial success, coupled with the failure of his more idiosyncratic solo records, led Ferry to direct the attention he once paid to images and ideas towards the less enticing process of recording. His live shows, once monuments to Roxy Music's power and irony, have now become leaden and dated paeans to badly prepared crowd pleasing. The music may be subtle and constructed with phenomenal grace, but it is not fun anymore.

Paul Feyerabend born 1924

FRENCH PHILOSOPHER OF SCIENCE

You may think science is a rational process, governed by a fixed method, but Feyerabend will convince you that it works best as an anarchist enterprise. And when he has convinced you, he will flip round and warn you not to believe his arguments. He fights the philosophers of science on their favourite territory – the Copernican revolution, early quantum theory and Newtonian mechanics. In *Against Method* (1975), he demonstrates that expecting new hypotheses to agree with old theories only preserves the older theory, not the better one. Great advances in science are made only when scientists, consciously or otherwise, disobey the rules, and the only principle that does not inhibit progress is 'anything goes'. Feyerabend's work is witty where others' is pedestrian. If he were not so playful, he would be arrogant. His aim is wisdom, saying there is no idea, however ancient or absurd, that is not capable of improving our knowledge. In *Science in a Free Society* (1978), he argues that the authoritarian nature of science is itself a threat to democratic society. To read his unfavourable comparison of the ignorant and contemptuous scientific attitude to astrology with the arguments of the Catholic Church against witchcraft is to get a feel for his remarkable technique. After reading it, you will always think twice about 'expert' opinion.

Richard Feynman 1918-88

AMERICAN PHYSICIST

This eccentric and likeable Nobel prize-winning physicist came to wide prominence in the last year of his life as a member of the committee reporting on the *Challenger* space-shuttle disaster. He differed publicly with the published findings, and is remembered for his dramatic demonstration of the reason for the explosion, when, on national television, he dunked a small rubber object in a glass of ice-water to show how subzero temperatures had destroyed the flexibility of an all-important sealing device. This cheerful simplicity of exposition was typical of a man who had worked all his life in the far reaches of nuclear physics, where common sense is usually not much use. With what would become known as 'Feynman diagrams' (probabilistic time-line maps of the life of a particle), he reformulated quantum mechanics by providing neat thought-pictures of what was 'going on' at particle level, which corresponded to established mathematics. But as well as such visual aids, he also introduced many profoundly counter-intuitive concepts. In particular, he came up with the idea that certain waves travel backward in time, and that particle/wave duality can be visualized by saying that particles take *all possible* paths between points, which can then be added so that different phase waves cancel each other out; what remains conforms closely to the predictions of classical mechanics.

Leslie Fiedler born 1917

& AMERICAN LITERARY CRITIC

Tagged the 'wild' man of American criticism, he scandalized academe with his proselytizing on popular culture. His witty and often vicious tome, *Love and Death in the American Novel* (1960), traces American fiction through the country's history, exploring American moral and cultural values. His often potent insights into the clashes of social and cultural mores betray a reactionary, aggressive dismissal of minorities that outrages other cultural commentators. His relevance arguably lies in the highly personalized nature of his observations and criticism, shaping his perspective to the point where one cultural study of 'freaks' draws largely on his own fascination with the concept of the physically deformed. While his political values can be insufferable, the dynamism of his lucid erudition has marked him as a key commentator on American letters, as well as an important standard-bearer for an assessment of populist culture, taking literary criticism out of its ivory towers and into more populist avenues. Together with Ihab Hasan, he has proposed a new post-modernist style as a reaction against post-modernist formalism – an art for the 'post-cultural' age that is anti-art, anti-literature and auto-destructive.

Karen Finley

born 1956

AMERICAN PERFORMANCE ARTIST

Finley is a performance artist whose foul-mouthed act involves what some regard as extremes of sexual degradation (a performance at London's ICA was banned: the police apparently told her she could not talk and show her body at the same time). She has been both championed as a courageous confronter of taboos and dispeller of myths, and vilified as a depraved abuser of First Amendment freedoms. America's atavistic Christian Far Right have turned her – along with Annie Sprinkle and others – into a symbol of confrontational sexual dissidence, and she has found herself a leader in the battle against censorship sparked by a ☛Mapplethorpe retrospective in 1989. As a result, she has become a hero to many, including those who used to sneer about her 'devalued shock-tactics'. Now the infamous yams-up-the-bum cliché (which always existed largely in the imaginations of hostile commentators who have never seen her act) has been replaced by the chocolate-smeared woman – she hasn't changed, but her context has. As a child, she was turned on to Michael Kirby's Happenings and Beat poetry, and would pay homage to ☛Claes Oldenburg at school, building plastic-wrap sculptures in corridors, doorways and schoolrooms, to create maximum havoc. Early work with her then-husband Harry Kipper (of the notorious Kipper Twins) gained her some attention; since then she has gone further down a route of populist solo fantasy-exorcism. To date her sunny, chatty common sense off-stage has made her work more disturbing rather than less: always in control, she redistributes the hierarchies of sexual symbolism and unsettles power relationships, provoking untamed and revealing reactions.

Shulamith Firestone

born 1945

CANADIAN FEMINIST

Firestone's ambition is dazzling: a theory of history based around the idea that the division of society into two sexes is more fundamental than that according to class – culminating in a call, in *The Dialectic of Sex* (1971), for women to take control of reproduction in order to eliminate the sexual classes. She found in Engels the insight that the division of labour between men and women was the prototype for all other forms of social division, and argued that this insight should lead to the conclusion that the liberation of women from responsibility for child-rearing would be the beginning of a real revolution. However, she pays too little regard to the complex interplay that has gone on between men and women through history, and many find distasteful her advocacy of artificial reproduction as a way to break down the 'tyranny of the biological family'.

Bobby Fischer

born 1943

AMERICAN CHESS PLAYER

In 1969, the US won the space race by putting the first man on the moon; in 1972, a 29-year-old American, Bobby Fischer, was pitched against the 42-year-old Boris Spassky in the first world championship match since 1948 to feature a non-Soviet player. Fischer, US chess champion since the age of 15, behaved appallingly – demanding a special chair, complaining about the colour of the chess board and refusing to turn up for his second game because the television cameras were upsetting him – but his consistently combative play and command of strategy secured victory. It was an extraordinary achievement, with Fischer winning seven games to Spassky's two, but those who predicted a great future for the American grandmaster had not looked very hard at the guy's behaviour. He spoke platitudes straight out of comic books, and seemed to see the tournament as an act of retribution for the Soviet Union's supposed injustices around the world. Fischer is now a drifter, moving around the flophouses of LA and hunting through anti-Semitic bookshops for reading material to feed his paranoia. Rumours of a comeback were stirred recently when he met up with Spassky in a Rotterdam bar, and he has also taken out a patent on a new chess clock, but it is difficult to imagine Fischer playing again. While his 1972 antics brought a worldwide audience to chess, they also established the game's image as an occasion for scandal and hysteria.

Ian Fleming 1908-64

■ BRITISH NOVELIST

With his James Bond novels, Fleming provided a bridge between the stolid closet-case, Fascist, public schoolboy spy stories of the 1930s and the heterosex-crazed working-class Pimpernels of the 1960s. There is a chapter in Kingsley Amis's book *The James Bond Dossier* (1965) simply called 'Small Firm Breasts' – it is a common Fleming phrase and one which illustrates his sparse *Bulldog Drummond*-style prose and his introduction of sex to the literature of snobbery with violence. Bond's sadism, racism, materialism and misogyny were too much even for the film studios to take, so they transformed the wooden character Fleming had created into the charming James Bond of Sean Connery, removing as they did so the soft pornography and the astounding violence: devotees will recall the scene in *On Her Majesty's Secret Service* (1963) where Bond is whacked about the testicles with a carpet beater . . .

Friedrich Flick 1883-1972

GERMAN BUSINESS EXECUTIVE

$ Flick was a Nazi supporter who, despite receiving a prison term at Nuremberg, recovered a leading position in post-war West German society. In 1939, he controlled 10 per cent of German steel output and was one of Hitler's richest backers; by 1945, he was said to be Germany's richest man. Convicted at Nuremberg for using Soviet slave labour and looting occupied states, he spent three years in jail. East Germany expropriated three-quarters of his holdings there; the Western powers forced the break-up of his residual interests on the other side. But he returned to industry with ease and, as far as one can tell, without any inhibitions, despite his age. He built a huge new coal and steel empire and moved into the car sector through acquiring a 40 per cent stake in Daimler-Benz; at the time of his death, he was again reputed to be the wealthiest man in West Germany. International punishments at Nuremberg broadly expired with the gaol terms of those convicted – no further domestic handicaps stopped an ex-convict making a comeback.

Fluxus see Macunias, George

Larry Flynt born 1942

AMERICAN PUBLISHER

Flynt's porn-rag, *Hustler*, epitomizes the extremist confusion of 1960s' American libertarianism as it enters middle age. Running rad-pol critiques of the state and the repressive right alongside vicious and bizarre satire, and all the while selling the magazine on its near-pathologically explicit girlie-spreads, Flynt seems to be committed to testing to destruction the American citizen's right to publish anything – based on the much cited Fourth Amendment. His convictions, however odiously contradictory, run deep: he has been jailed for refusing to name a source, and for a short while he employed radical yippie-undergrounder ☛Paul Krassner as *Hustler*'s editor, enjoining him to mock and subvert the very stereotypes of sexual exploitation on which the magazine seemed to be founded. Recently Flynt was embroiled in extensive litigation with ☛Jerry Falwell, after running a transparently fictional and extremely offensive 'interview' with the Moral Majoritarian. The consensus that emerged among observers seemed to be a hope that each would cause the downfall of the other. The actual outcome was distressingly inconclusive.

Dario Fo born 1926

ITALIAN PLAYWRIGHT

A lord of misrule, Fo describes himself as a 'maniac'. He creates a theatre that is inspired by the circus and the fairground, bringing together songs with slapstick and farce to explore hard social and political issues. His first theatre company, formed with his wife, Franca Rame, in 1957, was inhibited by state censorship, forcing him to début such plays as *Archangels Don't Play the Pintables* (1959) in Belgium. But when politics were allowed out of the Italian closet in 1962, he formed a new company, La Nuova Scena, to produce his bizarre reworkings of the Mystery Plays. It was his *Accidental Death of an Anarchist* (1970), originally written for the La Commune co-operative, that secured his international success (it has been staged in 41 countries). Both hysterically funny and deeply disturbing, it is an account of the torture of a dissident and the ramifications involved in disposing of his body – it was inspired by the 1969 Piazza Fontana bombs in Milan and the 'defenestration' of the anarchist Pinelli. Its successful production at London's Half Moon Theatre in 1979 led to the successful UK revival of his earlier *Can't Pay, Won't Pay* (1974), to which American audiences responded with horror, confusion and execration. Fo's talent is not easy to live with, but his theatre played a vital role in exposing the discontents of Italian society in the late 1960s and 1970s.

Surely, there is nothing more useless than an eternal problem.

Dario Fo

Richard Foreman born 1937

AMERICAN THEATRE DIRECTOR

Foreman was ☛Robert Wilson's main rival in New York's avant-garde theatre of the 1970s, forming the Ontological-Hysteric Theater which performed in his own downtown Broadway loft. As with Wilson, the emphasis was on visuals rather than narrative or dialogue, and the words spoken by the performers commented on the audience's perception of the action. This was taken to its extreme in *Pandering to the Masses: A Misrepresentation* (1975), in which the voice of Foreman, playing on a tape, gave the 'correct' interpretation of the drama. He collaborated with ☛Kathy Acker on a theatrical version of her *Great Expectations* and on his most controversial work, the *Birth of a Poet* (1985) extravaganza presented at the Brooklyn Academy of Music. For the latter show, the audience was bathed in blinding white light throughout while the company enacted a mannered ballet of obscenity. Seen as an attempt to bring performance to the yuppie market, it was greeted with boos and derision.

Norman Foster born 1935

& BRITISH ARCHITECT

If Foster is less well-known to the general public than his former partner, ☛Richard Rogers, it is not due to a lack of boldness, flair or productivity. The difference between the two architects lies in Foster's lack of interest in musing in public, and the fact that his buildings tend to be more broadly popular – both with those viewing them from the outside and those who work or live within. (An exception was his stylish Milton Keynes housing, which proved too flimsy for real-life rough-and-tumble.) What initially drew Rogers and Foster to work together was a shared interest in the external presentation of buildings, and this preoccupation has carried Foster through from the minimalist hi-tech of his 1970s buildings – with dazzling glass surrounds that made no reference to the floors or the pillars that held things together inside – to the fantastically expensive (£500 million) and extremely impressive Hong Kong and Shanghai Bank (1979-84). The first really radical office block built outside the US, this resembles nothing so much as a rocket launch pad. Foster has had more opportunity than Rogers to implement some of his bigger ideas for urban development. Starting out with a complex of buildings in Hammersmith, he has spent the last few years pushing through plans for the area around London's King's Cross railway station – trying to reconcile the interests of private investors, keen to maximize office space, with community demands for housing and greenery. The total projected cost of Foster's development is £30 billion.

Michel Foucault 1926-84

❍ FRENCH PHILOSOPHER, HISTORIAN

When invited to take up an academic post, Foucault made up his own title: Professor of the History of Systems of Thought. If there was a unifying concern in his work, it was with charting the development of our ideas as to what it means to be an individual in the late twentieth century. He asked us to look at the concept of a 'self' not as a concrete reality but as something constructed out of a web of social relations which articulate power. Foucault's works are histories or, as he called them, 'genealogies', of specific areas of rational thought which have moulded our contemporary identity. By investigating the ideas of individuality in the history of madness, medicine and punishment, he charted the way in which systems of power make us victims of specialized areas of knowledge. For Foucault, there was no deep or ultimate truth awaiting recovery. Not a Marxist, Freudian or structuralist, his aim was to record the development of humanity as the history of a series of interpretations. He seemed to be saying that, by living with a belief in a concrete 'self – i.e. we have certain concrete traits or characteristics – we have created a technology that subjugates us. We cannot see the power relations that define each of us, because we believe that we define ourselves. This is the trick that Western rationality plays upon us and, as tricks go, it is a pretty good one.

Francisco Franco 1892-1975

SPANISH POLITICAL LEADER

■ Ambiguity is the central theme in Franco's life. From a naval family, he became a military hero in the colonial wars of the 1920s. He was never a true Fascist, but colluded with the Axis powers in the first half of WW2 to recompense them for the help he had received before the war. His loyalty was to the Spain of Crown, Church and Army – yet he kept strict control over the ecclesiastical lobby. As Spanish dictator, he was, at heart, an anti-Communist – yet he did not find it easy to co-operate with the US, even in the pre-détente era of the Cold War. He had fought the Spanish Civil War brutally, but increasingly, as time passed, he sought ineffectively to heal feuds in a nation which had suffered millions of casualties. An extremely dull man who lacked ideas, charm or imagination, he ran a Mussolini-style 'corporatist' economy for most of his time as dictator, yet he radically reverted to *laissez-faire* when he saw the results of patronage, jobbery and corruption. He was a kind of Latin Napoleon – viciously suppressing critics and playing off interest groups against each other just as he had fought off Nationalist rivals in the Civil War – in search of an elusive idea of Spain as he held increasingly elaborate parades to mark the date of the uprising that sped him to power.

Robert Frank born 1924

SWISS-AMERICAN PHOTOGRAPHER

The documentary survey of small-town mid-America that Frank published in 1958 as *The Americans* revealed a vision of the country that most of its inhabitants did not want to see. Frank's attitude was ironic and sharp-eyed rather than clinical, well-intentioned or vapidly optimistic. In some ways, he was anticipating the New Journalism, by coming to his subject with a self-consciously detached commentary in mind and by refusing to take things at face value, depicting people at the edge of crowds, bored or at least disinterested, as American life passed them by. The book was described by ☛Jack Kerouac as 'a sad poem right out of America'. His subjectivity, however mild, was critical and unsettling once it combined with the revelations of his lens. Frank was also involved in semi-underground film-making that was substantially more subversive than his photography – for example, the documentary *Pull My Daisy* (1958), with narration by Kerouac, and *The Sin of Jesus* (1961), based on a short story by Isaac Babel.

Aretha Franklin born 1942

AMERICAN SINGER

Daughter of a preacher renowned for his impassioned and charismatic sermons, Franklin helped to initiate the route through gospel to pop, but her greatness lies in the way she put the rapture of gospel into pop – a far cry from the usual loud passion and rumbling enthusiasm. In doing so with songs such as 'I Say a Little Prayer for You' (1968), Franklin gave the female ballad both gentleness and strength; conversely, feminist discos have always rung to her smartly assertive twists on material such as 'Respect' and 'Think'. Reputedly a recluse and an agoraphobic, she should be an icon for pop fans as much as soul fans.

Rosalind Franklin 1920-58

BRITISH CRYSTALLOGRAPHER

The loner among those searching for the structure of DNA in the early 1950s, Franklin cut herself off not only from her competitors, ☛Crick and ☛Watson, but also from ☛Maurice Wilkins, her supposed colleague at Birkbeck College, London University. She was not an imaginative researcher, but it was her painstaking experimentation and careful rebuttal of the errors in their first model that enabled Watson and Crick to make the right intuitive hunches that led them to a solution – something they were not keen to acknowledge. Franklin herself came up with a double-chain helical structure for DNA, and published it in the same issue of *Nature* as that in which the Cambridge team unveiled their double-helix model, but she had not realized that the two chains ran in opposite directions. She moved on to investigate the structure of the less glamorous tobacco mosaic virus.

Alan Freed 1922-65

AMERICAN DISC JOCKEY

Freed has two claims to fame: he invented the phrase 'rock 'n' roll'; and he established the notion that a man who plays records can be as important as the people who make them. Indicted on payola charges, ie. receiving unofficial payment from record companies for promoting particular artists (he would also mysteriously acquire songwriting credits on certain rock records of the 1950s), he became the first high-profile financial victim of the rock music phenomenon. That a minor figure such as Freed could have so much influence shows not so much the power that one individual can wield as the medium's need for its own mythology.

Lucian Freud born 1922

▲BRITISH PAINTER

The grandson of Sigmund, Freud is best known for his interest in the body's formal expressiveness. His early pictures focused on close-ups of tense, wide-eyed people, isolated plants and dislocated dead animals. Under the influence of ☛Bacon, with whom he frequented the Soho demimonde of the late 1940s, he developed a more painterly style, with a looser and more expressive approach. His is not a world of the exotic, but one rooted in his immediate environment (a tatty and cluttered workroom) or his neighbourhood (the factories and wasteland around Paddington, London). Commissions for portraits are infrequent: he is unlikely ever to flatter or compliment his sitter, bringing out instead every mark and blemish; even the paintings of his mother, which he created in the early 1970s, are cold and impersonal. He adopts an analytical approach to his nudes, rendering them as frigid, desireless slabs of flesh. Freud despises the idyllic aims of art, but carries on painting all the same, in the process presenting the viewer with an image of life that is cold and passionless, but still compelling to look at.

Betty Friedan born 1921

AMERICAN FEMINIST ACTIVIST

The pioneer feminists of the 1960s reacted against the argument – actively propounded in the US and UK following WW2 – that a combination of biological destiny, housekeeping skills and nurturing abilities fitted women exclusively for the domestic sphere. Friedan led the way with her 1963 book *The Feminine Mystique*, which articulated the frustrations women endured, and which became a bestseller. The book's success plunged Friedan into action, setting up the National Organization for Women (NOW) and launching further campaigns on behalf of women. Although credited with setting off the feminist bandwagon in the US, Friedan soon became alienated from some of the new recruits – young radicals who attacked heterosexuality and the family. While defending the advances made during the 1960s, which she credits with having produced a new type of personality as well as humanizing both the family and business life, Friedan has pleaded latterly for communal values as an antidote to the sort of individualism that some schools of feminism have fostered.

The problem that has no name, which is simply the fact that American women are kept from growing to their full human capacities, is taking a far greater toll on the physical and mental health of our country than any known disease.

Betty Friedan, The Feminine Mystique

Milton Friedman born 1912

AMERICAN ECONOMIST

The 'monetarist' arguments that Friedman had been expounding since the 1950s found an audience in the 1970s as financiers and politicians in the US, Western Europe and Latin America, faced with rapidly rising prices, sought a cure that would not hurt them. His arguments for free markets and a particular definition of the 'free' man were welcomed by those who had become tired of hearing about 'welfare' and 'equality'. Friedman argues that the supply of money into the economy is the only explanation of future price levels: fast rises mean inflation. Prices are set by the interplay of demand and supply for money, as with any other item, and therefore governments should tackle rising prices through the pursuit of consistent monetary goals. The Keynesian view is that governments should fine-tune aggregate demand (chiefly by varying taxation and public-sector borrowing), whereas monetarism focuses on money and interest-rate policy, and has a rather simple balance-the-budget approach to fiscal policy. One problem for Friedman's theories is the question of the speed with which money circulates. He accepts that the price impact of one dollar changing hands ten times is equal to ten dollars doing so once, but he argues that the velocity of circulation is fairly stable in the long run. In fact, it is generally accepted that the long-run velocity of circulation is highly volatile. Although monetarism has been partially discredited, Friedman's idea that microeconomic supply-side factors determine a natural rate of unemployment, limiting governments' ability to ensure the Keynesian goal of full employment, is still widely held.

Elisabeth Frink born 1930

BRITISH SCULPTOR

Selling her first sculpture, a bronze bird, to London's Tate Gallery for £66 in 1952, Frink has ever since pursued a preoccupation with maleness through a repertoire of images that take in predatory birds, bird men, soldiers and mysteriously goggled heads as well as cats, horses and boars. Her only female sculpture is a Madonna, now standing in front of Salisbury Cathedral. Frink's adherence to representational values, even when contemporaries such as ☛Anthony Caro were taking up more strident and striking approaches to sculpture, has won her many public commissions, and her talent for enlivening traditional themes is evident in her horse and rider sitting outside the Aeroflot office in London's Piccadilly.

Erich Fromm 1900-80

✌ GERMAN-AMERICAN PSYCHOLOGIST

Fromm started out as a follower of Freud, but after spicing up psychoanalysis with lashings of Marxism, feminism and cultural anthropology, he went on to discard the fundamental Freudian insight that human beings, as the playthings of unconscious forces, can hope to contain, but never ultimately resolve, their inner conflicts. Fromm viewed Freudian insights as just one among several tools for understanding the human predicament, and his books never substantiate their general arguments with ideas gleaned from his own observations of patients. Nevertheless, his recognition of the extent to which the individual was influenced by social change produced some useful insights, and he achieved popular success with two books, *The Art of Loving* (1956) and *To Have or to Be* (1976). Like other thinkers who have analysed the problems of contemporary society from a psychoanalytic basis, he emphasized the importance of satisfying work and human relationships to individual fulfilment, as against the pursuit of power and material possessions, stating that people get tangled in emotional knots because they are not sufficiently concerned with the interests of their true selves.

Adrian Frutiger born 1928

SWISS TYPEFACE DESIGNER, SETTLED IN FRANCE

Beginning his career as a print apprentice in Switzerland, Frutiger established himself as a type designer, combining an aesthetic sense with mathematical ability and an understanding of technical processes. He moved to France in 1952, where he designed for the Peignot type foundry his most successful typeface, *sans serif* Univers. A modest man, Frutiger thinks of the letters of the alphabet as having basic personalities which he enhances. He once maintained that he clothed the letters rather as a couturier dresses a model: 'I do not create the body.' To prove the point, he did some tests on eight of the world's most widely read typefaces, laying all the faces on top of each other to reveal the basic 'skeleton'. Placing eight of his own designs over each other in the same way, he found that their skeleton was a shape closely resembling Univers: 'It is almost as if I never did anything beside Univers in my life,' he concluded.

Northrop Frye 1912-91

CANADIAN LITERARY THEORIST

The godfather of modern literary theory, Frye published his provocative *Anatomy of Criticism* in 1957. His study of mythologies – the pre-literary systems of deep beliefs, archetypes and conventions that shape writing even as it comments on them or strives to escape into more modern modes – provided the gateway for European critical thought to overwhelm American literary studies. (The idea that an unconscious body of mythic concerns has its hold over any particular rational speaker comes close to the basic structuralist belief that 'language speaks its subjects.') Also, he directed new attention to Romanticism (his *Fearful Symmetry* of 1947 is widely regarded as the best-ever commentary on Blake). Much concerned in particular with the (perhaps) inescapable hold that New Testament Christianity has had over literature and thought, his book *The Great Code* (1982) – a groundbreaking study of the Bible as literature and literary effector – is a demystifying secular masterpiece.

Klaus Fuchs born 1911

GERMAN MATHEMATICIAN, SPY, TEMPORARILY BASED IN UK

The hunt for Reds-under-the-bed really got going after the Americans discovered what this German exile had told the Soviets. A brilliant mathematician and physicist who never made any secret of his Communist sympathies, Fuchs let the high-ups in Moscow know that the UK was building its own nuclear bomb even before Prime Minister ☛Attlee had got around to informing his Cabinet. (A man of fine distinctions, Fuchs would not reveal certain things to a British policeman because that would have meant breaking security rules.) Part of various groups involved in building the atom bomb, and eventually head of the theoretical team at Britain's Atomic Energy Research Establishment, he started 'sharing' scientific knowledge with the Soviets when the USSR and the UK were allies. Although increasingly selective about what he sent, he carried on spilling the beans until shortly before his unmasking in 1949. The Soviets said he saved them two years' work on their atom and hydrogen bombs; it may have been more. After nine years in a British prison, he went back to a life of science and respect in East Germany.

Carlos Fuentes born 1928

MEXICAN NOVELIST

A peripatetic childhood that took him to the US in the entourage of his diplomat father sparked Fuentes' preoccupation with the face-off between cultures, particularly the lines that divide Latino from Gringo. His novels lift up a mirror to the polymorphous nature of all cultures, showing up the falsity of attempts to define one as the *opposite* of another. In the same spirit, he has explored the impact on Mexico of its revolution, where a nation rediscovered through violence a more ancient cultural heritage, which had merely been hiding under the normal constraints of bourgeois life. Influenced by Faulkner, Dos Passos and other American novelists as much as by indigenous Mexican traditions, Fuentes blends times past and future into epics of poetic density. His first novel, *Where the Air is Clear* (1958/60), presents a polyphonic

Elisabeth Frink

tapestry of voices from Mexico City. In *The Death of Artemio Cruz* (1962/4), a dying robber baron reflects upon the course of his life from the horrors of the revolution to the present, passing backwards and forwards across the tapestry of his progress from idealistic hero to corrupt capitalist. The sprawling epic *Terra Nostra* (1975/9) links Spain to Mexico and the Roman conquest to the end of the world in 1999. Fuentes has a lofty sense of the novelist's function as a moral legislator impelled 'to write everything that history has not said'. He was Mexico's ambassador to France from 1975 to 1977.

The great modern tragic novel has this major preoccupation of the disintegration of the human personality. Something we are seeing every day, it is mass communications, it is the atom bomb, it is AIDS, it is a million things that destroy the formal, formative bearings of the individual that is so precious a creation of Western civilization.

Carlos Fuentes

Athol Fugard born 1932

✌ SOUTH AFRICAN THEATRE DIRECTOR, SCREENWRITER

Fugard's plays are passionate indictments of South Africa's apartheid system, but their international success probably owes less to their political message than to the sense of humour that Fugard and his actors display in the face of absurdity and a senseless, repressive world run by a bureaucracy with which one cannot argue. As a merchant seaman in his twenties, Fugard came to appreciate the unacceptability of apartheid. That understanding was reinforced by six months spent as a clerk in a court which imprisoned 30 black men every hour. His plays show up the nonsense of a social system that treats a light-skinned boy differently from his dark brother, and condemns many blacks to a life of miserable vagrancy. His most unsettling play, *Sizwe Bansi Is Dead* (1972), was developed in association with actors John Kani and Winston Ntshona. Depicting a man from the country who can only survive in town by taking on the identity of another black man, it resonates with anger, pain and a zest for life. Fugard's solo work since has dealt (less satisfactorily) with broader issues. He opposes cultural boycotts of South Africa as denying the country access to foreign ideas which alone can feed the development of a more civilized society.

Buckminster Fuller 1895-1983

☆ AMERICAN DESIGNER, ECOLOGIST,
♦ WRITER

An American architect more concerned with the total human environment than with design fashions, Fuller's interest in cheap, prefabricated buildings (doing 'more' with 'less') culminated in geodesic domes – ingenious puffballs which many saw as representing an architecture of the future. He saw technology as a potentially benign force, and suggested that the problem of resource scarcity would disappear with the setting up of a world government to handle equitable distribution. 'Evolution,' he said, 'is integration of humanity.' Such ideas are utopian, of course, but Fuller made them seem attainable through his detailed blueprints for a better future. And they have become increasingly influential as people search for an antidote to the effects of technology. It has been suggested, for example, that enormous domes could control the problem of air pollution by containing the effluents from power stations, oil refineries and other sources. Geodesic principles have also been applied to the air-tight Biosphere II project being built in the Arizona desert, where eight astronauts will live for two years to test the problems of human survival on Mars. A one-time professor of poetry and a prolific public speaker on problems of planetary survival (he managed 120 engagements in one year), Fuller's writings sit on bookstore shelves alongside the works of such 'New Age' writers as Shirley MacLaine and Fritjof Capra.

Sam Fuller born 1920

⇔AMERICAN FILM DIRECTOR

The King of B-movies and a colourful character, Fuller trained as a journalist and brought some of the skills of that discipline to his films. By the time French critics spotted the qualities in *Underworld USA* (1960), Fuller's films were clearly defined by their startling images, sparse narrative and complex camerawork. His is a world where existence, according to a character in *Merrill's Marauders* (1962), is 'putting one foot in front of the other'. Love is either mutual dependence or a form of deception: the fiancé in *The Naked Kiss* (1963) is a child molester; the German heroine of *Verboten* (1958) marries her US benefactor out of financial need, but falls in love with him as he draws away from her. In Fuller's films, there is no triumph outside survival, and often the near destruction of his characters is brought about by the necessity of emotional alienation and programming – be they soldiers, the racist-bred 'white dog' or the reporter so determined to win a Pulitzer prize, by exposing a murder in the insane asylum of *Shock Corridor* (1963), that he loses his own sanity. Lionized by ☛Wim Wenders in Germany, and by the French New Wave, who recognized the implicitly 'filmic' qualities of his narratives, Fuller is a great cigar-chomping American maverick.

G

Peter Gabriel born 1950

BRITISH ROCK MUSICIAN

These days, Gabriel has short hair and dresses neatly in black turtlenecks. Fifteen years ago, he used to wear ludicrous giant head-dresses and appallingly stupid flowing robes; he also did his own make-up. Gabriel's Genesis epitomized the theatrical 1970s' student rock band, its every composition a ten-minute, time-changing platform for Gabriel's frighteningly fatuous lyrical conceits. Wisely, when Gabriel left Genesis for a solo career, he opted for a starker, simpler music (with clothing to match) and directed his intelligence into controlled experiment rather than rambling indulgence. Genesis meanwhile took a more accessible pop direction, resulting in their new vocalist Phil Collins becoming a fake Motown singer and professional Cockney. Gabriel retained his offbeat imagination, expanding it through influences as diverse as punk and African music.

Mu'ammar Gadaffi born 1942

99 LIBYAN POLITICAL LEADER

Under Gadaffi's rule, Libya has become a byword in Western circles for revolutionary terrorism. The leader of the Free Officers Movement that overthrew King Idris in 1969, he proceeded to remove American and British bases from Libya, and nationalized certain Western interests – the sorts of acts likely to start the hate-figure machinery rolling. Since then he has compounded the problem by supplying arms to the IRA, supporting Third World revolutions worldwide, sending hit squads after exiled critics of his rule, making war on neighbouring Chad and setting up an austere, teetotal regime for his people, who seem for the moment prepared to forgive him his authoritarianism because of the sense of purpose and independence he has given the nation. But in spite of the lucrative return on oil sales with which he has been able to bolster both Libya's prosperity and his own popularity, it is not clear whether he has carved out an identity for his people – certainly not one that would survive the removal of his own charismatic drive. Although he is hostile to any outcome in the Arab-Israeli conflict that favours the state of Israel (and he has provided material support for the Palestine Liberation Organization), he disassociated himself from Egypt's attack on the Jewish state in 1973. In 1986, the US bombed Tripoli, killing one of Gadaffi's children, as retaliation for an explosion in a West Berlin disco in which an American soldier died. Although evidence connecting this event to Libya was never forthcoming, Gadaffi, the 'mad dog', has been rather more circumspect in his anti-American proclamations ever since.

William Gaddis born 1922

☞AMERICAN NOVELIST

Gaddis intends his writing to be difficult, requiring the sort of close attention that can only be forthcoming when the mind has turned off the chatter of other media. His novels, which are long, require constant attention to tones, timbres and twists of speech: the characters in *The Recognitions* (1955) are constantly interrupted by inane radio announcements; his second book *JR* (1975), the story of a pre-teen tycoon, consists almost entirely of unattributed dialogue. None the less, apart from a slew of literary wannabees who drop out after a few pages, readers who persist still find him very funny. He has a vicious ear for chatter and the comic drama embedded in the American vernacular. The added kick of sustaining alertness through more than 700 pages can make him especially rewarding. His latest – *Carpenter's Gothic* (1985) – shows he is not prepared to make any concessions to the accessibility lobby.

Yuri Gagarin 1934-68

✈ SOVIET ASTRONAUT

❍ The first human to leave earth's atmosphere, Gagarin was launched into space by a Soviet rocket on 20 July 1961. A onetime anonymous test pilot, streets are now named after him and monuments have been erected to his memory. This is celebrity in its purest form, given that the scientific achievement which his mission represented – 'the genius of the Soviet people and the powerful forces of socialism' – had so little to do with the man who rode the spaceship *Vostok* as it encircled the earth. Only aloft for one hour and 48 minutes, the best Gagarin could offer to express his feelings about this moment in human history was: 'Flight is proceeding normally. I feel well.' But the Soviet's trip is said to have made ☛President Kennedy apoplectic, especially since it was completed only six days after the failure of the Bay of Pigs invasion. Searching for a dramatic riposte – a space effort 'which promises dramatic results in which we could win' – he committed the US to put a man on the moon by the end of the decade. Gagarin died in a plane crash just one year before ☛Neil Armstrong became the first man to step out on to the lunar landscape.

Hugh Gaitskell 1906-63

BRITISH POLITICIAN

A leader of Britain's Labour Party who never became prime minister, Gaitskell was once described by a rival as a 'dessicated calculating machine': trained in economics, he became Chancellor of the Exchequer within five years of becoming an MP. Exposure to the violent suppression of the left in Vienna was a significant influence in the development of his socialist convictions. An enigma to voters during the general election of 1955, he reached centre stage through his attacks on the Conservative government's actions at Suez in the following year. As Labour's leader, he became absorbed in arguments within the party, failing to end its commitment to a state-run economy, but winning the debate against unilateral nuclear disarmament, with a passionate speech to 'save the party we love from pacifists, Communists and fellow-travellers'. His stance on the European Economic Community turned Labour against it for a decade.

J(ohn) K(enneth) Galbraith

born 1908

CANADIAN ECONOMIST

A Canadian economist of a soft-left persuasion and an entertaining writer, Galbraith coined the phrase 'private affluence, public squalor' to describe what happens when the state surrenders its social responsibilities to large corporations. He has written a number of witty bestsellers, including his 1958 book *The Affluent Society*, to demystify his subject. In them, he argues that classical, pro-competition axioms have been rendered outdated by the industrial conditions of the late twentieth century. Free enterprise was justified by earlier, non-Marxist economists on the basis of the split between owner-shareholders and managers, but managers are now driven more by the momentum of the institutions they are running – sustaining market share, keeping things ticking along, perhaps expanding the firm's base – than simple profit maximization. As large firms increasingly control their particular market, competition gives way to mutual co-operation between the dominant institutions. Instead of price competition there is frantic product differentiation, backed up by the power of advertising. The result, he argues, is anything but economic efficiency.

John Galliano

born 1960

BRITISH FASHION DESIGNER

Galliano's clothes are beautiful in a traditional sense; he does not shock or outrage like ☛Westwood or ☛Gaultier. Manipulating unusual materials – black feathers into a bustier, a magpie nest into a wig – his work reflects a romantic ideal: beautiful female figures draped in soft, semi-transparent gauze and muslin, to produce a rippling and fragile effect; pasty white faces with dark eyes and lips seemingly stained with plum juice. He rejects the androgynous aspect of early 1980s fashion, emphasizing femininity and a nostalgic longing for the sensibilities of another era. Galliano claims to be influenced by everything, including the petrol station beneath his workshop, and one can only wonder when his first lead-free designs will take shape.

Ray Galton

born 1930

Alan Simpson

born 1929

BRITISH TV SCRIPTWRITERS

Galton and Simpson came out of such British post-war radio sketch shows as *Educating Archie*, created within a music-hall tradition of verbal slapstick and pantomime unreality, to develop the character-based, semi-dramatic TV comedy of *Hancock's Half Hour* (1954-61) and, later, *Steptoe and Son* (1964-73). Their main effect on British TV comedy has been make an institution of the writing duo (e.g. David Croft and Jimmy Perry, Ian La Frenais and Dick Clement), but their greatest contribution – taking comedy away from its reliance on the catchphrase or funny voice, and exploring the possibilities of depressing situations and anti-social characters – has been largely ignored as UK sitcom increasngly bases itself in an imaginary, nuclear family-addled suburbia.

George Gamow 1904-68

SOVIET-AMERICAN PHYSICIST

Gamow left his native Soviet Union in the 1930s, worked on quantum physics before WW2 and, in 1948, revived the theory that the universe began with a huge explosion. (Gamow prepared the paper with his student Ralph Alpher and it carried without permission the name of Dr Hans Bethe so that the authors' names followed the Greek alphabet – Alpher, Bethe and Gamow. Luckily Bethe thought the theory worth the joke.) Despite critics, including Fred Hoyle and ☛Tommy Gold, derisively dubbing it the 'Big Bang' theory, it became the standard model. Gamow also proposed that this explosion would have left a background trace of radiation, a suggestion that was confirmed in 1965. He went on to make significant discoveries in the field of molecular biology that would lead to the cracking of the genetic code of DNA. A capable popularizer, his *Mr Tompkins* stories plunged their hero into quantum and relativistic worlds for the edification of the non-technical reader.

Indira Gandhi 1917-84

➽INDIAN POLITICAL LEADER

The daughter of ☛Jawaharlal Nehru, Indira Gandhi was India's premier between 1966 and 1985, with one four-year gap. Party professionals chose her as someone they felt they could control, but in the end, they could not ride the tiger. A high-handed member of a semi-socialist dynasty, she was decisive and popular: she nationalized banks and abolished allowances to the Indian princes; she fought a war with Pakistan and secured her aim of an independent Bangladesh in the east. But she did not get to grips with India's economic problems, after the 'Green Revolution' ran out of steam. In the mid-1970s, the High Court said she had misappropriated state funds and should therefore lose her parliamentary seat. She retorted with a state of emergency – ruling by decree, jailing critics and, tacitly, allying herself to the Communist Party – the court's judgement was made void by law. However, she lost a long-delayed election, having over-rated her own magic. Her replacement could not rule effectively and she resumed office with a substantial majority in 1980. Inter-ethnic tensions in the Punjab led to her ordering the army to take over the Sikh shrine, the Golden Temple of Amritsar, in 1984; hundreds died. She was killed, in retaliation, by her Sikh bodyguards – an end like that of a Roman emperor. One of her sons, Sanjay, had been killed in an air accident; the other, Rajiv, succeeded her.

Gabriel García Márquez born 1928

COLOMBIAN NOVELIST

García Márquez has said of *One Hundred Years of Solitude* (1967/70) that it contains the stories of all the scripts he was unable to turn into films, thus making apparent both the superabundance of narratives at his disposal and the force of his desire to communicate. In Colombia, kids hustle his books at street corners, and he has recently reached out to a mass audience with his soap opera, *I Rent Myself Out to Dream*. The enchantment of *One Hundred Years* (apparently based on tales García Márquez heard from his grandparents) derives from its retelling of the deceptions that adults offer children as literal truth – for example, a barman is said to have a withered arm because he once raised it against his parents. But the book is far from being a pot-pourri. These stories are built into an account of an enchanted society, landlocked in time by its superstitions and populated by pompous landowners, brutal police, dull-witted peasants and stupid revolutionaries – a society that seems to epitomize the condition of Latin America, cut off from the main currents of history and the 'inevitable' linear progression of time, allowed to fester, breeding its own eccentricities until the intrusion of political conflict, revolution, civil war and massacre. In all of García Márquez's work, there is a fascination with the way the working out of small events can bring enormous consequences, dragging society down into decay, and he emphasizes that what we believe is as important as what happens, laughing off our attempts to divide reality from fantasy. That Márquez has lost none of his power to enchant the reader is evident from his latest novel, *Love in the Time of Cholera* (1985/88), where he follows a lifelong passion to final fulfilment with a degree of narrative fluency beyond that apparent in his early books.

Charles de Gaulle *see* De Gaulle, Charles.

Jean-Paul Gaultier born 1952

❞ FRENCH FASHION DESIGNER

With his impish good looks and cheeky smile, Gaultier epitomizes the essence of his fashion – fun, outrageous and naughty. Revitalizing the stagnant French scene, he became within ten years one of the world's top fashion designers. His clothes exaggerate the curves of the body – most famously in a tight velvet dress with conical breasts – and he developed the concept of bringing undergarments out into the open, with a series of devastatingly sexy corset dresses and bra tops. He did not neglect the male body either, allowing men to be provocatively sexy with a combination of tight leggings, gold lamé, pouches of chain mail worn over trousers, biker boots and backless T-shirts. In 1989, Gaultier also turned his hand to music, cutting a forgettable and forgivable kitsch record. Otherwise though, he will continue to shock and amuse with his boldly playful designs.

Marvin Gaye 1939-84

AMERICAN SINGER

Embodying the central contradiction in modern soul, Gaye was an extreme sensualist tortured by deep-rooted gospel faith. As a Motown artist he joined in the Sound-of-Young-America party, but his duets with Mary Wells, Kim Weston and (especially) Tammi Terrell, he slipped unspoken adult motives into the callow teenage emotions he sang about. Tammi's death from a brain tumour, at 24, shattered Gaye – she collapsed in his arms while on stage. He retired into the studio, which became the centre of his world. Albums such as *What's Going On* (1971), *Let's Get It On* (1973), *Here My Dear* (1979) and *Midnight Love* (1982) dealt with politics, sex, ecology, sex, divorce and sex with tortured honesty, passion and an openness that concealed deep confusion and self-hatred – much of the time he sought solace in a drug habit.

The first three records introduced important innovations into 1970s' music, and the fourth – a lushly sly synthesizer funk – totally transformed the R&B charts of the 1980s. And then, suddenly and shockingly, the double life came to an end when his father, a Pentecostal minister and fire-and-brimstone disciplinarian, shot him dead in the family home, claiming self-defence. Gaye's sweet, light voice – luxuriant in the pleasures it promises, seductive and suave – goes far beyond simple adult hedonism: somewhere in it there's the promise that sex can offer itself as a kinder and more loving religion than the one he grew up with.

Reinhard Gehlen

1902-79

GERMAN INTELLIGENCE OFFICER

Like ☛Werner von Braun, the space scientist and ☛Friedrich Flick the industralist, Gehlen was a leading Nazi who did a *volte-face* at the end of WW2 and, by explaining his utility to the allies, re-established an active career for himself. Gehlen's field was intelligence. Having joined the staff of the Nazi high command in 1940, from 1942 he ran espionage against the USSR. He foresaw Hitler's defeat and hid his files in 50 chests, which he turned over to the US at the end of the war; these gave the West access to the huge spy network he had established in Eastern Europe. Gehlen became head of West German intelligence in 1955, keeping the job for 13 years. An entirely anonymous figure – he was called 'Number 30' – he predicted the Soviet invasion of Czechoslovakia in 1968. Anti-Communism, and an addiction to intelligence work, were consistent motivating forces in his life.

Bob Geldof

born 1954

❞ IRISH ROCK MUSICIAN, EMERGENCY RELIEF CAMPAIGNER

An articulate rock singer who always seemed more at home with ☛Dylan and ☛Clapton than the naïve misanthropists who formed the vanguard of the New Wave in 1977, Geldof's band The Boomtown Rats rose to some prominence with a series of allusive social commentaries that lacked the ferocity displayed by either ☛The Clash or The Jam. Never remotely experimental, the Rats were notable mainly for the number one 'I Don't Like Mondays' (1979) and Geldof's success in capturing the wet-dream-laden affection of certain rock critics. Following a series of chart failures, Geldof exploded into zealous philanthopy when, together with Midge Ure, another pop singer who nursed dreams of credibility, he alighted upon the tragedy of starvation in Ethiopia in 1984. A commendably sincere essay in altruism, the star-studded ensemble single, 'Do They Know It's Christmas', prefaced a vast, seemingly non-stop rock concert, staged simultaneously in London and Philadelphia and televised worldwide. For a while, a flurry of middle-of-the-road super-groups and solo artists became synonymous with philanthropic ideals and even grandmothers could join with their progeny as they listened to mature millionaires singing about starvation, unrequited love and MTV.

Murray Gell-Mann

born 1929

AMERICAN PHYSICIST

Every time the romance at the heart of the atom seems to be ending, someone is on hand to give it a fabulous new twist. By the mid-1950s, the simple orbital picture – of electron, proton and neutron – was in complete disarray. A torrent of sub-atomic particles was being discovered in the debris of atom-smashing experiments, too many for comfort if they were all basic. Gell-Mann, working with George Zweig, rescued the model by proposing that, far from being 'fundamental', protons and neutrons were made up of three particles, called quarks, in three 'flavours' – *up*, *down* and *strange* – with three more – *charm*, *truth* and *beauty* – being proposed subsequently. This taxonomy helped explain such otherwise baffling properties as spin, and also why some particles were only selectively affected by the various attractive forces (strong, weak and electromagnetic), and it led, via group and permutation theories, to the successful prediction of new particles. Later, with Harald Fritzsch, Gell-Mann proposed a further system of classification, that quarks be divided into the 'colours' red, green and blue: the mathematics that this theory caused to be developed is called quantum chromodynamics. The quark-model encountered extreme resistance at first, but explanatory convenience eventually won through. The word itself is taken from a passage in *Finnegans Wake*; as a system, it is best thought of as a sophisticated mnemonic rather than as a picture of life inside the atom.

Uri Geller born 1946

ISRAELI PSYCHIC PERFORMER

Geller became a celebrity during the early 1970s with a 'psychic' party piece in which he caused forks and spoons to bend by the application of minimum force. Many thought him a fake and standard magicians replicated his feats, but some remained faithful. Geller summoned the mass concentration of people who considered themselves similarly gifted; as a result, clocks stopped, entire canteens of cutlery were hideously deformed and many a wedding present was ruined. Pontificating about the origin of his powers, he opted for a then-fashionable extra-terrestrial theory that was vague enough to allow the broadest possible interpretation. He represented the desire to believe in something, and his cod philosophizing was on the same level as ☛Erich von Däniken's multi-million-selling pieces of sophistry about how God was really a spaceman. The strangest thing about Geller is that he himself seemed to believe in his own power, agreeing to take part in tests he had no hope of passing. By the time his tricks were exposed, though, he was no longer news. It was not so much that people did not want to believe it was a set-up, more that, after the overkill, nobody cared.

Martha Gellhorn born 1908

AMERICAN JOURNALIST, BASED IN UK

An American war journalist who was present at most of the major conflicts of the late twentieth century, Gellhorn was a restless traveller whose talent lay in the vivid authenticity of her reporting. In the 1930s, she worked as an investigator for Federal Energy Relief, interviewing the unemployed to ascertain how acute their problems were during the fallout of the Depression, before journeying to Spain during the Civil War to make a tour of the central fighting fronts. She later covered the Sino-Japanese War with her husband, Ernest Hemingway, in tow and wrote up the trip in *Travels with Myself and Another* (1978). Gellhorn also reported on the Allied invasion of Normandy, accompanied the US army into Dachau, and went to Saigon to write on the effects of the war on the Vietnamese (she said later, 'It was the only war I reported on the wrong side'). More recently, she reported on the conflicts in El Salvador and Nicaragua.

Jean Genet 1910-86

FRENCH WRITER

Genet had been a tramp, a homosexual pimp, a prostitute and a convict before he turned writer on scatological and sadistic themes. The slumming glamour of his early life in and out of prison and the oblique force of his writing – poetry from hell – are irresistibly total because morally blank. His destructive scorning of social norms was complete. A writer who only wrote about what was alien to all his readers – his life was never theirs – and a dynamiter of the prison-houses of language, he spoke for Black Panthers and Palestinians when no one else would, and sympathized with their exile as inhuman 'others'. ☛Sartre's massive and implausible hagiography imposed on Genet one version of an outsider-self, an amorphous identity sketched only by the inadequate definitions of others. Genet and Hegel are represented as opposing poles of writing in ☛Derrida's most extreme project to date, *Glas* (1974): total irresponsibility against total rigour. Watching every new generation of critics polarize into fans or opponents of Genet has become a futile – if fascinating – pastime.

Stan Getz 1927-91

AMERICAN JAZZ MUSICIAN

His light, breathy saxophone was the soul of the *bossa nova* boom of the 1960s, and even though purists look down on his work then – in particular, 'The Girl from Ipanema' – Getz probably gave more pleasure to more listeners at this time than any other musician. One of the mainstays of West Coast Cool, Getz's melodic simplicity and intelligent inventions endeared him to dabblers as well as buffs ever since he first appeared in the 1940s, as one of the Four Brothers, with Al Cohn, Zoot Sims and the largely forgotten Serge Chaloff.

No Nguyen Giap born 1912

VIETNAMESE MILITARY LEADER

The hero of modern Vietnam, Giap was the author of both the French defeat in the 1950s, and the downfall of the US-backed Saigon government some 20 years later. Joining ☛Ho Chi Minh as military aide in 1939, he learned the basics of guerrilla warfare during the campaign against Japan from 1942 to 1945. The taking of Dien Bien Phu, a small mountain fort, from the French occupying forces was his supreme achievement. He was flexible – heavy artillery and siege tactics are not usual guerrilla staples – and he was willing to use Soviet professional advice. The US was worn down by a war of attrition in the jungle, masterminded by Giap, then vice-premier in Hanoi. His book on guerrilla warfare became a primer for people's armies round the world, who probably owe more to him than to ☛Che Guevara. It is also now required reading for US Marines, anxious to learn from their country's earlier mistakes.

William Gibson born 1948

♦ AMERICAN WRITER

▲ Gibson's novel *Neuromancer* (1984) took science fiction on from the Outer Space of the Golden Age (rockets and alien worlds), and the New Wave's Inner Space (altered states and parallel realities), into a third region: Cyberspace. This is fiction that links the brain to a global on-line network of electronic data, a kind of infinite video game jacking straight into the skull. The Cyberpunk genre he inaugurated takes its imagery from films such as *Blade Runner* and 1960s' writers such as ☛Samuel Delany, but the sardonic energy and tight dramatic organization of Gibson's three loosely linked novels are his own, alongside his preoccupation with prosthetic devices and his ear for brusque, hard-boiled dialogue. In *Neuromancer*, he introduced Cyberspace itself, with its dreams and its drives; in *Count Zero* (1985), he put ghosts and gods into the machine, letting them manifest themselves – with characteristic exoticism – as the Haitian voodoo pantheon; in *Mona Lisa Overdrive* (1987), which he insists is the last of the Cyberpunk novels, he wonders if human life itself can be stored on disk.

Edward Gierek born 1913

☞ POLITICIAN

A Polish miner raised in France, Gierek gained power in 1970 when workers protested at rising food prices, but lost it ten years later as worsening economic conditions drove workers to march for the right to form independent unions. His early life was troubled: his father was killed in a mining accident; and he was thrown out of France when he organized a sit-down strike in the mines. After emigrating to Belgium, where he also worked as a miner, he lay low in the early phase of Nazi occupation, but joined the Belgian Resistance in 1943. Even after beginning his rise through Polish political ranks after the war, he cleaved to his early career and took a degree in mining. Thanks to his background, he was seen as a figure sympathetic to Polish labour, but he was toppled by General Jaruzelski as events became too much for him. Perhaps he should have studied economics: the 1970s in Poland were marked by escalating fiscal problems, as the regime borrowed increasingly large sums from Western bankers. The rise of Solidarity, a new force he did not understand, led to his exit.

H(ans) R(udi) Giger born 1940

▲ SWISS GRAPHIC ARTIST

Imagine Dracula, Frankenstein, Van Gogh, Bosch and a slaughterhouse body-snatcher rolled into one and you begin to understand the creative world of H. R. Giger. A need to exorcize his nightmares (including one in which he was trapped in a toilet that became a contracting, decomposing vagina, festering with tiny creatures) led, via his discovery of the artistic possibilities of the airbrush, to *Necronomicon* (1972), the highly stylized images of which evoke Brueghel and Bosch while journeying into dark and potent realms haunted by womb-like effigies, demons and other creatures with enormous orifices. These caught the eye of screenwriter Dan O'Bannon, who got Giger involved in an abortive attempt to film *Dune*, and then in Ridley Scott's *Alien* (1979). Giger's designs for that film's eponymous creature, sculpted out of foam rubber and various parts of animal and human skeletons, and for the organic machinery inside the alien spacecraft, played a signficant part in *Alien*'s success and inspired a new look in mainstream science fiction. Since then Giger – who lists Poe, H. P. Lovecraft, ☛Frank Zappa and ☛Elvis among his influences, never takes off his black leather jacket in public and reportedly has the skeleton of a former lover who committed suicide suspended from his ceiling – has occasionally forayed into other media, from record covers to theatre design and fashion, without ever again causing quite the same stir.

Gilbert and George

Gilbert Proesch born 1943
George Passmore born 1942

BRITISH PERFORMANCE ARTISTS

Meeting first in 1967 as students at St Martin's School of Art in London, Gilbert and George have built their careers around presenting themselves as but a single person, sporting identical dark polyester suits and fixed po-faced expressions. For their most famous piece from the late 1960s, *Living Statues*, they stood motionless on a plinth for hours, with their faces painted gold. They moved on to large assemblages made from postcards, and from their own photographs – focusing upon urban aggression, squalor and deprivation. More recently, they have begun to express an obvious homo-eroticism – skinheads in Y-fronts portrayed as saintly figures and the like. At a retrospective exhibition of their work, they exhibited their joint self-portrait on bottles of Beck's Beer – part of the manufacturer's campaign to turn its product into a cult brand and Gilbert and George's attempt to transform a show, which most critics considered totally uninteresting, into a talked-about event. Tireless self-promoters, Gilbert and George seem to be pursuing iconic status as ☛Warhol acolytes, without ever going through the stage of critical engagement with the commercial culture of which they have now become a part.

Dizzy Gillespie

(John Birks Gillespie) born 1917

AMERICAN JAZZ MUSICIAN

Although his playing was, if anything, even 'further out' than that of ☛Charlie Parker – his trumpet smearing, skittering and screaming across chromatics that barely read – Gillespie's cheerful showmanship and organizational adeptness led bebop to some kind of early acceptability. With goatee and beret, 'Diz' could be just as much the weird hipster, but somehow whatever he did was less scary than the outer reaches touched on by Parker. To this day, he tends to be underrated, even while being fêted as a master, as if his interest in Cuban music, big bands or steady survival had somehow disbarred him from the highest artistic ranks. Hearing him duet with Parker ought to dispel such an idea – they were clearly soul mates.

Allen Ginsberg

AMERICAN POET

'I have achieved the introduction of the word "fuck" into texts inevitably studied by schoolboys,' noted self-confessed 'beat-hip-gnostic-imagist' performance-poet Ginsberg, the man who has done more than any other to define the image of the post-war modern poet. Timely rather than eternal, political rather than spiritual, his work – influenced by Whitman,

☛Kerouac and the rhythms of his personal mantra – was one of the key forces in the popularization of 'stream of consciousness' art. In his journey of the spirit via various ancient religions and consciousness-expanding drugs, he has taken from each culture that with which he empathized and integrated it into a hybrid concoction intended to reflect the spiritual truth of his soul (rather than any formalized version of organized religion). Ginsberg's poems may often be simplistic and frustratingly shallow (a common flaw in artists who assume that 'the first thought is always the best thought'), but the presence of the man lives through them and carries all in its wake.

Maurice Girodias 1919-90

FRENCH PUBLISHER

During the 1950s, Girodias provided an outlet through his Olympia Press for writing that would otherwise have fallen to the censor's axe in austerity Britain or McCarthyite America, thus continuing a tradition established by his father, Jack Kahane, who had published Henry Miller and Radclyffe Hall in the 1930s. Books such as ☛Beckett's *Molloy* (1951), ☛Nabokov's *Lolita* (1955) and ☛Burroughs' *The Naked Lunch* (1959), as well as the politically sensitive material contained in *The Black Diaries* (1962) of the Irish republican, Roger Casement, were published by Olympia. Girodias also commissioned pornographic works from young American and British writers who had come to Paris in order to live as bohemians, and adopted for the purpose such colourful pseudonyms as Marcus van Heller, Palmior Vicarion, Carmencita de las Lunas and Akbar del Piombo. As acolytes such as ☛Alex Trocchi, Terry Southern and Christopher Logue moved towards the mainstream, and the books he had launched crept on to the lists of establishment houses, Girodias gradually found himself without anything to do. He was left trumpeting the glories of complete artistic liberty, claiming in *The Obscenity Report* (1972) that the sexual revolution was 'the great motor of the moral, intellectual and political movement which is fast transforming the world'.

Sheldon Lee Glashow born 1932
Steven Weinberg born 1933
Abdus Salam born 1926

AMERICAN AND PAKISTANI SCIENTISTS

A perfect example of interdependently stimulated research and insight, Salam (from Pakistan), and Glashow and Weinberg (who had been contemporaries at the Bronx High School of Science) shared the 1979 Nobel prize for physics for their work on the forces that bind together elementary particles of matter. Operating independently, but in contact with each other, they had all been driving towards the 'grand unification theory', the still-elusive single explanation for the four nuclear forces (electromagnetic, strong nuclear, weak nuclear and gravity). In 1973, working from proposals that Glashow had made, Salam and Weinberg made the theoretical breakthrough that combined the electromagnetic and weak nuclear forces into the electro-weak force. Glashow went on to argue for a combined strong 'gluon' force with their electro-weak force, a suggestion that would determine the direction to be taken by further research on unification (leading to the inclusion of gravity). He is also responsible for conjuring up and naming the fourth quark – 'charm'. Weinberg is the author of the bestselling pop-science introduction to the Big Bang, *The First Three Minutes* (1977). The three scientists now take opposing positions over the 'superstring' controversy arising from the suggestion that an 11-dimensional extension of Kaluza-klein theory will provide the unified quantum model of gravity.

Philip Glass born 1937

♦ AMERICAN COMPOSER

■ A former taxi driver in New York, Glass's signature is so instantly recognizable – pulsating, repeated rhythmic modules of sound played on electric pianos and organs with amplified woodwind and voices – that he is almost too easy to caricature (there is a critic's joke that goes 'Philip Glass Glass, Philip Philip Glass . . .'). His music owes something to the procedures of Indian raga music, precluding any development beyond almost imperceptible modulatory shifts or the use of dynamic contrast. This sweetly haunting monotony put *Einstein on the Beach* (1976), the record of his collaboration with ☛Robert Wilson, in the bestseller charts for a few months. While he was instrumental in reuniting 'serious' music with an interested, committed audience, influencing such contemporary rock composers as Rhys Chatham and Glenn Branca, it began to seem as if the only new thing he could do with his music was to smear it over increasingly large-scale works, such as an opera about Gandhi, *Satyagraha* (1980). Recently, he has switched to composing music for dance pieces, and even worked on a pop album that featured Linda Ronstadt desperately trying to breathe life into his limp soundtrack. He has also written soundtracks for films, including Paul Schrader's *Mishima* (1985) and the documentary drama *The Thin Blue Line* (1989).

John Glenn born 1921

AMERICAN ASTRONAUT

Glenn was the most famous member of the Mercury Seven team, chosen not so much for his experience – 59 combat missions in WW2, 68 in Korea and a record-breaking supersonic flight from LA to NY in 1957 – as for his movie-star looks, all-American apple pie background and striking TV manner. He was the hot favourite to become the first American in space but lost out to Alan Shepherd and 'Gus' Grissom when he refused to play the publicity game. But his waiting ended on 20 February 1962, when he piloted Friendship 7 through what is still to many the most magical moment in the history of space exploration: the orbiting of the earth. On the first of his three orbits, all the lights in Perth were turned on to welcome him; on the last, his capsule was surrounded by thousands of tiny unexplained luminous particles. He was lucky to get back down – his heat shield had become loose – but he received a ticker tape welcome that matched the one for Lindbergh after he had flown the Atlantic in 1927. After escaping catastrophe a second time, in 1966, when the first attempted space-docking had to be broken off prematurely, he became a NASA consultant and then drifted into politics. Becoming a Democratic senator in 1975, he ran for the 1984 presidential nomination – but his simplistic view of world problems made him seem out of place even when compared with ☛Ronald Reagan.

Jean-Luc Godard born 1930

SWISS-FRENCH FILMMAKER

For the rest of us, Godard's tragedy – which does not seem to bother him – is the profound extent of his success; the technical innovations of his first 15 films have been so widely absorbed that you can watch them today and hardly sense any of what was once new. Starting with *Breathless* (1959), he spent the next decade scorching the flab off genre staples such as *film noir* and science fiction, and laced the cheap energy of Hollywood with a smart, impatient intelligence. His films had a quizzical, low-budget style that caught the spirit of the times and the same laconic verve that shaped his 1950s' film writing pushed a generation of film-makers into making movies new again. With as much daft zest as seriousness, he dissolved the barriers between fiction and documentary, between actors and the characters they played – performers would address monologues to the camera and people appeared as themselves in fiction films – while also building up an armoury of alienation tricks to keep us on our toes. But the world was changing, impelling Godard into 12 years of fragmented documentary and didactic experiment. He drove the medium way beyond its limits, aiming perhaps for a revolutionary audience that never materialized, perhaps just working for himself. Political disillusion set in along the way, and he took up the video camera for a series of (interminable) examinations of the nature of image communication, broken by flashes of innovatory brilliance. In his latest films, he has recovered his sense of humour, casting himself as a kind of uncle/clown in many of them. Some are accessible; others such as *King Lear* (1988) are recondite to the point of lunacy. For himself, Godard's tragedy seems to be that he was not able to get movies, his one and only love, to give him all that he once thought they could, and if he couldn't get them to, then no one could.

Bruce Goff 1904-82

AMERICAN ARCHITECT

If the problems of modern architecture derive from the fact that those who commission the buildings usually do not have to live or work in them, then the houses that Goff built provide an alternative approach. Considered vulgar by critics with an eye to architectural fashion, each design was tailored to the environment in which it was placed and the client who would live there (for a time at least). Often picking up objects from the site to incorporate into the buildings, he used materials in unusual ways – walls made of coal, ceilings of coiled rope, skylights fashioned from surplus airplane parts. Apart from a taste for complex geometry, there is not much stylistic continuity in the 140 commissions he executed in the American Midwest. Essentially, Goff gave schlock a good name.

Erving Goffman

CANADIAN-AMERICAN SOCIOLOGIST

Goffman's 1959 bestseller, *The Presentation of Self in Everyday Life*, argued that people were engaged in an elaborate theatre, choosing to define themselves before others, by gesture and word, in ways that irrevocably blurred fact and fiction. With more than half a million copies sold worldwide, this academic study appears to have connected with then-prevalent pop-existentialist theories about the 'phoniness' of conventional society. His non-judgemental conclusions were backed by research in the Shetland Islands, which provided just the right kind of hard scientific validation that ☛Sartre's and ☛Kerouac's similar, but highly judgemental claims lacked. Following up this work with a study of life within institutions from the point of view of the inmates – *Asylum* (1961) – he put himself in even further accord with the freedom-of-expression *zeitgeist* (radical psychiatrists ☛Laing and Cooper would inflate his implied critique into an actively anti-institutional fervour). Goffman keyed into a particularly significant 1960s' theme: the tension between public and private social relations. In the 1970s, however, his work was increasingly criticized for its uncritical user-friendliness (although, as ever, academic envy of the successful popularizer was not entirely absent).

Tommy Gold born 1920

AUSTRIAN SCIENTIST

In 1948, with Fred Hoyle and fellow Austrian Hermann Bondi, Gold proposed the 'expanding steady state' theory of the universe. The major rival to ☛Gamow's Big Bang (a name these three coined, in derision), this was a suggestion that the universe had always existed – rather than coming into being in a huge explosion. It expanded, in accordance with observation, in an endless series of localized 'Little Bangs', with constant creation of new matter to take care of the entropy that would otherwise ensue. This theory, now almost universally regarded as incorrect, was important in hastening cosmological research in ways that the Big Bang theory – at the time, somewhat ineffable – might well not have done. Gold went on to put forward the accepted theoretical explanation of pulsars as neutron stars spinning in such a way that the radiation emitted above their magnetic (not rotational) poles scans the universe like beams from a lighthouse. He has also speculated about what would happen after a finite universe reaches the limits of its expansion and starts to collapse in upon itself. Entropy, he suggests, will run backwards, and time itself will reverse as order tends to increase. Thinking animals will not notice, though – their thought processes will also be reversed, so they will still work on the assumption that their universe is expanding.

William Golding born 1911

▲BRITISH NOVELIST

Golding's visionary pessimism first found expression in *Lord of the Flies* (1954), which follows a group of marooned schoolboys as they revert to barbarism after a brief attempt at living in civilized imitation of what they had been taught about society. Standing out from the other British novelists of the 1960s, who turned simple style into aesthetic dogma, Golding developed similarly powerful narratives for subsequent novels – *The Inheritors* (1955), *Pincher Martin* (1956), *The Spire* (1964) – which all show that he is at his best when imagination gets the better of him. Unsentimental, but also rather humourless, he knows the pull of the bizarre, the primitive and the earthy, and does not believe much in civilization's ability to survive; his mythic world seems admirably vast, dark and old. But he has not had the influence one might have expected, perhaps because setting up the kids as the patsies in a retelling of man's fall was bound to limit his appeal to maturing generations. What they wanted to hear about was how all adults are fallible and how the kids are going to save the world. Plus there were no girls (now that would have been fun).

Albert Goldman born 1927

▲ AMERICAN BIOGRAPHER

Although he first came to the public's attention with his self-consciously hip biography *Ladies and Gentlemen – Lenny Bruce!!* (1974), Goldman is most notorious for his obsessively demythologizing works on ☛Elvis Presley and John Lennon. The books are the product of exhaustive research (carried out by others since he refuses to conduct interviews in person), but Goldman's insistence on illustrating – some say exaggerating – the gap between man and work, by going over the minutiae of their private lives with a fine tooth comb and drawing large theories from minor foibles and trivial incidents, infuriates both the fans and friends of his (for legal reasons, always dead) subjects. His biography of Lennon presented the Beatle-turned-proselytizer as, among many other things, a junkie and a purported man of peace who might have killed two people. The recognition that Lennon did have a dark side is fair enough, and Goldman's energy fills in much interesting detail, but the extent of his evident disillusion upon discovering the 'true nature' of his former idol may be evidence that he started out with a simplistic view of human nature. He is also under the impression that ☛Monty Python is a real person (he is probably thinking of the tall one).

James Goldsmith born 1933

$ BRITISH BUSINESS EXECUTIVE

Socially flamboyant, Goldsmith has made a fortune for himself without building up any significant enterprises. He left Eton after winning £8000 on the horses, and two years later he eloped with a Bolivian tin heiress. He is a buyer and seller of firms, a wheeler-dealer who, in late 1987, sold his stock-market holdings at a vast profit, just before the crash he had anticipated. In mid-1989 he made an unsuccessful bid for Britain's third largest business, BAT Industries. He may be shrewd and colourful, but he has contributed little to British economic prosperity, or to that of any other country. His smooth, sleek exterior invites satirical attack – hence the 'Goldenballs' saga when Goldsmith sued *Private Eye*, successfully, for libel. He has sometimes appeared to have designs on becoming a newspaper magnate – his weekly magazine venture, *Now!*, was a colourful, expensive fiasco.

Jerry Goldsmith born 1929

AMERICAN FILM COMPOSER

Graduating from television (but returning to write the themes to *Dr Kildare*, *The Man from U.N.C.L.E.* and *The Waltons*) to sign a contract with Twentieth Century-Fox, that studio's passion for widescreen epics in the 1960s gave Goldsmith the opportunity to move away from small-scale, emotionally complex scores to the heady romanticism of *The Blue Max* (1966). He began to experiment with atonal music, using various obscure instruments and objects to create the strange score of *Planet of the Apes* (1968). Changing the way films sounded became a habit in the 1970s, with

Goldsmith being the first to compose a synthesized score (rather than assembling a series of electronic sound effects) for *Logan's Run* (1976), and introducing Latin chants in *The Omen* of 1976 (ridiculously rumoured to be the text of a black mass), which rapidly became a cliché of the horror genre. Much of his best work has been on such turkeys as *The Swarm* (1978), *Inchon* (1982) and *Extreme Prejudice* (1987).

Barry Goldwater born 1909

AMERICAN POLITICIAN

A free-market anti-Communist, Goldwater was the Republican presidential contender who denounced ☛John F. Kennedy's 'quasi-socialist' policies and subsequently went down to ☛Lyndon Johnson by a massive margin in the 1964 elections. An authentic, consistent spokesman for conservatism for over 40 years, he thinks in broad, abstract terms – thus his supposedly election-losing line, 'Extremism in defence of liberty is no vice, moderation in pursuit of justice is no virtue.' Actually he lost the election largely through public fears about his foreign policy – he was felt to be trigger-happy. His Arizona department store background – he later became a major-general in the Air Force – made him a somewhat cranky Republican, analogous to a similarly rigorous British conservative, ☛Enoch Powell, an ex-brigadier-general from lower-middle-class West Midlands roots.

Anatoly Golitsyn born 1926

SOVIET INTELLIGENCE OFFICER, SETTLED IN US

Defecting to the West in 1961, Golitsyn succeeded in persuading CIA chief James Angleton that virtually every major international event since 1945 was the direct consequence of Soviet manipulation, and that nearly every Western government had been penetrated at the highest level – thus causing havoc in intelligence services worldwide and setting off numerous futile hunts for moles and double-agents. Although only a middle-ranking figure, Golitsyn did provide some invaluable data, including a missing link in the evidence which confirmed ☛Philby's guilt. His first-hand information was reliable, his interrogators felt, but when he strayed into politically contentious areas, he was erratic, even wild. His conspiracy theories were based on a top meeting he had attended in 1959, when the KGB unveiled a long-range master plan to spread disinformation to the West. He said that the Sino-Russian split was an elaborate subterfuge, aimed at undermining NATO's assumptions; and that Britain's Labour Party was little better than a Soviet fifth column – ☛Gaitskell, he insisted, had been murdered to make way for the Soviet plant, ☛Harold Wilson. ☛Dubček, he argued in 1968, was a Soviet agent – the invasion of Czechoslovakia was simply camouflage to hide the inside story of events. Golitsyn was treated with great respect by the Anglo-American intelligence community, but never secured a post as director of a NATO security service, as he had rather naïvely hoped.

E(rnst) H(ans) Gombrich born 1909

⇔AUSTRIAN-BRITISH ART HISTORIAN

Producing a bestseller in *The Story of Art* (1950), Gombrich has deployed his grasp of psychology and philosophy to defend the canon of great art and the notion of continuous development against claims that there can be *new* forms of artistic representation. In *Art and Illusion* (1960), he questions whether one can ascribe to the 'spirit of the age' those seemingly sharp breaks with tradition in artistic style. He argues that artists adopt different styles in order to attract attention to their work, but the underlying principles of visual expression shift only slowly, in response to new technical developments and long-term social shifts. There is no such thing as the 'innocent eye', whereby artists simply represent what they see, and the viewer concurs in that representation; artists are guided by the techniques they have mastered. Gombrich's shafts were initially aimed at art school courses which placed excessive emphasis on self-expression, at the expense of technical skills. The modernism he dislikes so much *is* part of a dialogue with tradition, even if acknowledging that is not going to make anyone, least of all Gombrich, like it.

Mikhail Gorbachev born 1931

❍ SOVIET POLITICAL LEADER

♦ ❀ Gorbachev presided over the disintegration of the Soviet Union but achieved international acclaim for freeing the countries of Eastern Europe to establish democratic governments and stopping the arms race that had shattered his country's economy. For Westerners, the mystery of Gorbachev's career was how he managed to develop such radical views while rising steadily to a position where he could implement radical changes in Soviet policies. A provincial background in the Caucasus partly explains his independent outlook, as does the fact that he witnessed Stalin's Great Purge and the German occupation during his formative years. He was the first leader of the USSR who seemed able to appreciate an outsider's view of his country, and not to share the values of the grim, drab, secretive elite that had run the place since Stalin's death – his vigour, openness and articulateness made an immediate contrast with the doddery figures who preceded him. His reforms aimed at an end to drift, low output and a byzantine bureaucracy, locked into under-investment, foreign adventures and escalating nuclear costs. He also saw that economic progress implied a more liberal, more open society. He was a pragmatist – thus the withdrawal from Afghanistan, offers of defence cuts and the loosening of state control over farming and services. But Gorbachev was in the end unable to acknowledge the full extent of the rottenness in the Soviet economy and he made the mistake of trying to retain reactionary support long after the necessity for a more radical approach was clear to nearly everyone else: he sent in the army to stop the Baltic states from seizing independence and largely failed to understand the desire for autonomy felt by many other Soviet republics. He also refused to expose the economy to market forces, never managed to deliver on his promise of more food and better consumer goods and established no new political structures to replace the Communist party apparatus – the source of his own legitimacy as leader. After Gorbachev's leadership team had staged a half-hearted coup in August, 1991, his rival ☛Boris Yeltsin pushed him out of power.

It's only by doing nothing that you avoid making mistakes – except that doing nothing is the biggest mistake.

Mikhail Gorbachev

André Gorz born 1924

& AUSTRIAN-FRENCH ECONOMIST

Unemployment is generally depicted as the bane of the post-industrial world, but Gorz looks beyond the political platitudes and builds a vision of utopia from his view that 'full-time, life-long work is the most vicious invention of capitalism.' The Keynesian notion that economic growth produces new jobs is wilting fast, but the continued pursuit of full-employment as an aim has led to large numbers of the population becoming marginalized into the ranks of the irregularly employed and the unemployed, as an élite fights to hold on to its fully employed status. Gorz argues that the work should be redistributed in smaller blocks, thus freeing people to produce for themselves, move away from obsessive consumption and create an area of production outside the capitalist market. It could be argued that, with the free time thus created, most people would just watch more television and drink more alcohol, rather than take up manual tasks. But Gorz, who in his 1980 book bade *Farewell to the Working Class* as the motor for social change, says that environmental anxieties are breeding new values and concerns that will render the crumbling of capitalism almost universally desirable. In his utopia, ecological health will be guaranteed by environmentally sound technology, and psychological well-being will result from involvement in production for oneself and one's community. Gorz does not begin to suggest how this vision might be realized, but by offering a concept of the future that is different from nightmare visions of a polluted desert managed by multinational conglomerates intent on profit-maximization, he does suggest a way ahead for radical politics.

Stephen Jay Gould born 1941

AMERICAN BIOLOGIST

Primarily a palaeontologist and evolutionary biologist, Gould also teaches geology and the history of science while writing theoretical and popular books on evolution, and debating with orthodox neo-Darwinists over the error of their ways. Ever since Darwin, one of the central pillars of biology has been the belief that evolution occurs as a gradual process over immense periods of time. To the argument that this is not reflected in the fossil record, orthodox biologists riposte that the geology is incomplete. Gould and Nils Eldridge point out that, where fossils do exist continuously in rocks of different ages, the most striking thing is that most of them look the same, but suddenly, in rocks only a few thousand years younger, quite different species appear. They propose that evolution occurs in fits and starts: sudden changes interrupt long periods of stasis. Their theory of 'punctuated equilibria' stirred up a big storm, with Gould accused by many of the more narrow-minded of shaping science to fit his Marxist beliefs. There is some contemporary evidence from African Rift Valley fish that punctuated equilibria do exist, but there seems to be no reason why they cannot be incorporated into a new Darwinian settlement: Gould has never proposed that evolution does not occur through natural selection.

Lew Grade
(Louis Winogradsky) born 1906

BRITISH TELEVISION AND FILM EXECUTIVE

A powder-monkey from the East End of London, who lit cannonballs to be fired at the populist mainstream in theatre, entertainment management, film and television, Grade's public persona is that of an indefatigable cigar-chomping impresario. In founding his ATV commercial station, the former Charleston dancer abandoned the traditional inform-instruct-enlighten edicts of British television for simple evenings of prime-time variety. The determinedly commercial format included soap operas, lavish adventure series (*The Avengers*, 1961-9, *The Saint*, 1963-8) and a variety show hosted by a popular comedian. His show-business empire foundered because of the almost uniformly unsuccessful products of his film company ITC, culminating in such box-office disasters as *Raise the Titanic!* (1980) and *The Legend of the Lone Ranger* (1981). Grade's legacy is as a deal-maker.

Billy Graham
born 1918

AMERICAN PREACHER

Graham took all-American fundamentalist evangelism into the television age. Converted as a 15-year-old schoolboy by revivalist preacher Mordecai Ham, he turned down a career in the movies to take up preaching, and by the 1950s was holding mass rallies on every continent. With his simple, direct, incantatory style, he undercut the mandarin chatter of liberal politicians, laying the ground for more extreme revanchists such as ☛Jerry Falwell and appealing to the religious emotions of white mid-America. 'I can't explain it all,' he says with a Bible in his hand. 'I accept it by faith.' A reactionary counterweight to ☛Martin Luther King, he became a cheerleader for ☛Richard Nixon – Graham's populist gospel-puritanism shored up support for the president's disgraced administration among the godly, even as moral revulsion at the seedy revelations of Watergate set in. Perhaps fortunate in that he is unable to emulate the lachrymose habits of his lately faltering rivals – he suffers from a deficiency of the tear ducts – he continued to attract large audiences in the early 1990s.

Martha Graham
1894-1991

♦ AMERICAN CHOREOGRAPHER

Generations have hailed her as the Mother of Modern Dance, yet she was initially shunned as a fanatical member of the avant-garde. An independent, from the formation of her company in 1929, Graham freed the body from classical rigidity to facilitate a more expressive style. Initially interested in abstract forms, she moved on to explore particularly dramatic myths. Her distinctive late style, blending avant-garde gymnastics with ritual or folk dance movements, was in some way a return to the abstractions of her youth, using spiral movements and linear stage patterns. Nearly every subsequent practitioner of modern dance was trained or influenced by her.

Ken Grange
born 1929

BRITISH DESIGNER

Through the 1960s and 1970s, Grange tried to persuade conservative managements in the UK to accord the same respect to innovative product design as did their competitors in Italy and Germany. He favoured simple designs, as did ☛Dieter Rams at Braun, but did not completely rule out ornament and frippery. The resulting aesthetic is less distinctive than that of his continental counterparts, but nevertheless Grange's designs became associated with such bestselling consumer products as the Kenwood Chefette and the Kodak Instamatic Camera. More recently, his creations have become ubiquitous: he designed British Rail's high-speed train and London's new parking meters. Grange's argument that designers should be closely involved in all aspects of the manufacturing process is now a truism, thanks partly to the evidence he has provided that the design approach can yield engineering breakthroughs: an impressive aerodynamic performance for the train, a lightweight sewing machine for a Japanese client.

Günter Grass born 1927

▲ GERMAN NOVELIST, POET, PLAYWRIGHT

Grass's childhood in the Third Reich and observation of the German people's mass self-deception led to his internationally celebrated novel, *The Tin Drum* (1958/62). This turned history into a sick fairy-tale about the childishness of all the grown-ups who believed in Hitler and later pretended it was just a phase they were going through – exemplified in a narrator who stopped growing for the duration of the war. The thread of displaced fantasy and symbolism runs through most of Grass's later work (including the speeches he wrote for ☛Willy Brandt). He exchanged the child's view for that of animals in *Cat and Mouse* (1961/3), *The Dog Years* (1963/5) and *The Flounder* (1977/8), and has explored not only the darker aspects of Germany's history, pre-war and post-war, by turning them into perversely realistic fables, but also the insanity and gullibility of those 'individuals' to whom common sense is a thing to be feared or ignored, and conformity something to be embraced – in short, most of us. Grass is out of step with many, though not all, of his countrymen in thinking that reunification may not be good for Germany.

Michael Graves born 1934

& AMERICAN ARCHITECT

❞ Lionized by architectural critic ☛Charles Jencks, Graves has contributed as much as anyone to the impression that the post-modern movement in architecture panders to the values of a consumer culture. He has done that not only by splashing colour on to his buildings, but also by becoming the sort of celebrity who does shoe commercials. One of the New York Five with Peter Eisenman and Richard Meier, the interest they shared in the (early International) style of the 1920s took his contemporaries towards hard-edged modernism but led Graves into pastiche. The pavilion he built on to a New Jersey house in 1969 – described by ☛Philip Johnson as 'a wonderfully sporty piece of lawn sculpture' – was packed with references to various modernist monuments. His Crooks House (1976) in Fort Wayne, Indiana, combined elements drawn from ☛Le Corbusier with allusions to Renaissance villa gardens. Gradually the quotations became increasingly less relevant to the buildings' functions, as Graves pursued an architecture whose 'general meanings are understood'. His public fame dates from the controversy over his Portland Building (1979-82) in Oregon with its ornamental façade of garlands, giant pilasters and huge keystone; one critic labelled it 'pop surrealism'. More protesting voices were raised in early 1985 with the unveiling of his plan for a pink expansion to Marcel Breuer's dark-grey granite Whitney Museum of American Art in Manhattan – a classic of high modernism. For Graves, remarked Eisenman, a building is no longer a social entity or an object in itself but rather 'a painting of an object'.

Alasdair Gray born 1934

▲SCOTTISH NOVELIST, PAINTER

The publication of Gray's first novel, *Lanark* (1981), opened the way for the current surge of interest in innovative Scottish fiction, particularly the work of James Kelman and Agnes Owen, with whom Gray collaborated on *Lean Tales* (1985), a collection of short stories. *Lanark* is an epic work of the imagination, taking its form from the old heroic myths and using autobiography, fantasy, science fiction and countless other literary techniques (including plagiarisms, all subdivided and listed in a dictionary which appears towards the end of the book) to construct a story that is as much about contemporary Glasgow as Kafka's works were about Prague. Also a painter, Gray decorates his work with illustrations and controls the use of typography. For his second novel, *1982, Janine* (1984), the many different voices in the head of a sales rep drunkenly masturbating his way through a night in a Scottish hotel are represented in different typefaces – at some points, exploding across the page – with the voice of God in the margin. The book also features a number of pages exclusively devoted to the word 'boak', onomatopoeiac Glaswegian for 'vomit', and has several blank pages to represent the character's moments of sleep, recalling not dissimilar experiments by ☛B.S. Johnson. Gray has said that he intends to give up writing – it remains to be seen whether he will keep this promise.

Michael Green *see* Schwarz, John

Peter Greenaway born 1942

▲BRITISH FILM-MAKER

& Greenaway has carved himself a specific niche within European cinema as a creator of painterly game-playing pictures. After a series of often fascinating experimental shorts, Greenaway broke into the art-cinema mainstream with *The Draughtsman's Contract* (1982), an ironic examination of his obsessions with sex, commerce and death. Set in Regency times, the film's elliptical plot culminates in a mysterious murder, establishing the piece as the sophisticate's whodunnit. The answer, of course, is that nobody knew, particularly not the actors who were shielded from any information as to motivation. With *A Zed & Two Noughts* (1985), the focus was again on death (as represented by some strangely moving time-lapse footage showing the process of decay in an angel fish and other creatures and sex (involving a woman with a varying number of legs and a pair of one-time Siamese twins eager to get back together). Its setting in the artificial, neon-lit starkness of a European urban zoo added an extra visual texture, which prevented the obsession from becoming wearing – but the acting was even more perfunctory than in *The Draughtsman's Contract*. Th

Peter Greenaway
Photo: James Park

Belly of an Architect (1987) was the first indication that the formula was spreading a little thin, with its Sunday supplement images of Roman opulence and spurious notions of male and female creativity. *Drowning by Numbers* (1988) underlined the fact that Greenaway's scripts were beginning to resemble geometric drawings. Equally, *The Cook the Thief his Wife and her Lover* (1989) failed to il luminate any emotional depth under its sumptuous set design, style-conscious costuming and carefully-orchestrated disgust. Far more interesting is Greenaway's ongoing collaboration with artist Tom Phillips on an an illustrated and annotated edition of Dante's *Inferno* for television.

Clement Greenberg born 1909

☞AMERICAN ART CRITIC

Greenberg's position in American art criticism is almost entirely dependent on his having discovered the painter ☛Jackson Pollock, and having championed abstract expressionism. Offering an alternative to the flowery art criticism of the 1950s, Greenberg confidently paraded his formalist conception of art through the journals of the period, occasionally with his foot firmly in his mouth. According to Greenberg, it was possible for painters to divorce themselves from everything that had gone before, and to create something unique. When a painter from one faction adopted approaches associated with another camp, Greenberg would mutter about how an artist would 'hunt about for new ideas under which to cover up the failure to develop his means'. Purity was the essential goal. Greenberg's refusal to modify his narrow, reductive view of art has led to fierce attacks upon him over the years, but his influence is undeniable – he is perhaps the closest the art world has yet come to producing a Bible-basher.

Graham Greene born 1904

▲✌ BRITISH NOVELIST, SETTLED IN FRANCE

For the best part of five decades, Greene has resisted the tendency of the rest of British fiction to drift into banality, provincialism and irrelevance. The qualities of his novels can be credited to his concern with spiritual issues (he converted to Catholicism in his mid-20s), his abilities as a storyteller (as a critic in the 1930s, he urged Britain's film-makers to strive for 'mass feeling, mass excitement, the Wembley roar') and a willingness to travel in search of new settings for his fiction (where the early books are set in a grey version of provincial England, later works explore more dramatic settings – Mexico, West Africa, Vietnam, Cuba, Congo and Haiti). He is also driven by a sense of anger at injustice and a commitment to political causes (the royalties of his 1982 book *Monsignor Quixote* are divided between a Trappist monastery and the FMLN guerrillas in El Salvador). His novels deal so consistently with men of quiet desperation who try to circumvent the demands of their consciences and throw off the sense of failure which the tackiness of life keeps highlighting, that the differences between them sometimes blur in memory, but no one could accuse Greene of merely repeating himself. For instance, he is the author of such diverse works as *The Power and the Glory* (aka *The Labyrinthine Ways* 1940), about priests in Mexico who embrace death rather than abandon their calling; the comic novel, *Our Man in Havana* (1958); and the script for *The Third Man* (1949), the best ever written for a British film.

Liz Greene

born 1935

☆ AMERICAN ASTROLOGER, BASED IN UK

Greene is offered to those who cannot take astrology seriously but feel they ought to, as the writer most likely to convert them. Trained as a Jungian psychoanalyst, she rejects the notion that astrology can provide substantial predictions about what will happen in a person's life, claiming only that her charts can show an individual's potential. Greene argues that astrology's 'accuracy' has been 'vindicated by statistical research and scientific investigation', and many believe her. It is when she takes on broader issues that even the most unwilling sceptic will have problems accepting her arguments. She says that humanity is currently undergoing a psychic transformation, moving into a new Aquarian Age (after the failure of that 'early and crude' Aquarian experiment, Communism) when everyone will set out on a search for inner knowledge. Where is the evidence for this? In the stars, perhaps.

Germaine Greer

born 1939

AUSTRALIAN WRITER, SETTLED IN UK

Because Greer always seemed more amused than angry, she is taken by all sides to be the Feminist that Won't Make Waves – periodically denounced by her more immoderate sisters and studiously ignored by the mainstream except by bookers for chatshows. The smartest in a coterie of Australian intellectuals who invaded London in the 1960s, her writings hide a formidable talent for gathering and examining information (she is perhaps less strong on analysis), to the extent that every one of her books – from the polemical *The Female Eunuch* (1970) to the recent semi-autobiographical *Daddy, We Hardly Knew You* (1989) – is about much more than it seems. The only writer for the underground magazine *Oz* to have secured an overground intellectual reputation, Greer is combative and able on camera, well used to manipulating her highbrow celebrity status to the advantage of her political positions, and a witty, embattled and somewhat isolated reformist figure whose tough, egalitarian, secular common sense has rarely been defeated.

Andrei Gromyko

1909-89

▲ SOVIET POLITICIAN

✓ Soviet foreign minister from 1957 to 1985, Gromyko was dubbed 'Dr No' at the UN Security Council for using the USSR's veto – '*niet*' – some 26 times in 12 years. Consistently dour, the model of negative anonymity, he was only sometimes a hard-liner – for example, while he vigorously opposed ☛Reagan in the 1980s, he had championed détente in the 1970s. He was by training an agricultural economist. Official convenience may explain his entrée to the apex of diplomacy: he spoke no English when he first joined the Washington embassy in the early 1940s, and was never linked to any doctrine of foreign policy except, arguably, the pursuit of Soviet self-interest. As he aged, the survivor elicited wry, admiring Western smiles. Shortly before his death, he was toppled as Gorbachev made a clean sweep of the party's 'old guard'.

Jerzy Grotowski born 1933

POLISH THEATRE DIRECTOR

Mainstream theatre increasingly emphasizes spectacle; Grotowski hones the medium down to the intimacy of a direct relationship between actor and audience. His response to clanking stage machinery is 'Poor Theatre', a transformation of theatre into ritual. The actors in his Polish Laboratory Theatre 'rehearse' for long periods, in a spirit of some solemnity, to become aware of their psychological stirrings which they then express through the fullest range of vocal and physical expression. Grotowski jumbles texts, and places the audience in unconventional relationships to the performers, in order to break through their commonplace assumptions about what theatre is and can do. For *Kordian* (1962), the audience sat on beds in a psychiatric ward; for *Faustus* (1963), they sat together, around two long wooden supper tables; for *Apocalpysis cum Figuris* (1968-9), performed to texts from the Bible, Dostoevsky and T.S. Eliot, they mingled freely in an empty room. This interest in the interrelationship between actor and audience eventually led Grotowski away from staged events; he set up retreats where non-actors could develop 'para-theatrical' events around outdoor activities, spiritual exercises and spontaneous acts of creativity. Grotowski shares with Antonin Artaud the paradoxical desire to create a theatre that will destroy theatre, bridging the gap between art and life.

Che Guevara

(Ernesto Guevara de la Serna) 1928-67

➳ ARGENTINIAN REVOLUTIONARY

✌ ♥ A radical guerilla leader in Latin America, Guevara had travelled around the continent before taking part in ☛Castro's revolt against Batista in Cuba in the 1950s, which led to him writing a manual on guerilla war which rivalled ☛Giap's. Guevara's targets were neo-colonialism and US policy in the Third World. Coming from a comfortable middle-class family in Argentina and trained as a doctor, he became director of the Cuban national bank under Castro, where he ruthlessly imposed a Soviet-style economy – treating it as a single unit, rather than the Chinese style of 'let a thousand flowers bloom'. He moved on to Bolivia, where he was shot by the government's army while attempting to foment revolution. In a sense, Guevara was a failure: no regimes were toppled through the implementation of Che's model of peasant revolution, which excluded the workers. His diaries show that he was a revolutionary because he liked the life (and the image) rather than from any sense of political urgency. But he did wonders for the poster industry and his photograph adorns many student bedrooms – or did.

Hans Gugelot 1920-65

WEST GERMAN DESIGNER

When Braun AG decided, in the mid-1950s, that the way to sell its electronic appliances was to pitch them to the top of the market with 'good design', it was Gugelot, working with ☛Dieter Rams, who came up with a grey-on-white, rectangular style that could be applied indiscriminately to radios, televisions and record players. For a

Germaine Greer

time this approach made the running as the Braun *Küchenmaschinen* picked up design awards through the late 1950s. Among Gugelot's important innovations (not always for Braun) were: the phono-super, which combined a record player and radio in one modular system; a sewing machine so arranged that accessories could be stored in the case; and the Kodak Carousel slide projector. However, the abstract aesthetic was wearing thin even during Gugelot's lifetime, and it is now too purist for much contemporary taste.

Thom Gunn born 1929

BRITISH POET, SETTLED IN US

The pugnacious, sharp style in Gunn's poetry of the 1950s and 1960s took English verse towards a new directness, unfettered by over-ornate structure or triflingly clever conceits. The son of a successful journalist, Gunn spent 12 years in San Francisco from 1954, writing verse that further fuelled the reputation established with his first collections, *Fighting Terms* (1954) and *The Sense of Movement* (1957). Unafraid to probe the personal arena of past or present, his vivid sense of the limits of mortality is allied to the strong instincts of a writer in tune with the passage of time as felt by people of the streets; his poem 'On the Move', captures the freedom of leather-clad bikers. Strangely marginalized by the critical establishment, Gunn remains one of the most honest British poets of the post-war period.

Helen Gurley Brown born 1922

AMERICAN PUBLISHER

'I have the same proportions I had at 16 and I have a reasonably flat stomach and I'm never sick,' Gurley Brown bragged at the age of 65. She is one of those women who have had so much done to their faces that you can no longer tell where the reality stops and the plastic surgery begins. So much for a relaxed old age (she does an hour's exercise before breakfast), but if you subscribe to the philosophy expounded by *Cosmopolitan* magazine since Gurley Brown became its editor in the early 1960s, then your body is the only key to success and happiness. She came to the job from writing a bestseller, *Sex and the Single Girl* (1962): the magazine's rising circulation was built on the idea that getting laid could be pleasurable for girls too. But just how far all this was from the feminist message some took it to be is made clear by Gurley Brown's more recent book, *Having It All* (1982), an instruction manual for women on how to 'mouseburger' their way into the arms of the most successful of men: do listen to what he says, darlings; and make love when he feels like it, even if you don't.

Gustavo Gutiérrez born 1928

PERUVIAN THEOLOGIAN

Gutiérrez's *A Theology of Liberation* (1971/3) laid the groundwork of a distinctive theology for Latin America synthesizing ideas that had been discussed at the Medellín conference of 1968. He developed a theological justification for priests who wished to side with the poor in their struggle against exploitation, challenging the assumption that there was a spiritual plane on which the church could remain 'above' questions of politics. The kingdom of heaven, said Gutiérrez, may be beyond history, but it is built up by partial realizations within history, and since the dictatorships of South America sustained themselves through violence, it was permissible to challenge them with violence. Gutiérrez saw that class struggle could not be smothered by appeals for the 'unity of the Church', and his writings encouraged subsequent liberation theologians to take an increased interest in Marxism. The resultant counter-attacks from the papacy and the established Latin American Church have become increasingly intense so that, except in Brazil and Nicaragua, liberation theology has largely been forced underground – preached by pastoral agents to communities of the poor.

Brion Gysin 1916-86

♦ AMERICAN PAINTER, WRITER

'Writing is 50 years behind painting,' Gysin remarked as he set about attempting to cut through the strait-jacket of language. Having exhibited with the surrealists when only 19 and having lived in Tangiers for over 20 years, studying Arabic calligraphy among other things, a trip to Paris in the summer of 1959 and a chance meeting with ☛William Burroughs led to one of the most inspirational artistic collaborations of recent times. With just a pair of scissors they literally liberated the text – cutting newspapers into sections and then rearranging the pieces one by one at random. The result of this first cut-up experiment – 'Minutes to Go' – brought to writing the collage methods of painters. By dislocating the harmony of the material, they allowed new truths to uncoil from the chaos. Gysin also constructed the 'Dreammachine', a cinematic contraption that can initiate a dream-like state in the mind of the participant. His innovations influenced such denizens of the contemporary music underground as ☛Throbbing Gristle and ☛Cabaret Voltaire.

H

Jürgen Habermas born 1929

☙ GERMAN PHILOSOPHER

The only significant second-generation Frankfurt School Marxist, Habermas has struggled – with some success – to steer a course between the pessimistic, humanist social analyses of his mentors, Horkheimer and ☛Adorno; and the non-Marxist critiques of historicism and power that ☛Foucault and ☛Derrida offer. A passionate rationalist, his project has been to rescue reason from its complicity in the technological oppressions and bureaucracies of modern industrial societies, but also from its own radical doubts and the necessary impossibility of authentic moralities – God-substitutes in a man-made world. He seeks to ground a solution in the 'normatively binding theory of intersubjective communication' that he outlined in his 1981 book *Theory of Communicative Action* (intersubjectivity would replace our present collapsing faith in the individual subject). Habermas is widely read in Europe and at American universities – and, typically, ignored in the UK, where his metaphysical pragmatism ought to strike a deep chord with a (supposedly) social democratic philosophical tradition.

Wolfgang Haken *see* Appel, Kenneth

H. R. Haldeman *see* Erlichman, John

Bill Haley 1925-81

AMERICAN ROCK 'N' ROLL MUSICIAN

Notable for being inextricably linked with the birth of rock 'n' roll while looking like the sort of person generally associated with its demise, Haley was smart enough to pick up on late 1940s' youth fetishes such as jazz and R&B, mix them with the ultra-conservativism of country music and get the result into the charts. The subsequent use of his music in such teen movies as *The Blackboard Jungle* (1955) meant that Bill Haley became the only chubby middle-aged man with a kiss curl ever to have incited riots in British cinemas. It is also his remarkable achievement to have put 'Rock around the Clock', which no one anywhere has ever liked, into the ledgers of great music.

Philippe Halsman 1906-79

LATVIAN-AMERICAN PHOTOGRAPHER

Halsman's best-loved series of pictures caught a variety of famous 1950s' names in the act of jumping –

everyone from an implausible, but very game, ☛Richard Nixon (then vice-president) to an enigmatic Salvador Dali, whose jump somehow also incorporated a still-airborne watersplash and a grumpily involuntary flying cat or two. Halsman often worked with Dali – they amused each other – and once photographed him standing elegantly beside a living sculpture that comprised seven nude models making up a death's-head; this kind of work, which combined technical ingenuity, weird imagination and striking composition, earned him the nickname of 'brainstorm-trooper'. A highly regarded portraitist, he shot 101 covers for *Life* magazine (more than any other photographer), including pictures of ☛Adlai Stevenson and Albert Einstein that were later used on postage stamps.

Halston

(Roy Halston Frowick) 1932-90

■ AMERICAN FASHION DESIGNER

Once America's best-known fashion designer, towards the end of his life Halston was paid a six-figure salary to produce absolutely nothing, and Revlon still makes millions out of the scent that carries his name. He started his career as a milliner, making hats for the likes of ☛Marilyn Monroe and Jacqueline Kennedy (who wore one of his pillboxes to her husband's inauguration in 1961). Later, as a New York-based party-giver and dresser of the glitterati (Lauren Bacall, Liza Minnelli and Bianca Jagger, among others), his success was based on a reputation for good taste (and stylistic conservatism), with his clothes being transformed into status symbols by the price tags. He declared himself 'the king of American fashion', and a monarchical ego may explain the distance he put between himself and what was going on in the rest of the fashion world, as well as the brickbats he received from some critics.

Richard Hamilton born 1922

BRITISH ARTIST

Earlier British artists had 'borrowed' ideas from comic books and pulp fiction in a half-hearted way; Hamilton tried to develop an art that would move with popular culture, pursuing an aesthetic that was 'popular', 'transient' and 'expendable'. By taking images from advertising and contemporary design – which he combined into collages such as his pioneering 1956 piece, *Just what is it that makes today's homes so different, so appealing?* – he celebrated, satirized and analysed the advertising and design images of the new consumerism. Despite the crowd-pulling surface appearance, a work such as *$HE* (1958-61) is a sophisticated account of the psychology that advertisers assume when pitching kitchen appliances to women. For Hamilton, Pop Art was essentially a surrender of art to popular culture; however, that should not detract from the message that artists need to seek out new ways of responding to changes in that culture.

Dag Hammerskjöld 1905-61

♥ SWEDISH POLITICIAN, DIPLOMAT

✈ The second secretary-general of the United Nations, Hammarskjöld was notably more active and effective than his predecessor, the Norwegian Trygve Lee, or successor, the Burmese U Thant, attempting between 1953 and his still-mysterious death to transform the UN from an assembly of hand-wringing observers into a significant force for world peace. To an extent he succeeded. His innovation was the idea of stationing neutral UN troops between opposing forces in Third World areas of military 'adventure' – thus offering an opportunity for negotiations. When this was effected during the Suez crisis of 1956, despite censure from both Soviet and British representatives, it was widely acknowledged to have reduced tensions between the power blocks. He was mediating during a crisis in the newly independent Congo between the central government and the state of Katanga, which wanted to secede, when his plane crashed near N'Dala in what was then Northern Rhodesia. Hammarskjöld proved that shuttle diplomacy by plausible neutral intermediaries could have an effect out of all proportion to their military status; since his death, however, the opposed blocs – and Kurt Waldheim – took it in turns to diminish the moral authority and global glamour of the post that Hammarskjöld held.

Armand Hammer 1898-1990

$ AMERICAN BUSINESS EXECUTIVE, PHILANTHROPIST

From his father, a founder of the American Communist Party, Hammer acquired sufficient grasp of ideology to charm Lenin and, in 1921, become the one capitalist that the Kremlin could deal with – although he never won over Stalin. Having made his first million by speculating in his father's pharmaceutical companies before graduating from medical college, Hammer visited the Soviet Union to provide famine victims with penicillin and other medical aid; Lenin then licensed him to export furs, minerals and Tsarist treasures in return for shipments of wheat, trucks and tractors. Although he made enough money from that trade to finance the post-Prohibition manufacture of whisky, Hammer's ascension into the ranks of the super-wealthy came only in 1955, when he bought into a rundown oil company that promptly struck oil with two wildcat wells: under Hammer's supervision, Occidental Petroleum has become one of the world's biggest oil companies. Lubricating his friendships with cash (he was convicted of illegal contributions to ☛Nixon's 1972 campaign), and establishing a reputation for substantial acts of philanthropy, he has become an international fixer: after the Chernobyl disaster, he flew America's top cancer specialists into the Soviet Union; in 1987, he shuttled between ☛Gorbachev, ☛Reagan and Pakistan's Zia, in search of a resolution to the Afghanistan conflict.

Peter Handke born 1942

☞AUSTRIAN NOVELIST, DRAMATIST, ▲SCREENWRITER, POET

Handke is a phenomenon. He lacks any sense of humour, refuses the narrative conventions that usually make for audience appeal and is grindingly pessimistic about modern life, yet his books repeatedly become bestsellers – in Germany, that is. With his first play *Offending the Audience* (1967), he proved that audiences love to be hated and abused, and his subsequent writings capture a sense of unease at the blandness of life in the shadow of the German economic miracle. His 1970 novel, *The Goalkeeper's Fear of the Penalty*, concerns a former goalkeeper who, having gratuitously murdered a cinema cashier, spends his time mooning around a provincial town all the while gradually losing his grip on the principles that govern norma human communication. ☛Wim Wenders filmed it two years later. Handke himself directed *The Left-Handed Woman* (1977) about a suburban woman's boredom, apathy and inability to communicate, in a world where there is no religion, politics, art or love to give meaning to life. Wenders and Handke collaborated again on *Wings of Desire* (1987), in which a modern, crumbling Berlin is inhabited by a melancholy population in search of hope. Despite working prolifically in many media, Handke has not done much to develop beyond his central insight into modern life, or to propose any route that might relieve the modern sicknesses he perceptively analyses.

An advertisement tells me that life is beautiful – a personal insult.

Peter Handke,
The Weight of the World

Hanna-Barbera

William Hanna born 1920
Joseph Barbera born 1911

AMERICAN ANIMATORS

Inseparable in fame and infamy, even Hanna-Barbera's one deathless achievement involved a partial recycling: their cat and mouse duo *Tom & Jerry* (1939-57) took their names from an earlier (human) cartoon pairing at the Van Beuren animation studios. H-B first capitalized on T&J's success with compendium retreads, wherein mouse or cat would contrive to 'remember' a clutch of past exploits. By the early 1960s, they had refined their style with such cheap (and not unlikeable) Saturday morning kids' television series as *Huckleberry Hound* (1958-62), *The Flintstones* (1960-6) – the first cartoon show ever to go out in prime time – and *Top Cat* (1961-2). Computer techniques further reduced scope for excitement in new cartoons such as *The Wacky Races*, 1968-9 and *Scooby Doo*, 1969-79, in which H-B reduced a potentially powerful form to its lowest common denominator and repeated this to exhaustion (although *Penelope Pitstop* and *Shaggy and Velma* did have their fans). By the mid-1970s, and the début of *Scrappy Doo*, however, even they were embarrassed about what they had done.

Duane Hanson born 1925

AMERICAN SCULPTOR

Critics have been hurling brickbats at Hanson ever since he abandoned abstract work in the early 1960s for life-size versions of real people, accurate in every detail. Modelling from life, he dresses the results in ordinary clothes and, like a make-up artist, brings out the most intricate details – body hairs, wrinkles, boils. In a sense, he is only doing what many a film-maker or photographer does whenever he or she points the camera: offering people a chance to have another, closer, look at observable reality. His early work in this style was preoccupied with violence and contemporary politics – for example, *War* grimly depicted four dead soldiers alongside one going through his final moments. In the 1970s, however, Hanson's focus shifted towards the small-town scene. Showing housewives stocking up with groceries in the supermarket or families on the beach hunting a tan, he implicitly criticizes the wastefulness of contemporary Americans who take for granted the culture of abundance and gleefully fill themselves full of junk.

Ray Harryhausen born 1920

AMERICAN ANIMATOR

The major figure in stop-motion animation, Harryhausen was entranced as a teenager by *King Kong* and went on to motivate dinosaurs, Medusas, Kalis and giant wasps in such films as *One Million Years BC* (1967), *Clash of the Titans* (1981) and *The Seventh Voyage of Sinbad* (1958). His moment of sinister genius – the battle of Jason's Argonauts with seven skeletons in his 1963 version of the story – took five months to produce. All of his films are remembered with fondness, not least because he obviously preferred small rubber-and-wire models to actors: invariably the monsters are the stars. Special effects have bypassed him, though, and with the Japanese *Godzilla* series easily out-manoeuvring him in the cheapo tack stakes, he is a genuine original caught in a middle-ground limbo, at once too serious and no longer serious enough.

Herbert Hart born 1907

BRITISH POLITICAL PHILOSOPHER

An ex-lawyer, now a professor of jurisprudence with a philosopher's perception, Hart's writing was shaped by the linguistic analysis current in Oxford during the 1950s, the utilitarian tradition and the detailed, daily problems of law in action. The distinction between 'self-regarding' conduct (to be left alone by the state) and other behaviour (apt for state regulation) was the basis for Hart's libertarian claim (in a debate with a senior judge, Lord Devlin) that society has no right to legislate for 'private morality'. Linked to that stance may be his view, expressed in *The Concept of Law* (1961), that the idea of duty is at the core of legal rules aimed at upholding society. Do women who engage in prostitution, say, have real duties to society, that it ought to apply if it is to survive? His distinction between 'primary' rules – naming these duties – and 'secondary' ones – that show how they are to be located, applied or changed – draws up a classic map for legal norms, winning for Hart a reputation abroad, as at home, and showing a way, later, for the work of ☛Ronald Dworkin.

Heinz Hartmann 1894-1970

AUSTRIAN-AMERICAN PSYCHOANALYST

The most striking initial consequence of the psychoanalysts' flight from Western Europe to the US, seeking refuge from Hitler's persecutions, was the development of ego psychology by Heinz Hartmann, Rudolf Lowenstein and Ernst Kris. Where Freud had concentrated on the study of the id, which he represented as a seething cauldron of instincts seeking an outlet, Hartmann and others (including Freud's own daughter Anna in London) turned their attention to the ego, the public face of the psyche. Although not initially presented as a challenge to the basic assumptions of psychoanalysis – Hartmann generally depicted the ego as being driven by the instincts rather than controlling them – the shift that ego psychology represented, by opening up the possibility that these unconscious drives could be tamed and neutralized, turned Freud's tragic vision of modern man into a practical therapy that would help its followers adapt to society's demands. The analyst aims to build up resistances in the patient, rather than interpreting past history so that it can be understood and dealt with. It was the reductivism of such a psychology that inspired the deconstructive work of ☛Jacques Lacan.

Václav Havel born 1936

CZECHOSLOVAK PLAYWRIGHT, POLITICAL LEADER

Havel started 1989 as a political prisoner and a dissident, much-victimized spokesman for Czechoslovakia's Charter 77 movement, but ended it as the country's apparently reluctant president, elected by popular demand and the unanimous vote of the Federal Assembly. This development was not altogether surprising since, for Havel, playwrighting and politics have always been one. His dramas are intense, black dissections of an absurd Communist system, and the consequences that follow when individuals surrender their reason to ideology. Havel touched a particularly raw nerve in the Czechoslovak authorities because he exploited so effectively the experiences that the State itself had put him through. His first play, for example, written while conscripted into the army, implies that a Czechoslovak soldier might fall asleep while on guard duty. A period working in a brewery resulted in a piece about a writer asked to inform upon himself, thus easing the work burden on a party stooge. *The Memorandum* (1965/7) satirizes bureaucracy, depicting its attempts to impose a new language, Ptidepe, in which a word's length would depend on frequency of use (317 letters in the word for 'wombat'), the aim being to iron out the ambiguous and the unscientific in language – thus ultimately tearing the heart out of literature itself. Eastern Europe is seen by Havel not as a unique manifestation of totalitarian power but a symbolic expression of how the modern world works. Having abandoned his sweater and jeans for a suit, it remains to be seen whether he will acquire a sufficient taste for power to dedicate himself to tackling his country's long-term economic problems.

The tragedy of modern man is not that he knows less and less about the meaning of his own life, but that it bothers him less and less.

Václav Havel

Robert (Bob) Hawke born 1929

AUSTRALIAN POLITICIAN

Hawke became Australia's prime minister only three years after entering parliament in 1980. He had been a brilliant trade union negotiator, winning settlements from arbitrators and wages indexation from the courts. President of his party from 1973, he already had a national reputation when he took up his seat. Unlike Gough Whitlam, whose earlier Labour government had been controversially dissolved after a budgetary crisis, Hawke has weathered storms by shifting, in economic terms, to the right: inflation has been controlled by a deal on prices and wages; he has sponsored tax reforms and deregulation of industry; strikes, always a risk from an ebullient union movement, are down. Economic growth has had results, and relations with the US are good. Hawke's personality is tough and genial, winning him easy popularity with machismo-minded Australians, thanks partly to his reputation as a former heavy drinker (while at Oxford, he entered the *Guinness Book of Records* for drinking a yard of ale in 11 seconds) and a sexual athlete – although he also has a tendency to weep both on television (over his infidelity to his wife) and at public ceremonies, such as the memorial service for the Chinese protestors murdered in Tiananmen Square. However, as debt and current account deficit problems grew, he began to look more like a skilful winner of elections than a totally convincing politician, and he was forced to resign in 1991, making way for Paul Keating.

Stephen W. Hawking born 1942

BRITISH PHYSICIST

Although one of the finest scientists of all time, Hawking's public reputation rests on his bestselling book, *A Brief History of Time* (1988), and the wasting disease which has confined him to a wheelchair for many years, latterly depriving him of the power of speech so that he has to communicate through a computerized voice-synthesizer. It is not clear that he altogether resents the attention this has brought; his aggressive confidence and willingness to challenge current scientific orthodoxy, even when this consists of his own previously accepted theories, suggests a personality that enjoys the limelight. Hawking's contribution has been to cosmology, in particular the development of the Big Bang theory – the study of the beginnings of the universe which involves considerations of mathematical singularities and quickly leads to black holes. In the 1960s he was involved, with ☛Roger Penrose, in the theoretical proof of the existence of collapsed stars – those scary but fascinating items whose gravity is so strong that even light cannot escape them. Over the past ten years, by applying quantum gravity equations to the theoretical edifice he had already constructed, he has shown to everyone else's astonishment that black holes do radiate energy after all; and he also put forward the idea that the acausal fluctuations at the subatomic level, which can bring virtual particles (basic to quantam explanations) into momentary existence, may also show that the Big Bang needs no first cause, that it blipped into being as a fluctuation that then ran away with itself – the universe as the ultimate free lunch, as one commentator has cheerfully put it.

Tom Hayden born 1940

☞ AMERICAN POLITICAL ACTIVIST, POLITICIAN

Brought up a low-to-middle-class Catholic, Hayden has been active on the left of American politics since the early 1960s. A leading theorist of Students for a Democratic Society, he was the principal author of the Port Huron Statement, which held out to SDS followers the prospect that they could secure personal fulfilment through political commitment: 'The goal of man and society should be human independence.' He also became famous for a trip to Hanoi as an anti-war campaigner and his meetings with North Vietnamese leaders, through which he sought the release of American POWs: three were set free. He also made news as one of the 'Chicago Seven', arrested during anti-war riots at the 1968 Democratic Party Convention. Since the heyday of student radicalism, only his marriage to Jane Fonda has kept him in the headlines – although he has been a member of the California State Assembly since 1982; with their separation, obscurity seems likely. The succession of issues on his agenda may be a paradigm for his generation: first, civil rights in the early 1960s; then anti-war protests; now, 'economic democracy' – which was not a problem for 1960s radicals.

Friedrich von Hayek 1899-1992

AUSTRO-BRITISH ECONOMIST

The guru of the libertarian movement, Hayek argued in his 1944 book *The Road to Serfdom* that the welfare state was a step towards tyranny rather than individual freedom, updating Adam Smith's suggestion that society will most effectively channel the means of production towards satisfying the wants of its members if it allows individuals to pursue their own goals. His three-volume *Law, Legislation and Liberty*, published between 1973 and 1979 was more influential. In it, he argued that the information necessary to run an economy is diffused through a modern society, so that governments lack the information necessary to achieve the results at which they aim. In addition, their actions deprive individuals of the capital required to take initiative, interfering with the ability of prices to indicate what is happening in the economy. Therefore, all blueprints for society – whether socialist or Fascist – must fail. Ignored in the 1950s and 1960s – one critic described his 1960 book *The Constitution of Liberty* as a 'magnificent dinosaur' – his espousal of the free market led to his being associated with ☛Milton Friedman and other thinkers of the New Right, while his argument that millions on the dole may be vital to cutting inflation gave him a demonic reputation in some quarters. He was, however, skeptical of the value of monetary targets, believing that governments lack the moral courage necessary to uphold them. Among his wackier suggestions were a plan for a legislative assembly of 40- to 50-year-olds, elected by those of the same age, to replace existing parliaments; and a proposal that banks should create private-sector money to replace the unreliable variety that governments issue and devalue at their convenience.

Seamus Heaney born 1939

IRISH POET

Based in Northern Ireland until 1972, Heaney is a self-conscious savage, whose poetry explores rustic backgrounds and farm life but avoids the purple prose of pastoral rhyme. For him, beauty and art have a price, and nature's magnificence hides dark secrets – like the sacrificial victim encased in the peat bog of 'Wintering Out' – that wait just beneath the surface, as does all the violence of Ireland's history which, together with his constant coupling of copulation and murder, is a recurring motif in Heaney's work. He deploys his pen as a weapon – in 'Digging', which links the poet's mental toil with a pen to his father's manual labour, he says 'The savage pen rests; snug as a gun'. His writing contains a frightening violence that is only qualified by his Catholic sense of redemption, seeming to imply that life must be endured until something better is offered.

Patty Hearst born 1954

AMERICAN VICTIM

Patty Hearst was the American dream turned American victim, her media profile going from innocent heroine to rich-bitch slut faster than that of the average rape victim. Heiress to the Hearst newspaper fortune, her kidnap on 4 February 1974 by a group of disaffected middle-class whackos calling themselves the Symbionese Liberation Army, who were already responsible for numerous acts of ill-planned and more-than-slightly psychotic violence, turned her into front-page news. But when she was caught on video a few months later at the Hibernia Bank in San Francisco, holding a gun on the terrified customers and reciting her new revolutionary name – Tania – in almost zombie-fashion as another member of the heavily armed gang kept a gun trained on her, the press had a field day. More armed robberies, kidnappings and a huge gun battle were to follow before her arrest, but Patty had already been tried by the American public. Her story was that she had been locked, blindfolded, in a tiny cupboard, bombarded with propaganda and death threats, then forced to have sex with SLA members: after 57 days, convinced that her captors would kill her otherwise, she chose to survive by joining them. The American public would not buy it – two-thirds of those polled said she had joined voluntarily and planned her own kidnap as a publicity stunt – and the jury did not buy it either, sentencing her to seven years' imprisonment (which was commuted by President Carter in 1979). Her 'crime' was not so much her betrayal of the capitalism that her family embodied, but rather her self-apostasy: she had accepted a fate worse than death – fucking with terrorists to save herself – rather than defending her honour with her life. The idea that torture, degradation, confinement and brainwashing might wear away even the most well-balanced mind was unthinkable to the public, who would never admit that in the same situation, they would be crawling on their knees and begging for their lives.

Edward Heath born 1916

BRITISH POLITICAL LEADER

Ever since his displacement as leader of the Conservative Party by ☛Margaret Thatcher, Heath has been a brooding presence in British politics, seeming to stand for a middle way that his successor had abandoned. In fact, his term of office was, in some ways, a dummy run for Thatcher's. The son of a builder, Heath was the first Tory leader not enrolled from the gentry or aristocracy, and he set out with a resolve to reduce inflation, clear out 'lame duck' industries and take on the seemingly all-powerful trade unions. However, he was deflected from these policies (due to a lack of guts, according to Thatcher's fans), and his regime ended in industrial strife and the three-day week. It was not all his fault: whereas Thatcher could draw upon the revenues from North Sea oil to finance her policies and strengthen political resolve, Heath had to cope with the fuel crisis that followed the Arab-Israeli War of 1973. He will probably never forgive Thatcher for failing to give him a post in her government, especially since she has ignored his vision of Britain as a leader in Europe, replacing it with an outdated concern for the Anglo-American alliance. He rightly interpreted her offer of a job as Britain's ambassador to the US as a rebuke, but had he taken the job, Heath might have been able to teach her a few lessons about the realities of international politics in the 1980s.

Hugh Hefner born 1926

$ AMERICAN PUBLISHER, BUSINESS
♦ EXECUTIVE

Hefner, whose mother would not hug him and whose fiancée forbade love-making, instigated his Playboy business empire in a spirit of libertine consumerism. *Playboy* magazine was the first girlie publication in which skin pictorials were not riddled with handy hints on how to annihilate small woodland animals; the sex was always mellow and fragile (compared with chief rival *Penthouse*), exploring the notion that it could be a mutually fulfilling experience – casual or otherwise – with the kind of girl who idolized ☛John F. Kennedy, enjoyed the novels of Erica Jong and always showered afterwards. For these reasons, and because of its commitment to serious writers and humanitarian causes, the magazine became irreplaceable for American men of a certain age. The comic-book iconography of the *Playboy* empire generated the phenomenon of 'bunny girls' with an easy-on-the-eye, pleasurable-to-pinch image that seemed at odds with the preponderance of female executives within the Hefner administration (daughter Christie later succeeded to the Hefner throne, becoming chief operating officer in 1984), or even with *Playboy* magazine's copious advocacy of issues such as abortion rights. The 1980s were not good times for the *Playboy* empire. When the UK authorities refused to renew their gaming licenses in 1982, the company had to sell its highly profitable casinos and bettings shops. And by 1986, when clubs in New York, Chicago and LA were shuttered, the only remaining *Playboy* outposts were in such unlikely locations as Des Moines, Omaha and Lansing. The magazine continues to move copies, although not in the same numbers as previously.

Robert Heinlein 1907-88

AMERICAN WRITER

Heinlein was to SF what ☛Ronald Reagan was to international diplomacy; for nearly 50 years, his combination of authoritarian and libertarian right-wing populism dominated the genre. Early short stories predicted transport and atomic difficulties in modern societies, and showed an imaginative interest in the paradoxes of time travel. However, in later books, square-jawed Republican heroes and heroines conquered space in the name of truth, justice and the galactic way. *Starship Troopers* (1959), for example, features an inter-galactic rapid deployment force of ruthless efficiency and macho camaraderie. Here, and in later books, Heinlein spells out his credo: respect for 'law and order', patriotism, self-discipline and individual freedom. Ironically, his 1960s novels propounding gentle ideas of free love made Heinlein a minor guru of the flower-power generation – a strange role for an unabashed authoritarian. The problem for those who find Heinlein's views repugnant is that his storytelling technique is so assured: you might not have liked what you read, but until the excesses of his last books, you were sure to keep on reading. The best antidote to his beguiling style is a story about the inter-galactic Camel Corps, an élite unit dedicated to cleaning up the universe on behalf of the 'right-thinking' citizen.

Joseph Heller born 1923

AMERICAN NOVELIST

Heller's novel *Catch 22* (1961) broke new ground in American literature with its skewed perspective on war as acid farce, successfully replaying the experience of global conflict in the blackest terms. Heller had flown 60 missions over Europe and it is out of this experience that he wrote about his protagonist, John Yossarian, as he struggles to survive and remain sane amid bungling bureaucracy and loss of life. *Catch 22*, with its brittle wit, is almost surreal in its imagery and in the savagery of its impact. It became the perfect symbol for the anti-war movement engendered by Vietnam, and the title, taken from US Air Force regulations, has entered the English language. Heller's later novels share the bleak pessimism of the first, but none has had the same impact.

Jimi Hendrix 1942-70

✣ AMERICAN ROCK MUSICIAN

Hendrix was an innovative genius working out of black music, who inadvertently created the worst and stupidest form of white music – heavy metal. He single-handedly brought the guitar out of its twiddling years – a wasp-like noise in the middle of otherwise exciting records – and made it into a bludgeoning instrument of terror; in doing so, he caused rock music to be defined as something other than merely youth music. Ironically, his death occurred at a time when he was moving away from the simple manipulation of rock's noise. By dying at the end of an era in which he had played a major part, he became an instant rock legend. He remains, paradoxically, an influence both on fans of bad heavy metal and on imitors of ☛Prince; Prince himself recognizes Hendrix's flamboyance and sexuality, as well as his unusual position as a black artist working in rock.

Hans Werner Henze born 1926

GERMAN COMPOSER, SETTLED IN ☞ITALY

Henze's 1976 opera *We Come to the River* sums up his originality, his political intensity and at least some of the reasons why he is not a household name. To perform it, you need two almost bare stages – one as a setting for the main drama; the other given over to a single performer, the percussion virtuoso as one-man orchestra, dashing from instrument to instrument. The opera itself is startling, distracting, harsh and deliberately anti-operatic – dedicated to creating 'the image and consciousness of the working class'. Henze's earliest influence was the chamber music he heard in the Jewish household of a friendly neighbour, and a youthful awareness of imminent peril firmly implanted the notion of music as something clandestine, dangerous and anti-authoritarian, which has remained an integral part of his creative thinking. His experiences during WW2 left him with a deep hatred of his native Germany which early success as a composer could not assuage. He left for southern Italy in 1953, and his music became more luxuriant and rich in orchestral colour. Moving to Rome in 1961, he began a period of self-questioning, from which he emerged with a commitment to revolutionary socialism, and wrote a sequence of political allegories which vividly express his contempt for bourgeois society.

Hugh Hefner
Photo: © Playboy

Frank Herbert 1920-86

AMERICAN WRITER

His fame rests on one SF blockbuster, *Dune* (1965), which he extended into a seemingly unending series, at the expense of new ideas (or perhaps as a way of financing them). With a fair gift for pulp narrative and diverting characters, he was adept at dramatizing sophisticated philosophical and political problems in tales of planet-wide social engineering and ingenious alien cultures; *Dune* itself is concerned with a drug-fuelled, desert-bound, fanatical theocracy. His lesser-known novels shift between elaborations of ludicrous alternative legal systems, and the directions in which his own anarcho-populist sympathies took him. (Several highly entertaining satires feature his idea of a governmental Bureau of Sabotage, whose entire purpose would be to slow up the operation of other government departments.) He was also interested in ecology and, in certain respects, anticipated the more speculative parts of ☛James Lovelock's Gaia theory: in *The Green Brain* (1966), he suggested that nature, operating as a single, self-protecting organism, would strike back at human attempts to tame it.

Zbigniew Herbert born 1924

POLISH POET

Growing up in the east of Poland and witnessing many of the worst horrors of WW2, then studying philosophy while Stalinism was a dominant force in intellectual life, Herbert has been preoccupied with finding a way to describe the world as it is, away from the lies churned out by the information-manipulation machinery set up by corrupt powers. His poems range through the past as he struggles to pull aside the curtain and gaze on the present without distortion or self-deception. The quality of his writing comes from his orchestration of these tensions, while avoiding cynicism and pretentiousness.

Hernandez Brothers

Gilbert born 1958
Jaime born 1960

AMERICAN COMICS WRITERS

The Hernandez brothers' cult comic *Love and Rockets* made its initial impact in 1982 through a surreal refusal to use many of the staples of the comic world. Through its 30 or so issues, the two main strips – Jaime's 'Locas', Gilbert's 'Heartbreak Soup' – have moved decisively away from the existentialist macho dynamism of most 1960s' comics into a magical-realist involvement with the concerns of the pinched 1970s. 'Locas' is a world of cool shadows and hot Californian indolence, a mostly female punk-Hispanic backwater that Jaime's art-trained eye makes funny, sexy and sad by turns. Gilbert's approach, by contrast, is fiercely mythological, and 'Heartbreak Soup', set in the crossborder town of Palomar, relates the loves and deaths of the townspeople through several generations. Although the brothers clearly influence one another, in technique as much as in manner of storytelling, their two strands work so well partially because they are different. Highly respected and aggressively opinionated, the brothers have brought a new dimension to comics without compromising their unrespectable verve.

Michael Herr born 1940

AMERICAN JOURNALIST, NOVELIST

Dispatches (1977), a drug-fuelled account of Herr's experiences as a journalist for *Esquire* during the Vietnam War, presented that conflict as a playground for the gung-ho theatrics of media parasites searching for the ultimate kick. Herr's book heavily influenced ☛Coppola's *Apocalpyse Now* (1979), although the film did not convey the tragedy that always seeped through the frenetic hilarity of Herr's own writing. One consequence of the book was the appearance of voyeuristic Nam freaks, who vicariously grooved at the spectre of riding Hueys into hot DMZs and going out on jungle patrols. Herr empathized not only with the GIs, but also with such war addicts as Errol Flynn's son Sean and photographer Tim Page, who both entered into the mythology of Vietnam through *Dispatches*.

Seymour Hersh born 1937

AMERICAN JOURNALIST

Hersh's *bêtes noires* are politicians obsessed with secrecy, especially ☛Henry Kissinger and ☛Richard Nixon, whose clandestine behaviour he depicts as an integral part of a foreign policy which involved the 'secret' bombing of Cambodia and the undermining of an elected (Marxist) government in Chile. Hersh made his name with the first detailed account of the My Lai massacre in Vietnam, and he became a speaker on the antiwar lecture circuit in the late 1960s. He was sniffing at the Watergate trail which led the *Washington Post* journalists ☛Bob Woodward and Carl Bernstein to fame and riches, but he seems to have been a graceful loser (playing squash with Woodward once a week while the story broke). More recently, apart from excoriating Kissinger, Hersh wrote *The Target Is Destroyed* (1986), a commonsense account of the destruction of a Korean airliner in Soviet airspace in 1983. Far from being on an espionage mission for the CIA, says Hersh, the plane simply flew off course. The Soviets made a mistake, and American intelligence *knew* what had happened, but it suited ☛Reagan's purposes to accuse the Soviets of malicious intent. Hersh has also reported on how members of the congressional hearings into the Iran-Contra affair ignored evidence showing that Reagan had known exactly what was going on.

Werner Herzog

(Werner Stipetic) born 1942

GERMAN FILM-MAKER

One of the few people ever to say 'I'll eat my boot' and actually mean it (marinated in hot oil for 24 hours, the boot was consumed in the normal manner with knife and fork), Herzog is best known for his nutter-in-the-jungle movies (*Aguirre, Wrath of God*, 1972; *Fitzcarraldo*, 1982; *Cobra Verde*, 1988) and a tempestuous collaboration with demonic actor Klaus Kinski. Looking for new forms of imagery in what is ugly and horrible, and in the process often seeming to expose the bestiality under the surface of civilized conventions, he specializes in bizarre tales of obsession set in timeless, remote lands. His heroes are grotesques, outsiders, victims of civilization or demented dreamers moving through a world where beauty exists only as a thing destined to be destroyed. He is especially concerned to show the effect that people and places have on each other: the pettiness of the villagers in *Woyzeck* (1978) turns a soldier's small jealousies into grand crimes; the alienation and moral hypocrisies of rural German life destroy the amnesiac in *The Enigma of Kaspar Hauser* (1974); the grandeur of the South American jungle inspires pathetic dreams of empire and cities of gold in *Fitzcarraldo* – the story of a man whose passion to build an opera house in the Amazon jungle necessitated the transportation of a full-sized steamboat up a hill. Whether because of remorse at the damage inflicted on native communities during filming, or because his obsessions have simply lost their force, that picture marked the start of Herzog's artistic decline and the loss of his earlier visionary intensity.

George V. Higgins born 1939

AMERICAN WRITER

The knowledge of Boston's underworld that Higgins brings to his novels was acquired as an attorney: he was a lawyer in the Organized Crime Section and Criminal Division of the Massachusetts Attorney General's Office and, as an assistant DA, was prosecutor at a series of murder trials during a war between Irish and Italian mobs in the city. Plotting is subsidiary to his skill in capturing the intonations of low-life speech, and in portraying modern monsters, hooked on power, money and sex. He made his reputation with *The Friends of Eddie Coyle* (1972), about a small-time crook who runs guns to a group of bank robbers while selling information to the cops in order to keep himself out of prison. Higgins is interested in people who destroy themselves by pushing their luck a little further than their talents will allow, and the way those who live in the muck, both lawyers and criminals, try in vain to preserve a clean area in their lives.

Patricia Highsmith born 1921

▲AMERICAN WRITER, SETTLED IN EUROPE

The poet of apprehension and fear, Highsmith is fascinated by the psychology of guilt. What makes her novels so chilling is the portrayal of how crime, once committed, can corrode the murderer's mental stability. In the case of Tom Ripley – the liar, psychopath and killer who glides through five of her novels – she has created a character sure enough of himself to kill, who still takes psychotic pride in outward respectability. The morally destabilizing effect of Europe (where she is based) on her American compatriots is also a recurring feature. Film-maker ☛Wim Wenders captured this in *The American Friend* (1977), a very loose adaptation of *Ripley's Game* (1974), and tied it to its mirror effect, the erosion of European identity by American culture. Anxiety is at the forefront in Highsmith's work – the twisted, obsessional but ultimately careful behaviour of those who kill, are going to kill or even those who think they might have killed. Her recent attempt to write satires of ecological and political disaster represents a classic case of somebody not playing to their strengths. And don't expect her to write convincing women characters.

Geoffrey Hill born 1932

⇔BRITISH POET

An individual voice in contemporary British poetry whose interest in the past, as evident from the titles of such sequences of poems as *Mercian Hymns* (1971) and *The Mystery of the Charity of Charles Péguy* (1983), is often misunderstood as simple nostalgia for another age. While Hill finds poetic resonances in history, as others do in myth, his vision of other times is dark, filled with death and blood. In *Mercian Hymns*, which juxtaposes the life of the eighth-century King Offa with scenes from a twentieth-century childhood, the contrasts are filled with ambiguity. Although a distaste for modernity is built into any romantic reference backwards, Hill's poetry does not rest on simple declarations but combines contradictory ideas within individual poems. He may seem to pine for simpler times, but he does not resist the complexity of the present.

Michinomiya Hirohito 1901-89

JAPANESE RULER, BIOLOGIST

Emperor of Japan from 1921 until his death, Hirohito was the first Japanese royal leader to travel extensively abroad. His lifetime passion was marine biology, about which he wrote several books. He could do little to prevent the militarist regime, which took over Japan in the 1930s, from launching aggressive foreign wars, culminating in their entry into WW2. Earlier views were that he sought in vain to restrain the regime; his death has led to claims that he bore an active responsibility for Japanese war crimes. Perhaps both versions are true. As the war ended, he emerged as a humanized figure in his own right, taking the initiative and surrendering in response to atomic attacks; afterwards, he de-deified himself and avoided trial as a war criminal. A ceremonial head of state, he brought the royal family into public view in the 1950s when he let his son marry a commoner and agreed to media coverage of the nuptials. Even as a human, he became a unifying national symbol, as Japan in the post-war era combined ancient and modern traits while pursuing material goals.

Alger Hiss born 1904

AMERICAN VICTIM

Hiss was one of the most significant victims of the anti-Communist witch hunts in the US of the early 1950s, and an important figure in the escalating paranoia over infiltration of the US State Department. He had been one of President Roosevelt's advisers during the 1945 Conference at Yalta, and a chief organizer of the San Francisco Conference that led to the birth of the UN, but was eased out of the State Department in 1947 because of suspicions about his political affiliations. He was thus easy prey for the unprepossessing Whittaker Chambers, a self-professed courier for an underground Communist cell in Washington, who accused Hiss of being a member of 'the apparatus' prior to WW2. Hiss was his own worst enemy, drawing attention to the case by suing Chambers for slander. The accuser, now working with the ambitious Senator ☛Richard Nixon, would not budge. Hiss – who, because of the Statute of Limitations, could no longer be taken to court for espionage, was indicted for perjury at Chambers' trial. Convicted, he served three years of a five-year sentence. One of the strongest arguments for believing that

Hiss was wrongly accused is the energy he has since put into campaigning to get his name cleared; suggestions of suppressed evidence have also surfaced to support his claims to innocence.

Alfred Hitchcock 1899-1980

BRITISH-AMERICAN FILM DIRECTOR

The director who gave people second thoughts about taking showers or feeding the birds, Hitchcock brought a then-unparalleled level of imagination and technical expertise to British cinema with such early classics as *The Thirty-nine Steps* (1935) and *The Lady Vanishes* (1938). He then departed for Hollywood, where he was to direct a series of precisely calculated thrillers. Off set, Hitchcock was a portly sadist with a penchant for sick jokes, and his dark side is reflected in some of his best work: *Strangers on a Train* (1951), in which a tennis player is invited by a fellow rail passenger to 'swap' murders; *Rear Window* (1954), a thriller about voyeurism; *Vertigo* (1958), an obsessive necrophiliac romance; *North by Northwest* (1959), in which a mother-dominated advertising executive is chased across America by sexually ambiguous foreign agents; and *Psycho* (1960), in which a mother-obsessed transvestite murders a thief. His movies were scrupulously planned and choreographed so that each set-piece stood out from the narrative at the planned moment, and tension was built to near breaking point at a stage when his characters – confused, harassed and pursued – reached an impasse. Thanks to cameo appearances in most of his films, and to his anthology TV series *Alfred Hitchcock Presents* (1955-61), he became one of the most publicly well-known directors. Although often highly innovative, his later films, with their unsympathetic characters and dark undercurrents of misogyny, made little impact on the new generation of filmgoers, and he strove too hard to live up to past glories rather than breaking any new ground. However, when compared to the works by François Truffaut, Brian De Palma, Jonathan Demme, Robert Benton and far too many others which he inspired, Hitchcock's films from 1935 to 1960 stand out as some of the finest examples of the thriller genre.

Eric Hobsbawm born 1917

BRITISH HISTORIAN, POLITICAL THINKER

A free-thinking Marxist historian, with his own schemas and insights, Hobsbawm's central focus has been the Europe of the nineteenth and twentieth centuries – matched by a zest for bandits. His edge is social – not political – as he brings out, say, the impact of economic trends through changing class constellations on taste and invention. His books have impressive titles – *Labouring Men* (1964), *Industry and Empire* (1968), *Revolutionaries* (1973) – and as with ☛Fernand Braudel on the sixteenth-century Mediterranean, a wealth of reference shoots through his texts: he is one of nature's cosmopolitans. Even so, his books are not, as Braudel's are, a dancing, kaleidoscopic vision; rooted in a world of work, he is a realist. Captured by the varied mysteries of evolving social forms, he possibly makes the past more complex than it is – he lacks ☛A. J. P. Taylor's flair for tight, set-piece narrative. Hobsbawm traces themes: he does not deploy a thesis.

Ho Chi Minh

(Nguyen That Thanh) 1890-1969

♥ VIETNAMESE POLITICAL LEADER

Ho was Vietnam's leader throughout its wars against the French and the Americans. In the final phase of his life, he acted merely as a symbol – a name for anti-war protesters in Europe and North America to brandish – and his death did not significantly alter North Vietnamese conduct of the war. Ho's family was already part of the anti-French movement in Indochina at the time of his birth. He travelled widely, working in a range of jobs – on a French liner, as a waiter in London, a hired labourer in Brooklyn, a cook in Le Havre (it is said that Escoffier told him he could become the greatest pastry cook of his time if only he gave up that silly political nonsense). His passions fired by the 1917 Russian Revolution, Ho vainly presented a demand for Vietnamese rights to the 1919 Versailles Peace Conference; he took part in the budding French Communist Party in the early 1920s, forming an Indochinese wing of the movement. As WW2 ended, he finally returned to Vietnam, sought US aid to establish a free state and announced a Democratic Republic in Hanoi. The French returned, having been displaced by the Japanese, and war followed until 1954. Ho became president of Communist North Vietnam in a time of division: Viet Cong resistance to the South's corrupt dictatorship led the North to become engaged in what turned into an anti-American war. Ho encouraged guerrilla attempts to control the countryside and strangle cities, sending teams into the villages in order to get his message across. He did not live to see Vietnamese reunification in 1975. Nationalism and Communism joined in his mind – there was no conflict: although his statements seem Maoist because of their peasant bias, Ho – mindful of the age-old antipathy between the Vietnamese and their immediate neighbours to the north – preferred Soviet help to Chinese. He fought the longest anti-colonial war of any twentieth-century revolutionary – and beat the most powerful nation on earth to a standstill.

David Hockney

born 1937

BRITISH ARTIST, BASED IN US

International acclaim came to this small mop-haired painter from Bradford while he was still a student at London's Royal College of Art. Partly through his colourful apparel and demeanour, he went on to become the modern art world's equivalent of ☛Elton John, engendering amusement and respect from people previously disinclined towards painting. Hockney's first major piece, *The Rake's Progress* (1963), was a series of 16 etchings (comparing his experiences in New York to those of Hogarth's profligate hero) that anticipated the colourful realism of his later work. Hockney was quick to challenge anyone who tried to co-opt him under the category of Pop Art; his originality and imagination displayed themselves in works of pictorial whimsy that owed little to trite celebrations of soda and candy or anything much else that has to do with the commercial culture that his contemporaries were busy embracing. During his first trip to Los Angeles (now his home) in the mid-1960s, he began a series of swimming pool pictures; culminating in *A Bigger Splash* (1967), they are notable for the dazzling effects of movement in still water. In the early 1980s, he temporarily abandoned painting in favour of photographic collages, but he has now returned to his position as the painter of good times and happy hedonism.

Dorothy Hodgkin born 1910

BRITISH CHEMIST

Winner of the 1964 Nobel prize for chemistry (only the third woman to be so honoured), Hodgkin's field was molecular biology, in which she specialized in crystalline structures. She began her career working on the X-ray diffraction of crystals of the digestive enzyme pepsin, and X-ray diffraction would become the core of much of her later work. Her most significant contribution was in determining the structure of the B_{12} molecule, a vitamin essential for the building of red blood cells and for treating pernicious anaemia. Having collected her first X-ray photographs of the vitamin in 1948, she pioneered the use of computers to carry out the necessary calculations and developed techniques to speed what was at the time an enormously slow process. Some idea of the complexity of the work can be deduced from the formula worked out for Vitamin B_{12} – $C_{63}H_{88}O_{14}N_{14}PCo$. Hodgkin also determined the structures of penicillin and insulin.

James Hoffa 1913-75

AMERICAN UNION LEADER

OFFICIALLY DECLARED DEAD IN 1982

The last nationally powerful union leader in the US, Hoffa was at the centre of a major scandal in America's labour movement in the 1960s. An ex-warehouseman, Hoffa was largely responsible for creating the International Brotherhood of Teamsters, a major trade union representing freight haulers. They were expelled from the umbrella union organization, the AFL-CIO, in 1957 – a move welcomed by Hoffa, who thought he could set up a rival force based on his union, which he ran on a Mafia-style basis. Robert Kennedy, Attorney-General under his brother, failed in an attempt to break his grip but, eventually, Hoffa was convicted of fraud, nobbling juries and looting union pension funds. He spent four years in jail before ☛Nixon commuted his term; he resigned as Teamsters' president in the same year, but then sought to regain control of the union. He disappeared from a Detroit restaurant where, it was said, he was due to meet two Mafiosi, and thus entered the American conspiracy consciousness alongside ☛John F. Kennedy and ☛Marilyn Monroe. The truth – that he was probably murdered by those who had taken his place in the union hierarchy – no longer really matters as much as the myth.

Abbie Hoffman 1936-89

AMERICAN POLITICAL ACTIVIST

'We Demand the Politics of Ecstasy! Rise Up and Abandon the Creeping Meatball!' With that and similar exhortations, Hoffman and anti-war activist Jerry Rubin sought to turn hippies into yippies (members of their Youth International Party) and divert a stampede to nowhere into radical political action. They were on to a loser. Just how difficult it was for Hoffman to make himself heard by the spaced-out inhabitants of the counterculture became apparent at Woodstock, when his appeal to raise funds for imprisoned activists was interrupted, and he was chased from the stage, by an acid-addled Pete Townshend of ☛The Who – who com

David Hockney
Photo: Jerry Sohn

plained that Hoffman was spoiling the fun. It was in pursuit of the yippie idea that you could make a revolution and still have fun that Hoffman applied his genius for comic subversion: he planted trees down the middle of Eighth Street in New York's East Village; organized the unloading of rubbish from the poverty-stricken Lower East Side on to the steps of the Lincoln Center during a garbage strike; and once nominated a pig to stand for the presidency against ☛Richard Nixon, pleading that his was a candidate you could at least eat. He was one of the 'Chicago Seven', radical leaders charged with conspiracy after the violent events of the 1968 Chicago Democratic Convention. Unlike several of his co-defendants, he went on getting himself arrested throughout the 1970s and 1980s, and performed his most impressive stunt when, while still on the FBI's most-wanted list, he met up with President Carter as the representative of an environmental action group.

Billie Holiday 1915-59

AMERICAN SINGER

'Angel of Harlem', 'Lady Day' – Billie Holiday has become a resting-home for clichés since her death, while her life – as played by Diana Ross in *Lady Sings the Blues*, Robyn Archer in *A Star Is Torn*, and various others – has been portrayed as a blueprint for 'The Woman Killed by Love'. Holiday's actual ability as a singer – the way she learned to use her voice, the way she wrote songs and created music – has been erased from the record to be replaced with a voice that is merely a vessel through which her pain and suffering flowed. The beauty of her songs – sad or otherwise, romantic or political – came as much from Holiday's talent as it did from her heart, from the sense of irony that could write 'Strange Fruit' as well as the amused resignation of 'Lady Sings the Blues'. She sang, at various times, with Benny Goodman, Count Basie, Lester Young and Ben Webster, and developed the crooning style of 1930s' swing into a taut, unpredictable simplicity all her own – no imitator even comes close to the weird, pared-down intelligence of her vocal style. A constant victim of racial prejudice and sexual abuse during her life on the road, she succumbed to drink and narcotics as an escape; even on her death bed, the New York police were unable to resist harassing her.

Buddy Holly
(Charles Holley) 1936-59

AMERICAN SINGER, MUSICIAN

Holly's music is the strongest contender for paternity of the modern pop song. Proficient in moving from gentle balladry and romance to raucous noise, he denied the separatism of the charts; and while only older listeners now remember the lyrics of songs such as 'Peggy Sue' (1957) with awed affection, the entire world can appreciate Holly's gift for marrying voice, melody and lyric to immense effect in early pop melancholy such as 'It Doesn't Matter Any More' (1959). He gave pop music subtlety, while avoiding the route back down Tin Pan Alley. Dying along with Richie 'La Bamba' Valens and the Big Bopper in a plane crash, he became the first posthumously marketed star; more recently he suffered the further indignity of pop canonization, when Paul McCartney not only bought the publishing rights to his songs but set up an unnecessary 'Buddy Holly Day' in his memory.

Jenny Holzer

born 1950

AMERICAN ARTIST

Holzer's work can be seen flashing across illuminated advertising boards, printed on baseball caps or available free in the form of stickers. Whatever the city's communications network, Holzer uses it to distribute her witty and inflammatory texts to the general public. *Truisms*, her first series of texts – containing the declarations AN ELITE IS INEVITABLE and MONEY CREATES TASTE – were flyposted around Manhattan in the late 1970s. More recently she has introduced a sophisticated combination of electronic message boards that dance her one-liners back and forth on street corners, as well as more gallery-based installation work where a crypt-like chamber is filled with neat slabs of concrete that have been engraved with her texts, kindling a sense of the apocalyptic and profane in an atmosphere of almost religious sanctity. It is still debatable, though, whether Holzer is anything more than an accomplished soapbox ranter who has swapped her wooden crate for an advertising board. Perhaps she had better take heed of her own words: IF YOU'RE CONSIDERED USELESS NO ONE WILL FEED YOU ANYMORE.

Tobe Hooper

born 1943

☞ AMERICAN FILM DIRECTOR

Landing himself in a cult limbo with his ferocious horror movie *The Texas Chainsaw Massacre* (1974), Hooper has never again been able to do anything else as striking. Evoking Z-movie cannibalism, the film pillaged freely from the American idiom of deranged-hick-murderer-as-folklore and was responsible for a vast output of nihilistic and brutal horror movies. *Chainsaw* revels in the humorous slaughter that ensues when five young Texans collide with a psychotic family who murder tourists and turn them into tasty comestibles. Hooper claims he was influenced by ☛Hitchcock, but he owes more than he might readily admit to obscure splatter veteran Herschel Gordon Lewis, who himself was similarly unconscious of the possibilities for social subtext latent in the genre. Hooper's subsequent cinematic forays include *The Funhouse* (1981), *Poltergeist* (1982) and *Lifeforce* (1985).

J. Edgar Hoover

1895-1972

✚ AMERICAN BUREAUCRAT, POLITICIAN

As director of the Federal Bureau of Investigation for 48 years, Hoover became an icon of American culture. To his admirers, he was a manly law enforcer; to his critics, a despot who blackmailed presidents and politicians, persecuted anyone with leftist political views, harassed blacks and undermined civil liberties whenever he had a chance. Always a fanatical Red-baiter, he was the first to suggest that there was something 'un-American' about Communism, and was largely responsible for the post-war anti-Communist hysteria. The American Communist Party was always tiny, but in 1956, Hoover set up a campaign of dirty tricks, involving sexual blackmail and disinformation, to destroy it. His real allegiance was to the organization he ran and sustained largely by fanning the paranoia of incoming presidents – providing fantasies about their enemies (everyone) at the same time as he let them know what he knew about their murky pasts. So obsessed did he become with his own survival that he was reluctant to admit the existence of organized crime or deal with drug traffickers: he wanted to keep the FBI small, and under his exclusive control.

Dennis Hopper

born 1935

AMERICAN FILM DIRECTOR, ACTOR

In *Easy Rider* (1969), the favoured parable for America's disaffected youth in the late 1960s – for which he was director and co-star – Hopper's hawk-like eyes and truculent demeanour expressed incipient hostility to the social hierarchy. The film, a phenomenal success, drew primarily from ☛Jack Kerouac's warped mythology of an American odyssey, populated with volatile rednecks anxious to persecute, deride and finally destroy the two good-guy riders. Its box-office receipts were parlayed into underground mainstream credibility, which Hopper then gambled away with his follow-up, *The Last Movie* (1971), a semi-autobiographical avant-garde exercise in drug-induced paranoia and indulgence which equated the making of a movie with capitalist destruction of Third World cultures. He escaped for a time into violence, narcotics and general sloth but, following a return to sobriety, was seen in ☛Wim Wenders' *The American Friend* (1977) and in a series of cameos of the mid-1980s as an anarchic, unrestrained icon of dementia, culminating in 1986 in a performance of stunning ferocity as the schizoid potentate of *Blue Velvet*'s underworld – which was counterpointed by his gentle, ageing, drunken basketball groupie in the same year's *Hoosiers* (aka *Best Shot*). He also made a directorial comeback in 1988 with gang-war drama *Colors*, by which time even *The Last Movie* had gained cult adherents.

L.Ron Hubbard

1911-86

☆ AMERICAN WRITER, CULTIST

Hubbard's 'church' of Scientology – based round his 'science' of Dianetics – is still winning converts, and is powerful enough to survive all the hostility it runs into. And for a while, its founder lived like a man-god, cruising the Mediterranean in a converted ocean liner, waited on by adoring teenage bimbos, while his pulp blockbusters outsold all others by huge margins. But by the time he died, he was on the run, his family torn apart by his paranoias, his son L. Ron Jnr denouncing him as a satanist, his once-colourful galactic buccaneer's con-trick of a religion run by sinister and ruthless drones. Dianetics was hatched in the late 1940s by this easily bored, talented SF writer, fedup at not getting on in a gullible and mediocre world. His artfully oversimplified mélange of psychoanalysis, hypnosis, future-tech humbug and Crowleyan adept-control (he had spent some time with a black magic sect in California) hinged on a pragmatically mass-marketable technique – 'auditing' – to cleanse the mind of 'engrams' (the blocks to total memory recall which, he claimed, caused most mental and physical maladies, from depression to asthma). It evolved into a full-blown religion packed with baffling pseudoscientific silliness, held together by Hubbard's own forceful imagination. In 1967, increasingly obsessed with abortion, homosexuality, buried treasure, smells, treachery, the 'evil that is woman' and – most pertinently – the unfriendly attentions of very many governments, he moved the labyrinthine core of his operation aboard a private navy. But the decade-long trials of the fabled Sea Org – meant to signal a new dawn for humanity –

turned Hubbard from an engaging charlatan into a senile megalomaniac; he returned to land, set up his own movie industry and succeeded in penetrating the IRS, the FBI and the CIA. They hit back forcefully: his wife went to jail and he into hiding where he died – no longer capable of distinguishing between fact and fantasy, his own most dramatic victim.

David Hubel born 1926

AMERICAN NEURO-BIOLOGIST

Torsten Wiesel born 1924

SWEDISH NEURO-PHYSIOLOGIST

Although the brain all looks the same, different regions do different jobs. For some time, only large-scale differences could be established, such as those between the different lobes. Working together at Harvard from 1959, Hubel and Wiesel found, by 'interviewing' the electrical output of single neurones in the visual cortex at the back of the head, that each neurone was only active if the animal experimented upon could see specific visual stimuli – mainly lines oriented at particular angles. Adjacent cells across the cortex were sensitive to oriented lines which progressed clockwise. There were also strips responding to stimuli in the left or right halves of the visual field. For the first time, the detailed organization of the brain seemed open to investigation. As their work progressed, they found cells that responded to more complex shapes and started to build circuit diagrams of the visual system. This helped computer scientists who thought that, since they were having no luck designing machines that could recognize things, perhaps they could learn from how the brain did it. Out of this came the constructivist model of the brain: the idea that different types of information are parcelled out to specialized systems and only subsequently recombined. In the visual system, different regions of the brain have since been found to handle colour, motion, stereoscopic vision and even faces (the fabled 'grandmother cells'). Recent complexities have muddied the beautifully clear picture that Hubel and Wiesel first developed, but they received a Nobel prize anyway.

John Hubley 1914-77

AMERICAN ANIMATOR

The cartoon industry and its innovators were mesmerized by the angular jazz modernism of Hubley's first cartoons for United Productions of America. Hubley had formed UPA in the 1950s as a company to house those toon industry workers who had been sacked following the notorious and angry Disney studio strike of the 1940s. He simplified lines, stylized backgrounds, and produced knobby little figures who demanded far less time-consuming in-between work: Gerald McBoing Boing, early Mr Magoo, as well as the characters in *Rooty Toot Toot* and *Oh My Darling Clementine*. His designs may well have helped those modern art luminaries they parodied and celebrated (Modigliani, Bonnard, even Picasso) to secure mass appreciation. In 1952 he fell out with UPA and formed Storyboard Inc. for his own artistic projects, including *Eggs* (1969) and *Voyage to Next* (1970), in collaboration with jazz-arranger Quincy Jones (who would go on to work with ☛Michael Jackson). Meanwhile, his simplifications were seized on by studios desperate to meet the challenge of television and, in no time at all, had degenerated into a jerkily arid cartoon hell, far from anything Hubley ever envisaged.

Howard Hughes 1905-76

AMERICAN BUSINESS TYCOON

Howard Hughes has become a byword for eccentricity of the obsessive, paranoid kind. Inheriting a sizeable fortune and a terror of heart disease from his father, it was his passion for aviation and movies that originally kept him in the public eye. He built the *Spruce Goose*, the largest and most useless plane ever constructed, and grounded it after a single brief flight (with himself at the controls); bought RKO Studios and ran it into the ground while attempting to screw or marry every female under contract; filmed a Genghis Khan epic *The Conqueror* (1955) on atomic test sites with the result that half the cast and crew, including ☛John Wayne, developed terminal cancer; and became a virulent anti-Communist, tapping the phones of all his employees to check for subversive behaviour. After a near fatal plane crash, he began to withdraw from day-to-day affairs, becoming more reclusive in the belief that contact with others would aggravate his heart condition (though many of his ex-wives doubted there was anything there to aggravate), until he disappeared into the penthouse of one of his hotels and into myth. There he saw no one apart from a few trusted Mormon aides who had to walk on the fresh toilet paper Hughes put his faith in, and handle everything with surgical gloves. His death caught everyone by surprise – many thought he had been long gone – and the first glimpse of the unkempt, long-haired figure with talon-like fingernails caught the imagination of a public that had forgotten him. Myths grew up overnight, alongside conspiracy theories and fights over his fortune (most notably that of Melvin Dummar, who claimed to have given a lift to Hughes under the impression that he was a tramp and was named as an heir in one of the wills that was produced, a story that was memorably filmed as *Melvin and Howard*, 1980). A pioneer who swept along the margins of American history without actually producing anything of value, Hughes took an epic journey from the role of Lindbergh-like idealist to monstrous tyrant to pathetic figure so afraid of death that he did not dare to live.

Langston Hughes 1902-67

AMERICAN POET

A leading figure in the Harlem Renaissance of the 1920s, this fanatically reserved African-American carried on his quiet war on racism and ignorance right through the zenith of the Black Power era. Isolated and, paradoxically, influential (regarded as seminal by the *négritude* movement), he built the language of black urban folk tales into a universal myth-making, invoking Africa, the Blues, and the great move from South to North in a poetry that is resonant, but also curiously impersonal, so that Hughes himself is someone we learn little about. A committed radical, for all his reserve, he was investigated by the House Un-American Activities Committee, and thereafter withdrew almost entirely into himself, making little alliance with succeeding generations of black writers or activists.

Ted Hughes

born 1930

∀ BRITISH POET

A Poet Laureate who is noted for sometimes seeming less than enthusiastic about rising to the royal occasion, Hughes looks to the natural world for metaphors to explore the inner drives and repressed fears of men. His red-blooded, sometimes simplistic, verse is collected under such titles as *The Hawk in the Rain* (1957), *Lupercal* (1960) and *Crow* (1970). For Hughes, a jaguar's magnificence is limited by the lack of soul that condemns it to exist only in the present until it becomes no more than a poundage of flesh and fat. Yet these beasts link us to a reality we deny through our aspirations to immortality: having lost all earthly love and glory, Hughes's Cleopatra says to the asp, 'I seek myself in a serpent.' More than just a link to this primal world of life and death, the serpent is also the true creator of the world – its gifts of evil and doubt are the ashes of Eden on which the world of lies, shadows and sorrows in which we live has been built. Even God, as in 'Logos', is dependent on the lower creatures to find his own answer and vindication in this spiral of despair, able only to conceive a son through man, who will not see the answer or hear the vindication. Married to ☛Sylvia Plath in 1956, he produced some of his blackest poems in the years after her death.

Barbara Hulanicki

born 1938

POLISH-BRITISH DESIGNER, BUSINESS EXECUTIVE, BASED IN US

Quitting Palestine at the age of 12, after her father had been assasinated by Irgun terrorists, Hulanicki acquired some of her distinctive aesthetic from the exotic aunt with whom her family lodged in London. When the innovative fervours of the 1960s began to wane, the first stopping point for those on the big retreat was a replay of the fashions associated with the 1920s and 1930s. After several years of designing cheap mail-order dresses, the success of a pink gingham number inspired Hulanicki and her husband, Stephen FitzSimon, to set up their first Biba shop in 1963; by the end of the decade, it had expanded to department-store size, following their take-over of the Derry and Toms building in High Street, Kensington. Everything they sold, whether furniture, make-up or clothes, reflected a camp sensibility that revelled in dark colours and slinky materials. The time for such super-sophisticated decadence was short, however, and the shop ceased trading in 1975, just in time to prevent its customers being laughed off the streets by the punk hordes. After a brief sojourn in Brazil, the FitzSimons settled in Miami Beach, where she designs clubs and recently wrote a novel, *Disgrace*, with a 1960s' London setting.

The Human League

formed 1977

Phil Oakey born 1955

Philip Adrian Wright born 1955

BRITISH POP GROUP

The Human League virtually defined pop music in the 1980s. They started as a fairly representative British would-be art synthesizer band with a certain self-deprecating humour and a quite advanced sense of kitsch: their instrumental EP *The Dignity of Labour* sported Nazis on the sleeve, which were coupled in live shows with slides of *Star Trek* and *Thunderbirds*. Minor critical and zero chart success led to the band's split in

1981. Survivors Phil Oakey (vocals and historic haircut) and Adrian Wright (slides and tack) went on to recruit teen female vocalists Joanne Catherall and Susanne Sulley and, with the glossiest production then available, they took on conceptually impeccable pop ideas and the charts. The new line-up's début LP *Dare* (1981) combines sexual tension and European dance melody (borrowed from Abba), 1960s' television and film kitsch obsessiveness (predating the late 1980s' fixation with trash television, comics and films), and the first proudly commercial use of all-electronic music; and it remains, along with ABC's *Lexicon of Love*, the nearest to a perfect realization of a conceptual pop record ever produced.

Nelson Bunker Hunt born 1926

✌ AMERICAN BUSINESSMAN

The son of a Texas oil billionaire, Hunt made headlines in 1980 as his bid to corner the market in silver futures collapsed in fiasco. From 1973 to 1980, following Libya's confiscation of his vast oil holding, he built up a stake until he held one-third of the world's silver – about $3 billion in cash terms – and tried to control the international price. Then new federal rules introduced a bias against such 'long' speculations. Panic swept the US stock and commodity exchanges: Hunt failed to pay up as his contractors demanded. He and his brother Herbert were forced to borrow $1.1 billion, and with his third brother Lamar, he filed for his oil firm's bankruptcy in 1986. He spent the rest of the decade selling off everything from oil wells and racehorses to his coin collection and a bargain-store teapot in an attempt to appease the tax man and aggrieved investors. He laughs a lot and is said to be amiable. Even so, he was active in the neo-Fascist John Birch Society and backs fundamentalist Christian groups. He winds rubber bands round his hands – his substitute for tobacco or alcohol – and he adores American football.

Hussein ibn Talal born 1935

KING OF JORDAN

King Hussein has been, for most of his reign, a vaguely benevolent despot in an artificial state containing an alien Palestinian majority. Defence spending has figured strongly in his budget: in 1967, he participated in an Egyptian-led war against Israel, which he lost (Israel took Jordan's West Bank); in 1970, he fought and won a civil war against the PLO. Smooth in manner, currently married to an American, and Sandhurst-trained, he is a minor hero to the British (despite his ejection of Glubb Pasha, the British officer who ran his army, in 1956). News programmes on Jordanian television feature him with an unintentionally comic constancy. However, he is an unpredictable figure, hemmed in by pressures: he gave signals to Israel that he would welcome peace, taking back the West Bank into a federation; in late 1988, he turned publicly against that option. And in 1990 he alienated European and American allies by refusing to take a vociferous stand against Saddam Hussein after the Iraqi leader's invasion of Kuwait – the caution was understandable given the strength of feeling among Jordan's poor against the oil-rich emirs whom Saddam had ejected. King Hussein remains a moderate force on the Middle East scene, in a royal version of what looks, however, very like a banana republic.

Saddam Hussein (Takriti)

❍ IRAQI RULER born 1935

⇔ The alliance which drove Hussein out of Kuwait in early 1991 included most of the governments responsible for creating his monstrous military might. Having risen to the top through assassinations, Hussein initiated a war with Iran in 1980 that eventually claimed a million lives and ruined 50 towns and cities. Western powers, anxious to counter the mullahs in Iran, supplied him with all the modern weaponry he could pay for. Once a peace had been brokered by the West, he deployed cyanide gas and bullets against the country's Kurdish minority, while developing a nuclear capacity aimed at Israel. Nevertheless, western arms companies still received government sanction to sell their lethal equipment to Iraq. The American-led alliance demolished the country's infrastructure and killed tens of thousands without loosening Hussein's grip on power or weakening his capacity to liquidate dissidents.

John Huston 1906-87

AMERICAN FILM DIRECTOR

Huston was a solid, unspectacular director who made his first film *The Maltese Falcon* in 1941, and by the end of the decade had become one of the most highly regarded American film-makers of his generation. He had written the screenplay for *High Sierra* (1941), which gave Humphrey Bogart one of his first major roles, leading to an ongoing relationship between Huston and the archetypal tough guy. Never one to toe the Hollywood line, he maintained his stubborn insistence on going his own way right to the end. Among many memorable pictures, he turned in such classics as *The Treasure of the Sierra Madre* (1948), about three gold prospectors disastrously driven by greed, and *Key Largo* (1948), notable for its sense of darkness and disillusion breeding in the heat of an approaching hurricane, as well as such portentous turkeys as *Moulin Rouge* (1952) and *The Bible* (1966). He gave striking acting performances in *Chinatown* (1974) and *Winter Kills* (1979), the latter written by ☛Richard Condon from his conspiracy thriller based on the Kennedy clan in which Huston played the unscrupulous head of the dynasty. Towards the end of his career, he completed a series of literary adaptations, including a 1979 version of Flannery O'Connor's novel *Wise Blood* (about religious extremism in the Deep South) and a version of Joyce's melancholy short story, *The Dead* (1987).

Aldous Huxley 1894-1963

BRITISH NOVELIST

Most of Huxley's pre-war novels inhabit the outskirts of modernism, doing little more than reflecting the bitter flatness of English smart society at the time. Huxley took the world to be as worthless as he felt himself to be: out of this grating despair, *Brave New World* (1932) builds a frightening dystopia around a future of generated satisfaction. Still much praised, the novel's world seems to resemble today less than any of Swift's scabrous satires, to which it is often compared. ☛Orwell thought the repressive agents of control of the future would be jackbooted militarists; Huxley believed that giving people what they want – 'the feelies' – would keep them tranquil more effectively than truncheons. Other Huxleys (brother Julian the biologist, grandfather Thomas the evolutionist) had made bright, positive contributions to science and our social well-being; perhaps feeling his own had so far been rather negative, Huxley began to experiment with hallucinogens in the mid-1950s, using his experiences with mescalin and LSD as the subjects of *The Doors of Perception* (1954) and *Heaven and Hell* (1956). A first step quickly superseded, these experiments led eventually to an upsurge of interest in hallucinatory drugs which continued into the 1960s.

I

Lee Iacocca

(Lido Iacocca) born 1924

❞ AMERICAN BUSINESS EXECUTIVE

$ Son of Italian immigrants, Iacocca personifies the American dream. A student of engineering, he turned to marketing, design and promotion after he joined Ford in 1946, where his successful models included the Mustang and the Fiesta. He became president of the firm in 1970. Personal tensions with Henry Ford II developed when Iacocca was made subordinate to an ex-General Motors man. He left in 1978, moving sideways and, in a sense, downwards, to run Chrysler, where he achieved a stupendous turnaround within four years. The company had been in bad shape, but through redundancies, rationalizations and a harsh negotiating stance with the unions (plus an aid package from Congress and some good design ideas from former Ford man Harold Sperlich), Iacocca turned a $1.7 billion loss for 1980 into 1984's $2.4 billion profit. He figured in the company's TV commercials and became a celebrity, opting to write his recipe for happiness in the bestsellers *Iacocca* (1984) and *Talking Straight* (1988), which celebrated hard work and loyalty to the US, hearth and home. Advocating such sentiments and sporting sideburns, big cigars, shiny cuff-links and a younger second wife, he was once even tipped as a presidential candidate. However, when Chrysler started making serious losses at the 1980s, it became apparent that Iacocca had not been following his own advice. Instead of attending to 'people, product and profits', he had been making big deals. With Japanese manufacturers stepping up their operations in the US, most commentators doubted whether Iacocca could again pull off a spectacular rescue.

Ivan Illich

born 1926

▲ AUSTRIAN SOCIAL CRITIC, BASED IN MEXICO

A polymath and anarchist, Illich has been a theology student in Rome, a history student in Salzburg, a priest in New York and a university administrator in Puerto Rico. He hit on his personal pitch while head of a Mexican think-tank, attacking society's received ideas on, *inter alia*, education, health and transport. His targets are the professions and the way they dispense their 'secret', expert knowledge. Illich focuses on how institutional structures can operate in such a way as actually to negate their intentions. Motorways aim to facilitate communication, but drive wedges between neighbours. Educational institutions fail to let learners teach themselves and each other, and do not foster challenges to society's ideas. Although Illich's provocative approach poses useful questions, his ideas can become vastly over-simplified conspiracy theories. His advice is sometimes better suited to Latin America than elsewhere. Western, affluent, industrial society has a greater need of standardized programming by institutions, say, in schools and hospitals; otherwise it would reject its base economic forms. Professions need to be kept in check, but it is a big step to conclude that the very idea of expert knowledge can be thrown out.

Eugene Ionesco born 1912

RUMANIAN-FRENCH PLAYWRIGHT

In his short plays of the 1950s, Ionesco takes a series of illogical ideas and stretches them to their ultimate logical extent. *The Chairs* (1952), for example, features two ancients who fill a room with chairs as if they are real people, thus depicting a world that has lost meaning and is truly absurd. Sensing a lack of audience involvement in his first full-length play, he created a comic hero – well-meaning but ultimately ineffective – for such later works as *The Killer* (1957) and the classic *Rhinoceros* (1960). The latter, with its tale of a man's refusal to believe the evidence of his own eyes (that people everywhere are turning into rhinoceroses) was an international success. However, despite the worldwide recognition that Ionesco received, audiences were more attuned to the farce-like comedic aspects of his plays than their serious themes, and such 1970s' pieces as *MacBett* (an individualistic reworking of Shakespeare) and *The Mire* (a groundbreaking montage of speech, image and sound) were received unenthusiastically.

No society has been able to abolish human sadness, no political system can deliver us from the pain of living, from our fear of death, our thirst for the absolute; it is the human condition that directs our social condition, not vice versa.

Eugene Ionescu

Alec Issigonis 1906-90

♦ BRITISH DESIGNER

Issigonis was hailed as one of the few British design geniuses of post-war industry. However, although the two cars he is best known for stand out as having character – the Morris Minor has become a quaint status symbol for young fogies, and the Mini has proved almost impossible to displace from the production line – it is difficult to see them as really important designs. For the Mini, initiated in the days of post-Suez fuel rationing and launched in 1959, Issigonis's most influential innovation was to mount the engine transversely across the car rather than have the cylinders in line, thus shortening the bonnet and allowing the design of much smaller town cars. Many manufacturers took up this brilliant idea, but none of them made cars that looked anything like the Mini. The rubber suspension damping system, which was the other innovation in the original design was eventually replaced by a more conventional arrangement. Issigonis really stands as a representative of the distressing tradition of British innovation: he had brilliant ideas, but through lack of support, negligible managerial foresight and, eventually, plain lack of capital, the industry he worked within never fully profited from his

Ivan Illich
Photo: Beverly Hall

brilliance. And Issigonis himself failed to adapt to changing tastes in car design. While most of the popular small cars in Europe have transversely mounted engines, it is Volkswagen, Fiat, Peugeot and Renault which sell most of them.

J

George Jackson 1943-71

➳ AMERICAN POLITICAL ACTIVIST

✌ A hero of the movement for black political rights in the US, Jackson died in jail after serving 11 years of a one-year-to-life sentence for petty theft. Largely uneducated when he entered prison, he devoted himself to intensive reading and developed the argument that the US was a Fascist state. His prison diaries, published as *Soledad Brother* (1971), reinforced black, radical and young people's negative perceptions of white law, white politics and a largely white-controlled political system. Jackson's case was taken up by ☛Angela Davis after he and two others were charged with killing a prison officer in Soledad prison. Jackson, being considered a 'lifer', could have been sent to the gas chamber simply for having assaulted the guard: he died on the day before his trial was due to begin, encouraging suspicions that he had been murdered. Ironically, his two co-defendants were later acquitted. His posthumously published *Blood in My Eye* (1972) was effectively a manifesto calling for civil war in the US; his death led to bomb explosions in the San Francisco area and the killing of a policeman.

Every time I hear the word 'law', I visualize gangs of militiamen or Pinkertons busting strikes, pigs wearing sheets and caps that fit over their pointed heads. I see a white oak and a barefooted black is hanging.

George Jackson, Blood in my Eye

Jesse Jackson born 1941

AMERICAN PREACHER, POLITICIAN

A one-time aide of ☛Martin Luther King, Jackson has become his *de facto* heir and the focus of all disenfranchised hope and semi-left rhetoric within the American system: no one else with any significant profile offers a programme so critical of mainstream politics. Born into a poor family in the Deep South, he joined the civil rights movement while at college, running 'Operation Breadbasket' for King – a project to persuade firms to employ more blacks. After King's murder – and a certain amount of controversy over Jackson's behaviour at this time – he formed PUSH, People United to Save Humanity, a black self-help organization. He became a Baptist minister, and has used his talents as a preacher to develop into the most charismatic speaker in US politics. In 1984 and 1988, he campaigned to secure nomination as the Democratic Party candidate for president, in each case galvanizing large sectors of the black and Hispanic community to register, only to be passed over; his

'Rainbow Coalition' was regarded as a liability and a vote-loser by the party elders, who twice allowed the party to pick faceless drones (first Walter Mondale, then Michael Dukakis) to run against ☛Reagan. But as non-whites, especially Hispanics, loom larger in a changing electorate, Jackson is now indispensable to the Democratic Party, if it is to win the presidency. He has been strongly attacked for his links with Louis Farrakhan, leader of the Nation of Islam, a separatist organization widely regarded as anti-Semitic. Jackson is trapped within the bankruptcy of the two-party system in America; but because he is intermittently willing to move outside its dictatorial consensus – for example, on the Palestinian question – he is unlikely ever to be given the opportunity to alter it. Meanwhile, as Hispanic and black confidence in the Democratic Party ebbs, the bigotry that he battled against with King in the 1960s is once again on the march.

Michael Jackson born 1958

❍ AMERICAN PERFORMER

Virtually born on stage, Jackson became the dominant voice in the Jackson Five, the classic late 1960s' vocal pop group. Their singles took advantage of the performer's youth to bring pre-pubescent vigour to songs also enhanced by his prematurely adult voice and energy. Moderate early-1970s' success was transformed at the end of the decade by the immense sales of Jackson's solo album, *Off the Wall* (1979). His reputed personal strangeness began to emerge at this stage, and by the time of the even more successful *Thriller* (1982), he was a myth in his own right. An alleged plastic surgery fetish, his preference for the company of children and animals to that of normal society and a growing list of reputed weird habits – bathing in Perrier, sleeping in an oxygen tent, trying to buy the corpse of the Elephant Man – culminated in the *Sun* newspaper's headline which summarized world speculation: 'IS JACKO WACKO'. Jackson's off-stage inaccessibility and on-stage brilliance – despite his permanent pre-pubescence, he is a superbly sexual dancer and adult singer – have sustained records of somewhat intermittent brilliance. Recently, videos playing with the Jackson mythology, involvement with massive commercial sponsorship and a brilliant business sense have begun to suggest that Jackson's *persona* of Walt Disney mind in Howard Hughes' bedroom is merely part of a PR strategy designed to make his admittedly great talent appear almost other-worldly. The idea that Michael Jackson may be just another talented rock singer with an image department is probably the most shocking of all.

Roman Jakobson 1896-1982

SOVIET-AMERICAN LINGUISTIC THEORIST

A leading theorist in the Prague School of linguistic theory, Jakobson became as important an influence on structuralist and post-structuralist thought as the school's great forerunner Ferdinand de Saussure, through the brilliant articulation of a single central theme: binary oppositions. It was his introduction of a framework for a flexible and attentive study of poetic language that caught the attention of critics such as ☛Roland Barthes and ☛Julia Kristeva. Jakobson, a contemporary of Mayakovsky and associated with the Russian Formalists, brought to light the operation of such rhetorical devices as elision, metaphor (one sign *substituted* for another) and metonymy (one sign *associated* with another). This last pair, whose binary opposition was first examined in his 1956 article 'Two Aspects of Language and Two Types of Aphasic Disturbances', and the supposed preference for metaphor over metonymy in poetic discourse, would become a basic – if abstruse – point of debate for Jakobson, and ultimately for the rogue psychoanalyst ☛Jacques Lacan, literary theorists such as ☛Paul de Man and a whole generation of *cinéastes*.

C(yril) L(ionel) R(obert) James

1901-89

✌ TRINIDADIAN HISTORIAN, WHO SETTLED IN UK

Born and educated in Trinidad, James's understanding of the syncretic cultural genius of the Caribbean brought vital new resources to exhausted First World Marxism. An early theorist of Trotskyism, he broke with the Socialist Workers Party in the 1940s when he realized that the nascent black independence movements were more politically advanced than the labour movement, and that similar roles for women and youth should also be developed. His earlier close associations with many of the post-independence African leaders, particularly Ghana's ☛Nkrumah, did not prevent him from being fiercely critical of their errors. Indeed, his acute mind and willingness to comment adversely left him somewhat isolated in old age, with no regimes living up to his severe, humanitarian-Marxist standards (although most important African-Caribbean and African-American cultural and aesthetic theorists are in his debt). His study of Toussaint L'Ouverture's slave revolution in Haiti, *The Black Jacobins* (1938), is one of the great works of radical history. A cricket fanatic and keen student of literature, he published many insightful articles on both. Living out his exile in London's Brixton, he saw and heard more in the world than most people a quarter his age.

Tove Jansson

born 1914

FINNISH WRITER, ILLUSTRATOR

Translating an ancient Finno-Ugric pantheon of animist cupboard-monsters into a modern child's quizzical, low-angle world-view, Jansson's *Moominvalley* stories have become internationally famous, probably as much for the illustrations as for her elusively magical imagination. With roots in theatre (she has a second career as a scene-painter and set-designer), Jansson demonstrates a genius for small-scale artistry. While it would be unwise to inflate her achievements beyond those she aims for, yet within a narrow, cosy framework – her stories centre round a happy, if eccentric, extended family of fat furry trolls – she can present a known world suddenly and subtly altered: the Moomintrolls experience dramatic summer floods; a comfortably hibernating Moomintroll wakes up by mistake in mid-winter, to confront a terrible parallel world of ice and snow. From her first book, *Comet in Moominland* (1946), to her most recent, *Moominvalley in November* (1971), she conjures a sense of dread in apparently jolly surroundings that is likely to stay with readers for many years.

Víctor Jara 1933-73

➳CHILEAN FOLK MUSICIAN

✌ Jara's highly charged songs spread radical protests against injustice as he became the focal point of Chile's 'new song' movement of the mid-1960s, initiated by folk singers Angel and Isabel Parra. A student scholar from a poor rural background, he had been theatre director at the Technical University in Santiago, putting on plays by Gorky and Brecht and touring the rest of Latin America. He turned, in the late 1960s, to music as a popular vehicle for protest themes, and home-grown melodies from the towns and villages gave his songs a native, Chilean air. His 'Venceremos' was taken up as the campaign anthem for ☛Salvador Allende's *Unidad Popular* during the 1970 elections, and he was tortured and killed after the military coup that toppled Allende in 1973. His murder contributed to the spread of hostility to the Pinochet regime in young, left-wing and student circles in the 1970s.

Derek Jarman born 1942

BRITISH FILM-MAKER, PAINTER

▲ If Jarman had never existed, the British film industry would have lacked the imagination to invent him. Trained as a painter, he looked for inspiration to the films of ☛Pasolini, with whom he shares a homosexual outlook, and to the ☛Warhol school of making films from the things and people that surround the film-maker. In 1976, the people around Jarman were minor stars of the early punk movement – Jordan, Siouxsie Sioux, Adam Ant – and the film he made with them, *Jubilee* (1978), is still his most intriguing. It is not so much a document of the time as an attempt to create a visionary fiction out of it. Buried beneath the nihilism of its surface ('Turn up the music, that way we won't hear the world falling apart') is a very English romanticism, which was further explored in his version of Shakespeare's *The Tempest*. His 1986 film *The Last of England* is a *Jubilee* for bleaker times, while the themes of death, loss of innocence and Englishness are explored in *War Requiem* (1989). Jarman himself, his own most cheerful critic, admits that some of his best work appears in pop videos.

Charles Jencks born 1939

& AMERICAN ARCHITECTURAL CRITIC BASED IN UK

Jencks' prolific writings are an extended celebration of the protracted dying of modern architecture, a finale which he suggests began with the 1972 demolition of the Pruitt-Igoe housing estate in St Louis, Missouri – a planned utopia which rapidly became a slum. He believes that pluralism leads to buildings that are popular because they can be easily 'understood', but it is not clear if 'radical eclecticism' does actually result in constructions any less 'obscure' than their 'modern' predecessors. Jencks' polemical stance makes him overly dismissive of the work of ☛Mies van der Rohe and ☛Le Corbusier; his portrayal of modern architecture as essentially meaningless and traditionless is a caricature, and it is not clear where he draws the line between kitsch and post-modernism. The distinctions he draws in classifying contemporary architects are often barely discernible to anyone but himself – they are certainly arguable – and his writings never convey any sense of the socio-political context from which the buildings he describes have evolved. It is doubtful, therefore, whether his work has significantly clarified the issues involved in current debates on architecture.

Arthur Jensen

born 1923

AMERICAN PSYCHOLOGIST

Jensen has been a notorious figure since a 1969 article in which he claimed that the generally lower IQs of American blacks should be attributed to genetics rather than social conditioning, and that progressive educational strategies were therefore doomed to failure. Studying with the equally controversial British psychologist, ☛Hans Eysenck, Jensen acquired from him an interest in the determinants of different behaviour patterns, and an obsession with quantitative and experimental research into personality types. All the same, the steps along the road to his conclusion were pretty dodgy ones. He claimed that his tests on children from minority groups were 'culture-free', and he worked from a conviction that 80 per cent of an individual's intelligence attainment could be explained by genetic factors. Jensen's evident puzzlement at the angry response to his paper – he was labelled a Fascist and his effigy was burned on university campuses – indicated the limitations of the laboratory-oriented research that had led him to develop his shattering thesis on such flimsy evidence. In any case, what educational policy conclusions could you legitimately draw from Jensen's thesis, given that some blacks secure the same high scores as the brightest whites? In the end, whether you commit yourself to nature or nurture, it is a fact that some pupils learn faster than others, and that all respond to good teaching.

Jiang Quing

1914-91

CHINESE ACTRESS, POLITICIAN

†

As ☛Mao's wife, Jiang Quing triggered the Cultural Revolution of the mid-to-late 1960s, but later, after his death, she was convicted of 'counter-revolutionary' crimes and gaoled. A former actress, she sponsored ballet at the Peking Opera, and insisted on injecting traditional themes with workers' concerns, a move that led to the cult of peasant values that swept through China. Students were forced to work on the land; 'bourgeois deviants' were persecuted. Jiang reached the apex of her influence in 1966, but her role waned as trends shifted. She re-emerged in 1974 to recommend a new shift – 'settling down', Mao's line. When he died two years later, the radicals were isolated, and wall posters, previously a technique of the Revolution, began to attack her. She and others in the 'Gang of Four', the name given to the left-wing faction in the Politburo, were subsequently arrested. Jiang was tried, ostensibly for whipping up civil unrest in the late 1960s. She fiercely defended herself, denouncing the court and Mao's successors. A death sentence was commuted to life imprisonment. With hindsight, it is hard to discern how much she was being used – first by Mao, then by those who wished to attack his policies through her. History is rarely kind to the surviving wives of strong leaders.

Steve Jobs born 1955
Steve Wozniak born 1950

○ ♦ $

AMERICAN ENTREPRENEURS

For a time, Jobs and Wozniak were the heroes of the enterprise culture, the sunrise kids just out of college who built computers in a garage and set up a company that became, within six years, one of the biggest in the US and a challenger to IBM's monolithic dominance. 'Woz' was the technical wizard, Jobs the visionary who saw the potential of their hi-tech invention; the name Apple was to symbolize the simplicity they sought. When IBM started to move in on the market, Jobs and Wozniak came up with the Macintosh, named after the reddest of American apples. It all ended less well than it began, for the company's founders at least. The profit figures of early years could not be sustained against competition; Wozniak dropped out first, while Jobs began to receive frosty responses from the new management to his quirky pet projects – he dubbed his office 'Siberia'. He left in 1985 to form a new company making machines for educational users.

Don Johanson born 1943

AMERICAN PALEONTOLOGIST

Every palaeontologist's dream – to find another link in the chain of evolution – came true for Johanson and his associate Tim White in 1974 when, on a dig at Afar in the Hadar Valley of north-eastern Ethiopia, they unearthed a 3.5 million-year-old skeleton. They named her 'Lucy' after the ☛Beatles song, 'Lucy in the Sky with Diamonds', which they played while they celebrated that night. Although her brain size was nothing to boast of, and she did not have a clue how to make stone tools, Lucy *did* walk on two legs. This blew apart the then-standard account of human development developed by the ☛Leakey family, who considered bipedalism as the final step away from an ape-like state, after the use of tools had generated larger brains. Johanson suggested that the human ancestors he dubbed *Australopithecus afarensis* stood on two legs in order to gather more food for their budding nuclear families, an idea that pandered to American sentimentality about family life. Some evidence for his hypothesis was provided the year after Lucy's unearthing, when Johanson turned up the adjacent bones of 13 individuals who had been killed in a simultaneous catastrophe. Perhaps, said Johanson, it was because these apes had learned to live together that they were becoming more intelligent. To Johanson's claim that 'Lucy' was the common root from which *homo sapiens* evolved, the ☛Leakeys riposted that Johanson's 'family' were just a curious blip on the evolutionary chart, outside the main line of human development. More recently Johanson has argued against Leakey that the so-called 'Third Man' – a 2.5 million-year-old 'gracile hominid' with a tiny brain found on the shores of Lake Turkana in Kenya – is just a stupid representative of *Homo habilis*, rather than a separate species as Richard Leakey maintains. It is said that Johanson and Leakey have not spoken to each other for ten years.

Pope John XXIII
(Angelo Roncalli) 1881-1963

ITALIAN RELIGIOUS LEADER

As Pope from 1958 to 1963, John XXIII did more to bring the Catholic Church up to date – '*aggiornamento*' – than any other, before or since. A peasant by birth, a diplomat by repute, he was a makeshift candidate for the job, initially expected to be only a caretaker. Although a conservative whose motto was 'obedience and peace', he appeared to be a liberal when compared to his forerunners. He has been credited with phasing out Latin from the liturgy, although this was already being planned at the time of his accession. The striking event of his tenure was the convocation of Vatican II (1962-65), which brought together bishops from around the world for the first Council since 1870 and redefined the Church's stance towards the modern world. Human rights and an end to the arms race were themes in his oratory, but he instituted no serious change in the Church's compromising links with the political regimes in Latin America.

Pope John Paul II

(Karol Wojtyla) born 1920

⇔POLISH RELIGIOUS LEADER, BASED IN ROME

You see him here, you see him there: the first Polish Pope, elected in 1978, is one of the world's great travellers, making some 40 foreign trips in the first ten years of his pontificate. He has visited Africa, the Americas, Europe – bringing fresh hope to some of the poor and oppressed by espousing the causes of social justice and human rights, while ensuring continued misery for many through his hostility to contraception, feminism and homosexuality. John Paul's first papal visit to his homeland, in June 1979, brought out the Catholic faithful in a manifestation of loyalty to the Church that was also a protest against the regime – a display that inspired Solidarity's challenge, led by devout Catholic ☛Lech Wałęsa, in the following year. John Paul undercut his support for the trade union movement by unrealistically declaring that it should remain 'non-political'. Offering Catholics a return to old certainties after two decades of liberalization, he has muzzled the intellectuals, tried to put a stop to liberation theology, filled diocesan sees with yes-men and done nothing to remove the stain left by the revelations of shady dealings by Vatican financiers. A paradoxical figure, he relies on performance skills and personal charisma (he was once an actor) for his appeal beyond the ranks of Catholics.

Elton John

(Reginald Dwight) born 1947

$ BRITISH POP MUSICIAN

John has achieved the near-impossible feat of moving from introspetive singer to living embodiment of the excesses of the music business in the 1970s, finally becoming a household name in the 1980s. A former session hack, working on everything down to supermarket cover version albums, he became famous during the singer/songwriter boom of the early 1970s and moved effortlessly through glam to become one of pop's richest and most flamboyant stars. The 1980s saw his position solidify; he now sports a cheerful millionaire persona which may have prevented him from being taken seriously as an artist but has ensured genuine popular affection. His decision to sue the *Sun* newspaper for allegations concerning his sex life at a time when that tabloid's ability to libel people was considered inviolate resulted in what was then called a 'famous victory'.

Jasper Johns

born 1930

AMERICAN PAINTER

'Take an object, do something to it, do something else to it.' This somewhat deadpan comment from Johns expresses much of what his work is about. His images are simple, cool and often banal – the American flag, targets, beer cans, numbers and letters of the alphabet – deliberately chosen as familiar images from everyday life. More careful viewing shows how much care has been taken to unsettle the casual viewer and coax more than a passing glance. The triviality of the content forces attention towards the work itself – its thickly layered and painted surface, the careful disposition of colour. Like ☛Rauschenberg, with whom he shares credit for laying the foundations of both Pop Art and minimalism, he would attach real objects to the canvas – rulers, brooms, spoons – but Johns always practised more restraint. It is his aesthetic coolness that accounts for the prices his work attracted in the late 1980s (the $17 million his 1959 canvas *False Start* collected at auction was a record for a living artist). His influence has been substantial – debts are owed from ☛Warhol to ☛Mach.

Betsey Johnson

born 1942

AMERICAN FASHION DESIGNER

Doyenne of the unexpected, Johnson is one of America's most unconventional and uninhibited designers. Working with neon nylon and other such novelty fabrics, she discovered the possibilities of combining cotton and Lycra spandex. In the late 1960s, she acquired a reputation as America's answer to ☛Mary Quant, as she brought out tight, clinging clothes at affordable prices. Opening her New York boutique, Betsey, Bunky and Nini, in 1969, she also reached a wider public by selling patterns of her designs. Today she still runs a successful mail-order business.

B(ryan) S(tanley) Johnson

☞ BRITISH NOVELIST 1933-75

✍ ✓ ▲ 'Why do so many novelists still write as though the revolution that was *Ulysses* never happened, and still rely on the crutch of storytelling?' wrote B. S. Johnson in *Aren't You Rather Young to Be Writing Your Memoirs?* (1973), and all the work of this brilliant, exploratory writer was based on that premise. One of his novels, *Albert Angelo* (1964), had a hole cut through the book to reveal a crucial event which Johnson wanted the reader to be aware of from the start; this led to the book being confiscated by Australian customs officials who believed the excision to be proof of some secret obscenity. *The Unfortunates* (1969) was a partially unbound novel, a collection of sections of varying lengths loose in a box to enable parts of the novel to be read randomly. Even his most accessible novel – the dry, macabre and hilarious *Christie Malry's Own Double Entry* (1973) – emphasizes its own artificiality at every turn.

Lyndon Baines Johnson

1908-73

AMERICAN POLITICAL LEADER

A man for whom ambition always came before principle, Johnson achieved his dream – the presidency – in the wake of ☛John F. Kennedy's assassination. A tough and astute Texan, his genius for political scheming had, by the early 1950s, made him

Jasper Johns
Photo: Hans Namuth

invaluable to his party, and he became a powerful Democratic majority leader in the US Senate. He took a perverse pride in encouraging rumours that he had rigged the 1948 election for Texas state governor by fraud: buying 200 votes in the notorious Precinct 13, according to legend, and possibly some 8000 to 10,000 votes all over the venal Tex-Mex districts. The first man to campaign by helicopter, the first to use detailed day-by-day polling, but by no means the first man to fight dirty, Johnson introduced modern technology to old-style smear tactics, and dominated Texan politics thereafter; as the democratic vice-presidential candidate, he played a vital role in JFK's narrow 1960 victory over ☛Nixon. As president, he secured the passage of major welfare and civil rights legislation through the early 1960s, but he split the country by escalating the war in Vietnam, thus losing his liberal aura. The conflict diverted money and attention from welfare programmes, and Johnson was frustrated in his attempts to secure the passage of a second Civil Rights Bill. Ill at ease with foreign affairs, misled by advisers, he saw the war in simple terms as an American commitment which he had to honour, and was confused by the venom he aroused in young radicals: 'Hey, hey, LBJ, how many kids did you kill today?' His behaviour began to resemble clinical paranoia as the US was beaten to a standstill by this tiny, far-off, peasant country, despite intensive bombing and the dispatch of increasing numbers of combat troops. Johnson declined to seek a second term and retired to his ranch in Texas. The sleaze he had modernize stuck around, however, to shape and finally end his successor Nixon's period in office.

History and our achievements have thrust upon us the principal responsibility for protection of freedom on earth.
Lyndon B. Johnson

Philip Johnson born 1906

☞AMERICAN ARCHITECT

✾ & Johnson is sometimes depicted as an architectural turncoat who steals avant-garde ideas from others and dilutes them until they are presentable to corporate patrons, and it is true that his museum-trained mind synthesizes the styles of past and present rather than establishing original territory of his own. The expectation that he might be something different derives from his having introduced the Modern Movement to American architecture while working at the Museum of Modern Art – establishing the reputation of ☛Mies van der Rohe and the style he brought with him from Germany. Johnson built his notorious Glass House (1949) in New Canaan, Connecticut, from a Mies project for a completely transparent building, and worked with his mentor on the 36-storey Seagram Building (1958) in New York, a bronze-and-brown glass office tower. But becoming bored with the limitations that Miesian concepts imposed and frustrated with minimalism, he set out in the early 1960s on the course that led to the classic of post-modernism, the AT&T building (1978) in New York – a glass-and-steel skyscraper clad in granite, with an arched entrance, colonnaded lobby and broken-pediment top. Johnson admits to plagiarism and will probably be remembered more for his provocative writings than for his buildings.

Virginia Johnson *see* Masters and Johnson

Allen Jones born 1937

BRITISH ARTIST

Jones's juvenile dreamworld of fantasy women and domination is designed to tease, shock and disturb. Associated with the Pop Art movement of the early 1960s, his most notorious work is *Green Table* (1972), which depicts a rubber-clad woman on all fours, balancing a sheet of glass on her back to represent a table. Responding to the verbal and physical abuse he received as a result, Jones feebly proffered the defence that the work was unreal, and that the proportions should never be attributed to a real woman. This presentation of woman as object – he has kitted out his fantasy females with coat-hangers and outstretched trays for drinks – is further developed in paintings displaying his fascination with the S&M scene and 1950s' erotica. Brightly coloured canvases feature long-legged women with pointed breasts, pouting lips and consistently bland expressions. Undeniably influential in commercial design and advertising, Jones helped inspire the TV commercials of the 1970s which featured high-stepping women with full lips.

Chuck Jones
(Charles M. Jones) born 1911

AMERICAN ANIMATOR

Chuck Jones's work at Warner Bros on the bulk of the toon-star pantheon (Bugs Bunny, Daffy Duck, Porky Pig *et al.*) made him the master of slapstick character-animation, but his formalist bent soon took short films beyond simple vaudeville fun into line-drawn metaphysics. *Duck Amuck* (1953), for example, takes a cartoon staple – the tension between an artist and his semi-independent creation – into a surreal war zone where backdrops are instantly redrawn, screen boundaries tumble and a duck's body is snatched away from him and altered for the worse. Jones crowned his career with a series as bleakly tragi-comic as *Waiting for Godot* when he introduced Roadrunner to Wile E. Coyote; the films are so awesomely perfect that many more cartoon fanatics pretend to love them than actually do, and Jones, the elder statesman of animation, is now revered wherever he goes. After *Who Framed Roger Rabbit,* he must regret that the studios never allowed him the resources to take on Disney with a full-length feature.

George Jones see Wynette, Tammy

Jim Jones 1931-78

† AMERICAN CULTIST WHO SETTLED
☆ IN GUYANA
✚ Setting up his People's Temple of the Disciples of Christ in a poor area of San Francisco, with declared aims that included ending the oppression of the poor and eliminating class distinctions, Jones deployed his personal charisma and mind control techniques to build up a devoted following. He made himself useful to local political figures and, in 1975, became chairman of the housing authority. However, when disgruntled former members alleged fake healings, beatings and extortion, Jones fled to Guyana with many of his disciples, and set up the agricultural commune of 'Jonestown'. Depriving his followers of all contact with the outside world, he frequently rehearsed their mass death in preparation for the Day

of Judgement. That day came on 19 November 1978, when Congressman Leo J. Ryan was murdered as he attempted to leave with a group of disillusioned converts. Jones then persuaded 913 men, women and children to take a cocktail of Kool-Aid soft drink and cyanide in what a final note described as 'an act of revolutionary suicide'. He then shot himself. The sign above Jones's throne read: 'Those who do not remember the past are condemned to repeat it.'

Leroi Jones *see* Baraka, Amiri

Janis Joplin 1943-70

✣ AMERICAN ROCK SINGER

♥ Joplin had an extraordinary, rasping blues voice which poured out a torrent of anguish, shifting from frenzied howls and shrieks to moans and whispers. She was the most powerful female rock singer of the 1960s, but for all their revolutionary trappings, these were not enlightened times for women entertainers. Joplin, who did not even have sexual glamour to protect her, was destroyed by the usual carrots of fame, money and drugs, and by the impossibility of her attempts to live a rock star life as a woman. A persistent drug abuser, she died of a heroin overdose at the age of 27. Posthumously, she has acquired neither the those-whom-the-gods-love glamour of a ☛Cochran or ☛Holly, nor the hero's death image of ☛Hendrix and ☛Morrison; rather, Janis Joplin is seen as a tragic victim whose life was merely an inevitable prelude to her overdose. Other rock corpses are mourned; Janis Joplin is pitied because she could not play the exciting rock star game. Being a woman, it seems, she was always unable to *get it right.*

Joy Division formed 1977
New Order formed 1981

Bernard Albrecht (Bernard Dicken) born 1956
Peter Hook born 1956
Steven Morris born 1957

BRITISH ROCK GROUP

Joy Division invented a music with few antecedents and no imitators of any significance, a closed world which only they seemed capable of exploring. The band started out in late 1970s' Manchester as a bleak punk noise and then, as self-taught players sometimes do, rapidly worked out a rock sound which owed little to American forms. An album, *Unknown Pleasures* (1979), emphasized both the strangeness of Joy Division's music and the lyrical concerns of impassioned singer Ian Curtis – death, urban chaos and doomed relationships. While Curtis's suicide in 1980 instantly gave the band a mythological status, it tended to confirm the integrity of his outlook. Critical consensus now underlines the degree to which their futurist-industrial image meshed countrywide with a then-prevalent adolescent ideal of crumbling, impassioned, independent Manchester as the cradle of tomorrow's art and aesthetics.

The remainder of the group took the name New Order. After a few failed attempts to re-infuse the music with some of Curtis's melancholy, they realized that, by using the voice as only a minor instrument, exploiting rather than bemoaning the anonymity of those left living, and eliciting mystery by cutting back publicity, they could not only survive as a group, but become one of the independent sales-phenomena of the 1980s. They did this first with the song 'Blue Monday' (1983), a crossover club hit of unprecedented proportions. Whether using rock, electronic or dance music, they have continued to produce self-referential and rootless music which has made them a respected dance band, a popular chart group and a critical obsession.

Donald Judd born 1928

AMERICAN SCULPTOR

Judd's work has been concerned with discovering, defining and expounding on the limits of what art can and cannot say. He helped establish the minimalist approach of the mid-1960s – constructing simple, baseless box forms out of a variety of industrial materials, colouring them brightly and then hanging them on walls, or placing them on gallery floors, where they rarely reached above eye level. These pieces were untitled: he wanted his work to convey no further meaning than its own existence in space and time, believing that art should be 'objective', and that in order to achieve this the artist must purge all autobiographical material, metaphor or reference. As he expanded from these primary formal concerns to include environmental ones, the scale of the work increased so that the viewer could now walk around or through some of the sculptures. At the time, his work was a reaction against art forms of highly expressive content and internal complexity; they now seem to present quite traditional visual concerns in their mathematical precision and use of contrasting textures.

K

János Kádár 1912-89

HUNGARIAN POLITICAL LEADER

Kádár gave Hungary a relatively high standard of living among Eastern European nations, and established what was commonly regarded as 'the happiest barracks in the Warsaw Pact'. But he was also the man who sold out his country to the Soviets. In November 1956, when ☛Imre Nagy's government declared its intention of leaving the Warsaw Pact, the Soviet tanks rolled into Hungary. Kádár gave the invasion legitimacy by forming an 'orthodox' government, presided over the state that executed Nagy and his associates, and created a workers' militia to prevent another popular uprising. In 1961, he pronounced his famous slogan of reconciliation – 'Whoever was not against us is with us' – and initiated a reform of the economy which brought a degree of economic and cultural freedom to Hungary. But Kádár's economic mini-miracle was based on massive loans from Western banks, and Hungary soon had the highest per capita debt in Eastern Europe. After being replaced as general secretary in 1988, Kádár saw his successors commit themselves to a genuine multi-party system and overthrow his decree that the stirrings of 1956 amounted to a 'counter-revolution'; they are now officially a 'popular uprising'. Kádár died shortly after Nagy's rehabilitation and state re-burial.

Pauline Kael born 1919

AMERICAN FILM CRITIC

Resident film reviewer at the *New Yorker* since 1967, Kael has established a much-imitated style that attends to the intensely personal as well as the broadly public emotions that watching movies entails. She delights in waspishly upending highbrow expectations while praising less exalted films for their pulpy energy. Her rigour as well as her mannerisms can become addictive – for example, her fondness for the neat critical paradox: 'Alan Parker has talent to burn, and that's what he should do with it.' (Parker is, in fact, one of the few directors prepared to fight back: describing Kael as a 'demented old bag lady', he has expressed pleasure in the fact that she will soon be dead.) Ostensibly a communicator rather than a theorist, her attitudes and judgements depend on the purest subjectivity, but she has a lifetime's film-going and a devouring love of the medium to back them up.

Pauline Kael
Photo: James Hamilton

Mauricio Kagel born 1931

ARGENTINIAN COMPOSER, FILM-MAKER, DRAMATIST, BASED IN GERMANY

Kagel's early music, such as the *String Sextet* (1953), demonstrates an awareness of serial music and willingness to experiment in electronic media. He went on, however, to display a taste for the bizarre and an interest in the theatrical potential of unusual performance situations – influenced by surrealism and ☛Cage – which distanced him from more serious-minded colleagues. He explores the means whereby ideas and forms can be transferred from one medium to another, making films that reflect his interest in the cinema of the 1920s and 1940s, and building on ☛Beckett and ☛Ionescu in his dramatic work, while continuing to develop a musical world marked by rampant fantasy, wide-ranging humour and a love of the esoteric. Winning a strong following among young composers, Kagel set up his Cologne New Music Ensemble in 1961 as a challenge to conventional opera companies.

Frida Kahlo 1910-54

♥ MEXICAN PAINTER

Crippled in a horrible accident as a teenager, and in constant pain, Kahlo turned herself into an icon in her paintings. With her glare, her moustache and her unlikely handlebar eyebrows, she was her own perfect religious subject – exotic and dynamically unsettling in an over-ripe world of pain, jungle fantasy and Mexican folkloric arcana. Married, twice, to Mexican revolutionary painter and liar Diego Riviera, she numbered Picasso, Trotsky and André Breton among her friends, but she was far more drawn to her Tijuana roots than to the cultural world of the gringos. She lived a wild, unconstrained bisexual life, which continued even after amputation confined her to a wheelchair, but had, in addition, an acute political instinct, so that she was notorious and much fêted by the time of her early death. For a long time after this, her reputation was subsumed under those of her (male) contemporaries, except in Mexico itself, but lately her visionary self-image (as proto-feminist Latino icon) has been increasingly acknowledged. She has been adopted in different ways as a role-model by a number of youth culture figures, ranging from the ☛Hernandez Brothers (who love her art) to ☛Madonna (who loves to party).

Louis I. Kahn 1901-74

& ESTONIAN-AMERICAN ARCHITECT

Defining architecture as 'a thoughtful making of spaces,' Kahn demonstrated to 1950s' America that grand building did not necessarily entail kitsch. He led a movement away from Miesian abstraction – wrapping everything up in one crystalline box – and established a more flexible way of thinking about large structure, an approach that has influenced such late modernists as ☛Richard Rogers and ☛Norman Foster. Kahn's Yale University Art Gallery (1954) established him as a monumental architect, but his distinctive personal style only became fully apparent with the Richards Laboratories at the University of Pennsylvania, completed in 1961. The strong formal distinction between the central service tower and the seven laboratory towers established a way of juxtaposing the public and the more private spaces, which he pursued through subsequent projects.

Kahn's towers may have evoked the buildings of medieval Italy, but they also expressed his subtle ideas about the way architecture should relate to social organization.

Tadeusz Kantor 1915-90

POLISH THEATRE DIRECTOR

Kantor built images of murder, riot and ceremony into dramatic spectacle – contemporary processions moving slowly across the stage. The repressed children initially seen at their desks in *The Dead Class* (1975), tentatively raising their hands to attract the attention of their teacher, are later transformed into a waltzing carnival, incorporating the diverse people they have become. With Kantor present to orchestrate each performance, his actors struggled with life-size puppets and other inanimate objects – beds, chairs and strange contraptions. The objects and machines were as much part of the conception as the actors, and there was a gradation, rather than a division, between performers and mannequins. Kantor seemed to acknowledge the result as more akin to moving sculpture than traditional theatre when he froze the movement on stage into images that broke into the normally frenetic pace and loud music. His first theatre work was developed in a mountain hide-out during WW2. After the war was over, he began to present productions in a cavernous café in Cracow, only beginning to develop his own pieces in the early 1970s.

Ryszard Kapuscinksi born 1932

POLISH JOURNALIST

Born to a poor Polish parents – his father never left Pinsk – this political journalist has been obsessively crossing and recrossing the globe since 1956 and claims to have been present at 27 revolutions to date. His international reputation comes largely from three studies of collapsing autocracies – *The Emperor* (1978/83) about Ethiopia's ☛Haile Selassie, *Shah of Shahs* (1982/4) about Iran's ☛Reza Pahlavi, and *Another Day of Life* (1976/87) on the disintegration of the Portuguese regime in Angola. He has been accused of being longer on readable impressionism than analysis, but then he is in pursuit of a more ineffable problem than what went on and why: the question of when absolute power becomes impotence. Some have suggested that his stories were the subtlest of coded references to a revolution that had not yet happened, in his native Poland, and the near-total absence of reportage by him on equivalent upheavals in the Eastern bloc has the weird eloquence of the dog that did not bark in the night.

Yousuf Karsh born 1908

CANADIAN PHOTOGRAPHER

Karsh is the sort of photographer that political leaders revere – they look strong and impressive in his portraits. His big break came at the beginning of WW2 when, during a photo-session, he asked Winston Churchill to put aside his cigar. The resulting picture showed the British bulldog looking, not piqued exactly, but sort of indomitable. That led to commissions from other British and American leaders, and he has gone on portraying the famous and powerful ever since. His tight compositions set against dark backgrounds almost idolize his subjects, and the result can seem pious as with his image of ☛John F. Kennedy in a gesture of prayer. Occasionally, however, a sense of humour does push its way through, as when Karsh caught ☛Khrushchev in a fur coat, creating a picture which played upon an American tendency to confuse Russians and bears.

Adnan Kashoggi born 1935

SAUDI BUSINESS EXECUTIVE

$ This Saudi middleman became an embodiment of super-wealth as he channelled the dollars of his newly rich countrymen in the direction of arms companies; some $5 billion was the value a former wife put on the resulting bank balance. Kashoggi spent his money ostentatiously – on yachts, planes, girls, parties and gambling (reportedly spending a night at the tables in Cannes with an Arab prince that cost the two of them some $5 million). Confidante of princes and presidents, friend to pop stars, he has been involved in nearly every significant recent political scandal, from Watergate to the Iran-Contra affair. Kashoggi's living expenses failed to contract when his compatriots learned to handle the West on their own and the flow of petrodollars into his pockets began to slow. His fund-raising tactics became increasingly desperate, and he was already staring at the prospect of bankruptcy when the American authorities went after him on charges of helping Ferdinand and Imelda Marcos to extricate embezzled loot from the Philippines. He rode to court on the subway, and secured his acquittal.

I've never felt poor and I've never felt rich. I am what I am.

Adnan Kashoggi

Rei Kawakubo born 1942

JAPANESE FASHION DESIGNER

Where many designers of the 1980s went in for nostalgia, Kawakubo offered innovation. Despite the name of her company, *Comme des Garçons*, it is the evocation of Japanese traditions – Sumo, Kabuki – in her clothes, together with scorn for traditional couture values, that have built her reputation as a visionary. Like the kimono, her garments ignore feminine curves – they are to be draped and wrapped – but their extremism owes nothing to traditional Japanese conceptions of woman. When initially unveiled in the West, her torn, slashed and creased designs, with missing sleeves and odd shapes, were regarded as ugly and absurd. It was also said that her long-time obsession with black would lead her into a dead end, until she moved into bright reds and floral patterns, as well as menswear that only seems conservative on first glance. Unlike some of her Japanese contemporaries, Kawakubo has remained firmly tied to Japan, still her most important market.

Elia Kazan

(Elia Kazanjoglou) born 1909

TURKISH-AMERICAN FILM, THEATRE DIRECTOR

A co-founder with ☛Lee Strasberg of the Group Theatre, Kazan found there the sense of belonging he was later to seek as a member of the Communist Party. He directed the first performances of ☛Tennessee Williams' *A Streetcar Named Desire* (1947) and ☛Arthur Miller's *Death of a Salesman* (1949), introduced to cinema the Method approach to acting, and went on to pillage his own experiences for his art after he had repudiated

Communism and named names to the House Un-American Activities Committee in 1952. A desire for moral exoneration led to *On the Waterfront* (1954), in which ☛Marlon Brando's Terry Malloy becomes a tarnished knight who betrays the corrupt labour union world that casts so many dark shadows over his clumsy attempts at self-improvement. Despite memorable scenes between Brando, Steiger and Eva Marie-Saint, the film also displayed Kazan's proclivity to heavy-handed allegory and a didactic tone that elsewhere led to hysterical melodrama, even though the performances of ☛James Dean in *East of Eden* (1955) and Montgomery Clift in *Wild River* (1960) kept Kazan's critical star in the ascendant for a while longer. A desire for self-exoneration is evident throughout his recent autobiography, in which he justifies his philandering habits as keeping him 'curious, interested, eager, searching, and in excellent health'.

George Kennan born 1904

AMERICAN FOREIGN AFFAIRS COMMENTATOR, DIPLOMAT

Now a commentator on foreign affairs and top authority on the USSR, Kennan played a leading role in post-war US diplomacy. Based in Moscow as the war ended, he noted the spread of anti-American propaganda and, in a 1946 memorandum, authored the doctrine of 'containment', which entails the use of economic and other means to stop the spread of Communism. The adoption of containment as official US policy led to the Marshall Plan, designed to rebuild the economies of Europe in order to obviate pro-Soviet subversion, and the ☛Truman doctrine, justifying American military intervention wherever American 'interests' were threatened. Kennan over-estimated the desire of Stalin and other Soviet leaders to expand the Communist empire – Soviet post-war moves were almost entirely defensive – but as Americans came to see the Communist bogeyman everywhere, US policy became less economic and more military than Kennan had originally intended. Briefly ambassador in Moscow, he was declared *persona non grata* by the Soviet government after he had criticized its treatment of Western diplomats. He retired from official service for a life in think-tanks, but returned, again briefly, as ☛Kennedy's ambassador to Yugoslavia. He has argued that relations between states should be seen in terms of self-interest, rather than ideology; lately, he has emerged as an opponent of the nuclear arms race.

John Fitzgerald Kennedy 1917-63

➳ AMERICAN POLITICAL LEADER

♥ ❍ The first Catholic president (1961-63) of the US, Kennedy's youthful vigour and charisma reflected a period of national optimism. He surrounded himself with an articulate and highly educated governing élite and delivered emotional speeches that captured the liberal progressive imagination. It is difficult, however, to pinpoint hard achievements: it was, after all, ☛Lyndon Johnson, his successor, who launched the 'Great Society' welfare programme that did so much to help the poor. Kennedy was stronger in crisis management, especially in the international arena, than in detailed institutional change: his insights into ☛Khrushchev's psychological state helped to avert nuclear disaster during the Cuban missile crisis of 1962. His decision to escalate the American role in Vietnam seemed marginal at the time, even though it subsequently had a devastating impact. His grasp of economics, never tested, would have become a key issue had he not been assassinated. Would he have been a hero in the 'Flower Power' era or a hate figure? Would he have had the courage to backtrack from Vietnam? And will we ever know what did or did not happen on the 'grassy knoll'?

Kenzo
(Kenzo Takada) born 1940

JAPANESE FASHION DESIGNER

The sense of adventure that Japan's fashion designers brought to the West is reflected in the names they gave their shops: Kenzo, the vanguard of their move on Paris, set up his stall under the banner of 'Jungle Jap'. The appeal of his work from the 1970s lay in the way he made the traditional seem contemporary, linking traditional Japanese designs to other ethnic influences – from Russian peasants, Chinese coolies and tribal Africans. His layered peasant-style dresses and folkoric styles appealed to a sense of cultural retreat without selling out to nostalgia or ceasing to innovate. He used bright lollipop colours and rich mixes of fabrics, and pioneered the oversize look by channelling an essentially Japanese lack of interest in body shape into drawstring pants and balloon dresses.

Jack Kerouac
1922-69

AMERICAN NOVELIST

Kerouac was the bibulous, long-winded, confused Prince of the West Coast Beat Generation, who made his name with *On The Road* (1958), which presented the first of his apolitical Zen hobos, his rôle model for a new America: the male drifter escaping narrow-hearted consumerism and narrow-minded parents in search of the lost frontier. At his best, Kerouac's uncontrolled, booze-fuelled floods of words ('That's not writing,' commented ☛Truman Capote, 'it's typing') celebrate escape from responsibility. His own responsibilities caught up with him, in the shape of the ageing mother he was always fleeing, always returning to. He found himself unable to shape his own fantasy, and consumed with self-hatred, he turned on it and tried to tear it up. The Beats were identified by the critical establishment as self-indulgent anti-American barbarians, and Kerouac, their chronicler, was consigned to infamy, which ensured veneration by all succeeding drop-out generations, even as he took to vilifying the civil rights movement and howling against the 'fairy Jewish Commies' who were stealing his dream from him. In the 1960s, no one was likely to listen to one drunken apostate trying again to sell them dreary old America the Beautiful. After all, this particular poet of the always open highway never even learned to drive.

Leila Khaled
born 1946

PALESTINIAN ACTIVIST

Khaled's success in hijacking a TWA Boeing to Syria in 1969 – she remained cool while her male accomplices suffered attacks of nerves – collapsed chauvinist assumptions as effectively as any of the feats with which women at the time established their competence. Educated at the American University in Beirut and already a successful political lecturer among Palestinian refugees in Jordan,

Khaled became a folk hero in the camps, and her reputation did not suffer the following year when a hijack attempt over the North Sea failed, landing her in a British prison. Keen to get her back, the Popular Front for the Liberation of Palestine threatened to blow up two more hijacked planes; after much dithering, Prime Minister ☛Heath dispatched his prisoner to Cairo. As an indication of her commitment to the cause, Khaled wore rings made from bullets, and she justified her actions by asserting that the 'friends of my enemies are my enemies.'

Ruhollah Khomeini 1901-89

♥ IRANIAN RELIGIOUS, POLITICAL
∀ LEADER
❍ For ten years, until his death, Khomeini ran a theocratic, vicious, war-like state in Iran. Adulated throughout the Islamic world, for many his name was synonymous with fanaticism, international terrorism and bloody revenge. From a dynasty of Shi'ite religious leaders, he was raised by his elder brothers after a local landlord ordered his father's death – an event that was possibly responsible for making him a permanently bitter man. He rose up the Shi'ite ecclesio-academic ladder, gaining the title of 'Ayatollah' in the 1950s. He was exiled from Iran in 1964 for attacking the Shah's policies of emancipating women and land reform, which reduced religious estates. He settled in a Shi'ite centre in Iraq; in 1978, asked to leave, he shifted to Paris, only to return to Iran after the revolution of 1978-9. Acclaimed as a religious leader, he named a government; and when a referendum in December set up an Islamic republic, he became not just religious, but also political leader for life. Khomeini was then and would remain a fourteenth-century philosopher with an acute understanding of late twentieth-century media manipulation – he knew how to enrage Western opinion productively, and he knew how to sway a secular revolution (against state corruption and human rights abuse) into forceful Islamic ultra-conservatism, wherein torture and execution could be justified by religious conviction. He introduced the strictest Islamic law: the veil for women, bans on alcohol and Western music. His opponents – including ex-monarchists, left-wingers, liberals and rival Muslims – were systematically gaoled or executed. Revolutionary committees were free to wreak terror. War with Iraq was the chief feature of the seven years from 1981, as Khomeini sought to export Islamic revolution throughout the Middle East. Daily executive decisions were not taken by him; instead he acted as an oracle – thus the order for ☛Salman Rushdie's assassination. In a cultural autarchy, he became insulated from alternative, critical approaches as he aged.

Nikita Khrushchev 1894-71

SOVIET POLITICAL LEADER

Joint secretary of the Communist Party at the time of Stalin's death in 1953, Khrushchev took real control two years later. His 'secret speech' of 1956 denounced the Stalinist order, in which he had played a leading role, a turnabout that made him a key personality in a new era. He proposed the idea of peaceful co-existence, as the Cold War became more cordial. An egotist, alternating between charm and bluster – he once banged the table at the UN with his shoe – in general, he opted for a high profile abroad, instead of seeking real, revolutionary solutions to pressing economic problems at home: his innovations in agricultural policy were *ad hoc* and mostly failures. His foreign trips did not win back ☛Tito or reduce tension between the USSR and China. However, despite his volatility, he kept his head when faced with the hysterical American threat of nuclear war during the Cuban missile crisis and backed down. Making policy 'from the hip', he alienated party colleagues, who plotted to oust him; 'bad health' was the official explanation of his exit in 1964. He had been the caretaker of post-Stalin adjustments: a demonstration of the difference he had made was the easy manner of his exit.

Anselm Kiefer born 1945

GERMAN ARTIST

A self-confessed recluse, Kiefer is also the most monumental of contemporary artists. Indeed, 'monumental' seems too slight a description for such a piece as *The High Priestess* (1985-9), which features two massive steel bookcases, 13 feet (4m) high and 26 feet (8m) long, filled with huge lead volumes. His ambitious and unquestionably awe-inspiring paintings examine themes from German history, which he interprets rather than illustrates. For Kiefer, German history is a series of illusions, false ideals and mistakes that he responds to by physically destroying the surfaces of his pictures – burning them, throwing acid at them, even exposing them to the elements. A typical image will feature a blackened, furrowed field or a stately burned-out building that Kiefer might embellish with stuck-on straw or painted railway tracks. He also produces staged photo works that he binds together into books, sculptures and wood-cuts. Kiefer's dense, complex, challenging and allusive vision provides a provocative antithesis to the international art market's current preference for immaculacy and an absence of ideas.

Kim Il Sung born 1912

NORTH KOREAN POLITICAL LEADER

Leader of North Korea from 1948, Kim was the son of a provincial schoolmaster and was brought up under Japanese rule. The family fled to Manchuria in 1925. He fought the Japanese as a guerrilla leader before and during WW2, taking his name from a legendary anti-Japanese fighter. Trained by the Soviet Union from 1941, he joined the Red Army and, with it, liberated Korea in 1945. His moment in world history came in 1950, as North Korea, with Chinese aid, invaded the South. Since then, he has systematically used the tension between North Korea and the South and the US to keep up a buoyantly pro-Sung mood; foreign 'paper tigers' act as excuses for high arms budgets. A quasi-religious personality cult bolsters the regime, and dynasticism has re-emerged in this time-locked Stalinist country: Kim's heir is his son.

B. B. King
(Riley King) born 1925

AMERICAN MUSICIAN

King is a Mississippi bluesman whose style draws on such diverse influences as gospel, country blues and jazz guitar. A prolific performer in black clubs and bars in the 1960s, notching up as many as 300 performances a year, white guitarists adopted him as a key influence on rock 'n' roll, and introduced him to a much wider audience. Rasping vocals – a sharp falsetto cry and gospel blues voice – balanced by guitar responses, were moulded into a distinctive style that has confirmed his longevity in the blues world.

Martin Luther King 1929-68

AMERICAN PREACHER, POLITICAL LEADER

King forced white America to question its attitudes towards segregation and inbred assumptions of racial superiority as his spellbinding oratory fired up the civil rights campaigns of the 1960s. Militants despised him for turning blacks into victims by not allowing them to strike back physically – he was a disciple of Mahatma Gandhi, though nowhere near as politically naïve – but he managed to put the appearance of a united front on the movement he led. He rose to fame as leader of the 1956 Montgomery bus boycott (when blacks nearly bankrupted the bus company by refusing to use the buses until they could sit anywhere, not just in the back), and became the nemesis of Southern racists and Northern appeasers as he organized mass protests in Birmingham, Alabama, during 1963. Despite rumours of his attractions to women who were not Mrs King, and attempts at blackmail by FBI boss ☛J. Edgar Hoover, his standing was undiminished. Nor was his concern limited to blacks – he focused on poverty regardless of colour or creed, articulating a 'dream' of a world without prejudice, poverty or injustice to a crowd of 200,000 people in Washington in 1963. In his last years, he was also opposed to the US involvement in Vietnam. The dream ended with an assassin's bullet on 4 April 1968, in Memphis, Tennessee. The nationwide riots that followed resulted in the deaths of 30 people, and the movement he led rapidly split into squabbling factions. It has never regained its former strength despite ☛Jesse Jackson's opportunistic attempts to depict himself as King's successor. Doubts about whether James Earl Ray, sentenced to a 99-year gaol term for the killing, was really responsible have increased with revelations about both the FBI vendetta and the CIA's convictions that King was under the influence of Peking-line Marxists. A Martin Luther King Day has been named as a national holiday in the US, reflecting the esteem in which he is now held.

Stephen King born 1947

AMERICAN WRITER

Front-runner of the gore-lit pack since his menstruating heroine, *Carrie*, moved on to the bestseller list in 1974, King's bulk-addicted word processor pumped a new populism into the horror genre throughout the late 1970s and 1980s. While James Herbert and Shaun Huston reached the limitations of graphic imagery, King has tried to promote more subtle thrills. His best work usually starts amid the inertia of small-town life. Benign family existence becomes the battleground for a protagonist's struggle with death-spawned adversaries and an internalized sense of decay, born from unconscious connections with the darker side of the night. His commercial instincts – supported by the use of such pop culture references as 1950s' Chevrolets and the lyrics of Springsteen songs (he now owns a radio station which broadcasts nothing but hard rock from the 1970s) – has pushed him towards extended narratives, built around communities of sympathetic characters as they wrestle with diabolic external forces. The lack of malign cynicism in his work betrays his affable nature, and occasionally leads to blandness.

The Kinks formed 1964

Ray Davies born 1944
David Davies born 1947
Mick Avory born 1944

BRITISH ROCK GROUP

Ray Davies's band The Kinks began as yet another Home Counties R&B group of little merit, produced a song generally seen as the parent of heavy metal – 'You Really Got Me' (1964) – and then mutated into the first rock group to explore the concept of Englishness. The Kinks managed to fit ideas of Empire and suburbia, small-town decay and mundanity into a form of music previously seen as merely America-obsessed. In doing so, Davies was to decline into whimsy and pretension, with musicals and songs about steam trains eventually replacing insight with nostalgia. At his best, he wrote songs which simultaneously celebrated and criticized lifestyles, and were far removed from the fictional Americana of his peers. In their brief period of popularity, The Kinks gave European pop music its first taste of regional identity, and also pointed out the pitfalls of rainy-London-melancholia as a musical mainstay.

Alfred Charles Kinsey 1894-1956

♦ AMERICAN ZOOLOGIST,
○ SEXOLOGIST

Kinsey took up the study of how humanoids behave in the sack as light relief from his day job, studying gall wasps. As he started conducting face-to-face interviews (eventually clocking up over 5000 – still an insignificant sample when compared to the 3.5 million wasps he had catalogued), the balance of his endeavour shifted. Hardly surprising given that his previous publications ranged from *Studies of Some New and Described Cynipidae* (1922) to *The Origin of the Higher Categories in Cynips* (1936). The Institute for Sex Research was set up in 1947, a year before publication of his team's first bestseller, *Sexual Behaviour in the Human Male*; their study of the 'other' sex came some five years later. By demonstrating just how various were the ways in which people enjoyed themselves with each other Kinsey encouraged the 1960s' assumption that anything goes – although this message reached the public largely through secondary literature, since the former zoologist's taxonomic approach kept him from examining what all the humping and pumping actually meant to its practitioners. The gap has been more than adequately filled by the numerous sexologists who have followed in his wake, from ☛Masters and Johnson in the 1960s to Shere Hite more recently.

Henry Kissinger born 1923

GERMAN-AMERICAN POLITICIAN, POLITICAL THINKER

Kissinger was among the first to recognize that the unchallenged domination of world politics by the two superpowers had given way to a multipolar situation in which power was divided not only between the US and the USSR, but also between China, Japan and Western Europe. His study of early nineteenth-century diplomacy, celebrating Metternich's bid for a stable European order through balance-of-power politics, provided the model for his 'Kissinger doctrine' which argued that Soviet control of Eastern Europe and American interference in Latin America were facts of life, and depicted any search for absolute security as utopian thinking. Coming to attention in the 1960s through such academic writings, Kissinger was introduced to power by ☛President Nixon, first as national security adviser, then secretary of state – he was the first man to go from one job to the other – and won acclaim as the architect of Nixon's historic rapprochement with China. But while his pragmatic approach may have contributed to a lessening of superpower tensions in any particular region, this was invariably achieved at the expense of those immediately involved: Chile's democracy sacrificed for Pinochet's brutal client-dictatorship; peace in the Middle East somehow to be bought by excluding Palestinian self-determination from the Egypt-Israel talks (now largely remembered for the razzle-dazzle of 'shuttle diplomacy'). With Le Duc Tho, he shared a Nobel peace prize for ending the Vietnam War, even though his singular diplomatic innovation had been the deployment of indiscriminate punitive bombing to shore up the US's superpower credibility after losing a war to a non-superpower nationalist guerrilla force. The chief victim of this action was Cambodia, which declined from a stable, insular, backward monarchy to ☛Pol Pot's genocidal regime as a result of cross-border terror-raids and the massive social trauma they induced. He has written prolifically about his years in power, but to date his most significant achievement may have been the way he has retained his own credibility with commentators worldwide. Known and envied as a ladies' man, this expert pundit-flatterer could still, unfortunately, effect a comeback.

Calvin Klein born 1942

❞ AMERICAN FASHION DESIGNER

The son of a Bronx grocer, Klein is the fashion designer who dared to be daring in the campaigns for his jeans and perfumes, with the result that he now has an annual turnover in excess of $1.2 billion. His break came when he met the vice-president of the New York clothes store Bonwitt Teller in a lift, leading to an appointment with the powerful Mildred Custin and an order for $50,000 worth of goods. Klein's name now calls to mind such memorable lines as 'Nothing comes between me and my Calvins . . .', the catchphrase of a campaign for jeans modelled by Brook Shields. His perfumes have becomes as famous as his clothes; they include 'Obsession' which ☛Bruce Weber's photographs depict at the centre of three entangled, naked bodies.

William Klein born 1928

AMERICAN PHOTOGRAPHER, FILM-MAKER, BASED IN PARIS

Klein introduced the idea of the photographic book with *New York* (1956) and, in the process, fired American street photography with new, much-needed energy. His images were to be read as part of a continuous account of modern city life and the realities of existence for New York's tired, tense inhabitants – abused by loud, brash music, bombarded with images from placards, billboards, neon signs and stray graffiti. He did not care for the perfect image, but used flash, wide-angle, blur and close-up to give the impression of people who had no time to hang around and satisfy the photographer's aesthetics. Klein went on to document, with more apparent affection, urban life in Rome, Moscow and Tokyo, and introduced some of his visual razzmatazz into fashion photography, but it was always clear where his approach to photography was leading. He moved to Paris and made his feature film début with *Who are You, Polly Magoo?* (1966), about a fashion model suddenly propelled to fame and the media circus that surrounds her. He has been working quietly in France ever since, and recently published a new book of photographs.

Yves Klein 1928-62

❞ FRENCH PAINTER, PERFORMANCE ARTIST

Among the earliest and most personally charismatic of a group who came to be called the Neo-Dadaists, Klein was one of the first performance artists, whose development of his own bizarre character and behaviour – as with ☛Beuys and, later, ☛Warhol – is his artistic legacy. One of his most famous art-pieces, in which naked women, who had been painted blue, threw themselves down on a canvas at his direction, appears in the cult exploitation movie *Mondo Cane* (1963, the first of the *Mondo* series which used anthropology as the pretext for prurient compilations of weird behaviour on film). His first all-blue exhibition was held in 1957 – the result, he said, of a search 'for the most perfect expression of blue'. As famous as his 'International Klein Blue' (IKB), though rather more alarming, are the extraordinary photographs of his performance piece '*Yves Klein saute dans la vide*' – in which he threw himself out of a first-floor floor window on to the pavement without benefit of wires or net. An acknowledged expert on judo and an unacknowledged jazz musician, Klein brought to his art some of the same dislocating poetry that ☛Cage brings to music, treating his spectator as a kind of collaborator in the irredeemably bizarre, as when he sold 'zones of immaterial pictorial senstivity' for portions of gold leaf, which he then threw into the Seine while the purchaser burned his receipt. Oddly enough, given his gift for the peculiar stunt, and the publicity that went along with it, he reputedly bribed the director to let him appear in *Mondo Cane*.

B(ernard) Kliban 1935-90

▲ AMERICAN CARTOONIST

✖ A reclusive Californian, Kliban drew cartoons for *Playboy* for more than a quarter century. In 1975, his collection *Cat* became a runaway cult bestseller in America, opening the way for the emergence into mainstream syndication of a distinctly underground sensibility – unrespectable by dint of its black humour and bizarrely surreal compactness, but made approachable by the simplicity of his cartoons – so funny and weird on their own that they can be enjoyed without the gags they illustrate. Kliban himself, as the first, best and perhaps the strangest of these one-panel sick humourists, has not been at the forefront of popular attention since, but several similar collections by others have appeared in the wake of *Cat*. Notable among these is Gary Larson's *The Far Side*, which began to make regular syndicated appearances in the national and eventually the international press: Larson also focuses on an animal kingdom though not so species-specifically, and keeps in broad view much of Kliban's double-take sophistication and comic nastiness.

Franz Kline 1928-62

AMERICAN PAINTER

Kline's switch to abstract art is said to have come about after he had projected his own drawing of a rocking chair on to the wall of his studio; the force between the black and white strokes impressed him. The switch was a sudden one: a year previously he had been painting realistic images in a boldly coloured manner; now he was wielding his brush with all the finesse of a house-painter. His huge black-and-white paintings bear large slashes of paint, shooting across the surface towards, and over, the edges in a manner reminiscent of oriental calligraphy. Like ☛Pollock's work, they could be read as an action made visible – the viewer can experience the physical gesture and vigour involved in the creation. They might look improvised and haphazard, but Kline refined and adjusted the work meticulously. Towards the end of his life, he reintroduced large slabs of colour, but this was akin to putting the brakes on his strengths. His legacy was popularized when the comedian Steve Martin commissioned an ink-splattered suit to resemble Kline's paintings.

Mark Knopfler born 1949

BRITISH ROCK MUSICIAN

Rock music has diversified enough in the past 30 years for its initial premise – music as sexual excitement for the young – to lose its centrality. Dire Straits, the group with Knopfler leads, are neither sexually exciting nor consumed primarily by young people. They provide entertainment for couples in their mid-30s who wish to consume music less bland than that enjoyed by their parents, but feel too mature to skip about the pop chart. Knopfler is respected for his impeccable guitar-playing, his instantly familiar reference points – ☛Bob Dylan, ☛Bruce Springsteen, ☛Eric Clapton – and his soothing melancholy. Dire Straits are rooted in the 1970s, but modern enough to eschew such cumbersome post-hippy vexations as epic instrumental work-outs, unfortunate drug/sexist lyrics and lurid clothes sense; their videos and record sleeves rarely even feature Knopfler's face, as if to confirm to the consumer that they are not collecting an image when they buy Dire Straits. What they are getting is their past, streamlined and reworked to be unobtrusive. Knopfler's soft, low voice and vaguely emotive guitar-playing provides the slightest edge to a music that is never quite bland. Reacting against the gigantism of contemporary Dire Straits tours, Knopfler formed The Notting Hillbillies at the end of the 1980s, as a semi-serious return to pub rock – just playing some gigs with his 'mates'.

Arthur Koestler 1905-83

† HUNGARIAN-BRITISH WRITER

☆ ✽ Koestler embraced ideas so passionately that reality could never live up to his expectations. He took up Zionism while studying science in Vienna, but discarded that idealism during his time on a collective farm in Palestine. His subsequent allegiance to Communism lost him his job as a political correspondent on a German newspaper; after he had eluded a death sentence handed out by ☛Franco's supporters in Spain, he broke away from the party, chronicling the dissolution of his revolutionary faith in his contribution to the multi-authored *The God that Failed* (1950) and such novels as *Gladiators* (1939), *Darkness at Noon* (1941) and *Arrival and Departure* (1943). He continued to write about the incompatibility of idealism with humanism and individuality, expressing the sense that Western civilization was being hurried to its end by barbarians and the spineless liberalism of its spineless defenders. But as Koestler turned to science for ways to better humanity, he found other ways to make sense of it all, coming to believe in an 'abstract' God as a vast, unthinkable Oneness; and its corollary, a systematic plan for nature. He also succumbed to the claims of parapsychological researchers (in his will, he left money for the endowment of the first British chair of parapsychology, at Edinburgh University). Despite the shoddy thinking generated by his urge to escape despair, Koestler developed many useful insights, and memorably observed that scientists were just 'Peeping Toms at the keyhole of eternity', who had barely glimpsed the immense subtlety of nature.

Heinz Kohut 1913-81

AUSTRIAN-AMERICAN PSYCHOANALYST

Kohut produced a version of psychoanalysis that now seems to have been tailored to the self-assertive 1980s' hunger for success. He argued, in books such as *The Analysis of Self* (1971), that the traditional picture of psychosexual development could not account for contemporary problems, thus seeming to demolish Freud's claims that he had produced a timeless picture of psychological development. Those who sought therapeutic help in late-nineteenth-century Vienna mostly sought to overcome inhibitions, so that they could become what they wanted to be; in the 1980s, many patients, lacking inhibitive obstacles, just do not know what sort of person they are, which leads to feelings of emptiness, depression and meaninglessness. To elucidate this new malaise, Kohut posited a narcissistic line of development that focused on the individual's need to develop self-esteem, de-emphasizing factors such as the need to satisfy instinctual drives. Changes in family structures, particularly parental absenteeism, have increased the prevalence of narcissistic disorders, and the job for the therapist is to build up a stable, integrated and mature self. The message that Kohut sought to get across was that narcissism is good for you: 'We should not deny our ambitions, our wish to dominate, our wish to shine and our yearning to merge with omnipotent figures,' he urged while executing a further dilution of Freudianism to render it yet more palatable for Americans.

Teddy Kollek born 1911

ISRAELI POLITICIAN

Pragmatic and dove-ish mayor of Jerusalem since before the 1967 war – Israel's moment of greatest self-confidence – right up to its present embattled and demoralized fragmentation, Kolleck has been fêted and reviled as a moderate and conciliatory voice for most of his years in power. The status of Jerusalem as a holy city to several religions is the centre of the problem, as is the fact that, in the years since the founding of Israel, Islamic and Jewish fundamentalism have made increasingly strident – and mutually exclusive – claims on it as the historical capital of their own faiths. Kollek, a secular Jew, has been almost alone among Israeli political figures in arguing that some new constitutional, geographical compromise *must* be found. The ultra-orthodox right revile him as an 'Arab-lover', while some on the left, and most radical Palestinians, argue that his moderation and peace-making instincts are being exploited by the state, as liberal gestures that can hide its absolute unwillingness to extend democracy to its most reluctant charges, the West Bank Palestinians. In 1989, Kollek lost his majority on the city council, which suggests his conciliatory influence is waning.

Willem de Kooning *see* de Kooning, Willem

Jeff Koons born 1955

$ AMERICAN ARTIST

Koons has enjoyed undoubted financial success, but the justification he offers for his 'art' – 'It's a good thing my work fetches such high prices because it shows I'm being taken seriously' – is very debatable. A former stockbroker, Koons is nothing if not business-like in his approach, seeking out craftsmen to execute his pieces – he will only dirty his hands counting the money – and arranging the dates of his shows. Unsure whether he wants to be ☛Warhol or Duchamp, Koons presents his mass-produced luxury items as confectionery for the meek and impressionable consumer to devour. His vulgar and garish porcelain sculptures and his giant teddy bears are too crass even to be called kitsch. Ever the media manipulator, his publicity photos regularly flood the art journals on the eve of his shows: Koons relaxing in his beachrobe flanked by sea lions with garlands of flowers about their necks; or acting as a punk school teacher in class, standing before a blackboard bearing the message: 'EXPLOIT THE MASSES, BANALITY AS SAVIOUR.' A child of his time, Koons has been allowed to play in the schoolyard too long.

Olga Korbut born 1956

✎ SOVIET GYMNAST

Terrorist assassinations apart, the 1972 Munich Olympics are remembered for Korbut's sparky performances. She won gold medal and reinvented gymnastics – previously a fairly prissy event – in the image of Soviet sex-teen as elastic pixie. She was 17. Four years later, in Montreal, she was knocked out of first place by the Rumanian Nadia Comaneci, who was tougher, more supple, remarkably composed and just 14. Comaneci mounted the podium to thunderous applause – but for Korbut, the silver medallist, after a moment of silence, as if the watching millions were suddenly struck dumb by their own fickleness, the applause doubled. By her late 20s, a senior coach to the Soviet women's gymnastics team, she was crippled by arthritis.

Josef Koudelka born 1938

CZECHOSLOVAK-FRENCH PHOTOGRAPHER

Koudelka's most famous pictures come from his years of obscurity, when he followed the routes of gipsies across central Europe, recording their traditional lifestyle. His pictures are mysteries inviting interpretation from the viewer: in one of the most striking images from *Gipsies* (1987), for example, the foreground is filled by a boy in chains while, a long way behind across ploughed earth, stand police and onlookers. Koudelka made his reputation with images of the Soviet invasion of Czechoslovakia in 1968, which focused on the passive resistance of the natives and the bewilderment of the young soldiers at the receiving end of hatred. Now working out of Paris as a member of the Magnum photographic agency, Koudelka's recent photographs (collected in the 1988 tome, *Exiles*) seem more distant from his subjects, more interested in surreal ideas and abstract geometries. His persistence in the search for images is attested in the five visits he made to the shrine at Lourdes in order to find the picture of a boy kissing the statue of the virgin while crowds look the other way.

Jannis Kounellis born 1936

GREEK SCULPTOR, BASED IN ITALY

Kounellis's work is concerned with the relationship between the natural and the artificial, expressing nostalgia for a lost wholeness. It was through his involvement with the *Arte Povera* movement in Italy during the 1960s that he evolved his aesthetic, rich in personal history and tensions. Kounellis uses an array of elements – ranging from steel, coal, rope and lamps to live participants – to express precariousness, ephemerality, fragmentation. *Parrot*, shown in 1967, had a live parrot sitting on a perch projecting from a monochrome canvas. For Kounellis, nature means not only earth, fire, water and the realms of animal and vegetable life, but coal and wool as well. Conjuring up the primal necessities of light, warmth and shelter, he brings his work close to the shamanistic approach of ☛Joseph Beuys. His recent work also draws upon texture and smell – paraffin lamps burn, illuminating a heap of coal buried beneath a gigantic panel of sheet steel, evoking an almost Victorian barrenness.

It is not possible to make paintings now.
Jannis Kounellis

Kraftwerk formed c. 1968

♦ GERMAN POP GROUP

Kraftwerk initially mixed electronic music with avant-garde *musique concrète*, but they moved towards pure electronics in the mid-1970s, producing spare, rhythmic and melodic songs. Despite an unlikely international hit single, 'Autobahn', in 1973, they were largely overlooked. It was a time for guitars and overtly sexual emotion; Kraftwerk had taken to wearing suits and clipped hair, and wrote about radioactivity and trains rather than sex and cars. Lacking rock and soul references, the music of Ralf Hutter and Florian Schneider became more popular when the similarly clean beat of disco appeared in the mid-1970s, but it was only in the early 1980s that a wide audience discovered that Kraftwerk were *funny*, and that their seemingly techno-obsessed lyrics were as relevant to pop life as any lachrymose lost-love ditty or breast-beating rock anthem. Unfortunately, Kraftwerk now found themselves as competitors in music, rather than innovators, and their creative processes became slower as every rhythm they invented was upstaged by a more radical sound from the American dance charts. The band's humour, simple melodies and sense of wonder at the modern world are still there, however, and it still is not too late for them to come back and trash the charts.

Paul Krassner born 1932

AMERICAN PRANKSTER, SATIRIST

A vital figure in the history of the underground from the early 1950s to the present, Krassner has kept himself so effectively in the background that, unlike his close friend ☛Abbie Hoffman, only a very few would recognize his name, and none his face. Satirist and prankster, occasional stand-up comedian and inventor of the word 'yippie', he has been publishing bizarre parodies and subversive disinformation ever since his *Tiny Tots* strips for EC Comics ran deadpan put-ons of True Love-type stories. His most important contribution was a magazine called *The Realist*, which he ran from 1958 to 1974, inventing scurrilous stories about the rich and the powerful as a way of running those stories which were known or assumed to be true, but which threatened court action and/or cowardice would always keep out of respectable papers. If the story was extreme enough – such as ☛Lyndon Johnson having sex with the wound in the dead ☛President Kennedy's head in Air Force One – the victim would be *too embarrassed* to deny anything, preferring to hope the story stayed buried. Krassner introduced radical politics and a spirit of self-parody to the hardcore porn rag *Hustler* when its publisher ☛Larry Flynt asked him to be its editor; he ran serious articles on abortion and the assassination of ☛Malcolm X before he was fired. In the mid-1980s, he began publishing *The Realist* once more, figuring that since ☛Reagan had managed to re-impose a 1950s' morality on much of the country, it was his job, once again, to punch the hypocrisy full of holes.

Julia Kristeva born 1941

& BULGARIAN PSYCHOANALYTIC, ☞LITERARY THEORIST, SETTLED IN PARIS

Ostensibly a second-generation semiotician, Kristeva quickly captured a circle of intellectual fans in late 1960s' Paris with her consistently provocative critical reappraisals. (☛Barthes said of her, admiringly: 'She always destroys the *last prejudice*, the one you thought you could be reassured by and take pride in.') Born and educated (by French nuns) in Bulgaria, she originally wanted to be a physicist, but became a journalist when she found that *nomenklatura*-culture barred her from the best education; travelling to Paris in 1966, she stayed. Her direct experience of intellectual stagnation under state socialism has impelled her towards independence ever since – she has argued that any semiotics must always be a critique of semiotics. As a result, her work is constantly pushing beyond itself, revising its last analysis, so that she has often seemed hard to place politically (she has been excoriated as far right, far left, over-Lacanian, post-Freudian, anti-feminist and ultra-feminist). *Semeiotiké* (1969) demonstrated her initial synthesis of linguistics (via ☛Bakhtin and ☛Jakobson), psychoanalysis and hardcore structuralism, and subsequent works have refined her studies of the production of meaning, desire and selfhood in language. Her fascination with the taboo and the controversial – in the social, in theory and in art – has probably given her work an edge over that of other writers just as abstruse, but *Powers of Horror; An Essay on Abjection* (1980) also shows her writing becoming more accessible. A member of the *Tel Quel* editorial board from 1970, she was part of that magazine's flirtation with abstract Maoism as long as it was helpful in fending off the remnants of the Stalinist left in Paris, but moved off into more obvious independence after ☛Mao's death allowed wider recognition of the realities of his regime. *About Chinese Women* (1974/7), her account of a trip to China during that time, remains a fascinating feminist study of the Cultural Revolution.

Ray Kroc 1902-84

AMERICAN BUSINESS EXECUTIVE

Kroc transformed his restaurant chain into a worldwide phenomenon, to such an extent that McDonald's is now almost a synonym for the American hamburger. He had spent almost two decades selling a device that could mix five milk shakes simultaneously, before moving into bread and beef. That move was sparked by a meeting with two brothers, Dick and Mac McDonald, who were doing exceptionally well out of hamburgers (and milk shakes): they had tapped into the family market after sacking the sort of young waitresses who had made California's drive-in restaurants into unsalubrious teenage haunts. Kroc acquired the right to franchise their name, opened his first outlet in 1955, bought out the brothers for $2.7 million in 1961 and, by the time of his death, was grossing over $8 billion a year. An important part of Kroc's success was the fact that he took the business of fast food very seriously indeed – putting franchisees through a tough training programme (which culminated in graduates receiving the degree 'Bachelor of Hamburgerology') and monitoring outlets to enforce the company's formula of 'Quality, Service, Cleanliness'. Kroc himself was so obsessed with hygiene that he once ordered all managers to have their nostril hairs clipped. When it comes to fast food, it seems that millions of people care less about what they are actually putting down their gullets than that the floors are clean and the staff can breathe freely through their nasal passages.

Peter Kroger
(Morris Cohen) born 1910

Helen Kroger
(Lona Petka) born 1913

AMERICAN SPIES, BASED TEMPORARILY IN UK

'Peter', born in New York, the son of Eastern European Jewish immigrants, became a Communist at university and married 'Helen', also a Communist. They vanished in 1951 after the disclosure of a nuclear spy ring, linked to ☛Fuchs and the ☛Rosenbergs, and reappeared in the London suburb of Ruislip under false names four years later. Their job was to act as 'housekeepers', transmitting radio signals, for another spy ring run by a Soviet agent. Their neighbours did not have the slightest idea what was happening. They were sent to prison for 20 years in 1961, but were swapped in 1969 for Gerald Brooke, a British business executive who had given out propaganda leaflets in Moscow. ☛Harold Wilson, the British prime minister at the time, was strongly criticized for the deal within parts of British intelligence, and it fuelled their suspicions about his patriotism.

Barbara Kruger born 1945

AMERICAN ARTIST

Starting as an art director on various women's journals in the 1970s, Kruger has gone on to produce witty commentaries on the sort of work she had been involved in. These combine existing photographs with the aim of forcing viewers to look again at an image they might otherwise take for granted: emblazoned across the image of a pig-tailed girl, pressing her finger on the flexed bicep of her boyfriend are the words: WE DON'T NEED ANOTHER HERO; 'I AM YOUR SLICE OF LIFE' is etched on to an image of several upright razor-blades. The clash of image with texts spins off a range of ideas and interpretations. Kruger seeks to uncover the unconscious manipulation exerted by advertising images, exploring their representations of power, work, sexuality and wealth.

Stanley Kubrick born 1928

■ AMERICAN FILM DIRECTOR, BASED IN UK

This expatriate American's talent is to synthesize, caricature and subvert novels parading big themes into highly stylized epics, often discarding the original narrative along the way. Working within a variety of genres, his films are dark commentaries on the misdirections of social evolution, laced with abundant panoramic photography and black humour. His science-fiction epic *2001* (1968) touches on the space program and mind expansion as well as implicitly referring to the LSD experience. Showing a talent for picking themes out of the headlines, *Doctor Strangelove* (1964) parallels the first wave of nuclear paranoia, while A *Clockwork Orange* (1971) is an intellectualized exploitation movie masquerading as moral parable. Kubrick likes to think he is heavy on moral parables; for some, he is merely big on overstatement.

Stephen Kuffler born 1913

HUNGARIAN-AMERICAN NEUROPHYSIOLOGIST

Kuffler was the first person to record the electrical signals from within an individual nerve cell, interviewing the nerves populating the brain, to find out what stimuli make them react, by poking an incredibly thin glass tube into the retina of the eye. Although there are 100 million nerve cells there, he showed that they only gave off a small number of basic electrical responses, and that each cell gets its electrical act together only if something appears in a certain small area of what the eye can see. After this initial success, many neuroscientists jumped on the bandwagon, poking these micro-electrodes all over the place. As they followed Kuffler from the back of the eye to the back of the brain, they found that ever more complicated things were necessary to get the neurones to 'fire'. The idea that the sensory systems were increasingly complicated pathways which process information became the basis of neurophysiology in the 1960s and 1970s. To a generation of students Kuffler is known as the co-author of *From Neurone to Brain* (1976), a title that perfectly sums up his approach: he hopes to understand the workings of the inside of the head by going to the individual nerve cells and working up. Kuffler's experiments did much to stimulate the later work of ☛Hubel and Wiesel.

Thomas Kuhn

born 1922

○ AMERICAN PHILOSOPHER OF SCIENCE

Most thinking by philosophers of science is devoted to elucidating the scientific method, but Kuhn argues, in *The Structure of Scientific Revolutions* (1962), that there is no such thing. He sees the development of science as a series of revolutions in which world views are transformed, resulting in the acceptance of new theories. For most of the time, scientists are engaged in 'normal science', conducting investigations within the boundaries of accepted theories. These periods are interrupted by revolutionary phases when, in addition to the accumulated anomalies thrown up by any set of experiments, whole new concepts of the world are constructed – which may become the bases of new paradigms. Where other philosophers stress sets of rules for choosing between theories – according to their accuracy, simplicity and ability to include all known information – Kuhn stresses that these are not rules but values. The way scientists employ them differs: Keplerian (sun-centred) astronomy was simpler than the Ptolemaic (earth-centred) system but actually less accurate; yet it triumphed. Far from offending some notional 'scientific method', this variability in judgement has been essential to scientific advance. Paradigm shifts, like that from biblical Genesis to evolutionary theory, or from consistent to quantum physics (where uncertainty reigns), show the intrusion of social values into science. Kuhn sees science as a social and political process, not one pursued by white-coated philosopher-magicians.

Normal science is a strenuous and devoted attempt to force nature into the conceptual boxes supplied by professional education.

Thomas Kuhn, The Structure of Scientific Revolutions

Milan Kundera

born 1929

CZECHOSLOVAK NOVELIST, BASED IN PARIS

A quirky approach to storytelling and a wry sense of humour characterize Kundera's writing – reflecting his earlier involvement with the film directors and screenwriters who created the Czechoslovak New Wave. He published his first novel *The Joke* (1967/82) – about a teenager imprisoned during the Stalin era for making an 'anti-Communist' witticism on a postcard – while still a teacher of screenwriting at the Institute for Advanced Cinematic Studies in Prague. After the Soviet invasion of the following year, Kundera lost his post and the opportunity to have his novels published in Czechoslovakia, and he moved to Paris. *The Book of Laughter and Forgetting* (1979/80) expresses an exile's sense of emptiness and alienation, and abandons straightforward narrative for a more open-ended form that incorporates historical and philosophical musings along with stories and anecdotes. The theme of exile was further explored in *The Unbearable Lightness of Being* (1982/4), in which the invasion of Czechoslovakia is counterpointed by a three-way romance, suggesting that love and sex are incompatible, and that knowledge of the impossibility of perfection can take the sense of ease or lightness out of existence. In Kundera's world, no one is what they seem to be, think they are or want to be. Their quests for freedom lead to the darkness of half-glimpsed self-knowledge, and characters are forced to seek happiness in the immediate world around them rather than in their ideals.

Hans Küng born 1928

GERMAN THEOLOGIAN

To call it an 'inquisition' was nonsense, but ☛Pope John Paul II's depriving Küng of his position as official theologian did reveal just how illiberal the Catholic Church had become. Küng's influential role in framing Vatican II had made him a significant target for the new orthodoxy. He challenges the doctrine of papal infallibility, believing that the Pope should not spend his time laying down rules for believers, but only present himself as a focus of unity in a Universal Church. He seeks to encourage belief in God by distancing the leap of faith that is required from clerical dogmatism, and argues that the laity is not in an inferior position to the clergy, just a different one. His opposition to compulsory clerical celibacy and the ban on artificial contraception has attracted a large following among liberal Catholics and non-believers.

Igor Kurchatov 1903-60

SOVIET NUCLEAR PHYSICIST

The significance of Niels Bohr's remark that the only secret of the atomic bomb was that it could be made is illuminated by the course of the Soviet nuclear project led by Kurchatov. The four-year gap between the explosion of an American device in the deserts of New Mexico and the Soviet test on 29 August 1949 owed less to scientific backwardness than to Soviet reluctance to believe that an atomic bomb was anything more than a distant pipedream, combined with a shortage of resources to play long shots. The discovery of nuclear fission in 1938 had encouraged research into ways of harnessing the chain reaction process, but it was a small, low-priority affair, which came to a halt when the Germans invaded the USSR in 1941. Even when one of Kurchatov's students realized why no articles on nuclear developments were appearing in British and American journals – they were now a top-secret military matter – Kurchatov was only allocated 100 scientists, a miniscule number by the standards of Los Alamos. When a bomb was exploded over Hiroshima, Kurchatov's project suddenly became top priority, leading to frequent invitations from the Kremlin for him to talk things over with Stalin and Beria, the secret police chief. Information from ☛Fuchs about American developments helped speed up development of the atomic and thermonuclear bombs (the latter being tested in August 1953), but did not solve the technological and organizational problems involved.

Akira Kurosawa born 1910

▲JAPANESE FILM DIRECTOR

Kurosawa's post-war films not only revitalized Japanese cinema, but much of European and US film-making as well – by inspiring *The Magnificent Seven* (1960) as well as ☛Sergio Leone's early westerns. In his turn, Kurosawa had adapted both John Ford's sense of landscape and

Jean Renoir's humanism to Japanese settings. His early films – such as the remarkable *Stray Dog* (1949), almost a love story between a detective and his stolen gun, and *Living* (*aka To Live*, 1952), about a terminally ill man's attempt to save a children's playground – were rapidly eclipsed by his Samurai pictures. *Rashomon* (1951), which explored a single horrific event through the eyes of each of four participants, was his first European hit, followed by *The Seven Samurai* (1954), which appealed to the Japanese as a revisionist account of an 'honourable' warrior culture in moral decline, and to the West because of its imaginative staging. Kurosawa went on to adapt Gorky, Thackeray, Dostoyevsky and Shakespeare, but as the films became longer, they made increasingly less commercial impact, and by the early 1970s, no Japanese company would finance him. Kurosawa found the money for *Dersu Uzala* (1975) in the Soviet Union, and went on to secure the support of American financiers for two stunning epics: *Kagemusha* (1980) and *Ran* (1985). Costs were kept down by shooting the battle scenes with several cameras and hastily editing them on an old moviola. But the results show such astonishing ambition achieved with so little apparent effort that, in comparison, the work of even his most accomplished disciples looks like amateurish doodling.

Harvey Kurtzmann born 1924

✍ AMERICAN COMICS WRITER

Kurtzmann is so very obviously the progenitor of the wilder side of modern comics that it is easy to be surprised at how tame much of his seminal work now seems. Working at EC during the early 1950s, when agitation for a 'comics code' was launched by those wishing to protect US youth (from, in particular, the perversely subversive extremes of EC's own horror line), he helped establish the near-surreal *Mad* comic for them, and went on to assure its later (much toned-down) success as *Mad* magazine, the leading satirical force in blandly suburban, boomtime America after the Code had forced EC out of business. Oddly enough, given his unshakable reputation among the furthest-out of the underground cartoonists, many of whom he gave their first break on *Help!* magazine in the early 1960s, his own most influential contribution may have been through introducing a degree of calm and decent humanism to EC's war genre – treating Koreans, for example, as human beings, rather than echoing earlier stereotyped depictions of the Japanese as screaming cartoony cannon fodder. Scrupulous research, an anarchic turn of mind and an engaging innocence give even the most outrageous of his chosen subjects something that was all his own, and it is notable that, in the 40 years he has been working, he really has not had to adapt his style to keep up with the times, providing a direct link from ☛Tex Avery through ☛Robert Crumb to punk moderns such as Pete Bagge of *Neat Stuff*.

Fela Kuti born 1938

✌ NIGERIAN MUSICIAN

Aggressively political, Kuti sings in a Nigerian-English pidgin which a wide audience understands, but which can also make hard-nosed points by dropping out of easy comprehensibility. His sound – AfroBeat – owes a little to rock and something to a jazz background (rare in West Africa). He knows far more about music theory than he lets on, but his music is basically his own – a snaky juggernaut that works in giant, rolling blocks, and eerie call-and-response to dramatize his witty, angry challenges. Successive Nigerian regimes have tried to keep him quiet, in spite of his close family connection with the ruling classes. Under one regime, his mother was thrown to her death from a window by soldiers ransacking Kuti's headquarters; under another, he was thrown in gaol for some years on a trumped-up currency charge. His music is not quite what it was – he is hard to work with and over the years his best players have left him – and he is taken more seriously outside Nigeria than in, but he has played an important role in formulating radical young Africa's modern sense of self: anti-colonial and anti-corruption. Despite his views on women, which alarm many, he is very astute.

L

Jacques Lacan 1901-81

FRENCH PSYCHOANALYST

Venerated by some as the agent of subversion, reviled by others for wilful obscurantism, Lacan's work articulates the surrealist belief that, to change society, you first have to change individuals. He pitched himself against those who would reduce Freud to commonsense psychology and argued for a return to the original texts that was partly a reinterpretation of the Viennese master's discoveries in terms of linguistic theory. After the events of 1968 had brought psychoanalysis into the centre of French intellectual life, Lacan's collection of papers, *Écrits* (1966/77), became required reading for thinkers in the social sciences and cultural studies. He argued that American 'ego' psychologists such as Heinz Hartmann – who considered it possible to build a stable ego that could withstand the psychic storms launched by the instinctive forces of the id – had diluted the impact of Freud's discovery of the unconscious. Rather than being a point of stability and self-control, Lacan saw the ego as the carrier of neurosis. There could be no such thing as a coherent, autonomous self because the ego was formed out of a network of symbols – 'de-centred', 'split' and 'alienated'. The 'I' that I am can never separate itself from the 'Other', seen in the mirror, through which it comes to know itself. Lacan, who split from existing psychoanalytic establishments but built his own substantial following, wrote in a style of magisterial impersonality, but he was a charmer and a brilliant teacher who saw the seminar room as a place to display his wit and status as intellectual *provocateur*. Although he has been adopted by a generation of French feminists, many of them appear to consider him a test case, tainted with male chauvinism, sexual essentialism and misogyny, which it is their job to challenge. His controversial habit of cutting off analysands' sessions after only a few minutes probably owed as much to a low boredom threshold as any theoretical justification.

R(onald) D(avid) Laing 1927-89

BRITISH PSYCHIATRIST

Laing's suggestion that it was the world that was mad, not the so-called lunatics, and his attacks on the family as the breeding ground of schizophrenia appealed less to psychiatrists than to lay people – especially disaffected 1960s' youth – who found in his writings a possible explanation for their own sense of internal conflict. We only accept the illusion that the world is 'real', Laing argued in *The Divided Self* (1960), in order to escape the conclusion that we have no stable identity. Schizophrenics, unable to make that pact, cannot see that they remain the 'same' at different places and different times. Their selves, being created out of fantasy, are always in the process of disintegration. Such psychosis often develops from the contradictory emotional attitudes of parents, who express hate while pretending to love, and conceal anger under a mask of gentleness. Laing extended his analysis to look at the sickness of society, which he felt had made 'camaraderie, solidarity and companionship' almost impossible, and he sought an antidote through involvement in a series of proto-hippy communes. His more lasting contribution lies in the challenge he presented to an attitude which cuts off the mentally ill from society. While this does not mean that he would approve a policy of dumping heavily drugged schizophrenics into bed-and-breakfast accomodation, this may unfortunately be the only lasting effect his writings have had on the profession.

Who poses the greater threat to society: the fighter pilot who droppped the bomb on Hiroshima or the schizophrenic who believes the bomb is inside his body?

R. D. Laing

Imre Lakatos

1922-74

HUNGARIAN PHILOSOPHER OF SCIENCE

Where ☛Popper follows a scientific approach to the philosophy of science, and ☛Kuhn emphasizes sociological factors, Lakatos sits somewhere in the middle. He treats science as a series of competing research programmes, each of which has a hard core of propositions which its protagonists decide are methodologically irrefutable – such as the laws of gravity and dynamics in Newtonian physics. Simple observational anomalies cannot threaten these central axioms. Around the core arise a belt of auxiliary theories which develop from the theoretical principles and are adjusted or replaced according to experimental evidence. Experiments which appear to contradict the central ideas of the research programmes are often shoved aside in the hope of being cleared up later when a theory becomes more developed. Popper's belief that science progresses by falsification suggests that well-established theories can be overthrown by a single crucial experiment. Lakatos agrees that refutation is vital, but he finds Popper's formulation naïve: no single experiment (except with very long hindsight) ever destroys a whole research programme. On the other hand, although Lakatos's idea of central cores resembles Kuhn's concept of paradigms, the former is opposed to the idea that large-scale shifts in scientific theories occur by anything other than rational processes. Here he comes dangerously close to denying any social context to the scientific process. While his model for scientific practice is sophisticated, he still seems interested in little more than theoretical physics.

Edwin Land

1909-91

♦ AMERICAN SCIENTIST, INVENTOR

❍ $ For 300 years, Isaac Newton seemed to have had the last word on colour vision – that the colour of an object depends on the amount of each wavelength it reflects to the eye. According to Land, Newton was wrong. Take the same object at the beginning and the end of the day. If Newton was right, then objects would change colour, because the wavelengths present in the different degrees of daylight vary enormously. In fact, an orange in the morning could reflect exactly the same wavelengths as a blue book in the evening; yet one always looks orange and the other always looks blue. With his extensive knowledge of the effects of coloured filters, Land initiated a whole new theory of colour vision. If the light falling on a set of objects varies and we can still tell the different colours apart, we must be making a comparison between the different wavelengths they emit, not checking off the reflected light against some absolute colour chart. Knowing that the three-cone systems in the retina act like three different colour filters, he proposed that, somewhere in the visual system, comparisons are made according to the brightness of the objects. Recently some neuroscientists have found cells in the brain which seem to be performing the kinds of computations that Land proposed – a process of relative differentiation. Land's extensive knowledge of filters – and the money to pursue his research – derived from his work on systems of colour photographic printing and the cameras needed for it: the company he founded to develop and exploit his inventions was called Polaroid.

Morris Lapidus born 1902

SOVIET-AMERICAN ARCHITECT

Everything Lapidus built, whether shops or hotels, was aimed towards pleasing mainstream public taste. His flamboyant designs were deliberately presented as the antithesis to what he saw as the cold and clinical approach of ☛Mies van der Rohe and his followers. His most striking gesture was the sweeping façade of his first major hotel, the Fontainebleau (1954) in Miami Beach (genuinely daring at the time, although much imitated after). There, as in several other hotels, he provided a lush and gaudy environment in which wealthy Americans could enjoy spending their money. The lobby for the Americana (1956), also in Miami Beach, boasted a tropical forest stuffed in a glass cone and a sweeping staircase modelled on the one in the Paris Opéra. 'My convictions,' he declared, 'are that good architecture and good profit are both possible, if we maintain a happy balance between convictions and compromise.'

Philip Larkin 1922-85

▲BRITISH POET

A novelist, librarian and writer on jazz, Larkin was also, as Clive James dubbed him, a 'poet of the void'. His early work, written in imitation of Yeats and Auden, attracted little attention, but when Larkin realized that he could write from his own life, the result was work of strong but restrained imagination. His was an individual voice amid the conformity of the 1950s, mixing mockery, compassion and bleakness without ever sinking to navel-gazing. What Larkin mourns is not a lost world, a common subject among writers of his generation, but the gradual ebbing away of life itself, and the inevitable failure of our attempts to ward death. 'The Building' is a hospital, admitting death and disaster every day, while 'The Old Fools' suffer senility until 'The Explosion' leads to a startling dream of resurrection and hope. Larkin's work has heart just as the man himself had a sense of humour, and one feels that he wrote for people rather than the cold demands of art.

Lyndon LaRouche

(Lyn Marcus LaRouche) born 1922

♦ AMERICAN CULTIST

Should one take seriously a man who believes the Queen of England is the mastermind behind one of the world's largest drug networks? Perhaps not, but when LaRouche stood for US president, in 1984, he secured 80,000 votes. Subsequently, in 1986, members of his National Democratic Policy Committee began to surface as Democratic candidates in various state elections, causing jittery observers to argue that this was a species of protest vote; the alternative – accepting that people were beginning to agree with him – seemed unthinkable. LaRouche's organization first appeared in 1968 as a Trotskyite splinter of the SDS, the student protest movement, and focused on the malevolent conspiracies allegedly being nurtured by the Rockefellers and the CIA. American society breeds conspiracy theories, and LaRouche seems determined to peddle the biggest and the best: he now indicts not only the British royal family and the European 'Black Guelph' aristocrats, but also the Knights of Malta, IMF officials, Zionists, bankers, the media and the Kremlin. He is currently serving a 15 year gaol term, after being convicted of conspiring to obstruct investigations into fraudulent fund-raising in his 1984 election campaign. His several thousand close supporters are well organized, with intelligence connections from the White House deep down into the anarchist underground. LaRouche will be back

I speak for the forgotten, the unrepresented majority – I speak for the people who want to stick it to Washington.

Lyndon LaRouche

Christopher Lasch

born 1932

▲ AMERICAN CULTURAL CRITIC

Lasch sees anxiety and rage as the characteristic psychological states of contemporary America. The post-war welfare state may have guaranteed material needs, he argues in *The Culture of Narcissism* (1978), but at the cost of frustrating the satisfaction of deeper longings. People have become obsessed with their individual 'survival' – fearing nuclear or ecological apocalypse. Bombarded by advertising that urges them to consume, by fleeting images that blur the distinction between fantasy and reality, and by 'experts' who have taken over the functions previously fulfilled by the community, people lose a sense of who they are and how they can shape their own world. Lasch started off by writing about the political movements of the 1960s – the New Left, feminists, blacks – and how they rendered themselves ineffectual by failing to develop a common radical programme. He has also analysed the way in which the New Right pays lip service to family and community values, but simultaneously undermines the very traditions it wishes to restore by offering unfettered licence to capitalist greed. Although dubbed a 'reactionary' by some on the political left, his analysis of the failings of liberalism provides the essential groundwork for a new politics, which acknowledges the concerns of contemporary conservatism, discards outdated notions about what divides the left from the right and takes account of the impact that the mass media have on the contemporary psyche.

Plagued by anxiety, depression, vague discontents, a sense of inner emptiness, the 'psychological man' of the twentieth century seeks neither individual self-

aggrandizement nor spiritual transcendence but peace of mind, under conditions that increasingly militate against it.
Christopher Lasch,
The Culture of Narcissism

Ralph Lauren

(Ralph Lifshitz) born 1939

99 AMERICAN FASHION DESIGNER

The archetypal Bronx kid who made good, Lauren took business studies before starting off in the fashion industry in the late 1960s with the four-inch kipper tie – a marked contrast to the then-current thin, dull and safe designs. Sold through Bloomingdale's stores, the ties marked the beginning of his popularity, barely interrupted since. His designs today represent what fashionspeak has dubbed 'lifestyle'. They are classic clothes – made of tweed, cashmere, silk and linen and alternating an American impression of the leisured life of the English aristocracy with lines that represent his nostalgia for the all-American 'life on the ranch', with its jeans, shirts and leather jackets. The Lauren image has been built up through advertising campaigns devised by ☛Bruce Weber – black and white evocations of a timeless world centred around picnics in the Hamptons and tennis parties against the backdrop of spacious houses and the great outdoors. Appropriately enough, Lauren designed the costumes for the film adaptation of *The Great Gatsby* (1973).

The Leakey Family

Louis Leakey 1903-72
Mary Leakey born 1913
Richard Leakey born 1944

ANGLO–AFRICAN PALAEONTOLOGISTS

The Leakeys' excavations in Kenya and Tanzania from 1926 onwards proved that East Africa was the cradle of humanity (and twentieth-century palaeontology). Louis laid the groundwork, with the finds that are detailed in *Stone Age Africa* (1936) – in particular a still hugely productive source of fossil remains at Olduvai gorge, which included traces of early hominids and their stone-age implements. Since Louis's death, his wife Mary has continued as director of operations at the gorge, and it has become clearer how much of the work that was attributed to her somewhat flamboyant husband was actually hers. In 1959, she spotted the skull that suggested that humans had evolved, in several branches, a million years earlier than previously believed. Three years later she began to expound the argument that a species of *Homo habilis* (tool-making man) evolved in parallel to several species of *Australopithecus*. Several subsequent finds have been taken to confirm this, but the case is controversial: the 1979 discovery by ☛Don Johanson and Tim White of remains at Afar in Ethiopia can be interpreted as indicating a hitherto unknown parent species. Johanson argues that Mary Leakey's 1959 discovery, for example, belongs to this parent species (*Australopithecus afarensis*) and not, as she maintains, to genus *Homo*. If they are right, hers is not, as was widely reported, the oldest 'human' fossil. Richard, born to Louis and Mary more or less on-site, has not had the opportunity to do more than elaborate his parents' path-breaking work. However, he did make the find, in 1974, of an unusually large-brained skull which had to be genus *Homo* with an age that proves parallelism. And he has argued that the so-called The Third Man, a 2.5 million-year-old 'gracile hominid' with a tiny brain found on the shores of Lake Turkana in Kenya is, in fact, a separate species, rather than a less intelligent representative of *Homo habilis*, as Johanson maintains. Richard has also shown himself to be an effective media communicator and, after a period running the National Museum of Kenya, has taken on the job of preserving Kenya's elephants from ivory poachers.

Timothy Leary born 1920

☆ AMERICAN PSYCHOLOGIST

An amiable college professor during the 1950s, the next decade saw Leary propel himself into social revolution as a proponent of sensory expansion. After experimenting with magic mushrooms, he was introduced to LSD in 1962 (by a biologist who had been investigating what the formula would do to the web-spinning of spiders). Excited by the experience, Leary helped set up the Castalia Foundation, dishing out licences and certificates in acid-dropping, and formulated his 'Turn Off, Tune In, Drop Out' mantra that caused panic among the parents of Middle-America, who came to equate Leary with Mick Jagger, ☛Charles Manson and other such agents of subversion. The FBI could have ignored him as a dotty professor with a talent for publicity, a perpetual smile and a very American tendency to utopian dreaming. Instead, they busted him for possessing marijuana (two cardboard roaches) and sentenced him to ten years in gaol. He was sprung by the Weathermen, made his way to Algeria and the protection of ☛Eldridge Cleaver (the two men hated each other on sight), and then carried on to Afghanistan. There he was recaptured, taken back to the US, put in the same prison as Manson and shunted around the penal system until his release in 1976. Since then, he has written about exo-psychology, neurologic, neuro-politics, re-juvenilization, neuro-geography and other silly subjects and has made a pile on the lecture circuit, debating the rights of the individual with his former nemesis, ☛G. Gordon Liddy. When he attempted to enter the UK in 1983 to promote his autobiography, *Flash Backs*, and the film, *Return Engagement*, he was re-fused entry as an undesirable alien. The convicted criminal, Watergate conspirator Liddy, however, was made extremely welcome. Leary's subsequent attempts to get through passport control at Heathrow Airport have been just as unsuccessful.

John Le Carré
(David Cornwell) born 1931

BRITISH NOVELIST

A former official in the British Foreign Service, le Carré has used the intelligence services as metaphor for the rigidity of Britain's class system, and the resilience of its establishment, in novels ranging from the Cold War dreariness of *A Spy Who Came in from the Cold* (1963) to the psychological acuities of *A Perfect Spy* (1986). In the process, he has popularized the word 'mole' to describe a deep-penetration agent burrowing into the Western capitalist system (he recently yielded to John Buchan his claim to have invented this usage).

Although all the novels are directed at the Soviet target, the Soviets themselves are almost totally absent – an unspoken other, neither devious nor dishonourable. Le Carré's novels define Englishness and parallel his personal involvement with the protection of that mythic place, rural England. For characters he chooses those in the most questionable positions – those who decide for themselves what is the national interest – hence the recurring worries about Britain's declining position within Europe and the post-imperial world. Le Carré has, however, changed with the times: his latest book, *The Russia House* (1989), is a test case for the future of the spy novel in the age of *glasnost*.

Le Corbusier

(Charles-Édouard Jeanneret) 1887–1965

○SWISS-FRENCH ARCHITECT

☞✾& Wherever people live in vandalized blocks of box-like flats, they have to blame not Le Corbusier himself but the cack-handed architects who imitated his innovations. He set out in the 1920s to replace nineteenth-century eclecticism and historicism with a new simplicity in architecture based around the use of modern building materials. His own designs from this period still impress with their balanced contrasts. For ten years from the beginning of WW2, he built nothing, and when he returned to architecture, his faith in machine-age technology and modernist purism had largely gone. Buildings such as the Notre-Dame-du-Haut chapel at Ronchamp (1950–3), with its sweeping curves, dramatic use of light and roughly textured concrete, display a sculptural approach, and an abandonment of modernist purism some 30 years before post-modernism became a fashion. A more ambivalent legacy is his Unité d'Habitation in Marseilles (1945–53) – a reinforced-concrete block containing 337 dwelling units, designed in 23 different types – a masterpiece of collective architecture which still challenges the assumption, bred by countless debased imitations, that all high-rise architecture causes social isolation. The emphasis he placed on the use of low-tech building methods for mass housing constructed by cheap labour has been influential in Third World architecture, and Le Corbusier himself designed the city of Chandigarh, a new capital for the Punjab.

Led Zeppelin

formed 1968

Robert Plant born 1948
Jimmy Page born 1944
John Paul Jones (John Baldwin) born 1946
John Bonham born 1948

⟿ BRITISH ROCK GROUP

It has become easy to forget the astonishment that greeted this drugged-up teenage foursome as they trailed their garish, stomping, dinosaur-squeal music around America in the last days of the 1960s. They led a second British invasion, to be met by critical derision and a wave of adolescent support that only Beatlemania dwarfed. They raped (no other word) the blues, they appropriated songs not their own and claimed the credit, and they chose to dress themselves and their lyrics up in a fantastically silly chivalry 'n' high magic mode. They were a disgrace. They were extraordinary. They were unforgettable, even though many observers may have needed to wipe them from their minds. Their legacy was a strong, loud, deeply unbalanced perversion of the blues, mixed with an unacknowledged debt to the ☛The Beatles.

Timothy Leary

They are popularly credited with having invented heavy metal, which they did not, but they did exacerbate a few too many of its surface idiocies.

Spike Lee

(Shelton Jackson Lee) born 1957

✍ AMERICAN FILMMAKER

Lee may be Hollywood's young-blood maverick, but like the mainstream, he works a cartoon aesthetic, albeit a defiantly African-American one. Lee's films emphasize primary colours in set-design and characterization, as well as improvised frame-to-frame intensity of drama. The result: no one comes out of one of his films with their minds settled. They're more likely to be poking each other in the chest and arguing loudly. His mastery of many-voiced, open-ended on-screen argument is probably his most remarkable talent, while his way with a more standard requirement like plotting is engagingly make-do. His first feature, *She's Gotta Have It* (1987), was basically a soft-core porn story dreamed up at the last minute to make sure that the actors and crew for an earlier failed project could get paid. But the ease with which he peopled it with black Brooklyn bohemia pushed it far beyond its exploitation origins. His second feature, *School Daze* (1988), a musical about in-culture rivalries in an all-black college, stirred up controversy about the value of warts-and-all portrayals. His third (and best), *Do The Right Thing* (1989), about the events leading up to a race riot in Brooklyn, stirred up debate throughout all communities in New York, and may well have contributed to the election of the city's first ever black mayor. *Mo' Better Blues* (1990), his characteristically oblique study of a modern jazz musician's tribulations, for the first time pulled some of its punches, as if Lee loved the music too much to throw it into the potent turmoil he got so much from before. Already a generation of similarly ambitious young black directors has formed in the wake of Lee's success.

Stan Lee

born 1922

$ AMERICAN CARTOONIST

Lee gave comic-strip superheroes the kinds of human sensitivities that ☛Buddy Holly brought to rock 'n' roll. While Batman's toughest problem in the 1960s was whether to buy run-resistant tights, and the last son of Krypton made the Son of God look like an underachiever, Lee's Spider-man was an insecure, financially impoverished youngster who could climb walls but could not do anything about his sinuses. The first superhero that geeks, wimps and weepies could identify with, the character became the cornerstone of Marvel Comics. Lee went on to amass a vast fortune with an array of cult figures inspired by primal urges (the Hulk), theogonistic memory (the Thundergod Thor), Californian psychedelic culture (the Silver Surfer) and even Walt Disney (the demoniacally wisecracking Howard the Duck). For all their super powers, these characters are losers, outsiders in a world they did not create and which will not accept them. They became part of just-out-of-the-mainstream American culture, even inspiring serious theoretical studies and leading the post-Woodstock generation to see an old form in a new way. Comic books have never been the same since.

Lee Kuan Yew born 1923

SINGAPORIAN POLITICAL LEADER

Lee held power for over 30 years in Singapore, until late 1990. For some time a liberal hero, as he turned the country into a model of self-reliant democracy with fast-rising incomes, he became the target of angry criticism as he developed dictatorial traits. His first language was English, despite his birth into a rich Chinese family; he only learned Chinese and Malay when he entered politics. Allying himself with other outsiders to break the hold of business on Singapore's colonial council, Lee won elections as a modern-minded, pro-Western socialist, carried out social reforms, sought to heal Malay-Chinese tensions, formed a bloc with Malaya against Indonesian attacks and took Singapore in, then out of, the Malaysian federation. Singapore became, with Taiwan and Hong Kong, part of the Pacific rim of booming market economies. One result of such economic change was the production of an underclass in the midst of skyscraper affluence and worsening inter-racial tensions. A *de facto* one-party state has evolved, with liberal opponents gaoled as Communist threats. Lee saw himself as a shrewd, tough fighter for the small, crowded island's integrity as a state, always under threat. Ultra-rationalist bourgeois norms, ruthlessly applied, are a feature of Singapore now – an odd policy of eugenics for graduates, hangings for hard drugs offences. A critic's cliché has been the compulsory trips to the barber imposed upon long-haired arrivals at the airport. A touch of paranoia may be to blame: as Lee aged, he did not take up new social challenges and he lost his democratic faith.

Marcel Lefebvre 1905-91

⇔ FRENCH RELIGIOUS LEADER

Many Roman Catholics were vaguely unhappy when the mysterious rituals of the Tridentine Mass were replaced almost overnight by a mundane modern-language version. They lobbied the Vatican for restoration of the 'real thing', but enjoyed little success. Some of those who preferred their prayers in Latin turned to the Fraternity of Pius X, which Lefebvre set up to carry on as if the liberalizing decrees of Vatican II had been just a big mistake – disapproving even of those which recognized religious liberty and freedom of conscience. Lefebvre argued that the new Mass was a surrender to the Protestant Reformation, having turned a sacred rite into a secular meal, and he saw himself as continuing the true tradition, to which the rest of the Catholic Church would eventually return. He blamed the evils of the modern world on the Reformation and the French Revolution. His enemies dismissed as a reactionary throwback with links to the extreme right in France (where most of his followers live), or else as a neo-Protestant. In 1988 he consecrated four bishops: he and they were promptly excommunicated.

Ursula Le Guin born 1929

AMERICAN WRITER

An elegant and controlled writer, Le Guin has always used science fiction to discuss questions about the meeting and cohabitation of incompatible cultures, exploring our own world in subtly altered states. *The Left Hand of Darkness* (1969), for example, depicts a race of androgynous humanoids in their first contact with humans, while *The Dispossessed* (1974) looks at a planet-wide anarchist society as it struggles to come to terms with its ordered, brutal and shamefully exciting parent-society. Very influential in the 1970s, especially on the various utopian feminist schools, her style is, in fact, cool enough for her to have largely escaped consignment to a despised genre-ghetto (and some SF critics consequently accuse her of an overly literary style). Her avowedly Taoist-anarchist slant on social crisis-management can make her seem preachy (her 1976 book, *The Word for World Is Forest*, is too transparent to be an effective critical allegory of the Vietnam War), but she is such an original writer that her faults rarely overwhelm the whole. Le Guin is also one of only a few adult writers who has successfully transferred her skills to children's fiction: the *Earthsea* series is as evocative and thought-provoking as any of her other works.

Mike Leigh born 1943

▲BRITISH FILM, THEATRE, TV DIRECTOR

Since the early 1970s, Leigh has been directing plays for television that take the post-war idea of kitchen-sink realism to a harrowing extreme – with both dialogue and action determined through techniques of improvisation at odds with the mainstream traditions of crafted drama. Works such as *Nuts in May* (1976), *Abigail's Party* (1977) and *Meantime* (1983) strip class uncertainty bare, playing out uneasy confrontations where inadequate, embarrassed and uncomprehending characters drive themselves into agonies of self-crucifixion. Because these are often simultaneously funny and excruciating, Leigh is much criticized as a mocking caricaturist. But he has extended the examination of ill-made language and the logic of the inarticulate far beyond such (now dated) pioneers as ☛Harold Pinter, laying down in the process the groundwork for a very British version of Method acting. It is fairly clear that this, along with his mastery of an unrespectable pop medium – television – has hampered his acceptance in the two most over-regarded middlebrow UK arenas: theatre and cinema. His work in both has been defensive by comparison with the avant-garde, soap-opera force of his television innovations.

Stanisław Lem born 1921

POLISH WRITER

Although Lem's novels have been widely translated, he has never really found a large English-speaking audience; possibly his work is too dense in neologisms and over-solemn philosophizing to win easy acceptance among readers accustomed to frenzied action. The pessimism that underlies Lem's visions of other planets, and the moral dilemmas they throw up for those who reach them, is a universe away from the writings of his Western contemporaries. To appreciate that difference, one only has to compare ☛Kubrick's *2001*, based on a story by ☛Arthur C. Clarke, with the film ☛Tarkovsky made in 1972 from Lem's *Solaris* (1961/70). The latter conveys the horror experienced by a young astronaut as the ocean on Solaris confronts him with the spectre of the girl who loved him on earth and then killed herself – the person he remembers with most guilt. In later novels, Lem shows a future in which computers have taken over from the men who created them, *and* records the destruction of these sophisticated man-made machines as they are pitched against the savage climates and geologies of alien planets. But his sharpest writing is found in his short stories, in one of which Lem's recurring character, the cosmonaut Ijon Tichy, is sent as a delegate to a meeting of the United Planets, where he has to present Earth's rather dubious credentials for admission. Tichy is also present at *The Futurological Congress* (1975), which throws up the intriguing notion of a drug called Dantine, which gives each user the illusion of having written *The Divine Comedy*.

Elmore Leonard

born 1925

▲AMERICAN NOVELIST

With thrillers such as *Stick* (1983) and *Bandits* (1987), Leonard has reflected the emergence of Miami as the new fashion centre of crime in the US. His feel for the rhythms of 'the street' brought a new grittiness to the crime genre, making the slick, gutsy novels in which he explored the shifting behaviour of small-time thugs and indifferent psychos instantly contemporary. His characters, on either side of the law, are subtle, broken ciphers for a constant redefining of the nature of evil amid the detritus of urban decay. At a rollercoaster pace, a metaphysics of action develops out of hard addiction in seamless narratives, peppered with a constant search for a code of survival. It is the endless failure of that quest which fuels his fiction.

Sergio Leone

1929-89

▲ITALIAN FILM DIRECTOR

'They call me the father of the Spaghetti western. If so, how many sons of bitches I have spawned.' Leone was also the man who made ☛Ennio Morricone's music and Clint Eastwood's poncho famous. His attempt to resuscitate the western resulted in long – very long – homages to malodorous, apocalyptic cigarillo-chewing characters who had not learned how to shave. ☛John Wayne razed Comanche villages and maintained the social equilibrium of America, all within a relatively innocuous 78 minutes; a couple could meet, marry, obtain a mortgage, have children, divorce and reconcile within the time it took for Leone's Arriflex to pass from Clint Eastwood's left retina to his right. Leone's eulogizing of the amoral lead that Eastwood played in his 1964 film *A Fistful of Dollars* (and its two sequels) appeased the good-time boys at the drive-ins who remained oblivious to the left-wing diatribes and anti-capitalist messages that the director concealed within three-hour celebrations of the days when 'men still had balls'. Abandoning the western, Leone took a 12-year sabbatical to prepare *Once upon a Time in America* (1983), the tale of a small-time gangster who betrays his friends, which was one of the most ambitious films of the decade. Unfortunately, Leone's moving examination of guilt and remembrance of times lost seemed to hold little appeal for the *Star Wars* generation; yet, once again, he had boldly reinterpreted and reinvented not just a jaded genre but the very idea of cinema.

Emmanuel Le Roy Ladurie

FRENCH HISTORIAN

born 1929

⇔History that aims to reconstruct the life of 'ordinary' people through detailed quantitative analysis of geographical, economic and other factors tends to bore non-specialists, who prefer their accounts of the past tinged with romance and clashing swords. Le Roy Ladurie uses the details of the daily grind as material for imaginative forays into French peasant life before the Revolution. His bestseller *Montaillou* (1975/8) shows the pattern of social conflict underlying the growth of heresy in the eleventh and twelfth centuries in a remote Pyrenean village, and the process of its extirpation. Also remarkable, for its sensitivity to the distinctions of social hierarchy and eye for the play of ritual and symbol, was *Carnival at Romans* (1979), an account of two weeks in a medieval town when a festival turned into bloody rioting. Despite his self-declared nostalgia for pre-urban life (which, one suspects, most of his readers share), Le Roy Ladurie builds a picture of peasant societies as settings for conflicts every bit as dramatic as those proceeding on the larger political stage.

Doris Lessing born 1919

▲ BRITISH NOVELIST

✾ ☆ Britain's cultural arbiters like to make sharp distinctions between realists and fantasists, and many of them have had trouble coping with Doris Lessing's shift from semi-autobiographical narrative to science fiction with a difference. But the continuities in her work are as interesting as the divergences. The early novels, set in colonial Africa or amid the seedy tenements of 1960s' Britain, reflect the pining for some 'alien' intrusion that would breathe new life into the dullness all around – as in her feminist-angled *The Golden Notebook* (1962). More recently, she has taken an extra-terrestrial perspective on the predicament of humanity in her *Canopus in Argos: Archives* series, articulating a gloom-and-doom view of the prospects for European civilization on its way to anarchy, dominated by rioting mobs with no respect for older values. This goes with a mystic belief that individuals can survive by developing higher mental powers so as to transcend both their biological limitations and emotional constraints. The real break is between the outspoken socialist-feminist position of her early years, and her current pessimism. *The Good Terrorist* (1985) – cast very much in the 'realist' mode – consolidates this position as it depicts the futility of radical politics through the eyes of a self-deluding woman who, willing slave to a radical group in a rundown London squat, seemingly understands nothing of the political content contained in the debates going on around her.

Richard Lester born 1932

◆ AMERICAN FILM DIRECTOR, SETTLED IN UK

Starting out in live television in the US, Lester was the first director successfully to bring out the latent surrealism of British comedy and translate it into films. Early work such as *The Running, Jumping and Standing Still Film* (1960) emphasized ☛Spike Milligan's Goon humour, while ☛The Beatles' films (*A Hard Day's Night*, 1964; *Help!*, 1965) showed how, imbued with pop excitement and advert-style editing, humour could become at once laconic and 'wacky'. *How I Won the War* (1967) and *The Bed Sitting Room* (1969)virtually defined British 1960s' black comedy. Later Lester projects, how-ever, have been far less interesting, although the opening sequence of *Superman 3* (1983) – ten minutes of sight gags all featuring great minor British comedy actors such as Graham

Stark and Gordon Rollings – recalls his best. Lester's tragedy echoes ☛Jean-Luc Godard's: he feels he is too intelligent for the medium he has ended up in; he is bored, and it has been showing for some 20 years.

Primo Levi 1919-87

† ITALIAN WRITER

The most respected chemist/artist since Borodin, Levi wrote novels which, although based on personal experience, were much more than autobiographies of his remarkable life. Graduating in chemistry from the University of Turin shortly before Mussolini's racial laws prohibited Jews from taking academic degrees, Levi continued to work as an industrial chemist through the pre-war years. He was later captured as a partisan and deported to Auschwitz. There his scientific knowledge made him useful to his captors, helping to save his life. He returned to Italy, resumed his career and began to write – trying to work through his experience so as to reaffirm the values essential to a civilized society. Grappling with the problem of how to forgive his wartime captors after the war was over, and the guilt of having survived camps where so many died, Levi continually asserts that it is only by looking horror steadily in the face that we can triumph over it. His writing is allusive and metaphorical but always crystal clear. In *The Periodic Table* (1975/84), he takes Mendeleyev's organization of the elements to contruct a narrative in which the properties of each chemical suggest an episode from the past. Structuring the book around the idea of work, Levi seems on the verge of suggesting a new way through the riddle of material being, yet he is always too calm and too self-deprecating to admit to such grandiose schemes. The books are luminous, intelligent and emotionally satisfying; his suicide disturbed many, as if a last act of despair invalidated his seeming triumph over the burden of survival.

We can and must fight to see that the fruit of labour remains in the hands of those who work, and that work does not turn into punishment.

Primo Levi

Claude Lévi-Strauss born 1908

FRENCH ANTHROPOLOGIST

Some anthropologists complain about the inadequacy of his field research, but Lévi-Strauss has transformed the way cultural activity is studied. Never interested in re-creating specific aspects of tribal life, he committed himself to discovering what can be learned from other cultures about human mentality in general. Myths, customs, linguistic practices and kinship systems are keys to the workings of the unconscious mind, reflecting psychological constants that cut across distinctions of time and place. It is Culture that separates humans from Nature, and from this opposition flows a series of binary oppositions through which humans explore and explain their world – village and jungle, animals and people, sky and earth. Since all symbolic structures reflect the same mental constants, it makes no sense to regard primitive peoples as backward (or modern ones as more advanced): each interprets the world according to the evidence on offer. Myths mediate the contradictions that are inherent in the human condition; since they attempt to impose meaning on seemingly chaotic Nature, they are proto-scientific rather than pre-scientific. Lévi-Strauss was kidding himself if he thought he could develop a theory that encompassed all local differences of language and culture, but the structuralist criticism he helped to inspire made possible a serious analysis of popular culture.

Sol LeWitt born 1929

☞AMERICAN ARTIST

More mathematician than sculptor, more draftsman than painter, LeWitt caused controversy when it was revealed that his wall drawings were painted over after their showing so as to deny the collector the 'right' to possess a particular piece of work. Refusing the traditional concerns of an artist, his sympathies lie more with philosophy and other abstract pursuits than emotions or the human figure. For him, the concept is the essential element, the planning more significant than the execution. LeWitt creates obsessive variations on conceptual art, evolving cubical forms with such imaginative titles as *Cube Structure Based on Nine Modules* (1976-1977), fragile black and white prints, and exacting sterile wall drawings which he meticulously plans and leaves others to execute. His systematic exploration of logic and space met its match in the other arts when he collaborated with composer ☛Philip Glass and choreographer Lucinda Childs on *Dance* (1979).

Alexander Liberman born 1912

SOVIET-AMERICAN PUBLISHER, PHOTOGRAPHER, PAINTER, SCULPTOR

The scale of Liberman's output is phenomenal – he has been a photographer, a painter and a sculptor as well as editorial director of Condé Nast Publications, exercising control over such magazines as *Vogue* and *Vanity Fair*. But it may be the distinctiveness of the work he creates as a 'weekend' artist that raises the most important questions about the way in which those with less economic freedom (not to mention self-confidence and creative drive) are controlled by critical fashion. During the 1950s, when wild paint-splattered canvasses were the rage, Liberman produced hard-edged geometrical images that played with the theme of circles. As soon as his form of minimalism began to attract critical approval, he moved on to paint-splashing in a manner reminiscent of ☛Pollock. Whether this simply reflected a sense of mischief, or was due to some alternative interpretation of the *zeitgeist*, a preoccupation with precise geometries is a prevailing theme in his sculptures. He sliced up ruined pipes, tanks and cylinders and welded them into abstract assemblages, which became increasingly complex, ornate and monumental. In 1972, ☛Richard Nixon, who is not noted for his appreciation of sculpture, dubbed Liberman's three-storey-high *Adam* a 'horror' and had it relocated from its original site opposite the Corcoran Gallery in Washington DC.

Roy Lichtenstein born 1923

♦ AMERICAN POP ARTIST

☛Warhol's pop art carried with it a weird, cold charge of dread; ☛Claes Oldenburg's had a wide streak of the bizarre; ☛Richard Hamilton's was directly critical of consumerism. But Lichtenstein's huge blow-ups of strip-cartoon panels, complete with enlarged colouration-blobs and lettering, were almost pure affirmation – his love for a despised medium in all its dumb, cheap-thrill glory was obvious. Beginning, like Warhol, as a commercial design and graphic artist, he moved through abstract expressionism before answering pop's siren call. It is clear that he respected the more technical aspects of strip-craft, and there is an open innocence in these works that is uncannily of its time: the early 1960s. At the same time, by putting such panels up in art galleries, he was mildly questioning conventional high art values. Fashion has moved on; disarming innocence no longer disarms. His work from the 1970s on seems cynical; when he parodies Matisse or Picasso, he is probably pointing out how total the commodification of 'greatness' and 'personality' has become – but this is a grown-up gripe, and no one wants to know. His market rating, however, is moving upwards, with *Torpedo... Los Angeles* being auctioned for $5.5 million in 1989.

G. Gordon Liddy born 1930

AMERICAN SECRET AGENT

Comical, robust American secret agent arrested for his part in the Watergate break-in, Liddy is also a kung fu practitioner, a firearms aficionado, an enthusiast of the writings of Nietzsche and an exponent of stoic witticisms. His sentence was commuted by President Carter in 1977 and he has since parlayed a high media profile, acquired through his bestselling autobiograpy, into a career on the American lecture circuit (where he often engages in feigned confrontational deadlock with amiable academic Timothy Leary), and more recently he has taken up calculated self-parody on prime-time television drama shows. John Cleese based the Kevin Kline character in his film *A Fish Called Wanda* (1988) on Liddy.

György Ligeti born 1923

HUNGARIAN COMPOSER, BASED IN AUSTRIA

A professor at the Liszt Academy in Budapest from 1950, and an exceptional teacher, most of Ligeti's compositions of the immediate post-war period were cast in a conventional mould – based on folk music in the tradition established by Bartók and Kodály. He was also, however, writing more adventurous works, using what he could learn about Schoenberg's innovations to develop his own style. He left Hungary in 1956 and the sudden exposure to new ways of musical thinking radically transformed his compositions. As a refugee in Vienna, he explored electronic and serial music in depth, focusing his attention on large formal shapes and gradually working towards an ideal of slow, seamless change which has come to characterize his mature works, which demand acute attention. He favours loud endings in which the music stops very suddenly: to the *Ten Pieces for Wind Quintet* (1968), he added a quotation from one of his favourite books: 'There was a long pause. "Is that all?" Alice timidly asked. "That's all," said Humpty Dumpty. "Goodbye."'

Don De Lillo *see* De Lillo, Don

Mario Vargas Llosa *see* Vargas Llosa, Mario

Raymond Loewy 1893-1986

FRENCH-AMERICAN DESIGNER

A Frenchman, Loewy was seduced to New York by advertisements in a magazine and went on to stylize the American dream. He designed, over three decades, the Lucky Strike cigarette packet, the Pepsodent toothpaste tube and the Greyhound bus, as well as redefining the dimensions of the Coca Cola bottle. These were all objects which, to Loewy, epitomized the grandeur of America. Initially, as a fashion illustrator, he appropriated the symmetry and elegance of his designs for Saks department store to impose an ethos of sublime beautification on commercial products. These were streamlined to convey the ultimate in subliminal aesthetics to consumers, who were eager to remain perfect in a country where the exterior has usurped the interior. The working equation that was reduced to MAYA – Most Advanced Yet Acceptable Design – became Loewy's gospel, producing a dual legacy of advertising as style and product as art.

Richard Long born 1945

∀ BRITISH ARTIST

Long's work says simple things about simple places. He is a romantic idealist who has created a new form of landscape art, making sculptures out of stone, driftwood and pieces of slate that he arranges in universally recognized patterns – spirals, straight lines and squares. He started off using photographs to record what he created in remote locations, along with maps, drawings and textual pieces that charted his walks in a kind of geographical shorthand, such as 'SCATTERED ALONG A STRAIGHT NINE-MILE LINE: 223 STONES PLACED ON DARTMOOR'. He then developed ways of preserving his 'natural' discoveries and putting them in galleries. Long has assumed the role of a modern primitive, respecting nature and at the same time wishing to leave his mark upon the earth. Cynics scorn the mud handprints on the wall and the stains upon the earth, but Long hardly appeased them when he had himself filmed creating a 'water piece' by pissing down the side of a mountain.

John de Lorean *see* de Lorean, John

Konrad Lorenz born 1903-89

♦ AUSTRIAN ETHOLOGIST

Laboratory-based scientists have been suspicious of Lorenz, who founded the science of ethology – the study of animal behaviour in the natural environment – out of his childhood enthusiasm for playing with geese, and tends to rely on such non-scientific tools as empathy for his most striking discoveries. His childhood experience taught him that a baby gosling who never sees its natural mother will 'imprint' the image of a human carer instead and follow him or her around as it would otherwise have pursued its parent. Working with Dutch ethologist ☛Nikolaas Tinbergen, Lorenz argued that every animal is born with certain pre-programmed patterns of response – such as bringing the egg back into the nest – and these are triggered by 'innnate releasing mechanisms' when they are needed. More provocative are the deductions Lorenz made from animal behaviour to human psychology. In *On Aggression* (1963/6), he argues that human aggressiveness is innate, and that it is the effectiveness of man's killing tools which has disrupted mechanisms that elsewhere confine aggression to species-preserving activities. The book's argument brought forth howls of outrage from those who wanted to believe, against all the evidence, that humans were fundamentally peace-loving until they were provoked, but it became a bestseller and inspired such books as Robert Ardrey's *The Territorial Imperative* and ☛Desmond Morris's *The Naked Ape*. In child psychology, ☛John Bowlby usefully applied Lorenz's ideas about 'imprinting' to his studies of the emotional ties that bind children to their mothers.

James Lovelock born 1919

○BRITISH CHEMIST, ECOLOGIST

◆ To understand life fully, Lovelock argues, we should consider the whole earth as a single organism, which he calls 'Gaia', after the Greek earth goddess. Lovelock is no fringe scientist: he trained as a chemist and formulated his ideas while working for NASA during a period when probes were being sent to Mars to look for life. He believed the search was pointless, as the atmosphere of Mars contains none of the reactive chemicals which have to be continually replenished and used if life is to develop. The atmosphere of the Earth is constantly in flux; without living organisms, it would subside into dead equilibrium. According to Lovelock's Gaia theory, life and the environment are mutually dependent: life regulates the atmosphere and the atmosphere provides the conditions necessary for life. Stars get hotter as they get older, yet the earth has managed to remain remarkably constant in temperature, at a level that is suitable for most of its organisms. The theory is designed to provoke speculation: what kind of drastic regulatory measures will Gaia take to combat the aberration of the manmade greenhouse effect? Will the planet take care of itself? Whether seen as a hypothesis or just a metaphor for the change of consciousness needed for planetary survival, the ideas flowing from Lovelock's house on the edge of Dartmoor are inspirational.

Frank Lowe born 1941

BRITISH ADVERTISING EXECUTIVE

As managing director of Collett Dickinson Pearce, Lowe played a significant part in the transformation of British television advertising in the 1970s, working closely with art directors and copywriters to come up with campaigns that have lasted. The two most famous CDP promotions – campaigns for Heineken lager and Hamlet cigars – have spawned endless sequels. For a long time no one has tried to stop them even though they claimed beneficial properties for both alcohol and nicotine – Heineken refreshes the parts other beers cannot reach; happiness is a cigar called Hamlet – in ways that were theoretically not permissible under the advertising code that came into force in the 1980s. Lowe left CDP to help found Lowe & Howard-Spink, which became, within six years, the third biggest advertising agency in the UK, largely thanks to ads from image-building corporations such as the Guinness Group and the Hanson Trust.

Robert Lowell 1917-77

AMERICAN POET

The muscular style of Lowell's poetry encompasses such themes as his conversion to Roman Catholicism, which he later rejected, and a sense of horror at the erosion of the values he held dear. Insanity and mortality became central to his work as his style moved towards simple directness. *Life Studies* (1959), opens up a series of intensely personal experiences, using his period in a mental hospital for some nakedly revealing poems. Concern with the destruction of values, relationships and traditions generated poetry that was both accessible and yet vulnerable in its honesty. By bringing in his passionate commitment to social responsibility – he served time for being a conscientious objector during WW2 and was an early public-figure protester against US involvement in Vietnam – his poems reflect an awareness of American history that gives them a poignant sense of loss.

Malcolm Lowry 1909-57

✣ BRITISH NOVELIST

Lowry hoped to make a great statement about the human condition but produced only two books during his lifetime, most of which he passed either bumming around the world or holed up in the Canadian wilderness, consuming hard liquor. He had to rewrite his first novel *Ultramarine* (1933), after the typescript had been stolen. *Under the Volcano* (1947), which followed, was a densely plotted tale of an alcoholic consul drinking his way through the Day of the Dead in Mexico while his wife pursues him with reminders of their failed marriage. The book shifts viewpoint several times, but the most powerful passages are those written from behind the eyes of the consul, for whom, through alcoholic mists, three disasters loom: world war and the end of the old way of life; the final failure of his marriage; and his own death. It is an apocalyptic work of great potency. His two other books, completed after his death from reams of intoxicated rambling prose, are attempts to strike a path through the disillusion that was the debris of *Under The Volcano*.

Patrice Lumumba

(Katako Kombe Kasai) 1925-61

➻ AFRICAN POLITICAL LEADER

♥ ▥ Many black African states discovered, when independence came, that they lacked national integrity – given tribal divisions – or a trained, indigenous middle class to run the country. The worst example was the Belgian Congo (now Zaïre). Lumumba, who had graduated through the local élite via spells as a postal clerk and head of a trade union, became a radical nationalist. He was gaoled after a riot in Stanleyville in 1959, led by the party he had formed. When the colonial regime announced elections, all parties required his release as a condition for taking part. Bypassing Belgian ploys, he won. A national leader at 35, he backed a strong, unitary state, but opposition quickly developed: a secessionist movement won control of the Katanga copper belt, Belgian troops landed to support them and Congolese army units mutinied over pay. Lumumba appealed to the UN for help; its army arrived, but could not quell the revolts. When he asked the USSR for transport planes, he was deposed, despite Parliament's backing, by the president, whose forces captured him and handed him over to the secessionists. They killed him, evoking a scandal throughout the continent: he was seen as a pan-African symbol and even his enemies later called him a 'national hero'. The Congo relapsed into violent anarchy for several years, and Lumumba's name haunts the country still. Joseph Désiré Mobutu, who ousted him, has been in power ever since – a violent and corrupt dictator.

Lydia Lunch born 1960

AMERICAN PERFORMER

Lunch staked her claim as plump Queen of the New York No Wave in the very late 1970s when her group, Teenage Jesus and the Jerks, transformed punk from a ☛Ramones-y condensed bubblegum sound to a brutally compact, squealing anti-music noise – barely endurable and certainly not meant to be enjoyable. They took dead-end nihilism and made it into extremist theatre. Somewhat surprisingly, in a notoriously self-destructive world, Lunch has survived and evolved into a tough and sometimes remarkable performer. Her innate sense of drama informs most of her records and readings, from the sublime (*Queen of Slam*) to the severe (*The Uncensored Lydia Lunch*) to the more or less impossible (*13.13*). Her capacity as a musician has always been delimited by extreme perversity; as a writer, however, she has unexpected resources; and as a controversial self-publicist in a milieu that ought to have become unshockable, she is still unmatched.

A(lexander) R(omanovich) Luria

SOVIET PSYCHOLOGIST 1902-77

The only Soviet psychologist to become well-known outside the USSR, Luria qualified in medicine during WW2 and worked on the rehabilitation of soldiers who had suffered brain injuries. Because of his wide interests, which ranged from psychoanalysis to Pavlovian conditioning, he was able to develop a set of multidisciplinary tests to chart the effects of wounds that damaged specific parts of the brain. His discoveries set neuropsychology on a strong footing, and his functional approach has been developed by many Europeans and Americans, but by almost no other Soviet scientist. Although he worked in many areas – attention, perception and the study of learning and forgetting – his two best-known works are short case studies. One describes the shattered perceptions of a brain-damaged soldier; the other the peculiar world of a mnemonist, a man who could remember almost anything, but could forget nothing without extreme effort.

Elisabeth Lutyens 1906-83

BRITISH COMPOSER

Lutyens' stylistic evolution as a composer was slow and arduous. One of the first English composers to use Schoenberg's serial technique, her exploration of 12-note systems during the 1940s and 1950s isolated her from an uncomprehending English musical establishment. Her output was large (over 150 works) and covered all genres, from opera to small-scale ensemble and instrumental music; to supplement her income, she wrote extensively for cinema, contributing scores to Hammer horror movies. Her music-theatre works are based around challenging ideas and radical subject matter: *The Pit* (1947) concerned trapped miners; *Infidelio* (1954) was the story of a broken love affair, traced back from the girl's suicide to a first meeting; and *Time Off? – Not A Ghost of a Chance* (1967) used riddles, puns and free associations to explore the nature of time and the working of chance. She was an influential teacher and friend of young British composers.

David Lynch born 1946

AMERICAN FILM DIRECTOR

Lynch has made only five films in 15 years, and one of them, *Dune* (1984), is a complete dud, but the other four incorporate such a powerful strangeness on or under their surface that no one doubts his importance or originality, only his mental health. *Eraserhead* (1976), from his own script, fused the factory hinterland of his native Philadelphia with the tactile and repellent inner world of the stumbling hero, Henry, an alienated worker bringing up his mutant baby while the electrics crackle and unseen trains shunt and groan. Achingly slow, it is a dread-filled horror one-off that reveals more lineage from ☛Burroughs and ☛Ballard than from the surrealists to whom Lynch claims affiliation, and it is the echoes of their black wit that made it a cult hit. By contrast, with *The Elephant Man* (1980), he took a staple horror-genre idea – the pathos of the hideous freak – and elegantly upended it in a film which never exploits Joseph Merrick's appalling deformities for shock effect. *Dune*, from ☛Frank Herbert's SF pulp blockbuster, proved Lynch incapable of tackling straightforward narrative – he travels by hints, jokes and misdirection, and has always been best at the points where explanations, psychological or otherwise, fail. What was disturbing, once again, about *Blue Velvet* (1986) was the refusal to accept certain basic film conventions in an overall framework so conventional that it is 75 per cent parody. Lynch tricks us into applauding violent death when it comes as retribution (a classic Hollywood device), but refuses to give us any clues regarding how to react to the married woman who demands to be beaten up during extra marital sex sessions. By the time *Wild at Heart* was released in 1990, Lynch had been adopted by Hollywood as its pet avant-gardist, and it was his work on the TV series *Twin Peaks* that seemed much the more daring. Lynch is mild-mannered to a fault, like the heroes of his scripts, and has pushed more ungodly avant-garde sensibility out into popular cinema than even ☛Godard. If he has inherited anything from the surrealists, it is an acute sense of psychological irresponsibility.

Loretta Lynn born 1935

▲AMERICAN COUNTRY & WESTERN SINGER

Married before her 14th birthday, and with four children before she was 20, Lynn went on to become the first woman in country music to join the millionaire ranks, rounding out a remarkable story of self-transformation and instinctive working-class feminism in a world where women rarely achieve any kind of control over their destinies. Unafraid to court controversy, she released a song called 'The Pill' in 1973, at a time when C&W was generally the last court of appeal for rednecks running from pop music's loose morals: several radio stations refused to play it. But she's no wild-eyed radical and put out an LP called *Who Says God Is Dead?* in the late 1960s. Her 1976 autobiography, *The Coalminer's Daughter*, was made into a film with the rather unlikely Sissy Spacek playing the lead role.

Jean-François Lyotard born 1924

& FRENCH PHILOSOPHER

One of the most original of the last wave of post-1968 Left Bank *philosophes*, Lyotard was at one time a militant member of the 1950s' anti-Stalinist movement, Socialisme ou Barbarie. The titles of his books, in particular *Dérive à partir de Marx et Freud* (1973), show him also to have been influenced by ☛Debord and the Situationists (*dérive*, meaning 'drift', was a word of huge importance to them). In the wake of the events of 1968, he had become disillusioned by any form of monolithic revolutionary resistance to capitalism, on the grounds that the faiths to which revolutionaries have recourse reintroduce only the most reactionary of pre-capitalist structures (hence, of course, Stalin as the feudal despot). For Lyotard, capitalism – cynical, vast, variegated – is so relentless a machinery for change (good and evil), so subtle and unstoppable an appropriator of value, that our only strategy can be what he called Paganism, the elimination of a drive for one truth in favour of a many-headed multiplicity of narratives, a recognition of local possibilities, and the (ancient Greek) Logic of the Occasion – which allows for no eternal truths, only strategic and parochial observations. An extensive summary of his position, as the advance guard of post-modern philosophy, is given in *The Differend: Phrases in Dispute* (1983/8), which begins with an examination of the philosophical meaning of Auschwitz, and goes on to make clear that wrestling with problems of naming and legitimation is pushing Lyotard towards arguments for formalized constitutions and provisional, but always debatable, structures for the 'Rights of Man' which are in advance of any presently adopted.

Trofim Denisovich Lysenko

SOVIET AGRONOMIST 1898–1976

Lysenko's willingness to bend genetic theory to fit vulgar Marxist-Stalinist precepts was one of the low points in twentieth-century science. An agricultural reformer, and a proponent of I. V. Michurin's Lamarckian model of inheritance (which allowed for inheritance of acquired characteristics), Lysenko hoped to announce that improvements in the environment – coupled with the speedy perfectability that Michurin's theories claimed for crops – would lead to a (much-needed) revolution in Soviet agriculture, magnificent harvests of wonder-crops and his own scientific deification. None of these was, on its own, a crime against science, even though the theories contradicted accepted Mendelian ideas of chromosome-heredity. What was wrong was his mode of proof: he would appeal to Stalin and dialectical materialism, denouncing those who disagreed with him, and rubbishing Mendelian theories as formalistic, bourgeois and metaphysical. Opponents were forced to recant publicly – one, N. I. Vavilov, the Soviet Union's leading Mendelian, was imprisoned for agricultural sabotage and died in a camp in 1943. Lysenko wrecked Soviet genetics for a generation, as his followers flocked to grab posts, degrees, honorary titles, prizes, dachas and private cars. None of their projects came to anything; the super-crops failed to materialize. Mendel was right and Lysenko was wrong. So, by a bitter irony, was Vavilov: Lysenko, though no more 'dialectical' than any of his victims, had found several errors in Vavilov's 'law of homologous series in variation'. But by appealing so disgracefully to the gallery where Uncle Joe sat, Lysenko managed to outlaw genuine scientific discussion. He was discredited when Stalin died, and what little he got right was not enough for him to retain any kind of reputation, although he held on to both his titles and his Michurinist beliefs right up to his death.

Yuri Lyubimov born 1917

SOVIET THEATRE DIRECTOR,
SETTLED IN WESTERN EUROPE

A pioneering Soviet theatre director as well as a canny political operator, Lyubimov's autocratic methods have not endeared him to performers in the West, where he has worked since 1984. He took over the Taganka Theatre Company in Moscow during the cultural 'thaw' instituted by ☛Khrushchev, and then maintained it as a steadily simmering cauldron of protest through the more oppressive times that followed. 'The theatre,' he said, 'is like an open fire in a very cold house. Everybody comes to sit near its warmth.' His modern-dress *Hamlet*, with the lead part taken by the late, extraordinary singer Vladimir Vysotsky (calling him 'Russia's ☛Bob Dylan' does not convey the radical anger his voice articulated), became a symbol for radical theatre throughout Eastern Europe. Lyubimov's survival is generally credited to his success in persuading the children of Yuri Andropov, KGB head and briefly Soviet premier, not to go on the stage. Following Andropov's demise, and an attack on the Soviet authorities that he delivered in London, he was banished. Since then he has roamed Europe, a brooding presence, staging productions of theatre and opera. In 1988, he was allowed back to Moscow on a ten-day visit.

M

Claire McCardell 1905-58

AMERICAN FASHION DESIGNER

When Americans emerged from WW2, somewhat less in love with things European than they had been before, it was McCardell who designed the clothes that defined their new mood. Her 'American Look' was the antithesis of the nipped waists, padded shoulders and tight skirts which marked pre-war styles in Paris and Rome. Dressed by McCardell, the American woman could be relaxed and comfortable; in advertisements, of course, she was also tall, slim, blonde and sporting a gorgeous smile. McCardell took ideas from men's work clothes, pioneered the use of denim in the Popover – a dress that was smart enough for social events but could also be worn around the house – and exploited traditional, simple materials to conjure an image of the Wild West in the rarefied world of fashion design. Her inventions reflected the new status that women had been given in the workplace and, although the factories were closed to most of them after the war was over, McCardell's clothing ideas are all around us still.

Eugene McCarthy born 1916

✌ AMERICAN POLITICIAN

A former candidate for the priesthood and an economics professor, McCarthy became a senator who, when he ran for the US Democratic Party presidential nomination in 1968, won the support of anti-Vietnam protestors. His success in the New Hampshire primary triggered the exit from the race of ☛President Johnson, who was losing confidence in his ability to bring the Vietnam War to a successful conclusion and had become disturbed at the way the issue was dividing the nation. Robert Kennedy, before his assassination, took over the liberal banner from McCarthy, but Hubert Humphrey, Johnson's man, won the nomination (but lost the election). McCarthy had managed, for the first time, to mobilize young radicals in a grassroots presidential campaign. It ended in tears and tear-gas at the Chicago convention, when his angry, bitter backers responded violently to his exclusion, calling down the wrath and the clubs of Mayor ☛Daley 's police. McCarthy was an also-ran in the 1976 presidential election, as an independent. He then retired from politics, to devote his time to writing poetry and journalism.

Joseph McCarthy 1909-57

AMERICAN POLITICIAN

A Republican senator, McCarthy gave his name to an 'ism' and to a brief twilight era, as he directed charges of Communist affiliation and treason against people in high posts. An obscure circuit judge, he won election to the US Senate in 1946, by making inflated claims about his role in the war. He was not a major presence in ☛Nixon's case against ☛Alger Hiss, but in 1950, with his career apparently on the wane, he said in a speech that he held in his hand the names of 205 Communists in the State Department. His claims stunned America and were the cause of much hysteria, playing on deep-rooted public hostility towards East Coast WASP and Jewish intellectuals. As chairman of a major Senate sub-committee, he initiated over 150 further probes of senior 'Communists', identified by data coming from his 'loyal American underground'. Hollywood was turned upside down in the hunt for Marxists, and many careers were ruined as McCarthy's flourished. Neither ☛President Truman nor ☛Eisenhower (from 1953) stood up to him. Ultimately it was television that destroyed the monster he had become when, in 1954, like those he had mercilessly pursued, he cited the Fifth Amendment as the reason for his refusal to disclose the sources for his allegations that the army was riddled with Communists. Publicly ridiculed, McCarthy ended his few remaining days staring numbly into the fire and blaming it all on the Kremlin. The spectre of his 'witch-hunts' is now routinely invoked by any hack politician under investigative pressure.

Don McCullin born 1935

▲BRITISH PHOTOGRAPHER

McCullin is an unremitting observer of the human cost of warfare. Although his subjects have ranged beyond war, it is the photographs from Vietnam that made his international reputation. Caught in the middle of the Tet Offensive of 1968, he was a key element in turning the media picture of the conflict from a noble endeavour to a fraught, homicidal nightmare, where mechanized slaughter proved no match for guerrilla warfare and ideological determination. Much of the power in McCullin's work comes from his seeming refusal to impose any formal aesthetic on his subjects; however, his calm compositions ensure that suffering, in all its horrifying squalor, stands unjudged and yet intimately embraced in the most desperate moments of unguarded revelation. In 1970, he photographed starving, disease-ridden Biafran children: his pitiful pictures of small bloated bodies, of eyes encrusted with flies and of a baby sucking vainly at a withered breast pile-drive through any form of complacency. In the 1980s and 1990s, he has turned his camera on to the British scene, recently producing a powerful series on the homeless in London's cardboard cities.

Ross Macdonald 1915-83

AMERICAN CRIME WRITER

Macdonald inherited Chandler's crown as a writer of West Coast crime stories, bringing a broken-backed humanity to the private detective genre. His most famous creation – the private detective Lew Archer – was a weathered reflection of the changing social and moral texture of the 1960s. Much of the despair of unfulfilled expectations that the denizens of Hollywood's underbelly display in the novels is balanced out by the corruption that underlies the incestuous networks of the *nouveau riche* families who call upon Archer to tidy up their affairs. The overhanging materialist obsessions of the 1950s fade away to the disillusion of the 1960s, where Flower Power oblivion and the morality of the new money continuously collide over the true casualties in Macdonald's novels: that generation's bewildered and lost children. Archer wearily patrols the wasteland of drugs, blackmail, promiscuity and homicidal resolution, where each case is a numbing education in human nature and its pursuit of oblivion in an emotional void.

David Mach born 1956

BRITISH SCULPTOR

Mach's work began to be noticed when one of his pieces, *Solaris* (1983), sparked a controversy pitching the sensitivities of taxpayers against the claims of artistic license. Such was the apparent public fervour stirred by his giant submarine built from disused tyres that a kamikaze protest by one irate member of the public led to the protestor's accidental death and the destruction of the work. This sad fiasco ignited Mach's career. He is an artist who rejects the isolation of the studio, preferring to work publicly as a kind of sculptural performance artist, and builds his works in shopping centres, parks, streets and car showrooms as often as in galleries or museums. Mach manipulates unorthodox materials – remaindered books, discarded shoes, unsold magazines – into a variety of sculptural forms such as a Greek column built out of plates, a head formed out of matchsticks or, his *tour de force, Fuel for the Fire* (1983), where billowing waves of stacked magazines poured through the gallery space, dislodging an upright piano, sofa and television in the manner of a hurricane. Intending the use of such materials as a commentary upon the wastefulness of consumerism, March builds monuments to the ruins of our post-industrial society.

The things I use are not dead like found objects. They are still part of life. The magazines will be shredded and repulped and will appear again next month – that awareness of a life cycle is an important aspect.

David Mach

Colin MacInnes 1914-76

BRITISH NOVELIST

Born in London and educated in Australia, MacInnes's celebrated trilogy of novels from the late 1950s – *City of Spades, Absolute Beginners* and *Mr Love and Justice* – catalogue his interest in the teenage phenomenon and popular music of the times. The effervescent protagonist of *Spades* is Johnny, a Nigerian pursuing excitement in the centres of London's low-life: pubs, drug emporia and illicit sex clubs. MacInnes intended Johnny's youthful ebullience to personify pop culture and an evolving multi-racial society, twin phenomena welcomed by the author as antidotes to the prim, constricting views of England's establishment. Since McInnes tried to analyse and popularize simultaneously, these tales of life, lust and love in the subtly discoloured environs of Tin Pan Alley retain their warmth and whimsy, although, through the processes of history and time, they no longer 'groove' in the manner intended.

George Maciunas 1931-78

LITHUANIAN-AMERICAN PUBLISHER, CO-ORDINATOR

Although Fluxus as an art movement is associated with such distinguished figures of the avant-garde as ☛John Cage, ☛Joseph Beuys, ☛Nam June Paik, ☛Yoko Ono and others, they would all acknowledge that it lived and died through the more obscure George Maciunas. Working as a graphic designer for the US army in West Germany, Maciunas had become adept at abusing their postal system for his own disruptive purposes. During the 1960s, he organized international multi-media events and underground news policy mailings which would forever blur distinctions between pop spectacle, disorientation course, demo and experimental music/art/performance workshop. But by the mid-1960s, tensions between the more culturally inclined avant-gardists and the more politically oriented activists had led to a breakdown of the movement's earlier jubilantly confused and confusing values, and the spectacles that developed from 1970 onwards – which included fluxshow, fluxmass, fluxhalloween – were dramatic, utopian and entertaining without being particularly subversive. Maciunas's death led inevitably – and therefore perhaps a little drably – to a fluxfuneral, and the movement wound down for good.

FLUX ART – non art – amusement forgoes distinction between art and non-art, forgoes artists' indispensability, exclusiveness, individuality, ambition, forgoes all pretension towards a significance, variety, inspiration, skill, complexity, profundity, greatness, institutional and commodity value.

George Maciunas

Malcolm McLaren born 1946

BRITISH IMPRESARIO, MUSICIAN

Managers have been almost as much part of rock mythology as the performers – Colonel Parker, Larry Parnes, Brian Epstein, ☛Andrew 'Loog' Oldham, Allen Klein and the Bowie/Bolan manager Tony De Vries epitomize their era of music nearly as much as their clients do – but the late 1970s saw this type of figure disappear from view. It was Malcolm McLaren – clothes-shop owner in partnership with ☛Vivienne Westwood and failed manager of the New York Dolls – who, with his group ☛The Sex Pistols, brought the job back into the realms of infamy once more. As The Pistols rose and fell, McLaren began the task of mythologizing his part in their story, aided by Julien Temple's marvellous pop film (but lousy biopic) *The Great Rock 'n' Roll Swindle* (1980). McLaren continued to create trends, inadvertently inventing Adam and the Ants as chart stars, making his own (sometimes influential) records and, occasionally, burying some failure (where is She Sheriff now?). Not as important as he says he is, McLaren's stories, true and false, nevertheless continue to fire up the imaginations of would-be pop stars and svengalis.

Marshall McLuhan 1911-80

♦ CANADIAN CULTURAL THEORIST

'The medium is the message' became the cocktail party cliché of the 1960s, and many thought that propounding this slogan gave them insight into McLuhan's complex theories about the way in which new communication media change the individual's understanding of time, space and the self. It is difficult now to get much sense out of the distinction he drew in *Understanding Media* (1964) between 'hot' and 'cold' media – the hottest medium being the visual and tactile gestures humans used to communicate before the development of speech – and easy to sympathize with the bullshitter in ☛Woody Allen's *Annie Hall* when confronted in a cinema queue by McLuhan saying, 'You have no understanding of my work.' McLuhan's point seems to be that the new electronic media would restore a (hot) sense of community and collectivity to a fragmented society, as in the period before the (cold) printing press, thus uniting all humanity in a 'global village'. It is a formulation that now seems simplistic as well as mystic, but McLuhan was clearly on the right track in arguing that new technologies would bring new ways of perceiving reality, and it was books such as *The Mechanical Bride* (1951) – an analysis of the way magazines, newspapers, comic strips, advertising, etc., affect readers – that helped determine the direction of contemporary media studies. McLuhan's eschewing of conventional snobberies about popular culture, as well as a talent for aphorisms, made him a celebrity even while one-time admirer Jonathan Miller accused him of offering up 'a gigantic system of lies'. McLuhan said that his books were just 'tentative probes' – which seems fair enough.

Harold Macmillan 1894-1986

✌ BRITISH POLITICAL LEADER

Despite early promise, it was only after Macmillan had reached his seventh decade that he came centre-stage politically. From then on, he was the supreme actor-manager, able to identify himself with ☛Eden's Suez venture, yet emerge unscathed from the ensuing crisis and secure the leadership of the Conservative Party. He went on to win an election on a consumer boom, persuading voters that they had 'never had it so good'. By the time he became prime minister, no clear, consistent ideas survived: hence the store he set by British entry to the EEC, denied him by ☛de Gaulle, as the cure for an ideological vacuum in the seat of power. In 1963, he resigned, supposedly because of ill health, although loss of momentum – as the political world saw through the vacuum – may have added to the pressure. The actor in him was at work when, following his elevation to the House of Lords as an hereditary peer, he warned against the ☛Thatcher government's privatization policy; 'selling the family silver' was his way of putting it. He had a gift for lasting lines, but also a flair for steering his country through troubled times – as it emerged from the comfortable 1950s, lost an empire and ran into major trade deficits. An impresario, he was not a dramatist in his own right: he did not know how to write the plot.

Robert McNamara born 1916

AMERICAN BUSINESS EXECUTIVE, POLITICIAN

Defence and managerial analysis have been the key interests of McNamara's life, stemming from his early years teaching management to the US Air Force at Harvard Business School. The first President of Ford Motors who was not a member of the family, his ability to predict shifts in popular taste derived from a grasp of the implications of rising affluence: a decision to change the company's Thunderbird from a two- to a four-seater trebled sales. He also promoted the idea of safety belts in cars, and came up with the concept of a 12,000-mile warranty. Both ☛ Truman and ☛Eisenhower approached him about a job in government, but it was for ☛Kennedy, in 1961, that he gave up his lucrative post to become secretary of defence. Civilian control, managerial efficiency and value for money were key themes of his period in office. 'Flexible response' – the idea of graduated, proportionate retaliation – was the key novelty he introduced into NATO 's war plans. He went along with the escalation of US involvement in Vietnam by both Kennedy and ☛Johnson, but was one of the first to become seriously disillusioned and argue that the US was on to a loser. During a long spell as head of the World Bank, he moved further in a liberal, dovish direction, and in the late 1980s he proposed halving US defence spending (currently six per cent of GNP) over the next eight years.

David McTaggart born 1948

CANADIAN ECOLOGIST, BASED IN UK

Once a building tycoon in Canada (where he made, lost and made a lot of money), McTaggart does not like to be called the 'founder' of Greenpeace, claiming he is just one among a group of American and Canadian friends who staged protests against ecological destruction during the early 1970s. But he did help to dream up the idea of a mobile flotilla – 'the first eco-navy in history' – to monitor or attack whale-hunts, nuclear tests and other sea-going threats to the ecosphere. The first Greenpeace campaign, in 1970-1, was aimed at atmospheric nuclear testing which threatened the island of Amchitka, off Alaska. In following years, McTaggart twice sailed into the French Pacific to challenge a ban on boats and to protest at nuclear tests; he was badly hurt the second time, when his boat was rammed. He has settled in the UK, running the Greenpeace HQ from Lewes, East Sussex.

Madonna born 1961

(Madonna Ciccone)

❍AMERICAN SINGER

$ Never as dirty as the hype suggested, Madonna's blend of emotionless sexuality with a refined, trash-based style secured her unparalleled penetration as a mid-1980s sexual icon. The image of consumer disposability that she created was timed to exploit the emphasis on visual packaging that MTV had introduced into the music industry, but underneath the wrapping of all-singing, all-dancing whore with a heart of videotape, Madonna had a highly commercial mind that synthesized black dance music into disco anthems of independence for girls seeking a new role model. The result, partially echoing the ecstatic reception of ☛Monroe in the 1950s, generated impressive sales. The hype machine was fuelled by her short-lived marriage to bad boy actor Sean Penn and by claims that she lost her virginity as a career move, but her film ventures to date have not recaptured the note of seductive indifference on display in her first picture, *Desperately Seeking Susan* (1985). Street smart, heartless and always ready to exploit her own sexuality, the bump and grind was less a come-on than an aggressive assertion of independence. None the less, it is hard not to assume she will secure some sort of longevity.

Madonna

Maharishi Mahesh Yogi

✚INDIAN CULTIST born 1911

☆Finding oneness with God was once a tough struggle to which only a few mystically minded monks and nuns dedicated their lives. Then the Maharishi came from India to offer an easily mastered shortcut – Transcendental Meditation – with such practical benefits as increased energy and 'creative intelligence'. TM was tailored to an irreligious and materialistic age, but it also pitched itself to an idealistic one; the Maharishi declared that, if everybody mastered his quick way to bliss, there would be no more social conflict, no more political haggling, no more wars. Impractical? If only one per cent of the world's population took up TM; their 'good vibrations' would quell the rancour and discontent. According to his Plan for Peace, the Governors of the Age of Enlightenment would visit those places where trouble threatened and start the mantras humming. The Maharishi himself travelled the world during the 1960s, but significant attention was forthcoming only after ☛The Beatles, seemingly traumatized by material success, came to sit at his feet. Ultimately, this brief liaison did not do his (or their) reputation any good: the Maharishi declared the failure of his mission after The Beatles had abandoned TM. But, unlike the Fab Four, he was to make a comeback: many people find TM a useful antidote to modern anxieties. The Maharishi's saving grace has always been his sense of humour.

Naguib Mahfouz born 1911

EGYPTIAN NOVELIST

Although he won the Nobel prize for literature in 1988, this giant of the modern Arabic novel is still largely unknown in any language but his own. He made his name with *The Cairene Trilogy* shortly after WW2, and has dominated Arabic writing ever since. The position of the Arabic novelist in a world still dominated by the teachings of the Koran is an uncertain one – Islamic teaching insists that Arabic is the language of God and law, so that even the idea of the modern novel hints at blasphemy. Mahfouz's 1959 trilogy, *Awlad Haritna*, was banned in Egypt on the eve of publication. Some commentators argue that his solitary dominance has held back a broader development of modern Arabic literature – as one younger writer put it, anyone who decided to write a novel would always first have to check that Mahfouz had not already written it. He is now held in such respect that even his modulated support for the Camp David peace accords, a treaty which enraged much of Egypt and the Arab world, could not diminish it, though it did lead to bans on his work for a time in some countries.

Norman Mailer born 1923

❞AMERICAN WRITER, FILM-MAKER

Power and the way it distorts private and public worlds are the recurrent themes of Mailer's writing. Developing an uneasy, blustering blend of 'improved' journalism – both fiction and 'faction' – he has written about boxing, the moon landings, the demonstrations at the 1968 Chicago Democratic Convention and ☛Marilyn Monroe, making himself and his tussles with his conscience, his urges and his image the centre and the driving force of any topic he lights on. Since the publication of his first novel, *The Naked and the Dead*

(1948), he has been renowned for a pugnaciously didactic and sometimes brilliant style, a penchant for violence on and off the page, his many divorces and his fine taste in haircuts. Mailer was one of the earliest and most influential American pop existentialists, and his essay 'The White Negro' had an enormous shaping effect on youth culture attitudes and philosophies of the individual-as-criminal-as-artist; he also helped fund the *Village Voice* in the 1950s, which gave the underground its first significant platform. His polemics on the theory and practice of violence-as-sex led to a famous feminist denunciation from ☛Kate Millett in the 1970s, and a peculiar series of showdowns that he was almost bound to lose. He has directed unwatchable films about himself and the world, written unreadable tracts about himself and the world, and tied himself into the most intractable public positions: one of his most exasperating and exhilarating tendencies is his need to tackle arguments from the loser's side. *The Executioner's Song* (1979), for example, investigated the wasted life and twisted soul of Gary Gilmore, the first man to be executed for murder in the US for over ten years. His relative silence during the ☛Reagan years has been regrettable – in an age when everyone else was so cautiously on the make, his incautious, self-indulgent, self-destructive bravura would have been instructive and inspirational.

Miriam Makeba born 1932

✌ SOUTH AFRICAN SINGER

When Makeba returned to her native South Africa in mid-1990, she had been in exile for more than 30 years. Twice a representative of her brutalized people before the Special Committee on Apartheid at the United Nations, Makeba has long embodied both the contradictions and the possibilities of combining politics with a career in pop. As an international success in the 1960s, under the auspices of Harry Belafonte, she became a symbol of what African music could offer: a new pan-global sound language of liberation and cultural independence. She married ☛Stokely Carmichael in the late 1960s, leading to her exclusion from the US as well, and has since made her home in West Africa. A diminutive, tough, battle-scarred woman, she returned once again to the world stage for a tour with Paul Simon in 1987. As always, controversy surrounded her decision, but judgements of her artistry were unanimous in their praise.

Bernard Malamud 1914-86

▲ AMERICAN NOVELIST

The experience of Jewish immigrants to the New World is the fulcrum around which Malamud weaves his tales of magic set in decrepit apartment blocks, and the Depression, seen from the 1950s, is the chief source of his stories. Love offers glimmers of redemption from the neighbourhoods in which his hard-working immigrants struggle through day-to-day life. In the gentle parables of his later work, Malamud often returns fleetingly to the flights of fantasy and the absurd that characterized his first novel, *The Natural* (1952). This tale of an ageing baseball player who finds he has miraculous powers is characterized by the poetry of Malamud's language, evoking a magical world where good and evil face off, and paradise beckons – only to be denied. The constant struggle of his characters to retrieve some kind of life from the ruins of the past brings a grey feeling to his writing, although flashes of humour and salty wisdom pierce briefly through the darkness.

Malcolm X 1925-65

(Malcolm Little/El Hajj Malik El-Shabbazz)

➳AMERICAN POLITICAL LEADER

✌ ♥ As a child, Malcolm Little saw his father murdered and his house burned by whites. The hate and anger this exposure to racism imprinted upon him was further nurtured during a period in prison, from which he emerged as an acolyte of Elijah Muhammad, subscribing to the rigid code of discipline and dress followed by the Nation of Islam (the Black Muslims) – plain dark suits, white shirts, close-cropped hair and general abstemiousness. His rich voice and charisma turned Malcolm X – the new name he adopted as a break from his oppressed past – into the leading spokesman for Muhammad's cause, advocating a rejection of the values of white society at a time when ☛Martin Luther King was emphasizing the transformation of those values by love and non-violence. His political aspirations frustrated by Muhammad, Malcolm separated from the Black Muslims in 1964, travelled through Africa and the Middle East, converted to orthodox Islam and made a pilgrimage to Mecca. Returning to the US, he formed the Organization of Afro-American Unity, but was assassinated by former associates before the organization had begun to take root. Malcolm's form of black consciousness – characterized by the idea that 'Black Is Beautiful' – was a legacy developed by ☛Stokely Carmichael, ☛Eldridge Cleaver and the Black Panthers.

David Mamet born 1947

AMERICAN PLAYWRIGHT, FILM-MAKER

Before Mamet took to directing for the screen (he claims he did this to defend his scripts), the Chicago-born playwright had built his reputation with a series of one-act plays, culminating in *Sexual Perversity in Chicago* (1974), which wittily and remorselessly examined the tissue of lies necessary to maintain a relationship. His first big hit, *American Buffalo* (1975), was the story of two foul-mouthed crooks whose dream of stealing a coin collection founders because of their limitations. The movie work started to come in after his play *Glengarry Glen Ross* (1987), resulting in his foul-mouthed script for *The Verdict* (1982) and the adaptation of *Sexual Perversity* into *About Last Night...* (1986). Mamet described the latter effort as an abortion, and also vented his spleen on Brian De Palma for adding a railway station shoot-out to *The Untouchables* (1986). He turned director with *House of Games* (1987), a complex story about perception, deception and gullibility, which was followed by the light and insubstantial *Things Change* (1988). His return to the theatre – and continuation of his revenge on Hollywood – with *Speed-the-Plow* (1987), features his usual brilliant dialogue wrapped up in an unbelievable plot (sleazebag producer is converted to message movies after sleeping with idealistic secretary), which was rendered half credible on Broadway by actor Joe Mantegna, but ultimately torpedoed by the much-hyped presence of a miscast ☛Madonna, a coup that seems indicative of Mamet's growing collusion with the 'package' mentality that has blighted American culture. Mamet has talent, cynicism and an ability to turn obscenity into an art form – no one writes an insult like Mamet – but his work is cold, distant and lacking in real sympathy.

Paul de Man, *see* de Man, Paul

Nelson Mandela born 1918

SOUTH AFRICAN POLITICAL LEADER

A black nationalist leader and hero of the movement against apartheid, Mandela spent over 27 years in prison before being released, in February 1990, as the man most likely to negotiate the seemingly impossible – a constitution that would give political rights to South Africa's black majority on terms acceptable to the whites. For most of those years, Western anti-apartheid movements had made calls for Mandela's release their rallying point – a touchstone for the Pretoria government's commitment to reforming the system. Son of an African chief, he had turned down the succession to become a lawyer and, from 1951 to 1952, led a 'defiance campaign' against discrimination under apartheid laws, as a member of the African National Congress (ANC). He argued for non-violent resistance until the Sharpeville massacre of 1960. Then, going underground to evade a government ban on the ANC, he began to espouse violence of a non-terrorist sort, aimed at state or military targets and not designed to spread civilian panic. He was convicted in 1964, with others, for incitement to sabotage, treason and violent conspiracy against the South African regime. The government initially refused to respond to Western demands for his release, unless he signed a pledge to non-violence, which he wouldn't do. Eventually, however, President F. W. de Klerk gave way out of a desire to lead South Africa back to international respectability, and bring an end to continuous police oppression. Inevitably, Mandela's release brought disillusion in its wake. His increasingly warm relationship with de Klerk, renunciation of violence and international globetrotting did not indicate a leader getting to grips with the problem of deteriorating public order in the townships, the result of murderous confrontations between supporters of the Zulu Chief Mangosuthu Buthelezi 's Inkatha movement and members of the ANC.

I believe that the overwhelming majority of South Africans, black and white, hope to see the ANC and the government working closely together to lay the foundations for a new era in our country in which racial discrimination and prejudice, coercion and confrontation, death and destruction, will be forgotten.

Nelson Mandela (1990)

Benoit Mandelbrot born 1924

FRENCH MATHEMATICIAN, SETTLED IN US

Mandelbrot's still controversial fractal geometry may represent the first important step for some 200 years in the oldest branch of mathematics. By focusing attention on the apparently innocuous question 'How long is the coast of Britain?', Mandelbrot emphasized the problems of magnification, self-similarity and approximation: however much you enlarge the map, the coastline will still be wiggly – and *in the same kind of way.* All you can do is choose an arbitrary scale at which to stop filling in further detail (the 'real', useless answer is that the coastline has infinite length). Going further, he drew comparisons with certain geometrical 'monsters' (Koch's Island, the Serpienski Sponge) that various nineteenth-century analytical mathematicians had come across and then had hurriedly hidden at the back of the cupboard. Working at IBM, Mandelbrot devised a technique for assigning these figures fractional dimensions that took account of this hitherto untackled anomaly. For example, a coastline, enclosing a finite area inside its infinite length, would be given a dimension between one (that of a line) and two (that of an area). His ideas are basic to modern computer graphics. Conversely, improved graphics have been essential in exploring such strange new worlds as the 'Mandelbrot set', something that was simply beyond comprehension in paper-and-pencil days. Fractal geometry has turned out to approximate many natural formations and processes – from lightning flashes and fern-growth to the chaotic turbulence patterns in clouds – far better than its predecessors.

Lata Mangeshkar born 1940

INDIAN SINGER

Mangeshkar has probably recorded more songs than any other human being: in the early 1980s, the number was put at some 25,000. Since the 1960s she has been the leading playback singer in the Bombay film industry – that is, she has provided the singing voices for the stars of countless completed or unfinished Hindi musicals (Indian actors are rarely also singers). With her sisters, Usha Mangeshkar and Asha Bohsle, she wields unprecedented influence in an industry that treats its artists in a distressingly conveyor-belt manner. She owes this in part to her longevity as a performer, but also to her voice, which retains a fiery and youthful flexibility. At home with traditional *ghazals* as well as the latest disco-pop, she is largely unrecognized outside her own worldwide community.

Charles Manson born 1935

AMERICAN MURDERER

Manson demonstrated that the fragrance of love hanging over the 1960s was mutating into violence and barbarity when he channelled his peculiar cocktail of black magic, drugs, sex and rock 'n' roll into homicidal mania. Having spent the first seven years of the decade in gaol (and most of the rest of his life in some form of institution), he tried unsuccessfully to break into the music business, then took to touring the roads of California in his converted VW 'love nest'. The 'Manson family', which he gathered around him, eventually comprised about 20 nubile drop-outs, all into sex, hallucinogenic drugs and Manson's messianic fantasies. On 9 August 1969, the gang brutally murdered the pregnant actress Sharon Tate (wife of film director ☛Roman Polanski) and four of her friends and then, the following day, Leno LaBianca, the president of a supermarket chain, and his wife Rosemary – victims chosen at random from among the wealthy inhabitants of Los Angeles – smearing the walls with blood and pseudo-political graffiti: DEATH TO PIGS, HELTER SKELTER. Gaunt of face, long-haired and with demonic eyes, Manson became the focus for speculation upon neuroses and decadent social mores, and he is still idolized as the ultimate outsider by satanists and neo-Nazis. Manson was sentenced to death in 1971, with his sentence being reduced to life imprisonment in 1972 when the California State Supreme Court abolished the death penalty.

Mao Tse Tung 1893-1976

CHINESE POLITICAL LEADER

Mao was one of the great non-European Marxists – a thinker and a leader. His heretical contribution to theory and practice was to stress the role of the peasantry, whom traditional Marxists, convinced that only industrial workers could foment revolution, had largely ignored. Mao realized that a Communist one-party state could only be built in China through the mobilization of the peasants. His idea of peasant-operated guerrilla war to topple pre-capitalist ruling structures, and his belief that peasant farming was a model occupation which all within society should experience influenced similar movements in Africa, the Far East and Latin America. Only under Mao did China in the modern era become a unitary, independent state which ranked as a world power, and that has remained his primary achievement. Despite a first decade of tentative co-operation with the USSR, China did not, as the Soviets had planned, become a reliable ally with a vast population under her wing. Mao ran China as a totalitarian dictatorship and was nearly as vicious as Stalin: exploiting his personality cult during the Cultural Revolution of the mid-1960s to assert his control; recruiting students into the 'Red Guards' to purge the Communist Party of his opponents; and imposing economic measures that were designed to increase productivity, without necessarily furthering social equality or democratic participation. But he gave the country a basis for building a viable, self-sufficient economy in the late twentieth century, with its chief problem – explosive population growth – under control. Some may have felt that the inbuilt cult of permanent revolution, as a basis for keeping the show on the road, had within it the seeds of the regime's break-up. None the less, Mao's leadership cult did not leave an ideological vacuum on his death; the veterans of the Long March who took over – his former opponents – had distinctive policies to implement. However, there was no provision for the members of a younger generation to move into positions of power, and when the gerontocracy sought to counter student campaigns for change, it did so in a very Maoist way: with executions and the dispatch of potential deviants to the countryside for re-education – much to the dismay of the real peasants, who did not welcome the disruption.

Robert Mapplethorpe 1946-89

AMERICAN PHOTOGRAPHER

Mapplethorpe built his reputation out of controversy – most notably with masochistic self-portraits and studies of genitalia – and even after his death, a retrospective of his work was cancelled under pressure from lobbyists. Precise, classical compositions, using stark lighting, belie the uninhibited poses that his subjects adopted and his work testifies to his passions, particularly in the way it presents the male body – aroused, taut, without shame. The celebrated *Man in a Polyester Suit* (1980), for example, shows a man in a suit and waistcoat, with a tuck of shirt and his large black penis protruding from his fly. An active participant in his dark, ritualistic world, rather than just a voyeur,

Mapplethorpe also created portraits of the rich and successful, as well as images of flowers which exhibit a sexuality and sensuality as strong as the nudes. One of his central preoccupations was with androgyny – his cover design for ☛Patti Smith's *Horses* LP depicts her in masculine drag and posture – but it was ultimately the combination of gender signs that interested him. There is still an aura of femininity even in his photographs of the body-builder Lisa Lyons. Perhaps the thing that hostile commentators find scariest about his work is how casually he domesticates the most unexpected behaviour.

Greil Marcus born 1945

▲AMERICAN WRITER

Marcus was one of the first writers to treat rock as art and himself as something more than the person describing it. His book *Mystery Train* (1975) attempts, with some success, to portray popular music as an epic thread in the national psyche, and with much less pretension than the work of many of his successors (and also without the crippling 'Gee, it's only music' homeliness of his opponents). Marcus articulated a sense that rock music was something more than a youth-oriented corner of the entertainment business, and his recent *Lipstick Traces* (1989) develops that argument to its furthest point, mixing ☛The Sex Pistols with the Dadaists in a pop-culture melting pot. His contribution to rock journalism is becoming more mythologized and less imitated, people being either too numbed by contemporary rock or too stupid to explore the routes of interpretation and criticism which he opened up.

Herbert Marcuse 1898-1979

GERMAN-AMERICAN

POLITICAL THINKER

☆ Thinkers are often defined by what they hate. Marcuse's main object of disgust was bourgeois, capitalist, industrial society, and his particular targets what he considered its trivial outlets for real discontents, its infatuation with science and technology and its suppression of human 'ludic' urges, as play was squeezed out by the quest for economic success. 'Repressive tolerance' was another bugbear – the idea of liberal norms that took the sting out of any protest by appealing to the transcending 'second-order' fact of formal freedom. Marcuse was a Marxist of an idiosyncratic sort, a German-Jewish refugee who had worked for US intelligence during WW2. He adulterated Marx with Freud, as his search to release the subconscious – erotic, without being phallic – in Westerners was taken up by those elements in the New Left of the 1960s who did not have the rigour or inclination to commit themselves to a traditional Marxist analysis and the disciplined, patient, time-consuming job of planning revolution. An unlikely guru, he argued for a return to the earlier, Hegelian Marx, whose youthful conception of the ideal life – the day spent thinking, working and playing – blurs into Marcuse's pastoral dream; like many other writers whose bias is anarcho-anthropological, he attacked the 'one-dimensional man' of the post-war West. Marcuse had little, real, lasting political impact. *That* would have required an interest in the dynamics of social change and the details of institutions as they evolve, and events as they move: the issue being what we want to do, not what we want to be.

Lynn Margulis

born 1938

AMERICAN BIOLOGIST

Each plant or animal cell contains subcellular organelles performing various functions vital to life. Mitochondria are essential to cells, providing their energy source, even containing their own genetic material. How did these sub-factories evolve? Margulis noted the resemblance of mitochondria to certain primitive bacteria and suggested that, at an early stage in the evolution of life, a unique co-operation took place. The organelles were originally discrete forms of life which developed a symbiotic relationship with the forerunners of modern cells by trading off energy production for a ready source of fuel and protection. Margulis has expanded the notion of the essential inter-dependency of living systems suggested by this symbiosis in order to supplement ☛James Lovelock's Gaia hypothesis: her thinking links the smallest organisms to planet Earth, situating us within the environment, neither above nor outside it.

Chris Marker

born 1921

✌ FRENCH FILM DIRECTOR

A writer, poet and Marxist critic before he started to make films, Marker first came to wide attention when his extraordinary, experimental short *La Jetée* was coupled with ☛Godard's 1965 film *Alphaville* in international distribution. Marker's film is a science-fiction story narrated entirely with stills (except in one shot, where a woman wakes), which pushes conventions to a surreal limit without driving its subjects – memory, time and history – beyond the reach of his audience. Marker's films before and since *La Jetée* are mostly essay-documentaries – on China, the Soviet Union and Cuba, for example – that return to these same obsessions. Despite the poetical quality of many of his works, he is no stranger to controversy: in the 1950s, he had worked with ☛Alain Resnais on a film about black cultures (*Les Statues meurent aussi*) which was banned by censors for ten years. In the 1980s, he wrote and directed his masterpiece, *Sunless*, a shimmering meditation on global communication, change, lost possibilities, sense of place, nostalgia and the eternal enthusiasm of the young. He has had a significant influence on avant-garde film-makers such as ☛Michael Snow.

Bob Marley

1945-80

♥ JAMAICAN REGGAE MUSICIAN

Marley took reggae from its status as a minor tropical diversion to a universal language, becoming the disillusioned spokesman for a global community predicated on Third World pride. His Rastafarianism (which reworks the story of the Jews taken to Babylon out of Israel as a metaphor for the enslaved of Africa) enabled him to forge a link between that continent's scattered exiles and the former colonies. Performing initially as one of the Wailers with the visionary Bunny Wailer and the volatile Peter Tosh, and later on his own, Marley transformed reggae into the vehicle for political protest. Thanks partly to clever marketing by Island Records, but also because this was a music sharing far more concerns with non-American blacks than soul or rock ever had, he became a huge crossover star – a position he held with amused dignity. After his death, reggae tumbled back to its previous position as a mainly regional concern, but its loping beat and many of its studio innovations still thread through pop.

Wynton Marsalis born 1961

⇔AMERICAN JAZZ MUSICIAN

Marsalis's rise in the early 1980s to the position of first pretender to the trumpet throne held by ☛Miles Davis might be seen as a triumphant return of jazz to public notice. On another reading, it is a sign that only the alarmingly retrograde can be sold in the present-day leisure-listening market. Marsalis himself is an icily brilliant player, and less narrow-minded than he presents himself, though perhaps not much. He is committed to a neo-traditionalist project that sidesteps Free Jazz and fusion, returning to the classic early 1960s' quintet sound of Davis's ESP as his jumping-off point. Initially, his fearsome rhetoric seemed to argue for technical mastery and a consequent retreat from avant-garde principles: this stirred up both enough support and hostility to justify his stance. Either way, he has found a path to making the music matter again.

Masters and Johnson

William Masters born 1915
Virginia Johnson born 1925

❍AMERICAN SEXOLOGISTS

It is hard now to believe that it was only in the mid 1950s that anyone thought to analyse scientifically what happens to the human body during sexual arousal and intercourse; or that before 1966, when Masters and Johnson published *Human Sexual Response* (a heavy medical tome that became an instant bestseller), many women had wasted their energies in a search for the El Dorado of full 'vaginal' orgasm – described by even the anti-Freudian ☛Simone de Beauvoir as the only 'normal satisfaction'. Masters the gynaecologist and Johnson the psychologist took copulating couples into the laboratory, and discovered that women could have experiences at least as intense as those of men, and probably more so given the capacity of some for multiple orgasms. As a result, sexual pleasure for women became a major talking point of the late 1960s, and every sort of magazine carried articles on the subject along with orgasm counts and quizzes. Masters and Johnson got married and started working as sex therapists. In *Human Sexual Inadequacy* (1970) they laid down some basic (behaviourist) guidelines for treating sexual problems.

Peter Maxwell Davies *see* Davies, Peter Maxwell

John Maynard Smith born 1920

BRITISH BIOLOGIST

The questions that interest Maynard Smith draw together evolution, behaviour and genetics. What has altruism got to do with evolutionary theory? Animals sometimes put themselves at risk to increase the chances of survival for others. But if natural selection is the story of survivors, this type of behaviour presents quite a problem, as does confrontation. Many animals gain access to mates by engaging in ritualized aggression. How are the rules maintained when there are obvious benefits for both fighters (hawks) and those who run away (doves)? To solve the problem of reconciling aggression with altruism Maynard Smith developed ideas o[n] kin selection. If an individual put[s]

Lynn Margulis
Photo: Contact *magazine, University of Massachusetts at Amherst*

itself at risk for the sake of its relatives, its own genes will survive in its kin. In evolutionary terms, it makes sense nobly to lay down your life for two children, four cousins, etc., according to the proportion of your genes they have inherited. To understand aggression, Maynard Smith looked to game theory, weighing up the costs and benefits of confrontation. There are pay-offs and risks in being a full-blown hawk – greater access to mates but a high possibility of injury – and a total dove – low mating but longer life. Working all the margins results in a model very like the ritual combats played out by animals: conflict progresses through a number of levels, where displays of increasing aggression are more important than actual physical harm. The best strategy, therefore, would seem to be that of the pseudo-hawk: act tough but be prepared to back down.

William Mayne born 1928

BRITISH NOVELIST

Although he causes no stir outside the world of children's books, Mayne is one of England's great writers. Quiet, lucid and a master of sharp, eccentric dialogue, he straddles the enclosed, infinitely dangerous world of childhood metaphysics and the plain workaday one of adult concerns. His oblique, plausible stories are told with economy, and a unique low-key drama that has led him to be compared, when noticed at all, to ☛Pinter, Brecht, Keats and Lawrence. A Yorkshireman, many of his stories have rural settings. Unsentimental, and far from idyllic, they sometimes drift, unsignalled, into a dark, dreamy folk-magic. Significant among his 70 odd books are *Sand* (1954), *A Swarm in May* (1955), *Underground Alley* (1958), *Earthfasts* (1966) and *A Game of Dark* (1971).

Albert Maysles born 1926
David Maysles 1932-87

AMERICAN DOCUMENTARISTS

Working with Richard Drew in the early 1960s, Albert and David Maysles were at the forefront of the new wave of real-life film documentary. Alongside ☛D. A. Pennebaker and Frederick Wiseman, they pioneered techniques of *cinéma vérité* and on-camera interview, making dramatic immediacy a major editorial criterion. The Maysles brothers went on to produce several commercially successful feature documentaries, including *Salesman* (1969) and *Grey Gardens* (1975). The latter revealed an eccentric mother and daughter, relations of Jackie Kennedy, living out their squalid, squabbling existence, reminiscing about long-dead days in Camelot, and generally behaving with uncomfortable intimacy to the cameras. The Maysles are much better known, though, for *Gimme Shelter* (1970), where events took a turn that opened the whole project of fly-on-the-wall to problematic moral questions. The brothers, along with Charlotte Zwerin, had been asked to make a *vérité*-spectacular based around a rock festival, headed by the ☛ The Rolling Stones, at Altamont, California; the proceeds of the film would help cover the costs of the event. Unfortunately, other costs were skimped: Hell's Angels were hired as stewards and paid in booze – and during The Stones' set, a young black, Meredith Hunter, was stabbed to death. The film captures all of this, as well as much of the grim paranoia, cynicism and despair that was dogging youth culture at the time; what it never satisfactorily addresses is the degree to which the stars and the directors may have been responsible for the events that ensued.

Margaret Mead 1901-78

♦ AMERICAN ANTHROPOLOGIST

Once the best-known anthropologist in the US, Mead has since become a figure of fun: her confident assertions about the peoples of Samoa, New Guinea and Bali seem based on pathetically little evidence, and her aim that Americans should be guided in how to live by the example of such native peoples seems fraught with pitfalls. But it was Mead who established the practice of the anthropological theorist being also a fieldworker (rather than relying on the reports of sundry clerics and adventurers); and her popularization of the idea that there were alternatives to the way in which American society then operated was enormously influential. Her account of the harmonious, sexually liberated adolescence of Samoan girls in *Growing Up in Samoa* (1928) questioned the assumption that transition into adulthood must necessarily be accompanied by stress, friction and rebellion. In *Male and Female* (1949), she queried the idea that the lines between the sexes were determined by biology rather than society. Along with Ruth Benedict, her teacher and sometime lover, Mead also challenged the 'melting pot' theory of American culture, which proposed that homogenized patterns of child-rearing and education could dissolve the linguistic, ethnic and social variety of the citizens of the US into a common American character, arguing instead that differences should be respected – a credo which informed and inspired her life's work.

George Meany 1894-1980

AMERICAN UNION LEADER

A plumber by trade, Meany was a US trade union chief who sported a big cigar and sought to make capitalism work for his members. A traditional Democrat, a fierce anti-Communist, a pragmatist on pay and a modernizer, he never led a strike as a union boss. In 1955, as head of the American Federation of Labor (AFL), he devised a merger with the other major labour group, the Congress of Industrial Organizations (CIO), which together made up 90 per cent of the unionized work force. He lobbied, pushed and negotiated for better wages and conditions, making the AFL-CIO a considerable power in society. Critics saw Meany as a Cold War figure, committed to the civil rights/welfare agenda of the pre-New Left Democrats, who put establishment politics before real pay rises. They also argued that Meany, who expelled ☛James Hoffa's Teamsters for corruption in 1957, acted as a dictator.

Peter Medawar 1915-87

BRITISH BIOLOGIST

Operations involving the transplants of internal organs have become so commonplace that it is hard to recall the time when the problems of tissue rejection seemed insoluble, unless perhaps through all-body X-rays – a horrific prospect. Working on skin grafts for burn victims during WW2, Medawar realized that the immune system was not fully developed at birth, but learned over time how to distinguish foreign cells and reject them. Since mice embryos injected at birth with tissues of a future donor were tolerant to any grafts from that donor, it seemed that the body could be taught to accept foreign tissue. The trick was to get those in receipt of transplanted organs to accept them for a sufficiently long 'learning' period, which mainly involved knocking out the immune system. This, of course, brought its own problems: Louis Washansky, the first man to receive another's heart, in 1967, died of pneumonia rather than of any form of coronary failure. After his groundbreaking immunological research, Medawar devoted much of the rest of his life to pursuing the chimera of a cancer vaccine. He called his autobiography *Memoirs of a Thinking Radish* (1986), a reference to his having been paralysed by a brain haemorrhage in 1969.

Roy Medvedev born 1925

✌ SOVIET HISTORIAN

Zhores Medvedev born 1925

SOVIET POLITICAL COMMENTATOR, ✌ BIOLOGIST, BASED IN UK

Roy is a historian of the post-1917 Soviet Union. His twin brother, Zhores, now based in the UK, is a biologist who doubles as a writer (he has written biographies of Andropov and ☛Gorbachev). They are sons of a Russian civil war hero, who taught philosophy and then vanished into an Arctic labour camp, dying in 1941. Zhores was head of a department at the Institute of Medical Radiobiology in Obninsk when he was incarcerated in a mental hospital for criticizing ☛Leonid Brezhnev. Having written about his experiences in *A Question of Madness* (1972), he was deprived of his citizenship while on a study tour in London. Working at the National Institute for Medical Research, he recovered his rights as a Soviet citizen in 1990. Roy, who has been a teacher, publisher and researcher, set out to retrieve the internal history of the USSR from the party hacks. His first study of Stalin argued that Uncle Joe had been the force which corrupted Communism; published in Paris, it led to his expulsion from the party. He has participated from afar in Western debates between Kremlinologists and other commentators about what is really happening in Moscow; his attack on ☛Reagan for describing the USSR as an 'evil empire', which Medvedev considered a 'direct insult', was typical of his role as a pragmatist who sought to stay on the right side of the authorities. His focus has been not just on the great figures of recent Soviet history – such as ☛Khrushchev, whom he has sought to rehabilitate – but also on current figures. He has played a cat-and-mouse game with the state: in 1981, his flat was ransacked and data was taken; in the Gorbachev era, he may be on the winning side at last.

Golda Meir

(Golda Myerson) 1898-1978

ISRAELI POLITICAL LEADER

Meir was the third woman – after Ceylon's Sirimano Bandaranaike and India's ☛Indira Gandhi – to become a modern national leader. As a woman, she was an unexpected choice as Israel's prime minister in 1969 but went on successfully to express Israeli angst to the world, making trips to see Pope Paul, Romania's ☛Ceauşescu and Germany's ☛Willy Brandt. Born in Russia, she was taken to the US as a child, where she became a teacher in Milwaukee. She did not Hebraicize her name until 1956, some 35 years after she and her husband had opted to settle in Palestine. She was a tough veteran of the Zionist movement, the Jewish Agency and several Israeli Labour governments. Heavily criticized for her failure to attack pre-emptively, once warned of the Arab attack which materialized in October 1973, her justification was that she did not want to provoke aggression. Even so, she won that war – after a close shave – but her perceived dovish line induced a swing against her in end-of-the-year elections and she subsequently lost power to Yitzhak Rabin.

Richard Meltzer

♦ AMERICAN WRITER

✍▲Meltzer's ridiculous, nearly unreadable, masterpiece *The Aesthetics of Rock* (1970) is ultimately responsible for the flood of garbage/genius foisted on popular music by illiterates, lunatics and others ever since extracts of the book – the first 'serious rock book' – were run in *Crawdaddy* during 1968. Regarded by many as an incomprehensible joke at the time, Meltzer's high-octane sarcasm and twisted erudition turned the premature ecstasy of rock 'n' roll into an arena where philosophy could celebrate its own collapse. Much of the writing's energy derives from the sense of a very clever, self-destructive intelligence revelling in the insights and liberation that total vapidity offered. In fact, in contrast to much of the utopian emptiness in the writing of the time, *The Aesthetics of Rock* now seems pretty sharp. ☛Lester Bangs learned from him, as did such British critics as Mick Farren, Charles Shaar Murray and Nick Kent. Meltzer began to hate what he had started, but went on to pioneer most of the more illicit and reprehensible techniques of LP reviewing (discussing one as if it was another; only talking about the sleeve; making up lyrics and then passing comment; not listening at all, and so on), and in spite of periodic retirements, he remains a fringe iconoclast, contributing offensive marginal gibberish to US fanzines such as *Forced Exposure*.

Jean-Pierre Melville

(Jean-Pierre Grumbach) 1917-73

FRENCH FILM DIRECTOR

Melville's film-making was shaped by his preoccupation with 1930s' Hollywood and all things American – he renamed himself after the author of *Moby Dick*. In *Bob le Flambeur* (1955), he deploys the US thriller genre in a film whose irony nevertheless marked it out as distinctively French. That, and the film's pioneering use of locations, natural light, improvisation and character actors established him as the father of the French New Wave. Melville, however, was not able to sustain the same level of creative freshness, making a succession of gangster films with the likes of Jean-Paul Belmondo, Alain Delon and Lino Ventura that, while often entertaining and sometimes big commercial successes, seem ritualized, often to the point of abstraction. At his best, however, as with *Second Breath* (1966), or *Army in the Shadows* (1969) – which draws on his own experience in the French Resistance – Melville went beyond trench coats and fickle girls, to create intense meditations on friendship, loyalty and betrayal.

David Mercer 1928-80

▲BRITISH PLAYWRIGHT, SCREENWRITER

Mercer, who had been a lab technician, naval recruit, art student, novelist, painting copyist and London supply teacher before turning playwright, arrived on the doorstep of his future agent so immersed in failure that he could hardly put two words together. His boldest stroke was to write television dramas that combined the intimacy and textural density of theatre with the flexibility of time and place offered by film. With plays/films such as *The Parachute* (1968), about a German aristocrat who seeks to escape from his domineering father during WW2 by volunteering for a team testing a new kind of parachute, Mercer established television as a medium for serious writing. In the process, he helped to build Britain's reputation for having the best television service in the world, which it has been living off ever since. His themes were politics – particularly the disillusion with Marxism best expressed by the writer in *On the Eve of Publication* (1968) – and madness. He drew on his own experience of a nervous breakdown for *A Suitable Case for Treatment* (1962, made into a feature in 1966), and on the writings of ☛R. D. Laing about family-bred schizophrenia for the Ken Loach-directed *Family Life* (1971). In his last play, a character refers to television as 'a window on the magnificence and pathos of man', then adds, 'I speak, you understand, of the science programmes and the documentaries.'

Maurice Merleau-Ponty 1908-61

FRENCH PHILOSOPHER

Regarded by some as the best philosopher of his generation in France, Merleau-Ponty's reputation has tended to increase while that of other existentialists has waned. He bypassed the wider, woollier concerns of ☛Sartre's mentor Heidegger, to take up where Heidegger's own teacher, Husserl, had left off; he rejected in particular the Cartesian tradition, with its clarity of argument that (he said) derived from doubting the existence of things in all their ambiguity (a position which led him to accuse Sartre, at one point, of 'cursed lucidity'; cue amazed collapse of all present). Interested in the idea of man-in-the-world, and the interaction of the body with the world, he broke with the ubiquitous post-war Marxism of the Left Bank (unlike Sartre, who had earlier been his co-editor on the immensely influential journal *Les Temps Modernes*) – setting a pattern for a resistance to the Communist Party's allures that would be followed by many in the next generation, particularly by ☛Derrida and ☛Foucault, even as they pitched themselves strongly against much of the rest of his thought.

Olivier Messiaen 1908-92

▥FRENCH COMPOSER

☞Messiaen's profound Roman Catholic faith, coupled with a personal interpretation of the musical developments made by Debussy and Stravinsky, led him towards a conception of music as static rather than dynamic: his most famous composition *Quartet for the End of Time* (1941) is based round texts from the Book of Revelations. He found parallels for this approach in the music of non-Western cultures less concerned with the classical idea of development and progress, as well as in bird song. Following WW2, which he mostly passed in a POW camp, he gathered a lively group of students around him at the Paris Conservatoire (including ☛ Boulez and ☛Stockhausen) and developed an unconventional curriculum that took in the study of Greek metric units and Hindu rhythms. His music explores not only the sounds that birds make, but also the colour of their plumage; like Scriabin and other mystically inclined composers, he claimed visions of color are induced for him by sound.

Grace Metalious

(Grace de Repentigny) 1924-64

AMERICAN NOVELIST

A largely forgotten writer, Metalious's potboiler *Peyton Place* (1956) spawned a film and, most interestingly, a television series (running twice weekly from 1964 to 1968) that took soap operas into primetime viewing and, as the genre evolved, led to the most lascivious forms of escapism dominating the American airwaves. The novel dealt with small-town relationships and minor ambitions. The television series was credited with spreading tolerance of extra-marital affairs and a view of monogamy as something unfashionable. Metalious's drinking and inability to cope with the combination of scorn in literary circles and monstrous success in middle America rubbed away her sense of creative identity and self-respect.

Christian Metz

born 1941

☞FRENCH FILM THEORIST

A seminal theorist of cinema whose importance lies in his detailed demonstration of how hard it is to impose systems on film, Metz started by attempting to develop a structuralism of the moving image. After sorting it all into signifiers and signifieds, *langue* and *parole*, he was quick to accept that film just would not play along. The relationship of signifier to signified, for example, is hardly arbitrary, as a structuralist approach would require; there is an obvious link between the film image and what it portrays. All visual images have the sort of expressive power that words only take on when placed in particular formations; therefore, in cinema, there can be no distinction between 'poetry' and 'prose'. Semiology can elucidate the iconography and forms of editing used in film, but alongside these processes, other non-cinematic codes – speech especially – are also operating: cinema is a multi-channel and multi-code system. Metz worked to unfold a detailed theory of narrative types, to the point where the richness of engagement became its own reward. His continued near-scientific concentration makes it clear that he does not believe he has exhausted his subject, or cracked the code. 'A film,' he acknowledges, 'is difficult to explain because it is easy to undestand.'

Russ Meyer

born 1922

AMERICAN FILM DIRECTOR

Where Cecil B. de Mille was a secret foot fetishist who shot his biblical epics in such a way as to conceal his perversion, Meyer is a self-confessed breast freak who shoots peculiar, home-movie soap-opera narratives to broadcast his. The films are neatly constructed, both funny and honest about suburban sexual hang-ups. However, once they get past castigating repression and the hypocrisy of traditional family values, they often seem to be viewing secondary problems as if they are the solution. There are a few Meyer films – *Faster Pussycat! Kill! Kill!* (1962) and *Beneath the Valley of the Ultra-Vixens* (1979) – where the story is bizarre and trenchant enough to repay repeated viewing, but like most trash, they can also be oddly enervating. Meyer coaxes lively, if amateur, cameos from his actors and actresses, and a few of these – Kitten Natividad, Tura Satana – have gained cult status for their anti-star glamour and eccentric 'womanly' strength, as well as their startling chest-size.

Duane Michals born 1932

AMERICAN PHOTOGRAPHER

Where some artists struggle to grasp reality, Michals dwells on the invisible, the things that photography is said not to be able to capture – loss, myth, spirit. Proving that photography can pin down our dreams as well as describe our environment, he strains against the leash of his chosen medium, showing us an angel falling from grace in *The Fallen Angel* (1968), or the afterlife in *Self Portrait as if I Were Dead* (1968). Many of his photographs employ texts that Michals handwrites beneath the image; sometimes he places images in a sequence, commonly relating some bizarre story, without beginning or end. These have varied from stories of love and loss, violence and death, where the text will complement the image, to pieces such as *A Failed Attempt to Photograph Reality* (1975) that uses no images, but instead consists entirely of a short written message. Though not always successful in his challenges to photographic convention, when thought and expression meet on equal terms, the results are at once unsettling, provocative and unforgettable.

Ludwig Mies van der Rohe

☞GERMAN-AMERICAN ARCHITECT 1886-1969

Mies van der Rohe is the architect who receives the rap for the 'glass boxes' that represent, for many, the ugliness of post-war architecture. Many of his buildings are, in fact, stunning in their refined beauty; it is just unfortunate that Miesian ideas appealed to corporate executives anxious to inflate their sense of importance, and to bureaucrats as symbols of supposedly rational planning, so that a bowdlerized approximation of Mies's steel-framed, glass-walled and flat-roofed style of construction became a standard for office and appartment blocks during most of the post-war period. Yet, there is something shocking about an approach to building that does not significantly distinguish (on the outside, at least) between living space and working space, and Mies does seem, in retrosp ect, to have become unhealthily hooked on a single formula. Reaching the US from Germany in the late 1930s, with an international reputation already established through the advocacy of ☛ Philip Johnson, the companies which commissioned the three dozen high-rises he designed in the last two years of his life must bear some responsibility for the relative sameness of the result. They all wanted a 'Mies', the badge of those who wanted to be 'with it' in modernist architecture.

Mike Milken

born 1947

$ AMERICAN FINANCIER

For a decade and a half he was America's Mr Financial Fixit. Based at the Wall Street firm Drexel, Burnham, Lambert and long legendary for his extended working hours, he provided the money with which business executives with seemingly insufficient credit ratings could still acquire major companies. He could raise millions in minutes, by selling the 'junk' bonds that came with his personal commendation and interest rates that older hands would have considered usurious. With his help, ☛Rupert Murdoch carried through a $2 billion takeover of the Metromedia television network, and ☛James Goldsmith became a billionaire. The shifts of power Milken initiated brought mayhem to boardrooms all over the US as terrified managements battled to fight off predators. It all ended in tears. After ☛Ivan Boesky had turned government informer, Drexel, Burnham, Lambert paid out $650 million to get the government and disgruntled investors off their backs, spent millions more on TV advertising to put the case that junk bonds had revived some of the oldest industries, and finally, in February 1990, filed for bankruptcy. Milken lost his job and was indicted on 98 charges of fraud, insider dealing and various other misdemeanours. He set about refurbishing his reputation with promises – to solve the problems of illiteracy, emotional disturbance in children, not to mention Third World debt – that were as grandiose as his earlier undertakings to liberate US business from corporate conservatism. Nevertheless he was landed with $200 million in fines, as well as payments of $400 million in restitution to defrauded investors, and a ten-year gaol term.

Arthur Miller

born 1915

AMERICAN PLAYWRIGHT

Miller was a golden boy of the 1950s, winning the Pulitzer prize, marrying ☛Marilyn Monroe and making a stand against ☛Joseph McCarthy, and he has never quite escaped the shadow of those glory days. He hit out at postwar smugness with *All My Sons* (1947), an explosive attack on war profiteering that ensured all eyes would be on his next – and finest – play. *Death of a Salesman* (1949) articulated the despair hiding beneath the complacency of the American Dream. Dealing with the destructive power of illusion by following the last days of Willy Loman, a salesman who refused to face the failure of his career and family relationships, it tapped a vein in every small-town guy who thought he had made something of himself, and then slashed it wide open. Miller went on to attack McCarthyism in his Salem witch-hunt play, *The Crucible* (1953). It seemed he could do no wrong, but mediocrity beckoned. Apart from his melancholy screenplay for *The Misfits* (1961), he seemed to be self-consciously looking for grand themes (anti-Semitism, man's relationship with God), and mainstream American theatre began to give Miller a wide berth, confining his new pieces to off-Broadway presentation.

Frank Miller

▲ AMERICAN CARTOONIST

❞ An apocalyptic writer-illustrator who claims to have rescued. mainstream comic books from the kindergarten to establish them as a medium for social commentary, Miller is a brilliant, irascible self-promoter. Originally intended as a mail-order-only collectors' item, his four-part *The Dark Knight Returns* (1986) turns Batman into an ageing, almost psychotic millionaire who fights crime with the aim of revenging his parents' murder. Compared with most of the DC/Marvel superhero output, *Dark Knight* seemed an apt social parable, and created a vanguard of New Wave comic-book followers, as well as inspiring the hit film of 1989. Miller writes and draws crime stories awash with the gratuitous violence so often found in the real world. His *Elektra Assassin* (1986, with illustrations by ☛Bill Sienkiewicz) combines the *Dark Knight*'s pyrotechnics with wry allegories on the CIA, nuclear paranoia, ☛Nixon and American militarism. In the wake of a hype that has dwarfed anything that went before, it remains to be seen whether Miller's revamped Batman has really been a boon to the comics industry. Heresy or no heresy, Marvel and DC are laughing all the way to the bank.

Lee Miller 1907-77

BRITISH PHOTOGRAPHER

Miller attained a rare level of inventiveness and personal resonance in her photography. Associated with Man Ray, to whom she became both lover and assistant after their meeting in 1925, she deserves part of the credit for developing the solarization technique that became his hallmark. Her early surrealist works of the late 1920s and 1930s led to commissions for both American and British *Vogue*, her fashion photos displaying a fresh and coolly sensuous look. As a photojournalist during WW2, she captured the defiant reality of destruction, witnessing the war on the Alsace border and the horrifying deadliness of Dachau concentration camp. These images – of children who seemed on the point of death – are striking for their combination of starkness and almost surrealistic magic. In later years, settled in England and married to art connoisseur Roland Penrose, she mixed with an influential group of friends – Picasso, Max Ernst, Colette, ☛Dubuffet and ☛Henry Moore – whom she captured in a series of candid poses. Acting as hostess and gourmet cook, she pandered to the whims and desires of these artistic figureheads, seemingly ignoring her own past status as an artist of merit and distinction.

Stanley Miller born 1930

AMERICAN BIOLOGIST

In 1952, as a young graduate student at the University of Chicago, Miller created life in a test tube. At least that is how the textbooks tell it. Having sent an electric spark through a mixture of gases in a sealed chamber, he analysed the contents several days later and found significant amounts of two of the 20 amino acids which are used by living cells to make proteins. When he and Harold Urey published the results, they made the cover of *Time* magazine. Their 'Frankenstein' experiment seemed to show that life (or, at least, its essential building blocks) could have been created by the action of lightning on the atmosphere of the primitive earth. If other planets have the same gases and electrical storms, then life in the cosmos should be plentiful. The Miller-Urey work is now taught as hard evidence of a mechanism for the creation of life, even though no subsequent experiment has ever yielded so much of the vital amino acids. So why did their discoveries have such an impact on the origin-of-life debate? Perhaps because they provided results to back up what might be called the 'predestinate view' – that, given enough time and the right conditions, there is an inherent tendency towards the creation of life. The response to their work reflects the desire of scientists to believe that Someone or Something Up There – God, laws of nature, call it what you will – cares about us.

Kate Millett born 1934

BRITISH FEMINIST, PAINTER, SCULPTOR, BASED IN US

The most significant theorist of the 1960s' generation, Millett transformed feminism into a movement with *Sexual Politics* (1970), which introduced the notion of Patriarchy – and the necessity for an engaged protest of a new kind – into a debate that had previously allowed itself to be obscured behind pressures for social change along class lines. Millett had been teaching at Columbia University and participating in the civil rights movement. When her radicalism lost her that job, she put together a devastating counterblast, showing that both the US and the USSR had failed in their promise to improve women's position in society: the corollary was that women must now agitate for the kinds of lives and society they wanted. Following this book, she published *The Prostitution Papers* (1976), which studied prostitution from a feminist angle; *Flying* (1974), her autobiography; and *Sita* (1977), a novel about a lesbian love affair. In 1979, she went to Iran to agitate for improved women's rights in the aftermath of the revolution there, but was expelled by ☛Khomeini's government. Throughout all this activity, she has exhibited as a painter and a sculptor, and now concentrates on this side of her work.

(Terence) Spike Milligan born 1918

BRTISH TELEVISION COMIC

Milligan's place in comic legend stems from such radio work as the *Goon Show* (1951-60) and *Puckoon*, and the *Q* television series, but also from his status as a total anarchist. He removes the dramatic conventions of plot, character and logic with an almost childish directness, and remains a legend in television for abandoning the concept of the sketch punchline. His occasional bouts of depression and his unreliability as a chat show guest (he once told a television interviewer than he 'never could stand' the then recently deceased Peter Sellers) make Milligan a completely fascinating character, as does the way his chillingly racist humour is mixed with tender compassion for all life, human or otherwise. Milligan, former idol of ☛Prince Charles, is one of the few comedians who can never be called 'safe'.

C(harles) Wright Mills 1916-62

AMERICAN SOCIOLOGIST

A maverick radical, Mills attacked fellow sociologists for merely protecting their status through the search for a value-free, objective way of analysing society. He also gunned for the grand theorists, whose speculations were so general as to evade empirical testing. What he was after was a committed discipline that was not afraid to prescribe solutions. *White Collar* (1951) surveyed the new middle-class in America: apathetic, caught up in their own lives and alienated in an increasingly bureaucratic, undemocratic world. *The Power Élite* (1956) developed his sceptical view of US politics through an analysis of the 'military-industrial complex', and replaced the Marxist idea of a 'ruling class' with the concept of a society modelled on the structure of 'mass' and 'élite'. With ☛ Marcuse, an important influence on the development of New Left ideas, Mills' humanist passion led him to undervalue patient, realistic stabs at objectivity made by academics with clear minds who were alert to their own possible bias.

By virtue of their increased and centralized power, political institutions become more objectively important to the course of American history but, because of mass alienation, less and less of subjective interest to the population at large.

C. Wright Mills

Czesław Miłosz born 1911

POLISH-AMERICAN POET

Miłosz combines novel-writing with political philosophy and literary criticism but his most significant work is as a poet. Much of his early verse, written during the Nazi occupation of Poland, expresses a sense of encroaching darkness which earned him the title of 'catastrophist'. But *The World*, a group of poems composed in 1943, stresses the power of values to withstand the interruption of war. The vision is child-like, based on an idyllic sequence of memories from his formative years and representing the war simply as a nightmare which is bound to pass. Following several years as a diplomat, he fell foul of the authorities and went into exile in 1951, reaching the US ten years later. While continuing to explore the past and all that has been lost, he can also express joy and wonder at the beauty of a rising sun or the sound of hummingbirds in his California garden. He denounced the Soviet dominance of Eastern Europe in *The Captive Mind* (1953), and argues that poets should be judged by their value for contemporary times. He won the Nobel prize for literature in 1980.

Lisa Milroy born 1959

BRITISH PAINTER

Milroy paints 'things' – everyday objects such as shoes, nails, screws, records and neatly stacked shirts – in a strongly detached style, more reminiscent of commercial illustration than traditional painting. Her eye lines up the repeated motifs in orderly little rows, creating the effect of flicking casually through a glossy catalogue. Milroy can be seen as the ☛Warhol of the 1980s – her choice of subject matter is equally inconsequential – but her presentation lacks the wit and heroic swagger of her guru. The 'disruption of the familiar' that Milroy excuses herself with has all the charm of a soiled nappy, and reveals more about the state of contemporary patronage than anything else.

Charlie Mingus 1922-79

AMERICAN JAZZ MUSICIAN

Irascible, embattled and free-thinking, Mingus led groups throughout the 1950s and 1960s that impressed and inspired his peers. Often spoken of as a father of Free Jazz, he largely despised the form himself, aggressively working towards a music that sprang from his (then-revolutionary) conception of collective improvisation – loose rhythm and a furious livewire energy that only his own disciplined bass-playing band-leadership could satisfactorily contain or showcase. With a gift for the dramatic, he worked through a series of aggressive set-pieces that are still rousing and daring – including 'Pithecanthropus Erectus' and 'The Black Saint & the Sinner Lady' – but he also recorded a series of delicate, impressionistic Cool Jazz collections which demonstrate his grounding in Ellington, the blues and Latin brass sounds. His autobiography, *Beneath the Underdog* (1971), roars and growls its very subjective way through an unlikely, contradictory life. It is one of the great studies of a creative career on the road.

Yukio Mishima

(Kimitaké Hiraoke) 1925-70

† JAPANESE NOVELIST

✌ Japan was startled when Mishima committed hara-kiri after he had overrun a military base with his followers and harangued the assembled soldiers to no effect (they responded with jeers and sarcasm) for 20 minutes. He was the country's best-known writer, but his vision of a return to the pre-war order which, with the God-Emperor dominant, would be free from intrusive Western influence, struck no chord with the wider Japanese public. In fact, his ideology probably alarmed and embarrassed genuine reactionaries as much as it did everyone else. He saw his death as a supreme work of art, 'the ultimate masturbation' – an attitude unlikely to slot into modern far-right political programmes. His appeal for Western youth derived from his unique mix of an aesthetic extremism, a body-fanaticism which drew on Samurai codes, a neo-Confucian philosophy of knowledge through action, Nietzsche and a certain amount of rock's flamboyant nihilism (live fast, die young, leave a good-looking headless corpse). These themes were expressed first in his obsessive novels and in his autobiography, *Confessions of a Mask* (1949/58), with which he made his name at the age of 24. His relationship to his homosexuality was as troubled as that to his national culture, and in the end he could only exorcize them both by formulating a programme of his own, less political than dramatically self-destructive, and assembling a private army – the Shield Society – devoted to fulfilling his loopy vision of a purified Japan.

When at last I came to own a beautiful body I wanted to show it off like a child. But the body is doomed to decay. I for one do not, will not, accept such a doom.

Yukio Mishima

Joni Mitchell

born 1943

CANADIAN SINGER, SONGWRITER

One of several Canadians who have been able to turn themselves into American icons, Mitchell rose to fame via Woodstock – even though she had not been present – assuring its status as a myth by providing an unforgettably sentimental anthem of hope. In the early 1970s, she was part of a wave of West Coast folk-confessional singer-songwriters who sold self-pity and self-examination to the Me Generation, but she rose above the rest by virtue of a sometimes-inspired jazz-sensibility. Throwing her inimitable voice across elegant and occasionally brilliant arrangements, which have at different times included Burundi drummers and the bass virtuoso Jaco Pastorius, Mitchell works at a music that is reflective, pessimistic and unusually well thought through: it is significant that she has survived into the 1990s when most of her Woodstock-era contemporaries – even the ones who *were* there – have long since disappeared.

Juliet Mitchell born 1940

✌ BRITISH FEMINIST, POLITICAL THEORIST

Inspired by ☛Althusser's theories on ideology and by the writings of Frantz Fanon, as much as by what then existed of feminism, Mitchell wrote *Women: The Longest Revolution* (1966) as an extension of ☛ Raymond Williams' then-influential *The Long Revolution*. Her book subsequently became one of the founding texts for the women's movement. Mitchell opened the way for the serious study of women as a group, unified by their shared experience of oppression, despite differences of class, race and nationality. Always an alert and informed reader, and one of the subtler minds of the New Left, she became deeply involved in psychoanalysis during the 1970s. Challenging the traditional feminist scorn for Freud, she argued that his findings had to be incorporated into a more rigorous analysis of the oppression of women. She has found common ground with French post-Lacanian analysts, such as Michèle Montrelay, Luce Irigaray and Hélène Cixous, on the need to develop a radical politics that takes account of theories of desire and the unconscious, and a Marxism that does not ignore the problems of patriarchy.

François Mitterrand born 1916

✓ FRENCH POLITICAL LEADER

Mitterrand is France's longest-surviving left-wing leader in nearly 120 years of popular elections; if he lasts until 1995, he will have been president for 14 years. He may also become the only genuine left-winger in European history to last this long as an executive, elected head of state. Trained in the fast-rotating rough-and-tumble of the Fourth Republic (1946 – 1958), he has learned to be a supreme politician's politician. Having lost to ☛de Gaulle, he managed to unify the left under his banner, but lost to Giscard d'Estaing. He kept on trying and finally beat Giscard in 1981. He won socialist majorities in two sets of legislative elections out of three – easing his presidency – and actually improved his reputation throughout the middle era of "cohabitation" with a right-wing premier, Jacques Chirac. High intelligence partly explains Mitterrand's success – he has degrees in law, literature and political science. So does a rootedness in France – he loves its literature, cuisine and countryside – since, if you are a socialist, it helps in elections if you are also a traditionalist. His critics excoriate Mitterrand as a French version of the UK's ☛Harold Wilson, who has betrayed the socialist principles to which he lays claim. It is true he has not delivered the "rupture with capitalism" that he promised in the 1970s and he has also defended French neocolonialism and nuclear testing, to the extent of tacitly endorsing the murder of a Portuguese photographer on board the Greenpeace flagship, *Rainbow Warrior*, which

French secret agents blew up in New Zealand. That said, he saved France from the worst excesses of monetarist economics, nationalized key firms, increased the minimum wage and did something to improve women's rights.

Issey Miyake born 1934

JAPANESE FASHION DESIGNER

By designing clothes that are firmly part of high fashion (prohibitively expensive and larger than life) but also reflect indigenous Japanese traditions, Miyake has gained international recognition and helped to establish Tokyo as one of the world's fashion centres. After an apprenticeship in the *haute couture* houses of Paris and New York, Miyake returned to Japan and began investigating the potential of Japanese materials. His creations range from 'Samurai' structures of bamboo and lacquered wood to dresses of pleated paper that resemble huge pieces of origami. Miyake's clothes are not made to be worn; rather they are angular sculptures – exaggerated, ballon-like and often semi-transparent – of which the wearer comprises a part.

Moebius (Jean Giraud) born 1938

FRENCH CARTOON ARTIST

Cofounder of *Metal Hurlant* with Philippe Druillet, Moebius is one of the great innovators of comic-book style, working in high fantasy/adventure mode on a vast scale, and helping to provide a space for styles other than those of the Hergé/Tin-Tin lineage to flourish. Moebius – who also works under another pseudonym 'Gir' – started as a hip and witty illustrator of strip-westerns, before moving towards an allusive and inventive space-age style more suited to the post-☛Godard modern world. Although *Metal Hurlant* lost much of its 1970s' verve as hippy-tech optimism began to fade, Moebius is still one of the most highly regarded narrative-cartoon artists in Europe, and perhaps more revered than imitated. His work influenced the set designs for the film *Blade Runner* (1982), which clearly inspired the Cyberpunk generation of SF-novelists, are a more solid mark of influence.

Meredith Monk born 1942

AMERICAN MUSICIAN, DANCER

Very much a New York artist in her versatility and enthusiasm for a range of media, Monk initially established herself in the late 1960s as a dancer and choreographer. Her dance pieces soon broadened into mixed-media events that included theatre, performance art and singing. It is her vocal pieces that have received most attention: with a lulling, sweetly simple electronic piano as the background, her voice explores the heights and depths of tonality. Harmonically simple, her work can nevertheless be highly expressive. Recently, Monk has devised opera pieces which reject weighty subject matter for autobiographical and domestic themes.

Theolonius Monk 1917-82

○AMERICAN JAZZ MUSICIAN

✍Monk was a master musician whose social awkwardness led many to chuckle behind their hands at him, even as they grooved to his stretched, quiet, angular piano playing. He was one of the most ambitious minds behind the bebop revolution, but almost no one played like him. Others preferred to baffle by taking corners at speed, with a lively mischief, while he cloaked his music in sharp enigma and exacting silences; he gave his compositions titles such as 'Crepuscule with Nellie' and 'Epistrophy'. Players such as ☛Parker and ☛Gillespie signalled their virtuosity; Monk was master only of his own style, and that allowed for no flash. He stopped composing long before he stopped playing, and he stopped playing a while before he died. Subsequent players, especially Steve Lacy, have delved into his compositions to develop a whole philosophy of playing and working.

Jean Monnet 1888-1979

○ FRENCH POLITICIAN

Monnet formulated the idea of European federalism as it emerged before and after the Treaty of Rome (which established the European Economic Community in 1958), and he was later founding president of the Action Committee for a United States of Europe. He also headed the committee whose ideas fuelled France's post-war economic revival, led by state intervention in key sectors. He was an economist, a planner and a diplomat with grand visions of the future. In 1940, he suggested Anglo-French union to Churchill and the concept was briefly espoused by the British premier as he sought to salvage something from the wreckage of the French collapse. Monnet had experience in diverse areas: shipping and supply in the 1914-1918 war, investment banking in the 1920s and, in the 1930s, a role as adviser on finance to various governments. He drew on his understanding of bureaucratic processes in drawing up a plan for the EEC, pursuing a belief that political union would be the inevitable result of economic co-operation between countries.

Jacques Monod 1910-76

FRENCH BIOLOGIST

A passionate, pessimistic commentator-philosopher as well as one of the greatest scientists of the century, Monod has been called the 'architect of molecular biology'. He did much of the pioneering work on the structure and mechanisms of genes, chromosomes, enzymes and proteins, and argued for the existence of messenger-RNA before it was discovered – incidentally throwing light on the whole problem of replication, the reproduction of viruses and the question of cancer. In spite of this depth-knowledge of the nuts-and-bolts mechanics of life, or perhaps because of it, he argued powerfully, in *Chance and Necessity* (1970/1), for the idea that life and evolution were purely the products of chance.

Man must at last finally awake from his milleniary dream and, in doing so, awake to his total solitude and fundamental isolation. Now does he finally realize that, like a gipsy, he lives on the boundary of an alien world. A world that is deaf to his music, just as indifferent to his hopes as it is to his suffering or his crimes.

Jacques Monod

Marilyn Monroe

(Norma Jean Baker) 1926-62

† AMERICAN FILM ACTRESS

♥ ○ Taken up since her death as a symbol of the destructiveness of fame and beauty, Monroe was a superstar like no other. The backwoods girl who never really knew either parent, she married first at 16, then parlayed her modelling connections into a job posing nude for a calendar in 1949. She showcased a dumb-blonde persona and lived her life so much under the intrusive eye of the mass media that she came to seem not only infinitely desirable, but also ultimately available. Her 'renaissance' year, 1953, produced *Niagara*, *Gentlemen Prefer Blondes* and *How to Marry a Millionaire.* Despite conveying both vacuity and voluptuousness, she strove for credibility and self-improvement – through marriage to playwright ☛Arthur Miller and tutelage under ☛Lee Strasberg at the Actor's Studio. But she consistently alienated serious film-makers by her unprofessional behaviour: Tony Curtis said kissing her was like 'kissing Hitler', while Billy Wilder warned the cast of *Some Like It Hot* (1959) to be perfect in every take because the first time Monroe remembered her lines he would print it. Her suicide may have secured her a place in showbiz mythology, but it also drew a convenient veil over the dead-end her career had reached (Fox had cancelled her contract in exasperation at the delays she had caused). While hers remains the blueprint for depthless blonde superstardom, many lesser figures – such as professional lookalike Kay Kent – have followed through to imitate her in death.

Monty Python's Flying Circus

formed 1969

BRITISH TELEVISION COMEDY TEAM

John Cleese, Graham Chapman, Terry Jones, Michael Palin, Eric Idle and the American Terry Gilliam worked their way through undergraduate revues, sketch shows and so forth before achieving the feat of destroying earlier television conventions and rooting small-screen comedy rock-solidly in their own soil for ever. *Monty Python's Flying Circus* (1969-74) quickly became obsessed with television itself, much of its 'surrealism' comprising a series of elaborate puns on the nature of the medium. The show's anarchy, all too often curtailed by the BBC's fear of masturbation and cannibalism, and its choice of 'silliness' over surrealistic terror, led to many weaker imitators in the 1970s and 1980s. While Cleese developed the immaculate but conventional *Fawlty Towers* (1975, 1979), the others parodied their own Python contributions for a few years. Animator Gilliam, however, transformed the genuine horror and weirdness which he had originally given to Python into the strange cinematic magic of *Time Bandits* (1981), *Brazil* (1984) and *The Adventures of Baron Munchausen* (1988).

Sun Myung Moon

(Young Myung Mun) born 1920

SOUTH KOREAN RELIGIOUS LEADER, BUSINESS EXECUTIVE, SETTLED IN US

One of several new messiahs who made an appearance in post-war Korea, Moon was unique in coming to believe that the way to rebuild the Kingdom of God lay through manufacturing armaments, agricultural machinery and pharmaceuticals. Developing his various activities into a politico-religious empire with an annual revenue of around $500 million, he has also persuaded around half a million unfortunate souls to view him as the perfect parent they never had and join his Holy Spirit Association for the Unification of Christianity. These 'Moonies' submit themselves to long hours of praying, chanting and singing as well as interminable indoctrination sessions, at which they learn to spout utopian clichés. Moving his base (and planned site for God's Kingdom) from South Korea to the United States, Moon has made himself indispensable to the anti-Communist right – 'Some say Communism is soluble in Coca-Cola, but it is only soluble in napalm' is typical of his contributions to political discourse, and his supporters seem prepared to overlook his idiosyncratic angle on the family values they hold so dear. He has also set up the *Washington Times* newspaper in the US capital to carry his arguments against détente and arms control and his support for such causes as the Nicaraguan Contras and the South African regime. (Attempts to spread his message through the cinema, including an abortive attempt to film the life of Christ with ☛ Elvis Presley and the disastrous $50 million *Inchon*, have so far been greeted with derision.) Moon is not very keen on paying taxes, but the gaol-term he received for laxity in this area clipped his wings for only a short while, and he is now moving into Britain through cultural and political seminars arranged through friendly members of the Conservative Party (who have promised him immunity from probes into his 'charity' status).

Michael Moorcock born 1939

BRITISH WRITER

Responsible for a lot of blood-and-thunder fantasy novels, Moorcock is one of the few hippy-influenced science-fiction writers of any note, his Jerry Cornelius novels being a genuine attempt to break out of the self-imposed limits of the genre. In the 1960s, as editor of *New Worlds*, he provided an essential space for the British New Wave to flourish; he also wrote much of his worst (and most popular) hack work at this time, to fund the magazine. What is unusual is that he improved so considerably during this period. He is also unique in almost any field of writing because, in the mid-1960s, he actively encouraged other SF writers to produce stories using the characters he had invented: this experiment could have destroyed fiction, but sadly, only ☛Brian Aldiss took up Moorcock's challenge. The only SF writer brave enough to mention the rock group Hawkwind in his work, Moorcock despises *Lord of the Rings* and is now embarking upon more 'conventional' writing.

Alan Moore

♦ BRITISH CARTOONIST

▲Along with the American ☛Frank Miller, Moore effected a big shot in the arm for the mainstream comics industry, developing just enough depth and subtlety of layered plot to justify the claim that comics had gone 'adult'. It is easy to overestimate the maturity and the originality of Moore's ecologically revamped *Swamp Thing* (1987), or even his dense, allusive and witty *Watchmen* (1987), which ambivalently mocked and celebrated five decades of the superhero genre. But although his writing style has clearly evolved from the desolate cosmic existentialism that Jack Kirby brought to the 1960s' cult-strip *The Silver Surfer*, Moore makes the most of a defiantly restless underground attitude, and of being vastly well-read in the weird reaches of feminist and ecological science fiction. Moore first came to attention on the British weekly *2000AD* in the early 1980s, producing the still fondly-remembered feminist space-opera *Halo Jones*, but in the end, he tired of IPC's miserly pay structure, and moved into the big league. Dissatisfaction with DC's and Marvel's very similar attitudes to their artists led him to set up, with Miller and others, a freelancers' pressure group which may make inroads into the corporate philistinism of the comics industry – but don't hold your breath. Moore is smart, influential and radically minded: he has published a comic book, *A.A.R.G.H!* (Artists Against Rampant Government Homophobia, 1988), in which a selection of the world's best comic artists tackle AIDS and homophobia, and another, *Brought to Light* (co-illustrated with ☛Bill Sienkiewicz in 1988), that uncovers details of the Iran-Contra affair.

Henry Moore 1898-1986

BRITISH SCULPTOR

Moore's work revolves around about half a dozen obsessively repeated themes. Very much a public artist, he is best known for his reclining figures – a series of chunky family groups. Admirers point to the breakthrough that Moore achieved with abstraction, but even with the most exploratory of his works, the shapes are still recognizably human. Moore was concerned with density and mass rather than depicting movement – his voluptuous women, captured in bronze, were drastically hollowed out to give them lightness. Moore only flirted with experimentation; while there is undeniable grace and grandeur in his works, the range of his forms was extremely limited.

Mary Tyler Moore born 1937

✓ AMERICAN TELEVISION, FILM ACTRESS, BUSINESS EXECUTIVE

A vivacious American comedienne, Moore's television shows have reflected the changing aspirations of American women. In her early commercials, she was the pretty young thing out to get the man of her dreams. Then, in *The Dick Van Dyke Show* (1961-6), she was the ideal wife every man wanted to come home to – supportive, understanding and a great cook. In *The Mary Tyler Moore Show* (1970-77), she was the go-getting professional woman coming to terms with liberation – a liberation that spilled over into real life as she set up MTM Television with second husband Grant Tinker in 1970. MTM revitalized American television, with safe shows such as *Rhoda* (1974-8) and *Newhart* (1982-9) boosting the less immediate appeal of *Lou Grant* (1977-81), *Hill Street Blues* (1980-8), *St. Elsewhere* (1982-87) and other experimental multi-character series dealing with social issues in an unsensational but dramatic manner. After an undistinguished movie career, Moore's image was transformed again when she took on the role of a mother whose neurosis drives her second son to attempt suicide, in *Ordinary People* (1982). Although the fortunes of MTM have declined since and an attempt to revive her solo show was unsuccessful, Mary Tyler Moore probably still has a few surprises up her sleeve.

Akio Morita born 1921

JAPANESE BUSINESS EXECUTIVE

A central figure in Japan's post-war industrial surge, Morita was the dynamo behind the Sony Corporation, which he set up with his friend Masaru Ibuka in 1946. Groomed to run the family *sake* brewery, he opted instead for electronics, developing his pre-war fascination for radios and sound. Part of his zest for electronics was a passion for miniaturization, the clue to such post-war coups as the world's first pocket-sized transistor radio and, 20 years later, the Walkman. MITI, the Japanese government planning department, initially tried to prevent Sony from making a transistor on the grounds that, if the product were any good, Mitsubishi or one of the other established firms would already be making it. There was opposition, too, to the Walkman: 'Everyone gave me a hard time,' Morita said. 'No market research predicted its success.' Sony's research and development is currently said to be a decade ahead of its (or anyone else's) marketing capabilities. An underlying vision of a peaceful, commercially successful state, as an alternative to earlier militarist dreams, may be central to Morita's psychology. On the other hand, by consistently exporting higher-quality hi-tech innovations than anyone else, Morita has found another way for Japan to invade and conquer the West, recently developing a plan to build up Sony as 'a total entertainment business around the synergy of audio and video hardware and software' through the purchase of such US media giants as CBS Records and Columbia Pictures.

Aldo Moro 1916-78

➼ITALIAN POLITICIAN

Ten years of political terrorism in Italy had resulted in national demoralization when the murder of Moro, one of the country's most influential post-war politicians, persuaded the country's high-ups to pull their socks up. Moro was a fixer. Chairman of the Christian Democrats, who had held power of a sort (through 39 regimes in 32 years) ever since the fall of the Fascists, he was, ironically, on his way to wrap up a deal with the Communist Party when members of the Red Brigades grabbed him from the streets of Rome. The aim of the terrorists was to 'break the military-bureaucratic machine of the state', but they achieved the opposite. Pursuing a policy of non-negotiation throughout the nine weeks before Moro's body was discovered, the quarrelsome factions of Italian politics showed rare unity: traditional Communists came out in defence of the state and Moro's own party was able to forget the rumours of corruption in high places. Portrayed at the time as a political martyr, it is possible that Moro was allowed to die as a result of infighting within the security services. As their commentary on his way of doing politics, the Red Brigades dumped his body halfway between the headquarters of the Communists and those of the Christian Democrats.

Ennio Morricone born 1928

ITALIAN FILM COMPOSER

The last time anyone tried to compile a complete filmography for Morricone, there were complaints of omissions, but no one could decide how many; even the genial maestro himself was not too sure (the best estimate of his output includes 350 titles). Fame came with his unique 'twangy' scores for ☛Sergio Leone's spaghetti westerns, which inventively combined haunting melodies for the flashbacks, modern tempos for the ritual set-pieces and a lot of wry humour in between. He has gone on to write a series of great scores in every conceivable genre, showing a particular sensitivity to lyrical Americana as in Terence Malik's *Days of Heaven* (1978) and just-out-of-mainstream pictures such as ☛Bertolucci's *1900*

(1976), Roland Joffé's *The Mission* (1986) and his final collaboration with Leone, *Once upon a Time in America* (1984). The latter, with its warmth, humour and elegiac yearning stands out as probably his finest work – incidentally exemplifying his tendency only to deliver the goods if the director does the same. Morricone may never turn away work, but unlike ☛John Barry or ☛Jerry Goldsmith, he keeps his finest efforts for the better films.

Desmond Morris born 1928

❞ BRITISH ETHOLOGIST

Zoo man and showman, Morris took the study of animal behaviour from the classroom into television and the tabloid press, and applied zoology to the study of human behaviour in a manner that often seems crudely determinist. In his hugely successful book, *The Naked Ape* (1967), he argues that humans are still governed by the same genetic controls that determine animal behaviour, seemingly ignoring the fact that the development of humans from the ape involved a loosening of just such controls. His sequel, *The Human Zoo* (1969), suggests that the behaviour patterns of wild animals in captivity resemble those of humans under the pressure of city life – meaningless activities, unnatural forms of sex *et al.* The bad zoology involved in some of these arguments was defended by Morris's teacher ☛Nikolaas Tinbergen with the claim that Morris was 'trying to shock people into an awareness of our ignorance of ourselves' and that this was 'a step in the important social process of cutting ourselves down to size'. Morris has gone on to popularize interest in body language – movements of the body that signal intentions, commands or comments – and has become a media pundit on every aspect of human behaviour.

Jim Morrison 1943-71

♥ AMERICAN ROCK MUSICIAN

As leader of The Doors, Morrison exposed himself on stage, performed a stage ritual called 'The Ceremony of the Lizard King', appeared on the cover of teen pop magazines, and died of a heart attack in a Parisian bath-tub. Both poseur and rebel, Morrison is one of the most ludicrous and most compelling of the great dead rock stars. He was important because he managed to make rock music 'serious' and glamorous at the same time; his lizard poems might have been meaningless, and monologues such as 'The End' overblown nonsense, but at its best, his schtick was grandiose, disturbing and, above all, sexy. Morrison managed to act the fool and still seem credible, as though taking your cock out on stage were a statement. Dying young-ish ensured that his image as a sex shag monster would outlast his overweight and unsuccessful last years.

Toni Morrison born 1931

AMERICAN NOVELIST

Until Morrison's extraordinary novel *Beloved* (1987), the early history of black Americans, in particular the experience of slavery, was subject only to troubled, angry, surface explorations: the social realist forms that her predecessors adopted could deal with the present powerfully enough, but this deep past posed different problems. In Morrison's earlier books, especially *Sula* (1974) and *Song of Solomon* (1977) – elliptical stories filled with near-magic and half-existence, all set in this century – the magic was the perilous symbol of a desire to reshape the world: to make things good that were not, to reclaim memory and find it happier than it was. But the evil of slave history cannot be remade in this way – so that Beloved, the book's eponymous central character, who is forced on a runaway family during the Civil War years, is one of the most potently terrifying ghosts in literature: a mother-murdered baby returned as a strange young woman. With her arrival, the story of the family's slave-existence and flight unfolds in quietly shocking fragments, leading to a point where the individuals can find some sort of centre to their miserably shattered lives. White America's greatness has been its constant remaking of its present. Morrison, by unearthing the bitter truths of its past and still allowing that there is healing in this, not just vengeful anger, is presenting the chance to turn that untreated hurt and fright into something richer, darker and better.

Van Morrison

(George Ivan Morrison) born 1945

⇔IRISH ROCK MUSICIAN

✍Van Morrison combines a visionary view of popular music with the apparent demeanour of a pathological park-keeper. He came out of Them, the Northern Irish 1960s' R&B group which was slightly better than most, and then departed for ever from the pop singles charts with solo records such as *TB Sheets*. Morrison took blues and soul into an almost completely personal realm; until he started adding stringed instruments and folk lyricism, no one had noticed even the remotest connection between Irishness and rock 'n' roll. The links between metaphysical poetry and jazz were similarly slender, but 'Rave On, John Donne' changed that. Morrison's invention of 'Celtic Soul', his way with the voice and language (most famous line: 'the love that loves to love the love that loves to love the love that loves'), and his ability to move from folk to jazz to blues make him one of the greatest, maverick, creative rock musicians. He is also arguably the most cantankerous man in the world; his comment on playing an open-air festival in the early 1980s was, 'All the hippies, lying in the mud, nothing's changed.' Apart from the hippies, Morrison's admirers have channeled his Celtic Soul ideas into much spiritually 'authentic' rock; The Pogues are currently his most prominent torch-bearers.

Paul Morrissey

born 1939

AMERICAN FILM DIRECTOR

Joining ☛Andy Warhol's entourage in August 1965, Morrissey's contempt for the art world and his aggressively reactionary opinions seemingly put him at odds with other members of The Factory, but he went on to spend almost ten years working on the production, distribution, exhibition and promotion of Factory films. He squabbled endlessly with Warhol during the shooting of *My Hustler* (1965), *The Loves of Ondine* (1967) and *Lonesome Cowboys* (1968), and went on to impose his own style on *Flesh* (1968), made while the pop art doyen was in hospital recovering from a would-be assassin's bullet. Rejecting the arbitrariness and detachment that had characterized Warhol's cinema until then, Morrissey continued in the same vein with *Trash* (1970) and *Heat* (1972), for which he drew his cast from the drag-queens and misfits that hung around Warhol, creating a star of the notoriously well-endowed Joe Dallesandro. Morrissey was probably leading Warhol in a direction he really wanted to go – away from his early minimalism and towards more conventional directorial assertion, but the two split up in 1975 after wrangles over *Flesh for Frankenstein* and *Blood for Dracula* (both 1973), Morrissey's flop attempts at mass-audience taste. Recent films such as 1985's *Mixed Blood* (aka *Cocaine*), about drug dealers on New York's Lower East Side, show Morrissey taking account of such old-fashioned values as characterization and chronology, without completely effacing the deadpan anarchy of his earlier work.

Degenerates are not such a great audience, but they're a step up from the art crowd; we would always rather play a sexploitation theatre than an art theatre.
Paul Morrissey

Franco Moschino born 1950

ITALIAN FASHION DESIGNER

Among the fashion crowd of the late 1980s, Moschino's became the hippest name to drop – the man who broke all the rules of Italian fashion design. The clothes are quite rock 'n' rollish – denim shirts covered in studs, etc. – but in the days when even the commonest high street shopper had heard of ☛Gaultier or ☛Galliano, and Chanel T-shirts were bootlegged by the score, Moschino's name confirmed the coterie's sense that they still knew something the others did not. His fascination with gimmicks makes his shows into circuses: the Italian flag appears in various guises; models appear on the catwalk on their hands and knees; surreal faces decorate his dresses; and Victorian swags and fringes appear in the most unlikely places. He appears in his own advertisements, sometimes wearing a curly blond wig, and his most expensive couture line carries the logo of a big, fat cow.

Robert Motherwell 1915-91

AMERICAN PAINTER

Although a leading light among New York's abstract expressionists, who created collages and prints as well as paintings, Motherwell was always a loner. There was no consistent theme in his work – he allowed the images to develop from within himself, and from his readings of the ideas around him. If, however, one image were to stand for Motherwell's work, it would be the motif of inter-related egg shapes, painted in black and white, that loom ominously over his *Elegy for the Spanish Republic*, which he began in 1949. For his collages, he used anything available – cigarette packets, stickers, matchboxes and notes – and the simple elegance of these assemblies contrasts with the work of his contemporary, ☛Robert Rauschenberg. Reflecting his interest in Eastern philosophies, one of Motherwell's aims was to translate sounds and sensations into visual language.

Jean Muir born 1933

BRITISH FASHION DESIGNER

'I prefer evolution or organic growth to revolution or grand idealistic concepts.' Muir, who regards herself as a craftswoman rather than an artist, embodies a reserved British approach to design. She is known as the designer who always wears black or navy but maintains that she is 'mad about good colour' when it comes to putting together her collections. Her style emphasizes good fabrics – she favours clinging silk jersey and fluid suede – and fine cut. An emphasis on simplicity produces clothes that are flattering, elegant and capable of being worn for years. She is probably one of the most widely respected of contemporary designers.

Russell Mulcahy born 1953

♦ AUSTRALIAN FILM, MUSIC VIDEO DIRECTOR

Mulcahy was one of the first to become famous for directing pop promos, along with Steve Barron and Tim Pope (and about 1000 others). He introduced a suitable pomposity to Ultravox 's New/Old Europe fantasies, made rock star travelogues with Duran Duran for a 'joke' and, with films such as *Razorback* (1984) and *Highlander* (1986), became the first film director to come to the job from videos. This is in contrast to Ridley Scott, who had at least worked with dialogue in his Hovis commercials, and Julien Temple, who might be considered a part-time video director, like ☛Nicolas Roeg or ☛Ken Russell, had he made some more feature films). Mulcahy's films were the first of which critics could say, 'It looks like a pop video.'

Gerry Mulligan born 1927

AMERICAN JAZZ MUSICIAN

✎A baritone sax player whose understated poise remains one of the miracles of breath-control over instrument size, Mulligan's compositions for ☛Miles Davis – 'Jeru', 'Godchild', 'Boplicity' – formed the elegant heart of the wayward trumpeter's *Birth of the Cool* as it first arrived, in the late 1940s. Miles moved on; Mulligan, still a very young man, stuck to his first strike, and became one of the formative innovators of the West Coast Cool School, before narcotics trouble blew his private world of sophistication to hell. Since the 1950s, Mulligan has been at the centre of a no-longer-unrespectable, pop-serious tradition, sidelined and unfairly criticized by the Free Jazz radicals who succeeded the Cool era.

Lewis Mumford 1895-1990

AMERICAN SOCIOLOGIST

Mumford predicted the emerging nightmare of life in New York and other modern cities, as housing became congested around skyscraper monuments to big finance, and he proposed sometimes utopian alternatives – cities that would be civilized places for people to live in. In *Culture of Cities* (1938), he argued that if the growth of cities was not controlled, the wealthiest inhabitants would flee to suburban regions, creating enormous problems at the centre. His solution was the delimitation of a green belt around each city and the construction of garden cities on the British model. He returned to the subject in *The City in History* (1961), but increasingly he also made holistic moves into philosophy, religion and economics. Mumford was one of the first to warn about environmental pollution, nuclear proliferation and the dehumanizing effects of urban deterioration. As contemporary politicians in the UK and US confront the problems of their inner cities, they must regret that their predecessors did not listen more carefully to what Mumford was saying from the 1930s on.

Rupert Murdoch

born 1931

$ AUSTRALIAN-AMERICAN MEDIA MOGUL

A flamboyant press proprietor with a worldwide newspaper empire, in the 1980s Murdoch widened into an all-round communications tycoon and turned his News International into the second-largest media group in the world. He is not alone in the move outwards from print media, but he is the most voraciously determined. He has made mistakes – losing $20 million on his first abortive pitch to launch a US satellite television network in the early 1980s, but he has the guts to pull out quickly, learn the lessons and try again. More recently he has poured money into the launch of the British Sky TV satellite service, and it is not clear that he yet knows how to match his flair for newspapers in the very different arenas of television and cinema (he owns the US major, Twentieth Century-Fox). He was born into the business – his father was a famous war reporter and publisher. At university, he was a socialist, something not reflected in the later editorial slants of his newspapers. A theme in many of his outlets is a strong focus on sex, sensation and sport – the *Sun*, which he has owned since 1969, is the most sophisticated and extreme example in the UK. He has reduced union power in newspaper printing; relocating his newspapers to new plant in 1986 made them vastly more profitable, and facilitated cost reductions on other journals – as well as encouraging numerous new launches. Unlike the barons of old, he refrains from daily interference in editorial decisions, but none the less appoints those who listen when money talks, so that he is widely blamed for turning the mandarin-independence of *The Times* into the Thatcherite sniping of just another newspaper. He probably does not so much want to change the world as to be seen supporting the party that is in power and the ideas that are in fashion. Determined to make his empire grow, he has lumbered himself with a heavy debt burden (around £5 billion at the last count), but he has probably borrowed so much that the banks could not possibly let him go under.

Muhammad Mussadegh

IRANIAN POLITICIAN

1880-1967

Seen in Britain as a Middle Eastern menace who nationalized the Anglo-Iranian oil company in 1951 and induced a fleeting, international crisis, Mussadegh is a central character in modern Iranian history – the one major, secular nationalist hero, directly elected, who could challenge the powerbases of the ruling dynasty and of the mullahs. Four decades later, he survives as a name to conjure with in Iranian exile circles. He trained as a lawyer in Switzerland, and as a member of a ruling family, he joined Iranian Cabinets in the 1920s. He opted out of public life when a new dynasty was established under Reza Khan, a Cossack leader, but he re-emerged in parliament as an enemy of oil concessions to the Soviets. His takeover of Anglo-Iranian led to a bitter dispute with Britain, making him a national symbol and triggering his choice as premier by Iran's parliament. A failure to find markets for the nationalized oil led to a deep economic crisis, and he was granted dictatorial powers, leading to strained relations with the Shah, as Mussadegh tried to carry out a social revolution which alienated both army and aristocracy. The Shah forced through another choice as premier and, backed by the West, used a coup to topple Mussadegh when he stood firm. The former premier was gaoled for treason – he spent his last 11 years under house arrest – and this led to a long and socially disastrous period of rule by the Shah, whose regime finally collapsed into the revolution that gave us the Ayatollah.

Gunnar Myrdal 1898-1987

SWEDISH ECONOMIST

Myrdal spent the war years probing the race problem in the US at the behest of the US authorities, and his book, *An American Dilemma* (1944), reflected his belief that economics could not be cut off from other factors. He was a 'holist', arguing that there are no specifically social, economic or political problems, only 'problems'. He never made any identifiable formal contributions to economics, but during the 1950s he became an expert on Third World development, which he analysed in terms of the the inter-action of variables that move a society away from 'equilibrium', either negatively or positively. He warned against economic planning which froze that equilibrium, and stopped it moving in response to other pressures. In 1974, he suffered the irony of sharing a Nobel prize with ☛Friedrich von Hayek, an economist of a very different ilk.

N

Vladimir Nabokov 1899-1977

SOVIET WRITER, WHO SETTLED IN SWITZERLAND

Nabokov's most notorious book, *Lolita* (1955), was inspired by an ape. The cosmopolitan writer, still resident in his native Russia, read of an experiment in which scientists coaxed an ape into producing a drawing – the bars of its cage. In a novella entitled *The Enchanter*, which Nabokov later discarded, the cage became madness, the bars desire and the ape an anonymous jeweller obsessed with a 12-year-old girl. It was not until political pressures led to his exile from Russia and his eventual settlement in the US that this 'first little throb' grew the claws and wings of the most notorious novel of the 1950s. Presented as the 'confession' of the pathetic Humbert Humbert, the book recounts his relationship with an under-age but far from innocent girl. Inspiring generations of sex symbols from Carroll Baker to Brooke Shields, *Lolita* differed from its prototype (which climaxed in its 'hero' accidentally ejaculating over the sleeping girl of his dreams and literally dying of embarrassment) in its marked absence of obscenity. Its success eclipsed Nabokov's later, much superior books such as *Pale Fire* (1962) and *Ada* (1969). Despite writing in English, he never lost his very Russian joy in language – nor did he escape the notoriety that moralists (who could not tell the difference between Humbert and Nabokov) heaped upon him.

Ralph Nader born 1934

❞ AMERICAN CONSUMER ACTIVIST

Nader carved himself a niche as the leading advocate of consumer rights in the US, capturing the imagination of the press in the 1960s. With an acute understanding of the effectiveness of good public relations, he used non-profit-making enterprises to horse-whip profit-worshipping multinationals through the streets of shame. Having blown the whistle on General Motors when it cynically put profit before car safety, he made campaigning consumerism respectable in the US; 'Nader's Raiders' took on everything from frankfurters stuffed with fat, through insecticides and baby food to policies on pipeline safety and pension reform. As American industry grew larger and increasingly less willing to make itself accountable to the American people, Nader built up a public platform for the right of individuals to question whether their interests were being best served. He made Americans realize they could question what had been taken for granted, fuelling a healthy paranoia that continued into the 1980s and 1990s.

Ernest Nagel born 1901

CZECHOSLOVAK-AMERICAN PHILOSOPHER OF SCIENCE

Nagel has defended the view of science as a process of steadily accumulating knowledge. The 'hypothetico-deductive' system, according to which fresh experimental data is continuously fed back to test, and develop, basic axioms, which become in consequence ever more adequate to explain natural phenomena – has come under increasing attack from the likes of ☛Thomas Kuhn and ☛Paul Feyerabend. Against them, Nagel argues that there is no such thing as a radical break in science. Einstein's theory of relativity, for example, did not totally replace Newton's physics; the old theory was just a limited version of the new. Science does not 'start' again, but builds on the past in such a way that it acquires the power to explain more things with fewer hypotheses. Nagel sees the 'scientific method' as the most viable tool for acquiring reliable knowledge of the world. What this view ignores is the degree to which scientists are pig-headed and self-deceiving in their use of data, and how much more is required to build new theorems than dutiful laboratory work.

Imre Nagy 1896-1958

➻HUNGARIAN POLITICIAN

✌ Nagy's execution by Soviet invaders – he headed Hungary's 1956 revolt against their control – was a tragic comment on the betrayed idealism of central Europe's left in the 40 years after the Russian Revolution. A POW from the Austro-Hungarian army, Nagy joined the Reds in the Russian Civil War, returned home as a radical critic of the regime and, later, moved to Moscow, his ideological home, to train and work as an agricultural economist. He played leading roles in post-war Hungarian regimes – in the end, as premier from 1953 to 1955, when he set out on new economic reforms. Thrown out, he returned to run the government in October 1956, pleading in vain for aid from the UN. When the Soviets moved in, the Hungarians were trapped; Nagy was arrested, tried secretly and hanged. Even in 1987, the authorities put down a demonstration at his grave in Budapest, but in 1989, as Hungary re-evaluated 1956, his rehabilitation led to the bitter irony of a belated state funeral.

V(idiadhar) S(urajprasad) Naipaul born 1932

⇔TRINIDADIAN NOVELIST

In spite of his frequent criticism of English life and culture, this Trinidadian of Indian extraction has become the most eloquent of apologists for the British empire. Undoubtedly a fine writer, Naipaul's early novels reflect his complex cultural and ethnic background; more recently, he has concentrated on travelogues. *Among the Believers* (1981), his Islamic journey, was well received, but it is clear that his views – in particular his negative attitudes towards fundamentalism – have gained undue attention simply because Naipaul is not a white European. The same may be true of his recent journey through the American South, appraising the legacy of the civil rights movement. By education and approach Naipaul is in every way the last English gentleman – more English (and more of a gentleman) than any of those on whom he models himself. In what seemed a suitable compliment to Naipaul's role in interpreting the non-white world, David

Hare drew a very similar character in his play *Map of the World* (1983). It seems appropriate that when this very English playwright took a rare excursion outside post-war Britain, he should choose a Naipaul-type voice for the aspirations of the Third World – a fitting tribute from one product of the post-imperial age to another.

R(asipuram) K(rishnaswami) Narayan born 1907

INDIAN NOVELIST

Whereas his most enthusiastic admirer, ☛Graham Greene, has wandered the world to find settings for his stories, Narayan is content to write about one invented South Indian place, Malgudi, through which he explores the endless conflict between past and present, the traditional and the progressive, the self-sacrificing values of Hinduism and the get-rich-quick attitudes of contemporary Indian youth. His characters typically start out as modest, prudent men, who are led astray by some crazy scheme, resulting in either self-destruction or self knowledge. The journalist in *Mr Sampath* (1949), for example, invests in a disastrous movie-making enterprise, while the railway station vendor of *The Guide* (1952) takes up with an exotic dancer, makes a pile, spends everything on extravagant living, endures a few years in prison, then emerges to find himself adopted as the region's spiritual leader. Narayan's clear, precise prose was the first to make India, as opposed to Anglo-India, known to an English-speaking readership.

Gamal Abdel Nasser 1918-70

EGYPTIAN POLITICAL LEADER

Egypt's leader from 1953, Nasser gave his name to an ideology – 'Nasserism' – which overlaps with Arab nationalism and which has latterly been eclipsed by Islamic fundamentalism. Nasser is recalled in the West for fighting two failed wars against Israel, and for triggering the Anglo-French landings at Suez through his decision to nationalize the Suez Canal, after the West had turned down his plea for aid to build the Aswan dam. In one sense, Nasserism was predictable anti-colonialism, as traditional imperialists were forced out of, or left, the Middle East; Nasser said that Israel was a surrogate for the colonialists. But he also aimed to make Egypt a leading power in three areas – the Arab Middle East, Africa and the wider non-European world – current, lasting tensions between Cairo, Baghdad and Damascus as rival centres of gravity in the Arab world have resulted from these ambitions. Nasser came to power following a young officers' coup against King Farouk. Initially a petit bourgeois revolution designed to restore uncorrupt, good government, Nasser turned it into a charismatic appeal to Arab youth everywhere. The revolution lasted as long as he was able to stave off a war by trumpeting his triumphs against Britain; when he lost to Israel, minds focused on a disastrous economy. Nasserism only lives now as a fringe movement.

Jawaharlal Nehru 1889-64

INDIAN POLITICAL LEADER

Gandhi's colleague through the years of disobedience campaigns, Nehru took over on the Mahatma's death in 1948 to steer India through its first 17 years. He cut a strong figure on the international stage, as a leading player in the movement of non-aligned nations. In 1956, he vigorously attacked Britain's Suez foray but stayed quiet about the Soviet Union's invasion of Hungary, defending his line by saying that he lacked 'full information'. He combined a Westernized manner – he was a British-trained lawyer, born into a high-caste family – with a homely, informal style of oratory that gave him instant access to Indian emotions. His major errors were deciding to wage a short but disastrous war with China in 1962 and failing to get to grips with India's booming population problem – the root explanation for its mass poverty. Even so, India survived as a parliamentary democracy. He made no serious efforts to set up a dynasty, and he died without naming a successor. His daughter ☛ Indira Gandhi took over anyway.

Pablo Neruda

(Neftalí Ricardo Reyes) 1904-73

✌ CHILEAN POET

Neruda was a politically committed poet, who travelled Chile reading his work at rallies and meetings of workers. He exploited all the tools of rhetoric – polemic, satire, eulogy, panegyric and lament – to build a profusion of vital imagery into multi-layered epics. His masterpiece, 'The Heights of Macchu Picchu' (from his 1950 collection, *Canto General*), articulates a history of suffering at the hands of tyrants, dictators and commercial enterprises, revealing both his sensitivity to the natural world and an ability seemingly to coax life out of stone monuments. Radicalized in Spain during the early stages of the Civil War, he became a Communist senator in 1945 and stood unsuccessfully as a Communist candidate for the presidency; he saw the accession to power of ☛Allende in 1970 as the realization of his dreams. Neruda's funeral, shortly after the Pinochet coup, occasioned the first public demonstration against the military government.

John Von Neumann 1903–57

♦ HUNGARIAN-AMERICAN MATHEMATICIAN

'Young man', said Von Neumann to an aspiring physicist, 'in mathematics you don't understand things, you just get used to them.' The man who published *The Mathematical Foundations of Quantum Mechanics* (1932) was pointing out that quantum mechanics would not support the commonsense assumption that its famous uncertainties were merely uncertainties of knowledge; he proved there was no mysterious hidden world that, once uncovered, could clear them up. A mathematical prodigy in his youth, Von Neumann's brilliance is best shown by the unwieldy range of his concerns and studies: apart from quantum mechanics, he made significant advances in number theory, information theory and the development of computers. His most far-reaching concept, among those which can be easily stated and considered, was the proof that machines could be constructed that could replicate themselves (in other words that no mystical force was necessary for self-reproduction). He showed this by transforming machine-language into a huge grid-array of lit and unlit squares, with a limited number of simple operations of change (which would later form the basis of mathematician ☛John Horton Conway's famous game, *Life*); configurations could be found that produced copies of themselves.

Louise Nevelson 1900-90

SOVIET-AMERICAN SCULPTOR

Nevelson was one of the first to take the flotsam and jetsam of garbage dumps and make something from them. Starting out with wooden bric-à-brac, she later used plastic, plexiglass and metal for her mysterious pieces. Always painted in one colour – black and gold were favourites – so as to obscure the source of the materials and give the pieces a unified look, the resulting monumental assemblages of abstract shapes suggest the ritualistic art of the Aztecs or the Mayas. *Nightscape*, which she finished in the early 1960s, incorporates bannisters, a chair-back and a coat-hanger under a thick coat of black paint, to evoke the mystery of the city of night, when a shroud of darkness has covered up all its multifarious activities.

Richard Neville

AUSTRALIAN JOURNALIST, PUBLISHER, TEMPORARILY SETTLED IN LONDON

One of a remarkably productive group of expatriate Australians based in London during the mid-1960s, Neville founded *Oz*, the paper that gave fullest expression to the cultural underground in all its incoherent splendour. The magazine was erratic, self-indulgent, peculiar, wide-ranging, obscene, funny, unreadable and important, providing a platform to every crackpot experiment and crazed opinion. *Oz* may have given ☛Rupert Murdoch the idea for the Page Three Girl, but also provided the impetus that led to *Spare Rib* and *Gay News*. A rampant Rupert Bear engaged in sex – in the Schoolkids' issue – earned all three editors the hostile attentions of British justice. An appeal ensured that establishment retribution amounted only to a few nights in gaol and brutal haircuts, but the money that went towards the defence had to be diverted from *Ink* magazine, Neville's follow-up project, which was intended to bridge the gap between overground investigative journalism and underground attitude. *Ink* folded, and that bridge was never built. What was important about *Oz* was that it was never safe, careerist or mealy-mouthed. Significantly, only a very few of its writers have ever been allowed into the grown-up press.

Arnold Newman born 1918

AMERICAN PHOTOGRAPHER

Newman's approach to portraiture – placing his subjects in relation to the artefacts they have created (he is keen on artists), or the places where they work – is generally saved from cliché by his painterly eye for abstraction and love of stark geometries. One of his most famous images, taken in 1946 for *Harper's Bazaar*, features Stravinsky at the bottom of a frame dominated by a raised piano lid. Sometimes the settings do seem a little easy, as when ☛Isamu Noguchi is caught peering through one of his sculptures, or playwright Shelagh Delaney pushes her back against a grimy wall in the north of England. At his best, however, Newman captures more of the spirit of an artist's work than its obvious surface. His 1942 picture of Max Ernst, for example, positions the artist in the lower right-hand corner of the picture, behind a puff of smoke, while a 1975 portrait of ☛Francis Bacon uses a naked ceiling light to convey the sense of claustrophobic horror that pervades the painter's own pictures. Newman does not always play up to his subjects' own vew of themselves, or hesitate to convey his own views – for instance, he made Nazi munitions industrialist Alfred Krupp look suitably demonic, and conveyed the pomposity behind ☛Franco's façade.

Barnett Newman 1905-70

AMERICAN ARTIST

At a time when most artists were spewing paint liberally over free-form canvases, Newman was more concerned with formulating a meditative approach to painting. He wanted, like his friend ☛Rothko, an 'art that would suggest the mysterious sublime rather than the beautiful', and believed that art is an intensely complex act of personal creation that deals with the mind's desire for expression. This led him to the creation of extremely large works – his *Vir Heroicus Sublimis* (1951) is more than 17 feet (5m) wide – that pulsed with a single glowing colour, typically cut by one or more thin vertical lines. The first of this series of works – *Onement* (1948) – in which an orange band severs a deep Indian-red canvas is about nothing but itself, simply an enigmatic pool of tranquillity. Newman's cosmic preoccupations relate him to the surrealists, but where they tended to amalgamate their dream worlds and reality in a kind of batter of creativity, he stuck religiously to his precise and spiritual ideals. The 'stripe paintings' remained his sole formal outlet for the remainder of his career, both anticipating and influencing the rise of minimalism in the 1960s.

New Order *see* Joy Division

Helmut Newton born 1920

GERMAN FASHION PHOTOGRAPHER

Newton found his niche in 1970s' fashion photography – a world of beauty, glamour and stars where he did not have to justify himself. In his limited vision, the female body is a sex machine, presented in a cold, calculated and yet refined manner. His work is all surface. Unlike ☛Robert Mapplethorpe, who documented the dark sexual world which he inhabited, Newton only dabbles in fetishistic imagery – corsets, furs, stocking tops, patent-leather boots, exaggeratedly high heels, phallic cigarette holders and leather gear – and ignores the distinction between pornography and eroticism. The effect is little more than titillation. How else can the viewer, or voyeur, respond to the image of a Barbarella embedded in a toilet seat with her toothy grin gleaming, or a woman squashed into a wheelbarrow and restrained by another rubber-clad seductress?

Huey Newton 1942-89

Bobby Seale born 1936

AMERICAN POLITICAL ACTIVISTS

Seale and Newton founded the Black Panther Party for Self-Defence in 1966, an organization set up to resist police brutality against blacks while initiating community services such as health clinics and a bus service for relatives of prison inmates. Propounding a mix of ☛Stokely Carmichael's black power rhetoric and Marxist-Leninist ideology, they were never as dangerous as ☛Nixon and ☛J. Edgar Hoover believed – it was their uniform of black berets and leather jackets (first displayed publicly in May 1967 when a group of Panthers disrupted the California State Assembly to protest a pending arms control law), and the fact that they recruited among Vietnam War veterans and the youth of the ghettoes, that placed them in the Washington establishment's demonology. The group became victims of a media scare campaign and FBI infiltration, leading to numerous shoot-outs, assassinations and arrests – the resulting standoff between black and white still sours race relations in the US. Seale was among the Chicago Seven arrested at the Democratic Party Convention in 1968, and spent four years in prison for contempt of court – he called the judge a 'pig', a 'liar' and a 'Fascist' and, as a result, was tied and gagged for the duration of his trial. He was freed in 1972 and wrote his autobiograpy, *A Lonely Rage* (1978). Trumped-up manslaughter charges put Newton behind bars for two years. Subsequently, he survived numerous attempts on his life before stopping the bullets that killed him; he had already lost the battle against alcohol and drug abuse. His book – *War Against the Panthers: a Study of Repression in America* (1980) – is a startling exposé of the subversive tactics employed by the FBI.

John Nichols born 1940

▲AMERICAN NOVELIST

Nichols is best known for his *Milagro* trilogy, set in a New Mexico township caught between poverty and development, with its memorable cast of villagers and outsiders – rough, frail and a little crazy. There are bastards on the loose in his books, but no villains, and the style is a species of realism that would have to be called Magic Dirt, owing as much to Steinbeck as ☛García Márquez. A Vietnam veteran himself, the distant rumble of the war makes for a sinister tremble of unease in the sunniest passages, but it was not until the late 1980s that Nichols found himself able to confront the psychological legacy he had been left with. The violent, furious, extraordinary *American Blood* (1987) charts the distortions in sexuality and the nihilism that men trained to be monsters will experience. If the hero comes to a provisional truce with himself and his own psychosis, the never-admitted hurt America did to itself is still in evidence, in a society of increasing bloody lawlessness. The book is unrelenting enough to terrify, but its control and political intelligence are significant, and Nichols is clearly one of America's major popular writers. His novels are easily made into films, though so far not especially good ones: *The Sterile Cuckoo* (1965) was filmed in 1969 with Liza Minelli (it was called *Pooky* in the UK); and Robert Redford's bland carve-up of *The Milagro Beanfield War* (1974) was released in 1988.

Oscar Niemeyer born 1907
Lucia Costa 1902-63

☞BRAZILIAN ARCHITECTS

Designing a city from scratch must be the dream/nightmare project of many architects, but Brasília, erected as Brazil's new capital in the late 1950s, now symbolizes the inability of any 'grand plan' to anticipate all the needs of those who will live in the buildings. It was Costa, progenitor of modern architecture in Brazil and Niemeyer's boss on earlier government-sponsored projects, who came up with the ground plan for the city – a model of geometrical simplicity whose beauty is (unfortunately) best appreciated from the air. But Niemeyer was the chief architect, responsible for designing the public buildings and supervising the overall project. The huge size of what he had taken on cramped his style somewhat, and his work for Brasília lacks the florid and fantastical originality of earlier designs. The city became, in time, a sociological disaster, as a squalid shanty town grew up around it: no one had thought to provide cheap housing for those whom Brazil's 'economic miracle' had yet to touch.

Robert de Niro *see* de Niro, Robert

Paul Nitze born 1907

AMERICAN GOVERNMENT BUREAUCRAT, DIPLOMAT

Established right-wing figures may have the sureness of touch, when change is necessary, to make radical moves. Nitze, an official rather than a statesman, had been Washington's leading post-war hawk, seeking an edge for the US in every arms area. But in the 1980s, he sensed a stalemate in the East-West Arms Control Talks being held at Geneva, and seized the initiative. As head of the US negotiating team, he took a quiet, one-to-one 'walk in the woods' with the Soviet envoy, cutting through the logjam and the ritual responses. The new formulae spun from that chat did not, as promised, instantly result in real weapons cuts; but they marked a real change in ideas, as chasms of debate between the powers became technical gaps, bridged by wit and sense. Nitze's insight presaged ☛Gorbachev's man-to-man talks with ☛Reagan. A public servant from 1940 and deputy secretary of defense during 1967-9, Nitze had been, as an investment banker, a 'prodigy'. Did this banking genius explain his keen eye for nuclear statistics in the 1950s and 1960s and a pragmatist's gift for a *volte-face* that paid dividends?

Richard Nixon born 1913

▯ AMERICAN POLITICAL LEADER

Even when the time came for Nixon to deliver his resignation speech, he was unable to admit that he had done anything wrong – although he had spent months trying to conceal the crimes he had committed or encouraged while holding one of the most important jobs in the world. His biggest problem was that he thought everyone was against him (and that the Soviets wanted to take over the world). He was secretive, not even consulting the US Senate before ordering bombers to drop havoc on to Cambodia ; and he played dirty – he used audits of tax returns against his enemies and put wiretaps on *everybody*. He became the first American president to resign from office, going down with no grace at all after the impeachment process had begun. Having trained as lawyer, he played a major role, after joining Congress, on the House Un-American Activities Committee, exposing 'Communists' in public life and winning a case for perjury against ☛Alger Hiss. Making his name as a ☛McCarthyite, he became vice president to ☛Eisenhower in 1953. On policy, he was always flexible – he wanted the Republicans in the 1950s to bid for the black vote – but with critics, he was ruthless. He lost the 1960 race against ☛Kennedy by a few votes; a defeat many blamed on his appearance in a television contest with his rival – Nixon's five o'clock shadow gleamed through his cheeks and lost votes. He lost again in the race to be governor of California, but he came back to win the 1968 contest for the presidency on a tide of moral panic caused by unrest among students and other radicals. A pragmatist abroad, he arranged a deal with China, the Salt I arms treaty with the Soviet Union and (eventually) the US exit from Vietnam. Since 1974, he has been a trenchant commentator on the US, much in demand as a lecturer. But the real mystery of his career is why he decided to record on tape every single word spoken in the Oval Office during his presidential term, and then considered this testimony to his greatness so important that he could not bring himself to destroy the evidence that eventually led to his downfall.

Others may hate you, but those who hate you don't win unless you hate them, and then you destroy yourself.
Richard Nixon

Kwame Nkrumah

(Francis Nwia Kafi) 1909-72

GHANAIAN POLITICAL LEADER

Nkrumah was leader of Ghana, the first black African country to gain its independence, becoming its president in 1960. His Marxist rhetoric and pan-African vision – he was the chief initiator of the Organization of African Unity in 1963 – hid an emerging dictatorship. Despite real economic advances and beginning as a genuinely popular leader, Nkrumah eventually imprisoned opponents without trial in much the same way as the old colonial regime had imprisoned him: the difference was that that he survived (and went straight from prison to become prime minister in 1952), while his critics died in gaol. The decisive shift away from legalism took place in 1963, after he had dismissed the chief justice following the acquittal of three leading figures arraigned for treason. His toppling by a military coup in 1966 was greeted by general jubilation, and he shifted to exile in Guinea. Although Ghana, a model for decolonization elsewhere, became a symbol of shattered dreams, Nkrumah remains an African hero. He had encouraged belief in his own immortality, but died in Romania.

Isamu Noguchi 1904-88

JAPANESE-AMERICAN SCULPTOR

Noguchi bridged cultures, living as much in the US as in Japan, and also challenged fixed ideas of what it is that a sculptor does. He was an impressive all-round designer, who had studied medicine as well as cabinet-making, drawing and pottery. He designed 'Akari' paper lights to rescue the paper-making industry of the town of Gifu from commercial exploitation, as well as stage sets for leading contemporary choreographers, but he also constructed monumental stone sculptures which he described as part of dialogue between himself and 'the primary matter of the universe'. Setting highly polished stones against rough surfaces, his favourite shapes were thin and elongated. Beyond that, he was concerned with the way his work was experienced in space – he carefully organized the placement and juxtaposition of objects for the Isamu Noguchi Garden, his museum in New York.

Eliot Noyes 1910-77

AMERICAN DESIGNER

The story goes that Noyes was standing outside the Olivetti showroom in New York with the president of IBM, shortly after the end of WW2, when the latter asked him to do for the American office-machine company what ☛Sottsass and Nizzoli were already doing for the Italian outfit. So was born a post-war commonplace: good design equals good business. Noyes kept the typewriters for himself, but gathered a team of designers to work on other aspects of his masterplan for IBM. This involved going beyond what the Olivetti team had done in giving a coherent image to the Italian company's product range and building a corporate identity that would be reflected in every visual manifestation of IBM – from graphics to building interiors and advertising.

Robert Nozick born 1938

AMERICAN PHILOSOPHER

As the ambitions of the modern state have grown, so many have become increasingly attracted by the idea of reducing government activity. Nozick, who has written upon a broad range of philosophical issues, argues for the 'minimal' state and espouses a passionate individualism (he abandoned socialism at high school). Arguing that attempts to redistribute incomes for egalitarian ends involve unacceptable interference in people's lives, he insists that the state should confine itself to protecting its citizens against force, theft, fraud and such like, and not seek to compel some citizens to assist others, or to prevent people from harming themselves. In case this vision of society seems a little uninspiring, Nozick proposes that we dream about a 'utopia' where individuals can each realize their *own* vision of the good life. This view has something in common with proposals that the political future lies in the establishment of space colonies – a supermarket of societies from which people can make their own choice – and does not take account of the fact that what many in the Western world feel they are missing is belonging to a community which will help them develop values to live by. With pragmatic inconsistency, ☛Thatcher and ☛Reagan both combined 'sweeping back the powers of the state' with appeals to 'old-fashioned' morality. Nozick's arguments, by contrast, are insensitive to psychological needs and the complex strategies necessary to sustain modern societies.

Julius Nyerere born 1922

TANZANIAN POLITICAL LEADER

As Tanzania's president from 1962 to 1985, the central idea in Nyerere's plan for his country, which turned into a one-party state after independence, was 'African socialism': the party was designed as an umbrella, absorbing tribal factions and interest groups; rural units for small-scale economic development were stressed; nationalization of the most important industries acted as an alternative to reliance on multinationals. Despite a war to topple Uganda's ☛ Idi Amin, which was successful, Nyerere was able to give his country peaceful, slow change – he had never been a violent opponent of the British – and sharp rises in literacy. His was a one-party state that avoided becoming a vicious or aggressive dictatorship. It lacked economic momentum though; self-reliance may have been taken too far. Nyerere was a father-figure for his own people, and a powerful force not only in the East African federation but for all ex-colonial Africa. He left power voluntarily.

O

Michael Oakeshott 1901-90

BRITISH POLITICAL THINKER

Oakeshott was a Tory with a difference – one foot in political theory, as he analysed the preconditions of action; the other in idealistic philosophy, as he attacked the distinction between observer and object. An iconoclastic hero for the traditionalist wing of the New Right, he is still little-read in leading circles of the Conservative Party. That is partly because his Hegel-inspired philosophy does not accord with the Conservative temper, and also because a superficial kinship with ☛Hayek – Oakeshott too wrote about the poverty of corporatism – sits ill alongside his scorn for economics and his rejection of prosperity as a criterion of social change. Scepticism is the common key to his matching interests in ideas and action: life is much, much more complex than it is said to be. He writes elegantly, if often obscurely, with an air of a dandy and a poet, luxuriating in the rhythms of his prose. He argues that politics is about keeping the state afloat – a ritual, a game with its own skills, learned from its own stock of experience. A self-sufficient activity, it is not an enterprise with 'substantive' goals. Oakeshott drew his attack on 'rationalism' – the new ideas that would overturn the traditional English way of doing things – from the same source as ☛Orwell's attack on Communism, and his dismissal of all the social legislation of the post-war world seemed to have more to do with dyspepsia than dystopia.

Flann O'Brien

(Brian O'Nolan) 1911-66

IRISH JOURNALIST, NOVELIST

An *Irish Times* columnist and civil servant, O'Brien combined immense academic and literary knowledge with an overpowering, absurdist imagination. His books, whether written in English or Gaelic, owe some debt to Joyce in their subversion of narrative and sharp detailing of Irish character. His relentlessly bleak plots and harsh treatment of characters are reminiscent of Kafka, but the beautifully argued illogic of O'Brien's theories and raging creative powers are his own. *The Third Policeman* (1967) posits his own Atomic Theory, suggesting that any object which spends too much time in physical contact with another object takes on that second object's characteristics, and vice versa; thus Ireland is full of men who are more than half bicycle. The newspaper column he wrote under the name 'Myles NaGopaleen' simultaneously commented on Irish daily life, included meticulous character sketches and played host to some of the worst puns ever inflicted on the reading public. Every writer since to whom the tag of 'surrealist comedy' could be applied has been compared to O'Brien, but it was his ability to take the impossible and make it utterly convincing – and, generally, somehow threatening – which makes his work more than just great comic novel-writing. He could put his nonsense into the mouths of credible characters, argue the impossible and place his action in any hell from history.

Flannery O'Connor 1925-64

AMERICAN NOVELIST

O'Connor's few novels and short stories are probably read more for their Southern 'eccentricity' than for their humour and religious conviction: an atheistic reader not raised in the Deep South will find a book such as *Wise Blood* (1952) more unsettling than enlightening. But O'Connor's dry style, matching her eye for sticky Southern afternoons, ultimately draws everyone in. Her stories shift the spectre of evil into the foreground, surround it all with arid humour and conclude that God is salvation. O'Connor found Christianity in the Southern states 'painful and touching and grimly comic', a description which fits her writing. The vein of aggressive puritanism in her prose accounts for its current appeal. Ex-Birthday Party singer Nick Cave's first novel, *And the ass saw the angel*, draws on O'Connor's mix of religious obsession and mocking violence.

David Ogilvy born 1911

BRITISH ADVERTISING EXECUTIVE

A Scot, who showed that outsiders could penetrate the hallowed halls of Madison Avenue, Ogilvy built Ogilvy & Mather into one of the world's leading advertising agencies even as he tried to maintain there the cosy gentleman's club atmosphere that had long prevailed in the British ad world. A believer in scientific research, he also introduced new marketing disciplines to an industry that sometimes misunderstood his desire to entertain. His theories regarding the long-term value of the brands he advertised continue to influence the industry, and his book, *Confessions of an Advertising Man* (1963), was essential reading for several generations of entrants to the industry. Among those who did service as O&M copywriters (in London) were Fay Weldon and ☛Salman Rushdie, who share responsibility for such famous copylines as 'Drinka Pinta Milka Day', 'Go to Work on an Egg' and 'At 60 miles an hour, the loudest noise in this Rolls-Royce comes from the clock.' Ogilvy despised the financial engineers who built up huge advertising agency empires, and O&M began to lose its sparkle as new boys (notably the ☛Saatchis) followed him across the Atlantic. The company was bought in 1989 by Martin Sorrell (whom Ogilvy had earlier described as 'an odious little jerk') and appended to J. Walter Thompson, Sorrell's earlier purchase.

Georgia O'Keeffe 1887-1986

AMERICAN ARTIST

O'Keeffe gained early notoriety as a subject for portraits by her photographer husband, Alfred Stieglitz, who was also an enthusiastic promoter of her paintings. She explored the American landscape, from the hills and prairies of Texas to the skyscrapers of Manhattan, and blazed a trail for an art that was more abstract than figurative, and definitely 'American', combining explorations of unbroken horizons and endless skies with lush, erotic closeups of flowers, stones, skulls and leaves. Having presented her first exhibition in 1916, O'Keeffe's reputation enjoyed a renaissance in the 1970s through the proselytizing of feminist artists and art historians who interpreted her designs and shapes as symbols of female sexuality – generally to the dismay of the artist herself. After Stieglitz's death in 1945, she lived a solitary life in an artists' colony in Taos, amid the open deserts of New Mexico. The one important relationship of this part of her life was with Juan Hamilton, a potter some 60 years her junior, who became her amanuensis and to whom she left nearly all her possessions. Her final will was contested by O'Keeffe's family, leading to the establishment of a charitable foundation to distribute the pictures to museums.

Arthur Okun 1928-80

AMERICAN ECONOMIST

Based at the Brookings Institute, the leading policy think-tank in the US, Okun attempted to reformulate Keynesian economics in response to the criticisms of ☛Milton Friedman. His argument – that supply and demand are brought into a state of equilibrium by adjustments in output, rather than cuts in prices – is based on a study of American gross national product in the 1950s and 1960s: he found that a one per cent rise in unemployment was linked to a three per cent fall in the ratio of actual GNP to the potential figure if there was full employment. In other words, a downturn leading to unemployment is much more costly to an economy than unemployment levels on their own suggest. Okun's correlation may only be true for lower unemployment levels – as the level rises, it is subject to diminishing marginal returns. Also, it may not apply to job losses due to automation.

Claes Oldenburg born 1929

& SWEDISH-AMERICAN SCULPTOR

Oldenburg's brightly coloured 'soft' sculptures demand that we take the objects of our materialistic culture seriously – by recognizing that we live in an unheroic age, and finding something appropriate to fill the spaces once assigned to equestrian statues. Why not, he once suggested, a peeled banana for Times Square, a King-Kong-size teddy bear for Central Park or a giant lipstick for Piccadilly Circus? Unlike most of his Pop Art contemporaries, Oldenburg was directly connected with subversive underground activity, and his Happenings, conscious engineerings of the environment, were often documented by the New York film avant-garde (☛Robert Breer, Stan Van Der Beek) – they come cheerfully close to home movies starring Claes and Pat (his wife). Some of his sculptures are commissioned celebrations of what is going on in the environs: *Balanced Tools* in the grounds of a West German factory; a steel-mesh baseball bat fo Chicago; *Hat in Three Stages of Landing* for a town with a rodeo. Recentl he has been drawn to imagery that h sees as having a more universal reso nance – a giant toothbrush outside German museum, a screw bent into a arch for Rotterdam.

Andrew Loog Oldham born 194

BRITISH POP IMPRESARIO

British pop's first teenage tycoon, a manager of ☛The Rolling Stones fro

1962 to 1967, Oldham helped the group to develop the disagreeable and disreputable identities that carried them to world popularity. Imitator of American ☛Phil Spector's magisterial excess, Oldham himself was a thwarted popstar who immersed Mick Jagger and Keith Richards in controversy. Revelling in the tabloid chaos that produced such far-from-spontaneous headlines as 'WOULD YOU LET YOUR DAUGHTER GO WITH A ROLLING STONE?', Oldham similarly paraded The Righteous Brothers and Marianne Faithfull before an undiscerning public. Dissatisfaction with his incomplete participation in the creative process was Oldham's downfall. In the mid-1970s, another aspiring entrepreneur, ☛Malcolm McLaren, would try to do the same thing all over again.

Charles Olson 1910-70

AMERICAN POET

Writing on an epic scale, Olson became an influential poet/teacher at the experimental Black Mountain College of 1951-6, where he was a famously impressive lecturer. He also took part in the very first collaborative Happening in 1952, a multi-media event which also featured ☛Merce Cunningham and ☛John Cage. In his short prose texts – *Call Me Ishmael* (1947) and *Mayan Letters* (1953) – he explored mythical-historical aspects of American history, using them to provoke new kinds of knowledge that have a critical bearing on the present. His chief legacy to poetic theory was the concept of 'breath', whereby the phrasing of a poem should contain the 'voice' of the writer, so that reading the poem has the same effect as hearing it read by the author. His writing stirred such oppositional American poets as ☛Robert Creeley, Edward Dorn and Robert Duncan, as well as influencing such British names as Donald Davie, J. H. Prynne and Andrew Crozier.

Michael Ondaatje born 1943

SINGHALESE-CANADIAN NOVELIST

In *Coming through Slaughter* (1979), Ondaatje's clipped and dreamily displaced style perfectly suited his subject – the legendary dawn-of-jazz trumpeter Buddy Bolden, whose short life and lost sound are beyond possible recall, though still endowed with extraordinary mythic potency. Historically specific without being trapped in a too-well-known biography, the book breaks with the outsider-as-singular-authentic romanticism that Beats and existentialists (☛Mailer especially) foisted on their bebop heroes, catching instead some of the same hallucinatory density that is ☛Burroughs' best feature, shorn of his brutal pessimism. Born in Sri Lanka, educated in the UK, settled in Canada – a classic late twentieth-century extra-territorial – Ondaatje always bases his novels on, as he puts it, 'history which has yet to be finished'. *In the Skin of a Lion* (1987), for example, is set in modern Toronto, amid the cool swirl of an immigrant polyglot on the edge of settled society.

Yoko Ono born 1930

☆ JAPANESE-AMERICAN
& PERFORMANCE ARTIST,
$ BUSINESS EXECUTIVE

Possibly the most famous widow in the world, Ono came to international public attention in 1969 as the most hated woman in the world – the woman who 'split ☛The Beatles'. Arguably, though, it was they who ruined her career; for Yoko Ono was a noted conceptual artist of ten years' standing before she met John Lennon. From presenting avant-garde events and shows by the likes of ☛LaMonte Young in 1961, she had gone on on to develop, both alone and in association with New York's Fluxus group, work that was dramatic and imaginative, from the hilarious *Bottoms* film to *A Piece for Strawberries and Violins* of the late 1960s – in which a dancer stood or sat behind stacks of plates and ended the piece by smashing them. Her meeting with Lennon coincided with her interest in film, and work such as *Smile*, a 51-minute film of Lennon's three-minute smile, shows an optimism and beatitude concomitant with the later 'bed-ins' and the worldwide 'War is over if you want it' agit-pop campaign. As a musician, her edgy, semi-psychotic LPs of the early 1970s have acquired a belated respect and encapsulate what one critic has noted as her peculiar combination of 'serenity and rage'. She continues to hold retrospective showings of her work; in the decade since her husband's death, it seems that Ono's reputation is finally emerging from under the shadow of a popular rock group.

Marcel Ophüls born 1927

FRANCO-GERMAN DOCUMENTARY FILM-MAKER

Born in Germany, son of Max (director of *Lola Montes* and *Madame de . . .*), Ophüls was six when his family fled the Nazis – and all his adult life has been an attempt to understand how ordinary people could have so betrayed themselves and their neighbours. His remarkable documentary *The Sorrow and the Pity* (1971), which ran for four-and-a-half hours, presented the facts of French collaboration to a nation still hiding behind the myth that every citizen was a member of the Resistance, and brought into play Ophüls' remarkable skills as a sympathetic, wily, ironic interviewer, able to draw his subjects out into unlikely self-revelation. In 1972, *A Sense of Loss* underscored the intractability of the civil war in Northern Ireland, while drawing comparisons between the black civil rights movement in the US and the Catholic movement in Ulster. A second four-and-a-half-hour documentary, *The Memory of Justice*, re-examined the Nuremberg trials in the light of American atrocities and injustice in Vietnam. This film demonstrated, for the first time, a certain moral indecision, as if Ophüls had not entirely made up his mind about still-unfolding events. In 1988, *Hotel Terminus: The Life and Times of Klaus Barbie* presented, once again at the same long length, the grim story of a Nazi butcher spirited away to South America with the connivance of the allied secret services. To reveal the contempt he feels at humanity's capacity for self-deception, the approach Ophüls increasingly adopts is to allow his interviewees to speak on, revealing their own prejudices and terrible mediocrity.

Peter Opie 1918-82
Iona Opie born 1923

BRITISH FOLKLORISTS

The Opies wrote several books about the games children play and the stories they tell each other. *The Lore and Language of Schoolchildren* (1959) was the first collection of playground rhymes, children's jokes and tricks, and it proved that, despite the early incursions of television, the basic rituals of childhood remained much as they had been for centuries. By influencing a generation of precocious baby-boomers into learning chunks of their book by heart, the Opies showed that the artificial creation of folklore is not merely an adult pastime.

Robert Oppenheimer 1904-67

AMERICAN SCIENTIST

Director of the Los Alamos project to develop the atom bomb, Oppenheimer went on, when his opposition to work on the hydrogen bomb became public knowledge, to become a victim of ☛McCarthy and of his one-time colleague ☛Edward Teller's implacable anti-Communism, and he was disallowed from further involvement in a project he had no wish to continue. An intriguing, attractively melancholic figure (though by repute an excellent and efficient director at Los Alamos), he had moved into bomb-making from earlier work on neutron stars and quantum mechanics, but now is as much remembered for quoting from the *Bhagavad Gita* after the first atomic detonation as for any of his significant, purely scientific discoveries: 'I am become death, the destroyer of worlds . . .' He is often seen as a tragic figure, the seeker-after-truth caught up in a sordid politics of war that he regrets but cannot escape, with Teller cast as the opposing symbol in this drama.

Roy Orbison 1936-89

AMERICAN SINGER

Orbison took the most unlikely elements – the sentimentality of Don Gibson's country music, the utter desolation of Johnny Ray, the histrionics of opera and the exhilaration of rockabilly – and invented a version of rock 'n' roll which made him a legend. His early records were the best: the lonely tenor voice over sparse guitars and orchestration brought dignity to rock music. Orbison, always wearing sunglasses (to hide allegedly piggy eyes), was never as frivolous as his contemporaries: his occasional tiger growl or cry of 'Mercy!' was all the more effective for it. In the 1960s, his career was virtually frozen by the death of his wife in a motorcycle accident and, two years later, the deaths of two of his children in a fire. His influence and importance continued, however: ☛Presley confessed that he dared not share a concert bill with Orbison; the infinitely more braggart ☛Springsteen claimed him as an influence; in the 1980s, ☛David Lynch and ☛Nicolas Roeg rediscovered his voice for film soundtracks. At the end of his life, after a series of concerts and the recording of a new LP, released posthumously, full of contributions from respectful rock star fans, Orbison had become one of the few early rockers to reach middle age with a sizeable degree of respect, credibility and success.

Joe Orton 1933-67

BRITISH DRAMATIST

A convivial, sceptical guttersnipe, Orton's plays laid into England's class-ridden, socio-sexual hypocrisy. He gleaned his cynicism from his socially-aspiring mother and from excursions around the toilets of Islington and Tangiers, whose comical sordidness provided much material for his writing. With pantomime diatribes such as *Loot* (1958) and *What the Butler Saw* (1969), every line was another brick launched at the double-glazed, Venetian-blinded screen that protected middle-class England from a world full of blood and shit. Orton was a working-class Oscar Wilde who had fought too long for the right to improve and redeem himself through his celebrity status to inveigh with the same degree of fervour as ☛Osborne or ☛Pinter, although he was as original and resonant as either. In time, the democracy of stardom that turned council-house tenants into RADA-trained superstars proved too attractive for Orton, and too elusive for aspiring author Kenneth Halliwell, who turned into his lover's nemesis, with a hammer.

George Orwell
(Eric Blair) 1903-50

▲BRITISH JOURNALIST, NOVELIST

Orwell's notorious dystopia, *1984* (1949), gained its shock impact at the time of publication from the fact that so many on the left were still starry-eyed about Stalin's regime. The book provided a sort of spurious support for ☛McCarthyism and the Cold War, but it is simplistic to see it as just an anti-Communist tract. In the real 1984, the state that bore the closest comparison with Orwell's was Iran, a brutal theocracy where repentant sinners went on television to confess their crimes, and mass hysteria was sustained by a war against neighbouring Iraq. And when the Communist states crumbled in 1989, it became obvious that *no one* had really believed in the various versions of Big Brother that were on offer. Orwell's major concern was the way language could be distorted to express untruth – the sort of 'Newspeak' that substitutes peace for war, strength for ignorance, slavery for freedom – so as to make freedom of thought impossible by taking away the words to think differently. His belief that language could be transparent, giving a direct account of reality, is muddle-headed and even dangerous, but that has not stopped it from becoming widely accepted.

Almost certainly we are moving into an age of totalitarian dictatorships – an age in which freedom of thought will at first be a deadly sin and later on a meaningless abstraction.

George Orwell

John Osborne born 1929

⇔BRITISH DRAMATIST

▲Osborne once wrote a diatribe entitled 'I Hate You, England' and his scathing view of middle-class mediocrity and fascination with non-conformism mark all his writing. A volatile, vitriolic figure, resolute in his sense of self-importance and hatred of women, he had left school after striking his headmaster. His theatrical reputation was established with *Look Back in Anger* (1956), a rant on behalf of disaffected English youth who had been elevated by education to a no man's land of inane middle-class values. It is said that the play is performed somewhere in the world every night of the year, and a black gay version was presented in San Francisco. His best play is a metaphorical study of the decline of the empire as represented by the fading grease-paint world of music halls – *The Entertainer* (1957). But it is his vibrant, caustic script for Tony Richardson's film *Tom Jones* (1963) that best illustrates the depth and vivacious amusement he could extract from his obsessive exploration of the rebellious spirit. Osborne's plays have become less interesting as he has withdrawn into a Blimpish middle age.

Nagisa Oshima

born 1932

JAPANESE FILM DIRECTOR

Writer, director, poet and game-show host, Oshima's tendency to subvert the expectations of whichever medium he adopts has kept him at the forefront of Japanese cinema since the 1960s. Cutting his teeth on routine Samurai programmers, into which he incorporated social themes, he lost his job after an attack he had made on the impotence and confusion of left-wing opposition was blamed for the assassination of a socialist minister. He set up his own company to make a series of pessimistic attacks on the establishment, including *Death by Hanging* (1968) and *Diary of a Shinjuku Thief* (1969), which brought him to the attention of Western critics. The exposure helped him raise French money to make *In the Realm of the Senses* (1976), an allegorical tale revolving around a suicide pact and almost non-stop bonking in the final days before Japan's invasion of China. He reached a wider audience with *Merry Christmas Mr Lawrence* (1983), a complex examination of conflicting martial and cultural codes in a Japanese prison camp, where the machismo of the Samurai ethos and the repressive guilt of the public school are both confirmed and outraged by a (male) kiss that simultaneously unites and destroys its protagonists. Oshima has kept a low profile since – partially due to the failure of his dreary *Max, mon amour* (1986), in which Charlotte Rampling is bedded by a chimpanzee. The political activist seems to have found himself in ☛Kurosawa's position of prophet without honour.

Rifat Ozbek

born 1954

TURKISH FASHION DESIGNER

Ozbek's collections are a pageant of rich colour. Brought up in Istanbul, he arrived in England to study architecture and then fashion design. After working for Trell in Milan and Monsoon in London, he launched his own label in 1984. Much admired by pop stars such as ☛Madonna and Whitney Houston, as well as the actresses Cher and Michelle Pfeiffer, Ozbek made a name for himself as *the* designer for the well-formed 1980s' woman. His collections demonstrate a preoccupation with ethnicity: beginning with an African theme, he has offered the Mexican matador, the Turkish fez and tassel and Arabian djellabas. More recently, he has adopted a sumptuous harem-look, epitomized by his bras decorated with gold coins. His use of black models, coupled with such simple ideas as gold embroidery on moiré jackets and sequined lips on black rayon, combine to create a unique effect.

P

Jack Paar born 1918

AMERICAN TV PRESENTER

If television is a medium designed only to cultivate the disposable, then ☛Orson Welles was right: the live chat show – purpose-designed for the mass broadcasting of aimless bar, or laundromat, gossip – is a concept that could only have been developed for television. America's NBC network launched *The Tonight Show* in September 1954, and between its original host (Steve Allen, who lasted two years) and Johnny Carson, who soon became omni-present, the capricious and volatile Jack Paar tried and failed to turn this format-pioneer into something of more lasting social value, ruining his own career in the process. Reclusive and introverted, Paar was uncomfortable with crisp vaudeville-derived *badinage*. He had a genuine concern for the show and the issues he sought to raise through it, but his liberal politics elicited only contempt, and his faintly scatological sense of humour did nothing to help. After Paar's relegation, Carson's format dominated for almost two decades, spawning many less able imitators, before David Letterman's loose and effortlessly snide 1980s' presentation brought a little underground verve back to guest-choice, attitude and celebrity chat. Anyway, by the end of the decade, Phil Donahue and Oprah Winfrey had pushed the issue-dominated live show far beyond anything a chat-format could have come up with, and Arsenio Hall – crisp, glib, liberal and faintly scatological – had broken with the past for good.

Vance Packard born 1914

AMERICAN CULTURAL COMMENTATOR

The Hidden Persuaders (1957), Packard's classic study of amoral advertising practices – which focused attention on the supposed shaping of American consumer consciousness by unscrupulous media 'depth manipulators' – did as much to overestimate the effective power of the advertisers as any of their own PR. Fears that commercial interests are invading people's minds – always some other person's, never yours or mine – have persisted, while two decades of semiological journalism have made most of the successful tricks public, and have taught us that our own hard-to-admit complicity is far more important than any subconscious sleight-of-hand. Advertising has made us aware of many shared inner yearnings – given what some of them are, of course, it is not surprising that Packard's first readers were so alarmed.

Muhammad Reza Shah Pahlevi

SHAH OF IRAN 1919-80

The mystery of Muhammad Pahlevi's reign is why, after 38 years in firm control, he gave way so easily to the ☛Ayatollah Khomeini in 1979, going into exile in Egypt where he died the following year. The only previous gap in his reign, which combined modernization, secularization and industrialization with strong-arm dictatorship and ambitions to cut a figure on the world stage, had been a span of three days in 1953 when his nationalist premier ☛Mussadegh had launched a coup, which was ended by a CIA counter-coup in the Shah's favour. The key factor in his downfall was the alienation of his people from the regime. Oil wealth had freed him to build up an economic power-base for his international aims, but had not encouraged him to build strong popular support. When his oil revenue and, with it, the economy came under pressure from inflation, the regime – and the Shah as a man – collapsed. In the 1970s, he turned his attention abroad – convening a think tank on the international order, hosting foreign visitors and channelling funds to back Gerald Ford's 1976 presidential campaign in the US. Meanwhile, his secret police, SAVAK, acted viciously to repress dissidents at home and abroad. Liberalism in the economic and social sphere – measures, for example, to emancipate women and for land reform to give plots to peasants – were not matched by liberalized political institutions. Land reform misfired as it angered Islamic forces and drove peasants into the cities. A brutal massacre of protestors in Tehran at the end of 1978 triggered unrest across the country, manipulated by Khomeini as he played on atavistic Islamic emotions. When even the army turned against him, the Shah had nothing to fall back on, not even his own fragile will.

Nam June Paik

born 1932

☆KOREAN-AMERICAN VIDEO ARTIST

The original video freak, Paik laid his hands on the first portable camera that Sony let out of its factory, in 1965, and has been playing around with electronic imagery-producing machines ever since. As a composer and 'cultural terrorist', he was credited by ☛John Cage with taking his ideas further than anyone else would have dared (probably around the time Paik cut Cage's tie off in public). His 'action concerts' were more theatre than music: Paik might smash a piano or have cellist Charlotte Moorman remove her clothes while playing Bach. The same spirit of mischief underlies his messing around with television sets, producing sculptural pieces that he sees as a commentary on the omnipresence of the 'box'. And his videos deploy the techniques of avant-garde film-making, along with every possible electronic image-distortion device, to produce results that are often extremely tedious, but do have the value of demonstrating just how monotonous is the bulk of what exudes from the cathode tube. Associated from the early 1960s with the Fluxus movement, Paik has helped a global community of critical art to flourish.

Olof Palme

1927-86

SWEDISH POLITICAL LEADER

Palme established an international reputation as an advocate of aid to the Third World, an opponent of the US in Vietnam and a man with strong views on European disarmament. His assassination, as he walked down a Stockholm street, shocked his country: Scandinavia has rarely been a venue for political gunmen. He was prime minister from 1968 to 1976, and from 1982. Sweden under his leadership made a name for itself as a major, aggressively neutral power, but one with a very potent arms industry. Relations with the US became tense when Palme gave refuge to Vietnam deserters. He was chosen as UN Special Envoy to try and negotiate an end to the Iran-Iraq war while he was out of office: the 1976 polls had ended his Social Democrat Party's 44-year tenure of power. The failure of the Swedish police to solve Palme's assassination – the alcoholic dropout Christer Pettersson, who was found guilty in 1979 after being identified by the prime minister's widow Lisbet, was later released – has encouraged many journalists to claim that they can do better and pin the blame on, among others, Iranian terrorists and Kurdish exiles.

Gary Panter born 1953

AMERICAN CARTOONIST

Panter's cartoon-wildness takes him to the jittery edge of America and beyond, his style a post-punk appropriation of fascinated terrors, SF garbage and modern art history. Originally working for two extreme avant-garde papers, within five years Panter had graduated to the front cover of *Time*, and then beyond this to on-set designer and Dada-conceptualist for the television show *Pee Wee's Playhouse*, from where he could damage a whole generation irreparably and for ever. *Pee Wee, Invasion of the Elvis Zombies* and *Jimbo*, his long-running strip for Art Spiegelman's *RAW* magazine, all add up to an allusive, perceptive but deranged sensibility. Whereas his colleagues ☛Lynda Barry and Matt Groening have focused their talents into prominent and widely syndicated simplicity, Panter is content to travel fast and let the world catch up with him.

George Papadopoulos born 1919

GREEK ARMY OFFICER, POLITICAL LEADER

Papadopoulos was a career soldier, catapulted to power by the Greek army coup of 1967 which unseated a democratic government in a country still riven by WW2-induced tensions between far left and far right. He was initially minister to the premier's office, but a failed counter-coup by King Constantine, who then left for exile, led to his premiership. The junta he ran lacked a clear sense of direction: in an ideological vacuum, they banned beards and mini-skirts. The torture and arrest of critics followed, as the regime acquired a reputation for extremism. Five months after the introduction of a republic, in 1973, a student revolt led to Papadopoulos's exit. He was tried for treason; the death sentence was commuted. 'Fascist' may be the wrong term for the regime, which was unique in post-war non-communist Europe for having taken power illegally. Fascism, which represents violence as a goal in its own right, is a movement by civilians; the junta stood for militarism in office – for its own sake.

Charlie Parker 1920-55

AMERICAN JAZZ MUSICIAN

'Everything obvious,' ran the bebop motto, 'gets left out.' Bop was black modernism, with Parker's alto sax its motor force. It was the signal musical achievement of the 1940s, developed by an élitist coterie of deliberate outsiders who set the style for every underground upswell that followed. Parker's music burst out of nowhere – Kansas City – as a sharp retort to the commercialism of swing, demanding recognition of black art while mocking the mediocrity of what was then praised. Parker became a star even to bop's enemies because of his playing, which was faster than anyone else's but wholly unhurried. Bop was about passion, but its authenticity was cut with a studied intent to baffle: it was difficult, which was its pride and its curse – there was no noble primitivism in its rawness. It would end in cheerfully warring egos – a brilliant canon of note-mastery and speedy chord negotiation that was also a series of dead-ends. Parker himself would surely have shifted elsewhere, trading with ☛Stockhausen or rock or something. And his speed of reaction, his massively alert mind, his urge to absorb conflicting traditions and his ability to transcend those conflicts would all have worked together to take his music who knows where?

Evan Parker born 1944

♦ BRITISH JAZZ MUSICIAN

☞Evan Parker's saxophone technique – complete with circular breathing and an astonishing multiphonic range – is a prodigy in itself, so that he is gripping to watch even for those whose commitment to the outer reaches of avant-garde sound study is otherwise slight. Coming up out of the generation of British players who took the legacy of African-American Free Jazz and ☛John Cage's aesthetic renewals as their starting point, he is one of many who have devoted themselves to a study of ☛Coltrane, but only one of few to have emerged from the other side with an individual programme. Although it is a constantly evolving sound, his playing, especially on the soprano, is a powerful and startling many-voiced cry that comes forward best when he is playing solo. A player who has to be heard to be believed, Parker's influence is still small – the discipline required to work out a technique of this kind is all too clearly fearsome – but he is one of a very few musicians in the world who can transform a listener's understanding of music in one sitting. A long-standing partnership with guitarist ☛Derek Bailey is presently in abeyance, although few observers suppose they will remain apart for good.

Talcott Parsons 1902-79

AMERICAN SOCIOLOGIST

Parsons introduced the work of his German, Italian and French predecessors to the US but led sociology away from the analysis of tight issues – suicide, élites, myths – towards broad theories about the basic structures of society. He saw sociology's task as being to explain the development of order from the seemingly random multiplicity of individual actions. Society runs, he argues, on a biological model. It is homeostatic; its institutions, forms and patterns of conduct all reinforce its survival system. The interplay of self interest leads to benign results. His normative claim that people should pliably accept the 'givens' of the world around them, ensuring equilibrium, may have encouraged American psychology's search during the 1950s for that chimera, the 'integrated' personality. Parsons' critics, who include ☛C. Wright Mills and ☛Ralf Dahrendorf, point out that his theory is unable fully to explain social conflict and change.

Arvo Pärt born 1935

⇔ ESTONIAN COMPOSER

✖ In some ways the 1950s' equivalent of Finnish composer Sibelius, Pärt owes his popularity to a tie-up between a very recognizable stylistic signature, an extreme conservatism in compositional practice and a surge of interest in 'modern' classical music. He is exotic (a profoundly religious and reclusive Estonian) and his music is not particularly demanding to listen to – melody, timbre and structure sit happily inside a tradition that most serious Western composers have felt compelled to break with. But almost all serious Soviet composers have been persuaded of the advisability of sticking within classical conventions, with permitted ethnic or nationalist flavourings their only freedom. For Pärt, music is the breath of the holy, a means to reverence and the sacred; member of a faith that has not changed its mind for over 1000 years, he is naturally little concerned about questioning things, including the respective social roles of artists and audience. Meanwhile, the calm, cool density of his *St John's Passion* (1982) is soothing and attractive; the pitch at which he chooses to work – mystical, minimalist melancholy – is remarkable enough to justify at least a part of the attention he diverts from more forward-looking composers.

Harry Partch 1901-74

☞ AMERICAN COMPOSER

Partch described himself as 'a music man seduced into carpentry', which just about captures the esoteric quality of his work. After living as a hobo on the railways in the Depression years, he committed himself to developing a unique form of music that ditched conventional concepts of pitch and harmony in favour of his own grandiose 43-tone scale. This necessitated building his own instruments, many of which almost defy description – from the exotically titled Quadrangularis Reversum to his Mazda Marimba. These instruments convey a powerful visual aesthetic over and above the sounds themselves, but the fragility of the materials used – wood, glass, metal, bamboo and gourds – has tied performance of the work almost exclusively to its creator, so that only through rare recordings and films can his unique, almost mystic, vision now be captured. Nevertheless, Partch influenced the motor-rhythmic music of the minimalists and such latter-day sound corrupters as Tom Wait and ☛Einstürzende Neubauten.

Dolly Parton born 1946

❞ AMERICAN COUNTRY SINGER, ACTRESS

The best-known country singer of all, Parton's cheerful self-promotion makes great play with her dirt-poor roots and the troubles woman is heir to. Associated with Nashville at its most sap-headedly showbiz, she easily transcends its excesses, being funny and smart, as well as a dynamic interpreter of pop, rock and country songs. Little of the dark, tragic romance of an earlier era of country remains in her routines – her world is as nine-to-five modern as anyone's in pop, and her link with singers such as ☛Patsy Cline or ☛Loretta Lynn is purely nominal (Sissy Spacek played

Lynn on celluloid – Parton would have to play herself). 'Jolene' is, of course, a camp classic, carrying with it everything that is trivial and thus deeply affecting about big-money C&W. Parton is good value in the most trying circumstances.

Pier Paolo Pasolini 1922-75

ITALIAN FILM DIRECTOR, POET, NOVELIST, PAINTER

Pasolini's painting, novels, poems and films explore a vision of a civilization in ruins, where street urchins embody the glories of the classical age. He referred to himself as a Catholic Marxist, but references to religion in his work were usually semi-mystical. He felt a passionate identification with the Italian peasantry, and members of the urban underclass: his first film, *Accatone*, was a portrait of a Roman pimp. As the problems involved in financing his films and fighting off the censors increased, so his work became progressively darker, culminating in *Salo, or The 120 Days of Sodom* (1975), in which the action of De Sade's novel (chiefly sodomy, coprophagia and mutilation) is transported to the short-lived Italian Fascist republic of Salo. Pasolini was murdered shortly after the film was completed, in violent and mysterious circumstances, by a couple of street hustlers.

George Passmore *see* Gilbert and George

Boris Pasternak 1890-1960

SOVIET POET, NOVELIST

Pasternak's poetry brought him national acclaim, while his novel, *Dr Zhivago* (first published in Italian in 1958), led to a Nobel prize, expulsion from the Union of Soviet Writers and social exile within his own country. This epic, soaked through with spiritual despair, recounts a story of love during the Russian Revolution, symbolizing the tragedy and sacrifice that echoed through Pasternak's own life. Unwilling to forego creative individuality in favour of revolutionary rhetoric, he took a stand as an outsider in the artistic community during Stalin's reign, thus maintaining the integrity of his vision, at the price of a constant, if finally unrealized, fear of being singled out during the purges. The poetry of his early years uses traditional rhymes and metres but is completely modern in the way it builds a complex vision out of fragmentary observations.

Linus Pauling born 1901

♦ AMERICAN CHEMIST

Winner of the 1954 Nobel prize for chemistry for his work on the structure of the chemical bond, Pauling had gained such a reputation as the pre-eminent intuitive genius of the field that, when ☛Crick and ☛Watson were trying to uncover the structure of DNA, they were terrified he would beat them to it: if even the slightest detail of their approach leaked through to him, they thought, he would see what they could not. Pauling's early work on crystal structures of various minerals led to the treatment of atoms as tiny spheres of definite radius, and he went on to expand theories of valency and bonding by applying sophisticated quantum methods. He also provided much of the groundwork for modern molecular biology, including a proof that hereditary disease can be biochemically explained. Having been an official inspector of defence projects during WW2, Pauling became increasingly critical of US nuclear defence strategies from the mid-1950s, setting the tone for Western scientific dissidence with his *No More War* in 1958. He became the first person to win two full Nobels when he was awarded the 1962 Nobel peace prize. He went on to argue the case for vitamin C as a cure for the common cold and cancer, involving himself in bitter confrontations with biochemists and clinicians. He may still surprise us with some thoughts on his current preoccupation: low-temperature superconductivity.

Octavio Paz born 1914

MEXICAN POET, CRITIC

Paz, who analysed what he saw as Mexico's crisis of identity in *The Labyrinth of Solitude* (1950/61), regards his native culture as like no other. He has, however, drawn eclectically on many cultures and traditions in his poetry – including an interest in Asian religions that blend magic and sexual ecstasy, in which he developed an interest while living abroad as a diplomat (he was Mexico's ambassador to India in the early 1960s). A significant formative influence on the young Paz was his attendance at the 1938 Writers' Congress held in Madrid during the Spanish Civil War. A celebrated poem 'Sun Stone' (1957/63), modelled after the Aztec calendar stone, links personal reminscences from wartime Madrid to general reflections on love and society. Founder of numerous journals, Paz now publishes *Vuelta*, an important Latin American cultural magazine.

There was the other culture, a culture destroyed, but still inside us, alive. In this sense I knew, not only with my intellect, I knew with my senses and my body that the West was not the only civilization.

Octavio Paz,
The Labyrinth of Solitude

Mervyn Peake 1911-68

BRITISH NOVELIST, GRAPHIC ARTIST

Peake's reputation as a writer rests on a trilogy of fantasy novels – *Titus Groan* (1946), *Gormenghast* (1950) and the unfinished *Titus Alone* (1959). Gormenghast is a huge, rambling, crumbling ancestral home, into which an heir, Titus, has been born at the very moment when a demonic and dynamic kitchen boy, Steerpike, has started his rise to sinister prime mover in the ancient, ridiculous hierarchies of the castle's utterly enclosed society. Peake's gothic imagination is inventively dense; his characters, in name and manner, are Dickensian. As an unfixed allegory of unchanging Britain, the books come to mean increasingly more: Jon Savage has made provocative and insightful play with the idea that Steerpike and ☛The Sex Pistols' Johnny Rotten are one and the same. Peake also has a reputation, different but equal, as an illustrator, particularly of children's books. Once again, it rests in large part on his character invention and a grasp of physiognomy that borders on the nightmarish. Having spent his childhood in China, Peake seems to have developed an alien's eye for the

Pier Paolo Pasolini
Photo: Roloff Beny

weirdness under the bland surface of British life. As a result, he has never quite been taken to its heart.

Pelé (Edson Arantes do Nascimento) born 1940

BRAZILIAN FOOTBALLER

Pelé's status as the greatest footballer of all time was undoubtedly cemented by his luck at being the world's most loved player just when the game was beginning to secure worldwide TV coverage. Nevertheless, the degree of his popularity remains remarkable and unchallenged: a two-day truce was called during the Biafran civil war so that both sides could watch him play. During another match, a major riot ensued when he was sent off for dissent. The referee had to be hustled off the field, and in the end – just to keep the peace – Pelé was allowed to return. Crucial to the success of Brazil's team throughout the 1960s, Pelé scored 1363 goals, more than any other modern player, and he perfected an astonishingly fluid athleticism and intelligence as a striker in the revolutionary four-two-four formation that the Brazilian team pioneered.

Oleg Penkovsky 1919-63

➳SOVIET DOUBLE AGENT

A Soviet secret service-man, who had won medals for bravery during WW2, Penkovsky became, in 1961, a double-agent working for the West; he was later uncovered, tried and executed. The West did not protest; a major Soviet intelligence overhaul followed. His contact, a British businessman, was gaoled, but later exchanged. Penkovsky changed sides because he considered that ☛Khrushchev's foreign policies were likely to lead to nuclear war. His period as a double-agent brought him to London, where he was allowed to walk around the City in a British officer's uniform. Between April 1961 and August 1962, he passed on more than 5000 copies of classified military, economic and political documents to US and British intelligence, and his data on Soviet forces played a part in ☛Kennedy's stance over Cuba, where, Penkovsky's information said, the USSR planned to station a rocket base. His journal, *The Penkovsky Papers*, was published in 1965.

Irving Penn born 1917

AMERICAN PHOTOGRAPHER

Penn won acclaim as a fashion photographer, earning a reputation for serenely stylish and elegantly controlled images. He has also taken his portable daylight studio tent to such places as Peru, Cameroon and New Guinea, and he approaches everything he does in much the same spirit. His fashion pictures sometimes look more like portraits, while his portraits often have the feel of fashion shots; the petal of a dying flower is treated with as much attention as a model's lips or fingernails. Something of a technical fetishist, he re-created an antique studio and revived the archaic platinum process of photography, a method which provides images of absolute clarity and brilliance.

D(onn) A(lan) Pennebaker born 1930

♦ AMERICAN DOCUMENTARIST

The mythic power of Pennebaker's pioneering *cinéma-verité* rock-documentaries derived directly from the thrilling sense that they were demystifying their youthful subjects – and that these same subjects (☛Bob Dylan, ☛Otis Redding, ☛Jimi Hendrix) displayed a nerve and a raw political zing that no public figure had previously offered. Rock in 1966 had achieved an extraordinary news-flash intensity, and Pennebaker's films – in particular *Don't Look Back* (1966) with its back-of-a-taxi portrait of the hip, snide, speeding Dylan – underscored this. In retrospect, Pennebaker, with his laconic impatience and fascination with unprettified energy, happened to be in the right place at the right time, and you only have to compare his portrait of the young outsider-star with the dopey poet-joker-guru-god Dylan in his abysmal self-directed *Renaldo and Clara* ten years later, to see the inevitable shift from fly-on-the-wall truth to home-movie indulgence. Once first-generation rock stopped being the outsider, it got flabby fast, and its court recorder seems to have lost interest. He returned to the fray in 1988 to work with likeable suburban dance-*naïfs* Depeche Mode, a group as unlike Dylan, early or late, as it is possible to imagine.

Roger Penrose born 1931

♦ BRITISH MATHEMATICIAN

Working with ☛Stephen Hawking in the mid-1960s, Penrose provided the arduous mathematics to show that singularities in space-time were possible, given certain quite likely conditions – specifically, strong enough gravity. In other words, he proved the possibility of black holes (as collapsed stars) before they were either named or found, and gave us a reason also to believe that the normal rules of space-time no longer apply within them. Singularities are the 'edge' of the continuum under study: beyond this edge, predictions fail. Penrose also proved that classical general relativity required a singularity at the beginning of time: a problem – since this primordial black hole would be unlikely to develop into the rule-bound universe we occupy – that was not solved until Hawking showed how to apply quantum theory to the equations. Penrose, a lecturer in non-Euclidean geometry who is currently working on 'Twistor' theory, has also made several fascinating minor discoveries, including the optical illusions of the eternal waterfall and staircase made famous by ☛Escher's prints.

Georges Perec 1936-82

& FRENCH NOVELIST

✍ Perec's work has only recently been translated into English – *Life: A User's Manual* in 1987, *W, or The Memory of Childhood* in 1989 – and his most notorious book may never reach it: *La Disparition*, a 'lipogram', avoids the letter 'e' throughout. Perec was the youngest member of a group founded by ☛Raymond Queneau, among others, in 1960. Called 'OuLiPo' (*Ouvroir de Littérature Potentielle*), it was dedicated to the invention of new ways to write, through the application of eccentric algorithms and outrageously arbitrary rules. Perec followed *La Disparition* with *Les Revenantes*, in which the only vowel was 'e'. He can also make claim to the discovery of a palindrome some 5000 words long. His books are elaborate, witty, self-referential and playful beyond mere play; their formalist construction comes from some deep commitment in him. Although the youngest OuLiPian, he was quickly recognized as the most inventive; he is also, in an oblique but palpable way, the most political.

Fritz Perls
(Frederick Perls) 1894-1970

AMERICAN PSYCHOTHERAPIST

Psychologist-in-residence at the Esalen Institute in California during the 1960s, Perls coined such buzzwords as 'the here and now' and 'awareness', dressed the part of the guru, with long white hair and beard, beads, sandals and flowing robes, and slept with some of his patients. Whereas psychodynamic practice traditionally encourages quiet talking and contemplation-filled silence, the characteristic mode of the Gestalt therapy that Perls developed with his wife Laura is one of confrontation – for instance, one therapeutic method involves chair-hopping, as the patient carries on an aggressive dialogue between the different parts of his or her personality. Gestalt uses such polarities as success/failure or dominant/submissive to focus on splits in the personality and stimulate self-awareness, encouraging the individual to discover his or her own core of uncorrupted desire. As with other consciousness-raising techniques, the emphasis that Gestalt places on self-responsiblity leads to such a fervid individualism and denial of the needs and desires of others that it ends up as an impoverished view of human possibilities.

But how do we open the ears and eyes of the world? I consider my work to be a small contribution to that problem which might contain the possibility of the survival of mankind.

Fritz Perls, Gestalt Therapy *(1969)*

Juan Perón 1895-1974

ARGENTINIAN POLITICAL LEADER

A populist, with Fascist leanings, who took over after a coup in 1943, Perón is now famous because of the uninspired Tim Rice/Andrew Lloyd Webber musical *Evita* (1978) about his wife. Eva won over the masses through her involvement in union organizations, and Juan would have been lost without her: he was toppled three years after her death in 1952. She looked after the home front while he looked outwards – a national symbol, an anti-American. Civil liberties were ignored during Perón's rule; he had won election in 1945 by strong-arm tactics. In 1973, he staged a comeback from Spanish exile by appealing to his wife's memory. He died soon after, and his second wife took over for two years. Peronism – a mixture of anti-Anglo-Saxon nationalism, hostility to the Church and populist economics – lives on as a movement in Argentina, and a Peronist, Carlos Menem, was elected as the country's president in mid-1989.

Lee Perry born 1939

JAMAICAN RECORDING ENGINEER

Perry – who also calls himself 'Pipecock Jackson', 'The Gong' and 'Scratch the Upsetter' – is an astute self-publicist, as well as Jamaica's genius of the mixing desk. Deliberately fostering a reputation for unhinged behaviour, he can claim credit for finding ☛Bob Marley and the Wailers their breakthrough sound, and thus for taking reggae out of small-time parochialism into an unsettling, surreal sonic jungle of beats, delays, echoes and other effects – the subtle studio reconstructions of familiar rhythms and known songs that came to be known as 'dub'. His techniques of alteration, editing and fading, insertion, subtraction and distortion, belong in a broader Caribbean tradition, and others – such as Studio One's Coxsone Dodd – deserve mention, but Perry's astringent plays on the idea represent it at its most sophisticated.

Worship me! Prostrate when you enter my domain 'cos I'm the Red Ninja who's got no time for prissy hypocrites.

Lee Perry

Kim Philby

(Harold Philby) 1912-88

✚ BRITISH SPY,
WHO SETTLED IN USSR

Philby's father was an Arabian explorer who nicknamed his son 'Kim', an apt one as it evoked a spy tale by Kipling (the security service did not take the hint). Philby junior met Donald MacLean, ☛Guy Burgess and ☛Anthony Blunt in the early 1930s, before Hitler gave Marxism its anti-Fascist credentials. Socialist leanings became Communist loyalties, as in turn they enrolled as long-term Soviet agents. Philby was the toughest and the most serious, working for 11 years in British intelligence and diplomacy. His real value to the USSR may have been overplayed; even so, a leak may have upset the West's plan to infiltrate Albania with émigré agents in 1950. MacLean and Burgess, fearing exposure, fled East the following year, as Philby's real role began to emerge. From 1951 to 1963 he was in limbo; officially cleared, he was nevertheless a target for suspicion, and he left the corridors of power and secrets to become an SIS field officer, using journalism as a cover. From Beirut, he defected to Moscow in 1963, and spent the next 25 years giving advice to Soviet publishers while reading *The Times* at breakfast. Unlike Kipling's Kim, he did not see spying as a 'great game': his memoirs reveal that he had been deadly serious about his role as a double-agent.

Jean Piaget

1896-1980

SWISS PSYCHOLOGIST

'The ideas of a genius, such simplicity,' remarked Einstein of Piaget's theories on the child's development of reasoning powers – and psychologists have criticized him ever since for leaving out everything that is important. Nevertheless, Piaget's theories remain enormously persuasive, offering insights into the qualitative differences between infantile and adult ways of thinking. He showed that the increasingly complex schemas that children use to explain reality evolve out of a very few simple reflexes – sucking, grasping and other 'action schemas'. At around the age of two, mental schemas are transformed into symbolic ones: children acquire language when logical thinking is still a long way off. The infantile world view is egocentric, and everything is seen in animistic terms – e.g. the sun is going to bed. Only when the child's world view has become de-centred, at around the age of six or seven, does logical thinking become possible. The suggestion that children's natural curiosity carries them through these successive stages differentiates Piaget's approach from the carrot-and-stick style of pedagogy favoured by behaviourists. He said it is not for teachers and parents to hustle their kids into becoming mathematicians, or whatever; they should provide a sympathetic environment and the necessary tools, but then accept that children have to do the job on their own.

Renzo Piano born 1937

ITALIAN ARCHITECT

Piano's light and playful designs reflect a fascination with the creative potential of modern materials; there is a fun element to many of his buildings. But he is also sufficiently hard-headed to have been entrusted by the Japanese with a £1 billion airport project for Osaka: it is to be built on an artificial off-shore island, which will sink a metre or so in the first year or so of operation and may have to tolerate earthquakes. Piano made his reputation through working with ☛Richard Rogers on the Beaubourg (Pompidou) Centre in Paris, where the glass exterior and decorative passenger tunnels established them both as 'hi-tech' architects. Piano seems to have a special fascination for roofs – for the De Menil museum in Houston he designed one with 300-leaves hand-carved out of reinforced concrete, lit by an intriguing diffuser. With offices in three countries, he nevertheless does half his work in Italy, where he is involved in plans to remodel cities and make them 'work' socially, in part through community involvement.

T. Boone Pickens born 1928

$ AMERICAN CORPORATE RAIDER

Pickens' attempted takeovers of various oil and mining companies in the mid-1980s nurtured such euphemisms as 'shark repellents', 'poison pills' and 'golden parachutes' to describe the tactics deployed by those attempting to frustrate him. His was a no-lose strategy: by buying up undervalued stock in companies whose managements did not want to be cast into the maw of Mesa Petroleum, the company he had built up since 1964, Pickens either secured the company and its assets, or got to sell his stock at a price considerably higher than the one originally paid. The first time he tried, and failed, to take over a company – Gulf Oil – his consolation was a profit of some $760 million. He went on to work the same trick several times elsewhere. Although he justifies his raids as benefiting shareholders, who, he says, are the 'victims' of inefficient management, the size of his rewards makes such claims unconvincing. He has a point when he states that executives are more concerned about their survival on the promotional ladder than about the real interests of their companies, but it is hard to see Pickens' panic-sowing tactics as a healthy stimulus to corporate decision-making. More recently, he turned his attention to the Japanese motor industry, taking an $800 million stake in the Koito Manufacturing components firm – a move which some interpreted as an excuse for a spate of Japan-bashing to promote his candidacy for the governorship of Texas.

Gregory Pincus 1903-67

AMERICAN BIOLOGIST

When Pincus developed the contraceptive pill with the aim of holding back worldwide population growth, he did not anticipate that his invention would be adopted by a generation of young people as the licence to limitless carefree sex. Responsible for bringing about the first virgin birth, in 1939, when he fertilized the egg of a rabbit through hormone treatments, it was in 1951 that Pincus started to look for a synthetic hormone to prevent fertilization. After clinical trials in the slums of Puerto Rico and Haiti, the pill was licensed for use by the affluent in 1960. For a decade and more, many made love to whomsoever they liked whenever it was mutually agreeable. But as possible links between the pill and cancer and various circulatory diseases were revealed, women began to wonder whether the pleasure was worth the disturbed menstrual cycles, the headaches and weight problems. Some asked whether the pill had not perhaps been a male conspiracy against the bodies of women, others whether the pill did not foster a sexual hunger that could never be satisfied. Since then, scientists have worked to limit the pill's detrimental side-effects by lowering hormone doses, but with the coming of AIDS and the 'new celibacy', that piece of rubber which most had thought the pill would replace forever has come back into fashion.

Harold Pinter

born 1930

▲BRITISH THEATRE, FILM WRITER

Through the 1960s, Pinter wrote shadowplays of humanity at its most insecure and deceitful, conveying comic menace and brutality. He had grown up in London's East End, a community exposed to some of the worst bombing of WW2, and a sense of impending violence was to permeate his writing. The threatening emotions and sardonic humour of his first major play, *The Birthday Party* (1958), were greeted with confusion and furrowed brows by London audiences, but Pinter's reputation was secured by *The Caretake*r (1963), in which an ex-mental patient introduces a tramp into his brother's home. A more commercial edge emerged in his elliptical scripts for Joseph Losey's *The Servant* (1963), *Accident* (1967), and *The Go-Between* (1969). Pinter's ability to peel back the layers of his characters' personalities and to expose, through dialogue and silence, the incongruity that exists between utterance and intentional meaning, created stark, chillingly opaque theatre. His sense of contemporary language has frozen somewhat, and his theatre work has faltered, although he is still a competent screenwriter. Perhaps to cover up the gap in his creativity, he has established a reputation for his political views, specifically for the passionate anti-Americanism which sprouted after the US-backed coup against the Chilean leader ☛Allende in 1973, and for convening a circle of anti-Thatcher writers under the grandiose title of the June 20 Group. 'We have a precise agenda and we're going to meet again and again until they break all the windows and drag us out,' was Pinter's overblown retort to those who ridiculed the group as Champagne Socialists or Claret Comrades.

Sylvia Plath

1933-63

† AMERICAN-BRITISH POET

▲For most of her life, Plath presented herself as the wholesome all-American girl – winning prizes and scholarships, getting her stories and articles published. Nevertheless, she harboured self-destructive inclinations. The nervous breakdown she suffered at the age of 20, which led to her first suicide attempt, is recounted in the semi-autobiographical novel, *The Bell Jar* (1963). Afterwards, she moved to England, studied at Cambridge and married another poet, ☛Ted Hughes. Plath injects a feeling of darkness and doom even into poems that deal with such domestic matters as bee-keeping or a finger cut while cooking, and her poetry is lacerating in its honest picking-over of wounds: in 'Daddy', she articulates her ambiguous feelings towards an authoritarian father who died when she was eight; 'Lady Lazarus' chronicles her impulse towards annihilation. It was shortly after the breakup of her marriage that she gassed herself; the poems produced in the few months before her death, collected in the volume *Ariel* (1966), are some of her strongest.

Roman Polanski born 1933

POLISH FILM DIRECTOR, WORKING IN UK, US, FRANCE

Polanski chisels away at the psychological walls whose steady erosion prefaces insanity, paranoia and a highly internalized, often manic, approach to life's horrors. For Polanski, real-life tragedies – wartime atrocities in childhood, the murder of his pregnant wife Sharon Tate by the ☛Charles Manson gang – fortify his position as the tabloid stereotype of mad-director-as-good-copy. Usually working with screenwriter Gérard Brach, his movies have exploited various genres. *Repulsion* (1965), a dissection of a young girl's descent into lunacy, remains symptomatic of the parallels in Polanski's work between picturesque images and rancid, discordant thematic treatment. In *Chinatown* (1974), as in many of his films, evil ultimately triumphs over good. As a voyeuristic performer in many of his works, he has signposted his own persona: an elusive, diminutive *bon viveur* and cradle-snatcher (he was charged with drugging and raping a thirteen-year-old girl in 1977) whose skill in both containing and expressing his angst proves that he learned a long time ago that a dark, musty cinema is the safest place to hide.

Jackson Pollock 1912-56

AMERICAN ARTIST

Pollock's early attempts at a revolution in American art, during the 1930s, were coloured by surrealist influences. A decade later, two divergent styles had emerged – one an expression of linear elegance, the other articulating a more ebullient romanticism. The latter triumphed and developed in later years into a stream-of-consciousness style that led to Pollock's elevation as a pioneer of what became known as abstract expressionism. He was dubbed 'Jack the Dripper' as he poured paints from cans or dripped it from sticks, to form an interlacing of fine lines and interwoven forms on the huge canvases he had placed on the floor or hung on the wall. Painting between bouts of drinking and depression, Pollock was the first pictorial iconoclast that modern America had to call its own – although he was toppled from that position by ☛Warhol and ☛Lichtenstein. He was killed in a car crash.

Pol Pot (Saloth Sar, Tol Saut, Pol Porth) born 1928

CAMBODIAN POLITICAL LEADER

Without the massive destabilization brought to the whole of the South-east Asian peninsula by the Vietnam War, Pol Pot's tiny clique of genocidal ultra-Maoists would never have come remotely close to seizing power in Cambodia, let alone reducing that isolated, backward nation to a traumatized ruin – a process only partly halted by the Vietnamese invasion of 1979. In the 1960s, Cambodia was under the fairly benign rule of the eccentric playboy Prince Sihanouk, and discontent was held in check by his somewhat idiosyncratic Marxist monarchism. Pol Pot had gone to Paris in 1949 to study radio electronics, and there fell under the influence of the ultra-Stalinist French Communist Party. Back in Cambodia, he worked as a teacher and journalist until, in 1963, he left Phnom Penh to begin an insurrection in the northern jungles. After ☛Kissinger and ☛Nixon's 1969 terror-bombing had devastated the western reaches of the country, Sihanouk was overthrown in a CIA-backed coup by the incompetent and venal Lon Nol, who proceeded to oversee a total collapse in national confidence and economic viability. Pol Pot's Khmer Rouge guerrillas took advantage of Hanoi's 1975 victory in neighbouring Vietnam to invade the capital Phnom Penh and instigate their project of national renewal – an urgent task which involved driving all city-dwellers out into the fields, and starting civilization all over again. 'Year Zero' was to mark the inauguration of a peasant-agrarian utopia. Within three years, with all doctors, scientists, engineers and other technocrats and intellectuals either murdered or silenced, many dead from starvation or starving, fratricidal warlordism between regional party organizations rife, the utopia was littered with unburied bones – estimates of the number of victims range between 0.5 million and 3 million. The Phnom Penh government installed by the Vietnamese invasion has never been recognized as legitimate by the West. Always a shadowy figure, Pol Pot has moved even further into the background, even while his Khmer Rouge again seem close to recapturing the country as part of a US-backed resistance coalition, led by the irrepressible Sihanouk. An interview with Pol Pot has become the Holy Grail for journalists wanting to make a name for themselves.

Gillo Pontecorvo born 1919

✌ ITALIAN FILM DIRECTOR

Few directors have built a reputation so considerable from one film, but Pontecorvo's *Battle of Algiers* (1966) is a still-astonishing account of a popular uprising. With documentary-feel authenticity, the film makes its case for the Algerian rebels with such force because its depiction of the conflict seems so even-handed, and, as such, it provided the prototype for mainstream radical films made by Costa-Gavras and ☛Francesco Rosi in the 1970s, as well as being (unwisely) claimed by British producer David Puttnam as an inspiration for *The Killing Fields* (1984). Pontecorvo, a commander of partisans during WW2, was an active member of Italy's Communist Party from 1941 to 1956, and all his films are concerned with the fight against oppression: *Kapo* (1964) concerned a young Jewish girl's battle for survival in a Nazi concentration camp; *Ogro* (1979) recounted the assassination of ☛Franco's prime minister by a group of Basque terrorists. Since the failure of *Burn!* (1969), his attempted break into Hollywood which had ☛Marlon Brando starring as a British adventurer, Pontecorvo has worked in relative obscurity, calling into question his argument that a capitalist film-making system can make space for radical messages on a regular basis. But he resurfaced in 1990 as a possible director for *Siege of Leningrad*, the film ☛Sergio Leone had been preparing at the time of his death.

Iggy Pop

(James Jewel Osterberg) born 1947

∀ AMERICAN ROCK MUSICIAN

❃ Iggy Pop represents rock as madness and threat, survival and integrity. He formed The Stooges, performed aggressive, minimalist proto-heavy metal and took performance outrage to its limits. He retired hurt, had his career revived by his biggest fan, ☛David Bowie, and went on to perform aggressive, slightly less minimalist proto-HM. Retiring even more hurt, this time to a mental hospital, he had his career revived again by Bowie, performed aggressive, minimalist proto-European alienated rock, slid into American rock music again with little success and diminishing creative returns, had his career revived for a third time by Bowie, performed fairly aggressive transatlantic rock pop, then returned to proto-HM, this time retaining his sanity and self-respect. Iggy Pop excelled in two very different forms of music, to both of which he brought the isolated and very messed-up sensibility that much great rock needs in order to be convincing. Unlike his biggest fan, he has also had the ability to make personal, individual music without destroying his personality.

Generoso Pope Jnr

1927-88

AMERICAN PUBLISHER

Pope inspired junk journalists the world over by buying up the *New York Enquirer* in 1952 and turning it into the tabloid *National Enquirer* , a scandal-and-strange-phenomena sheet that secures shelf-space near supermarket check out desks and sells millions of copies across the US. Although following in the tradition of Hollywood's *Confidential* in publishing every last insider rumour about this or that celebrity and his or her sex life, the *Enquirer* had to tone down its salaciousness to get the supermarket franchise. Owned by the same company, and covering the really far-out stories, is the ineffable *Weekly World News*, which cheekily claims to be the 'only UK-style tabloid available in the States', and was responsible for such headlines as 'TWO-HEADED WOMAN PREGNANT: SAYS ONE HEAD, "I'LL HAVE THE BABY"; SAYS THE OTHER, "NO WAY!"' The *Enquirer* has not done an alien-stole-my-baby article since it went glossy; its photos-of-freaks quotient is now way down, and its famous sales pitch – 'Enquiring minds want to know' – has become a countrywide in-joke. The headlines have always been better than the text, and everyone knows it – all snide cynicism to one side, this is a far from boobishly innocent readership. In the late 1980s, as if to prove this, Britain's *Sunday Sport* began to steal and run many of *WWN*'s wilder stories, and to make up its own pitiful imitations – which revealed an almost total lack of understanding of the playfully punk sophistication of this market.

Karl Popper

born 1902

○ AUSTRO-BRITISH PHILOSOPHER

When Popper first gave us the invaluable phrase 'pseudo-science', his aim was to cut Marxism and psychoanalysis off from the oxygen of a higher scientific authority that he felt they were never entitled to claim. Living in Vienna before the *Anschluss*, he had seen the Austrian Social Democrats fail to resist Nazism: the anti-democratic parties had made much of their progressive scientific basis and Popper was passionately committed to building a philosophy of science that could protect democracy by unmasking such claims. By analysing science as a process of conjecture and refutation, he developed a definition that excluded both 'scientific Communism' and Freud's theories (as well as areas of mathematics, zoology, history and sociology). His *The Open Society and Its Enemies* (1945, 1966) made it easy to equate Fascism with Communism, forming the theoretical backbone for the Cold War conceptions of totalitarianism, so that Popper gradually became a guru of the New Right, associated with ☛Hayek and the free-market liberals. His major works – *Objective Knowledge* (1972), *Conjecture and Refutations* (1963), *Unended Quest* (1976) – elevate the methods of the physical sciences to an absolute degree. The effect has been to give one species of scientist an excuse for ignorance of their own broader social contexts – not only did they live in ivory towers throughout the 1960s and 1970s, but they happily sold the leases to every big business or military-industrial complex that happened along.

Oliver Postgate born 1925

✖ BRITISH ANIMATOR

Reading out a list of Postgate's creations is a surefire way to plunge the children of the 1960s into nostalgic catatonia: mention 'Olaf the Lofty' or 'Nogbad the Bad' and watch adult eyes glaze over. Obsessively reclusive, director of his own independent company, Smallfilms, Postgate's career as the foremost fabulator/animator in children's television – often in collaboration with artist Peter Firmin – spans the golden age of British television: from *Ivor the Engine* (1960) to *Bagpuss* (1972), passing through *Pogles Wood*, *The Clangers* and no fewer than 12 series of *Noggin the Nog*. The amiably puppet-jerky simplicity of the animation tied in with neatly comic touches of observation, tapping into a generation's sense of child-like wonder. Never cute or sugary, Postgate's genius for the scaled-down transplanted classic suburban commonsense into prosaically detailed fantasy settings – from the deep historical romance of the Land of Nog (where the men of the Northlands would sit by their great log fires to tell tales of the days of old . . .) to the artfully enclosed space-age ecosphere of the Clanger planet.

Dennis Potter born 1935

BRITISH TELEVISION WRITER

Potter, perhaps the only unreconstructed modernist anywhere to have committed himself so wholeheartedly to television, combines an élitist disdain for the stupidity of the medium with an unending fascination for its cheap powers. His television plays push narrative structure to surreal limits, via flashback, dream-vision and bizarre pulp parody interruption. He obsessively runs through aspects of his own life – as a writer, as a child in the Forest of Dean, as a sufferer from horrific skin complaints – to pour scorn on the elaborately rigid social strata of English society. His use of 1930s and 1940s radio-pop – most impressively in *Pennies from Heaven* (TV 1978; feature film 1981) and *The Singing Detective* (1986) – probably softens his rage rather than dramatically heightening it, and sometimes, as in *Brimstone and Treacle* (TV version 1976, transmitted 1987; feature film 1982), the flights of nostalgia sit uncomfortably with the wrath. The latter film, in which a demonic young stranger exposes suburban hypocrisy and liberates, or 'cures' a crippled girl through sexual assault, highlights his most troubling reactionary characteristic: the unapologetic misogynism which also marred his recent, self-directed *Blackeyes* (1989). Furious, intelligent and isolated, Potter remains the television iconoclast that television loves to cultivate.

Anthony Powell born 1905

■ BRITISH NOVELIST

Before WW2, Powell was a satirist and light comedian, dealing with the seedy, pleasure-loving, party-going life of London. Realizing subsequently that the world in which he had been brought up could not continue, he sought to describe the collapse of what he had once mocked, in the 12 volumes that comprise *A Dance to the Music of Time* (1951-75). Named after a Poussin painting (with which it shares a classical severity and structural rhythm), the sequence's narrator, Nicholas Jenkins, belongs to the generation that grew up in the shadow of WWI. His world is full of literary hangers-on, politicos, derelicts, drop-outs, socialists and phoney gurus, dominated by the ruthless Kenneth Widmerpool who journeys from rather ridiculous obscurity to a sinister apex of power. Humorous, melancholy, sometimes very funny, with an intricate interweaving of personal relationships, there are still enough moments of genuine insight amid the snobbery to justify Powell's contention that 'All human beings, driven as they are at different speeds by the same furies, are at close range, equally extraordinary.'

Enoch Powell born 1912

☞BRITISH POLITICIAN

⇔Only moderately well-known before the late 1960s, Powell was a zealous advocate of *laissez-faire* who resigned over high expenditure when a junior finance minister, and came a bad third in the 1965 Tory leadership poll. Fame – and infamy – followed in 1968, when he made rabid speeches against black and Asian immigration, quoting Virgil to proclaim his vision of 'The Tiber foaming with blood'. Dockers marched through London to back him; the nation was divided. If it was a calculated bid for power, it failed – Prime Minister ☛Heath sacked him immediately, and he has never regained a significant position of influence. Powell claimed to be driven by his own irresistible logic – his demon. He expressed vigorous hostility to Britain's entry into the Common Market – advising Tories to vote Labour in 1974 so as to avoid this terrible fate – and went on to espouse Ulster Unionism, and become a Unionist MP in the late 1970s. A constitutional scholar and pedant, he has recently argued that Britain should ally itself with the Soviet Union, the other great continental power, since the US poses a threat to the nation's autonomy. Enthusiasts, and some critics, claim he has a massive intelligence – he was a professor of Greek at 25. Even so, there are a wide range of issues, arguments and insights that pass him by. His prose and oratory, compelling in a way, can be dry, tortuous and pedestrian. He takes himself very seriously – almost no one else does.

Michael Powell 1905-90

✍ BRITISH FILM DIRECTOR

Powell's assertion that he was 'English as a Worcester Pearmain' might seem odd given that his film-making apparently owed more to Disney and German expressionism than any indigenous cinematic tradition, and his dream of a total cinema in which 'music, emotion and acting made a complete whole, of which music was the master' could not have been more un-English. But Powell drew his mysticism from an English Romantic tradition in literature that the nation's cinema had largely ignored until he came along. The astonishing sequence of pictures from the 1940s, made by Powell and his screenwriting partner Emeric Pressburger (1903-1988), combine elegies to rural England in *A Canterbury Tale* (1944) with explorations of the emotional storms that rage beneath the veneer of civilization and good behaviour, as among the quarrelsome nuns of *Black Narcissus* (1946). After reaching a peak with *The Red Shoes* (1948), the tale of a dancer who cannot reconcile her desire to dance with her husband's wish that she give it all up for married life, the creative fires were dulled and the partnership split up. Powell, however, went on to direct *Peeping Tom* (1960), a dark account of voyeuristic murder which made him *persona non grata* for many years among Britain's prissier cinema critics and assured his ostracism from the industry. For British film-makers of the late 1970s and early 1980s, the 'rediscovery' of his work provided the only evidence that might suggest the possibility of creating a national cinema of riotous fantasy and turbulent emotion. Unfortunately, none of these epigones came anywhere near rivalling Powell's achievements.

Swami Prabhupada

(A. C. Bhaktivedanta, Abhay Caran De)

1896-1977

✚ INDIAN RELIGIOUS LEADER,
☆ WHO SETTLED IN US

The founder of the Hare Krishna movement had been a business executive in Calcutta, who channelled the profits from pharmaceuticals into his own religious magazine before he took the vows of an ascetic. Six years later, in 1965, he arrived in New York, carrying a suitcase full of translations of his books and the addresses of people who might welcome his spiritual guidance. The International Society for Krishna Consciousness (ISKCON), which he founded, grew rapidly through the 1970s, leading to the establishment of 200 teaching centres to which his followers withdraw from normal life. There they follow a daily regime that involves rising at 3.30 a.m. for a day of prayers and active proselytization in the wider community – approaching people on the street to sell religious books, and parading through city streets in saffron-coloured robes, banging drums and chanting the name of Krishna. Their high public visibility accounts for the passionate opposition of anti-cult groups, particularly in the US, who resent the Krishna movement's rebuke to contemporary individualism. ISKCON provides a haven for those who prefer the emotional warmth of community life to the strains and stresses of modernity.

Elvis Presley 1935-77

✤ AMERICAN ROCK MUSICIAN

Presley remains the embodiment of *everything* there is to say about rock music. As the poor white Southern boy who managed to combine black music with white country and rockabilly, he invented rock 'n' roll. As a young performer, he made it sexual; his above-the-waist performance on the Ed Sullivan Show pointed up the conflict between establishment entertainment and anarchic youth. His belief in God and his gospel recordings illustrated the contradictions which riddle pop music and make it potent; and his emergence as a family entertainer showed up another contradiction – the way that the system dilutes the 'threatening' aspects of culture. His complete subservience to manager 'Colonel' Tom Parker, and the subsequent near-destruction of his talent, testify to the music industry's ability to destroy its own best features; and his death at only 42 – obese, drug-addicted and cocooned from the world – is still the ultimate horrible rock death. Presley represented the sexual chaos of rock music and its bland antithesis; his cabaret years, sweating in Las Vegas and imitating his imitators, now fascinate almost as much as his early explosions, because both are landmarks in the history of rock. The more time that passes, the more people refuse to believe that Presley is dead, as if the things he stood for, real or imaginary, are so virtuous and good that their creator should be able to share in them.

Ilya Prigogine

born 1917

○ SOVIET-BELGIAN PHYSICIST

Prigogine's 1955 book, *Thermodynamics of Irreversible Processes*, sparked a revolution by observing the limitation in classical thermodynamics, that it was restricted to reversible processes and equilibrium states. Prigogine holds a chair of chemistry at the University of Brussels where he has nurtured a substantial cross-disciplinary team who help apply his work on dissipative (dealing with states far from equilibrium) biological and chemical structures to a variety of fields, including diffusion, quantum theory and the social behaviour of ant colonies. His fascination with, and significant clarification of, those large non-equilibrium systems which spontaneously evolve from chaos to order through instabilities, fluctuations and other states, and which were once deliberately – almost superstitiously – ignored by scientists, have generated a transformation in what it seemed possible to know, a shift so basic and so enormous that it is already importing its powerful effects into art and philosophy.

Prince

(Prince Rogers Nelson) born 1960

AMERICAN ROCK MUSICIAN

Prince refuses to make merely 'black' music, acknowledging pop's nature as a mixture of anything and everything. He also chooses images which reflect his progenitors: ☛Hendrix, the black guitarist who invented white rock; Sly Stone, the black soul singer who moved from bubblegum soul to the most frightening and desolate rock music; ☛Little Richard, the sexually ambiguous and vulgar rock singer who oscillates between profane rock 'n' roll and pure gospel. Prince uses both blatant sexual imagery and devout Christian belief. He has made records such as 'The Cross', a song about redemption based entirely on the music of ☛The Velvet Underground; '1999', a thundering party dance anthem about Armageddon, and 'Paisley Park', a jaunty psychedelic pop-rock song about the dead. He has also created some of the best music in any of the American genres, taking in arena rock, funk and the soft soul ballad. His eclecticism and ☛Michael Jackson-style weird-hermit image often make Prince look too much of a cartoon rock figure and he rarely seems genuinely subversive, but everything he does has greater musical intelligence and diversity than is to be found almost anywhere else in contemporary rock music.

Gilbert Proesch *see* Gilbert and George

Psychic TV *see* Throbbing Gristle

Public Enemy formed 1984

AMERICAN ROCK GROUP

◆▲ Public Enemy have lived in controversy since the moment Chuck D and Hank Shocklee were persuaded to move out of their influential slot as radio DJs by rap pioneers Run DMC and Def Jam label boss Rick Rubin, and to transform a popular and innovative 1984 radio mix, 'Public Enemy No. 1', into a record that fused a torrent of confrontation into a suitably protean noise. Furious, lunatic, untrammelled, fiercely political and far and away the most original hip-hop group, PE have consistently sought to mould genuine street violence and neighbourhood anger into a music that is fragmented, visionary and dangerous. They are constantly under pressure to atone for the wilder claims and statements made by some of their number (especially those of the almost-unhinged Professor Griff, who at times espouses an unreconstructed anti-Semitism), but for good or evil, they have refused to compromise, unwilling to give up on rap's genius for expressing otherwise silenced opinions. Dynamic street-heroes by dint of intelligent intransigence, brilliant media-dogging, hard-nosed musical excellence and a willingness to live out at the edge of provocative contradiction, they disbanded in 1989, ostensibly in response to a more than usually offensive outburst from Professor Griff, but came together again the following year – *sans* Griff.

Manuel Puig 1932-90

ARGENTINIAN NOVELIST, BASED IN WESTERN EUROPE

Puig's novels are built around comically desperate characters, and the dreams they learned in celluloid palaces; their garrulous outpourings, shaped from the clichés of mass culture, leave them trapped in the emotional knots they have tied around themselves. Diverse narratives are run alongside each other, the fantasy world generated by a distant America often set against the emptiness of 'ordinary' life in Argentina. Radical politics sometimes seems to provide a bridge between the two, but its roots in irreality condemn it to failure, and Puig embraced the tension between the two worlds: he was certainly not a simple-minded critic of Hollywood's tinsel reveries. When the imprisoned homosexual in *Kiss of the Spider Woman* (1976/9) retells the plots of B-movies to his radical cell-mate, he transforms them into a commentary on their situation, deploying them to influence, and change, his companion. Puig recognized that the meaning of films is altered by viewers, in accordance with their own positions; and that fact seems to render Hollywood dreams (almost) as valid as any others. His fascination with the images he replayed, and the way they imprinted themselves on his consciousness, was evidence of his own ambivalence about cinema's brainwashing activities.

Thomas Pynchon born 1937

✖ AMERICAN NOVELIST

Gravity's Rainbow (1973), perhaps the only novel to encapsulate the whole of the post-war world as opposed to just hinting at parts of it, is a masterpiece of allusive conciseness and imaginative wanderlust. Its 750 pages are filled with learned diversions, paranoid transitions, hip coincidences, conspiracies and tragi-comic mini-biogs, all relating to life under the shadow of the Bomb. Opening in the final months of WW2, it traces the rise and fall of the anarchic Zone that flourishes before political order (and the nations that go with it) is restored. The reclusive Pynchon writes as if everything is connected to everything else, and detours so obsessively *en route* through his story that even the revelation that there is actually no revelation seems extraordinarily significant. If *Gravity's Rainbow* and the earlier *The Crying of Lot 49* (1966) are mostly about the necessary futility of reading – not just novels but the astonishing proliferation of codes in the late twentieth century – they are also about the difficulty of pleasure and the pleasure of difficulty. In 1990, after a 17-year silence, Pynchon published *Vineland*. Expectation had been screwed so high that a critical backlash was inevitable, even though the book became an instant bestseller. American writers generally have to live their lives as high public drama. Of Pynchon, there exists only one known photo – from his high school yearbook.

Q

Mary Quant

born 1934

♦ BRITISH FASHION DESIGNER, BUSINESS EXECUTIVE

Originator of the 'Chelsea' fashion style, Quant's dress designs of the early 1960s were adopted by young people seeking a banner with which to defy their parents. She is best remembered for the scandal-provoking, leg-displaying mini-skirt, which suggested a new kind of sexual freedom after the constrictions of the 1950s. Her boutique in the King's Road was the start of a business empire which, within seven years of its opening in 1957, had spread through Europe and the US to become a multi-million pound enterprise. Quant's name is now known largely through her cosmetics.

Quay Brothers (Stephen & Nicholas)

born 1947

BRITISH ANIMATORS

The uncannily tactile sensibility of the twin Quay brothers has taken model animation way beyond children's video into surrealist dread, where dolls, bird skulls, brass screws and dead insects lurk, creep and roll in peculiarly repellent imitation of life. Establishing a wide reputation with *Street of Crocodiles* (1986), they do not conceal their debt to the Czechoslovak ☛Jan Svankmajer, but they have, in fact, made far more of the very Eastern European tradition of life in inanimate objects: the Golem, Karel Capek's robots, Kafka's organisms of bureaucracy and folk tales of the Undead all prefigure the Quays' precisely modelled world. Although they have increased the scope of music video techniques, their importance lies in their invocation of more abstruse animations.

Raymond Queneau

1903-76

FRENCH NOVELIST, POET

Queneau's *Un Cent Mille Milliard des Poèmes* (1961) – a sample-book for would-be poets that works on the heads-bodies-legs principle of certain children's books, with each line on each page separately articulated – actually constructs rather more poems than the title suggests: it is conceivable that a reader could open up at a combination never before reached, and it is certain that no one will properly read or absorb in a human lifespan all the possible combinations. Fascinated by the arbitrariness of language, Queneau was founder in 1960 of OuLiPo (*Ouvroir du Littérature Potentielle*), an organization dedicated to the discovery of new ways to write, which built on the early lead of Raymond Roussel, a turn-of-the-century eccentric whose inability to write as if words meant anything has made him one of the century's more enduring figures. Queneau, a brilliant parodist, is not much known outside France, simply because the force and humour of his writing defies translation. But Louis Malle tried to find visual equivalents for Queneau's syntax for his adaptation of *Zazie dans le Métro* (1959; film and translation, 1960), in which a young, foul-mouthed girl from out of town unleashes a torrent of comment on her planned ride through Montmartre.

Willard van Orman Quine

born 1908

AMERICAN PHILOSOPHER, BASED IN UK

Quine's significance derives more from the intellectual debates his writings have encouraged than from the number of people who agree with him. His early preoccupation was with the problem of whether we can know that words mean what they seem to mean: can one word act as a synonym for another, or reliably translate a word from another language? Quine argues that no firm distinction can be drawn between a sentence which expresses information drawn from the world and a sentence such as 'All bachelors are unmarried' which seems true as a result of internal logic. The same thinking underlies his ideas about translation. Even when a word used in one language seems to refer to the same thing in another, there is no justification in assuming that the meaning ascribed will, in fact, be the same. For example, a word translated as 'rabbit' might in fact mean 'the condition of being a rabbit'. Since it follows that no hard line can be drawn between the facts, and what we project on to them, we can build our philosophical theories of the world as we choose, subject only to the constraints of logic. Quine sees philosophy as the abstract wing of science, exploring a human capacity to build complex conceptual structures from sensory inputs received. He does not accept that what people say should be attributed to inner and unobservable mental states, seeing mind as a matter of nerves, and language as a response to what people see, touch and hear.

R

Bhagwan Rajneesh

(Mohan Chandra Jain) 1931-90

INDIAN GURU

Since the days when you could not go out without being buttonholed by smiling dropouts in orange, each with their neck-charm photo of Bhagwan ('Blessed One') Rajneesh on prominent display, this remarkable fraudster-guru has been regarded as the archetypal cult figure – an Indian far, far smarter than the thousands of upper middle-class dropouts he seduced from the West. They flocked to him as he sold them New Age religion packaged as pure, unguilty orgasm (he came to be dubbed the 'guru of the vagina'), and they made him a millionaire. A socialist and an atheist in his youth, he recognized what many more sincere Asian gurus never had – that the ascetic mysticism of a genuine oriental religion had little or no Western appeal: hippies would never tumble for fasting and celibacy. So he put together an idiosyncratic philosophy that blended deliberate irrationalism, pop psychotherapy, vulgarized existentialism, (very debased) Buddhist/Hindu jargon, free love, self-love and Bhagwan-love. At various times he insisted that he was God, that his followers should laugh for three-and-a-half hours a day, and that their psychic and spiritual salvation lay in total surrender to his teachings: for a young girl in his community, the highest honour was the opportunity to sleep with this ageing, wheezing, whispering old man. His ashram in Poona became a focal point for belated Aquarians in the 1970s, until the Indian authorities objected to the unbridled sex-activities and expelled him in 1981. Then they moved to the small town of Antelope in Oregon, where Rajneesh opted out of direct control, and handed over to his secretary Sheela, a brittle, harassed, intelligent woman who cracked completely under the pressure of local politics. While she popped pills, put wiretaps on everyone, including the Bhagwan, and attempted to poison the population of Antelope, the Bhagwan amassed 93 Rolls Royces and kept quiet. The storm broke – Sheela went to prison and the Bhagwan was expelled from the US in 1985, leaving crowds of leaderless worshippers bewildered, disillusioned and penniless.

The Ramones formed 1974

Dee Dee Ramone (Douglas Colvin) born 1952
Joey Ramone (Jeffrey Hyman) born 1952
Johnny Ramone (John Cummings) born 1952

♦ AMERICAN POP GROUP

Formed somewhere between teen bubble-gum pop and punk, The Ramones melted down American sounds from the time before the slow death years of hippy and rock – The Beach Boys, ☛Phil Spector, surf bands, garage bands, trash bands – and occasionally perverted them with sicko joke imagery. British rock in 1976 appreciated the speed and the cartoon aggression; British punk kept the shapes and the more accessible parts of the humour. The Ramones continued for years with only a few, slight changes, occasionally acknowledging the times with a slightly out-of-date record whose lessons were ignored. A brief liaison with Spector hinted at potential glory, but generally The Ramones encircled popular music on an elliptical orbit, never having quite invented punk, never quite making the link with their bubble-gum forebears.

Dieter Rams born 1932

GERMAN DESIGNER

☛Hans Gugelot ran the team, but Dieter Rams did much of the penwork involved in developing the Braun house style, and later shifted away from the stylistic influence of his mentor. Chief designer at the company for 25 years, he experimented with plastics and came up with design solutions that blended his admiration for Japanese aesthetics into the austerity associated with Braun – sleek, matt-black finish and compact casing. The formula was applied to clocks, stereo units, kitchen equipment as well as shavers, hair dryers and electric toothbrushes. Some mock the practice of placing beautiful objects amid the chaos of day-to-day domestic activity, but Rams' designs were also practical. Form and function did meet, here at least.

Ayn Rand

(Alice Rosenbaum) 1905-82

SOVIET-AMERICAN NOVELIST, SCREENWRITER

This lonely, gifted Russian émigré fled the Soviet Union and a miserable childhood to become a pulp-novelist, Hollywood screenwriter and pop philosopher so right-wing that, for most of her life, even conservatives shunned her. As total a convert to self-help capitalism and the American Way as there has ever been, she spent 40 years on the development of her philosophy of pure individualism, free markets and free minds – which, for some reason, she called 'Objectivism'. Her novels *The Fountainhead* (1943) and *Atlas Shrugged* (1957) are Mills & Boon with a libertarian agenda; her obsessions were the threat of Communism and the conspiracy of mediocrity that always blocked genius. A total inability to operate socially – to compromise or empathize – rendered her uniquely bad at understanding the thoughts of others (it is not clear whether she even understood Nietzsche, her prime influence); the mark of her intelligence is the degree to which, ignorant of precursors, she reinvented the *laissez-faire* wheel and passed it off as her own. She was a witness against 'Communists' at the House Un-

American Activities Committee hearings, and always thought of herself as a warrior for modern rationality. She despised conservatives, including ☛Ronald Reagan – but began to influence the far right in the 1970s, when economists such as ☛Friedman and ☛Hayek contributed articles to the journal she published. Always totally lacking in humour, she took to wearing a flowing black cape and a dress covered in dollar signs, and treated any disagreement, public or personal, as a sign of jealousy on the part of the 'conspiracy of mediocrity'.

Robert Rauschenberg born 1925

♦ AMERICAN ARTIST

Notorious for having encased a stuffed ram in a car tyre and splattered it with paint in one of his 'combine' paintings, Rauschenberg opened the door to many artistic movements of the 1960s by re-establishing contemporary bric-à-brac as material for art. His paintings, however, offer an unfocused sensuous complexity – very different from the work of the Pop artists who were influenced by him. He drew from ☛John Cage the idea that art should represent the confused complexity of the world, and his creative trajectory took him from (dull) all-black paintings to (intriguing) collages of modern imagery. Initially working with newspapers, rusty nails and scraps of rag, Rauschenberg became more sculptural, as he moved through Coca-Cola bottles and stuffed animals, towards such items as an electric clock, a blinking light, a radio set. One could say that his vision never fully absorbed such imagery: by keeping his distance, he emphasized it as just one part of the contemporary babble. Never content simply to rework a formula, he also developed his own variations on the silk-screen process developed by ☛Warhol, and has worked with laser scientists, under the auspices of a group he helped set up, to foster collaborations between artists and engineers. Often associated with ☛Jasper Johns during the 1960s, it is the latter's star that has risen in the eye of collectors. The immediacy of response that Rauschenberg offered to his times makes him seem less relevant to now.

John Rawls born 1921

BRITISH POLITICAL PHILOSOPHER

Rawls argues in his 1971 book, *A Theory of Justice*, for a political philosophy that balances individual liberty against the quest for economic and social equality. He does not believe that the general good justifies ignoring individual claims – most of the people who sound off about Rawlsian 'socialism' have not read him – but nor does he believe that a free-for-all provides the best option. Drawing sophisticated conclusions from a fairly simple hypothesis, he argues that, if a group of people were asembled to decide the rules of society, unaware of where they would eventually stand in the economic and social hierarchies of that society, they would agree on two basic principles: first, that each individual would have an equal right to the basic liberties (speech, assembly, thought, etc.); second, that inequalities can be permitted if they produce economic growth whose benefits filter down even to the least advantaged members of society. The principles of justice, he says, define the constraints which institutions and joint activities must satisfy if the persons engaging in them are to have no complaints against them. The resulting distribution, whatever it is, may be accepted as just (or at least not unjust). Rawls felt that the best argument for such principles was that they would generate their own support. He can hardly have suspected, when he wrote his book, how tough would be the resistance to even his limited egalitarianism.

Nicholas Ray 1911-79

AMERICAN FILM DIRECTOR

☛Jean-Luc Godard almost got it right when he said, 'The cinema is Nicholas Ray.' Certainly few directors of the 1950s managed so consistently to transcend the limitations of their material. Coming out of television, Ray set the trend for his later work with his first film, *They Live by Night* (1948), a tale of doomed outsiders who escape into a world of darkness where their love is forced to hide in the shadows. Despite his romanticism, Ray's characters are often characterized by latent violence – as with the mild-mannered teacher of *Bigger than Life* (1956), whose addiction to cortisone turns him into a paranoid madman, or the confused Sal Mineo who inadvertently instigates the tragic climax of *Rebel without a Cause* (1955). Never on the best of terms with Hollywood or the critical establishment, Ray's directorial career was all but rounded off by two of the finest epics of the 1960s. *King of Kings* (1961), ridiculed in its day as 'I Was a Teenage Jesus', placed Christ firmly in his social and political context while boasting some moving set pieces, while *55 Days in Peking* (1962) gave Charlton Heston the best role of his career as a soldier unable to cope with human relationships in other than military terms ('Go in, seize the objective and pull out with minimum casualties'). Both were heavily cut by the studios (*King* even lost its main character), and the heart attack that prevented Ray completing *Peking* led to his semi-retirement. It was not until the 1970s that his films, for years regarded as glossy production-line items, received the attention they deserved.

Satyajit Ray 1921-92

INDIAN FILMMAKER

Pather Panchali, the unforgettable account of a Bengali boy's childhood which was Ray's first film, stirred excitement at the 1956 Cannes film festival: here was an Indian film that looked European. Ray's aesthetic and working methods derive from the Italian neo-realists and owe nothing to Bombay's spectacular musical fantasies, but he made productive use of the tensions between East and West that are embedded in Indian life. These can result in a film such as *Charulata* (1964) – an account of a woman's unrequited love for her neglectful husband's poet cousin – that can seem, depending on one's point of view, either quintessentially Bengali or completely English. Ray had some uncomfortable run-ins with Hollywood, being asked by the producer of *Gone with the Wind* whether he would be interested in making an Indian version of *Anna Karenina*, and almost eliciting studio finance for a script about a humanoid splashing down in a Bengali village that bore more than a passing resemblance to the film later made as *E.T.* But, for the most part, Ray was content to work with limited resources, pursuing his own vision of India. His influence on such film-makers as Shyam Benegal and Mrinal Sen is inestimable.

Ronald Reagan born 1911

AMERICAN ACTOR,
POLITICAL LEADER

When considering the career of Ronald Reagan, it is worth remembering that Orson Welles turned down the Democratic Party nomination because he felt a divorced actor could never make it in politics. Reagan, once married to Jane Wyman, won the presidency for the Republicans in 1980 – at 69, the oldest man ever to take over the Oval Office. He remains an enigma even after two terms in the White House and a quarter of a century in far right politics. Beginning as a radio sports announcer, he was given to brilliantly energized and convincing commentary on games he wasn't actually watching at the time. His career in Hollywood was not a distinguished one; all the same, the fact that he had been an actor was proof to certain critics of the absolute inauthenticity of his politics. Reagan's success derived from a phenomenal ability to project himself as a likeable, bumbling relative – surely no politician has ever before got so much mileage out of errors, incompetence and mis-speaks. People felt they were on his level: he made the mistakes that they might have made, he no more understood the meaningless complexities of economics and international diplomacy than they did and his cheerful simplicity cut through, they felt, to the heart of the matter. The far right agenda that his populist vagueness hid was in fact only partly put into practice: although welfare programmes were rolled back, and wealth was redistributed to the rich, his staff were unable to make the lasting changes that his reactionary Californian sponsors had been agitating for. As governor of California in the 1960s, he had waged a war on youthful anti-Vietnam dissidents; as leader of the Free World, he continued to wage war on proxy Vietnams, becoming in the end so committed to backing the Contra terrorists in Nicaragua that he allowed his underlings (through the Iran-Contra conspiracy) to subvert the US Constitution – only the most adroit mumbling and smiling got him off the hook. His policies reflected an uneasy mix of libertarianism (which hooked many voters) and authoritarian moralism (which attracted the religious fundamentalists). He made America feel great about itself, but gave it nothing substantial to feel great about – unless you count the largest budget deficit in any nation's history.

Otis Redding 1941-67

AMERICAN SOUL SINGER

As The Supremes symbolize Motown, so Otis Redding is the artist one associates with Atlantic Records; his ability to put pop into the gritty Stax style has meant that his records have lasted. From his posthumous 'Dock of the Bay' – a record which would have gained mythic status even without Redding's untimely death – to his versions of Rolling Stone's and Beatles' songs, he was the most successful (commercially and artistically) crossover act of the mid-1960s. His first (definitive) LP, *Otis Blue*, assimilated the culture of the period – style, soul, pop, nostalgia, advertising – into the sagas of Mod.

Ishmael Reed born 1938

AMERICAN NOVELIST

Mumbo Jumbo (1972), Reed's hip, allusive allegory of the impact of jazz on Western civilization is one of the lost works of 1970s' literature – too far out to be respectable, but still warmer than his mocking fury initially suggests. Working up a pulp of modern urban folk tales that cohere around the absurdity of racism, he pushed down a line that was too demanding for less experimental readers, unpicking and insulting everything, from Hollywood to the high arcana of Masonry. His novels – critical, conspiratorial and street-witty – are just too much for some, and that may be why he moved towards a more realistic style for his most recent book, *Reckless Eyeballing* (1986), the story of a black playwright who has been 'sex-listed' and is trying to get back into favour with the feminist power-brokers. Explosive, and unarguably somewhat misogynistic, he has fallen out with everyone at some time over the years: his enraging gift for satire-out-of-paranoia unearthed a touch too much nasty fun from the 1970s' wave of black feminist fiction. *Reckless Eyeballing* is the barbed coda to all that; it will not do him any good where he is already excoriated, but it has kicked his furious, contemptuous daemon back into motion.

Steve Reich born 1936

♦ AMERICAN COMPOSER

Minimalism has been a success in music because it locked into the pop accessibility of high volume and mesmeric repetition. Based in New York, Reich has always been minimalism's most interesting exponent because he retains some of the characteristics that the public never warmed to in serialism – theoretical rigour and astringency. His work is guided by abstract considerations – for example, the rhythmic patterns of *Clapping Music* (1972) – but always directed towards emotional intensity. This began early, with the timely baldness of *Come Out* (1966), which used tape-looped voices as the primary sound source, and dealt with police brutality during the 1964 Harlem riots. Throughout the 1970s, as minimalism gained audiences by soothing them, Reich studied the limits of innovation through economy, travelling to Ghana to gain a better understanding of non-Western rhythm. Emotional intensity burst out with force in *Tehillim* (1981), a choral setting of the Psalms in the original Hebrew, as Reich began to move deeper into personal history. *Different Trains* (1988) uses train sounds and voices to montage his own journeys as a Jewish-American child in the 1940s against those of Holocaust victims being transported through Europe at the same time.

Wilhelm Reich 1897-1957

AUSTRIAN-AMERICAN

PSYCHOANALYST

☆ In his lifetime, Reich came to be regarded as an increasingly dangerous spouter of gibberish, but seekers after nirvana have acclaimed him as a prophet and a visionary because of his insistence on the importance of intense sexual activity. His books *The Function of the Orgasm* (1927/42) and *The Mass Psychology of Fascism* (1933/46) stimulated discussion among 1960s' radicals about the relationship between sexual liberation and politics, while the emphasis Reich placed on the need to throw off repression has influenced primal therapy and bioenergetics. Reich started off as an argumentative member of Freud's inner circle, while also being a member of the Communist Party – both groups eventually expelled him. He fled to the US from the Nazis and there expanded on his idea that the

Steve Reich

elimination of sexual repression was the way to free the masses. Claiming to have discovered electrochemical particles which controlled sexual energy, he built a machine that would collect these 'orgones'. The US Food and Drug Administration began an investigation after Reich started to market his 'orgone box' as a way to universal health and happiness. Clearly hovering on the edge of insanity – he wondered whether he might not be a spaceman, and suggested that aliens from outer space were interfering with his experiment in 'orgonic weather control' – he was gaoled for failing to appear in court, and died in prison.

Whatever you have done to me or will do to me in the future, whether you glorify me as a genius or put me in a mental institution, whether you adore me as your saviour or hang me as a spy, sooner or later necessity will force you to understand that I have discovered the laws of the living.

Wilhelm Reich,
Listen, Little Man *(1949)*

Jamie Reid born 1946

BRITISH GRAPHIC ARTIST

Reid's ransom-note graphics induced astonished and malicious delight at the time they were first shown, defining ☛The Sex Pistols, their era and their locality (sleepy and unswinging London town, and the punk rock movement that would alter it for ever), as well as his own lazy, limited, brilliantly refusenik sensibilities. While at art school, he evaded the blanket adoration of Pop Art that others fell for, being more impressed by ☛Jackson Pollock and ☛Charlie Mingus. He met ☛Malcolm McLaren in 1968 and became caught up in the worldwide uplift of revolt and resistance. Working at *Suburban Press* in Croydon during the early 1970s, he distilled situationist theories about urbanism and momentary disorientation into work that still stands up – instant, tacky and untainted. When McLaren became involved with The Sex Pistols, Reid found himself at liberty to take his approach much further. In retrospect, the late days of *The Great Rock 'n' Roll Swindle* pushed points as cynical as any ever made by the capitalism that the punks had mocked so bitterly. But, for a while, Reid's framing – his notorious safety-pinned Queen in Jubilee year, for example – ensured that this most successful of pop's outrage-scams would always retain at some level a jagged, dense resonance, with a permanently ambivalent attitude to the suburbia from which it sprang. Trapped, by the successes of this time, Reid has done nothing notable since.

Ad Reinhardt 1913-67

AMERICAN ARTIST

Reinhardt approached his ambition to produce 'a painting that is simply a black painting and nothing more' with polemical seriousness. Beginning his series of *Ultimate Black Paintings* in 1960, he achieved his goal of creating pictures with lives of their own, independent of the artist, subject matter, colour and form. Mapping the furthest point from reality that art could reach, Reinhardt presented the viewer with square canvases formally divided into nine smaller squares of black, so subtly distinguished as to appear imperceptible. Taking his cue from oriental art and Western minimalism, these works were devoid of any meaning other than that suggested by their very presence, reminding viewers of Gertrude Stein's line 'A rose is a rose is a rose' – or, in Reinhardt's case, 'A black square is a black square is a black square.'

The one work for a fine artist, the one painting, is the painting of the one-size canvas – the single scheme, one formal device, one colour monochrome, one linear division, one symmetry, one texture, one free-hand brushing, one rhythm, one working everything into one dissolution and one indivisibility.

Ad Reinhardt

Edgar Reitz

born 1932

▲GERMAN FILM-MAKER

⇔It seemed appropriate that Reitz – who, with Alexander Kluge, was one of the prime motivators of the New German Cinema in the 1960s but missed out on its glory days – should announce the movement's mellow middle-age with *Heimat* (1983). This 15-hour film portrait of a small German village between 1919 and 1982 indicated a more sympathetic stance towards Nazism and the post-war economic miracle than had been apparent in the angry films made by the likes of ☛Fassbinder, ☛Herzog, ☛Wenders and ☛Syberberg. Also, after long years of friction between the television companies (who provided most of the finance) and the directors, it seemed extraordinary that a film, which most people would see in 11 parts on the box, was so calmly accepted as being cinema. Inspired by anger at the debased romanticism of the 1978 NBC television series, *Holocaust*, *Heimat* secured its cinematic status through Reitz's eye for the way people relate to landscape, and his sensitivity to the complexity of emotions aroused by major events. But no one really answered the question as to whether it is very good television or a very long movie, or whether the question really matters at all.

Alain Resnais

born 1922

☞FRENCH FILM DIRECTOR

Older than most of the New Wave *cinéastes* who first raved about him, Resnais is a technical innovator of genius, but in the end, that is more or less all his talent amounts to. Since his 1958 collaboration with ☛Marguerite Duras on the hauntingly sinister dream poem, *Hiroshima mon amour*, his work has seemed continually to miss its own best opportunities. Resnais shared little of ☛Godard's enthusiasm for the potential in Hollywood pulp or genre material, and he has never rid himself of a rather airless high modernist aesthetic sensibility which, from the 1960s onwards, would read more and more like nostalgic snobbery. Its appeal lay in its refusal of any of popular cinema's anarchic drive. *Last Year in Marienbad* (1961) arrived at a time when European art-house cinema still seemed to offer a map of refreshing new possibilities for the movies, and Resnais' narrative ambivalence, his cool play with flashbacks and his obsessive concentration on such abstractions as time and memory at the expense of conventional movie staples (as well as his undoubted formal brilliance and the coldly opulent look of the film) gave it the air of mystery that made it a hit. His only real hit, in fact – none of his work from then on has had anything like the same impact. ☛Robbe-Grillet used to claim that character-psychology and narrative were nineteenth-century relics which now only flatter the bourgeoisie. In Resnais' films, dream-like stillness and frozen ambiguity have probably come to do much the same, unfortunately.

Syngman Rhee 1875-1965

KOREAN POLITICAL LEADER

A veteran Korean nationalist, Rhee was introduced to Western ideas by Methodist school-teachers, and acquired Christianity together with a hatred of Korea's status as a satellite of either Japan or the Soviet Union. Gaoled by the authorities for seven years in the 1890s, on release he went to the US, studying at Harvard and Princeton. He spent two years back at home, where the Japanese were now in control, and then fled back to the US, spending 33 years there. As president of the Korean Republic-in-exile, he developed a massive ego, and began to see himself as the pivot of Korean independence. He was flown back to Korea clandestinely in an American aircraft and, despite opposition from virtually all other political forces in the country, became president of the South in 1948. His oppressive domestic policy and determination to reunite the peninsula under his own control led the Americans to view him with distrust. However, having already lost China, they were compelled to support Rhee in a war against ☛Kim Il Sung. Originally a civil dispute which threatened no one, the Korean conflict became a central episode in the Cold War. Rhee massacred his own people, objected in vain to a UN peace plan that confirmed partition, and tried hard to get the war restarted. He was dictatorial and paternalist: purging the national assembly, banning the opposition and executing its leader. Student protests in 1960, attacking electoral fraud – he had claimed 90 per cent of the vote – and corruption, forced him out. He had held senior political status for 64 years.

Boyd Rice born 1956

AMERICAN MUSICIAN

'King of Noise', practical joker and film scholar, this engaging Californian has operated off the deep end of punk since the late 1970s. Rice's first record bore the notorious instructions 'multi-speed multi-axis for play at 16/33/45/78 at home maximum volume suggested', as well as having extra holes drilled here and there on the disc: the distress and/or entertainment you experienced at the damage to your hi-fi tended to make the listening experience secondary. This may have been a blessing, since Non, his pop operation, takes the principle of dissonance to cheerful extremes of volume and formless distortion unknown elsewhere. Apart from a tiresome obsession with ☛Charles Manson (which he shares, after all, with every other West Coast punk), Rice is a pleasant individual who carries out archive work on the marginal and the rejected from the underbelly of the film world: he says his aim is to uncover the mechanisms that form and fix values. A collection of interviews, *Pranks!*, has become a textbook for assaults on the status quo.

Adrienne Rich born 1929

AMERICAN POET

Rich became active within the women's liberation movement in 1970 and her work since has engaged in the struggle to articulate 'the experiential grounding of identity politics' as 'Jew, white, woman, lesbian, middle class'. Two collections of her prose record this angry effort, and as 'a woman sworn to lucidity', her collections across three decades have sustained their focus on relations, identity and sexual politics: 'Poetry never stood a chance/of standing outside history,' she says in 'North American Time' (1983). A poem such as 'The Images' from 1976-8 speaks eloquently against the prejudice and violence experienced by women in the cities: 'Two women sleeping/together have more than their sleep to defend . . . I am remembered by you, remember you, even as we are dismembered/on the cinema screens.'

Cliff Richard

(Harry Webb) born 1940

✓ BRITISH POP MUSICIAN

Cliff Richard's beginnings as the British Elvis could well have led, via jolly family entertainment movies and television shows, into mediocrity – increasingly middle-aged records, pantomime or games shows. However, his conversion to Christianity and sickening eternal youth (now slightly fading) meant that Cliff suddenly took on a fixed vigour and unending self-confidence. No one with his rightist Christian views and unlimited stamina could be expected to stay long in BBC light entertainment; nor can he be described as 'bland', no matter how bad his records can be. An inexorable voice of youthful passion and age-old 'morality', Cliff Richard is sexless, self-righteous and unique. He is lost in some long-gone Britain, outside any conventional version of popular music.

Little Richard

(Richard Penniman) born 1932

AMERICAN ROCK MUSICIAN

No one apart from Jerry Lee Lewis better exemplifies the contradiction in rock music between God and devilry: Little Richard (the real-life version of ☛Prince) has been both a practising minister and a partying bisexual love monster. His records, though beyond good and evil, are only a part of his gigantic charm. Not even the thunderous sex of 'Tutti Frutti' (1956), with its pumped-dry piano and screams, come close to the wailing excess of Richard himself – the man who suggested, as parents often do, that pop music was a garden of non-heterosexual, drug-taking weirdness. Without him, rock music would be an endless parade of dating and straightness, brutality and wistfulness. Little Richard – gospel and rock, preacher and sinner, king of raunch and camp space queen – contains almost every aspect of pop's ambiguity.

Bridget Riley

born 1931

BRITISH PAINTER

Philosophers sometimes ask whether what the eye sees is what is really there; Riley's pictures play optical games to prove that it does not – deluding the eye with waves, dots, triangles and zigzags that transform themselves before the viewer's gaze. Initially working in black and white, Riley laid lines or undulating waves against each other in such a way that, as one looks, they seem to vibrate. Moving through greys into colour, she exploited the way the after-image of one coloured stripe can affect and modify its neighbour. Spontaneous these pictures are not – the work is done by assistants working from detailed drawings and instructions – but the sense of a world seen through a heat haze is alluring, even moving. By undermining our confidence in the stability of things – secured precisely, her works are not kinetic (objects that really do move) – Riley reminds us that everything is in flux. To mark its difference from Pop Art, the movement Riley began was called Op.

Terry Riley born 1935

AMERICAN COMPOSER

A photograph of Riley typically depicts a man who might have dropped out of a 1960s' photo album – bedraggled, long-haired and sitting cross-legged on the floor before a keyboard. Though normally linked to such minimalist composers as ☛Philip Glass and ☛Steve Reich, Riley is unique in his willingness to accept improvisation. His seminal work, *In C* (1966), consists of a series of repeated sound blocks that each performer has the freedom to adapt, to repeat or even to cease playing – Riley does not even specify what instrument each performer should use. He is is reported as saying that his lush, pulsing music is 'the oriental way of being able to get far out. You can get as far out as you want if you relate to a constant.'

Max Roach born 1925

♦ AMERICAN JAZZ MUSICIAN

✌ An unsurpassed drummer-innovator who, while in his early 20s, probably gave more to bebop than any other player except ☛Charlie Parker himself, Roach is still one of the most open, challenging rhythm-performers in the world. His armoury of understanding about beats, timing, pulse and punctuation has made it possible for him to work with everyone from avant-gardist ☛Anthony Braxton to Brooklyn rapper Fab Five Freddie, without sacrificing his identity or his dignity, but equally without swallowing up each co-performer's art in the vastness of his historical knowledge. His comparative invisibility today stems from a studio blacklisting in the 1960s, when the outspoken intelligence of three successive records (*Freedom Now Suite*, *We Insist!* and *Percussion Bitter Sweet*) came to be seen as a kind of premature anti-racism by the music business. Roach's politics still drive much of his work.

Alain Robbe-Grillet born 1922

☞FRENCH NOVELIST, FILM-MAKER

As literary director of the Éditions de Minuit publishing house, and author of the critical treatise, *For a New Novel* (1963/5), Robbe-Grillet acted as spokesman for the *nouveau roman* movement that brought together Michel Butor, ☛Claude Simon and ☛Nathalie Sarraute. What made him a suitable figurehead was the clarity with which his own novels illustrated the contention that there was an irresolvable gap between external reality and what the mind projected on to it. An agricultural scientist before he turned to writing, Robbe-Grillet juxtaposed the weavings of his characters' imaginations against precise, geometrical descriptions of every tomato, paving stone or gunshot wound they confront. In *Jealousy* (1957/9), the fantasies of a banana planter whose wife has gone on a shopping trip grow in intensity until they are cut short by the return of a patently unentwined

Alain Robbe-Grillet
Photo courtesy of John Calder (Publishers) Ltd

couple. *Project for a Revolution in New York* (1970) gathers images from countless B-movies to construct a picture of the city as a continuous succession of muggings, police sirens, tortures and rapes. But having pared his writing down to a point of complete simplicity, and made his philosophical point, there was nowhere for Robbe-Grillet to go except back into the messy, complex world of the imagination, and away from critical respectability.

Paul Robeson 1898-1976

AMERICAN ACTOR, SINGER, POLITICAL ACTIVIST

A victim of America's post-war anti-Communist fervour, Robeson had been in the 1930s a towering screen presence with a resonant bass voice and personality to match. The son of a runaway slave, he was denied promising careers in football (his own, white, team-mates at college would tackle him) and the law (he was told that 'no sane white man would want a nigger pleading his case'), and demanded civil rights for blacks before politicians were willing to take such things seriously. In response, ☛Joseph McCarthy and ☛J. Edgar Hoover arranged things so that concert halls were barred to him and he could not leave the country for ten years. Although he never joined the Communist Party, he was a fan of the USSR: only on the streets of Moscow, he said, did he feel truly a man. He was thrown out of ☛Truman's office when he challenged the president on America's failure to pass anti-lynching laws to protect blacks. By the time the civil rights movement really got going, Robeson's fervour had been banked down – with electro-shock treatment and sedatives – and his continuing commitment to the Soviet Union ensured that he was kept at arm's length from leaders such as ☛Martin Luther King.

Smokey Robinson

(William Robinson) born 1940

AMERICAN SOUL SINGER

Writer of the best self-pity songs ever – 'Tracks of My Tears' (1965) and 'Tears of a Clown' (1970) – Robinson possesses an impossibly sweet voice. Even more than ☛The Beatles and the teen-fixated ☛Chuck Berry, he was responsible for the idea of the intelligent, witty and moving lyric; ☛Bob Dylan was winding them up when he told a press conference that Robinson was America's greatest living poet, but Robinson is an extraordinary verbal (and musical) articulator of desire. His other contribution to Motown's position in pop is dubious: as a director of the company, he was responsible for the factory-style pop production ethic of melody-as-commerce, and he seems to have done little to introduce his own high standards into Motown's later repertoire.

Nicolas Roeg born 1928

BRITISH FILM DIRECTOR

Roeg is a once-innovative British filmmaker whose hallmark was an unusual approach to time, evidenced by cutting techniques which seemed to misplace key points in the drama. Related to this is a preoccupation with extra-sensory perception, and the deeper realms of the psyche. He began as a cinematographer, and seems to have drawn from his work on ☛Roger Corman's *The Masque of the Red*

Death an interest in that colour as a motif representing danger, blood and sexuality. *Performance* (1970), set in the London of the late 1960s, captured the period's violent curdling of peace and love. Since then, he has made films in a variety of exotic locations – Venice, Marrakech, Australia, The Great Lakes – and pursued a preoccupation with exile and characters who were literally as well as metaphorically out of place. More recently, since the cruel treatment meted out to *Eureka* (1982) by its financiers, Roeg seems to have lost his nerve. The visual style remains striking, but the films promise more than they can deliver.

Richard Rogers born 1933

& ITALIAN-BRITISH ARCHITECT

With only two major buildings to his credit – the Beaubourg (Pompidou) Centre in Paris (on which he collaborated with ☛Renzo Piano) and the Lloyd's Building in London – it is the passion with which Rogers defends architecture from those who want to drag it back to a nostalgic neo-classicism that has kept him in the public eye. Detractors note his inadequacy with a pen (he is dyslexic and a poor draughtsman), but the limitations may give him the space he needs to develop his ideas. A concern to open up the dividing line between the world inside a building and the public realm outside is a recurring preoccupation. Deploying new technologies (his style has been dubbed 'hi-tech') to create fresh forms, he 'reveals' the structures of his buildings – a great steel-tube frame, for example, encloses the glass exterior of the Beaubourg Centre, and the exposed lifts at Lloyd's, like the escalator ducts in Paris, emphasize that these are places used by people. He is also a planner, looking for ways to reclaim the public spaces in large cities from the intrusive motor car: his plan for an extension to London's National Gallery would have linked Trafalgar Square, currently a 'dead' area only occupied by tourists feeding pigeons and occasional protesters, with Leicester Square – in a forlorn attempt to make London as friendly to pedestrians as Rome or Paris.

The Rolling Stones formed 1963

Mick Jagger born 1943
Brian Jones 1942-69
Keith Richard born 1943
Bill Wyman (Bill Perks) born 1936
Ian Stewart 1938-85
Charlie Watts born 1941

$ BRITISH ROCK GROUP

'☛The Beatles,' said ☛Tom Wolfe, '"want to hold your hand", the Stones want to burn your town'. The distance between the two groups was never so extreme, but The Stones deliberately pumped up the idea of rock music as threat. After starting out as another blues-obsessed pub group, they began to introduce demonstrative sexuality into their records and performances, then went on to spend the 1960s in various kinds of drugs-and-sex debauchery through court cases, trans-sexual promo films and increasingly exaggerated versions of Mick Jagger as a penile Satan. Their concert at Altamont in California, at which a young black was murdered by Hell's Angels, officially sealed the decade. The Stones went on to represent the bloated, drugged sexuality of 1970s' rock, veering from genuinely frightening records such as *Exile on Main Street* (1972) to concert appearances in which a ludicrously effeminate Jagger rode a giant dildo. The end of that decade saw them epitomize the naffness of a bored music: New York fashion discos, meeting Princess Margaret, one LP every three years and musical self-parody (although 'Miss You' is one of the funniest disco songs ever). Their relevance to the 1980s and 1990s seems fairly minimal, but The Rolling Stones have been a barometer of pop trends, the most imaginative interpreters of black music (but for them, the 1960s would have been filled with anaemic British blues guitarists), and a cumbersome dinosaur with the occasional ability to revitalize itself. If one group had to represent the joy and horror of 'rock', they would be it.

Sonny Rollins born 1930

AMERICAN JAZZ SAXOPHONIST

Rollins is probably the greatest straight-ahead soloist in jazz. Never truly an innovator, or any kind of jazz theoretician, he has survived periods when importance tended to be associated with one or the other (or both), into an era when he can be fêted as much for his old-fashioned solid individualism as for his exemplification of the great tradition. Like ☛Coltrane, Rollins has made performance the absolute centre of his music-world, and has garnered a lifetime's respect for the results, starting with the aptly named *Saxophone Colossus* (1957). However, unlike Coltrane, Rollins' study of the possibilities of an instrument have never driven him towards the outer limits of musical quest. As a result, he is more accessible and less daring – comparisons which hardly diminish his mastery of the sax.

George A. Romero born 1939

AMERICAN FILM DIRECTOR

The zombie trilogy that Romero launched in 1968 with *Night of the Living Dead* no longer seems particularly startling; gore and 'body horror' having been absorbed into the film mainstream. It is the second and third in the series (*Dawn of the Dead,* 1971; *Day of the Dead*, 1985) that get the most airing – they are in colour, more obviously funny-scary, with standardized production values, and only people who never go to the movies would be alarmed that they might corrupt the kids. *Night of the Living Dead* is another matter. Arriving when it did, before Splatter had formed into a genre, it melds the watch-the-skies McCarthyism of the 1950s invaders-genre with the low-key *vérité* shock of 1960s' radical docudrama. The undifferentiated risen mass has not yet been given its cheerful fun-face, and the end of the film is strikingly ambivalent: the black hero is casually shot by his redneck rescuers. The film is frightening in a way that owes something to low-budget-constraints-turned-virtues, but more to its amorphous morality. It killed off the market for vampire movies; decadent blood-sucking aristocrats simply were not as frightening – or as pertinent – as mumbling mobs. The dead, after all, are the only real silent majority.

Oscar Romero 1939-80

➻SALVADORAN RELIGIOUS LEADER

A turbulent archbishop, Romero was guaranteed instant martyr status (although the Pope ostentatiously refused to bestow the official variety) when one of the most brutal regimes in Central America had him shot in a hospital chapel, and then claimed the deed as the work of left-wing guerrillas seeking to provoke an uprising. Romero opposed violence in a country where murder had become government policy, and although neither a supporter of El Salvador's guerrilla resistance nor a blanket advocate of 'liberation' theology, he interpreted the generalized brutality as 'the product of an unjust situation in which the majority of men and women and, above all, the children in our country find themselves deprived of the necessities of life'. The more vocal he became in speaking out against injustice (he used to read out the names of the 'disappeared' during his radio sermons), the more he provided a focus for the hopes of the poor and desperate. A few days before his own assassination, trade unionists on the run from death squads were killed on the steps of his cathedral.

Richard Rorty born 1931

AMERICAN PHILOSOPHER

Through forging links with the various sceptical philosophies expounded by such Continental thinkers as Nietzsche, Heidegger, ☛Wittgenstein and ☛Derrida, Rorty has attempted to take further the tradition of American pragmatism which William James and John Dewey had established. Taking shots at many species of naïve realism – which he finds not only in the surface conversation of our society, but embedded in most of the recent intellectual heritage – means, for Rorty, isolating and attempting to defuse those studies of truth that assume it to be 'something out there' that we can discover or reach by naming it. Pragmatists tend to insist that ideas of knowledge be limited to those of instruments for action; they are also deeply suspicious of elaborate metaphysical theories, eternal Platonic forms and the like. Rorty makes an intriguing case for the contingency of everything significant (self, language, community) and, further, the importance of our recognizing the same and acting on it: truth is something we make. Widely (and deeply) read, with an interest in the play of ideas at least as strong as his stated positions on the meaning and purposes of truth, Rorty is also – thanks to an exemplary clarity of exposition that does not defer to some of his more wayward models – becoming a valued modern commentator on the history of philosophy.

Eleanor Rosch

COGNITIVE PSYCHOLOGIST

The questions that interest Rosch concern the ways in which we categorize things. What is it that defines a chair? Is it the number of legs, the shape or the materials it is made of? Is there an archetypical chair in our minds to which we compare all other chairs? Earlier theorists produced two models, either ideas of archetypical objects or checklists of conditions that have to be met to qualify for the title of 'chair'. Rosch thinks differently. We categorize objects according to their functional properties – what we can do with them. 'Sit-on-able-ness' is more often a property of sofas than cats, though both normally have four legs supporting a fairly horizontal surface. Most objects are also situated in a hierarchy of classifications. Cats are also pets, mammals and animals. Tables are also furniture and so on. In large numbers of experiments in different cultures, Rosch has found that classification follows similar lines no matter where it occurs. Like most good ideas, all this sounds blindingly simple, but it is really quite different from the Platonic or empiricist models of mind that have gone before. And like all trendy varieties of cognitive psychology, it can claim the back-up of brain science: after certain types of brain injuries, some patients display problems with thinking and talking about objects that are used in a similar way even though they do not look very similar.

Ethel Rosenberg
(née Greenglass) 1915-53
Julius Rosenberg 1918-53

AMERICAN (ALLEGED) SPIES

Anti-Americanism developed worldwide when the gentle-seeming Rosenbergs, a dentist and his wife, were sent to the electric chair – the first US citizens to be executed for espionage committed in peacetime. Heightening the emotional pitch was the fact that a US court had never before ordered the executions of both husband and wife, and the Rosenbergs left two children to face the horrible emotional consequences. It was claimed that they had formed part of a complicated spy network, and were personally responsible for relaying secrets from the atomic bomb project in Los Alamos to the Soviets. The Rosenbergs consistently maintained their innocence even while President Eisenhower thundered about the 'millions of dead whose deaths may be directly attributable to what these spies have done'. Tried in 1951, when anti-Soviet feeling was running high, they were convicted on circumstantial evidence. Papers subsequently released suggest that, while Julius was involved in a minor capacity, Ethel had no part in it – and was indicted purely as a lever to make her husband crack. The ploy failed, and while other conspirators received lengthy gaol sentences, the Rosenbergs were executed. One lawyer remarked at the time that the executions showed that the US was 'living under the heel of a military dictator garbed in civilian attire'.

Harold Rosenberg 1906-78

AMERICAN ART CRITIC

Clement Greenberg and Harold Rosenberg together popularized the term abstract expressionism, but the sourness of the relationship between these two aesthetic arbiters of the 1950s can be seen in the title of a Rosenberg essay – 'How Art Writing Earns Its Bad Name'. While Rosenberg championed the action painting of De Kooning and Pollock, he rarely wrote about individual artists – being more concerned with exploring the raw and brutal qualities of the action itself. He argued that artists defined their unique identity through the eruption of gesture upon gesture – the unwilled actions guiding the painter into some sort of 'self-transformation'. Others, of course, saw things differently. Critics dubbed Rosenberg 'silly' and expressed concern that he had led artists to an art 'outside of art'. Even those he wrote about had some reservations about his conception of what they were doing, seeing Rosenberg as a critic obsessed with foreplay, and seemingly indifferent to the climax of the act itself – the canvas.

Francesco Rosi born 1922

ITALIAN FILM DIRECTOR

Rosi's recent career is a case history for what has gone wrong with Italian cinema in the 1980s. His early films were caustic inquiries into human doubt and deceit: *Lucky Luciano* (1974) and *Illustrious Corpses* (1976), both set in Sicily, deal with the conflict between Mafioso morality and the civil society with which it co-exists. But Rosi's adaptation of Carlo Levi's *Christ Stopped at Eboli* (1979) marked a turning point in his film-making. The politics and humanity of the original, which tells of a cultured anti-Fascist doctor's visit to barren Calabria, is subverted with glorious photography. This trend away from political awareness has continued in Rosi's more recent films, particularly his picturesque but vacuous treatment of ☛García Márquez's *Chronicle of a Death Foretold* (1987). Rosi has become yet another director dealing only in wishy-washy tales of human emotion, working on ever bigger international co-productions with ever more muddled multi-lingual casts.

Roberto Rossellini 1906-77

ITALIAN FILM DIRECTOR

Tagging Rossellini the founder of cinematic neo-realism obscures his achievement as much as the Hollywood brouhaha that resulted when ☛Ingrid Bergman opted, adulterously, for his Italian charm. *Rome, Open City* (1945), the film credited with reintroducing reality to post-war Italian cinema, is an angry, jagged, sometimes melodramatic chronicle, wrenched from lived experience, of the German occupation and its effect on the psyches of those who endured it (filming was begun when the occupying troops had barely left the city). Bergman's arrival into his life drew Rossellini to stories about the difficulties of human relationships, although he was always as interested in the backdrop as the individual. *Stromboli* (1949), in which an East European refugee struggles to reach an understanding with the uneducated fisherman she has married, and *Voyage to Italy* (1953), which follows the dismantling and reassembly of an English couple's marriage, deploy natural phenomena – the slaughter of tunafish off Stromboli, a visit to the catacombs of Naples – as guides to the characters' inner states. Each film is a journey through shifting emotions towards a climax reasserting the need for solidarity between unhappy humans. In later years, Rossellini made a series of television films on crucial epochs in human history – *The Rise to Power of Louis XIV* (1966), *Augustine of Hippo* and *Blaise Pascal* (both 1972) – and set himself against a cinema that 'only allows for small variations within a basically standardized product'. A continuing source of critical controversy, his films show the way to complexity through simplicity – a contrast to much contemporary work, whose bombast too often leads to cold banality.

Walt Rostow born 1916

AMERICAN ECONOMIC HISTORIAN, POLITICAL ADVISER

Rostow became policy adviser to the US State Department in the early 1960s after his phrases, 'the new frontier' and 'Let's get this country moving again' had been adopted as banner slogans for ☛John F. Kennedy's election campaign. Getting countries moving again was Rostow's theme as an economic historian, as he argued in *The Stages of Economic Growth: A Non-Communist Manifesto* (1960) that societies pass through five economic stages: a 'traditional' stage; preconditions for take-off; take-off as growth becomes normal; a drive to 'maturity'; and 'maturity' itself, reached through high mass consumption. It was in the third stage, with its traumatic changes, that societies were susceptible to Communism, whose adoption ruled out any further development. This formulation seemed to justify the US taking any sort of action to repress the Commies – it was for their own good. As a member of Kennedy's staff, Rostow advocated escalation of the Vietnam War – blocking the Ho Chi Minh Trail, introducing ground troops in the South and bombing the North. In 1966, he supported a plan to bomb the petroleum installations near Hanoi and Haiphong and, in the following year, advocated a US invasion of Laos. After his time in office, he returned to the teaching of economic history, but has never written about the sixth, throw-back stage reached by Vietnam, as it was bombed (in the graphic words of General Curtis LeMay) 'back into the Stone Age'.

Theodor Roszack 1907-81

☆ AMERICAN PUBLISHER, CULTURAL COMMENTATOR

Roszack's editorship of the sober but seminal *Peace News* is now overshadowed by the underground publications it anticipated. He is remembered best for his of-its-time document-polemic, *The Making of a Counterculture* (1969), which laid out his intoxicated vision of the post-pop future: he expected the underground (being anti-technological, anti-materialist, dissident, pleasure-loving, unrepressed, individualist and, because of all these things, more moral than establishment culture) to form the basis for society to come. It would do this by organizing, networking, agitating cheerfully and seceding, in every possible way, from the overground – with its false and normative sense of self, its bogus scientific claims and its overall obvious sickness. While young Americans were still dying in Vietnam, young people poured their energy into the kinds of resistance and refusal he had hoped for – but by the time the war ended, there were enough get-away-from-it-all entrepreneurs with New Age solutions (☛Sun Myung Moon, ☛Bhagwan Rajneesh, ☛Jim Jones) to make dropping out a decidedly perilous action. The addled titles of Roszack's subsequent books tell a sad story: *Unfinished Animal: The Aquarian Frontier and the Evolution of Consciousness* (1976) and *Person/Planet: The Creative Disintegration of Industrial Society* (1979). Networking subculture still exists in many important forms in the US – from ultra-conservative political direct-mailing to the punk-rock fanzine circuit – but Roszack's own optimistic and free-form brand of counterculture, far from inaugurating a new politics, went on to foster apolitical lifestyles, escapism and self-absorbed, quasi-spiritual eco-mysticism.

Philip Roth born 1933

▲ AMERICAN NOVELIST

Jack off, feel guilty, write books to feel better. Become successful, feel very guilty, sleep with students to feel better. Thus Roth's four Zuckerman novels (1974, 1979, 1981, 1983). He is not the only author whose plots condense so easily, but the days are long gone when narratives about writers which contrast private fantasy and public conformism were the bold future of literature. *Portnoy's Complaint* (1969), in the form of a patient's confessional diatribes to his analyst, deals with masturbation, abortion and modern (read 'dated') sexual manners.

It is acerbic and uncompromising, and garnered much shocked attention in its day, but it could only be hailed as radical by those who sought to avoid the more pressing aspects of sexual and racial dissidence beginning to surface in 1960s' literature. Drawing on his early life, including periods at various universities, Roth's work rarely pushes beyond the thought that God is cruellest in middle-class Jewish New York (or Chicago or wherever). However, the possibility of cultural identification with the hero-as-*schlemiel* and the hero-as-*nebbish* has been one of the most valuable gifts of American urban Jewish culture, and Roth's wise-cracking sensitivity has been important in broadcasting this.

Mark Rothko 1903-70

✚ RUSSIAN-AMERICAN ARTIST

† Rothko's early work had strong links with surrealism, but by 1949, the totemic objects which characterized those paintings had given way to the formula he was to use until his death: a large rectangle with one large and one small rectangle within it. The method of painting that he used – many light films of colour laid on top of each other – gives the pictures an ethereal and contemplative air. He worked with large canvases, saying 'To paint a small picture is to place yourself outside your experience, to look upon an experience with a reducing glass. However you paint the larger picture, you are in it.' His work culminated in a series of triptychs for a non-denominational chapel attached to Rice University in Houston, each composed almost solely of one colour – black, dark red or purple. Because of antagonism between Rothko's daughter Kate and the executors of his will, whom she accused of a conflict of interest, it took over nine years, and £1.6 million in legal fees, to settle his estate, comprising some 798 paintings.

Salman Rushdie born 1947

ANGLO-PAKISTANI NOVELIST

Rushdie's career illustrates that most exacting of punk assumptions: he who responds angrily to one's insults proves himself only too worthy of them. *Midnight's Children* (1981) and *Shame* (1983) were triumphs of outraged political venom and provoked more than satisfactory responses – bans in India and Pakistan – but they were as nothing alongside *The Satanic Verses* (1988) – with its fabulist philosophies and Bombay-movie maybe-history of the Koran – which had a devastating effect on an Islamic world in turmoil, and led the ☛Ayatollah Khomeini to sentence the author to death from Tehran. Rushdie became an author-in-hiding, only occasionally participating in the debates about censorship, racism, blasphemy and many other issues that the Ayatollah's *fatwa* had provoked. His books crackle with multi-cultural friction, and ask how much we need to know before we can even agree to differ, and their overloaded Hindu/Muslim/Western pop-mandarin idiolect (a jagged Anglo-Asian version of magic realism) throws up a mocking challenge to moral and religious grandstanders, professional purists and last-ditch fundamentalists everywhere. The common British response – 'Call me stupid, but I find his books unreadable' – is as pitifully narrow as was the Ayatollah's.

Joanna Russ born 1937

AMERICAN WRITER

The most challenging and disruptive of the radical feminist science-fiction writers who emerged in the 1970s, Russ has came up through the New Wave to challenge and disturb the casual sexism of her male peers with tight, shocking tales of active female characters and gender-transference. *The Female Man* (1975) was her most nakedly political work – strikingly innovative in structure and developing a peculiarly disturbing theme – but she finds strong ways to subvert cliché even in her lesser sword-and-sorcery stories. The wave of feminist-utopian fiction now seems to have lost much of its momentum, declining into a slackly separatist sentimentality, so that the Cyberpunkers were unaware of how much they were working through its influence. However, ☛William Gibson's *Molly Million* is, in fact, a direct descendant of Russ's *The Adventures of Alyx* (1983).

Bertrand Russell 1872-1970

BRITISH PHILOSOPHER, POLITICAL ACTIVIST

Russell's status as Britain's greatest living (though by then non-practising) philosopher gave credibility to the Campaign for Nuclear Disarmament (CND) which he helped launch in 1958, but his Committee of 100, a schism from the rest of the movement, publicized the cause of civil disobedience more than nuclear disarmament. Like many abstract thinkers involved in politics, Russell came up with unsound ideas – arguing shortly after WW2 that bombs could be used to establish a world of peace and justice under one government, and building his campaign against US intervention in Vietnam around a naïve anti-Americanism. However, his contribution to the anti-nuclear case was considerable. While American hawks were casually proposing Hiroshima-style solutions to all international problems, Russell argued that nuclear weapons had not only changed the nature of war, but made it useless as an instrument of policy. If nuclear weapons were retained, he said, they would inevitably be used – through mistake, panic or a brinksmanship gone out of control. Unilateral action was the only way to cut through the political obstacles to disarmament. Some of his theses have, fortunately, yet to be proved.

Ken Russell born 1927

BRITISH FILM DIRECTOR

Working in television from 1962 to 1968, Russell made a series of documentary biographies about composers that were characterized by a restraint completely lacking when he moved into cinema. Hollywood's reverential approach to the biopic was swept aside to make room for a unique species of pomp-rock opera. Silver-haired, raucous and porcine, Russell is cinema's de Sade; his capriciously baroque movie romps left critics aghast. He is committed to cinema as a visual medium: when you learn he dismisses the bulk of 1980s' Brit-film as 'radio with pictures', you may become perversely fond of him. But his iconoclasm is now very self-derivative and his primitive film technique no match for his visual imagination. Pop video, which often occupies similar territory, has helped make a lot of his work look much worse than it once did. His stupidest film, which many think his best, is *Women in Love* (1969), an attempt-

Ken Russell

ed 'interpretation' of the D. H. Lawrence novel. His funniest, and probably actually his best, is the goofily stunning trip-thriller *Altered States* (1980).

Gilbert Ryle 1900-76

BRITISH PHILOSOPHER

Ryle believed that clarifying the content of concepts bandied about in debate would resolve most of the problems of philosophy – a common view in the universities after WW2, when many wanted to rein in philosophers from their wilder flights of metaphysicial fantasy. On this basis, Ryle did advance some provocative ideas, most notably with his 1949 book, *The Concept of Mind*, in which he argued that it was a sign of sloppy thinking (a 'category mistake' in his own jargon) to present mind and body as fundamentally distinct entities. What is presented as talk about the mind should be understood rather as an account of what people did, or how they behaved. There is no 'ghost in the machine', as Ryle put it. Everything about a person can, in principle, be discovered by others. This limited view of human beings, seemingly excluding any interior angst or joy that is not visible as behaviour, may have been appropriate to its times, but now seems like playing safe.

S

Saatchi and Saatchi formed 1970

Maurice Saatchi born 1943

Charles Saatchi born 1946

IRAQI-BRITISH ADVERTISING EXECUTIVES

With Maurice providing the business brains and Charles the creative acumen, Saatchi and Saatchi started out in 1970 with the declared aim of offering a 'new kind of advertising'. The brothers acquired their reputation by taking on controversial, government-sponsored contracts. They kicked off an anti-smoking campaign with a commercial that intercut lemmings on their way over a cliff edge and commuters puffing cigarettes as they walked across Waterloo Bridge, and followed up with the pregnant man (to promote family planning) and the first ad, for British Airways, to be launched simultaneously around the world. They also promoted the British Conservative Party during the 1979 general election (and two subsequent campaigns) with a 'Labour Isn't Working' poster that showed long queues of the unemployed snaking into the distance; this gave credence to the idea that oppositions do not win elections, the government of the day simply loses them (rising unemployment was soon to become a thorn in the Conservative Party's own side). Saatchi and Saatchi became for a while the biggest advertising group in the world, while also expanding into other business service areas. They bought companies on both sides of the Atlantic, launched a (disastrous) attempt to become the world's number one management consultant and cheekily inquired, in 1987, whether they could put in an offer for the Midland Bank. Meanwhile, the reclusive Charles and his then-wife Doris went shopping in the art world – building the reputation of ☛Julian Schnabel and many others of dubious talent by bulk purchase of their work. The Saatchis epitomized the go-getting approach that the Tories advocated, and like other businesses which had been caught up in the ☛Thatcher boom, they endured corporate retrenchment at the end of the 1980s. Evaporating profits forced the brothers to relinquish their executive responsibility for the company, leading some to conclude that the ad men had become as smug and complacent as those they had once usurped.

Anwar Sadat 1918-81

EGYPTIAN POLITICAL LEADER

An Egyptian army officer – classmate of ☛Nasser – Sadat was tried and gaoled by the British after WW2 for his role in a conspiracy to kill a pro-British official; during the war, he had been court-martialled for pro-Nazi plotting. He was party to another plot to overthrow King Farouk and, as a result, became Nasser's vice president in the 1960s. President from the death of Nasser in 1970, he expelled Soviet advisers, brought in technocrats, appointed himself military governor, issued a war budget and launched an attack on Israel in 1973. Convincing himself and his people that brief moments of success in the war added up to a face-saving military victory, he was now satisfied that it was timely to seek a lasting peace with the Israelis. This – the Camp David accord – was secured under the auspices of President Carter and ☛Henry Kissinger, following Sadat's dramatic trip to address the Israeli parliament. Egypt retained Sinai, but became isolated from the rest of the Arab world: Sadat was shot by an Islamic extremist while reviewing an army parade.

Carl Sagan born 1934

❞ AMERICAN ASTRONOMER

Best known as the man in the polo-neck sweater who led television viewers on a guided tour of the universe, Sagan is no mere presenter: he has received more medals than a military dictator; he has won a Pulitzer prize for his book on the evolution on the human mind; he is an expert on the seasonal changes of Venus and Mars; and he has even received an award 'for distinguished contributions to the welfare of mankind'. Sagan was also largely responsible for the message about ourselves being carried by the *Voyager* probe out of the solar system on its way to other stars and, just possibly, other civilizations, and he came up with the idea of 'terraforming' nearby arid planets by introducing algae into the upper atmosphere to absorb carbon dioxide, thus producing oxygen and organic materials. There are many scientists with expertise beyond their own special field, but few have Sagan's talents for communication. A cynic might say that the role he performs is one of public relations for the orthodox scientific community. When he denounces various pseudo-sciences or the comet theories of ☛Velikovsky; he does so with the authority of scientific orthodoxy. He has a romantic view of science, and his essays on famous scientists make good reading but sound increasingly old fashioned and inflexible in a world beset by doubts about the bounty of science's more wonderful creations, such as genetic engineering, nuclear power, computers and toxic waste.

Edward Said born 1935

✌ PALESTINIAN-AMERICAN LITERARY THEORIST

Born in Jerusalem, Said is one of the most articulate advocates of Palestinian nationalism outside Israel. Living in the US since 1950, he has spent much of his academic career trying to shore up Arabic and Middle Eastern cultures against the pressures of dominant Western attitudes. In his most important book, *Orientalism* (1978), he argues that, for two centuries, Islamic culture has been systematically distorted or misrepresented by explorers and commentators – who have presented prejudice and the complex ideological agendas of imperialism in the guise of objective academic expertise. *The Question of Palestine* (1979) and *Covering Islam* (1981) both deal with modern-day problems in the way the Middle East is discussed. As a highly engaged post-structuralist critic, Said clearly sees his role as one of demystification – picking up on forms of language, clichés of commentary and buried subtexts, then showing where they come from and how they operate. He has also been a vigilant critic of the canonization of 'great literature' in university courses, and the easy way that non-Western works get pushed off into branches of anthroplogy. An expert on Arabic literature, he also has a valuable familiarity with the philosophies and critiques of ☛Derrida, ☛Foucault, ☛Bloom and ☛Barthes, which he dealt with in *The World, the Text and the Critic* (1983).

Yves Saint Laurent born 1936

ALGERIAN-FRENCH DESIGNER

The 'King of Couture', having arrived in Paris from Algeria at the age of 16, had become chief designer at the house of Dior by the age of 21 and started his own house in 1962, before moving quickly to his current status as a living legend. He has had his work displayed in New York's Metropolitan Museum of Art, but he is camera-shy and known for his sensitivity to criticism; after a bitter response to his 1971 collection, he said he would no longer design couture. He displayed his admiration for Van Gogh by having sunflowers embroidered (using pearl beads of 60 different colours) on just one outfit.

Andrei Sakharov 1921-89

SOVIET PHYSICIST, POLITICIAN

His career as a 'dissident' having somewhat eclipsed his brilliant earlier work as a physicist, it is important not to forget that Sakharov, a member of the team which developed the Soviet hydrogen bomb, was a 'Hero of Socialist Labour' before he began to trouble the authorities. His work in the 1960s included proposals concerning necessary conditions in initial states of the universe that answered questions about observable predominance of matter over anti-matter. The requirements – which included the necessary existence of a process that produces baryons out of non-baryons – were calculated from purely theoretical positions, and by the time experimental confirmation caught up with him in the mid-1980s, he had already been locked in battle with the Soviet authorities for well over a decade. Through his work on nuclear weapons, he became aware of the unscrupulous use that Soviet leaders were making of the formidable technologies at their disposal, and began to argue that, only through the government becoming accountable to a people allowed to express itself freely, would dangerous abuses of power be avoided. Exiled to a remote part of the Soviet Union with his wife Yelena and, until shortly before his death, subject to constant harassment by the security services, he became a supporter and critical adviser to ☛Gorbachev in his drive for political reform. In 1989, he was appointed to the Supreme Soviet, where he immediately outraged almost everyone by denouncing the war in Afghanistan and calling for an end to Communist one-party rule.

Abdus Salam *see* Glashow, Sheldon Lee

J(erome) D(avid) Salinger born 1919

AMERICAN NOVELIST

It is hard to imagine one of today's teenagers reading *The Catcher in the Rye* (1951) and not feeling that it is set in the Dark Ages. But then 40 years is a long time, and Salinger's untarnished reputation relies heavily on the uncritical first impressions of adolescents who think they are his hero, Holden Caulfield – alienated, put-upon, vaguely disgusted. His style, elegant and economic, has been overtaken by events. Salinger left the world behind to pursue Zen enlightenment, and the only things he has done to allow us to revise our opinions are to sue a biographer so that he could not use information derived from private letters, and be tricked into having a photograph taken of himself, which showed him to be a scared little old man, arm thrown up as if to ward off a blow.

David Salle born 1952

✎ AMERICAN ARTIST

A Californian artist who became one of the biggest and most bankable names in the New York art world of the 1980s, Salle often represents naked women as objects – flat, coldly studied figures. These basic images are then painted over or juxtaposed with found images, thereby suggesting some kind of new reading to the images and drawing out metaphorical levels that previously lay dormant. One is constantly disconcerted by the rather poor execution of the canvases and Salle's apparent wish to become an illustrator for *Playboy* with his tiresome depictions of the female form, but the work is only pornographic in the sense that it is so dull. Salle belongs with other artists of his generation such as Eric Fischl, Robert Longo and ☛Julian Schnabel, whose preoccupation with other creative forms – the rock song, the film, the novel – has led them towards empty formalism.

Paul Samuelson born 1915

♦ AMERICAN ECONOMIST

❍ A titan amongst contemporary economists, Samuelson has been influential in almost every branch of the subject and has written an influential basic textbook. He developed the use of mathematics as a framework for expounding economic theory, and also made crucial contributions to the analysis of government monetary and fiscal policy, putting forward a theory that an increase in government spending, matched by a corresponding increase in taxes, will generate an identical increase in national income under some circumstances. He radically simplified the analysis of consumer demand by freeing it from theories that entailed consumers making assessments of how useful goods were to them. His thesis is that demand emerges from the known spending patterns of consumers in different price-income situations, which assumes that they act rationally, not erratically – their choices do not contradict each other. Economists do not neeed to postulate abstract models for the value set by individuals on items. Philosophically, Samuelson's approach lines up with behaviourism in psychology: there is no 'ghost-in-the-machine'; demand is what it is.

Thomas Sargent born 1943

AMERICAN ECONOMIST

Sargent is a black US economist who espouses market-led solutions to the problems of urban poverty, especially black ghettos. He argues that vast welfare programmes – such as ☛President Johnson's 'Great Society' formula – only throw money at problems and create a 'dependency culture'. The answer, instead, is to encourage slum-dwellers to direct native energy, skill and wit towards achieving upward mobility. 'Self-help' has a big appeal to Americans. One spin-off is that slum-dwellers who start firms will employ other slum-dwellers, who can build up skills and savings through paid work. A riposte to Sargent is that, even with 'self-help', the state should be an 'enabler' and there should always be a safety net: the ill, the elderly, the house-bound and, often, the unemployed cannot work themselves out and up; they have just to survive. In most industrial societies with welfare systems, the big money goes on inescapable, universal benefits – not, say, housing programmes or special payments, where Sargent, arguably, has a case. It might be possible to evolve forms of welfare, given to citizens as of right, which, when matched with incentives, will not entail dependency as a state of mind and will encourage self-reliance. Sargent's ideas correspond to trends in development economics, which now stress Third World aid to help people work out their own means of survival through capital investment, not as income-streams.

Nathalie Sarraute born 1900

FRENCH NOVELIST

Tropismes (1939), the title of Sarraute's first book and a reference to the involuntary movements made by organisms responding to external stimuli, could refer to all her writing. She probes the area where waves of past hurt and experience interact and combine to become actions, whose origins elude the categories of everyday language. Placing her under the umbrella of the *nouveau roman* or calling her *Portrait of a Man Unknown* (1948) an 'anti-novel' (☛Sartre's term), misleadingly suggests that she aimed for a clean break with literary tradition. But her arguments were with Balzac, not Proust or Dostoyevsky, whose explorations of the turbulent unconscious she has pursued in her almost plotless fiction. She writes precise, poetic prose, but is much less cool than some accounts suggest. She propagandized through the 1950s for a literature that would reflect the changes in our understanding of consciousness, discarding old ideas about stable and consistent characters. She takes from science, not its method, but the metaphors it offers to explain strange rumblings of the psyche that could not otherwise be made intelligible. And she showed in *The Planetarium* (1959) – an account of the the efforts made by an ambitious young intellectual to deprive his aunt of the apartment he covets – that her style could be turned to comic and satiric effect.

Jean-Paul Sartre 1905-80

FRENCH PHILOSOPHER, NOVELIST, PLAYWRIGHT, POLITICAL ACTIVIST

Sartre's early works – *Nausea* (1938/48), *The Roads to Freedom* trilogy (1945-49) and the metaphysical treatise *Being and Nothingness* (1943/56) – offer the excitement of a philosophical system grounded in the torment of human experience. But later, less achieved writing makes it clear that the urge to explain every facet of human life must dissolve under its own impossibility. If Sartre believed in the possibility of combining sociology, philosophy and psychoanalysis into a total account of experience, then the intellectual contortions that resulted were simply silly. But assuming he realized that the work could never be finished, but was worth trying anyway, then there is something admirable in the energy he put into writings that ranged from political journalism and drama to psycho-biography and materialist analysis, and the bravado with which he changed his mind – flinging himself into political activism with seeming insouciance about the extent to which he was turning himself into a figure of fun. The existentialist philosophy with which he made his name after WW2 traced human suffering to people's doomed attempts to find some rational grounds for existence, and proposed the recognition of this unresolvable contradiction as the key to a new, never written, moral philosophy. As human beings, he argued, we are totally free. Nothing, but the way in which we circumscribe ourselves, prevents us from doing *anything*. Elements of this approach continue in later writings, but Sartre's realization of the extent to which personal freedom is qualified by the pressures of living in an exploitative society, and his embrace of Marxism, led him increasingly further away from his early individualism and, many feel, from common sense.

Gerald Scarfe born 1936

BRITISH CARTOONIST

The high estimation Scarfe has of himself is deserved, but he has poor judgement about who to work with and what to work on. His violent deformations of famous faces are astonishing revisions of shape, making over-familiar mugs into flow charts so alien and distorted that it is amazing they can be recognized at all. They connect up with primal evils – mired venality, hypocrisy, moral rot and mania – and scared responsible editors witless. Apart from ☛Ballard's psychosexual celeb-dissections, no one else had achieved analysis so palpably hurtful. How then could such a fiercely exacting critic of character and banal evasion allow himself to become involved in such a meagre and self-pitying exercise as Alan Parker's film, *Pink Floyd: The Wall* (1982)? Scarfe's energy took him beyond the quality newspaper world in which he came to prominence, but it turned out there was nowhere else to go except rock opera.

Leonard Schapiro 1908-83

BRITISH SOVIETOLOGIST

Schapiro was an important influence on the 'totalitarian' school of post-war Soviet studies, which played a vital part in forming Western policies towards the USSR. Trained as a lawyer in Britain, he argued that the central role of the Communist Party of the Soviet Union, with its dictatorship of power and its alienation from legal norms, is the base fact of post-1917 Soviet history. The USSR after ☛Khrushchev is predominantly a result of, and should in the end be explained by, the Bolsheviks' ideology and the way in which they seized power. A longer-term nineteenth-century Russian preference for organic ties (based on love and loyalty) ove[r] liberal, legal links between state and subject accounts for easy Communis[t] control. Schapiro's heroes wer[e] Turgenev and the late-Tsarist 'liberal conservatives', who had offered a[n] alternative to despotism by left o[r] right. Revisionists argue instead tha[t] the USSR is the scene of competin[g] interest groups, ultimately equiva[-] lent to the Western model. Schapir[o] often showed an appealing range o[f] responses to key Soviet figures, suc[h]

Natalie Sarraute
Photo courtesy of John Calder (Publishers) Ltd

as Lenin and Bukharin, at odds with his reputation as a one-track 'determinist'.

Dore Schary 1905-80

AMERICAN FILM PRODUCER

Soft-spoken and self-effacing, Dore Schary was to earn his place in cinema history as the man who took on legendary studio tyrant Louis B. Mayer – and won. He was also one of the few producers to survive the ☛McCarthy witchhunts with his integrity intact. He joined MGM as a screenwriter in 1937 and went on to turn out a series of low-budget popular movies dealing with all the liberal causes that Mayer hated. Moving to RKO in order to secure more freedom and less Louis, Schary was responsible for *Crossfire* (1947), the first film about anti-Semitism to come out of an industry dominated by Jews. In 1948 Schary was invited back to MGM as head of production, a job that guaranteed daily confrontation with his would-be nemesis. Although he could not stop ☛John Huston's *The Red Badge of Courage* (1951) from being re-cut, and nearly lost his job over the same director's 1950 film, *The Asphalt Jungle*, (described by Mayer as 'a movie I wouldn't cross the room to see'), the success of the latter, along with *Singin' in the Rain* (1952), *An American in Paris* (1951), *Julius Caesar* (1953), *Seven Brides for Seven Brothers* (1954) and *Bad Day at Black Rock* (1954), secured his position. When the final conflict between the two men took place, over *Battleground* (1959), Mayer pulled out all the stops to get the production halted, but the New York financiers sided with Schary and his record of profits plus artistic respectability. By 1956 Mayer was a retreating memory and Schary had ushered in a golden age of independent film-making in a world over which the moguls no longer held sway.

Jonathan Schell born 1943

▲AMERICAN WRITER

A journalist on *The New Yorker*, and author of many of its anonymous columns attacking the Vietnam War and the conduct of government since the 1960s, Schell wrote a major best-seller, *The Fate of the Earth*, in 1982. In this, he argues, in apocalyptic terms, that the risk of nuclear war, if realized, poses a series of strikingly novel threats to the earth's ecological balance – from nuclear winter and attacks on the ozone layer to the vanishing of the planet. The title of his first chapter – 'A Republic of Insects and Grass' – describes the humanity-free post-nuclear world he envisages. Writing in a highly emotive way, he uses a barrage of scientific data, which, however, is not classified on any analytically serious basis. His view is that we have completely to rethink global values and institutions to deal with the danger. Others have posed an alternative to his prescription: analyse the scope and scale of nuclear weapons in the world, assess the risks and do what can be done to minimize the risk of war. But the people with the power to effect changes may be too far mired in current practice to be responsive to such pragmatism, and nightmare visions such as Schell's draw attention to the horrible consequences of failure.

Julian Schnabel born 1951

✎AMERICAN PAINTER

$ Schnabel's publicity photos present him as the lone hero in the outback, all muscle and angst in a white vest. He drives around New York in a Cadillac, creates his work in an adapted tennis court and makes outrageous statements which reveal that modesty is not a character trait upon which he places much value. Whether painting his eclectic array of images on smashed porcelain, velvet or tarpaulin, the bombastic aspect of the whole enterprise is evident in the titles: *Maria Callas No. 2, Prehistory: Glory, Honour, Privilege, Poverty* and even *Portrait of God*. Schnabel pilfers his ideas from everywhere – Indian miniatures, graffiti, Renaissance painting – and paints them in an explosive manner that has led some critics to dub him a 'neo-expressionist'. A creation of the contemporary gallery scene – ☛Leo Castelli sells him, ☛Charles Saatchi has bought his work – Schnabel has undeniably established his presence in contemporary painting, not only by his high-spirited behaviour, but also because of the precedent he has set with the price of his paintings.

I can go where I want, eat whatever I like, make a pig of myself and will continue to do so as long as I've got money.

Julian Schnabel

Paul Schrader born 1946

▲AMERICAN FILM DIRECTOR, SCREENWRITER

Hollywood – and corrupting, senseless, pleasure-crazed urban America – lured Schrader away from the extreme austerity of his Calvinist upbringing in Michigan, and since then he has been simultaneously celebrating and savaging its lazy, sleazy surface attractions and hunting for new routes towards love and order. First noted as the writer of ☛Martin Scorsese's *Taxi Driver* (1976) and later his *Raging Bull* (1980), Schrader brought to life hell-driven crazies who sought redemption through extreme violence, adding a Teutonic darkness and weight to Scorsese's manic Catholic/underground rhythms. Turning director himself, he focused on the same tensions – between mid-American puritan morality and the exotic libertarian hedonisms of the city – in the real-life horror plots of *Blue Collar* (1978), *Hardcore* (1979) and *American Gigolo* (1980). Drawn to a version of the Samurai ethic ever since his dopey script for *The Yakuza* (1975), Schrader found in the life story of the Japanese novelist ☛Yukio *Mishima* (1985) a way of resolving at least some of the contradictions dogging his work.

Ernst Schumacher 1911-77

WEST GERMAN ECONOMIST, ECOLOGIST

Schumacher gave the Green movement its resonant jingle – 'Small Is Beautiful' – in a book of the same title, whose anti-growth arguments were well timed to coincide with the repercussions of the 1973 oil price hike. His writings reflected 25 years of experience as economic adviser to the allies in West Germany and – a rare European in a very British firm – the Coal Board. His target was not economic growth itself, but its energy-intensive, mass-output, humanity-hostile spin-offs. He called for radically reduced units of production, even in bigger firms. The experiments at Sweden's Volvo plants, which allow small groups of workers to make individual cars, rather than dividing up the labour between isolated production lines, may mirror his influence. Presciently, he also warned against the consequences of allowing Third World countries to accumulate heavy debts.

Delmore Schwartz 1913-66

▲ AMERICAN POET,
SHORT STORY WRITER

A poet and writer of stories who never recovered from initial success, Schwartz's own life, with its lurid descent to a fatal heart attack in a Manhattan hotel, has tended to obscure his literary achievements. His first book, *In Dreams Begin Responsibilities* (1938), combines poetry with a short story – about a boy in a cinema who watches his parents' courting and wishes to change the course of events – and the wistful sense of loss evokes deep despair beneath its technical bravura. Schwartz's work deals with Jewishness, the conflict between immigrant parents and their New World-educated children, and the insecurity born of an unsettled family background. Teaching for a while at Syracuse University – where he made a lasting impression on Lou Reed – his last years found him suffering from a persecution mania that drink and drugs only served to heighten. His life story was the inspiration for ☛Saul Bellow's *Humboldt's Gift*.

John Schwarz

♦ AMERICAN PHYSICIST

Michael Green

♦ BRITISH PHYSICIST

The search for a 'grand unified theory' – a theory of everything – has been pursued in cosmology since Einstein developed his famous energy-matter equation. Most eagerly sought is a theory that could connect the four basic cosmological forces (gravity, electromagnetic, strong and weak nuclear) while still being compatible with quantum physics and general relativity. In the early 1970s, the suggestion that gravity could be explained *geometrically* began to excite interest, leading to the dusting off of the long-forgotten Kaluza-Klein hypothesis, which proved that gravity and electromagnetism were the same in a universe of five dimensions or more. A favoured argument was that we lived in no fewer than 11 dimensions, three visible, one the time-line, the other seven of a closure of subatomic measure (in other words, to travel along one of them would be to travel on a tiny loop far smaller than the radius of an atom's nucleus). Although the original formulations proved not to work out, John Schwarz of Cal Tech and Michael Green of Queen Mary College, London, began in 1980 to explore models that posited, not particles, but strings, as basic subatomic building blocks – waves vibrating round these other-dimensional closed loops. Their still controversial 'superstring theory' has solved many difficulties that earlier theories had foundered upon, and though far from universally accepted, it has become a particularly important field of theoretical study since the mid-1980s.

Leonardo Sciascia 1929-89

ITALIAN NOVELIST, JOURNALIST,
POLITICAL COMMENTATOR

Sciascia's reputation outside Italy is built around a series of chilling crime novels, especially *The Day of the Owl* (1961), in which the clues the detective unearths only draw him closer to the failure of his own investigation. These narratives focus on the rotten state of contemporary politics in Sicily, exposing the lies and self-deceptions that smudge over the network of corruption that links the island's Mafia to the Cabinet in Rome. Known in Italy for his hard-hitting criticism of the Church, the police, the Christian Democrats and the Communist Party, Sciascia's novels express a fascination with his native Sicily, and acknowledge the ways in which its deluded people obstruct any attempts to remedy the island's perennial problems

Martin Scorsese born 1942

▲ AMERICAN FILM-MAKER

With two films in the mid-1970s – *Mean Streets* and *Taxi Driver* – Scorsese brought a violent, pulpy new rhythm to popular cinema. In the process he drew upon his apprenticeship with exploitation king ☛Roger Corman, his own complex and driven personal vision of rot and redemption, and all the subversive emotions of junk culture. *Mean Streets* (1973), the story of two minor Italian-American hoods, was only a breath away from underground cinema in its gliding, delirious, crimson-lit, hand-held technique. *Taxi Driver* (1976), the story of a confused Viet vet turned psychotic vigilante, was, if anything, bolder in its layering of molten pop sensibility. In both films, Scorsese worked with ☛Robert De Niro to expose the inside of uncharted manias – and subsequent, less commercially successful films continued this two-man project (*New York, New York*, 1977; *Raging Bull*, 1980; and *The King of Comedy*, 1983). Intense and intelligent, Scorsese in interviews talks at machine-gun speed, but many of his subsequent films seemed more well-made than emotionally motivated. In the wake of John Hinkley's copycat assassination attempt on ☛President Reagan, performed as an extension of a fan-crush on *Taxi Driver* teen star Jodie Foster, Scorsese seemed reluctant to be as uncannily prescient again and to be backing away from his own insights into urban craziness. The completion of his long-nurtured *The Last Temptation of Christ* (1988) sparked half-baked protest from the fundamentalists, but the film marked no advance in Scorsese's work. But having got that out of his system, he came close to his claustrophobic best with *GoodFellas* (1990), which drew again on Scorsese's knowledge of New York's mean streets for its account of Mafia violence.

Bobby Seale see Newton, Huey

Haile Selassie 1892-1975

♥ ETHIOPIAN POLITICAL LEADER

⇔ ➳ Revered by Rastafarians as the Lion of Judah, Selassie was crowned emperor in 1930. Five years later, Ethiopia was successfully invaded by Italy, and the exiled Selassie upheld with dignity the claims of his people until he was restored to his throne in 1941 by the British. In the latter phase of his reign, he did his best to carry out superficial modernization, relaxing feudal taxes, setting up schools and, in 1955, introducing a written constitution. He also ended Ethiopia's isolation by fully identifying with the best of the new Africa, and in 1963, the Organization of African Unity made its headquarters in Addis Adaba, his capital. But the obverse of his fierce dignity and proud defiance was resistance to genuine change, and patronage and graft turned Ethiopia into a grotesquely feudal state. He refused, despite pressures, to allow his son to take over power; people starved; nothing was done. Selassie was finally toppled in a 1974 coup led by a Marxist, Colonel Mengistu, after a series of mutinies, strikes and demonstrations. Mengistu, a tyrant with no more idea of how to manage an economy than the monarch he replaced, has sent Ethiopia sharply backwards from where it stood in 1974. The famine has worsened – a consequence of drought but also of bad agricultural planning, civil war and cynical superpower interference.

Amartya Sen born 1933

INDIAN ECONOMIST

Sen has sought to widen the scope of economics, which he feels has been limited by narrow views of such concepts as welfare, choice and resources. Taking a particular interest in development issues, he has argued that a breakdown in the ability of individuals to buy food explains the oddity that the 1943 famine in Bengal coincided with higher available supplies than in 1941, when there was no famine. He has broadened the study of investment decisions by stating that governments should take into account far-reaching results of labour policies – the long-run spin-offs, the 'shadow cost of labour'. In consumer choice, he has argued that there is no one-to-one equation between urges to be satisfied and real levels of demand: people in markets pay heed to social, not just personal, factors. A wide-ranging abstract curiosity, allied to an urgent sense of real problems, makes Sen an entertaining and provocative thinker.

Léopold Senghor born 1906

✌ SENEGALESE POET, POLITICIAN, POLITICAL THEORIST

An exponent of *négritude*, the movement for black political awareness and pride that grew out of existentialism, Senghor became the first president of Senegal when it secured independence from France in 1960, and he went on to rule for 20 years as a near-dictator. He was born into a rich Catholic family in a largely Muslim area, and studied at the Sorbonne. In Paris, with other black students – Léon Damas from Guinea, Aimé Césaire from Martinique – he developed the concept of *négritude*, retrieving a unique, civilized African tradition and, at the same time, affirming it as a prescriptive response to Western colonial values. As a teacher in France, Senghor also became a noted poet, who evoked African culture with striking imagery. Returning to Senegal, he played an active part in the movement for independence, holding a seat in the French national assembly. He wanted a West African federation – his group was hostile to the Balkanization of the continent. As president, he kept close ties with France, and became the first black member of the French Academy in 1984.

Rod Serling 1924-75

AMERICAN TELEVISION WRITER, PRODUCER, PRESENTER

A former paratrooper and boxer, Serling initially enrolled in a writing course to shake off the war's effects. He went on to produce *The Twilight Zone*, a long-running fantasy anthology, launched by CBS in 1959, which like a lot of golden age television, hit harder and deeper than we are quite prepared to acknowledge. The show never needed cheap devices to sustain tension, and Serling, who wrote some 90 of the 151 episodes, seemed to have a perfect understanding of the subversive potential of the genre, quickly winning critical praise (though never huge audiences or reliable sponsorship) as he assaulted prejudice, ignorance and a wide range of semi-political issues. After *Twilight Zone* was cancelled in 1964, Serling co-wrote the script for *The Planet of the Apes* (1968) before the début of *Rod Serling's Night Gallery* (1970-73). By now, the demand for thrills was greater, but also for more escapism, and Serling's turnabout paradoxes could not compete with monsters, special-effects gore, gun-battles, car chases – or the Black Panthers and Vietnam. Although the show was sold on his reputation, he had little control over its content, and probably was not unhappy when it was cancelled in 1973. He retired to teach writing.

Richard Serra born 1939

AMERICAN SCULPTOR

Serra is dubbed a 'cowboy' in New York to indicate his macho, frontiersman attitude. His work is big and monumental, his ethic is 'go out and do it' and his great enemy is 'prettiness' in whatever form. The enormous sculptures, utilizing mass-produced lead and steel plates, depend precariously upon gravity and balance: on several occasions, assistants installing the works have been crushed to death beneath them. For his early work, he compiled a 'Verb List' which comprised directions – to fold, bend, crease, etc. – for manipulating materials. Today, however, he is more widely known for his controversial *Tilted Arc*, a massive slash of steel embedded in a New York street and dwarfing passers-by, which became the subject of heated controversy. In August 1989, it was finally removed: Serra had failed to understand that public art required some sort of collaboration between artist, architect, environmental planner and the public at large.

Michel Serres

❀ FRENCH PHILOSOPHER OF SCIENCE, LITERARY CRITIC

An intriguing philosopher of science and literary critic, still little known or remarked on outside France, Serres works a pitch that resembles ☛Foucault's concept of the *episteme* – the period of time dominated by a certain conceptual structure – examining the links and analogies between ideas in writing and prevailing paradigms in the sciences. His commentary can seem both slight and irrelevant, in the light of its interdisciplinary focus. But his insights into mythologies of flow, turbulence, distribution and interference leave an imprint, none the less – he is a more subtle writer than he seems. An expert on mathematical structure – in the mould of ☛Bourbaki – and widely read in all branches of the history of science, he aims to bring into being an overall history that would explain, for example, how, in the classical age, the pervasive concentration of all disciplines on 'the fixed point' shifted, in the modern age, to become a consistent obsession everywhere with the 'steam-driven engine' – what came first, what affected what? He has published a five-volume series of essays on science and literature, *Hermes* (1968-77), of which only extracts are presently available in English.

Jean-Jacques Servan-Schreiber
born 1924

FRENCH POLITICIAN

Servan-Schreiber has been an insider-outsider in French politics and the press for 40 years. A wartime pilot in the US Air Force, he has had a love-hate affair with the US, leading to his bestseller, *The American Challenge* (1967). The book's line is that American industry in Europe, as of 1968, looked set to become the world's third force, with the US and the USSR, wrecking Europe's autonomy. His remedy was for a united Europe to modernize itself, developing EEC ideas. As Europe has become, with 1992 on the horizon, more of an economic unit, with Japan and the UK moving into the US economy, his thesis now seems wrongheaded – which may attest to his influence. Servan-Schreiber is also noted as the founder of *L'Express*, a *Time*-style magazine, and for winning the release from gaol of Mikis Theodorakis, the Greek composer/singer, in 1969.

Doctor Seuss
(Theodor Seuss Geisel) 1904-91

✓ AMERICAN WRITER

Since their first appearance in the 1950s, Doctor Seuss's large-format, primary-coloured learn-to-read books have been dividing teacher from parent and parent from child. The old rote approach was wiped away for ever by Seuss's rash and sinister masterstroke of a character, 'The Cat in the Hat' – a tall, dark stranger who bursts into a suburban home on a boring rainy day and creates delirious havoc. Less cat than weird rampaging monster-from-the-id, this creation brought down howls of excoriation, and instantly sold millions worldwide. Seuss's drawing style owes something to George Herriman's legendary Krazy Kat, pumped up in size and volume, although obviously reduced in metaphysical scope. Seuss's surrealistic verse-for-kids is memorable in sleep-murdering snatches ('There once was a woman called Mrs McCave who had 35 sons and called all of them Dave', for example, or 'I, I, I-I-I, Ichabod is itchy and so am I', from an alphabet book that only he could have written). Although he wrote many other books, including *Green Eggs and Ham* and *Hop on Pop,* none had an effect quite like the first, but his sensibility is probably responsible for such 1980s' adult phenomena as *Pee Wee's Playhouse.*

The Sex Pistols
1975-79

Sid Vicious (John Beverley) 1957-79
John Rotten (John Lydon) born 1956
Paul Cook born 1956
Steve Jones born 1956

BRITISH ROCK GROUP

The most mythologized group since ☛The Beatles, The Sex Pistols made rock records short and obstreperous again, introduced anarchist ideas into the charts, outraged lots of people, created a space for thousands of new bands to form and illustrated once more that pop music can only change the world if it is allied to a mass revolutionary movement. Their impact was partly due to luck (the music scene in 1976 was so stale that singing hamsters could have revitalized it), partly to genius (Johnny Rotten/Lydon is one of the most charismatic performers in rock's history) and partly to skilful promotion (☛Malcolm McLaren was its manager/publicist/conceptual artist). Although The Sex Pistols failed to destroy rock music, they made life in late-1970s' Britain worthwhile and inspired any number of musicians, writers and artists. They enjoyed a quite spectacular decline, with the death of Sid Vicious and the degeneration of their post-Lydon work into exploitative (but often wonderful) pop. Lydon re-emerged as a wilful and self-indulgent artist of immense ability, and McLaren launched himself as the world's first manager-cum-popstar. Rock music since The Pistols has been completely fragmented, referring to the past rather than growing organically out of it.

The Shangri-Las 1964-66

AMERICAN POP GROUP

Created from thin air by the suitably eccentric George 'Shadow' Morton, The Shangri-Las were a mixture of ordinary 1960s' girl pop, ☛Phil Spector, teen-mag melodrama and unfathomable melancholy. Morton used dramatic Spector sound, sound effects, vocal interjections and the Weiss sisters' keening Brooklyn voices to produce records that could soar with joy ('Train from Kansas City') or, more usually, trawl the depths of despondency ('Betty . . . is that Jimmy's ring you're wearing?). 'Past, Present and Future', their strangest and greatest record released in 1966, uses Beethoven's *Moonlight Sonata* to back the oddest and most ominous line in pop music: 'But don't try to touch me/ 'Cos that will never . . . happen . . . again.' Only in the experimental 1960s could such melodramatic and daring pop have happened. The Shangri-Las say more about young love than any other pop group has done since; they were innocence, maturity, silliness and rapture all at once.

Claude Shannon born 1916
Warren Weaver 1894-1978

♦ AMERICAN MATHEMATICIANS

The speed with which computers sprang up, evolved and multiplied makes it difficult to remember how recently the theory that made them possible appeared. ☛Von Neumann and ☛Turing did much of their important work in the 1940s; Shannon and Weaver's *The Mathematical Theory of Communication*, which first articulated the concept of information as a quantifiable abstract, appeared in 1949, and introduced ideas of message, redundancy, noise, storage and transmission by treating information as (in one description) 'a specialized, value-free term without the usual connotations of facts, learning, wisdom, understanding, enlightenment.' Shannon, employed originally at the Bell Telephone Company's research department, produced the original paper on communication; Weaver developed it, examining the implications of Shannon's technical innovations in the light of semantic and social theory.

Sam Shepard born 1943

✎AMERICAN PLAYWRIGHT, ACTOR

While ☛Bob Dylan and Lou Reed attempted to write the Great American Novel in three-minute pop songs, Shepard stole the rhythms of rock music and applied them to prose. Tramping the wilderness and scoring on America's main streets, Shepard came back to attest to the mysteries of life on the road, but without the naïveté of ☛Kerouac or the Beach Boys. With a keen ear for the phonetic inflections of American blue-collar speech, his plays typically depict

American families as they tear each other apart by raking over old griefs, losses and resentments. His characters are modern cowboys, drifters and farmers nostalgic for a simpler past that may never have existed, caught between a mystical world of prairies, Indian spells and superstitions and the mechanized realm occupied by the motor car and modern technology. All these concerns are evident in his script for ☛Wim Wenders' *Paris Texas* (1984), about a loner who tramps the wilderness after his marriage has come apart, and then sets out with his son in a futile, and extremely sentimental, attempt to put things back together again. Shepard, the son of a wartime pilot, joined the higher ranks of Hollywood stars when he took the part of flyer Chuck Yeager in *The Right Stuff* (1983) – even though, in life, he refuses to travel by plane.

Cindy Sherman born 1954

▲ AMERICAN PHOTOGRAPHER

Sherman's work is a woman's obsessive search for identity, although she has gradually widened out from concentrated investigations into the self to examine broader questions. Her early black-and-white pictures depicted a woman, the artist herself, in isolation – a frightened victim waiting on a lonely country road or cowering on a motel bed. Reminiscent of countless movies and film stills, Sherman's pictures play ambiguously with pin-up images of women. When she moved into colour, the images grew more exotic, and became exaggerated depictions of fashion photography – with Sherman deploying elaborate costumes, false plastic buttocks, a pig's head or an elongated tongue lapping at the air to create a fairy-tale-like mythology. Lately she has been concerned with images of disease and sickness, expressing her sense of the stain that AIDS has spilt on society through unsettlingly garish displays of festering food and rotting (human) waste. Sherman shows the body at its extreme, stripped of humanity.

Dmitri Shostakovich 1906-75

✓ SOVIET COMPOSER

Before the details of his life under Stalin were known, Shostakovich tended to be reviled by Western commentators as no more than a talented but subservient hack. The notorious tag he appended to his fifth symphony after he had been hauled over the coals for the crime of formalism – 'A Soviet artist's practical reply to just criticism' – was considered proof of his spinelessness. Now he is often held up as a paragon of aesthetic resistance. With a bold melodic and tonal sense, but also an absolute willingness to pass more than twice over the same ground (the same tunes, structures and experiments often appearing several times in as many different projects), Shostakovich is, in retrospect, as difficult a composer to categorize as the shifting attitudes to his politics would suggest. In fact, although his supposedly formalist work is often striking, his more self-consciously prole-friendly music is just as powerful and rich in tensions between rural folk-lyricism and acerbic modernist juxtaposition; in a sense, after all, he was being forced, daily, to resolve the contradictions between mass and high art that Western musicians would not encounter until well after WW2. His output was large; the constant social pressures he was under may have embittered him, but they did not block his creativity. Inevitably, he now seems a nineteenth-century figure, but the pop drama of his best work, like the political soap opera of the story behind it, remains compelling.

Bill Sienkiewicz

☞COMICS ILLUSTRATOR

The degree to which a new generation of mainstreamers have made comics 'adult' is questionable: the undergrounds, like *Zap* and *Weirdo*, had already explored more porno/politico topics than your average adult would care to be caught examining. With Sienkiewicz's illustrations for ☛Frank Miller's *Daredevil* (1986) revamp and *Elektra Assassin* (1986), the lurid subuniverse of psychosis that Marvel heroes and villains have always inhabited leapt into relief as a mirror of power politics in the real world. Sienkiewicz started as a standard Marvel realist, but by the time he came to do *Elektra Assassin* and, going solo, *Stray Toasters* (1988), he had created a unique amalgam of space-opera impressionist mysticism, Japanese Samurai dynamism and classic Marvel action-shot, along with touches of his own – collage, fake Xerox, zip-gun editing. In 1988, he teamed up with ☛Alan Moore to illustrate *Brought to Light*, a comic book examination of the Iran-Contra affair and 30 years of CIA malfeasance. His style brings a nightmarish hyper-reality, bad-trip *cinema vérité* to an ugly story: this goes far beyond the 'comics have grown up' sales pitch.

Dave Sim born 1956

✎CANADIAN CARTOONS WRITER, PUBLISHER

Sim is the pioner of modern cartoon DIY independence. He edits, publishes and distributes his *Cerebus* strip entirely through his own company and aggressively challenges anyone he considers is limiting his artistic freedoms. His work is appropriately eccentric and original. *Cerebus*, originally a parody of *Conan the Barbarian*, is no muscle-bound he-hunk, but a small, plump, grey, scowling aardvark, lost in a world he did not make and hates: a moronically primitive hinterland, where fun boils down to whoring and warring. Cerebral, cynical and horny – Pooh Bear as Pa Ubu – the aardvark originally began when Sim was inspired and empowered by the ☛The Sex Pistols to challenge comics orthodoxy. Since then, in the course of some 120 issues (on the way to a projected 300), it has become an extended, laconic, dense meditation on power, feminism, religion, politics and integrity. Sim gets bored quickly, and he does not suffer fools at all: his characters, his readers, his critics or those who stand in the way of his by-now lucrative self-help masterplan.

Georges Simenon 1903-89

■ BELGIAN WRITER,

✓ WHO SETTLED IN SWITZERLAND

Simenon's career is not easy to summarize in statistics, unsurprisingly given that he once wrote pulp fiction under 17 pseudonyms, and estimates of his fictional output vary by a factor of 100 (420 tomes is the best guess). Also, his claim to have bedded some 10,000 women was disputed by one of his ex-wives, who put the figure at closer to 1200 (he ascribed his dealings with prostitutes to his desire to 'penetrate humanity'). Simenon's contribution to the detective story was to replace the calculated, well-shaped plot with a detailed account of the milieu through which criminal and detective moved, and their symbiotic relationship. Jules Maigret, who featured in 84 books, was a relatively placid man, comfortable with the pleasures of domesticity, but Simenon seemingly felt closer to the losers driven to self-destruction who people such 'hard' novels as *The Man who Watched the Trains Go By* (1938) or *The Stain on the Snow* (1948). Retiring from novel-writing in 1972 after what he claimed was his first experience of writer's block, Simenon devoted himself to a series of self-indulgent memoirs, including his wretched *Intimate Memoirs* (1981) – his revenge on his second wife for her own account of their relationship and a lament for their daughter, Marie-Jo, who had shot herself.

Claude Simon born 1913

▲ FRENCH NOVELIST

Simon is one of the most important contemporary French novelists. He is interested in simultaneity – the idea of 'so much happening in a single moment', and so remorselessly philosophical that he has been identified with the *nouveau roman* school, although he began writing before it became fashionable. Constantly interrupting the narrative of his books with temporal disjunctions and with the use of other genres and other texts, his method is more Cubist than cut-up in the way it approaches different angles to his subjects; his aim is to oppose the customary view. His work frequently draws on his experience of capture and escape during WW2, as well as a love of nature and a certain breed of pacifism. His latest book, *The Georgics* (1989), is about an artillery officer who threw in his lot with the French Revolution, kept away from Paris during the height of the Terror and eventually became one of Napoleon's generals. It is also about ☛George Orwell in Barcelona, and his own experiences as a cavalryman ordered to attack Rommel's tanks in Flanders in 1940. Simon was one of the few who survived.

What has been imagined, been lived, been dreamed, the important, the unimportant, the decisive, the trivial, are for me terribly difficult to disentangle.

Claude Simon

Alan Simpson *see* Galton, Ray

Nina Simone
(Eunice Waymon) born 1933

✌ AMERICAN JAZZ, ROCK MUSICIAN

Her husky voice, precise piano playing and general air of melancholy placed Simone high in the canon of moody jazz entertainers; her records epitomized popular sophistication. She moved towards R&B, and thence towards strangeness; her involvement in the Black Power movement kept her away from the respectable status she was close to achieving. Simone's return in the 1980s brought with it a reputation for outright weirdness and general public bafflement; people shelled out to see the woman who sang 'My Baby Just Cares for Me', and they got a woman who sang an emotional and dark version of Gilbert O'Sullivan's 'Alone Again Naturally' and then abused the audience. Sadly, Simone's continuing refusal to conform to *anybody*'s standards has denied her the respect she deserves.

Claude Simon
Photo courtesy of John Calder (Publishers) Ltd

Frank Sinatra

(Francis Albert Sinatra) born 1915

AMERICAN SINGER, ACTOR

Sinatra has been a big band singer, the first teen idol, a youthful movie star, a has-been, the supreme singer of a certain kind of song, a (rumoured) Mafia fellow-traveller, a Hollywood roustabout, and the true king of show business. Certainly, little that Sinatra has done professionally has been bad: his singing with the Harry James Big Band in the 1940s was acceptable; his 1950s' films, whether musical (*Guys and Dolls*) or serious (*The Man with the Golden Arm, From Here to Eternity*), developed his superbly tough-innocent persona; and even his later work, such as 'Something Stupid' with his daughter Nancy and 'It Was a Very Good Year', has the style and wisdom of a singing genius. Sinatra will mostly be remembered for his 1950s' Capitol albums: the trilbied loser in the bar singing over Nelson Riddle's tremulously sympathetic strings. Sinatra virtually invented melancholy as a musical form, and his phrasing on those records is nearer to the understated emotionalism of jazz than the slick crooning of Sinatra's showbiz peers. Even now, despite increasingly glitzy records and shows, despite books condemning his reputedly unpleasant personality, Sinatra appears cool and worldly-wise, ineffable and sassy.

Isaac Bashevis Singer 1904-91

POLISH-AMERICAN NOVELIST

Singer dealt with the plight of European Jewry in the twentieth century, often focusing on the situation that confronted the Jews in Warsaw when the Nazis occupied the city. His work is both a celebration of his religious roots and a magnificent alliance of beauty with the grotesque. His father and grandfather were both rabbis, and he was educated at the Warsaw Rabbinical Seminary. The influence shows in the way religious debate and philosophical contemplation flavour his writing: he plugs into the individual's relationship with his God. Emigrating to America in 1935, Singer's writing found its tone and texture by drawing on the fantastic and grotesque for tales of religious and personal awakening. His works fascinate Jewish artists – hence Barbra Streisand's 1983 film (which Singer tried to stop) of his 'Yentl, the Yeshiva Boy', a short story involving gender confusion, lesbianism and Hassidic law. Its haunting evocation of love unspoken and lost is a quintessential analysis of the patriarchal nature of the Hassidic religious order, lit through with Singer's sense of the marvellous and the ethereal found in the struggling aspirations of those who yearn to live out their ideals. More recently, Paul Mazursky made a film from *Enemies, A Love Story* (1966/72), about a weak-willed Holocaust survivor who cannot make a choice between his three wives.

Douglas Sirk 1900-87

DANISH-AMERICAN FILM DIRECTOR

Even in his German movies of the 1930s, Sirk displayed a reverence for small-town values and humanitarian ideals – juxtaposed with luxurious sets and histrionic lead performances from traumatized females. He went on to inject sensitive imagery and middle-class glamour into such movies as *Magnificent Obsession* (1954) and *All that Heaven Allows* (1955), which were essentially dime-store potboilers elevated to the level of epic drama. A supremely moral denizen of an upmarket version of Norman Rockwell's universe, his films flaunt the inability of affluent people to enjoy life, recovering their sense of belonging only through philanthropic endeavour and self-sacrifice. He re-established Hollywood trash as social consciousness, and anticipated the enormously popular idiom of television soap opera (*Dallas*, *Dynasty*) that created an industry out of angst and voyeurism. To everyone's bemusement, including probably his own, the French New Wave film critics adopted Sirk as their mascot.

B(urrhus) F(rederic) Skinner 1904-90

AMERICAN PSYCHOLOGIST

Skinner rejected the idea of an inner world, arguing that behaviour is completely determined by environmental pressures, and that psychology should restrict itself to the study of observable behaviour. He developed the 'Skinner box', equipped with a lever and a light: an animal placed in the box soon discovers that, if it presses the lever when the light is on, it will receive a reward in the form of food. From observing rats in this context, Skinner developed the principle of 'operant conditioning' – which basically states that we learn to repeat behaviour which is reinforced and replace that which is punished. Upon this starting point, he built a theory which sought to cover all humour behaviour: his critics diagnosed this as a case of severe over-stretching. Even among his supporters, there are few who defend his most extreme work, *Beyond Freedom and Dignity* (1971), which considered methods of applying operant condition to society in an attempt to cure all its ills. Perhaps even more alarming is his novel, *Walden Two* (1948), in which he sets out his idea of utopia. Skinner wants to tidy up the psyche, with all its messiness and internal conflicts, and seems willing to accept a benign totalitarianism as the way to cure humanity of its aggressive drives. Liberals may mock, but only at the cost of ignoring the way behaviourism takes the ambitions of a therapeutic culture to its most extreme point.

Josef Skvorecký born 1924

CZECHOSLOVAK NOVELIST, SETTLED IN CANADA

Skvorecký's first novel, *The Cowards* (written 1948, published 1958/70), is an autobiographical story of a jazz-loving youngster living in a small town during the Nazi occupation, who is caught in political crossfire when his only real concerns are bebop and the opposite sex. In jazz, he finds a freedom that goes beyond political creeds, but to impress the girls, he has to take up a posture of resistance that relates ill to his instinct for self-preservation. Skvorecký has continued to pursue similar preoccupations, with his work becoming increasingly less humorous and more bitter. Closely involved with writers and film-makers of the Czechoslovak New Wave, he left for Canada after the Soviet invasion of 1968. His memories of Czechoslovakia and his experiences of exile are recounted in the epic novel, *The Engineer of Human Souls* (1984).

David Smith 1906-65

AMERICAN SCULPTOR

Smith did for sculpture in the 1950s what the abstract expressionists were doing for painting. He forged subtly balanced, often colourful, abstractions out of pieces of scrap metal in an artistic shift that owed something to Picasso's experiments with found objects in the 1930s but a lot more to a personal fascination with technology and the craftsmanship of industrial production. He had been a welder on an automobile production line while a student, and spent much of WW2 screwing rivets into tanks, but when he said, 'I'm just a welder,' it was simply a bluff to wrong-foot critics and screen out tedious art-talk. The critics fell for it, calling Smith an unimaginative primitive, but there was nothing crude or clumsy about his *Agricola* series: montages of metal farm tools suggesting the figures of those who work the land. Smith wanted to create contemporary symbols. Through his influence on the work of ☛Anthony Caro, he helped shift the direction of British sculpture in the early 1960s. He was killed in a car accident.

Eugene Smith 1919-78

AMERICAN PHOTO-JOURNALIST

The father of modern photo-journalism, Smith worked at *Life* magazine for years, only leaving when he felt it was moving towards glamour and away from fact. His speciality was the photo-essay and he shot definitive stories on, among other things, the industrial city of Pittsburgh (*Labyrinthine Walk*), the British election of 1950, and the working day of a black Southern midwife. Utterly unwilling to be directed by picture editors towards any preconceived narrative, he would demand to oversee the choice, layout and captioning of his photographs, and made sure that nothing crept in which did not fit in with what he had seen. Already wounded as a war correspondent at Okinawa, he was violently beaten and lost an eye while shooting *Minimata* in the 1970s. There, after staying and working undercover for three years, he exposed the grotesque and tragic effects of mercury poisoning on the children of a small Japanese village – a story which led to extensive legislation controlling the disposal of commercial chemical waste.

John Maynard Smith *see* Maynard Smith, John

Patti Smith born 1946

✎AMERICAN ROCK MUSICIAN

Women in rock were just token chicks in a boys' world playground until, in 1975, Patti Smith opened an LP called *Horses* with the ☛Van Morrison love song, 'Gloria'. She had been working up her New York act for some years before she actually surfaced, mixing long bouts of improvised poetry with chillingly propulsive cyclic punk-rock. That LP, with its ☛Mapplethorpe cover shot of her, dyke-icy, transformed everyone's ideas of what could be sung and how. Smith became pretentious and second-rate astonishingly fast, but this hardly mattered to a generation of sexually confused teens who welcomed her wildness and her arrogant confidence in her own stream-of-consciousness. Her faults – extreme self-indulgence, mainly – were her strengths for long enough to deflate an old myth and pump up several new ones. By the time she had been reduced to falling off stage and breaking her neck, or marrying her bass-player, almost everyone had lost interest, and she retired for ten years. When she reappeared, the world fell over themselves to get the interview, but she seemed to have become a quiet, intelligent, rather nice woman. No one changes the universe twice, even in pop.

Robert Smithson 1938-73

✈ AMERICAN SCULPTOR

Deliberately creating work that could not be owned, either by museums or private patrons, Smithson's pieces are created out of the land and usually situated in remote places. They aspire to have the same impact as ancient earthworks. His largest and most famous work, *Spiral Jetty* (1970) – a curling spiral of rock which projected a quarter of a mile into the Great Salt Lake in Utah – required an expedition to reach. Once there, the impression was that you had come upon some mysterious object from an ancient civilization. Ironically, the level of the lake rose and submerged *Spiral Jetty* under water. Smithson was killed in an aeroplane accident while surveying sites for later work.

Michael Snow born 1929

♦ CANADIAN EXPERIMENTAL ☞FILM-MAKER

Although Snow belongs to the 1960s' wave of New York avant-garde cinema, his attitudes mesh more convincingly with 1970s' minimalism than with the previous decade's pop. He secures his effects by withdrawing stimulus rather than increasing it, which is presumably why his influence has been less than that exercised by some of his more manic contemporaries. Most notoriously, *Wavelength* (1967) features an uncut 45-minute zoom through a single sunlit New York loft, focusing finally on a still photo (of waves) hanging up on the wall. According to taste and patience, it is either film poetry concentrating on the nature of time and the role of the camera, or an interminable experimental indulgence. Snow has designed sophisticated camera equipment to free it in space, which he used most effectvely in *La Region Centrale* (1972), when automated machinery allowed him to map (over-three-and-a-half hours) the whole sphere of possible vision by rotating the camera in every direction round a fixed point, recording exhaustively every distance and close-up available in a barren, rocky mountainscape in wilderness Canada – except, of course, the camera machinery at the centre of the whole operation.

Valerie Solanas 1936-88

✌ AMERICAN FAILURE

Solanas is remembered as the victim of the man she tried to gun down in 1968, ☛Andy Warhol – as with ☛Reagan, bullets could only enhance so timely a spectre as Andy. A brief member of his Factory, as an actress who never even rose to his invented rank of 'superstar' (she appears in *I, A Man*), Solanas had formed the Society for Cutting Up Men (SCUM) of which she was the sole member, and issued a furious manifesto, prefiguring the most rejectionist of radical feminist tracts (the Velvet Underground's John Cale said of her that 'she was so full of rage, she could hardly speak'). Her intended target's art set the tone for the 1970s, with its disturbing apolitical emptiness and cool self-concern – the fascination with the glamour of death and the death-glow of glamour had already led to another Factory-hand pumping bullets into a pile of

☛Marilyn screenprints. But with this sole piece of gestural politics – Dada-gone-bad – Solanas foreshadowed many other aspects of the *zeitgeist* to come, with its misdirected radicalism and soured propaganda. She barely survived Warhol by a year, dying in obscurity, of bronchial pneumonia.

Alexander Solzhenitsyn born 1918

▲SOVIET NOVELIST,
POLITICAL COMMENTATOR,
✓SETTLED IN THE US

The shock effect of Solzhenitsyn's writings, as they emerged in the 1960s, was immediate enough for him to be hailed as the Tolstoy or Dostoyevsky or our age. His defiant courage was obvious – he risked life and liberty in order to expose Stalin's criminal legacy from inside the Soviet Union. Having already spent time in prison camps for criticizing the dictator to a friend in 1945, the force of his early novels came directly from this lived experience of repressive mundanity. He demolished the old clichés of the all-seeing monolithic state and its malevolence: the dominant mode of evil in Solzhenitsyn's study was the uncultured and desensitized incompetence of a godless system's commissars. His three-volume account of the network of Soviet labour camps, *The Gulag Archipelago* (1973/5, 1974/8), was a significant influence on theorists such as ☛Foucault, showing that systems of incarceration developed their own self-contained logic and a momentum that was independent of economic infrastructures. Soviet sympathizers and centralist Marxists were driven on to the defensive. But Solzhenitsyn, an isolated figure even in Moscow's tight-knit dissident culture, has always also been a tool in others' hands. ☛Khrushchev used the publication of *A Day in the life of Ivan Denisovich* (1962/3) as a force in de-Stalinization; the West used Solzhenitsyn's dignified courage and his 1970 Nobel prize as propaganda against the Soviets; and ☛Brezhnev used the writer's later calls from exile for a return to tsarist theocracy in Russia as a weapon against other less severely anti-socialist dissidents. After some ill-conceived historical novels, he largely fell silent – a soured doom-watch spectre at the feast of tremulous reconciliation between East and West – until, in September 1990, a Soviet newspaper published his 16,000-word article, 'How We Are to Rebuild Russia', in which he called again for a return to old values and traditions.

Anastazio Somoza Debayle 1925-80

NICARAGUAN POLITICAL LEADER

A father and his two sons, the Somozas ran Nicaragua as dynastic dictators from 1936 to 1979, with minor gaps. The father, Anastasio García, rose via the National Guard and masterminded the assassination of guerrilla leader Augusto César Sandino, before taking over the presidency. He built up vast wealth and established close ties with the US before he was assassinated. His elder son, Luis, extended the family fortune, but ruled more gently than his father. Anastasio Debayle won the presidency at a general election in 1967. The cash holdings carried on increasing; foreign protests at human rights abuses also mounted. He was attacked for embezzling enormous sums when international aid was sent after the devastating earthquake of 1972. By 1979, he had lost the support of President Carter, and he was overthrown in a revolution led by the Sandinistas, leaving the country with $100 million. He fled to Paraguay, haunt of war criminals, where he was assassinated. Despite their infamous reputation, the Somozas probably helped Nicaragua's economy to diversify.

Sonic Youth formed 1981

AMERICAN ROCK GROUP

A 1980s' guitar-rock vehicle, Sonic Youth drew on the tonal knowledge of minimalist experiments in tuning, volume and distortion, particularly those of composer Glenn Branca, to create sexy, speedy, obsessive, avant-garde pop that is crass and subtle, mobile and creaky. Their LPs are dense and obscure on first hearing, but increasingly addictive and sensual thereafter. Deliberately impenetrable in interview, this inscrutable and unusually democratic foursome offer something close to the ideal of rock that its earliest iconoclast theorists, ☛Richard Meltzer and ☛Lester Bangs, had demanded: an art that is post-everything and subtly political in understanding, but still prehistoric in sound. Sonic Youth came out of the aftermath of New York punk nihilism armed with player-resources far beyond those of most groups, and they promise to be to the early 1990s what ☛The Ramones were to the late 1970s – an inimitable role model. That is, as long as arrogance at their own success does not trip them up along the way, of course.

Susan Sontag born 1933

♦ AMERICAN CULTURAL
☞COMMENTATOR, NOVELIST

'Probably the most intelligent woman in America', Jonathan Miller called her, with an olde worlde chivalry that seems an age away now. In the 1960s, Sontag's gift was the critical re-expression of European high culture as a thing of urgent concern, paralleled with a playful veneration of all things pop. Almost alone, she found reasons to dovetail the great lost past into the energies of upheaval all around, but increasingly her tendency to venerate the pensive and the melancholic gave the game away – this is a doomed love affair with a dying lover. Much too smart to be unaware that the mandarin citadel has tumbled, given her sympathetic rad-lib politics and the energy she once put into polemics such as 'On Camp' and 'Against Interpretation', she now maintains a curious indifference to new values rising outside the European canon. Her importance is not lessened by this. When she brings all her New York seriousness and intelligence to bear on a pressing political/cultural subject – as with *Illness as Metaphor* (1976) and, more recently, *AIDS as Metaphor* (1988) – she is still a forceful voice, whose care and debunking alertness matter.

Ettore Sottsass born 1917

♦ ITALIAN ARCHITECT, DESIGNER

As an architect who, in the late 1940s, turned to designing small-scale pieces such as tables and vases, Sottsass's work was spotted by a member of the Olivetti family and, after a period of producing 'thick, very expensive aluminium cabinets' for huge computers, he was given the job of coming up with a design for the first electronic typewriter. In association with other designers such as Marcello Nizzoli (who created the Lexicon 80 typewriter in 1948), Sottsass went on to evolve a design vocabulary for the company's new technologies, including small computer systems and calculating machines. While retaining control of the Olivetti house style, he was also, in the early 1980s, the driving force behind Memphis, a Milan-based design movement which set out to challenge accepted notions of 'good taste' with anti-modernist furniture – rejecting the maxim that form follows function. Decoration was in, as Memphis sofas appeared, covered with the kinds of colours and patterns associated in the UK with punk graphics. Steeped in intellectual designer-speak, Memphis started out as a statement for rebellious people with a lot of money to spend on expensive furniture, but its legacy was mere style-mongering.

Thomas Sowell born 1930

AMERICAN ECONOMIST, JOURNALIST

An economist doubling as a right-wing columnist, Sowell has evolved a novel framework for analysing the differences between left-wing and right-wing views of the world – running through responses to a typical spectrum of issues from law and order and the economy to defence and international aid. The basis, he argues, for these patterns lies not in a different range of sympathies, nor in diverse models of relationships between state and citizens, but in views of human nature. 'Conservatives' adopt a 'constrained' vision; liberals, the reverse. Conservatives seek a society built round a common faith in the process of resolving arguments into outcomes, not an explicit commitment to end-results. They also see 'constraints' – social, legal, moral – as vital, to stop human wants running ahead of the resources at hand and inducing an interplay that leads to intolerable psychic pain. Sowell's is an elaborate scheme, but it may add up to nothing more than a distinction between 'optimists' and 'pessimists'.

Wole Soyinka born 1934

NIGERIAN PLAYWRIGHT, NOVELIST, CRITIC

Soyinka's writings have been disgracefully neglected by many First World literary establishments, largely because the keepers of the canon have been unsettled and embarrassed by his triumphant ease with structures that they wanted to reserve for their own, and his sardonic mastery of the multiplicity of voices and political demands associated with the modern novel. Even his 1986 Nobel prize for literature excited less attention than it ought to have done. Much of his work has involved deep-mining his Yoruba roots, beginning with a series of village-life comedies and moving into experiments at mapping the subtle and introspective Yoruba mythology on to its Greek analogue – brilliant and difficult cross-cultural cross-fertilization that has earned him a certain hostility from some African commentators. In the late 1960s, during Nigeria's ruinous and brutal civil war, he was imprisoned for pro-Biafran activity (his 1979 memoir, *The Man Died*, is an embittered account of his two-year gaol term), since when his work has become markedly less celebratory, while the intellectual demands on his readers have increased.

Wole Soyinka

Phil Spector born 1940

♦ AMERICAN RECORD PRODUCER

✖ Spector was gifted with melody and the ability to create sound, producing and writing records for The Ronettes, The Crystals, Ike and ☛Tina Turner, The Righteous Brothers and Darlene Love which reproduced the excitement of pop music simply by their apparent unremitting loudness and crashing hooks. (His 'wall of sound' production technique took the simplest tunes into canyons of holy thunder.) Spector raged through the 1960s, destroying talk show hosts and record companies by an almost megalomaniac conviction in his own abilities. His career is often reckoned to have been halted when radio DJs, tiring of his seeming dominance of pop, killed 'River Deep, Mountain High' in the US; the image of Spector as unhinged recluse began to appear soon after. Despite later superb work with John Lennon and Leonard Cohen, Spector found his style out of fashion as the creative producer became identified with record company manipulation and non-authentic music. (Spector's 'back to mono' campaign of the 1970s suggests also that he is uncomfortable with developing technology.) Sadly, as the age of the Svengali-producer returns, the man who epitomized that role has become just another 1960s' icon, brought in occasionally to add a 'Spectoresque' sound to a record. (He also tends to wave guns at artists and shout at them – another bad career move.) Spector, who created so much of what pop has become, has now been left behind by his monster.

Johnny Speight born 1921

▲ BRITISH TELEVISION WRITER

British television normally divides the political from the comic, keeping social comment for the serious end of the evening; satire is equally strongly aimed at the 'establishment'. The sole exception to these rules is Speight's Alf Garnett series. *Till Death Us Do Part* (1964-74) offered accurate and hilarious comment on the English bigot at home, a demon of ignorance and stupidity, and it had no peers as a vision of all that is appalling in England and the English. After some poor attempts at a 1970s' revamp, Speight wrote *In Sickness and in Health*, a series beginning in 1985 which took on the facts that his characters were now pensioners, poor and outmoded, crippled and dying. In the process, it acknowledged the similarly changed state of the nation. Garnett's prejudices are now more clearly the result of fear, his life less that of the jolly Cockney at home and more the old man trapped in poverty and neglect.

Dale Spender born 1934

✌ AUSTRALIAN FEMINIST

Unlike fellow Antipodean ☛Germaine Greer, Spender has chosen a low profile and no consorting with the foe. Her work, which is closely argued and rigorously academic, leads with absolute confidence towards a body of knowledge aimed at presenting a solid political challenge to patriarchy – a woman's history that exposes forgotten oppressions and celebrates unacknowledged contributions. Her most important book, *Man Made Language* (1980), makes a very convincing case for the existence of sex-specific symbolism (in religion, politics, literature and daily life), and the need for the development of an alternative set of symbols that shift towards feminist meanings and requirements.

Steven Spielberg born 1946

■ AMERICAN FILM DIRECTOR,
$ PRODUCER

Starting out as a competent television director, Spielberg quickly gained access to multi-million dollar budgets and went on to direct some of the most successful movies of all time. Influenced by cartoons and apparently intent upon emulating Disney's humanitarian themes and mainstream appeal, Spielberg's penchant for action, comedy and adventure – generally diluted with sentiment and the affirmation of the child in all of us – is most successfully encapsulated within *E.T.* (1982), whose central message is that children are closer to God due to their familiarity with innocence, fantasy and esoterica. Thus he restructured ancient mythology into a twentieth-century epic, stressing homespun platitudes. He moved on to tackle grown-up subjects, imposing a similarly well-meaning but hollow thematic on such films as *The Color Purple* (1986) and *Empire of the Sun* (1987). Spielberg's ultimate value is as a zealot who has restored the public's faith in the whole idea of going to the movies. And he has persuaded a whole new generation of film school graduates to ignore the rudiments of film theory and ☛Robert Bresson, stressing instead such contemporary wisdom as fun, love, money, agents and development deals.

Mickey Spillane born 1918

▲ AMERICAN NOVELIST

A hard-boiled detective story writer who began by writing comic books in the 1940s, Spillane invented Mike Hammer, the doyen of modern American vigilantism and bane of liberal critics, oblivious to the metaphorical subtexts and resonances scattered through such books as *I the Jury* (1947). Although Spillane's novels, in particular those featuring Hammer, have been vilified as one-dimensional, violently right-wing clichés, the books were voraciously consumed, elevating Spillane to a bestseller strata where, for critics, popularism equals bad taste. This is unfair. Hammer was a surreal precursor of other disillusioned, corroded heroes who willingly embraced fatalism – an emotional, confused yet cathartic figure for whom the anomalies of right and wrong may get in the way of physical vengeance. Such a moral tenet was highly relevant at the time, given America's response to the aftermath of WW2 and the moral dichotomies that James Bond and Dirty Harry have pursued ever since. Spillane twice retired from literature: in the 1950s to cultivate religion; and from the late 1970s, when he was largely content to collect the royalty cheques from the spin-off *Mike Hammer* television series and promote Miller Lite, that most macho of North American beers. But, after 20 years of silence, he recently published *The Killing Man*, in which Hammer takes on drug dealers and the CIA.

Benjamin Spock born 1903

AMERICAN PAEDIATRICIAN, POLITICAL ACTIVIST

Spiro Agnew, ☛Nixon's first vice-president, held Doctor Spock personally responsible for the anti-Vietnam protest movement. It may be overstating things to credit one man with fundamentally influencing a generation, but Spock's *Baby and Child Care* (1946) is up there with The Bible as one of the bestselling books of all time, and was referred to more frequently than the religious tome by many a post-war family. Addressing itself to the Victorian concept of parental discipline, Spock's book provided a strategy for more liberal times and stressed consideration for the child as an individual. In recent years, he has seemed to agree with his critics that children need stronger parental discipline than he recommended. Spock was also very active in the anti-war movement, and his image as godfather to the hippies was reinforced by his penchant for advising draft evasion.

Axel Springer 1912-85

$ WEST GERMAN PUBLISHER

In view of his later reputation as a press baron and ruthless exploiter of his power, it is entertaining to remember that one of Springer's first sales gimmicks involved handing out posies of white flowers to women at street corners. Like ☛Rupert Murdoch later in Britain, he owned both a scandal sheet and a 'respectable' newspaper: *Bild*, which he set up in 1952, was Germany's first successful tabloid, building its circulation figures on a diet of sport, crime, sex and innuendo; the following year, he took over *Die Welt*, the newspaper established by the British after WW2. Both were outspoken in their advocacy of Springer's views, particularly his desire to see West and East Germany reunited. In 1958, he pleaded the case for reunification in Moscow, and it was the failure of that mission which fuelled the passionately anti-Communist line he espoused thereafter. He accused ☛Willy Brandt of giving too much away to the Soviets during his time as chancellor, and published accounts of Brandt's bohemian lifestyle. Springer began to symbolize the unacceptable use of press power, and students marched on his offices after an assassination attempt on ☛Rudi Dutschke, who had been much vilified in the Springer press. By the time of his death, Springer controlled the largest press empire in Europe.

Bruce Springsteen born 1949

AMERICAN ROCK MUSICIAN

After years of bad poetry, woollen hats and unpleasant straggly bearded rock, Springsteen took note of the working class as portrayed by US cinema, assimilated the lot (from ☛James Dean to *Badlands,* from *Blue Collar* to *Wise Blood*), and trundled it out in simple language and cumbersome, loud rock. By now he had realized that ☛Phil Spector had a stronger grip on American mythic pop than ☛Bob Dylan, and that dance music would sell better; in 1984, 'Dancing in the Dark' became the first factory floor disco hit and Springsteen went on to conquer the world by complaining about Vietnam with 'Born in the USA' (1985). Springsteen took a set of views on American post-war culture and attached them to a supposed working man's version of democracy and integrity; in his favour is his apparent political sincerity, his taste and his genius for welding together disparate musical elements.

Set against that is his irritatingly bluff persona – rock star of the people – the fact that he apparently owns only one set of clothes, and his belief that a four-hour concert is not only 'good value' but also 'good rocking'.

Peter Stein born 1937

GERMAN THEATRE DIRECTOR

As director of West Berlin's lavishly state-funded Schaubühne Theatre through the 1970s, Stein was able to produce deconstructed versions of classic texts (resulting sometimes from three years' intensive research) that genuinely surprised, even while the 'message' – something about modern man's need to abandon individualism in favour of the collective – might seem to have been pre-ordained by the theatre's ensemble approach and political outlook. Stein's aim was to create pieces that combined the intellectual weight of Brechtian theatre with an emotional pull that owed more to Artaud, although he is willing to acknowledge that most audiences will swallow the spectacle without noticing the argument. Working now as a freelance, Stein recently staged a production of *Titus Andronicus* in an urban wasteland version of ancient Rome, resounding to the babble of air-raid sirens, ambulance wails and traffic noises, that demonstrated his ability to create resonant images, his painstaking approach to detail and his ability to make ancient texts relevant to today in a way that goes a long way beyond the sort of modern-dress updatings presented on the London stage.

Saul Steinberg born 1914

☞ AMERICAN CARTOONIST

A remarkable cartoonist for *The New Yorker*, whose work began to appear in the 1940s, Steinberg specializes in near-abstract comedies of meta-logic, where style itself – decoration, handwriting and the drawn line – is subject, object and butt of the joke. Cartoon people jostle with apt and unexpected word-picture representations of, for example, the days of the week, or the streets and avenues of New York. Steinberg's laconic, ink-scratch style echoes some of the obsessions of New York high art (☛Warhol's repetitions, ☛Johns' numerals), but for all his ease with abstraction, he is just as much amused by the borderline between the purist vision of it, and what happens when it fails (as when a member of the public, confronted by a ☛Jackson Pollock, says 'hey, I can see a face in that').

Gloria Steinem born 1934

AMERICAN PUBLISHER, FEMINIST

Steinem has been alternately acclaimed and derided as the gentle face of the feminist movement in the US. Starting out as a writer of photo captions on ☛Harvey Kurtzman's magazine *Help!*, she went on to make her name with her 1963 article 'I was a Playboy Bunny' (based on two weeks undercover as a bunny girl in one of ☛Hugh Hefner's clubs), and with a series of campaigning pieces that came out of her work for the civil rights movements. Writing up a meeting about abortion in 1968 as 'Black Power, Women's Liberation', she announced her conversion to the feminist cause. Her particular contribution in this area lay in the way she deployed her glamour and popularizing abilities as a way of alleviating male paranoia when discussing women's issues. In 1971, she was a founding editor of *Ms.* magazine , which publicized issues such as why women fear success and love between women, and spawned numerous imitators. Hardline radicals responded by attacking Steinem for 'backsliding bourgeois feminism', and viciously raking over her past – alleging early ties to the CIA. But Steinem weathered these storms, even though the magazine she founded retains little of its early influence.

George Steiner born 1929

⇔FRENCH-AMERICAN LITERARY
❞ CRITIC

Whatever it says on his passport, Steiner is normally referred to as a polymath, and his erudition is dazzling. He writes both to lament the passing of the notion of literature as a civilizing force, and to celebrate what remains from the past. The lament now comes with a warning, against allowing the density of literature to be submerged into science, oriental philosophies or mass culture. Unsympathetic to, and probably completely ignorant of, contemporary culture, he is still an appealing figure because of his evident passion for language and literature in its (historical) diversity, and his uncertainty as to whether that passion should be recommended more widely. He took a scythe to the agonizings of linguistic philosophers in *After Babel* (1975), arguing that it was the ambiguity within language which made it such a fine vehicle for fiction, generating metaphors and symbols to describe alternative worlds – dreams of freedom. More recently, in *Real Presences* (1989), he tried unsuccessfully to circumvent problems thrown up by deconstruction with the argument that literature should be approached with a sense of religious awe. A dazzling rhetorician, Steiner argues for the polymorphousness of culture against those thinkers, from Freud to ☛Lévi-Strauss, whose accounts of art as the manifestation of psychic traumata or structural constants he sees as attempts to constrain it.

We know now that man can read Goethe or Rilke in the evening, that he can play Bach or Schubert, and go to his day's work at Auschwitz in the morning.

George Steiner

Frank Stella born 1936

AMERICAN ARTIST

Stella secured rapid recognition, and the patronage of ☛Leo Castelli, in the late 1950s with precisely ruled black stripes laid on to his canvases with a housepainter's brush, a style that led the minimalist reaction against abstract expressionism. Nothing he has done since has matched the force of his initial impact, even though every shift in his approach involves a logical development from the original idea: aluminium and copper replaced black; new geometries took the place of lines; canvases were shaped to echo the configuration of the stripes; the original sparseness was replaced by a more lyrical, fluid style – culminating in the exotic, gaudy, garish *mélanges* of the *Exotic Bird* series of 1976 or the *Indian Bird* series of 1977-8. Since then, he has reversed back into simplicity with three-dimensional wall reliefs, but the ease with which he changes style makes it increasingly apparent that Stella sees himself as working new product lines rather than making any sort of statement about art or life.

Adlai Stevenson 1900-65

AMERICAN POLITICIAN

Hero of the liberal tradition in US politics, as Democratic Party candidate for president in 1952 and 1956, Stevenson summed up the humane values and zeal for public service of the Ivy League, even though he hailed not from the East Coast but from California. He was not linked to a programme, but to a style, and an approach – elegance, wit, thought. The phrase 'radical chic', without its negative associations, is applicable. He lost twice against a national hero, ☛Eisenhower, because he did not have the 'killer' instinct. That had been in his favour at the Democratic convention of 1952, when he was drafted for the nomination that he had never sought, but the Greek ideal of the philosopher-king, chosen for power against his will, did not appeal widely enough to middle-America. In fact, he won only one election in his life – to be governor of Illinois, by the biggest majority in the history of a state that was later to be noted for another tradition in Democratic politics: Mayor ☛Daley's hard graft. Stevenson spent his last four years as US ambassador to the UN, an apt post for an international idealist.

James Stirling born 1926

☞BRITISH ARCHITECT

& Stirling draws fruitfully from architecture's past but always makes from it something distinctively his own. He packs his buildings with historical references – heroic machine-age architecture for the Engineering Building at Leicester (1959-63), libraries of the nineteenth century for his History Faculty Building at Cambridge (1965-7), the whole history of art for the gallery in Stuttgart (1980-3) – but combines these within brazenly modern overall structures. The hard, shiny, brick-and-tile exteriors of the university buildings that he put up in the 1960s were designed as a riposte to the bland surfaces that characterized the British version of modern architecture. It required no 'conversion' to turn him into one of the most creative post-modern architects, circumventing the movement's nostalgic tendencies by ensuring that classical elements are always challenged by the new. The open circular courtyard of his Stuttgart Staatsgalerie may remind one of ancient Rome, but a colourful steel construction disturbs the original configuration. The eclecticism – Romanesque arches for the sculpture court, Egyptian cornices for the painting galleries – is always under firm control.

Karlheinz Stockhausen born 1928

♦ GERMAN COMPOSER

☞One of the first composers to utilize ☆ the potential of electronic music, Stockhausen's compositions blend purely abstract electronics with more recognizable sounds. In *Gesang der Jünglinge* (1956), for example, children's voices and nursery rhymes penetrate through an electronic mêlée. That piece ends with an act of praise, highlighting a religious sensibility that is characteristic of Stockhausen. A lapsed Catholic, he sometimes seems to see himself in the role, if not of deity, at least of ministering saint, an evangelist of the new world, preaching a vision of left-wing political rebirth from the furnace of the post-nuclear age. A sense of spiritual discipline emerges in the later works, as in *Aus den sieben Tagen* (1968), which contains no notation, simply an instruction for the performers to starve themselves in solitary silence for four days and then, 'late at night, play single sounds, without thinking you are playing.' Stockhausen was at least talked about, if not necessarily listened to, by most of the experimental synthesizer bands of the 1970s.

Edward Stone 1902-78

AMERICAN ARCHITECT

Stone's early adherence to the tenets of architectural modernism may account for the viciousness with which critics greeted his designs for the American Embassy in New Delhi in the 1950s. Its colour and ornament – a water garden, steel columns lined with gold leaf, an elephantine Great Seal above the entry – reflected Stone's feeling that austerity and restraint were appropriate neither to the setting nor to the building's function. The controversy sharpened his convictions, and enough people were persuaded that he had tapped the beginnings of a 'new architecture', to ensure that his career flourished. His Huntington Hartford Gallery of Modern Art (1965, now the New York City Department of Cultural Affairs), with its arches and curved windows reminiscent of Islamic architecture attracted such epithets as 'kitsch for the rich' and 'marble lollipops'. Stone did not really know where to go from there, and subsequent output eroded his reputation. There was no theory behind his ornamental invention, no convincing explanation as to why his was a road along which anyone else might want to go.

I(sidor) F(einstein) Stone 1907-89

AMERICAN JOURNALIST

Stone published his first magazine at the age of 14; called *The Progress*, it supported the League of Nations and Gandhi. He never stopped. For 19 years, until ill health forced him to shut down in 1972, he brought out *I. F. Stone's Weekly* on his own. It was a muck-raking broadsheet that exposed the contradictions between different government publications and proclamations. A radical-liberal democrat and life-long defender of free speech, at times Stone provided the only critique of particular White House and Pentagon mendacities. After his retirement, he settled down to write a complete history of free speech, a mammoth task that he soon narrowed down to a study of one of its earliest trials: the execution of Socrates during the golden age of Athenian democracy. The resulting book, *The Trial of Socrates* (1988), is a striking piece of politico-historical detective work which reaffirms Stone's commitments (very much at the expense of Socrates, whose worst anti-democratic tendencies are repeatedly flayed), and deploys his well-honed bullshit detector to enlarge our understanding of an event that has cast its shadow across the whole history of Western culture. Stone's belief was that close attention and acid comment can unearth a great deal of the wrongs that the powerful do. Much of the fierce contempt that disciples of his method, such as ☛Noam Chomsky, feel towards the press stems from a comparison between what Stone achieved with his one-man show and what the Fourth Estate, with their huge resources, seem continually to dodge.

Sly Stone

(Sylvester Stewart Stone) born 1944

AMERICAN POP MUSICIAN

♦ Sly and the Family Stone gathered up all the exuberance and optimism of late-1960s' pop and soul, made records that celebrated harmony, joy, unity and love, and then crashed the lot into a numb black wall of fear and despair. Sly Stone came through pop music as an eclectic genius, absorbing jazz, rock and soul; The Family Stone were the nearest to a collective that the pop charts had seen. Their records were parties and included everyone; they became the darlings of the teen-mags and the Woodstock audience. Sly responded by becoming rich, with drug problems. After a protracted silence, he returned with *There's a Riot Going On* (1971), a record which was not only unlike any of his previous ones, but was (and is) unlike anything else ever. It wails and screams and twists and sneers and occasionally lunges into apparently pretty pop, which is either sardonic or resigned. At a time when a 'statement' in rock music meant an acoustic guitar and a bad version of a ☛Dylan lyric, *There's a Riot* put a hole through rock music as a serious force. It also effectively wrecked Stone's career: a few LPs and minor hits later, he vanished from the pop scene, and only occasionally surfaces on compilations or backing vocals. Such is the reward for honesty in rock.

Tom Stoppard

(Thomas Straussler) born 1937

CZECHOSLOVAK-BRITISH PLAYWRIGHT

Born in Czechoslovakia but raised in India, Stoppard was briefly a journalist before his first play, *A Walk on the Water* (1960), led to various radio commissions and his breakthrough with *Rosencrantz and Guildenstern are Dead* (1967). Fitting in between the demise of The Goons and the birth of ☛Monty Python, the play poses questions about the meaninglessness of life and free will through the non-adventures of two minor characters from *Hamlet* during their absence from the action of the play. They discover they have no real existence, prompting the suggestion that, if Shakespeare is their god, deciding their actions and life and death, might not someone very similar be our God? This perfect marriage of ideas and farce led to further surrealistic forays: *The Real Inspector Hound* (1968) draws two theatre critics into the action of the play they are watching; while *Jumpers* (1972) satirizes logical positivism by looking at the disillusion felt when the moon, subject of so many romantic songs, is landed on by a group of Americans. The beginning of a move towards a more naturalistic style was marked by *Travesties* (1974), which found a perfectly logical motive for uniting Lenin, James Joyce and Dadaist painter Tristan Zara for an amateur production of *The Importance of Being Earnest* in Zürich during WWI. Stoppard's recent work has been more generic and less able to contain the weight of its ideas so that he now seems more comfortable adapting books into screenplays, and real events into television drama.

Lee Strasberg

(Israel Strasberg) 1901-82

❍ POLISH-AMERICAN ACTOR, THEORIST

Described by ☛Elia Kazan as having 'the aura of a prophet, a magician, a witch doctor, a psychoanalyst, and a feared father of a Jewish home', Strasberg brought the 'Method' to the US and helped to shape some of the most intense and overblown performances ever seen on the silver screen. The Method, as developed by Konstantin Stanislavsky, involved actors drawing upon their emotional experiences to feel their way inside their parts, rather than simply putting the characters on with their make-up. As artistic director of the Actors Studio from 1948, Strasberg coached such diverse talents as ☛Marilyn Monroe, ☛Marlon Brando, Rod Steiger, Dustin Hoffman and ☛Robert De Niro. Brando's performance as Joey in *On the Waterfront*, with his angst and despair externalized in fumbling, cramped gestures and mumbled, self-conscious dialogue, is the archetypal Method performance. Equally, De Niro's physical changes to meet the external demands of his characters in films such as *Raging Bull* and *The King of Comedy* are the style's extreme contemporary form. But the Method's potential for an almost mechanical form of self-parody often resulted in a character's identity becoming lost amid the mannerisms. Strasberg himself made an electrifyingly controlled cameo appearance as mobster Hyman Roth in *The Godfather II* (1974).

Leo Strauss 1899-1973

⇔ GERMAN-AMERICAN POLITICAL THEORIST

A teacher at the University of Chicago through the 1950s and 1960s, Strauss drew disciples to his analysis of the malaise in contemporary political thought, although his almost total disdain for the realities of modern society necessarily limits his influence. The source of the quasi-religious awe in which he is held came from his offer of a return to such ancient and comforting concepts as 'absolute truth' and a notion of 'natural right' – a high point on which students could take refuge from the moral relativism, scepticism and nihilism that 'modern' thinkers, from Hobbes to Nietzsche and beyond, had espoused. Strauss expressed distaste for egalitarian democracy, mass culture and what he saw as the contemporary cult of mediocrity, preferring instead a classical regime that made people 'civilized' by enthroning reason and virtue above base human passions and desires. It is a significant irony that ☛Ronald Reagan, the leader whose ascent went hand in hand with the rising fashion for Straussian ideas, was so far from being the sort of philosopher-king that Strauss's adherents seek. Recently, Allan Bloom's indictment of American university life, *The Closing of the American Mind* (1987), popularized Straussian arguments against value relativism – Bloom usefully shows how European intellectual ideas have been deboned in the US, producing 'nihilism with a happy ending' – and for restoring the humanities (particularly the study of Plato) to a prominent position in the curriculum. If Strauss's name is not particularly well known, it is partly because his followers revere it so much that they do not like to mention it, lest their own failings cast the teacher in a bad light.

Alfredo Stroessner born 1912

∀ PARAGUAYAN POLITICAL LEADER

Paraguay, like other Latin American states, has traditionally been run by military dictators – with brief, democratic interludes. General Stroessner, son of a German immigrant, was chief of the army staff when he came to power via a coup in 1954. He ran the country under an iron grip, 're-electing' himself via rigged polls every so often until February 1989, when he was forced into exile. He offered hospitality to Nazi war criminals and ran Paraguay as a family business: the general who toppled him was the father of his son-in-law. Contraband, including cocaine, made up more than half of Paraguay's trade, but his rackets did little to end the country's semi-feudal languor. A tough anti-Communist, Stroessner kept close relations for most of the time with the US, which has never been choosy about its Latin American allies.

Achmed Sukarno 1901-70

INDONESIAN POLITICAL LEADER

Sukarno was an aggressive, despotic Indonesian dictator, the first president of the state which won its independence after 1945 as the Dutch failed to regain pre-war control. Trained as an engineer, he began his career as leader of the anti-Dutch, anti-colonialist movement and, during WW2, he co-operated with the Japanese puppet governments. After taking power, he used theatrical oratory to exaggerate often fictitious external threats, mixing together Communism, Islam and nationalist ideas as a substitute for institutional mechanisms to tie together a racially heterogeneous archipelago; the economy took a back seat and island independence movements were suppressed. An enthusiast for an Indo-Malay empire, stretching from Malaya to Australia, Sukarno fought and lost a war against the British-backed Malaysians. One-man rule by Sukarno took over from parliamentary institutions in 1959 under the *1984*-ish slogan, 'Guided Democracy'. Suppression of a Communist coup attempt led to his butchering 300,000 rebels in 1965; but the rebel leader, General Suharto, was to ease him from power in 1968. Events since (especially in East Timor) have not shown Suharto to be much of an improvement.

Sun Ra born c. 1910

✍ AMERICAN JAZZ MUSICIAN

☆ ✓ Ra, whose exact name and birthdate are still kept under wraps, has maintained a mystical, baffling, highly entertaining avant-garde presence on the outskirts of jazz for over half a century. Dressing in robes and outlandish headgear, invoking all things spacey, he claims that he was born on Saturn millenia ago, and that he was kidnapped by aliens in the 1940s and trained as the Messiah – an honour he has since declined. Brought up in Birmingham, Alabama and, by his own account, sheltered from the worst racial prejudice of the times, he showed immediate promise as a musician, reaching his first audience by playing piano in Fletcher Henderson's popular swing orchestra and writing futuristic music that left many of his colleagues only reluctantly impressed. By the 1950s, he had evolved an independent community lifestyle, which was financed (just about) by the records he made with his own band, The Arkestra, a remarkable collection of players whose innovations – including his own on the synthesizer – deeply influenced the Free Jazz generation, and whose proto-New Age nuttiness somehow manages to be profound, political and theatrical at one and the same time.

Survival Research Laboratories

formed 1980

AMERICAN PERFORMANCE ARTISTS

Survival Research Laboratories is an eccentric and sometimes dangerous long-term performance project which has involved a guinea pig driving a giant flame-throwing metal spider, knife-wielding robots and the accidental explosive destruction of founder Mark Pauline's right hand. Their legendary performances involve monstrous machines, which often incorporate dead animal parts (though the guinea pig was alive and well and enjoying himself). Targeting bored Californian teens with such titles as *A Cruel and Relentless Plot to Pervert the Flesh of Beasts to Unholy Uses*, the three members of Survival Research Laboratories devote their considerable design and machine-construction skills to spectacles of extreme theatrical impracticality. Generally successful in amazing audiences, they present themselves as 'the vaccine for the virus of total destruction'. Pauline, the son of a Miami mobster, previously made a reputation for himself as a 'hoarding doctor', defacing billboard ads in offensive and socially valuable ways.

Mikhail Suslov

1902-82

SOVIET POLITICIAN

A shadowy figure, Suslov was for 35 years the chief ideological spokesman for Marxist-Leninism in Moscow. He joined the party in 1921, and rose rapidly through the era of the the Great Purge: after the war, he was in charge of sovietizing Lithuania; in 1946, he was chosen to run a department of agitation and propaganda; two years later, he took control of the Cominform; he was briefly, soon after, editor of *Pravda*. The late 1940s were his heyday. From Stalin's death in 1953 onwards, he was fighting a defensive war. He helped ☛Khrushchev to resist a palace coup in 1957, but stayed independent; he went on to organize Khrushchev's overthrow and replacement by ☛Brezhnev in 1964. As a symbol of orthodoxy, he has been succeeded by Yegor Ligachev – not quite in the same class.

Jan Svankmajer

born 1934

CZECHOSLOVAK ANIMATOR

Heir to the full darkness of turn-of-the-century Czechoslovak surrealism, Svankmajer has pushed model animation out to the dankly nightmarish limits of childish fantasy. In a short called *Dimensions of Dialogue* (1982), lovingly crafted clay statues claw lumps out of each other, and a parade of weird heads chew on each other, vomiting up an increasingly homogenized paste that blossoms into further parading, chewing heads. In *The Flat* (1968), a man is assaulted by everything in his tiny stone cell – the furniture, the walls, the lightbulb, the food, the water in the taps. The White Rabbit in Svankmajer's recent version of *Alice* (1988) is stuffed, and takes his watch out from a hole in his chest which continually leaks sawdust. Svankmajer's animation is simple compared to the sophistication demanded by the Hollywood horror mainstream, but because it evolves right at the heart of the still-infant adult unconscious, it occasionally cuts deep, as he recovers the sublimated domestic nastiness in tales-for-kiddies. *Alice* is a *tour de force* recap of the tricks he has been evolving over three decades; and the earlier works are generally more interesting. In *Down to the Cellar* (1983), for exam ple, the heartbreaking courage of a child sent to fetch potatoes from the bin in the basement in coal-dust darkness, facing in the process not only several bad dreams made real, but two very sinister neighbours, pushes at the limits of the genre.

Hans Jürgen Syberberg born 1935

☞GERMAN FILM DIRECTOR

Syberberg's early films were erratic forays in search of a theme and a style, but he had found his way by the time he came to make three controversial pictures exploring German history, in which his fellow countrymen are depicted as liars and hypocrites. After *Ludwig, Requiem for a Virgin King* (1972), about the mad visionary and builder of impossible castles who became Wagner's patron, and *Karl May* (1974), came the 12-hour *Hitler: A Film from Germany* (1977), which explores the Hitler that Syberberg finds inside us all. Using various techniques – puppets, circus rings, slides, theatrical settings, monologues – and presenting the Führer in numerous disguises, from Chaplin's Great Dictator and Frankenstein's Monster to a ventriloquist's dummy, the film explores the ways in which the multifarious messages purveyed by the mass media end up trivializing and distorting reality. Characterized by ☛Susan Sontag as 'a spectacle about spectacle', *Hitler* aimed to escape the 'pornography' of the standard war movie and to rescue the spirit of High Romanticism from its Nazi associations. Syberberg followed *Hitler* with a film of Wagner's *Parsifal* (1982), in which he subverted the militarist subtext of the Führer's favourite opera by replacing the lead figure with a woman.

Thomas Szasz born 1920

HUNGARIAN-AMERICAN PSYCHIATRIST

Szasz propounds a view of psychiatry that sends professionals into fits of apoplexy, but brings on screeches of 'right on' from others – or rather it did in the decade after he first laid out his argument in *The Myth of Mental Illness* (1961). His radical line built from the looseness of psychiatric language and the difficulties involved in defining, let alone treating, schizophrenia to the argument that the very concept of mental *illness* was a phoney. Psychiatrists were not curing disease, he said. They were social policemen, sent in to enforce a definition of normal behaviour. The initial enthusiasm for Szasz's writings waned as it became clear that he was not particularly concerned about throwing off social shackles, nor complaining about the power wielded by psychiatrists; his position was that individuals should take responsibility for their own actions. Today, he is cited as an authority for the policy of moving mental patients out into their non-existent communities. And while it is all very well for professors to argue that psychiatrists should deal only with 'voluntary' patients, helping them to reach their full potential, try telling someone who is living with a violent schizophrenic to rely upon their powers of verbal persuasion. As Szasz has gone on propounding the same idea, without significant development, for almost 30 years, it has become disturbingly apparent that he is just a one-trick academic.

Psychiatrists are not concerned with mental illnesses and their treatments. In actual practice they deal with personal, social and ethical problems of living.

Thomas Szasz

T

Toru Takemitsu born 1930

& JAPANESE COMPOSER

Takemitsu's unusual teenage desire, to become the new Debussy, was at first ruled even further out of bounds than most teen-dreams. WW2 and militant Japanese nationalism demanded that the only acceptable Western music was German and, in fact, the most Teutonic of the Romantic era. But when the war ended, and American culture flooded into Japan, Takemitsu wallowed in it. Even now, with a reputation as the subtlest of latter-day Impressionist composers, his range of technical explorations suggests a man unprepared ever again to be forced to dream within limits. He has experimented with the full spectrum of post-war innovations, including unusual instrument combinations (Japanese and Western), unconventional performing techniques, electronics, free improvisation and graphic notation, as he concentrates on building a sound world that is no longer wholly Japanese or wholly Western. Many of the Western composers who come closest to him in global outlook – including ☛Stockhausen, who Takemitsu first brought to Japan for the fabled Tokyo Expo – are familiar names to people who have never heard a note of their music. Takemitsu, by contrast, has provided the music for such international art-house film successes as *Women of the Dunes* (1964) and *Ran* (1985), and seems happy to make that last populist connection that the seniors of the Western avant-garde frown upon.

Talking Heads 1976-88

David Byrne born 1952
Chris Frantz born 1951
Jerry Harrison born 1949
Tina Weymouth born 1950

& AMERICAN POP GROUP

Talking Heads were the ones you could dance to with the 1977 cult monster, 'Psycho Killer'. David Byrne moved the band toward ethnicity, and from there they shifted for a decade back and forth between art and America, Europe and Africa, art and parody. Somehow they also began to have occasional hit singles and be allocated movie budgets. Talking Heads became immensely successful, simply because they had the curiosity to try everything. They never knew whether they were above pop or just part of it; their solo projects reveal conflicting truths, from the Tom Tom Club's eternal summer pop tunes to Byrne's hilariously unsettling *Music from the Knee Plays* (1985). Talking Heads, in short, were everything.

Andrei Tarkovsky

1932-86

▲ SOVIET FILM-MAKER

Like the novels of ☛Solzhenitsyn or the music of ☛Arvo Pärt, Tarkovsky's films, with their intense mystic imagery, come out of a Russian Christian tradition. A consistent vision runs through his pictures, from *Ivan's Childhood* (1962) to *The Sacrifice* (1986) – of a personal spiritual quest illuminated by images of icons, fire and water, and a fluid transition between time and place. His lionization in the West as an oppressed Soviet film-maker is an ideologically crude attitude which ignores the fact that, for all the bureaucratic problems he faced and the sporadic opportunities he had for working, he was at least allowed to realize his vision in film – resulting in such extraordinary pictures as *Solaris* (1972), his riposte to ☛Kubrick's *2001*, and the partly autobiographical *Mirror* (1975). He came West for his final films, *Nostalgia* (1985) and *The Sacrifice*, but although the images came from the same source, they seemed dessicated when cut off from the culture which had shaped them.

Frank Tashlin

1913-72

AMERICAN CARTOONIST, FILM DIRECTOR

Furiously inventive, Tashlin nourished America's pepsi 'n' popcorn crowd with movies such as *Hollywood or Bust* (1956), *The Girl Can't Help It* (1957) and *Cinderfella* (1960), turning the caricatured personas of Jayne Mansfield, Bob Hope and Jerry Lewis into live-action cartoons with outrageous sight gags. His protracted apprenticeship with animation supremo Max Fleischer, and later associations with ☛Tex Avery, ☛Chuck Jones and Bob Clampett, helped him develop a profoundly visual sense of comic timing. Despite directing a vast number of cartoons, he will be remembered for creating the absurd-for-its-own-sake school of comedy that would indirectly produce such diverse alumni as ☛Monty Python, ☛Richard Lester and Julien Temple.

A(lan) J(ohn) P(ercival) Taylor

1906-90

■ BRITISH HISTORIAN

A prolific historian of modern Europe, Taylor's genial, quirky, machine-gun style may be explained by his experience as a columnist on the *Daily Express* newspaper. He was a radical who sympathized with the Soviet Union but was at odds with schematic, Marxist 'conspiracy' theories. He explained the past through happenstance and inconsequentiality, favouring the 'cock-up' line: 'Whatever can go wrong, will.' His reputation developed after publication of *The Origins of the Second World War* (1961), in which he argues that Hitler, with no long-term plan for world mastery, was a gambler who seized chances and probably did not know his own mind. Taylor's passion for paradox led him to make many fast judgements that resist detailed proof; he relied on his 'green fingers' – his intuitions, his eye for the surprising detail, his gift for a racy story.

Cecil Taylor

born 1933

◆ AMERICAN JAZZ MUSICIAN

☞One of the cornerstones of the Free Jazz movement, Taylor's piano technique can seem bewildering – an unending torrent of notes, runs, flourishes and hammered chords. Looking for the underlying form in his work can be like looking for patterns in a snow-storm. Although classically trained, Taylor argues that he has returned to the blues – that since all music came from Africa anyway, what matters is to give what he does an African-American inflection. The result is a music that has been compared to a man playing 88 tuned drums – his work is highly percussive, and he has worked fruitfully with ☛Max Roach, the prince of the avant-garde drum kit. Taylor abstracts from conventional sources, but there is little point in trying to follow his music back to them. He is a significant original and his playing demands maximum stamina from sidemen, listeners and, most of all, himself.

Edward Teller born 1908

HUNGARIAN-AMERICAN PHYSICIST

Father of the hydrogen bomb and prophet of Star Wars, Teller is a brilliant, inventive scientist whose political imagination has been eroded by his position of power in the military-industrial establishment, where his personal hostility to Communism – born in Hungary, he became a naturalized American citizen in 1941 – has turned into a fixation with the rhetoric of the arms race. Starting his career under ☛Oppenheimer at Los Alamos, in 1945 Teller withheld his name from an appeal to have the atom bomb demonstrated openly before any use; nine years later, he gave the US Atomic Energy Commission details of Oppenheimer's opposition to the development of the H-bomb, which led to the latter's forced departure and subsequent ☛McCarthyite press-hounding. A masterful exponent of the necessity to modernize US nuclear arsenals, who once expressed the belief that radioactive fallout was an acceptable price to pay for freedom, Teller's scientific credibility was as sharply questioned as his politics in the wake of his Strategic Defense Initiative (SDI) proposal. This, a speculative suggestion of a nuclear defence umbrella of orbiting computer-run, laser guns designed to shoot incoming missiles out of the sky, was warmly taken up by ☛President Reagan, despite its many unsolvable problems and consequent ludicrous aspects.

It won't be until the bombs get so big that they can annihilate everything that people will really become terrified and begin to take a reasonable line in politics.
Edward Teller

Mother Teresa
(Agnes Gauxha Bojaxhiu) born 1910

ALBANIAN NUN, SETTLED IN INDIA

Standing for the Christian ethic at its most pietic and unassuming, Mother Teresa has spent more than 40 years going out from the relative comfort of her Calcutta convent to dispense food, medicine and hope to the abandoned and orphaned children of the slums. She has also sponsored more than 700 shelters and clinics around the world. Many see the work that she and her nuns, the Missionaries of Charity, perform as little more than a theological band aid – superficially dealing with the effects of overpopulation fo which her Church's opposition tc birth control is partially responsible – and her pro-life stance has certainl contributed to the problems witl which she deals. Providing a favourit photo opportunity for world leaders she has exploited her high profile t draw attention to world poverty, an has the knack of turning up at majo disasters – the Israeli invasion c Lebanon, the Armenian earthquake at the same time as the television cam eras. She embarrassed ☛Margaret Thatcher by going straight from the British prime minister's residence to help out at a London soup kitchen.

Studs Terkel born 1912

AMERICAN SOCIAL HISTORIAN

Jazz fan and DJ, Chicago radio-journalist and writer Terkel belongs to an older tradition of American populism than the one that is currently smothering his country. Since the mid-1960s, he has been using his tape-recorder to uncover what people are really thinking, and editing the results into his remarkable series of oral histories, wherein large numbers of US citizens unburden themselves of their worries, prejudices and memories. To date, he has given us *Hard Times: An Oral History of the Great Depression* (1970), *Working* (1975), *Division Street America* (1976), *American Dreams Lost and Found* (1982) and *The Great Divide* (1988) as forays towards a true history of the Silent Majority. Nothing in the evidence he uncovers suggests that things have got better since he began; equally, nothing suggests that people have got worse, even though the level of frustration, hopelessness, racial resentment and uncorrected ignorance have clearly risen since ☛Reagan came and left so blithely.

Glen Tetley born 1926

AMERICAN CHOREOGRAPHER

Tetley began training when almost in his 20s, but soon became one of America's top male dancers. The late start may explain his willingness, as a choreographer, to fuse the techniques of classical ballet to the innovations of the avant-garde. He worked briefly with ☛Martha Graham, but became prominent for the work he did with the Nederland Dans Teater in the 1960s, developing an eclectic style that drew upon such diverse sources as Japanese theatre, the movement of silent film comedians and the mime styles of Marcel Marceau. His first significant piece of choreography was *Pierrot Lunaire* (1962), a contest between innocence and experience. Sharp dramatic contrasts continue to characterize Tetley's work, together with a taste for savage themes: in *Mythical Hunters* (1965), a series of primitive, ritualistic sequences depict the male hunter's pursuit of his female prey. Increasingly he has taken an interest in non-narrative, 'pure' ballet. *Dithyramb* (1967) was an almost plotless juxtaposition of static poses and fast-moving dance; *Field Figures* (1970), set to music by ☛Stockhausen, contrasts male and female movements.

Twyla Tharp born 1941

AMERICAN CHOREOGRAPHER

When young, Tharp learned tap, ballet, jazz, contemporary, baton twirling, piano, violin, theory, composition, shorthand and typing. Unsurprisingly, her dance work has embraced a wide variety of styles and she has worked in a range of fields, from pop cred with her David Byrne-soundtracked *The Catherine Wheel* (1983) to baroque archness in the film version of *Amadeus* (1984). She started out as a dancer in the Paul Taylor company, but frustrated by the lack of opportunities for personal expression, she left in 1965 to set up her own company, creating pieces that were self-consciously aggressive and belligerent. As her company grew, Tharp moved sharply away from the staples of post-modern dance, limiting her movement vocabulary and dropping such standard routines as the task dance. A professional linkup with Mikhail Baryshnikov was established with the vaudevillian *Push Comes to Shove* (1985). That her career survived having worked on the movie of *Hair* (1979) is strong testament to her ability.

Margaret Thatcher born 1925

♦ BRITISH POLITICAL LEADER

Although Thatcher is an intellectually unimpressive figure, cowed thinkers have named an 'ism' after her. She has used a forceful personality to make a dynamic impact on a lazy political scene. Non-conformist and *petit bourgeois*, with narrow class fixations and obscure convictions at odds with the 'consensus' prevailing at the time of her elevation to leader of the Conservative Party, she won control of a party torn between High Tory tradition and market liberalism: no one, in fact, is less '*laissez-faire*' and she has never hidden her contempt for the languid aristocrats of the old order. She went on to win the premiership, and to transform political attitudes, although lasting changes were harder to discern. State-owned industries and council houses were sold off, trade union freedoms were curtailed, but economic growth was modest by post-war European standards. Inflation nudged back up, above the European average; unemployment, which tripled under her government, only briefly fell below the two million mark; and her early monetarist squeeze may have permanently damaged the UK's industrial base. It is debatable whether she can take the credit for the new enterprise culture which is said to have emerged in late 1980s' Britain, and which, with all the excitements it provides for insiders, has done little for a growing underclass of homeless and otherwise disenfranchised citizens. Her image of invincibility owed most to her performance on the world stage – earning the title of 'iron lady' from the Russians for her anti-Communist views; hectoring EEC ministers to secure rebates in Britain's contribution to the community budget; establishing strong friendships with ☛Ronald Reagan and ☛Mikhail Gorbachev; and leading the UK into the 1982 war against Argentina over The Falklands. But taken overall, hers was not a spectacular performance; nor is she a spectacular personality. Impervious to debate or the idea of non-partisan agreement ('perspective' is not, perhaps, a quality you would expect from someone who reputedly only needs five hours sleep a night), she survived for eleven years as prime minister by diverting her opponents into micro-class wars with one another. But her ideas, once shocking because she alone dared articulate them, left her seeming increasingly isolated and cranky. A mix of saloon-bar ideas and a passion for winning, combined with ruthlessness, respectability and gaps on the sympathy front do not really put her in line for a twentieth-century political Oscar.

Wilfred Thesiger born 1910

∀ BRITISH EXPLORER

Thesiger's writings are a hymn of hate to everything that modern technology has created: even as a boy, it is said, he hated aeroplanes for taking the effort out of travel. The last relic of an English aristocratic tradition which holds that the hard life is the only good life, he followed up an unhappy spell as a civil servant with five years among the bedouin of Arabia's Empty

Quarter – travelling on camels, participating in raids on other tribes, learning the ways of trade in the desert and enduring extreme privation. For some the resulting book would have been the *raison d'être* for such hardship, but Thesiger had to be cajoled into writing *Arabian Sands* (1959), which turned out to be the last eyewitness account of a lifestyle little changed since the time of Muhammad, now swept away by oil wealth. Equally impressive was his subsequent account of the less dynamic, but equally tough, life of *The Marsh Arabs* (1964), found among the high reeds growing in the flood waters of southern Iraq. Since then, between journeys, he has gone on lamenting the fact that the modern world no longer cares about heroic savagery and barbarian splendour.

René Thom

born 1923

FRENCH MATHEMATICIAN

Thom's 'catastrophe theory' has been applied to explain every sort of drastic event – including mental breakdowns, prison riots and the collapse of ecosystems. Where traditional calculus assumes continuous processes, Thom's theory provides a model for sudden flips that occur in continuous systems, following an accumulation of small inputs. Having first outlined the theory in 1968, he explored its broader implications in his 1972 book, *Structural Stability and Morphogenesis*, and thanks to the work of such popularizers as the charismatic Christopher Zeeman, Thom went on to acquire the reputation of a philosopher-mathematician. But many supposed applications of his theory make almost no use of his precise mathematics, and most of the sudden changes to which it has been applied can be described perfectly well by other forms of mathematics. As a result, many consider that the popularity of catastrophe theory should be ascribed almost wholly to its name – so appropriate to the temper of the times.

E(dward) P(almer) Thompson

born 1924

✌ BRITISH HISTORIAN, POLITICAL THINKER

Always maintaining a distance between himself and the academic establishment, Thompson transformed the way in which British history is written about. He also helped to shift perceptions of Britain's relationship to the two Europes, East and West, by keeping similarly aloof from radical political groupings. This low regard for cliques, and the dogmatism that sustains them, make him a very 'English' non-conformist figure. He argued through the late 1950s that inappropriate Continental ideas were being grafted on to British Communism, making inevitable his eventual expulsion from the party. His most influential book, *The Making of the English Working Class* (1963), opened up a new way of looking at the Industrial Revolution – by describing English radicalism in relation to working-class culture. Having sharpened his polemical powers through the late 1970s with attacks on the police, government ministers and others who were scything their way through traditional British liberties, Thompson emerged in 1980 as the spokesman for the revived Campaign for Nuclear Disarmament. An earnest, harassed, white-haired figure, Thompson mustered sufficient public opposition to the stationing of US cruise missiles on British soil to stave off the factionalism that had dogged the movement in the early 1960s. Politicians scoffed at his insistence that there was no moral difference between US foreign policy and that of the USSR, and mocked his scenario for a reconciliation between the peoples of Eastern and Western Europe. However, the events of the late 1980s, when the cruise missiles did go home and Eastern bloc countries began to envisage a future without the Communist Party, showed Thompson to have been a more reliable prophet than he, or anyone else, might have anticipated at the beginning of the decade.

Hunter S. Thompson born 1939

AMERICAN JOURNALIST

The social upheavals of the mid-1960s, inaccessible to the mandarin weightiness of traditional US journalese, brought with them the 'New Journalism' – subjective, hip and speeding on its own irresponsibility. Thompson's basic pitch is that only a spirit wholly immersed in the post-Vietnam, gun-ridden, drug-fuelled rot of America can chronicle it accurately, and his fried, psychotic, paranoid semi-fictional document, *Fear and Loathing in Las Vegas* (1972), is thus his best-known work. Thompson's wired energy is backed by a phenomenal ability to grasp complex facts and report them coherently, which led to accounts of Watergate and the Democratic Party Convention of 1972 which are unmatched for laying out the seamy drama of byzantine political situations. Thompson – the mad, dogged analyst of the ☛Nixon years – seemed to lose his grip in the surrealism of the Daydream Nation under good-time Ron. As George Bush offers a return to old-time rampant hypocrisy, Thompson is once more on the prowl – older, weirder, a rogue frontiersman with his own peculiar sense of honour. And the guardians of the status quo are out to get him, having arraigned him on six charges relating to drug use, possession of explosives and drugs, unlawful sexual contact and assault.

He speaks for the Werewolf in us; the bully, the predatory shyster who turns into something unspeakable, full of claws and bleeding string-warts on nights when the moon comes too close.
Hunter S. Thompson on Nixon

Throbbing Gristle/ Psychic TV

formed 1976

☆ AMERICAN UNDERGROUND GROUP

Rock's desire to seem a threat to Western civilization has been turned into a masterful little crusade by Genesis P. Orridge, a sweetly sinister and engaging family man. With the theatre of Throbbing Gristle, he used repetition, ritual and shock to short-circuit the consumer's expectation of being managed towards certain approved pleasures. TG became the focus for a number of low-budget electronic groups who developed concurrently with the emergence of punk; it also spearheaded the 'Industrial' movement, an international network of artists who derived their force from the arcane research carried out by ☛William Burroughs into power/control mechanisms, tribal cultures, modern primitivism and many of the darker undercurrents of society. Inevitably they ranged from intelligent explorers to mumbo-jumbo occultists, and the latter received the most publicity. When TG imploded Orridge inaugurated Psychic TV, to carry on the work in different ways and at different levels – his stated aim now is to bring about a better world with his own religion: Thee Temple Ov Psychic Youth. PTV is the rel gion's erratic pop spearhead, which lurches from hypnotic trance-rock to clumsily experimental self-parody and back. Half the things you hear about Orridge are not true – as for the other half, he has left a lot of hostages to fortune over the years, by accident or design. Some continue to dismiss him as a very ordinary man hungry for publicity; others would argue that, simply by combining the particular contradictions he exhibits in one project and one personality, he may really be as extraordinary as he wants to seem.

Nikolaas Tinbergen 1907-88

♦ DUTCH ETHOLOGIST

☛Konrad Lorenz and 'Niko' Tinbergen founded modern ethology by taking the study of animal behaviour out of the lab and into the field, and opening up the sorts of questions about the consequences of evolutionary histories and the function of particular activity patterns that had simply been bypassed by those who looked only at rats pressing levers in boxes. Tinbergen's own field studies emphasized the richness of animal repertoires. Through detailed observation of how similar species deal with particular problems, he came to understand how adaptation to specific environmental circumstances shapes behaviour. Why, he asked, do some seagulls remove the eggshell remnants from the nest after the chick has hatched? The answer is that some have predators who see the eggshells as a sure sign of a bite-size meal, and others do not. Like Lorenz, Tinbergen was also interested in the combined effect of different levels of behaviour and the way they might be organized into hierarchies. At the lowest level are small, relatively consistent packages, but the way these patterns are combined is very flexible and allows animals to build extensive, seemingly unpredictable, repertoires to suit changing circumstances. Like many ideas that change the course of a scientific discipline, Tinbergen's now seem obvious, almost simplistic. Only in the context of the dogmatic attitudes prevailing at the time can their significance be appreciated.

Dmitri Tiomkin born 1899

RUSSIAN-AMERICAN FILM COMPOSER

Despite an early and distinguished career scoring film classics for the likes of Frank Capra, ☛Alfred Hitchcock and Howard Hawks, Soviet refugee Tiomkin's main contribution to motion pictures was the creation of the hit single as a selling tool. Following disastrous previews of a low-budget western, Tiomkin tried to salvage his investment (he had taken a percentage rather than his full fee) by selling the title song he had built the score around to a record company. The resulting 'Do Not Forsake Me, Oh My Darling' was such a phenomenal hit that the film, *High Noon* (1952), was taken off the distributor's shelf and went on to do tremendous business. Theme tunes folowed for *Gunfight at the OK Corral* (1957) and *The Alamo* (1960). His attempts to repeat the formula outside the western genre were often embarrassing, but Tiomkin's ability to convey a sense of epic grandeur without losing human intimacy, as in *Red River* (1948), *Giant* (1956) and *The Fall of the Roman Empire* (1964), made him the top man in the business for the best part of three decades.

Michael Tippett born 1905

BRITISH COMPOSER

That a man who can title an aria 'Motherfucker' – from his opera *The Ice Break* (1977) – can also be a knight of the realm suggests that opera's deadening social respectability will not be gainsaid. Tippett, a natural social dissident (pacifist, atheist), made his name with the oratorio *A Child of Our Time* (1941), an account of the Nazi terror that deals with the classic themes of the twentieth century: the individual beset by desolation, violence, persecution and isolation. Although essentially an epic work of condemnation, it bears formal relationships to the affirmative religious tradition of works such as Handel's *Messiah* and Bach's *St Matthew Passion*. Tippett's youthful affinities with Stravinsky's neo-classicism and Hindemith's jazz-inflected eclecticism, combined with an abiding fascination for his most unmistakably English forebears (Purcell, the madrigalists), probably denied him the attention less political but more formally radical (and anti-Romantic) composers gained. In the 1950s and 1960s, they steered away from the mixed-media demands of theatrical music, but in his drive for pan-cultural reconciliation, Tippett worked (productively) with little else, dealing with personal, social and universal themes in operas such as *The Midsummer Marriage* (1955), *King Priam* (1962) and *The Knot Garden* (1970). Remarkably, he has carried on writing operas into his mid-80s, picking and mixing today's musical sounds with pop-culture references in *New Year* (1989), the story of a child psychologist terrified to set foot outside her room and enter the chaos of Danger Town.

Richard Titmuss 1907-73

BRITISH ECONOMIST

Titmuss was dubbed the 'high priest of the welfare state' in Britain. Although he became professor of social administration at the London School of Economics, he had never taken an exam in his life, coming to the post from working as a book-keeper. His special interest was social statistics, the predominant theme in his major studies of the social services. He argued that traditional British statistics left out the social dimension – he wanted 'humanistic accounting'. His most famous case-study looked at the private market for blood donors. It wasn't good enough, he felt – commerce undermined social integration and a 'Gresham's Law' of selfishness applied. He established social administration as an important subject in universities, and matched his studies with practical work on supplementary benefit tribunals.

Tito

(Josip Broz) 1892-8[illegible]

YUGOSLAV POLITICAL LEADER

Yugoslavia has always been a fragil[illegible] federation, inviting break-up. For 4[illegible] years, Tito, a Croatian Communis[illegible] leader of the anti-Nazi resistance an[illegible] subsequently head of state, skilfull[illegible] and ruthlessly upheld it as a uni[illegible] against German or Soviet outsider[illegible] and internal attacks. Other Croats sid[illegible]ed with Hitler in the war; Tito wa[illegible] driven by a fierce nationalism. Th[illegible] son of a peasant, he was a youn[illegible] mechanic who fought in the Austria[illegible] army during WW1, was captured b[illegible] the Soviets and joined the Red Arm[illegible] He was the first Communist leader t[illegible] break with the USSR, in 1948, rotatin[illegible] between pro-Western and neutrali[illegible] axes as counters to Soviet pressure. Worker self-management evolved as a Titoist device to give Yugoslavia, at home, a novel economic twist. Unlike Hungary's ☛Imre Nagy, Tito was not a Marxist victim of history; unlike Romania's ☛Nicolae Ceauşescu, another independent Eastern European, he did not let a dynastic leadership cult and Stalinist convictions cancel out progress.

Alvin Toffler born 1928

❃ AMERICAN SOCIOLOGIST

Being a futurologist is fun, given that, in the late twentieth century, almost anything can happen, and no one is going to mind if you get it wrong as long as your account is apocalyptic enough to grab attention. Toffler spews out theories, wields dubious statistics and accumulates the sort of clumsy neologisms that do not stand a chance of reaching the dictionary – such as 'indust-reality', 'blip culture', 'psycho-sphere' – but his theories never add up to a very clear picture of where we are going. In *Future Shock* (1970), he suggested that society was on the point of a breakdown because of the stress and disorientation resulting from rapid change – of the sort that shifts values, destroys communities and overturns institutions – and, in the process, begged countless questions about how adaptable humans are to the changes he described. Ten years later, he seemed to turn the argument around to posit that *The Third Wave* (1980), the result of all the new technologies, would make everything in the garden rosy if only we would embrace it fast enough: the mass media would fragment, the proletariat would break up into small cottage-industry units, individual time would be freed up for creativity and leisure and the old political formations would be shattered. A lot of what Toffler talks about is happening, but there are also forces pulling very hard in the other direction. Whether prophesying crackup or utopia, he seems overconcerned to offer his readers a pathway to some brighter future – the weakness of the compulsive popularizer. In the early 1970s, when Toffler sent ☛Harold Wilson two of his articles to introduce his ideas, the British prime minister responded by saying that he was not interested in talking to a man who had written for *Playboy*.

J(ohn) R(onald) R(euel) Tolkien 1892-73

☞ BRITISH NOVELIST

An academic philologist, Tolkien must have been surprised and embarrassed when his novels were adopted by Disney-weaned sectors of the Flower Power era. In bald summary, the story of hobbit Frodo's quest to cast the One Ring into the Cracks of Doom and end for ever the evil power of Sauron the Great can seem both twee and irritating; it inspired the science-fiction 'Sword and Sorcery' genre that uglified the 1970s. However, the naïveté is also a strength, and the extraordinary depth of his background invention – he thought up not one, but several complete languages in the course of developing his mythologies – takes his work beyond the workaday. Regarded as avant-garde when the various volumes first appeared in the 1950s, *The Lord of the Rings* can now be clearly seen for what it is – a bluff, cheerful translation of Norse and Old English archetypes into the language and attitudes of middle-class Home Counties Britain in the 1920s. The absurd vastness of his imagined world gives him a firm place at the forefront of fantasy construction.

Kwame Touré *see* Carmichael, Stokely

Michel Tournier born 1924

FRANCO-GERMAN NOVELIST

Tournier is fascinated by relationships between grown men and infants, and his novels serve as reminders that there is no escape from the experiences of childhood – which he commonly depicts as a mysterious ritual out of which infinite potential is reduced to destiny, which decides whether the result will be a saint or, more interestingly, a monster. Originally trained in both French and German philosophy, Tournier has used his bicultural understanding, notably in *The Erl-King* (aka *The Ogre*, 1970/2), to explore the attractions of Nazism's perversions to a maladjusted Frenchman. Despite some similarity in their concerns, he would have shocked J. M. Barrie with his declaration that the novelist should practice perversity since 'there is nothing comparable to the exploratory and polymorphous suppleness peculiar to infantile sexuality.' Those critics who charge Tournier with immaturity overlook his message that we have to do more than 'come to terms' with our dark side.

Robert Towne born 1936

AMERICAN SCREENWRITER, FILM DIRECTOR

As well known for the scripts he has rewritten (*The Godfather* 1972, *Marathon Man* 1976) as for those he wrote himself (*The Last Detail* 1973, *Chinatown* 1974, *Shampoo* 1975), Towne is a rarity: an American screenwriter who is not only a skilled craftsman when it comes to sustaining audience interest, but also brings to his work a deep grasp of character, vernacular idiom and the possibilities of cinematic expression. And he has sufficient regard for the medium not to see himself, like so many others who feel they have 'sold out' to Hollywood, as a novelist or playwright *manqué*. The dip that Towne's career seems to have undergone during the 1980s is generally credited to his 'mistake' in seeking to build a career as a director with *Personal Best* (1982) and *Tequila Sunrise* (1988). Perhaps it is rather that the American film industry, hooked on one-dimensional storylines and formulaic scripts, can no longer make a comfortable space for such a writer. Or it may be that Towne himself is having problems living up to his own mythical reputation.

Arnold Toynbee 1889-1975

BRITISH HISTORIAN

Toynbee told the British that their empire was doomed, and bestowed on Americans a mission to save Western civilization. While other professional historians considered his writings largely bunk, Toynbee acquired prophet status in the US and commanded such substantial fees for lecturing there that one malicious observer remarked that he must 'rank second only to whisky' as a post-war dollar-earner. His 12-volume *A Study of History* (1934-61) argued that civilizations grew by reacting constructively to the demands of small groups of special, talented leaders. Tyrannical cliques as well as militaristic and nationalistic tendencies undermined the forces for expansion, since they were unable to act intuitively or imaginatively. It was this account of the cyclical rise and fall of civilizations that drew flak from Toynbee's peers, who perceived the work as a product of soggy mysticism rather than analysis: a long article in 1957, written by Hugh Trevor-Roper and published in *Encounter*, labelled him 'fundamentally anti-rational and illiberal' and 'moved by a detestation of human reason and its works'. Toynbee's vision of world history was undoubtedly wrong, but the erudition remains astonishing.

Lionel Trilling 1905-75

AMERICAN LITERARY CRITIC

Trilling set up literature as an antidote to those forces in modern culture that crushed the idiosyncratic individual perspective in favour of dull convention and group-approved moralities. He staked his ground with *The Liberal Imagination* (1950), in which he argued that writers should deal with hard facts, and reveal to readers the intractibility of human existence. Writing is an act of courage that involves tolerance of uncertainty and resistance to the allure of ideology – demonstrating 'that one may live a real life apart from the group, that one may exist as an actual person not only at the centre of society but on its margins, that one's values may be none the less real and valuable because they do not prevail.' All this was as much anathema to the 1960s' generation as the crudities of the progressive spirit were to Trilling, who became increasingly aggressive in his defence of moral liberalism and intellectual standards. The 'free play of mind' was his clarion call; pop and the mechanistic attitude to sex incorporated in the ☛Kinsey reports were among his bugbears. He attacked thinkers such as ☛Laing and ☛Foucault, whose work he saw as a glorification of irrationality, and his final, sour book, *Sincerity and Authenticity* (1972), was an onslaught on those who offered routes to an experience of the divine which did not involve the inconveniences of 'reasoning with rabbis, or making sermons'.

Alexander Trocchi 1924-84

SCOTTISH-ITALIAN POET

Trocchi fled to Paris in order to escape Scotland's 'turgid, petty, puritan, stale-porridge, Bible-class nonsense' and became involved with the Beat movement. Responsible for coining the catchy phrase, 'cosmonaut of inner space', he proselytized for a non-political revolution in consciousness. His two 'serious' novels are both marked by the *sang-froid* of their prose style and rejection of conventional morality. Both also deal with the theme of the wanderer: across the canals of late-1950s' Britain in *Young Adam* (1954, under the pseudonym of Frances Lengel); through the dockland underworld and drug subculture of New York in *Cain's Book* (1960). He also wrote a series of 'dirty books' for ☛Maurice Girodias's Olympia Press imprint, and his contributions are worth reading for other than prurient reasons. *Thongs* (1967), with its combination of Glasgow noir and S&M fantasy, almost certainly influenced ☛Alasdair Gray's *1982, Janine*. From the mid-1950s Trocchi was associated with ☛Guy Debord and the Situationist International and shared much of their resistance to convention and routine. A heroin addict for more than 30 years, it is hard to decide whether he ended up victor or victim.

Garry Trudeau born 1948

AMERICAN CARTOONIST

Trudeau is widely acknowledged as America's leading political cartoonist, even though *Doonesbury* is produced in a strip format that is often banished to the funnies pages. Since its début in 1969, his strip has dramatized events of the day – as well as fashions and social shifts – by weaving standard shots at major political personalities with the changing lives of a group of former campus buddies. Anti-war, anti-authority, critical and alert, named for its quietest character, *Doonesbury* has been simultaneously loved and feared by the political élite since the ☛Nixon years. At times, it has showed inspired prescience: representing Bush as a mobile mumbling vacuum with an evil twin brother, Skippy; and having Nixon send no less a reprobate than Trudeau's friend ☛Hunter S. Thompson as his ambassador to China, thinly disguised as the character Duke. More than any other artist, Trudeau has been responsible for giving 1960s' underground attitudes a mainstream outlet.

Pierre Trudeau born 1919

CANADIAN POLITICAL LEADER

Canadian prime minister for 15 years between 1969 and 1984, Trudeau stood for a moderate French-Canadian stance against the nationalists of Quebec, and helped Canada to survive testing domestic tensions. Sophisticated and modern-minded, he also represented Canada's desire for some measure of autonomy: he ushered through the severance of constititutional ties with Britain; and he opposed the siting of US nuclear arms on Canadian soil. His charismatic and flamboyant style gave him a ☛Kennedy-ish air, but he was less conventional; thus, his image as a late-1960s' 'swinger', with sports cars, girlfriends in mini-skirts and, after he married in 1971, a wife who dallied with a member of ☛The Rolling Stones. He campaigned, Swedish style, for a new world economic order and redistribution in favour of the Third World.

François Truffaut 1942-84

FRENCH FILM-MAKER

At this distance in time, it is difficult to understand how two film-makers as different as Truffaut and ☛Jean-Luc Godard could ever have worked on the same magazine, *Cahiers du Cinéma*, or have given commentators the impression that they were arguing about the same things. Truffaut's qualities as a critic derived from an all-embracing passion for cinema which enabled him to respond both to the romantic realism of Renoir and to ☛Hitchcock's misanthropic suspense tactics, and his film-making was an attempt to reconcile these conflicting influences. When Hitchcock's influence was dominant, as in *The Bride Wore Black* (1967), the result lacked the *élan* that characterized more obviously personal films: *400 Blows* (1959), his semi-autobiographical story of a juvenile delinquent's early life; *Jules and Jim* (1961), a chronicle of an impossible three-cornered love; and *Day for Night* (1973), his account of the craziness that making a film involves. Truffaut's early roots in a vibrant critical culture ensured that he had a good crack at putting his personal concerns on to the screen in films that nevertheless communicated something to an audience, demonstrating that the *politique des auteurs* for which he had argued as a critic, did not necessarily lead to self-indulgent tosh. But as he became increasingly divorced from his former colleagues, Truffaut became the first victim of that lack of creative challenge which too often follows the successful bid for directorial independence, and is the bane of contemporary cinema.

Harry S. Truman 1884-1972

AMERICAN POLITICAL LEADER

A tough, modest fighter, unexpectedly picked as US vice-president in 1944, Truman became president as unexpectedly, on Roosevelt's death in April 1945. Among other things, he will go down in history as the man who used atom bombs against Japan when he could have tested them on an empty atoll to shock the enemy into surrender. Born on a Missouri farm, Truman pursued an erratic career as a Kansas haberdasher before joining the state's Democratic Party machine as a civic official. Elected as a senator, he made his name by exposing graft in WW2 defence programmes. As president, he swung the US into an interventionist line abroad, overseeing the Marshall Plan for Europe, the formation of NATO and the giving of aid to states menaced by Communism, under the 'Truman doctrine'. As the US 'lost' China to the Reds and failed to prevent the Korean War, his administration was attacked by right-wingers, such as ☛Joseph McCarthy. He gave way to pressure over 'Communists' in official posts but, in 1951, sacked General McArthur as head of his forces in Korea for posing the threat of nuclear war against China. Truman lacked strength in Congress to realize promised welfare programmes, and he oversaw the breakup of Roosevelt's Democratic Party coalition of workers, blacks, liberals and the South. He was a conformist president, who was determined to resist the Soviet Union at all costs. But the world needed a chance to emerge from the Cold War sooner, if not later. Truman lacked Roosevelt's will or imagination, and he did not (or could not) create the conditions at home for a lasting, liberal order abroad.

Alan Turing 1912-54

† BRITISH MATHEMATICIAN

⚣ ❍ ♦ The key figure in the development of digital computers, Turing is the twentieth century's most likely candidate for elevation to the super league of scientific history. As a cryptographer in WW2, he designed Colossus, the first practical program computer, which broke the German secret codes. He also proposed a theoretical test for assessing whether machines possess intelligence. Originally called 'the imitation game', although now more commonly known as the Turing test, it proposes a way of determining if a simulation of the human mind can be successful. Two subjects, a man and a woman, sit in different rooms. An investigator in a different room asks them questions to which they reply via a teletype. The investigator's job is to find out which replies are from which person without asking questions about physical attributes. The next step of the game is to substitute a machine for one of the humans. Can the interrogator distinguish the machine from the remaining human? If not, the machine has truly simulated a 'mind'. The major objection is that the test is behaviouristic. Turing's answer is twofold: he stresses that the important questions are not what minds are made of, smell like or look like, but whether they act intelligently. Second, he says that though this is a 'black box' test, we treat each other every day as black boxes, as we cannot get inside another human being to have direct contact with their conscious experience. The game proposes a clear test, demanding but possible, and crisply objective in its judging. In his original paper, Turing left open the question of whether we should assume that any machine which passes the test is conscious. But perhaps that is another story. Turing's suicide was the result of medical treatment aimed at 'curing' his homosexuality, which he was forced to undergo in order to evade a prison term.

Tina Turner

(Annie Mae Braddock) born 1938

✓ AMERICAN ROCK PERFORMER

In the 1960s, despite a reputation as a belting soul singer, Turner was really known as the women who sang 'River Deep, Mountain High'. In the 1970s, despite having appeared at Woodstock and played the Acid Queen in ☛Ken Russell's *Tommy* (1974), she was the woman who sang 'Nutbush City Limits'. In the 1980s, she seemed set to be known as the woman who Ike Turner used to abuse, but instead she became the first person to benefit from British pop's 1980s' fetish for rehabilitating icons. She was relaunched as a survivor – a frighteningly raunchy older woman of rock who will never actually make a good record again. It is as if pop music did not know what to do with her when her career ended and she did not die in poverty, so they kicked her so far up into the category of 'living legend' that she became a genuine star – vastly rich and distant. In 1988, the women who two decades earlier would have been fifth on the bill to Diana Ross, played in Rio to the biggest concert audience yet recorded. This is how history rewrites itself.

Amos Tutuola

born 1920

∀ NIGERIAN WRITER

Tutuola's *Palm Wine Drinkard*, published in 1952 and the first novel from tropical Africa to secure a wide non-African readership, showed up the inadequacy of Western critical categories when it comes to dealing with texts from outside its own traditions. While Welsh poet Dylan Thomas admired Tutuola's highly idiosyncratic use of English, others dismissed the book as quaint and primitive. Meanwhile many Africans were dismayed that such an 'unsophisticated' piece of writing was being promoted as the new voice of the continent. Subsequent reactions to *Drinkard* and Tutuola's four subsequent novels have not done much to clarify the issues, with Western critics trying to squeeze his books within established critical pigeon holes and making comparisons to Kafka's stories of quest or to André Breton's surrealism, while many Africans now celebrate Tutuola as the only completely *African* writer. What commentators seemed to miss was just how rich was Tutuola's language and deployment of Yoruba myth, as he fused native supernaturalism into an unsophisticated narrative. He seems to draw nothing from European traditions, but then, if that is the case, what have two-and-a-half millenia of Western civilization been for? Tutuola have had no imitators, but he has been translated.

Aleksandr Tvardovsky 1910-71

✓ SOVIET PUBLISHER

All dissidents in the Soviet bloc have had to play a cat-and-mouse game with the authorities. Their role became especially ambiguous if they were attached to a group or outlet which was on the inside track. Tvardovsky is a classic case. A popular, talented poet, he took over in 1952 as editor of the literary magazine *Novy Mir* ('New World'), a position from which he was twice expelled. In 1954, during the twilight era between Stalin's death and ☛Khrushchev's clear emergence as a leader, he ran pieces which argued for further liberalization. He lost his job; the magazine survived. In 1958, he won the post back again, as Khrushchev loosened literary controls, and took the chance to publish ☛Solzhenitsyn's *One Day in the Life of Ivan Denisovitch* (1962). The authorities stopped publication of *Cancer Ward*, but allowed a new Solzhenitsyn short story to appear in 1966. Under ☛Brezhnev, Tvardovsky lost his job again, in 1970; but *Novy Mir* continued. Official tolerance of the magazine implied an interest in allowing some sort of independent voice.

Ken Tynan 1927-80

BRITISH THEATRE CRITIC

The two things most people know about Tynan – that his *O Calcutta!* (1969) put nudity and sex back on the London stage for the first time in several centuries, and that he was the first person to say 'fuck' on television – are a fairly precise summary of his legacy. 'Rouse tempers, goad and lacerate, raise whirlwinds' could have been the motto of this bastard son of the English aristocracy. His work as a critic restored controversy to theatre and writing in the 1950s and 1960s, but *O Calcutta!* was an ill-conceived revue-romp which proved that his artistic judgement needed to be driven against the solid presence of others before things could spark. He had given up criticism because he was tired of the role of spectator and professional groupie, but once free of them, he seemed to prefer mixing with the glitterati than out-creating them. As a result, he is remembered as an anarchic social commentator, raconteur and enemy of timid mediocrity rather than as any kind of artist.

U

U2 formed 1979

Paul 'Bono' Hewson born 1960
Dave 'The Edge' Evans born 1961
Adam Clayton born 1960
Larry Mullen born 1962

IRISH ROCK GROUP

Bono Hewson and Dave Evans invented a music which drew on ☛Joy Division's desperate passion and took U2 out of Ireland into the world of rock. Their discovery of America and its stadium outlook gelled perfectly with Bono's Christian sense of awe and grandeur. On their way to phenomenal success, they traded their European sensibilities for American glory, going straight from anti-rock to rock 'n' roll. U2 have come to be perceived as being as significant as ☛Madonna or ☛Michael Jackson, when really they sell less than Def Leppard. They appear big through making big music. At their best, they can hold back their grandiloquence just enough to create tension, but too often they will let rock's self-importance ride them. The best music is so vague that it can say everything; too often, U2 are so grandly vague that they say nothing. Even Bono's insistent examination of his faith, which for many performers sets up exciting contradictions and complications, seems ultimately too self-assured to bring any force to the music.

Walter Ulbricht 1893-1973

EAST GERMAN POLITICAL LEADER

East Germany was the Soviet Union's most loyal post-war ally in Eastern Europe. Ulbricht, the man responsible for putting up the Berlin Wall and an archetypically loyal Bolshevik, partly explains why. A cabinetmaker by trade, he joined the German Social Democrats in 1912 and helped to organize the German Communists into cells during the 1920s. Becoming a member of the Weimar government, he fled on Hitler's accession to power, and worked as a Communist agent abroad, liquidating anti-Stalinists on the republican side in the Spanish Civil War. During WW2, he worked with German POWs in the Soviet Union, seeking converts to Communism. Returning to Germany, he was asked to establish an administration in the Soviet-occupied zone, which although in Communist hands, would be behind a non-Communist façade. He was a key organizer in the new East Germany from 1949, even if he was not officially in charge. For 11 years from 1960, he was head of state. Policies linked to him include the collectivization of agriculture and the establishment of a police state on Stalinist lines – it has been revealed that he secretly had 62 political prisoners guillotined and their bodies burned.

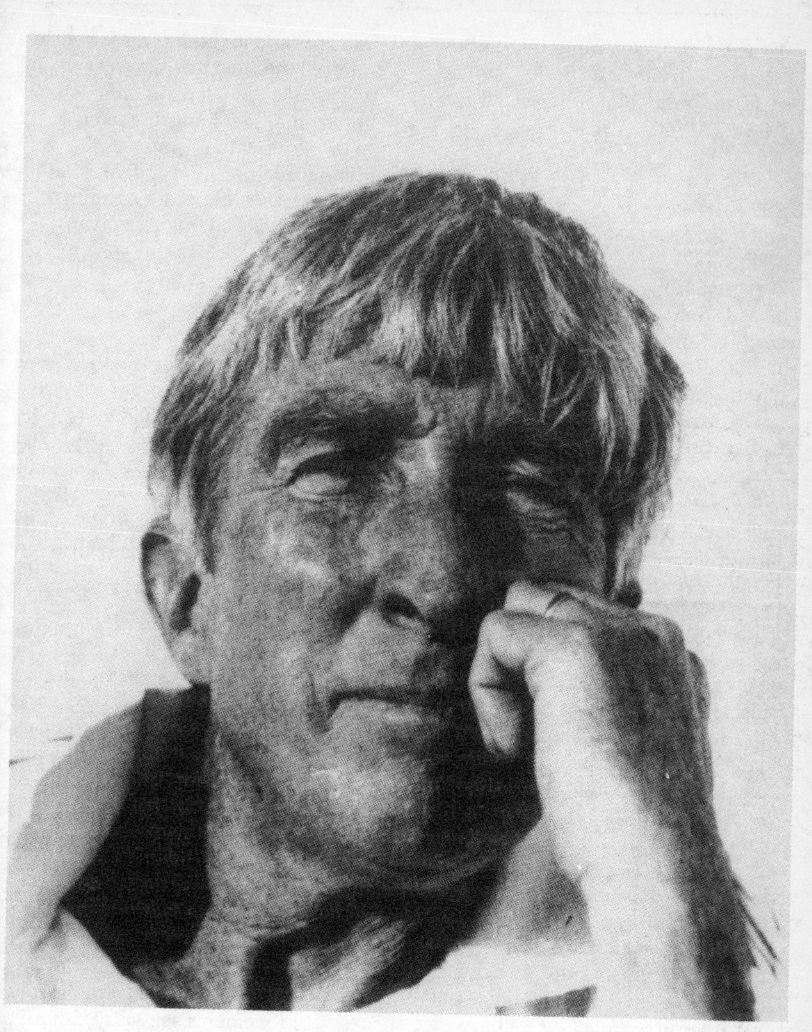

John Updike

With the Wall stemming the outflow of skilled refugees, East Germany became, under him, one of the Top Ten industrialized states.

Edgar Ulmer 1900-72

AUSTRIAN-AMERICAN FILM DIRECTOR

Reaching Hollywood in 1930, Ulmer turned financial expediency into a near art form of despair and fatalism. While many of his 128 films are undoubtedly mediocre, he gave them a stark imagery that revealed his roots in German expressionism (he was the designer on Murnau's *Sunrise*). *The Black Cat* (1934) was Ulmer's only film with a major budget or significant cast (Boris Karloff and Bela Lugosi). For the rest of his career, he had to make the most of distinctly unstellar leads, virtually no money and minimalist sets. In *Detour* (1945), Ulmer's camera and lighting frames one of the most desperate stories in *film noir* – the tale of a hitch-hiker and a *femme fatale* – which he transformed into a valentine to despair and inevitability: when his hero tries to end his nightmare by phoning the police, he inadvertently strangles the 'heroine' to death with the phone cord. *Beyond the Time Barrier*, shot back-to-back with *The Amazing Transparent Man* in 1960, features a pilot breaking the time barrier and landing in a post-WW3 world peopled by mutants and princesses. Using space-age exhibits from the Texas State Fairgrounds in Dallas as sets for both films, he encapsulated the magpie-like scavenging talents that gave a distinctive flavour to all his low-budget exercises in genre exploitation, and on the way influenced the independent production initiatives of the 1960s and 1970s that fostered talents as diverse as ☛Altman, Carpenter and ☛Coppola.

John Updike born 1932

AMERICAN NOVELIST

An observer of the nuances and emotional corruption of small-town American life, Updike has explored the evolution of social and sexual mores from the 1950s to the 1980s. After graduating from Harvard, he began a relationship with *The New Yorker* that has continued. He first attracted national attention with *Rabbit, Run* (1960), the story of a former star athlete fleeing responsibility and a tedious marriage, who is unable to recapture the dreams of a gilded past. This was followed by *Rabbit Redux* (1971), *Rabbit is Rich* (1981) and *Rabbit at Rest* (1990), comprising a history of middle America since the 1950s. Updike's persistent concern with sexual morality is evident in the pain that the bed-hopping husbands and wives of *Couples* (1968) inflict upon each other. In *Witches of Eastwick* (1954), he offered a more sympathetic portrayal of women's sexuality, fantasies and frustrations.

V

Van Halen formed 1977

David Lee Roth born 1955
Eddie Van Halen born 1957
Alex Van Halen born 1955
Michael Anthony born 1955

AMERICAN ROCK GROUP

Van Halen can be seen as a slick repackaging of a music that was threatening to die of moronic stasis. In the late 1970s, heavy metal was still popular thanks to its lumpen stupidity, but it did not seem to have anywhere to go. The Van Halen brothers – Alex the drummer and Eddie the guitarist – brought a sharp sense of speed-rhythm that retained the skeleton of the beat while adding an attractive witty energy. They were funky, and still heavy metal. Thanks also to their charismatic front-man, David Lee Roth, they exploded into popularity and astounded critical esteem (Eddie was even asked to contribute to ☛Michael Jackson's *Thriller* – a coup for a metalman). Roth left, for a solo career as rubber-limbed macho front-man for no one in particular; the brothers abide, as tight and straight as ever, a perfect example of the squeaky-clean amiability of packaged rebellion. The designer-eccentricity and consumer-friendliness of the whole project is best summed up thus: when on tour, instead of drugs, drink or women in the dressing room after the show, they demand M&M sweets, with all the brown ones removed.

Laurens Van Der Post born 1906

SOUTH AFRICAN EXPLORER, WRITER

Van Der Post's accounts of journeys into the African heartland intertwine mysticism with political concerns. Born and brought up in South Africa, he set up *Vorrslag*, a journal that attacked racist thinking and values. After serving with the British army during WW2, and being captured by the Japanese, he farmed in South Africa and travelled throughout the rest of the continent for the British. Travel books such as *Ventures to the Interior* (1951), an account of his search for the vanishing bushmen of the Kalahari desert, reveal both a vivid, descriptive talent and a central theme: explaining racism as an attempt to suppress man's own primitive instinct. The spirituality that Van Der Post finds in the African continent reverberates in other ways through his novels, where age-old myths and cultures are replaced by rites of passage and elusive political allegories, as in *The Heart of the Hunter* (1961) and *The Hunter and the Whale* (1967). Although sometimes swept away by poetic portentousness, he often hits upon imagery and symbolism that penetrate to the heart of the African continent.

Edgar Varèse 1883-1965

♦ FRENCH COMPOSER

'Every age has its characteristic sounds,' wrote Varèse, who gave form to what the futurist Luigi Russollo called the 'art of noise'. Varèse studied science before turning to music, and used this background as a key to open up new methods of composition – deciding in the 1950s that the way ahead lay through electronics and a music made up of 'beautiful parabolic and hyperbolic curves'. Idiosyncratic to the last, Varèse sought sounds that kept up with thought: he spoke of music as being 'spatial', as 'sound set free' yet 'organized'. He dealt with sound as a raw phenomenon, deploying it in great blocks of percussive assault and rhythmic layers – and as a result, he probably has more in common with contemporary rock musicians than with more traditionally oriented composers. An attempt to produce something truly 'modern' that used none of the techniques, media or themes of the past, his work still challenges the listener. Many feel the way a *New York Times* critic felt on hearing Varèse's piece *Hyperprism* in 1923, an experience he compared to 'a catastrophe in a boiler factory'.

Mario Vargas Llosa born 1936

✌ PERUVIAN NOVELIST, JOURNALIST,
❞ POLITICIAN

An urbane Peruvian charmer, Vargas Llosa is a football enthusiast whose failure to secure his country's presidency in 1990 – he lost to Japanese-Peruvian agronomist Alberto Fujimuri – provoked audible sighs of relief from all those who love his novels. The bleak tone of his early works reflected a leftist stance (he was a member of a Communist cell in Lima), but Vargas Llosa shifted towards the liberal right following Castro's disappointing revolution and the USSR's 1968 invasion of Prague. This shift showed up in the more satiric, ironic and playful approach that he took in such books as *Captain Pantoja and His Regiment* (1973/78) and *Aunt Julia and the Scriptwriter* (1977/82). The former concerns a diligent young army officer sent into the jungle to organize a team of prostitutes who will ease the lot of lonely soldiers stationed in a remote outpost. Captain Pantoja's deficient imagination, puritan zeal and analytical approach to the job make a great nonsense out of an enterprise that was always ridiculous. Vargas Llosa's disillusion with radical politics resonates through more recent work, as he examines – in books such as his monumental epic *The War of the End of the World* (1981/84) – the disasters that seem the only possible outcome of blind ideology. Intense reflections on literature and history influence the shifts in Vargas Llosa's approach to writing – meanwhile, his country crumbles into polarized violence, corruption and hyper-inflation.

Victor Vasarély born 1908

& HUNGARIAN-FRENCH ARTIST

Artists have adapted in various ways to the omnipresence of mass culture imagery, but the idea that art itself could be mass-produced, and yet remain 'art', still offends some sensibilities. Vasarély wants to do away with the concept of the 'unique' art object, and with it much of the self-importance that attaches to the 'artist'. His idea – that the artist should be a 'craftsman' purveying art for everyone – harks back to pre-modern traditions, but Vasarély's own pictures aim to break with the themes of the past. You do not have to swallow the rhetoric to respond to the images. He combines geometric shapes – circles, squares, rectangles – and uses striking contrasts of tone to give an impression of movement, and of other shapes that are not really there. His pieces are ambiguous and disturbing but also calculated towards appreciation. Vasarély advocated a new sort of city where art would be 'kinetic, multidimensional and communal', and certainly the idea of streets lined with hoardings that are not trying to sell something, or murals that are not simply naïve, is appealing.

I(mmanuel) Velikovsky 1895-1979

✍ SOVIET-AMERICAN
☆ MYTHOGRAPHER
An orthodox Jew who studied medicine in Moscow and reached New York in 1939, Velikovsky stopped off along the way in Vienna, and picked up just enough psychoanalysis to back up his wacky theory that the Old Testament's account of the sufferings endured by the people of Israel reflected enormous planetary upheavals. Noah's Flood, he claimed, was the result of the earth and moon passing through a great cloud of water following an explosion on Saturn. It was a giant comet breaking out from the planet Jupiter and passing close to the earth that caused the Red Sea to divide for Moses, scattered manna along the route followed by the Israelites and then returned in time to help Joshua when he wanted the sun and moon to stand still (the comet eventually settled down and became the planet Venus). A curious attempt to convince people hooked on science, and therefore irreligious, of the Bible's literal truth, Velikovsky's theories involved riding roughshod over almost every tenet of modern astronomy, physics, chemistry, geology and archaeology. That did not seem to worry his numerous readers, or his publisher, who kept both *Planets in Collision* (1950) and *Worlds in Chaos* (1952) in print for over 20 years.

The Velvet Underground

formed 1966
Lou Reed (Louis Firbank) born 1944
John Cale born 1940
◆ AMERICAN ROCK MUSICIANS
∀ While John Cale was working with ❍ ☛LaMonte Young, Lou Reed was writing 'Do the Ostrich'. The result of combining Cale's avant-garde origins with Lou Reed's roots in Tin Pan Alley was The Velvet Underground. No previous group had possessed sufficient understanding of both forms of music to blend them successfully. ☛Andy Warhol's brief patronage acknowledged the pop and the art in the group, and it did their reputation no harm to have songs about transvestism and drugs in their repertoire. Their position as the antithesis of hippy – East Coast, dressed in black, sun-hating and writing songs which explored love rather than vaguely exalting it – also ensured their complete commercial failure. Cale's departure and Reed's increasing affair with the E chord turned The Velvet Underground into the first great urban rock band, but by 1970, very few people were interested. By then, Maureen Tucker, one of a handful of drummers in rock to understand the power of relentless simplicity, and probably the first female singer not called upon to be seductive or raunchy or passive, had also departed, and Reed left the group's name to the mysterious Yule brothers. His subsequent career in the 1970s saw him taking out a Velvets

parody show, all needles and Warhol characters; now he is able to make sparse rock records about New York. Cale continues to explore the strangeness of life; Tucker has returned as a cult figure; and The Velvet Underground's records have influenced the best of rock in the 1980s.

Robert Venturi born 1925

& AMERICAN ARCHITECT

'Less is a bore' – his retort to ☛Mies van der Rohe's 'Less is more' – is perhaps Venturi's most famous slogan, but the spirit of his shift in the architecture he proposed is better conveyed by the formula: 'Main Street is almost all right.' He felt that putting up 'heroic' buildings in a silly decade, or heading off along the path of functionalism and geometrical purism, was nonsense; architects should become part of the cultural ferment and diversity going on around them. Venturi's ideas developed out of his training with ☛Louis Kahn, but his fascination with vernacular styles, especially the electric signs and billboards standing around the parking lots of Las Vegas, made it natural to dub his work Pop. In his 1966 manifesto, *Complexity and Contradiction in Architecture*, he argued for 'messy vitality' over 'obvious unity' and a hybrid approach to architecture, using ornament, decoration and colour. A subtle theorist, he failed to find any large-scale opportunity to develop his ideas as the first wave of post-modernism gathered momentum in the late 1970s, but a commission to design the extension to London's National Gallery has enabled him, for the first time, to go beyond the scale of private houses and minor public commissions. The chance came too late to be anything but a disappointment.

Hendrik Verwoerd 1901-66

SOUTH AFRICAN
POLITICAL LEADER

South Africa's prime minister from 1958 to 1966, and native affairs minister from 1950 to 1958, Verwoerd was more closely linked to the inception of apartheid than anyone else. He was not born in Africa but came from Holland as a child. Before WW2, he edited an Afrikaaner newspaper, attacking 'British-Jewish imperialism'; during the war, he sided with Hitler. The central policy moves he devised were the institution of tribal areas for blacks – the seven 'Bantustans' – and South Africa's exit from the Commonwealth. The key event of his premiership was the massacre at Sharpeville of blacks demonstrating against the pass laws, an event which provoked the first real, global hostility to apartheid. In a sense, he was an academic in politics – aloof, unassuming, fanatical. He was stabbed to death by a deranged white assassin, pretending to be a courier, on the floor of parliament – an end like Caesar's.

Gore Vidal born 1925

AMERICAN WRITER,
POLITICAL COMMENTATOR,
BASED IN ITALY

No one holds a higher opinion of this novelist, scion of Washington's political aristocracy, than Vidal himself. America's greatest sin in his eyes may simply be that it is not the kind of place where he – aesthete, satirist, historian, highbrow bruiser – could ever achieve the high office he is convinced he could hold so well. All the same, he is one of few living writers prepared to tackle past and present on an equal footing, and to deal with the great issues of state, power and social purpose. When he puts Lincoln in a novel, for example, it is a historical re-creation and a dramatization of the concerns of the day – however controversial – but it is also alert, readable and moving. By maintaining an amused superiority to everything, in particular the orthodoxies of the middlebrow, he seems to have given himself the space to remain both radical and coolly accessible, where others have drifted either to the right or into safe little ghettos of opposition. His essays are elegantly provocative, if deeply cynical, and even his weakest books are entertaining. His barbed humour has led to heated exchanges with ☛William Buckley, ☛Norman Mailer and ☛Truman Capote, among others.

Paul Virilio born 1932

FRENCH POLITICAL PHILOSOPHER

One among several post-1968 French political philosophers who have taken a lead from the Situationists, Virilio is an unusually lucid and provocative innovator – with a knack for titles that perfectly summarize his realignments of conventional thought: *Bunker Archaeology* (1975), *Speed and Politics* (1977), *Pure War* (1983). His interest in military organization, and the effect on society of military and guerrilla technologies of movement, communication, threat and resistance is what sets him apart from the Marxists and quasi-Marxists he would otherwise resemble. Like ☛Foucault, he reads intentions in structure and in architecture. He takes institutions seriously, recognizing how they can act to alter and even determine their surroundings – so that he reads Clausewitz, Sun Tzu and their modern equivalents in depth, and brings to bear a social critique of military establishments, and of the society their philosophies have colonized. He argues that the superpower blocs have effectively been on military alert for 40 years, and that most of the world lives in a state of 'pure war' as a consequence. For Virilio, the state *is* war, where any act is absorbed into a logic of attack and defence (without necessarily erupting into overt violence or bloodshed), and where politics and the possibilities of debate and compromise are driven into narrower and narrower areas of operation.

Luchino Visconti
(Count Don Luchino Visconti di Modrone)
1906-76

▲ITALIAN FILM-MAKER

♉ Despite a formal aristocratic upbringing (horses and classical literature), Visconti's early interest in music and theatre led to a career in film. His début was *Ossessione* (1942), an adaptation of James Cain's *The Postman Always Rings Twice*, which is now seen as a forerunner of neo-realism – a movement that his post-war work was to disavow, leading to much criticism from his contemporaries. The backlash to the operatic romanticism of *Senso* (1954), a portrait of destructive passion amid shifting social loyalties, was answered by *White Nights* (1957), in which a realist attempts to win a woman away from her romantic dreams, only to lose her when they come true. Visconti continued his fascination with Italian history and the inevitable decline of his class with *The Leopard* (1963), and various excursions into the politics of corruption, including *Death in Venice* (1971), which turned the inadvertent object of the protagonist's fatal attraction into a sexually ambivalent flirt. His later work generally disappointed both his admirers and backers, preventing realization of his long-nurtured plans to film Proust's *Remembrance of Times Past*.

Kurt Vonnegut born 1922

AMERICAN NOVELIST

Vonnegut has applied the pessimism he shares with ☛William Burroughs to tales of mankind ensnared in altruistic beliefs that are often as dogmatic, mechanical and dehumanizing as the automated civilizations from which his characters endeavour to liberate themselves. His recounting of his experiences during WW2, *Slaughterhouse-Five* (1969), was popular during the Vietnam War, another time of violent social upheaval. The pivotal event of the novel – the destruction, by fire bombs, of Dresden, which Vonnegut witnessed as a member of a POW work force – illustrates his view that chaos is a prerequisite of human history. This view reached its absurd zenith early, in *The Sirens of Titan* (1959), in which earth defeats a Martian attack, and the forces of goodness and normality manifest themselves in the shape of a new religion: 'The Church of God the Utterly Indifferent.' Vonnegut appreciates that laughter remains our only antidote to death or fear in a Darwinian universe where evil will probably emerge as the ultimate survivor, and his works abound with humour, satire and benign fatalism. His almost cartoonishly simple style polarizes critics, and is in danger of becoming formularized; his popularity, especially among students, is not under threat.

Johannes Vorster 1915-83

SOUTH AFRICAN POLITICAL LEADER

South African prime minister from 1966 to 1978, Vorster was a 'strong man' at home, but a would-be conciliator abroad. Gaoled during WW2 for neo-Nazi activity, as a tough minister of justice from 1961 to 1967 he oversaw the Sharpeville massacre. He did not take apartheid in any new directions, except to set up quasi-autonomous black homelands such as the Transkei. These were not part of a basic rethinking of apartheid; they were a logical result of it. The aim was to win black African friends, but he had only one real success, when the leader of Malawi paid a visit. Vorster sensed that South Africa was becoming increasingly isolated – an untenable future, especially economically – but he was not ready to make more than cosmetic changes to the structure of white supremacy. Vorster's era marked the consolidation of an entrenched, near-global, anti-apartheid movement and he became synonymous with South Africa's highly negative image abroad. He was promoted downwards to the symbolic post of president in 1978, leaving even that when his role in a corruption scandal was exposed.

W

Andrzej Wajda

born 1927

▲POLISH FILM DIRECTOR

Wajda's films explore Poland's history and culture in a spirit of bleak pessimism. At the end of *Kanal* (1957), the second film in his trilogy about the Polish resistance during WW2, a wounded fighter staggers through the Warsaw sewers towards the light at the end of the tunnel – only to turn the corner and find light, life and liberty barred to him by a thick grating. Wajda's subsequent work was fairly minor until *Man of Marble* (1976), which shows a documentary film-maker seeking the truth about an officially ostracized worker hero of one of Stalin's Five-Year-Plans. Its sequel, *Man of Iron* (1981), is set against the glory days of the Solidarity trade union's rise to prominence. Wajda took up residence in France, turning the tale of the French Revolution's sacrificial lamb, *Danton* (1982), into a verbose allegory on the conflict between ☛Lech Wałęsa and General Jaruzelski in contemporary Poland. Away from his native land, Wajda seemed unable to make the most of his material. In 1989 he went home to build a political career.

Derek Walcott

born 1930

WEST INDIAN POET, PLAYWRIGHT

A native of Santa Lucia who now divides his time between Trinidad and Boston, Walcott turns the many defeats of the Caribbean's colonial past into a cultural victory as he moulds the English language into rhythms more vital and urgent than anything now being created by the old oppressors. The tensions inherent in the words and phrases he uses, together with his ear for rhythm and his sensitivity to nature, shape poems that concentrate upon the plight of islanders haunted by ancestral wrongs and the beauty of their native country. Founder of the Trinidad Theatre Workship in 1959, Walcott uses the Creole idiom in his plays as a way of drawing a popular audience for his probes into possible futures for the West Indies. *The Dream on Monkey Mountain* (1969), for example, concerns an old charcoal burner who comes to town, gets drunk, lands up in gaol and hallucinates about being the king of a united Africa.

Lech Wałęsa

born 1943

POLISH TRADE UNION LEADER

Wałęsa led the 1980 strike in the Gdansk shipyards which forced ☛Edward Gierek out of power but ended in martial law under General Jaruzelski. Under Wałęsa, Solidarity, a trade union group with 10 million members, entered into an on-off partnership with the state. In August 1980, the government admitted the right of Polish workers to form independent unions and to strike – Solidarity's supreme achievement. Wałęsa was an electrician at Gdansk and, after a spell in gaol, he returned to work there. Part of his secret was a close rapport with the Catholic hierarchy, together with his self-image as a socialist, in a non-ideological sense, who accepted the norms of the post-war order, but appealed from it to policies that related to Polish national tradition and tackled basic working-class grievances. Solidarity was suppressed under martial law, but later reached an accord with the regime and went on to triumph in the free elections held during 1989, arguably the first in Poland this century. The movement will be a fixture in Polish society from now on, but Wałęsa has increasingly found himself under attack from the intellectuals within it, and at odds with other new leaders steering Eastern Europe towards democracy. Nevertheless, he was elected president at the end of 1990.

Alice Walker born 1944

AMERICAN NOVELIST, POET

Walker's reflections on the experience of black women are coloured by her natural lyricism. Influences on her writing range from the Gothic irony of ☛Flannery O'Connor to the ornate delicacies of Japanese *haiku* and the work of such black writers as Jean Toomer and ☛James Baldwin. Her first novel, *The Third Life of Grange Copeland* (1970), recounts several generations in the life of a sharecropper's family, oppressed by racism but victims also of each other's violence and cruelty. *Meridian* (1976) tackles the distance between political commitment and needy reality. But it is *The Color Purple* (1983), the tale of a young girl's journey to self-understanding constructed as a series of letters to God, that fully reveals Walker's virtuosity. In her narratives, the men are always unyielding and destructive; the women struggle for freedom and finally triumph, to rise beyond cramped, violent, patriarchal and colour prejudices to intense, painful release.

George Wallace born 1919

AMERICAN POLITICIAN

A radical Southern campaigner for racial segregation, Wallace has been confined to a wheelchair since an assassination bid in 1972 left him paralysed from the waist down. He had been a circuit court judge before he went into politics. He was also a Democrat – the party of the South until the 1970s – and achieved his reputation, or notoriety, in 1962 when, as governor of Alabama, he 'stood in the door' and physically confronted federal marshals set on integrating the University of Alabama. He stood as a third party, right-wing candidate for president on a law-and-order ticket in 1968, winning nearly 10 million votes – the strongest challenge to the two-party system for many years. He was governor of Alabama on and off between 1970 and 1982, but he has modified his racist stance, and attracted black votes, as segregation has become a dead issue.

Andy Warhol (Andrew Warhola) 1927-87

AMERICAN ARTIST

From 1960 onwards, this shyly intuitive iconoclast was the purest celebrity embodiment of Pop Art. Through his silk-screened repros of icons such as ☛Marilyn Monroe and Jackie Onassis, multiple Coca Cola bottles and piles of Brillo boxes, he effected a guileless high-art affirmation of contemporary mass culture at a time

Andy Warhol
Photo: Constantin/Connex

when high art, and even most pop art, was still taking shots at it. His graphic sense had been honed in the world of commercial advertising, and he realized that, by appropriating, framing and formalizing such slim pleasures, he could celebrate the cheap energy of the modern world at the same time as he forced it to accept and proclaim his values. For many, radical and conservative alike, he was the modern vampiric nightmare – powerful, amoral, vaguely likeable, militantly shallow and, in a peculiar sense, incorruptible: even as he courted the wealthy and grooved to their fame, he turned them into his creatures. Studious, skeletal, adorned with uncombed silver-blond wigs and surrounded by the pseudo-bohemian habitués of the Manhattan counter-culture, he oversaw his Factory's outpouring of Warhol prints, experimental home movies (many in collaboration with the sporadically brilliant ☛Paul Morrissey), and Happenings – including the legendary 'Exploding Plastic Inevitable', which showcased ☛The Velvet Underground, that impossibly seminal rock group. By the mid-1980s, he had lost touch with the heart of what critic Kenneth Silver called his 'blue-collar, gay, American art', and survived as a presence conferring modish approval on nightclubs, rock concerts or restaurants. Although this still-devout Catholic could cause minor tremors by, for example, admitting that he masturbated to photos of Duran Duran, his most significant interrogations of the canons of art were long over. The first fully to grasp the import of Walter Benjamin's prophetic ambivalence about the age of mass production, and the absolute pluralism of values it brings with it, he became his own best publicist/analyst by insisting that all that was significant in his work could be read on the surface; but he was never taken at his word, by apologists or detractors. No one has discomfited so many by being so positive, and had so much that was negative, even nihilist, read into his work. For everyone but him, it seems, the celebration will always be tinged with dread.

Art? Isn't that a man's name?

Andy Warhol

Earl Warren 1891-1974

AMERICAN JUDGE

Warren's name will live on in the annals of whitewash, as head of the commission that investigated the killing of ☛President Kennedy and ended up supporting the on-the-spot theory that Lee Harvey Oswald acted alone and fired all the fatal shots – despite considerable evidence (which now seems incontrovertible) that the bullets came from at least two different places. To understand how a committee of the great and good could reach such an improbable conclusion, and argue their case through many (unindexed) volumes of testimony and argument, it is necessary to appreciate how much easier it was for shocked Americans to credit the crime to a lone nutcase than to come to terms with the possibility of dark conspiracy. Warren, chosen by ☛Eisenhower to serve as chief justice in the US Supreme Court, introduced an era of liberal verdicts which had a decisive impact on American society; Eisenhower later remarked that his biggest mistake had been 'the appointment of that dumb son of a bitch Earl Warren'. In 1954, Warren presided over *Brown vs. Board of Education*, which attacked the apartheid-style defence for racial segregation in schools as 'separate but equal'; it means, he said, 'separate, but unequal'. Other judgements extended integration to parks, restaurants and buses. 'Legislators represent people, not acres of trees,' he argued, as he made population the test for equal representation in state legislatures. Another novelty was to make the police supply a lawyer to an arrested person, as they probed for admissions of guilt. His era preceded a more contentious phase in the 1970s, as hanging, abortion and 'affirmative action' on race, made up a new agenda for liberal lawyers. Son of a railway worker, he held public office for 50 years.

John Waters born 1946

❞ AMERICAN FILM-MAKER

Labelled the 'Ayatollah of Crud', the 'Pope of Trash' and the 'Disciple of Dirt', Waters pursued the low-rent showmanship of ☛Russ Meyer to produce primitive but ambitious black comedies made for the underground culture that was spurned by Midwesterners in his native Baltimore. Often preoccupied with the very dregs of American pop-trivia (☛Charles Manson, Jayne Mansfield, sleazy tabloid journalism, junk food-induced obesity and lurid sensationalism), Waters beatified the spirit of America's blue-collar grotesques with *Pink Flamingos* (1972) and *Female Trouble* (1973). Both featured the prominent comic talents of elephantine transsexual actor/singer Divine (Glen Milstead) whose visual flamboyance, whether as a criminal in *Female Trouble* or as a gangleader who dines on dog shit in *Flamingos*, never fails to delight and disgust a vast contingent of sleaze-absorbed cinema-goers. Recently, Waters has headed towards the mainstream with *Hairspray* (1988) and the disappointing *Cry-Baby* (1990).

Muddy Waters 1915-83

AMERICAN BLUES MUSICIAN

The uncrowned king of Chicago blues, Waters was the foremost influence on the white R&B explosion of the 1960s. Breaking with country blues, he used an electric guitar, with strong dance rhythms and his shouting vocal style, to capture a mood that was punchy and threatening. His lyrics shifted from sexual bravado to a mournful approach. Although overtaken in sales by Little Walter, the harmonica player in Waters' first and most famous group, Waters remains the most prominent proponent of City Blues.

James Watson born 1928

♦ AMERICAN MOLECULAR BIOLOGIST

❍ The American who came out of nowhere, never did an experiment but discovered the genetic code, then secured the Nobel prize and wrote a best-selling book, *Double Helix* (1968), to congratulate himself, Watson set out in the 1950s to find the chemical substrate of the hereditary material of living cells. Working with ☛Francis Crick, he concentrated on building theoretical models informed by the experimental data of others, particularly ☛Rosalind Franklin, rather than deriving the structure from intensive experimentation, which neither he nor Crick had the expertise to perform. The double-helix structure they proposed has become part of contemporary scientific mythology. Though it has become fashionable to talk cynically of this achievement, anyone who can identify a game and win against competition that includes people as bright as ☛Linus Pauling is pretty impressive. Watson is now in charge of the 15-year Human Genome Project, which aims to map the hundreds of thousands of gene sequences found in humans, with promised insights into cancer, psychiatric diseases and the ageing process.

This structure was of such simplicity, such perfection, such harmony, such beauty even, and biological advantages flowed from it with such rigour and clarity, that one could not believe it untrue.
James Watson on DNA

Alan Watts 1915-73

† BRITISH-AMERICAN ZEN
☆ PROSELYTIZER

As a schoolboy visitor to London's Buddhist Lodge and Magic Bookshop in the 1930s, Watts started early on the path that took him from a traditional Anglican upbringing in Chislehurst, Kent to become, in the 1960s, a purveyor of diluted Zen Buddhism to mystically inclined members of California's counter-culture. He travelled to the US for training as a minister in the Episcopalian Church, but eventually turned to revamping Eastern wisdom into a version that Americans could consume with ease. Not for him the ascetic life of the traditional Zen Roshi; Watts drank, smoked, loved good food, used LSD, believed in free love and spoke about ecstatic communion with nature in a way that possibly owed more to D. H. Lawrence than Eastern holy books. And whereas contemporaries such as Krishnamurti adopted the traditional Buddhist's tone of gentle irony, Watts won the hearts of Americans as a self-confessed spiritual entertainer, known for his belly laughs and view of worship as 'spiritual whoopee'. His genial style made people listen, and few who came could fault his indictment of modern pre-packaged culture, but Watts never quite hit upon a path that others could follow which would give them a share of his own seeming equanimity. Perhaps he just wasn't letting on.

Evelyn Waugh 1903-66

BRITISH NOVELIST

Waugh's early novels, such as *Decline and Fall* (1928) and *Vile Bodies* (1930), caught the brittle, cynically determined frivolity of the inter-war generation with light-hearted banter and high comedy. But darkness began to set in with *A Handful of Dust* (1934), written after a bitter divorce, which was followed by Waugh's conversion to Catholicism. In *Brideshead Revisited* (1945) and *The Loved One* (1948), he mourned the world that WW2 had destroyed, while at the same time becoming the very thing he used to parody – an eccentric adopting the life of a country squire, who felt so alienated from the modern world that he refused to own a television or radio. He answered his critics in *The Ordeal of Gilbert Pinfold* (1957), a portrait of a man who tries to escape to a land where the twentieth century is just a rumour, a trip that ends in redemption and the kind of excessive Catholic nostalgia that marred his later work. Waugh was a tremendous stylist, and a one-time great satirist, who set out to re-create a world he once ridiculed in a golden image he knew had never been.

John Wayne 1907-79

(Marion Michael Morrison)

AMERICAN ACTOR

Airports are named after him; there are more statues of him in the US than of any other non-presidential figure; ☛Ronald Reagan quoted him extensively. Yet John Wayne was only an actor who believed that, if you can kick the crap out of someone, God and moral right must be on your side. He helped to create the American myth of a nation made with the blood of two-fisted, hard-drinking, fast-shooting men of few words, becoming in the process the icon of the right and the National Rifle Association: 'God, guns and guts made American great – let's keep all three.' He could question that image, producing one of the most chilling portraits of racism's dehumanizing effects in John Ford's *The Searchers* (1956), but the propaganda for America's role in Vietnam contained in *The Green Berets* (1968) proved that his image was incompatible with 1960s' social awareness. By the time he appeared in *The Shootist* (1976), as a dying gunfighter who takes the tram to his final shootout, Wayne knew that he had outlived his time and the western genre that had made him famous.

Warren Weaver *see* Shannon, Claude

Bruce Weber born 1951

AMERICAN PHOTOGRAPHER

Imagine a world populated by beautiful men and women, sublime examples of heroically flawless stature – a world of sandy beaches, at peace with itself. Welcome to the world of Bruce Weber, who began his career as a successful male model but turned to commercial photography, as his looks faded, in order to capture these impossible images of perfection. His pictures found an outlet in the European fashion magazines of the 1970s where he displayed photographs of young, clean-cut, athletic male nudes. His more daring work from this period showed sailors celebrating together on shore or the shaved heads of sportsmen. Surprisingly, it was Y-fronts that brought Weber to a wider audience, after he received a commission from ☛Calvin Klein that led to an ongoing collaboration. More recently, Weber has taken up filmmaking – exploring the career of a small-time boxer in *Broken Noses* (1989), and the tragic life of Chet Baker in *Let's Get Lost* (1989).

Steven Weinberg *see* Glashow, Sheldon Lee

Orson Welles 1915-85

❞ AMERICAN ACTOR,
✍ FILM AND THEATRE DIRECTOR

Welles was a master conjuror, whose overriding love was to trick an audience into taking the outraged ride they all longed for. His *Citizen Kane* (1941) is a sly, vulgarly melodramatic slice of nothing much at all, but somehow Welles got it driven to the top of all the 'Best Films of All Time' lists and parked there permanently: one in the eye for every other film-maker (especially the ones who could get their work financed and finished). His best films – the studio-recut *Magnificent Ambersons* (1942), the ineffable *Lady from Shanghai* (1948), the ridiculous *Touch of Evil* (1958), the nightmarish *Chimes at Midnight* (1966) – are distorted and fragmented Hollywood B-movies, with the Falstaffian Welles himself inflating visibly at centre-stage. A brilliantly cranky and reactionary innovator, he reforged the artifice of the best nineteenth-century theatre back into the cinema. In the 1980s, a thousand empty video scene-sets (neon reflected in wet dark streets) have been born out of the angled glitter of his style. As an actor, his presence was overwhelming, from his voiceovers for sherry commercials in the 1970s to his uncanny domination of the best film he never actually directed, Carol Reed's *The Third Man* (1949). On screen for only a few minutes in this, Welles effects the most extraordinary entrance and exit scenes; his Harry Lime is a despicably charming, murderously unscrupulous conman, preying on the weak and sick, but his death leaves us desolate -- the achievement of a master illusionist.

Wim Wenders born 1945

GERMAN FILM-MAKER

Wenders' films are a vindication of his own assertion that 'the Americans have colonized our subconscious.' A series of revisionist road movies, they present images from an American Germany, where a post-war generation that distrusts the advice of their parents and looks elsewhere (and anywhere) for guidance attempts to reclaim the old country – only to lose themselves through an inability to recognize their own identity. Unresolved journeys feature in all his films, from *Alice in the Cities* (1974) through *Kings of the Road* (1976) to *The American Friend* (1977) and *Paris, Texas* (1984). One of his most recent, *Wings of Desire* (1987), is the story of two angels in Berlin drawn to people by compassion and curiosity, and into humanity by pain (the moment one of the angels, Bruno Ganz, becomes human, he starts to die). Filmed mostly in striking black and white, the film's warmth suggests the beginning of a new direction in Wenders' work.

William Westmoreland born 1914

AMERICAN GENERAL

Since his retirement from the army in 1972, Westmoreland has pounded the lecture circuit arguing that the US could have won a victory in Vietnam had it not been betrayed by the civies back home. Taking over in 1964 as commander of all military forces in Vietnam, he presided over a colossal increase in American ground forces (from 16,000 to over 0.5 million men), the first bombing raids into North Vietnam, and the initiation of 'search and destroy' missions in the jungles. His pitch to Washington was that victory was certain, given increased firepower, more troops and more ammunition. But the body bags being shipped home told a different story, as did the near-success of the Viet Cong's Tet Offensive of 1968. Having become a despised symbol of an ugly war, Westmoreland was replaced by General Creighton W. Abrahams and went back home to spend four years as chief of staff. In 1982 he launched a libel case against CBS television over a documentary, *The Uncounted Enemy: A Vietnam Deception*, which suggested that he had produced deliberately misleading figures about the scale of the enemy forces: The CIA had said there were 500,000 enemy combatants; Westmoreland had put the figure at 300,000. At issue was not simply whether it was misleading to distinguish between well-armed regular soldiers and guerrilla fighters, but also questions of psychological determination and political will that Westmoreland's statistical approach simply left out of the account. But the case was dropped; the risk of losing that contest, Westmoreland concluded after the initial hearings, was just too great.

Vivienne Westwood born 1941

BRITISH FASHION DESIGNER

Collaborating for a time with ☛Malcolm McLaren, Westwood was the guardian aunt of punk fashion who brought bondage and rubber fetishism out of the closet. Although the clock above her shop, World's End, may whirr madly backwards, Westwood continues to forge ahead. Each year she creates a new pastiche – such as a garish juxtaposition of tartan and chiffon or ringlets and Sherlock Holmes hats – the effect of which often seems one of purposeful ugliness, and a challenge to those unthinking fashion victims who will dish out fistfuls of money for anything so long as it has a designer label. Westwood was one of the first to promote underwear as outer-wear, and she manages to suggest a strong sexual charge, along with naïve playfulness, in many of her designs.

Edmund White born 1940

AMERICAN NOVELIST

White's *A Boy's Own Story* (1982) took gay experience into the publishing mainstream. A semi-autobiographical account of young man's unfocused longings and fantasies of enslaving an older man, the book explored White's political interests as much as sexual questions, and it could be easily assimilated into the American tradition of novels about inarticulate adolescents who invent themselves through a series of intense experiences. Its alluring, overblown style won White the reputation among French critics of being the American Flaubert. A similarly burnished prose style was in evidence for *Caracole* (1985), decorous high porn about two nineteenth-century country lovers who, when forcibly separated, turn to sexual escapades in the big city.

Patrick White 1912-90

▲BRITISH-AUSTRALIAN NOVELIST

A childhood spent shuttling between educational establishments in England and his father's sheep ranch – where he encountered what he has called 'the great Australian emptiness, in which the mind of man is the least of possessions' – gave White the particular slant on the conflict between civilized manners and the primitive which he explored in his highly poetic novels. His first published book, *Happy Valley* (1939), reflects the rural elegiac of some English writers, but White went on to develop a distinctive use of allegory and symbolism with which to probe beneath the colonialized topsoil of white manners and morals – as in *Voss* (1957), the account of an ill-fated expedition led by a megalomaniac explorer. White's novels explore the continual struggle of men and women to suppress their sensuous and elemental instincts. It is only, for example, when Mrs Roxburgh in *A Fringe of Leaves* (1976) has been shipwrecked and captured by Aborigines that she locates in the midst of that violent, bewildering society, a near-eroded personal truth. He won the Nobel prize for literature in 1973.

The Who

formed 1964

Roger Daltrey born 1945

Pete Townshend born 1945

Keith Moon 1947-78

BRITISH ROCK MUSICIANS

The Who represent the danger of authenticity. From their rebel pose as Mods destroying the very instruments of their trade, they came to write introspective songs of pop alienation with huge riffs, played at Woodstock and wrote the most horrible thing ever to happen to pop music, *Tommy* (1969) – a 'significant' musical about a deaf, dumb and blind boy who achieves grace through pinball. Strangely, their career recovered after this, and Pete Townshend continued to write introspective songs of pop alienation with even larger riffs. Young rock fans bought their records because of the rock in them, and critics wrote about The Who because of Townshend's search for integrity. After *Quadrophenia* (1979), a reasonable film about the Mod life that Townshend never had, The Who became increasingly less interesting. Their drummer, Keith Moon, had been almost single-handedly responsible for the image of rock stars as drivers of cars into swimming-pools, and his death effectively destroyed the balance of the group's psychological make-up. The Who are now dragged out for charity events and nostalgia LPs, their 'significance' forgotten. Pete Townshend is associated with the London publishers Faber & Faber.

Norbert Wiener

1894-1964

♦ AMERICAN MATHEMATICIAN

A mathematical child prodigy and pupil of ☛Bertrand Russell, Wiener took a post at the Massachusetts Institute of Technology (MIT) in 1919, where he remained for the rest of his life. Early in his career, he found it hard to focus on a single concern, and published important work on a variety of topics, including logic, quantum mechanics and relativity theory. However, after a series of personal breakthroughs in guided missiles, feedback control and electronic information processing during WW2, he founded the field of cybernetics (publishing *Cybernetics* in 1948), which demonstrated that the distinction between organic and inorganic 'machines' was essentially mistaken. His multidisciplinary studies of the use and developments of control systems were of immense value to the US government, but Wiener grew to distrust their attentions and, in the last decade of his life, devoted his time to critical essays on the manipulation of society (*The Human Use of Human Beings*, 1950). He was worried by the possibility that machines could be built with capabilities beyond the expectations of their makers, and was in part responsible, with a series of post-war articles, for inculcating the American public with a distrust of the robots he had largely made feasible.

Torsten Wiesel *see* Hubel, David

Maurice Wilkins

born 1916

BRITISH BIOPHYSICIST

☛Crick and ☛Watson may have been the most successful at self-promotion, but Wilkins, too, was awarded the Nobel prize for discovering the structure of DNA. Undoubtedly a brilliant X-ray crystallographer, it was his unflagging interest in DNA as a possible genetic material, at a time when there were still other contenders, that made possible the proposal of a structure by Crick and Watson. Wilkins kept on bashing X-rays at crystals of the right material, but in his analysis of their diffraction patterns, the elusive double-helix structure was not immediately apparent. His success was recognized by the establishment of a special Institute of Biophysics in London under his command, but as has happened to so many other supremely competent scientists whose work contributes to what seems a major advance, no discoveries quite so startling were ever made again.

Hank Williams 1923-53

AMERICAN COUNTRY MUSICIAN

Looking like Franz Kafka in a Stetson, Williams encouraged people to see him as a melancholy cowboy. He often recorded under the name of 'Luke the Drifter', and became a country and western star just in time to prefigure rock 'n' roll, where his lyrics – witty, wry, depressed songs with titles such as 'I'll Never Get Out of This World Alive' – and his loner persona, fitted the new, self-aware music. Artists such as Johnny Cash picked up on his more maudlin or silly songs ('My Son Calls Another Man Daddy') but the only lesson modern country artists seem to have learned from Williams' fate is that money and fame must be handled with caution. In a genre full of artists who came from extreme poverty to find wealth, success and ample opportunities for self-destruction, Williams is one of the only ones who died a rock 'n' roll death, in a car crash. His songs are still covered by singers in nearly every field of music, but Williams' own recordings are invariably superior. The dry, keening voice is still melancholy and powerful 40 years later.

Raymond Williams 1921-88

BRITISH CULTURAL HISTORIAN

A Welsh miner's son, Williams became a Cambridge professor and the glum avatar of British Marxist literary criticism, and though respected, he was never as influential as he should have been. He was one of the first critics to recognize how diverse media interract, and in particular how newspapers, television and cinema have altered perceptions of literature, ending the suzerainty of high art attitudes. He was concerned to develop a view of art as 'cultural materialism', in which the recognition of the role of material production in aesthetic and critical evaluation would be assured, and argued for the introduction of social studies of communication. However, from the beginning he tended to resist the pop and mass culture that was flooding in from the US – like many on the left, he pinpointed the bad but failed to recognize the good in it. With ☛E. P. Thompson and Stuart Hall he attempted to rally the New Left in 1967 around the *May Day Manifesto*, but their arguments were largely adrift from the times. His work on socialism, especially *The Long Revolution* (1961), was accurately pessimistic about Britain's cultural and economic future. In time the complacency he diagnosed became obvious to all, but it is not clear that Williams ever articulated a genuine alternative; optimism of the will was absent, crippled by nostalgia for the working-class communities of his childhood.

Richard Williams

born 1933

CANADIAN ANIMATOR, SETTLED IN UK

Until the success of *Who Framed Roger Rabbit?* (1988), Richard Williams was known only to other animators. Among them, however, he was a legendary recluse, the true inheritor of the advanced comic genius of ☛Chuck Jones and ☛Tex Avery. The winner of a trip to the Disney Studios at the age of 15, Williams went on fully to absorb the traditions of the Hollywood cartoon, in comic timing and character creation. However, all the signs were that he had arrived too late: Disney was restricted to fine-tuning and overselling earlier format-successes; television demanded no more than a palely imitative shadow of the skills Williams boasted; and European art-animation had very self-consciously avoided what it regarded as Hollywood's technical slickness. Williams ended up animating for commercials, and financing an underground project of his own, *The Cobbler and the Thief*, which he has now been working on for almost a quarter of a century. Occasionally surfacing to work on such high-profile projects as the opening sequence to *The Pink Panther*, or ad characters such as the Cresta bear, he garnered a huge subterranean reputation for his abilities and his integrity, so much so that when Robert Zemeckis and ☛Steven Spielberg began planning *Roger Rabbit*, Williams was the obvious choice as animator. Now back working on *The Cobbler and the Thief*, he is hoping that its release will kick-start cartoon animation's best possibilities.

Tennessee Williams

(Thomas Lanier Williams) 1911-83

AMERICAN PLAYWRIGHT

Williams's plays so effectively established the American South as a land of fierce, frustrated sexuality and passionate Christian zeal, barely concealed behind a mask of gentility, that none who come after can wander into that same territory without first giving him a reverential nod. With plays such as *A Streetcar Named Desire* (1947), in which a woman struggles to hold on to the last traces of her refinement as she steadily goes to pieces, *Cat on a Hot Tin Roof* (1955), about the family of a former champion athlete who cannot face up to his father or accept his subsequent failure, and *Sweet Bird of Youth* (1959), in which a gigolo who has infected a senator's wife with the clap ends up being castrated, Williams focused on characters ravaged by anxiety and appalled by the trashiness of their own lives. His own decline through booze and drugs (the latter administered by Dr 'Feel Good' Jacobson) was probably the result of pushing too far the conflicts and confusions of his own life into his writing. As his later plays failed to find an audience, declining creative powers and the struggle against insanity became the only things he could memorably write about.

William Carlos Williams

1883-1963

AMERICAN WRITER

A novelist, essayist and obstetrician, Williams was largely responsible for the great change which has come over American verse in the late twentieth century. He drew his style from the direct language of common speech, stripped poetry to its essentials and wrote about rather mundane subjects – his patients, the weather, his garden, his wife – in such ordinary terms that he risked being dull, and often was. But, as he introduced more of his own personality into his later work, the writing became richer. His dedication was sometimes comic – he would pull his car off the road while on a house-call so that he could jot down a poem on his prescription pad, and he concealed a typewriter in his office desk to compose between patients. Many of his pieces are forgettable, but the openness with which he shared his life and emotions, and his vivid observations of the ordinary, account for his influence.

Brian Wilson

born 1942

AMERICAN POP MUSICIAN

The inventor of surf music – the sound of tanned and fit youths cruising about with their 'girls' around the beaches of California – Wilson developed into a bona fide musical genius and then became another ruined eccentric. Without him, The Beach Boys would have been just another straight and clean West Coast rock group with good close-harmony vocals. With him, they took studio technology and ideas of the pop song into bizarre and often wonderful areas, vying with the ☛The Beatles as the only successful pop experimentalists of their time. However, Wilson's personal insecurity and increasing drug use in the mid-1960s resulted in him leaving music and, apparently, sanity behind for a decade, returning to both only in the late 1980s with an album made in collaboration with his analyst, Dr Eugene Landy. The record itself, though sketchy, received massive critical praise but sold little. Meanwhile Wilson's creation – The Beach Boys – continue to tour and chart.

Colin Wilson

born 1931

BRITISH WRITER

Wilson's brief canonization as Britain's answer to ☛Sartre, with the 1954 publication of *The Outsider*, was more a mark of existentialism's success as the first pop philosophy than of any special merits of the book itself. In Britain, existentialism manifested itself in an even more tight-assed and reactionary form than the worst aspects of the American Beat movement: Wilson became one of the best known Angry Young Men, and *The Outsider* articulated a classic AYM sentiment – the claim that the author deserved immediate elevation into the ranks of the revered Great (on the grounds, perhaps, that he was a spokesman for his generation). Basically a warmed-over list of romantic modernists of known stature (Nietzsche, Dostoyevsky, Lawrence, etc.) with the hardly hidden implication that Wilson was the next and the greatest in this line, the book was a phenomenon with so inevitably built-in a backlash that Wilson seems never really to have recovered his poise. Since his late 1950s' heyday, he has devoted himself to the production of inventories: his encyclopedias of murder and dictionaries of the occult fill the murkier sections of all big bookshops, and not the slightest hint of critical or moral attitude is to be found in any of them. They are undoubtedly the best written of such books, but Wilson's inability or unwillingness to judge the truth or falsehood of any claim is not so much a courageous transvaluation of values as an indication of the corner he long ago painted himself into.

Edward O. Wilson born 1929

AMERICAN SOCIOBIOLOGIST

Professor of zoology at Harvard, Wilson stirred considerable controversy when he published *Sociobiology: The New Synthesis* in 1975. Modernizing the famous aphorism that the chicken is the egg's way of making another egg, Wilson argued that the organism is only DNA's way of making more DNA. Basing his work on W. D. Hamilton's pioneer studies of kinship selection and the possibility of evolutionary (gene-based) development of altruism in species, Wilson examined several further behavioural traits that he argued could be gene-transmitted, and looked for evolutionary advantages that such behaviour could bring about. The sociobiological way of thinking sees an animal's behaviour as adaptive only if it ensures the survival of that individual's genes in future generations. This has led to the idea of 'reproductive success': the best strategies – those that will survive through natural selection – are those which maximize the chances of an animal transferring its genetic material to the largest number of offspring. This argument encourages sociobiologists to talk as if the genes, rather than the organism, were the point of the whole exercise. Controversy centred on the final chapter of Wilson's book, in which he outlined future studies of all human social behaviour – such as xenophobia, homosexuality and (behavioural) gender differences – which might have been arrived at through natural selection. Early critics pointed angrily to the political irresponsibility of such speculations. Coming in the wake of ☛Arthur Jensen's notorious claims for the heritability of IQ, work that based itself on biological determinism of any kind was seen as an attempt by the racist right to reclaim lost ground. Detailed rebuttal followed, from fellow Harvard zoologist Philip Kitcher, in his exhaustive *Vaulting Ambition*.

Harold Wilson born 1916

☟BRITISH POLITICAL LEADER

A strikingly young member of the British Cabinet at the age of 31, Wilson won (by narrow margins) four out of the five elections he fought as Labour's leader from 1964 to 1974, and showed himself a supreme pragmatist by holding together his party through successive identity traumas. On the party's left in his early phase – he resigned, with ☛Aneurin Bevan, over charges for National Health dental work and spectacles – he later drifted to the right. His style as premier was marked in the 1960s by intense activity, but he later reverted to the role of 'soccer schemer' – 'feeding balls' to ministers, as he put it. Failure to devalue the pound until 1967 led to constant trade crises; a seemingly pro-US line on Vietnam won the odium of the young. His return to office in 1974 was a surprise; Labour solved the miners' strike but triggered wage-push inflation. His exit in 1976 was, equally, a shock – but it is unlikely to have been due to an MI5 plot, as has been suggested. His cheeky style, pipe and quick mind earned Wilson real popularity; he was a whizz-kid with transatlantic impulses and simple tastes, such as Gannex macs. Major flaws were his Mitty-ish fantasies and his constant itch to defend himself. The character of his Cabinets and the contexts in which he held power made for acute problems – he had a tough ride, and his reputation did not survive.

Robert Wilson born 1944

AMERICAN THEATRE DIRECTOR

Wilson's protracted, gargantuan spectacles draw upon all the theatrical arts. He pitches towards the subconscious, building dramas around the logic of dreams, and works out from a distrust of language. His emphasis is instead on communication through bodily movement and sensational imagery, with enormous casts focusing attention on the grotesque and the mentally crippled. He reverses the normal theatrical process of compressing time, and stretches out minor actions to extreme length. It took seven days and nights to create *Ka Mountain and Guardenia Terrace* (1972), for which cast and audience had to wind their way up the slopes of a mountain in Iran. *The Life and Times of Joseph Stalin* (1973) ran for 12 hours and the title gives no suggestion of the range of *dramatis personae*, which take in a chorus line of 'mammies' waltzing to 'The Blue Danube' and a shrieking Queen Victoria as well as Freud, Ivan the Terrible, the Pope and Marie Antoinette. Despite their separate titles, his plays inbleed into each other, with mythic and iconic figures from one putting in appearances in others. Wilson's stress on the musical aspect of his creations led naturally towards 'opera', and in 1976, he wrote *Einstein on the Beach* (1976) with ☛Philip Glass.

Tuzo Wilson

(John Tuzo Wilson) born 1908

♦ CANADIAN GEOPHYSICIST

Although the idea of Continental Drift had been kicking around since the beginning of the century – inspired by the fact that Africa and South America could be so exactly 'fitted together' – it was not until the 1940s that the technology existed to study the matter, and it was not until the 1960s that a sizeable part of the scientific community began to pay attention. During WW2, Princeton geologist Harry Hess, then commanding a ship in the Pacific, had used echo-sounding equipment to map the sea-bed, and discovered not only a rash of mysteriously sunken volcanoes, but also a central ocean ridge. He suggested – so speculatively that he decided to call it an 'essay in geopoetry' – that the sea floors were spreading away from this ridge, constantly renewed by molten rock bubbling up through the rift that remained. Tuzo Wilson combined with Hess to produce magnetic readings that turned the speculation into a convincing case, and went on to chart hitherto unnoticed 'transform faults' which proved the reality of sea-floor spreading. Tumultuous sessions followed at the 1967 meeting of the American Geophysical Union as the received conventions of a century's geophysics withered under the assault. As many as 70 papers backing up the theory had been submitted, many by sceptics who had started out intending to disprove the claims but ended up converted by the evidence they had uncovered. Several respected authorities of an earlier generation woke up to find their life's work undermined. In 1974, Wilson was appointed director general of the Ontario Science Centre.

Donald Winnicott 1896-1971

BRITISH PSYCHOANALYST

It was Winnicott, the child analyst dubbed a 'pixie' by his friends, who coined the the phrase 'good enough parent' in the hope of encouraging people to give their children the freedom they needed to develop inner strength and 'the capacity to be alone'. Some considered his arguments 'sloppy' as he sought to shift psychoanalysis away from its strict biological base, and the straight-forward manner in which he expressed them often distressed his colleagues. But the 1951 paper that defined his distinctive line – 'Transitional Objects and Transitional Phenomena' – was hugely influential. It focuses on the child's use of familiar and unchanging objects – the corner of a blanket, a bundle of wool – as defences against anxiety. The emotions stirred in the child by such an object, which it recognizes to be neither the absent parent nor a representation of that parent, help encourage feelings of inner security which then foster a sense of independence. This transitional object is discarded once the child feels confident enough to take an interest in the wider world, but the relationship established with the blanket or whatever becomes the source of feelings stirred by other symbolic, 'cultural' experiences. An empiricist with an intuitive grasp of children's feelings, Winnicott has had a considerable influence on 'object relations' theorists who consider that children's need to relate to other persons or the symbols of other persons is central to their development.

Ludwig Wittgenstein 1889-1951

✍ AUSTRO-BRITISH PHILOSOPHER

Wittgenstein's oblique domination over British philosophy is a mystery. He transformed it not once but twice: first with the *Tractatus Logico-Philosophicus* (1922), which initiated the Vienna Circle of logical positivists on the Continent; and then, when he launched (posthumously) the whole Anglo-American linguistic analysis school with *Philosophical Investigations* (1953). In fact, both books, accurately read, signal the end of any possible philosophical project – let alone two such conflicting (and barren) schools. Wittgenstein was a gloomily tortured anti-metaphysician whose lack of faith in his own calling was legendary (he rejected his own arguments in the *Tractatus* just as the relevant faculties were getting to grips with them). His effect has been largely to innoculate British philosophy against any significant developments in European metaphysics, from Heidegger through to ☛Derrida; an exclusion which is variously portrayed as a triumph of common sense and a disastrously insular snobbery. The latter is probably closer to the truth – valuable work has been done by Wittgenstein's heirs, but at the expense of wider political or critical significance. Wittgenstein, deeply influenced by Nietzsche's radical doubts about any quests for truth through logic, seems the oddest possible candidate for use as such a quarantine device – if so many did not stand to lose so much face, he would be the obvious point of reconnection for the two traditions.

Tom Wolfe

(Thomas Kennerly Wolfe) born 1930

❞ AMERICAN JOURNALIST, NOVELIST

Along with ☛Hunter S. Thompson and a few others, Wolfe brought a new dynamic to reportage in the 1960s and early 1970s. Their New Journalism grew out of the innovations that ☛Truman Capote and ☛Norman Mailer had introduced, rejecting what they considered fraudulent objectivity for material moulded round the personality and attitudes of the writer.

Wolfe's contribution was a mix of epigrammatic verve and epic volubility that brought to life the profound (and the superficial) changes that society was going through from the mid- to late-1960s. His dandyism, his seductively hip and aggressive style, his genius for dramatic titles (*The Kandy-Kolored Tangerine-Flake Streamline Baby* 1965; *The Electric Kool-Aid Acid-Test* 1968; *Radical Chic and Mau-Mauing the Flak-Catchers* 1970) and his willingness to examine counter-culture events all disguised the cold distance he actually put between himself and the targets of his exposés – but by the mid-1970s, it was fairly clear that Wolfe was at best agnostic about any of the possibilities for change that America should have been demanding of itself. *Radical Chic*, in particular, had an undertone of hostility to claims the black community was making at that time. The publication of his novel, *The Bonfire of the Vanities* (1987), proved that he had lost little of his near-prescient ability to encapsulate the absurdity of current life, but it also showed that, if anything, he had become even more conservative and resistant towards the perceptions and demands of minority groups.

Edward D. Wood, Jr 1922-78

AMERICAN FILM DIRECTOR

Often acclaimed as the worst film-maker of all time, Wood's commitment and courage in the most dismal of circumstances (total lack of funding, a world that rejected him, his long-retired star Bela Lugosi dropping dead on the set) were matched only by his ambition. Unconcerned by continuity or convincing settings, his sublime disdain for craft conventions, hackneyed Hollywood subjects or the basics of audience-pandering might have turned him into the first among the aesthetic rebels if he had been working a decade or two later. The zenith of his no-budget anti-technique is represented by *Plan Nine from Outer Space* (1959), while *Glen or Glenda* (1953), a somewhat ambivalent study of the trials and pleasures of transvestism and transsexuality, shows him at his most passionate. His assaults on good taste are somewhat erratic, and he ended up directing dead-zone sexploitation cheapies. As a pioneer of a primitivist sensibility, his work retains a demented integrity.

Bob Woodward born 1943

AMERICAN JOURNALIST

Forever associated with the Watergate story, which he broke with Carl Bernstein at the *Washington Post* in 1974-5, Woodward was the one who capitalized on a dogged and remarkable piece of journalism: he could play office politics and had the right connections. Both Woodward and Bernstein were unknown when they received the assignment, and the recognition they won as the most significant and courageous cogs in the machine that toppled a corrupt president was deserved. Now a superstar journalist, Woodward is still drawn to stories of sleaze and failure. His publications include *Wired* (1983), the story of comic John Belushi's life and death from a cocaine habit, and *Veil* (1987), a study of William Casey and the CIA, which included a (much contested, somewhat inconclusive) death-bed confession about the arms-for-hostages negotiations with Iran that came to be known as 'Irangate'. Revealed also is something that *All the President's*

Men (1974) and *The Final Days* (1976) only hinted at: Woodward, good at ferreting out stories, is poor at interpreting them. A pedestrian stylist, he never addresses the question of why we want to know about Belushi and talent burn-out, or what was really at stake in Watergate or Irangate.

Stevie Wonder

(Steveland Morris) born 1950

♦ AMERICAN POP MUSICIAN

Wonder was the blind child-star whose genius proved too much not only for the label-grooming that Motown was giving him in the 1960s, but probably also for Berry Gordy's whole paternalist project. When he first appeared, frenetically singing 'Fingertips' at the age of 12, and playing a peculiar broken-bird harmonica style that remained his and his alone, Wonder was a novelty. By the mid-1970s, his wide listening and significant musical intelligence had become so obvious that he secured his demands for complete artistic freedom – against Motown tradition. Initially this seemed all to the good: *Music of My Mind* (1972), *Innervisions* (1973) and *Fullfillingness First Finale* (1974) were filled with highly original music, synthesizing most of what was best about great mid-1970s' pop. He followed these up with an impressive, though overlong double LP, *Songs in the Key of Life* (1976), and a disastrous triple concept album, *The Secret Life of Plants* (1979), where sensibility and obsession combined to produce a huge wodge of half-baked piffle. Since then, he has never achieved quite such consistently innovative results, preferring to consolidate and mould a personal style that diverges increasingly from the R&B chart mainstream. He occupies a position so like that of ☛Ray Charles that it is almost uncanny – the two blind keyboard players from different generations as solo guarantors of the soul-jazz tradition. Both of them caused a huge shift in the course of pop, and both of them remain, aloof and adored, after pop has moved on.

Steve Wozniak *see* Jobs, Steve

Charles Wright Mills *see* Mills, Charles Wright

Tammy Wynette born 1942
George Jones born 1931

AMERICAN COUNTRY MUSICIANS

Wynette and Jones were country music's most noteworthy married couple and lived their lives accordingly. They got divorced in 1975 and Tammy recorded 'D.I.V.O.R.C.E.'; before that, they had had a good patch and she had recorded 'Stand By Your Man'; a previous bad patch had resulted in Jones's 'Good Year for the Roses'. The fact that the last two are great songs merely emphasizes the way that country music attacks the emotional jugular: full on, with no thought of false modesty. The greatest moment in this couple's marriage has not, as yet, been reported in song: when his alcohol problem had reached a particularly bad stage, she took his car keys away from him; he drove into town on their motor mower.

X

Malcolm X *see* Malcolm X

Yannis Xenakis born 1922
☞GREEK COMPOSER,
♦ BASED IN FRANCE
The fact that Xenakis has occasionally worked with another displaced Greek musician, the scream-diva Diamanda Galas, places him accurately enough – once again, post-war classical music is being forced to face the legacy of political terror (and the possibility of the end of Western civilization) left behind by Hitler's regime. A fighter in the Resistance who was horribly wounded, losing the sight of one eye, Xenakis arrived in Paris from Greece after WW2 and studied architecture with ☛Le Corbusier at the same time as he was studying music with ☛Messiaen. His music reflects a conviction that 'all things are numbers,' and he has chosen to apply the laws of physics and stochastic probability theory to the problems of composition – surprisingly, in view of this, his works are intense and emotionally powerful. A pioneer in the use of computers in composition, he has had to wait years for players of sufficient calibre and will to tackle much of his music satisfactorily. Though his use of mathematical models provides a highly abstract frame, his music is infused with his political humanity. His choral piece, *Nuits*, carries the dedication: 'For you, unknown political prisoners and for you, the thousands of the forgotten whose very names are lost.'

Y

Yohji Yamamoto born 1944

JAPANESE FASHION DESIGNER

One of the first Japanese designers to make it in the West, Yamamoto was also central in moving the all-black style from the realms of rock outsiders into the inner coteries of the supposedly sophisticated. In the West, his garments sell for ludicrous prices – presentation in his shops is minimal and there is nothing so prosaic as a pricetag in sight, fostering the 'If you have to ask, you can't afford it' attitude. In Japan, where the exoticism factor is lower, the prices correspond. Most of the clothes are oversized and baggy. The early lines were made of good fabrics, but once the name was established, a higher ratio of synthetics crept in.

Boris Yeltsin born 1931

❞ RUSSIAN POLITICAL LEADER

Yeltsin's reputation as a political hooligan was enhanced in late 1991 by his success in engineering the crackup of the Soviet Union and the fall of his long-time rival ☛Mikhail Gorbachev. Sacked as Moscow party boss in November 1987, Yeltsin took revenge on the old guard in March 1989 by securing election (with a vast majority) to one of Moscow's seats in Congress. He went on to become leader of the first opposition group in the Soviet Union since just after the Revolution and then head of the Russian Federation, the USSR's largest republic. His popularity was rooted in revulsion against corruption, privilege, bureaucracy and the status quo's failure to deliver the goods, and was enhanced when, the first democratic president of Russia, he took a stand against the timid hardliners who attempted a coup in August 1991. He went on to topple Gorbachev, but his own career is likely to flounder on the lack of any political institutions to replace a discredited Communist Party. Yeltsin is good at tearing things down but shows few signs of being a skilful strategist who has the measure of his country's problems and some ideas about possible solutions.

Yevgeni Yevtushenko born 1933

SOVIET POET

A poet who for a long time wanted to be a footballer, Yevtushenko is sometimes treated with suspicion because of his 'independently minded loyalist' stance and capacity to get his work published whatever regime is in power. But he has been popular in the USSR since the mid-1950s, having established his reputation with the autobiographical 'Zima Junction' just as the shadow of Stalin's regime retreated. A magnetic, driven charisma fuels his abilities as a public speaker, and his capacity to convey public emotions in poetry with a conversational style is impressive – as in his recounting of the massacres of Babi Yar. His poems – harsh, outspoken and potent in their harking back to early poets of the revolutionary era – suggest a streetwise personality open to the nuances of youth culture, who treats emotional themes that had long been taboo.

LaMonte Young

born 1935

♦ AMERICAN MUSICIAN

☆ A constant of New York's avant-garde for four decades, Young is generally associated with the minimalist composers, whom he influenced greatly in the early 1960s. In fact, his interests derive more from Asian mysticism and ritual. Developing the kind of confrontational Zen theatre that ☛Cage and his pupils bought to music the decade before, his work pushes out beyond the uptown respectability that ☛Glass and ☛Reich have achieved. As the man who once stuffed a violin with concert programmes and torched them in front of an audience, it seems fair to suggest that he is happy with his present status. Significantly, he was involved with the agitational art group Fluxus, an association (with what Fluxus kingpin ☛George Maciunas dubbed the 'mixed media neo-baroque happening') that brought him into the orbit of ☛Warhol's 'Exploding Plastic Inevitable'. It was the noise and monotony of his extended drone works, performed at high volume, that became such a crucial influence on the ☛The Velvet Underground and the history of rock; while his 1970s' work with Indian singer-guru Pandit Pran Nath did as much to inspire such ambient mood composers as Brian Eno and more especially Jon Hassell. Young, a shadowy but fascinating presence, has to date resisted the lures of commercial success that almost everyone he has influenced seems able to tap into.

Neil Young

born 1945

⇔ CANADIAN ROCK MUSICIAN

⊶ Young is one of those Canadians who act both as guardians of America's historical myth and a penetrating critic of the same, following a line that stretches from distorted dream-nostalgists The Band to manic metal-Cassandras Voivod. Young's success with archetypal West Coast super-group Crosby, Stills, Nash & Young might have led to early fossilization. In fact, he managed to retain his audience along with a New Wave credibility, despite a flirtation with clumsy, post-*Star Wars* electro-pop (a kind of burnished and cynical ☛Reaganism) and a tendency to flip-flop from project to project which makes him look like some sort of redneck ☛Bowie. His group Crazy Horse were distortion maniacs during the blandest rock-aristocratic era, and Young seems to cast the same kind of spell that Clint Eastwood does in film – the intelligent reactionary who ignites a sexual attraction in his strongest critics, smiling his way out of trouble and off into the realms of mysticism.

Z

Frank Zappa born 1940

▲AMERICAN COMPOSER,
☞ROCK MUSICIAN

Emerging in the middle of the 'summer of love', Frank Zappa and The Mothers of Invention, his band, set out to satirize and antagonize the hippy movement. Their first LP title *We're Only in It for the Money* (1968) was at odds with the hazy idealism of the age. In the year of Woodstock and salvation through sex and universal togetherness, Zappa asked the question, 'What's the ugliest part of your body?' and came to the conclusion that it was 'Your mind'. Musically, he used time signatures and key changes unknown to conventional rock, thus betraying his avant-garde origins – he studied contemporary music in Germany alongside ☛Boulez and ☛Stockhausen, and claims ☛Varèse as an influence. The height of his musical invention came with *Grand Wazoo* (1972). After that he descended into would-be outrage that seemed increasingly juvenile, and as a result never lacked an audience.

John Zorn born 1954

&AMERICAN ROCK MUSICIAN

The last man in the alphabet is not the last man in music, although he sometimes writes, plays and talks as if he would like us to think he is. Zorn's obsession with style collision is a product of New York's polyglot city-never-sleeps culture, and his strength lies in the sheer cheek of his cut-up, fold-and-blast strategies. He will take the idea of feeding ☛Ornette Coleman's free blues into hardcore punk form, and then short-circuit scepticism by virtue of his alertness, his impatient Dada brutality. He will trace his influences through to the cartoon composers at MGM and Warner Bros: apart from his shared wit and speed, what he is referring to is a need to quote, to parody, to distort, to irritate and to be amused. An organizing force in the New York downtown scene for over a decade, he is a capable bebop saxophonist and an experienced free improviser. Innovative in terms of allowing tired distinctions to collapse and eccentric cross-fertilizations to bloom, the question of whether he is just going round and round, or *out*, will stick with him as long as he keeps moving. On the surface, at least, the energy is the thing.

Index